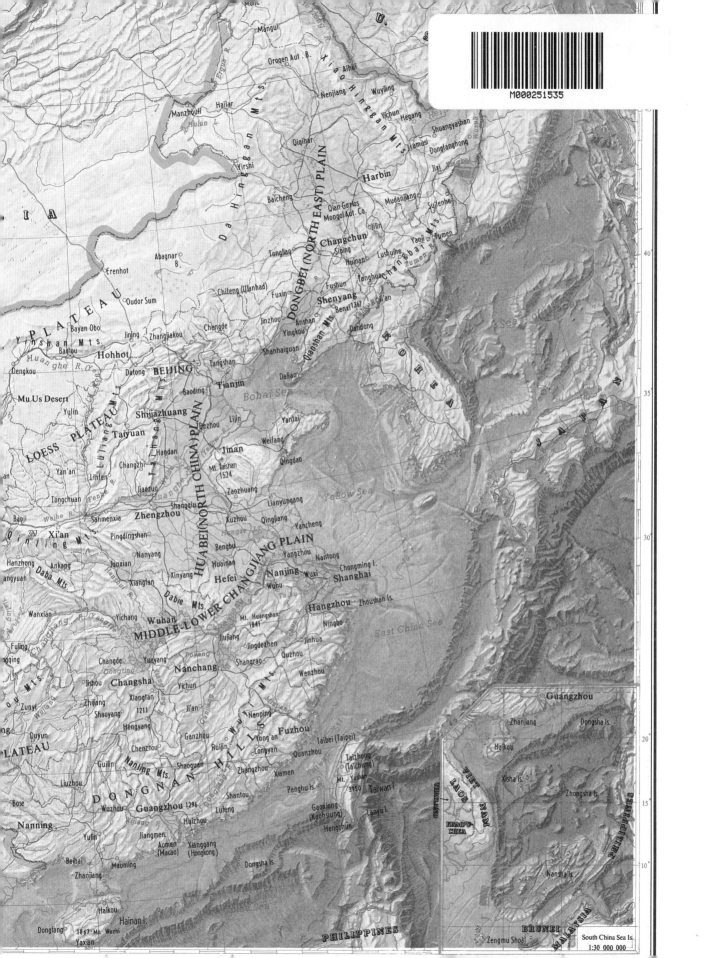

Geography of China

ENVIRONMENT, RESOURCES, POPULATION, AND DEVELOPMENT

WILEY SERIES IN ADVANCED REGIONAL GEOGRAPHY

John Wiley & Sons, Inc. is pleased to announce the availability of these other excellent Advanced Regional Geography titles for you classroom use and personal reading and enjoyment.

REGIONAL LANDSCAPES OF THE UNITED STATES AND CANADA, Fourth Edition, by Stephen Birdsall and John Florin.

LATIN AMERICA AND THE CARIBBEAN: A SYSTEMATIC AND REGIONAL SURVEY, Second Edition, edited by Brian Blouet and Olwyn Blouet.

EUROPE IN THE 1990'S: A GEOGRAPHICAL ANALYSIS, edited by George Hoffman.

PHYSICAL GEOGRAPHY OF CHINA, by Zhao Songqiao.

LATIN AMERICA, Fifth Edition, by Preston E. James and C. W. Minkel.

Geography of China

ENVIRONMENT, RESOURCES, POPULATION, AND DEVELOPMENT

ZHAO SONGQIAO

Institute of Geography, Chinese Academy of Sciences

JOHN WILEY & SONS, INC.

New York   Chichester   Brisbane   Toronto   Singapore

Acquistions Editor	Barry Harmon
Marketing Manager	Cathy Faduska
Production Editor	Bonnie Cabot
Designer	Laura Nicholls
Manufacturing Manager	Andrea Price
Illustration	Edward Starr
Copy Editor	Elizabeth J. Leppman

This book was set in 12 pt. Galliard by General Graphic Services and printed and bound by Hamilton Printing. The cover was printed by The Lehigh Press.

Library of Congress Cataloging in Publication Data:

Chao, Sung-ch' iao.
  Geography of China : environment, resources, population, and development / Songqiao Zhao.
     p.   cm.
  Includes index.
  ISBN 0-471-57758-8
  1. China—Geography.   I. Title.
DS706.7.C36 1994   93-34414
915.1—dc20   CIP

Printed in the United States of America

10 9 8 7 6 5 4 3 2 1

Foreword

China is a fascinating country with a rich history, a legacy of cultural superiority among Asian countries, a large area and an immense population, and a landscape that varies from the hot and humid lowlands of the east coast to the forbidding deserts and towering peaks of the west. For Westerners, China still carries the aura of mystery that was whetted by the stories of Marco Polo, the search by Columbus for a direct route to the Orient, and the isolation that the last dynasty of rulers imposed on the nation.

As China transformed itself in the twenty-first century from a developing country into a developed one, its influence on world affairs is certain to increase. Anything that brings change to one fifth of the world's population is bound to affect the lives of people everywhere. The task of modernizing China is a monumental challenge, if for no other reason than the sheer mass of humanity involved. Fortunately, the ethnic composition of the nation is overwhelmingly a single cultural entity, the Han Chinese, amounting to over 93 percent of the population in 1982 or over 91 percent in 1990. However, saying that less than 9 percent consists of 55 minority groups should not obscure the fact that 9 percent in China means about 100 million people. That is more than the population of all but eight other countries of the world.

Professor Zhao Songqiao has undertaken the very difficult charge of preparing a comprehensive geography of China. He is admirably qualified to do so because he has been intimately involved in a wide variety of geographical studies of the natural resources of his country while at the Institute of Geography of the Chinese Academy of Sciences. He has traveled to nearly every part of China, observing at first hand the human and environ-mental conditions he describes so well. Moreover, his personal interest in the developmental history of agriculture has allowed him to relate geographical data to human occupancy of the regions of the country. Professor Zhao's national and international stature makes him uniquely able to write this authoritative book.

There are several features of the book that warrant special mention. Professor Zhao has related the historical development of China to its natural resources and has included that theme in his descriptions of the geography of the seven divisions of the nation. One of the most interesting chapters discusses the occurrence and significance of environmental hazards. It includes natural and human-induced hazards such as droughts, floods, land degradation, earthquakes, typhoons, environmental pollution, and others.

Of particular interest is the analysis and interpretation of the direction, magnitude, and significance of population growth on the compositon of the urban and rural sectors of the economy, on the standard of living in the twenty-first century, and on the probable impact of future natural and human-induced environmental stresses. Barring a catastrophe of unprecedented magnitude, the population of China will be about 1.3 billion by the end of this century. Family planning has been reasonably effective in urban areas but much less so in the rural areas, where 80 percent of the populace resides. Given the inertia built into the system by the continuing influx of women of child-bearing age, the population curve will inexorably go on rising well into the twenty-first century, no matter how effective the birth control policy may be. That rise is sure to place greater and greater stress on natural and economic resources.

China is an agricultural country. It faces the future

with a cropland base of about 100 million hectares and little potential for increase. Despite the great strides made in recent decades in raising yields, food grains must be imported to meet internal demand. That situation is likely to worsen even in years of normal crop production. It will become much worse in drought or flood years. There is little room for increasing the efficiency of the food chain because the Chinese diet already is heavily vegetarian and livestock live largely on waste plant products. There is undoubtedly some opportunity for increasing crop yields but probably not enough to represent an agricultural revolution, at least for the foreseeable future. Nevertheless, it is well to remember that the Chinese have demonstrated that they are industrious and resourceful. They have managed to produce most of the food for 1.1 billion people, using low-technology practices, on a cropland area only two thirds that of the United States, where the population is 260 million.

Professor Zhao believes that the first 25 years of the twenty-first century will be the critical time for the land–food–population equation. That period will be weathered successfully if population growth is controlled and economic development is strong. If success is not achieved, the entire world is likely to feel the effects. If it is achieved, living conditions for the 1.5 or 1.6 billion people who will occupy the country then will be better than it is now.

Understanding a country as large and populous as China will not be achieved by reading one book, but *Geography of China* is an excellent place to begin. It contains a wealth of information that has not been published before, as well as an analysis of the interplay among natural, social, and economic forces within the country. The insights it provides will help reduce the cloak of mystery that has surrounded the country and the people.

H. E. Dregne
Lubbock, Texas
July 9, 1992

Preface

For many students, teachers, and people interested in the great land of China the need for up-to-date information has not been filled by outdated books or those written by outsiders. This volume is written by an authority, a senior scientist in the Institute of Geography, Chinese Academy of Sciences, Dr. Zhao Songqiao. I first met Dr. Zhao many years ago when he attended an annual meeting of the American Association for the Advancement of Science (AAAS) as a member of a China Association of Science and Technology delegation. Our friendship was assured when I found that he was the representative for the arid lands of China and I was the chair of the AAAS Committee on Arid Lands. Since then we have been close professional and personal friends.

Much of this book on the geography of China was written during the author's stay in the United States as a visiting professor for the 1991–1992 academic year at Weber State University and the University of Utah. Even though considerable planning and organizing of data was done in advance, completing a book of this magnitude in less than a year is in itself a testimonial to the scholarship of Dr. Zhao. I had the honor of reviewing the text in its early draft. Although I have traveled to China several times as an international scholar and have seen the vast areas of northern China, I must confess to being a novice in China's geography. Yet, I can attest to the authenticity of the work.

The reader can be confident of the accuracy of the information given in the text, tables, figures, and photos. Dr. Zhao has provided us with a comprehensive picture of official population numbers, of land and resource use in the face of sobering population increase, and a pattern of historical and economic development over China's long and interesting history. Even so, there may be many unanswered questions that would require more data and, particularly, answers to questions of why and how things have happened geographically, in China during recent years.

During some of my long discussions with Dr. Zhao I have raised some questions about the geography of China. His answers have been a model of simplicity, honesty, and directness that require him to maintain a "freedom of silence." Perhaps in future editions there may be more answers and more data. For the present we may be assured that we have seen a panorama of the great changes in the cultural landscape of the third largest land area and the most populated country in the world.

Cyrus M. McKell, Dean
College of Science
Weber State University

Acknowledgments

I wish to express my deep gratitude to the Weber State University, the University of Utah, and Texas Tech University for inviting me to visit the United States from May 31, 1991, to September 30, 1992. I am also extremely grateful to my uncle, President Tewu Wong (United Daily News) for giving me financial support. All this help made writing this book possible. I am especially obliged to Professor Harold E. Dregne (Texas Tech University) and Dean Cyrus M. McKell (Weber State University) for writing the Foreword and the Preface, respectively, for the book. The University of Hawaii at Manoa kindly gave me a chance to lecture on my manuscript of this book during the 1992 Summer Session.

I must pay homage to President Bradford Wiley (John Wiley & Sons, Inc.) for his support and encouragement for writing this book. Barry Harmon, geography editor, and his colleagues at John Wiley & Sons have worked laboriously in its editing and publishing. I should also thank Professor Ka Lu Fung (University of Saskatchewan), Professor Ronald G. Knapp (SUNY College at New Paltz), Professor David Nemeth (University of Toledo), Professor Clifton W. Pannell (University of Georgia), Professor Roger M. Selya (University of Cincinnati), Professor Gregory Veeck (Louisiana State University), and Professor Jack F. Williams (Michigan State University) for constructively reviewing and revising the manuscript.

In preparing my manuscript, I have drawn scientific data and figures freely from my previous book, *Physical Geography of China* (in English, published jointly by John Wiley and Science Press) which, in turn, drew freely from my still earlier publication, *Physical Geography of China: General Survey* (in Chinese, published by Science Press). I have also received help from Professor Lu Dadao (Chinese Academy of Sciences) in writing the chapter on modern industry, from Professor Yeh Shunzhang (Chinese Academy of Sciences) and Professor Sen-dou Chang (University of Hawaii at Manoa) in preparing the chapter on urban development, from Dr. Liu Weidong (East China Normal University) in preparing the chapter on central China, and from Professor Su Yingping (Chinese Academy of Sciences) and Mr. Lang Deng (University of Utah) in drawing a couple of figures. To all these publishers and colleagues, I am grateful. Finally, I appreciate with affection the numerous services (including computer word processing work) by my wife Xiaoyou Zhu and daughter Xuyun Zhao, son-in-law Baocai Zhang, and granddaughter Tianyi Zhang.

Zhao Songqiao (Sung-chiao Chao)
Salt Lake City, Utah
July 20, 1992

Contents

Tables

Introduction

China is the third largest country in the world with an area of 9.6 million sq km, occupying about 6.5 percent of the world's total land area. It is endowed with varied physical environments and rich natural resources. China is also the world's oldest continuous civilization, with agricultural development uninterrupted for 80 centuries. It still carries the banner of oriental civilization, one of the greatest civilizations in the world. In addition, China is the most populous country in the world and the only one with more than a billion inhabitants. With a total population of more than 1,143,000,000 in 1990, China accounts for about 22 percent of the world's total population, or more than double the total of seven Western industrialized countries: the United States, the United Kingdom, France, Germany, Italy, Canada, and Australia. Consequently, China is of global significance and deserves attention from the world community.

On the other hand, China has been reduced to the status of a poor, "developing" country in modern times. Per capita income on the Mainland is only about U.S. $300 (1990).[1] Rapid population growth has resulted in a population explosion, which in turn exerts great stress on the physical environment. Consequently, although China's natural resources and economic production look enormous, on a per capita basis, both are much lower than world averages. Again, natural hazards and other environmental problems occur frequently and widely, causing disorder in the environment–resource–population–development system. China is now standing at a dangerous crossroad: to survive and to make a new start, or to sink still deeper in poverty and misery. All intelli-gent Chinese are anxious about such a stark dilemma and try to consider remedies. The world community also watches with great concern.

Geography is a basic science as well as an applied science. In general summary, geographers start by conducting basic studies, topically and comprehensively (systematically), on all physical and human attributes at different scales (regional, national, global) of areas on the earth's surface. Then, based on results of these in-depth studies, they suggest relevant strategies and actions to make better use of all natural and human resources as well as to deal effectively with all natural hazards and environmental problems.

Geographers are thus competent to identify and solve difficult problems involved in the disordered environment–resource–population–development system in China. Many Chinese geographers have already tried their best to solve resource productivity problems. Colleagues from other countries are also welcome to lend a hand. However, they must be well versed in the geography of China. It seems that each major geography department in the world should teach at least one course on the geography of China, using modern textbooks. An advanced course is also quite useful. Foreign geographers are also welcome to do fieldwork and research in China. To do so, they need quality references and guidebooks.

Geography is both an old and a new science in China. As early as the fifth century B.C., the classic *The Tribute of Yu* (*Yu Gong*) subdivided China into nine regions and made, for each region, an inventory of mountains, rivers, lakes, swamps, soils, and chief economic products. About the same time, *Record of the Rites of Zhou* (*Zhou Li*) classified China's land into five

---

[1] Per capita income in Taiwan is more than U.S. $8000 and that in Hong Kong is U.S. $11,500.

major types, while the *Book of Master Kwan* (*Kwanzi*) offered a systematic hierarchical classification of the land with 3 first-level types (plain, hill, mountain) and 25 second-level types (determined chiefly on the basis of ground surface materials and soils). These schemes were certainly among the earliest systems of geographical regionalization and land classification in the world. Later, a series of well-known studies appeared, including *The Geographic Book in the Han Chronology, Yuan Hu Reign Period Regional Geography, Diary of the Travels of Xu Xia-ke, Comprehensive Geography of the Chinese Empire under the Qing Dynasty*, and *Essentials of Historical Geography*. In practically every ancient dynastic chronology, there is a chapter on the geographical environment; for most provinces, prefectures, and counties, there are regional geographical studies. In all, more than 9000 regional studies are known to have been produced by Chinese chroniclers.

Since the middle of the nineteenth century, modern physical, human, and regional geography have gradually been introduced into China. Many topical studies of different physical and human elements as well as modern regional studies have been conducted.

Since the founding of the People's Republic of China in 1949, great strides have been made in physical geography. A series of integrated investigations into resource inventories and agricultural potential as well as comprehensive regional plans have been launched for many parts of China. This is especially significant in the frontier areas where scientific information was hitherto unavailable. Many basic and theoretical studies, including *Physical Regionalization of China* (8 volumes, compiled by a special committee of the Chinese Academy of Sciences, 1953–1959), *Physical Geography of China* (12 volumes, compiled by a special committee of the Chinese Academy of Sciences, 1979–1988), *National 1:1 Million Scale Classification and Mapping of Land Resource* (64 sheets, including land type, land evaluation, and land use, conducted by three separate committees of the Chinese Academy of Sciences, 1978–1990), and a series of topical and regional studies have also been produced. However, during the 1950s, the 1960s, and even the 1970s, human geography, except agricultural geography, was rather neglected, and comprehensive studies on physical, human, and regional geography had even been flatly rejected. However, since the adoption of the "opening up" and "modernization" policies beginning in 1978, all branches of geography, including human geography and comprehensive geography, have been revitalized. The present book is one of the pioneer works on the comprehensive geography of China.

To date, because China is such a vast country with a huge population and a long history, geographic information and research are still far from adequate. What we now know is still far less than what we need to know, and good textbooks and research references are especially needed. Moreover, most research, including field trips, have to be conducted inside China, and most available publications are written in Chinese, which seems to be rather difficult for non-Chinese-speaking people. There is also a wide cultural divergence between the East and the West. Consequently, comprehensive, in-depth textbooks on the geography of China written by Chinese scholars in English are much needed.

My textbook, *Physical Geography of China*, appeared in English in 1986. In this revision I try to present broader, more comprehensive coverage in English. This book might be used as an advanced textbook, a research reference, or as a guidebook for tourism and business. During the last half-century, I have had the opportunity to carry out fieldwork virtually throughout China and to conduct research in all aspects of physical, human, and regional geography. I also have diligently pursued library work, learning from and analyzing information contained in a large number of relevant publications. Particularly, I have maintained a "warm heart" for both nationalism and globalism, eager to present faithfully the geographic realities and problems of my country to the learned publics of the world. I believe that I am qualified to do so. Of necessity, I may seem to rely too much on Chinese sources and my own personal observations, and to present many events from a traditional Chinese viewpoint. Consequently, the true picture of China might sometimes need clarification for English-speaking readers. There is an old Chinese saying, "One cannot see the true picture of the Lu Mountain if one views it from inside only."[2] However, I have studied in the United States and have traveled widely in the world. I have never become a member of any party and was never involved in any prejudice. "Outside," objective views of China are carefully maintained in this book.

The present book focuses on the environment–resource–population–development system of China, including the component factors and the integrated whole. It is divided into two parts and 18 chapters. Part I includes 11 chapters, offering a general topical survey of China's environment–resource–population–devel-

---

[2] Lu Mountain, or Lu Shan, is a scenic site and a summer resort located on the southern bank of the middle-lower Chang Jiang (Yangzi River). Many people have visited it, and hence, it is usually mentioned as a typical mountain area.

opment system. Chapter One, based on a revision of the earlier *Physical Geography of China*, sketches the physical features of China's geographic environment. Chapter Two takes stock of China's natural resources. Chapter Three recalls the long history of China's political, economic, and social development. Chapters Four, Five, and Six discuss China's modern economic development in agriculture, industry, and transportation and foreign trade, respectively. Chapters Seven and Eight describe China's ethnic groups and population dilemma. Chapter Nine presents briefly China's urban development. Chapter Ten portrays the widespread and frequent natural disasters and other environmental problems in China. Chapter Eleven attempts a tentative assessment of the land–food–population system in China, which lies at the

core of China's environment–resource–population–development system.

Then come the seven regional geographic chapters of Part II, discussing each of China's seven traditional, natural divisions: Northeast China, North China, Subtropical China, Tropical China, the Inner Mongolian Grassland, the Northwest Desert, and the Tibetan Plateau, including their physical conditions, historical background, social and economic development, as well as areal differentiation and regional development. The whole book is illustrated by 63 figures, 59 tables, 32 color photos, and 42 black-and-white photos.

A brief introduction to China's present administrative units and some commonly used geographic terms may be helpful for English-speaking readers. Broadly

TABLE I.1
Natural Realms, Traditional Divisions, and First-level Administrative Units in China

| Natural realm | Traditional division | First-level administrative units | | |
		Province	Autonomous region	Municipality
Eastern Monsoon China	Northeast China	Liaoning Jilin Heilongjiang		
	North China	Hebei Henan Shandong Shanxi Shaanxi		Beijing Tianjin
	Central China	Jiangsu Anhui Zhejiang Jiangxi Hubei Hunan		Shanghai
	South China	Fujian Guangdong Hainan Taiwan	Guangxi	
	Southwest China	Sichuan Yunnan Guizhou		
Northwest Arid China	Inner Mongolia Northwest China	Gansu	Inner Mongolia (Nei Mongol) Ningxia Xinjiang	
Tibetan Frigid Plateau	Qing-Zang	Qinghai	Xizang (Tibet)	

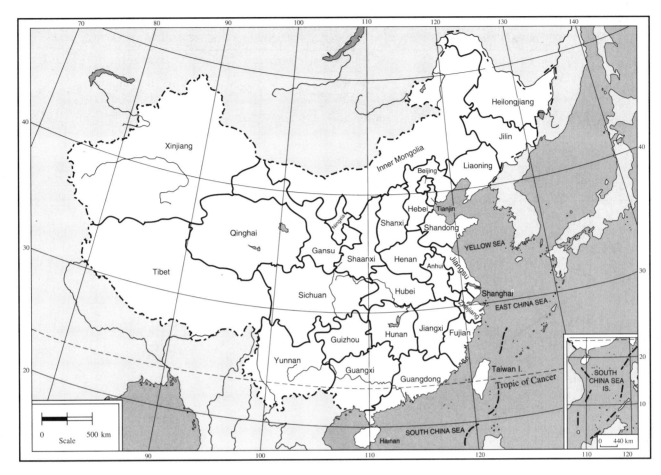

Figure I.1 China's administrative regions (1990)

speaking, China can be divided into three natural realms: Eastern Monsoon China, Northwest Arid China, and the Tibetan Frigid Plateau. Eastern Monsoon China contains five traditional divisions: Northeast China, North China, Central China, South China, and Southwest China. They roughly correspond to the four natural divisions (temperate humid and subhumid Northeast China, warm temperate humid and subhumid North China, subtropical humid China, and tropical humid China), but they are not entirely coincident. For example, tropical China includes only the southern parts of South China and Southwest China while subtropical China takes in all of Central China as well as most of South China and Southwest China. Again Northwest Arid China is traditionally subdivided into Inner Mongolia and Northwest China, corresponding roughly to the semiarid grassland and the arid desert respectively.

There are now 31 first-level administrative units (provinces, autonomous regions, and national munici-

palities) in China. They may be roughly grouped within natural realms and traditional divisions as shown in Table I.1 and Figure I.1.

The romanization of Chinese words and place-names can sometimes be quite confusing. For this book, the official *pinyin* system is generally adopted, with the Wade-Giles system shown in Table I.2 for reference. Again, Chinese names can be rendered both phonetically and literally. There are also many traditional names such as the Yangtze River (phonetically Chang Jiang or literally Long River), the Yellow River (phonetically Huang He), the Tibetan Plateau (Qinghai-Xizang Plateau in *pinyin*), Inner Mongolia (Nei Mongol in *pinyin*), the Greater Hinggan Mountains (Da Hinggan Ling in *pinyin*), and others. Furthermore, a decision has to be made about Chinese nomenclature, particularly in the terms for (1) mountain (in Chinese: *shan*, *ling*, *feng*, and others; in Mongolian: *ula*; in Tibetan: *daban*; in Uygur: *tag*); (2) river (in Chinese: *he*, *jiang*, *shui*, *xi*, and others;

TABLE I.2
Commonly Used Chinese Words with their Romanization and English Meaning

| Chinese characters | | Romanization | | |
Traditional	Simplified	Pinyin	Wade-Giles	English meaning
一	一	yi	i	one
二	二	er	erh	two
三	三	san	san	three
四	四	si	szu	four
五	五	wu	wu	five
六	六	liu	liu	six
七	七	qi	ch'i	seven
八	八	ba	pa	eight
九	九	jiu	chiu	nine
十	十	shi	shih	ten
百	百	bai	pai	hundred
千	千	qian	ch'ien	thousand
萬	万	wan	wan	ten thousand
億	亿	yi	yi	hundred million
東	东	dong	tung	east
南	南	nan	nan	south
西	西	xi	hsi	west
北	北	bei	pei	north
中	中	zhong	chung	center
上	上	shang	shang	up
下	下	xia	hsia	down
大	大	da	ta	large, great
小	小	xiao	hsiao	small
天	天	tian	tien	heaven
地	地	di	ti	earth
山	山	shan	shan	mountain
嶺	岭	ling	ling	range
峰	峰	feng	feng	peak
砂	砂	sha	sha	sand
石	石	shi	shih	stone
河	河	he	ho	river
川	川	chuan	ch'uan	river
江	江	jiang	chiang	river
水	水	shui	shui	river
湖	湖	hu	ho	lake
海	海	hai	hai	sea
洋	洋	yang	yang	ocean
橋	桥	qiao	ch'iao	bridge
口	口	kou	k'ou	mouth
省	省	sheng	sheng	province
國	国	guo	kuo	country
縣	县	xian	hsien	county, district
市	市	shi	shi	municipality
京	京	jing	ching	capital
紅	红	hong	hung	red
黃	黄	huang	huang	yellow
藍	蓝	lan	lan	blue
白	白	bai	pai	white
黑	黑	hei	hei	black
沙漠	沙漠	shamo	sha-mo	sandy desert
戈壁	戈壁	gebi	gobi	stone desert

TABLE I.3
Conversion of some Commonly Used Chinese Units into the English and Metric Systems

	Chinese	English	Metric
1	*mu*	1/6 acre	1/15 hectare (ha)
1500	*mu*	640 acres	1 square kilometer (sq km)
1	*li*	1/3 mile	1/2 kilometer (km)
1	*chi*	1.09 foot	1/3 meter (m)
1	tael	0.13 pound	50 grams (g)
1	catty (10 taels)	1.33 pound	1/2 kilogram (kg)
1	picul (100 catties)	133 pounds	50 kilograms

in Mongolian: *moron*); (3) lake (in Chinese: *hu*; in Mongolian: *nur*; in Tibetan: *co*; in Uygur: *kol*); and (4) sea (in Chinese: *hai, yang*). For the convenience of English-speaking readers, they are essentially converted to English terms, although for phonetic consideration, any place-name with only one Chinese character has its Chinese term repeated in English; for example, Qinling Mountains, Tianshan Mountains, Nanling Mountains, Huaihe River, Hanshui River, and Bohai Sea. Appendix 1 is a glossary of geographic place-names. As not all place-names mentioned in the text could be included on the small-scale maps, readers are advised to use an up-to-date Chinese atlas (in *pinyin*) for additional reference.

Table I.3 contains conversions of some commonly used Chinese units into the English system and the metric system. However, with a few exceptions (e.g., "*mu*" in the tables), the metric system has been generally used in this book.

REFERENCES

Buchanan, K. 1970. *The Transformation of the Chinese Earth.* London: Bell.

Cannon, Terry, and Jenkins, Alan (eds.). 1990. *The Geography of Contemporary China.* London and New York: Routledge.

Chinese Academy of Sciences. 1953–1959. *Physical Regionalization of China*, 8 volumes. Beijing: Science Press (in Chinese).

Chinese Academy of Sciences, 1979–1988. *Physical Geography of China*, 12 volumes. Beijing: Science Press (in Chinese).

Chinese Academy of Sciences. 1978–1990. *Natural 1:1,000,000 Classification and Mapping of Land Resources.* Beijing: Science Press (in Chinese).

China State Statistical Bureau. 1991. *Statistical Yearbook of China.* Beijing: China Statistical Publishing House.

Commission of Integrated Survey on Natural Resources, Chinese Academy of Sciences. 1990. *Handbook of Natural Resources in China.* Beijing: Science Press (in Chinese).

Cressey, G. B. 1934. *China's Geographic Foundations: A Survey of the Land and Its People.* New York: McGraw-Hill Book Co.

Goodman, D.S.G. 1989. *China's Regional Development.* London: Routledge.

Pannell, C. W. and L. Ma. 1983. *China: The Geography of Development and Modernization.* London: Edward Arnold, New York: Halsted/Wiley.

ousons. Géographie universelle, tome d Colin. (in French).

phy of China. Beijing: Higher Education: Culture University Press, 1990 (in

ina: A Geographical Survey. New York:

. Physical Geography of China. Beijing: w York: Wiley.

PART ONE

General Survey: The Environment–Resource–Population–Development System

The geographical factors in China, both physical and human, are interrelated in a dynamic environment–resource–population–development system. In the following eleven chapters we shall discuss and analyze, one by one, the major component factors: physical features, natural resources, historical background, agricultural development, modern industries, modern transportation and foreign trade, ethnic groups, population dilemma, urban development, environmental problems and natural hazards, and the land–food–population system.

CHAPTER ONE

Physical Features[1]

Characteristic of the physical environment of China are mountainous topography, monsoon climate, many big rivers, and conspicuous areal differentiation.

MAJOR FACTORS SHAPING CHINA'S PHYSICAL ENVIRONMENT

China's physical environments have been shaped chiefly by the interaction and integration of five major factors: vast area, mid-latitude and east coast location, mountainous topography, complex geological history, and the significant impact of human activity.

Vast Area

China has a land area of 9.6 million sq km, occupying 6.5 percent of the total land area of the world. Only Russia[2] and Canada are larger, but both of them are located near frigid Arctic regions. Only the United States has approximately the same land area as well as similarly favorable natural conditions. Table 1.1 shows the land areas of some selected countries and their percentage of the world's total.

From the confluence of the Heilong Jiang and its tributary, the Wusuli River, westward to the Pamir Plateau is a distance of more than 5200 km. When the noon sun shines brilliantly over the Wusuli, it is still early morning on the Pamir. From midstream in the Heilong Jiang north of Mohe southward to the Nansha Islands near the equator the distance is more than 5500 km. When blizzards still threaten the Heilong Jiang in winter, spring sowing is underway on Hainan Island, while the Nansha Islands remain hot and humid all year around.

Besides a vast land area, China also has extensive neighboring seas. One territorial sea—the Bohai—and three neighboring seas—the Yellow Sea (Huang Hai), the East China Sea (Dong Hai), and the South China Sea (Nan Hai)—together have an area of about 4.73

TABLE 1.1
Land Areas of Selected Countries in the World

Country	Land area (in 10^4 sq km)	Percentage of total world land area
USSR* (in 1990)	2240	15.0
Canada	995	6.7
China	960	6.5
USA	936	6.3
Brazil	851	5.7
Australia	770	5.2
India	295	2.0
Saudi Arabia	240	1.6
Indonesia	190	1.3
France	55	0.37
Japan	37	0.25
UK	24	0.16

*The former USSR ceased to exist at end of 1991. The largest of its succesor states, Russia, has an area of 1710×10^4 sq km.

---

[1]This chapter is essentially a summary of the author's former book, *Physical Geography of China*, with some updating and revision.

[2]The former Soviet Union (USSR) had a territory of 22.4 million sq km; the present Russia has 17.1 million sq km.

million sq km. Both the vast land area and extensive sea area provide a large spatial basis for different geographical elements and geographical processes as well as rich natural resources (see Chapter Two).

Mid-latitude and East-coast Location

China has a geographical location for temperate and subtropical climates. Latitudinally, the country stretches from 3°50′N up to 53°31′N. With the cumulative temperature during the ≥ 10°C period as the chief criterion (Figure 1.1), from south to north, six temperature zones might be identified (not including the Tibetan Plateau), as shown in Table 1.2. As about 98 percent of the land area is located between 20° and 50°N, the temperate zone (including cool temperate and warm temperate) and the subtropical zone are most extensive, accounting for 45.6 percent and 26.1 percent of the total land area, respectively.

China is sandwiched between the largest continent (Eurasia) and the largest ocean (Pacific). Consequently the monsoon climate is very well developed. During the summertime, high temperatures together with plentiful rainfall make agriculture quite productive. The extensive subtropical zone in a planetary wind system should be characterized by little precipitation. However, in China this region has favorable temperature and moisture conditions for agricultural production. As moisture in the atmosphere over China comes mainly from the warm and moist summer maritime monsoon, precipitation is closely related to distance from the sea. The greater the distance from the sea, the less plentiful is the precipitation and the drier the climate. The Physical Regionalization Working Committee of the Chinese Acad-

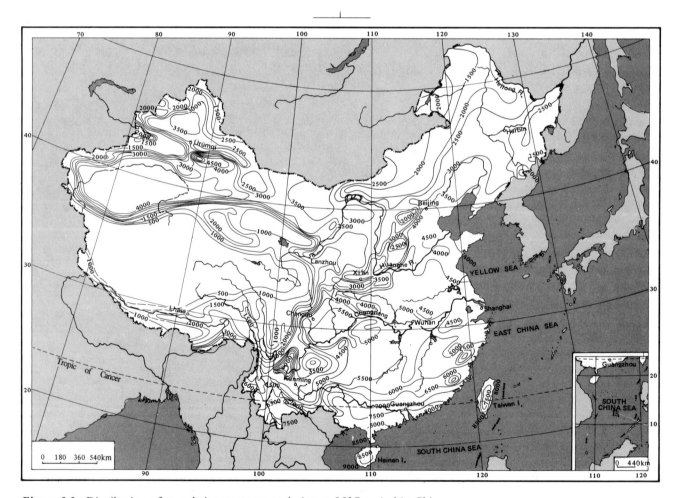

Figure 1.1 Distribution of cumulative temperature during ≥ 10°C period in China.

TABLE 1.2
Temperature Zones in China (From South to North)

Temperature zone	Accumulated temperature (during ≥ 10°C period)	Features
Equatorial	Around 9500°C	Hot and humid all year round; rainforest; laterite
Tropical	8000°C–9000°C	Coldest month > 16°C; monsoon forests; lateritic soil
Subtropical	4500°C–8000°C	Coldest month 0°C to 16°C; evergreen forests
Warm temperate	3200°C–4500°C	Coldest month −8°C to 0°C; deciduous forests
Temperate	1700°C–3200°C	Coldest month −24°C to −8°C; mixed broad- and needle-leaved forests
Cool temperate	Around 1700°C	Coldest month < −24°C; Taiga forests

emy of Sciences in 1958 adopted the aridity index (the ratio between potential evaporation and precipitation)[3] as the chief criterion to divide China into four moisture zones from southeast to northwest (Figure 1.2):

1. *Humid:* aridity index (k) < 1.0, dominant natural vegetation being forest, occupying 32.2 percent of the total land area.

2. *Subhumid:* k = 1.0 to 1.5, dominant natural vegetation being forest-steppe, occupying 14.5 percent of the total land area.

3. *Semi-arid:* k = 1.5 to 2.0, dominant natural vegetation being steppe, occupying 21.7 percent of the total land area.

4. *Arid:* k ≥ 2.0, dominant natural vegetation being desert-steppe (when k = 2.0 to 4.0) and desert (when k ≥ 4.0), occupying 30.8 percent of the total land area.

Furthermore, a vast inland area and an east coast location lead to a conspicuous continentality in climate, even in the coastal area. Influence of the westerlies is usually negligible in any amelioration of the warm Kuroshio Current during winter, owing to offshore winds, and the Coriolis force deflects away from the Chinese coast. Hence, a continental climate is well developed in China, generally with warmer summer and much colder winter when compared with west coast

areas at similar latitudes. For example, Huma in Heilongjiang Province lies at about the same latitude as London (51.5°N), but Huma has a mean January temperature as low as −27.8°C, whereas London, with 3°C, is similar to Shanghai, which is located at about 31.2°N.

Mountainous Topography

China is a mountainous country, with hills, mountains, and high plateaus occupying about 65 percent of the total land area (Color Plate 1). According to an estimate (Table 1.4), land of less than 500 m in elevation above sea level occupies only 25.2 percent, while that above 3000 m occupies 25.9 percent. In the world, there are 12 high peaks higher than 8000 m; 7 of them are located in China. The highest peak in the world, Mount Qomolangma (8848 m),[4] stands majestically on the border between China and Nepal (Color Plate 2).

China is remarkable not only for its absolute relief, but also its relative relief; consequently, vertical zonation is often conspicuous, sometimes even overshowing horizontal zonation. The second-lowest land in the world (−155 m) lies in Ayding Lake of the Turpan Basin, which is located at the southern piedmont of the 5445 m high snow-capped Mount Bogda of the Tianshan Mountains. Another contrast is in the Medog area of the southern Tibetan Plateau, where there are differences in elevation of more than 7000 m in a horizontal distance of less than 40 km. A tropical, humid forest landscape dominates in the Yarlung Zangbo valley, while on top of nearby mount Namjagbarwa (7756 m), there is eternal snow. Generally speaking, changes of 100 m in vertical

---

[3]The aridity index (k) is calculated by the following empirical formula:

$$k = 0.16 \frac{\Sigma t \geq 10°}{\Sigma r \geq 10°}$$

where $\Sigma t \geq 10°$ is the cumulative temperature during the ≥ 10° period, in °C; $\Sigma r \geq 10°$ is the cumulative precipitation during the same period in mm; 0.16 is a constant under Chinese climatic conditions.

[4]Also known as Mount Everest in the Western world. In Tibetan, *Qomo* is the name of a fairy, while *langma* is a young lady.

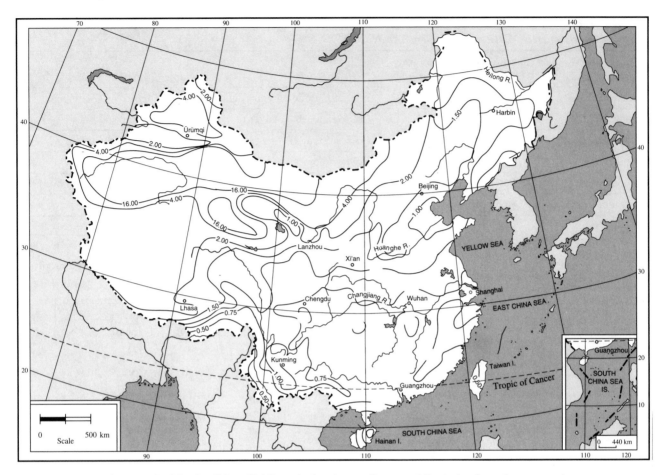

Figure 1.2 Distribution of aridity in China. (Aridity calculated according to aridity index formula; see text.)

relief correspond to horizontal (latitudinal) changes of about 100 km in their impact on geographical environment.

There are five major mountain systems in China (Figure 1.3):

1. ***The east–west trending mountain system:*** the Tianshan–Yinshan–Yanshan mountain subsystem, the Kunlung–Qinling–Dabie mountain subsystem (Color Plate 3), and the Nanling mountain subsystem. All are important geographical barriers and divides.

2. ***The north–south trending mountain system:*** mainly controlled by the so-called longitudinal structures system, including the Helan Mountains, the Liupan Mountains, and the Hengduan (Traverse) Mountains.

3. ***The northeast-trending mountain system:*** mainly determined by the so-called cathaysian structure sys-

tem and located east of the longitudinal structure system. Examples include the Greater Hinggan Mountains, the Taihang Mountains, and the Wushan Mountains.

4. ***The northwest-trending mountain system:*** mainly determined by the so-called west-domain structure system and located west of the longitudinal structure system. Examples include the Altay Mountains and the Qilian Mountains.

5. ***The arc mountain system:*** located mainly along the southeastern margin of the Eurasia Plate. Examples include the Himalaya Mountains and the Taiwan Mountains.

These mountains, together with numerous intermontane plateaus, basins, and plains are interwoven into three macro-scale landform complexes in China:

1. ***The gigantic Tibetan Plateau (Color Plate 4):*** with an area of about 2.5 million sq km and an

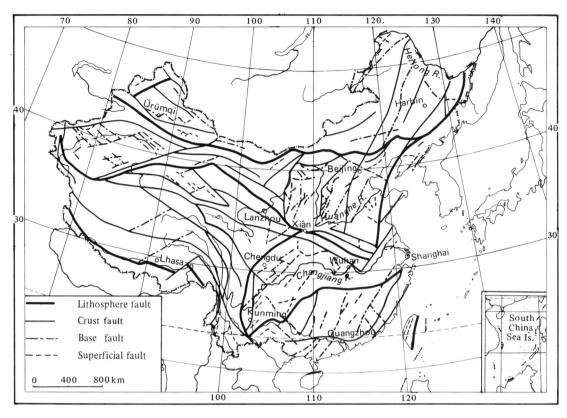

Figure 1.3 Distribution of major fault structures in China.

average elevation of about 4000 m, uplifted and located in the southwestern part of China.

2. The land areas in most parts of China are interwoven checkerboards of mountain ranges, plateaus, basins, and plains of different size and elevation.

3. The continental margin, which is composed of hills, plains, coasts, islands, and continental shelves.

Such mountainous topography makes China quite rich in mineral resources but comparatively poor in arable land (see Chapter Two). The mountainous topography also exerts a great influence on climate and other physical elements. Relief causes redistribution of temperature and moisture, which in turn, leads to vertical zonation of climate, soil, and vegetation. Furthermore, in the flow of energy and matter in a physical environment, mountains act as barriers and detainers. For example, the Qinling Mountains act as a barrier to the southward advance of cold waves and can be distinguished as the greatest divide between northern and southern China. In January, Ankang (about 33°N), on the southern flank of the mountains, compared with Xi'an (about 34°N), on the northern flank, has a mean temperature that is

higher by 4.2°C and an absolute minimum temperature that is higher by 11.1°C. In comparison, on the eastern coastal plain, which does not enjoy the protection of the Qinling, Bengbu and Xuzhou with a similar difference in latitude display temperature differences of only 1.6°C and 3.0°C, respectively.

The huge impact of the lofty Tibetan Plateau on the Chinese geographic environment should be emphatically pointed out. The formation of the monsoon climate and the accelerating desiccation of Northwest China have been closely correlated with the uplifting of the Tibetan Plateau, which has been caused by the Himalayan tectonic movement that has continued since the Miocene epoch. In the late Pliocene epoch, when the Tibetan Plateau attained an elevation of about 1000 m above sea level, the Chinese monsoon system was not yet formed, and there was only a weak high pressure belt near present-day Lhasa (about 30°N). At the end of the Tertiary, the Tibetan Plateau, together with its neighboring region, was violently uplifted. The plateau surface attained an elevation of 3000 m, and the weak high pressure belt near Lhasa was strengthened and pushed northward to the southern rim of the Tarim Basin, about 40°N. Yet, not until the late Pleistocene to early Holocene, when the Tibetan Plateau and its neighboring areas underwent violent uplifting again and the plateau surface attained its present elevation of more than 4000 m, did the modern Chinese monsoon system and the extensive desert areas in Northwest China fully develop. Since then, the Siberia-Mongolia high pressure has been pushed northward to its present position at about 55°N. Today, the Tibetan Plateau still exerts a great influence on the climate of surrounding regions. Its thermodynamic effects cause the peculiar plateau monsoons over the eastern part of the Tibetan Plateau: a northeastern monsoon during winter and a southwestern monsoon during summer. The west wind currents passing through the plateau are also bifurcated into southern and northern branches during winter.

Complex Geological History

The physical geographical environment is a function of latitudinal, longitudinal, and vertical dimensions as well as time. Thus, the present Chinese physical environment is an end product of a long, complicated geological history. According to plate tectonic theory, China is mainly situated on the Eurasian Plate bordering the Indo-Australian Plate on the south and the Pacific Plate and the Philippine Plate on the east. China's geological history is essentially a long, complex process of tectonic movement and interaction both between the Chinese Platform and its surrounding folding belts inside the Eurasia Plate and between the Eurasia Plate and its neighbors.

The Indo-China tectonic movement during the early Mesozoic era began a new epoch for the Chinese mainland; henceforth, it became essentially a continuous, vast land area. The Yanshan tectonic movement during the late Mesozoic era had even greater impacts on the Chinese physical environment; it determined the broad geological structures and macro-geomorphological features of China. After this tectonic movement until the early Tertiary period was a relative quiet, stable time in China. Most of the land area was peneplaned, with level and undulating topography predominating. The climate was much warmer than it is now, with the northern limit of the subtropical zone pushing northward more than 7° to 10° in latitude. However, the modern monsoon system was not yet established.

The supposed thrust of the Indo-Australia Plate underneath the Eurasia Plate and the impacts of the Himalayan tectonic movement since the Miocene epoch have been the dominant forces in shaping the modern Chi-

nese physical environment at its most recent stage. The Himalayas and the Taiwan folding belts have thus been formed. The Tibetan Plateau has also been uplifted, and in turn has been the major cause in the formation of the modern monsoon system in Asia. Consequently, three great natural realms have been identified in China: Humid Eastern Monsoon China, Northwest Arid China, and the Tibetan Frigid Plateau. In Eastern Monsoon China north of the January mean 0°C isotherm, which runs approximately along a line extending from the mouth of the Chang Jiang westward to northwestern Yunnan Plateau, the climate has become much cooler, changing from a subtropical to a temperate environment, with landforms exhibiting a remnant reddish weathering crust distributed as far north as the southern slopes of the Greater Hinggan Mountains and the Altay Mountains. South of this line, the climate has shifted from a semiarid trade wind to a moist monsoon climate.

Significant Impact of Human Activity

China has a very long agricultural history and a huge population; hence, humans have made very significant impacts on the physical environment. As early as 1.7 million years ago, there already were tribes of *Homo erectus* in Chinese territory. Agricultural activity on the Loess Plateau and its surrounding areas started 7000 to 8000 years ago, and on the southeastern coast, more than 7000 years ago (see Chapter Three). Table 1.3 shows a brief outline of Chinese history. At present, China has about 100 million ha of cropland and more than 1.1 billion inhabitants. Practically no more virgin land or primary vegetation still exists in China, and humankind has made a significant imprint nearly everywhere. Hence, G. B. Cressey once aptly remarked, "The most significant element in the Chinese landscape is thus not the soil or vegetation or the climate, but the people. Everywhere there are human beings. In this old, old land, one can scarcely find a spot unmodified by man's activities."[5]

In a country with an agricultural history of about 80 centuries and with almost four-fifths of the population still engaged in agriculture, agricultural development is naturally the most important human activity and exerts the heaviest impact on the physical environment. Chinese farmers in the hundreds of millions have worked upon the Chinese physical environment, making a living

---

[5] G. B. Cressey, *China's Geographic Foundations: A Survey of the Land and Its People.* New York: McGraw-Hill Book Co. 1934, p. 1.

TABLE 1.3
A Brief Outline of Chinese History

Stages (Dynasties)	Age
Yuanmou Man	About 1.7 million years ago (B.P.)
Peking Man (Lantian Man) (*Homo erectus*)	About 0.7–0.2 million years ago
Upper Cave Man (*Homo sapiens*)	About 18,000 years ago
Dadiwan (Cishan, Peiligang, Hemudu) Culture	About 8000–7000 years ago
Yangshao Culture	About 6000–5000 years ago
Longshan Culture	About 5000–4000 years ago
Xia Dynasty	?2206–1766 B.C.
Shang Dynasty	1766–1126 B.C.
Western Zhou Dynasty	1126–771 B.C.
Spring and Autumn Period (Eastern Zhou Dynasty)	771–403 B.C.
Warring States	403–211 B.C.
Qin Dynasty	211–206 B.C.
Western Han Dynasty	206 B.C.–A.D. 9
Eastern Han Dynasty	A.D. 25–220
Three Kingdoms	A.D. 220–289
Western Jin Dynasty	A.D. 280–316
Southern & Northern Dynasties	A.D. 317–589
Sui Dynasty	A.D. 589–618
Tang Dynasty	A.D. 618–907
Five Dynasties	A.D. 907–960
Northern Song Dynasty	A.D. 960–1126
Southern Song Dynasty	A.D. 1126–1279
Yuan Dynasty	A.D. 1279–1368
Ming Dynasty	A.D. 1368–1644
Qing Dynasty	A.D. 1644–1911
Republic of China	A.D. 1911–1949
People's Republic of China	1949–present

Zhao Songqiao, Geography of China

from it and transforming it tremendously (for details, see Chapters Four and Ten).

CLIMATIC FEATURES

The Chinese climate has three features. First, the monsoon climate is dominant, with significant changes or even reversal of wind direction between winter and summer as well as seasonal variation in precipitation according to whether the maritime monsoon advances or retreats. Second, continentality is rather conspicuous.

Third, there are many climatic types in China, some of them unique.

The Monsoon Climate

During the winter, the polar air mass controls China's climate. There is a high pressure ridge over the upper troposphere between 90° and 100°E. The cold air mass behind it moves incessantly southward and deepens the cold high pressure near the ground—the Siberia-Mongolia high pressure. Consequently, the cold, dry northern monsoon dominates the lower troposphere in China.

On the other hand, during the summer, the Chinese mainland is chiefly controlled by the tropical and subtropical maritime air mass. There is a low pressure trough in the upper troposphere between 70° and 80°E and a shallow high pressure ridge along the coast; the pressure systems near the ground are represented by the Indian warm low pressure over most parts of Eurasia, coupled with the maritime high pressure over the Pacific and Indian oceans. Hence, the warm, moist southern and southeastern monsoons dominate the lower troposphere over China.

The location of the main rain belt is closely related to the advance and retreat of the summer monsoons in China, and the beginning and ending of the rainy season are closely correlated with these monsoon systems. Whenever the front of the summer monsoons arrives, the rainy season begins. Generally speaking, the dividing line between the southeastern (Pacific) and the southwestern (Indian) monsoon lies from 105° to 110°E. To the east, the southeastern monsoon begins in South China as early as March, moves to Central China in June, to North and Northeast China in July, and then retreats rapidly southward during late August and early September. It takes only one month to retreat entirely from the Chinese mainland. In close correlation with the advance and retreat of the summer monsoons, the rainy season starts in early April in South China, early June in Central China, and early July in North and Northeast China. In Southwest China, the southwestern monsoon dominates; it bursts northward in late May when the rainy season in Yunnan and western Sichuan begins. It does not stop until October when the southwestern monsoon retreats rapidly southward.

Chief Climatic Elements

Temperature

The distribution of temperature in China is chiefly determined by latitude and topography. China has a vast area; hence, there is a great difference in temperature between the south and the north. Annual mean temperature in the Nansha Islands is about 25°C, whereas in northern Heilongjiang Province it is below 5°C. In Eastern Monsoon China, following the sequence of temperature belts from south to north, the annual mean temperature is above 20°C south of the Nanling Mountains, about 10°C in the Chang Jiang valley, between 12° and 14°C in the Yellow River basin, below 10°C north of the Great Wall, and below 0°C in the Greater and Lesser Hinggan Mountains. In Northwest Arid China, the annual mean

temperature ranges from 0°C to 10°C. The Tibetan Frigid Plateau has an annual mean temperature below 0°C, while its northwestern part, the Qingtang (Changtang) Plateau (elevation 4500–4800 m) has an annual mean temperature below −8°C.

As China is essentially a monsoon country, seasonal change in temperature is pronounced, and annual mean temperature has little significance for illustrating the true climatic condition of an area. Therefore, it is preferable to discuss climate in terms of the seasons, especially conditions during January and July, which represent the conditions of winter and summer, respectively. Figure 1.4 shows the distribution of mean January temperatures in China. The isotherms run generally latitudinally, closely paralleling each other. From Heilongjiang Province to Hainan Province, the temperature differs about 1.5°C for each degree of latitude. The January −6°C isotherm (the boundary between spring and winter wheat) runs roughly along the Great Wall, and the January 0°C isotherm is approximately at the Qinling–Huai He line. The minimum January temperature has been recorded as low as −52.3°C at Mohe. In South China, the absolute minimum temperature might also drop below 0°C. Even in northern Hainan Island and southern Taiwan Island, freezing temperatures might occasionally occur. Hence, low temperature and frost are frequent hazards to agriculture in China.

Figure 1.5 shows the distribution of mean July temperatures in China. The influence of latitude on temperature is reduced to its minimum, with a difference of only 0.2°C in temperature for each degree of latitude. Isotherms are widely spaced. They are arranged in a longitudinal pattern, generally paralleling the coast. Most parts of China have a mean July temperature of between 20° and 28°C. There are two high temperature centers: one around Poyang Lake and another in the Turpan Basin, both with a mean July temperature above 30°C. Hence, four big cities in the middle and lower Chang Jiang valley—Wuhan, Changsha, Chongqing, and Nanjing—are known as the "four ovens" in summer, while the Turpan Basin with the highest recorded temperature in China (47.6°C), was called Fire Prefecture as early as 1000 years ago.

Precipitation

Figure 1.6 shows the distribution of annual precipitation in China. The isohyets run generally parallel to the coast, and annual precipitation decreases from southeast to northwest. The 500 mm isohyet is a rough dividing line: northwest of it, precipitation is scarce, resulting in

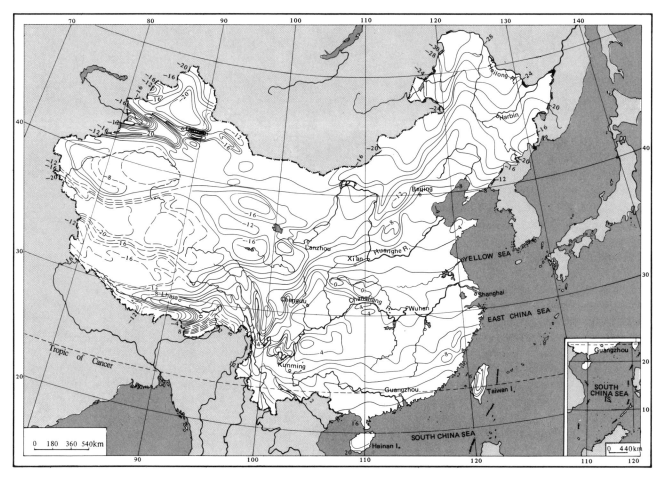

Figure 1.4 Distribution of mean January temperatures in China.

chiefly pastoral areas; southeast of it, precipitation is abundant, giving rise to the chief farming areas of China. The 750 mm isohyet generally follows the Qinling Mountains–Huaihe River line; it is the divide between the paddy rice areas in southern China and the dry farmlands in northern China. The heaviest precipitation occurs along coastal hills and mountains with more than 1500–2000 mm annually. The highest annual precipitation in China has been recorded in Haoshaoliao (northeastern Taiwan Island) with a mean annual precipitation of 6570 mm (a record of 8408 mm in 1912). The driest area is the mountain-enclosed heart of the Eurasia continent, the eastern Tarim Basin, with a mean annual precipitation of less than 50 mm; the lowest record in China is 3.9 mm (a record of 0.5 mm in 1968) at Toksun in the Turpan Basin.

Seasonal distribution of precipitation is uneven. Most areas have their annual precipitation concentrated in summer when the warm, moist maritime monsoon dominates. Precipitation in one month usually accounts for more than one-quarter or even one-half of the annual total. In southern China, because of the earlier arrival of the maritime monsoon, spring is the most important rainy season, followed by summer. In northern China, however, summer rain comprises more than one-half of the total annual precipitation, and there is a pronounced spring drought. In Southwest China and the southern Tibetan Plateau, where the southwestern Indian monsoon is the chief moisture source, there is a clear-cut rainy and dry season. The rainy season begins in May and ends in October, accounting for 80–90 percent of the total annual precipitation. Only a few areas in China have a rather even seasonal distribution of precipitation, such as the Ili Valley and the Altay Mountains in Xinjiang, with about 20–30 percent of the total annual precipitation occurring in each season. Even fewer areas have a winter maximum; the most famous example being northeastern Taiwan Island where the northeastern con-

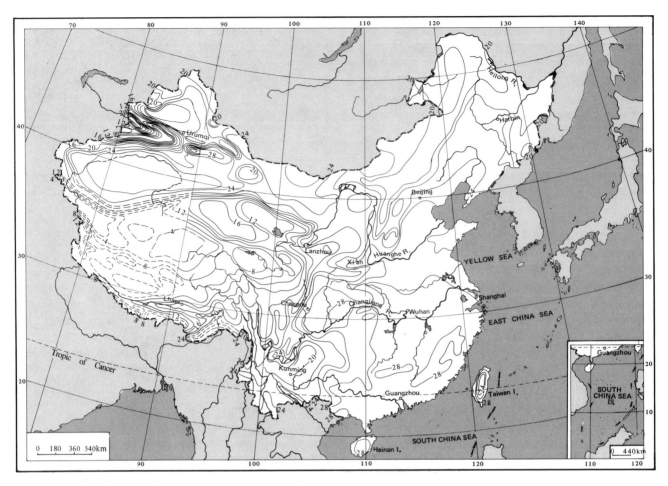

Figure 1.5 Distribution of mean July temperatures in China.

tinental monsoon, after traveling a long distance over the sea, brings the chief moisture source with more than 30 percent of the total annual precipitation occurring in winter.

Annual variability in precipitation is also great, often leading to disastrous droughts as well as floods. As a rule, the more abundant the annual precipitation, the smaller its annual variability, and vice versa. The humid coastal areas usually have less than 20 percent of annual variability, but Northwest Arid China generally has more than 30 percent, or even more than 50 percent in the eastern Tarim Basin. In the extreme case of Turpan, August precipitation in 1958 totaled 42.1 mm, which is 2.5 times the mean total annual precipitation.

Wind

The distribution and velocity of near-ground winds are chiefly determined by pressure systems in the atmo-

sphere. In winter, continental high pressure dominates the atmosphere over southern Siberia and the Mongolian Plateau. From that sector blow the northwesterlies in Northeast and North China, as far south as the lower reaches of the Chang Jiang. Due to the Coriolis force, they become northeasterlies in South China and even easterlies or southeasternly winds on the Guizhou Plateau. In summer, the Chinese mainland becomes a thermal low pressure center, and southeasterlies dominate the coastal areas, turning to southerlies inland.

As a rule, North China has higher wind velocities than South China, the coasts higher than inland, the plains and plateaus higher than the mountain areas. The southeastern coast and northern Inner Mongolia have an annual mean wind velocity higher than 4–5 m/sec. Wind velocity is generally greatest in spring and winter and least in summer. Yet, in coastal areas south of 30°N, because of frequent typhoons, mean wind velocity is

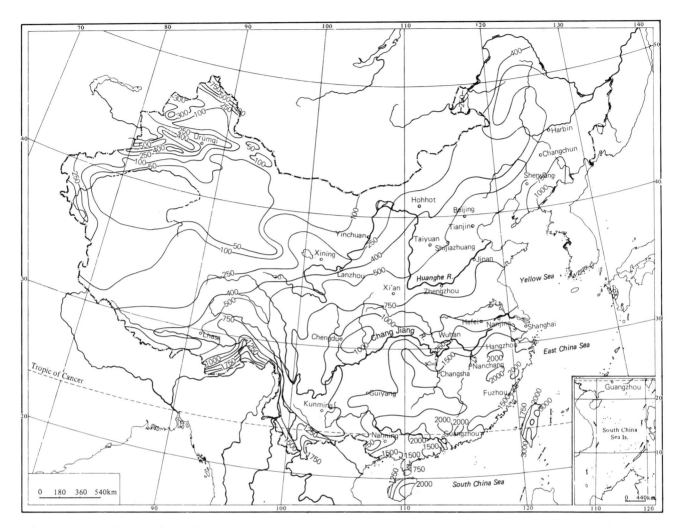

Figure 1.6 Distribution of annual precipitation in China.

highest in autumn, but in Northwest Arid China it is highest in summer.

Some Special Weather Phenomena

Following the advance and retreat of the monsoons, a series of special weather phenomena occurs; the following three are the most outstanding and relevant to agricultural production.

Cold Waves

Cold waves are a frequent, large-scale atmospheric phenomenon, occurring on the average of once every 10 days during late autumn, winter, and spring. The cold wave front usually "bursts" with strong northwesternly winds. At first, there are sandstorms or snowstorms in North and Northeast China, heavy precipitation (rain or snow) in Central China, and continuous rain in South China. Then, when the polar continental air mass controls the whole region, the weather is cold, warming up gradually until the arrival of the next cold wave.

A cold wave together with its accompanying strong northernly wind and sharp decrease in temperature is unfavorable, sometimes even causing great harm to agricultural production. It increases the frost hazard and restricts the growing season. Even as far south as northern Hainan Island (about 18°N), a strong cold wave can break through a series of mountain barriers—the Yinshan Mountains, the Qinling Mountains, and the

Nanling Mountains—and inflict great havoc on cold-sensitive tropical crops. Therefore, good weather forecasting and effective measures for protecting crops and livestock are of paramount importance in winter.

Plum Rain

The plum rain is a special weather phenomenon occurring in the middle and lower Chang Jiang and the Huai He river basins during late spring and early summer. Its name comes from the rain's arrival at the time when the plum fruit is ripening. The weather is continuously rainy, with moderate temperatures, low wind velocity, and high relative humidity. It feels stifling and uncomfortable, and clothes and other belongings may even become moldy.

In June, the planetary wind system moves northward, and tropical maritime air mass reaches the Chang Jiang valley. The polar front, which is a product of interaction between the polar and tropical air masses, is located over the Huai He basin and the lower Chang Jiang valley. When newly arrived northwestern cold air forms a cyclone or low pressure trough along the polar front, its further eastward movement is blocked and prolonged rainy days occur in this area. Total precipitation during this period is determined by frequency and intensity of newly arrived northwestern cold air; the stronger and more frequent the cold air, the more plentiful the precipitation, and vice versa.

Plum rain usually starts with the onset of the summer monsoon in this area in early or mid-June. The total duration is about one month, with the rain generally ending in early or mid-July. Yet, the dates of its commencement and conclusion can vary greatly. For example, the statistical data of five cities (Shanghai, Nanjing, Wuhu, Jiujiang, and Wuhan) show that between 1885 and 1974 the earliest starting date of the plum rain was May 26 (1896); the latest, July 4 (1954). The earliest and latest concluding dates were June 16 (1961) and August 1 (1954), respectively.

As this is the greatest paddy rice-producing area in China, the plum rain is a very significant factor in agricultural production. It is especially favorable for paddy rice growing. If it fails to come on time, and thus does not bring the all-important moisture, the local farmers express their complaint in a proverb, "Little rain in plum rain month means disaster for the next six months."

Typhoons

Originating mostly in the western Pacific Ocean and sometimes in the South China Sea, these tropical cyclones hit the Chinese coast during the summer and autumn. According to statistics for the 30 years between 1949 and 1979, there were 276 typhoons that struck the Chinese coast. Among the coastal provinces Guangdong (including Hainan) ranks first with 48.2 percent of the total landed typhoons; Taiwan is second, with 20.1 percent; Fujian third, with 18.1 percent; and all coastal provinces north of Shanghai account for only 6.2 percent. As for the seasonal distribution, 79.7 percent of the typhoons strike China from July through September. In October and June, they are much less active, and are restricted mostly to Guangdong, Hainan, Guangxi, and Taiwan. In November and May, they appear only occasionally in southern coastal provinces. The earliest recorded typhoon struck Hainan Island on May 11, 1954; the latest, Taishan (Guangdong) on December 2, 1974.

Typhoons bring not only high winds but also heavy rain. Between September 9 and 12, 1963, one strong typhoon landed on Taiwan; the montane meteorological station near Taibei (elevation: 1936 m) recorded total precipitation of 1684.0 mm in four days, of which 1172.2 mm fell in one single day (September 2). The maximum downpour for 24 hours was 1247.9 mm. The typhoon rains play an important role in Chinese coastal provinces; they make up more than 20 percent of the total annual precipitation south of Wenzhou (Zhejiang) and nearly 40 percent in southern Hainan. North of Wenzhou, they account for about 10 percent. From July through September, the typhoon rain is even more important, comprising more than 50 percent of the monthly precipitation in Fujian and southern Zhejiang coast.

High winds and heavy rains that accompany typhoons are a great hazard to coastal fishing and shipping, but more important, they can inflict a toll on human life and produce heavy flooding in the areas where they strike. Hence, reliable forecasting and effective precautions are absolutely necessary. On the other hand, the typhoons are sometimes quite beneficial. When the polar frontal rain belt has already moved northward to northern China, the middle and the lower Chang Jiang valley, the most important farming area in China, is controlled by subtropical high pressure, which subjects it to mid-summer drought. The heavy typhoon rains bring a most welcome relief. The hundreds of millions of Chinese who live in southern China endure oppressive summer heat and find the typhoon with its high wind and heavy rain a great, although temporary, relief.

GEOMORPHOLOGICAL FEATURES

In the vast domain of China, topographical and geomorphic conditions are quite varied. Not only are there numerous high mountains, extensive plateaus, enclosed inland basins, and fertile low plains, but there are also long, curved coastlines, thousands of sea islands, and broad continental shelves. Landforms of China have three major geomorphological characteristics.

The Four Great Topographic Steps

The topography of China from the mighty and towering Tibetan Plateau eastward, is broadly arranged into four great steps (Figure 1.7).

The Tibetan Plateau

The Tibetan Plateau with an area of about 2.5 million sq km, is the westernmost great topographic step. Its eastern and northern borders roughly coincide with the 3000 m contour line. The plateau generally has an elevation of 4000–5000 m, and hence is called the "roof of the world." On the plateau, there extend many east–west or northwest–southeast trending mountains of enormous height, usually more than 5000–6000 m. Some are even more than 7000–8000 m high, such as the Kunlun Mountains, the Gangdise Mountains, the Nyainqentanglha Mountains, the Tanggula Mountains, and the Himalaya Mountains. The last-named range, with an average elevation above 6000 m and containing the world's highest peak (Mount Qomolangma) at 8848 m, form the highest mountain range in the world. Between these lofty ranges, there are extensive rolling basins studded with numerous saline lakes. On the southeastern border of the Tibetan Plateau, however, all mountain ranges turn southeastward or due north–south, forming the famous Hengduan Mountain system with deep gorges cut by the upper reaches of the Chang Jiang, the Nu Jiang (the Salween River), the Lancang Jiang (the Mekong River), and their tributaries. The gorges are tightly sandwiched between high, steep mountain slopes.

The Central Mountains and Plateaus

The second great topographic step lies eastward of the Tibetan Plateau north to the Greater Hinggan Mountains (the eastern margin of the Mongolian Plateau), the Taihang Mountains (the eastern margin of the Loess Plateau), and the Wushan Mountains (the eastern mar-gin of the Sichuan Basin). It is composed mainly of plateaus and basins with elevations of 1000–2000 m above sea level, such as the Inner Mongolian Plateau, the Ordos Plateau, the Loess Plateau, the Yunnan–Guizhou Plateau, and the Tarim, Junggar, and Sichuan basins. On the borders of these plateaus and basins are generally uplifted mountains with elevations of more than 3000 m, such as the Tianshan Mountains, with their highest peak (Mount Tomul) at an elevation of 7435 m.

The Plains

The third great topographic step extends eastward from the mountains and plateaus to the coast. Here lie the largest plains of China, such as the Northeast China Plain, the North China Plain, and the middle and lower Chang Jiang valley. They lie generally at elevations below 200 m. However, south of the Chang Jiang are extensive hilly lands, usually composed of red beds and igneous rocks with elevations below 500 m. Along the coast and between these plains and basins is a series of hills and mountains, generally with elevations of 500–1000 m.

China's coast—starting from the mouth of the Yalu River (the border river between China and Korea) and extending southwest to the mouth of the Beilun River (the border river between China and Vietnam)—has a total length of more than 18,000 km, not including islands and their coasts. Coasts along the Liaodong and Shandong peninsulas and south of the Hangzhou Estuary are rocky.

The Seas

The fourth great topographic step is composed of the neighboring seas together with their continental shelves. The depth of the seas is generally less than 200 m. There are more than 5000 islands in China's neighboring seas; many of them are rocky and uplifted. The largest island in China, Taiwan Island, is located in the arc mountain system along the southeastern margin of the Eurasian Plate and has 62 peaks towering above 3000 m, the highest (Mount Yu) at an elevation of 3950 m.

Mountainous Topography and a Checkerboard of Landforms

As we have mentioned, mountainous topography is one of the major factors shaping China's physical geographical environment. Five main mountain systems serve as

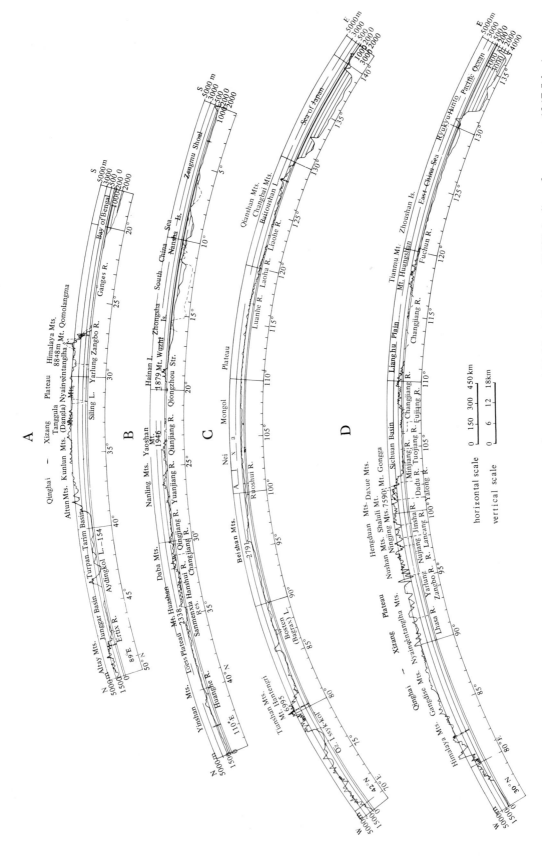

Figure 1.7 Topographical profiles in China. N–S: A. Along 89°E (radius of curvature 6367.5 km); B. Along 110°E (radius of curvature 6367.5 km); W–E: C. Along 42°N (radius of curvature 4730.7 km). D. Along 30°N (radius of curvature 5514.2 km).

TABLE 1.4
Land Area at Various Elevations in China

Elevation (m)	Area (10,000 sq km)	Percentage of total land area
<500	241.7	25.2
500–1000	162.5	16.9
1000–1500	174.6	18.2
1500–2000	65.3	6.8
2000–3000	67.6	7.0
>3000	248.3	25.9
Total	960.0	100.0

the backbones of China's three large-scale landform complexes and the four great topographic steps. On the Tibetan Plateau—the first topographic step—the Kunlun, Karakorum, Gangdise, Tanggula, Nyainqentanglha, Hengduan, Himalaya, and other high mountain systems form the backbone. In combination with intermontane basins they form the numerous elongated checkerboard landforms.

The second and the third topographic steps are also essentially composed of different-sized checkerboards of mountains, hills, plateaus, basins, and plains, in which mountains and hills usually dominate the landscape. All inland plateaus and basins are encircled and divided by high mountains and hills. Even in the Sichuan Basin, a part of the second great topographic step where the elevation is comparatively low, mountains and hills still dominate. Along the coast, southern Zhejiang Province is aptly described by the Chinese as "mountains with their enveloping clouds extending hundreds of kilometers, where thousands of families live amid pine forests and bamboo groves." The amount of land area at different elevations above sea level is shown in Table 1.4.

Chiefly on the basis of their elevation, mountains in China are classified into four categories:

1. *Extremely high mountains (higher than 5000 m):* generally covered year-round by snow and well-developed modern glaciation; located primarily on the first great topographic step.

2. *High mountains (between 3000 and 5000 m):* summits generally below the snow line but above the tree line; snow and ice process predominate, with well-developed periglacial landforms and ancient glaciation; located primarily in the second great topographical step.

3. *Middle mountains (between 1000 and 3000 m):* generally below the tree line; the process of erosion dominates (the process of desiccation dominates in arid zones), with conspicuous vertical zonation; most located in the second and third great topographic steps.

4. *Low mountains (elevations from 500 to 1000 m):* the process of erosion dominates (the process of desiccation dominates in arid zones), with vertical zonation not conspicuous; most located in the third great topographical step.

"Hills" generally have a relative relief less than 500 m and are scattered among all the four mountain types.

Broad Continental Shelves and Shallow Neighboring Seas

The fourth great topographical step in China is composed of the broad continental shelves and extensive shallow neighboring seas. Table 1.5 shows the chief features of the four neighboring seas. Except for the eastern margin of the East China Sea and the central sea basin of the South China Sea, all are located on broad continental shelves, with a water depth of a few dozen to a little more than 100 m. The extensive Yellow Sea–East China Sea continental shelf is one of the broadest and richest petroleum-bearing continental shelves in the world, with a width of more than 300 nautical miles. This continental shelf is a natural extension of the landmass into an

TABLE 1.5
Chief Features of Neighboring Seas

Sea	Sea area (sq km)	Water depth (m) Average	Water depth (m) Maximum
Bohai Sea	7,000	−18	−70
Yellow Sea (Huang Hai)	380,000	−44	−140
East China Sea (Dong Hai)	770,000	−370	−2,719
South China Sea (Nan Hai)	3,500,000	−1,212	−5,559

ocean basin; hence, its geological and geomorphological features are closely linked with the landmass. China's continental shelves generally have a level or rolling floor, gently dipping toward the southeast, and they feature many drowned deltas and ancient fluvial channels near the coast. Recent investigations have found that sea level has risen nearly 100 m since the late Pleistocene and early Holocene with the present sea level having been formed about 3000–5000 years ago.

SURFACE WATER AND GROUNDWATER

Water is an active and movable element in the physical geographical environment. It is also a natural resources essential to varied and intense agricultural and industrial activities (see Chapter Two). For example, total food production in China has more than tripled since 1949, and probably the most important ameliorating measure has been the construction of a series of hydroengineering works to improve the use of water resources. Since 1952, the amount of irrigated farmland in China has more than doubled.

Surface Water

Surface water consists chiefly of rivers and lakes, although it might also include glaciers and marshes. Glaciers are widely distributed on the Tibetan Plateau and in the lofty mountains of Northwest China with a total area of about 57,000 sq km and an estimated total water volume of about 2964 billion cu m. Marshes are also extensively distributed in Northeast China and on the northeastern Tibetan Plateau, with an area of more than 110,000 sq km. However, a detailed discussion of them will be omitted in this book.

Rivers

According to a recent estimate, the total length of all rivers in China amounts to about 420,000 km, and more than 5000 rivers have a drainage area of more than 100 sq km each. The annual discharge of all rivers totals more than 2600 billion cu m. Chief features of China's major rivers (each with a drainage area of more than 100,000 sq km) are listed in Table 1.6.

Rivers in China, owing chiefly to areal differences in climate and geomorphological conditions, can be divided into two great types of systems: oceanic and inland (interior). Oceanic systems include numerous large riv-

TABLE 1.6
Chief Features of Major Rivers in China *

River	Area (sq km)	Length (km)	Discharge Annual total ($10^8 m^3$)	Discharge Annual average (m^3/sec)
Heilong Jiang	888,502	3,101	1,181	3,740
Songhua Jiang	545,594	1,956	706.4	2,240
Nen Jiang	283,000	1,374	240.9	764
Liao He	219,014	1,390	144.8	459
Hai He	264,617	1,090	232.6	737
Yellow River (Huang He)	752,443	5,464	574.5	1,822
Wei He	134,766	818	98.0	311
Huai He	189,000	1,000	459.0	1,460
Chang Jiang	1,808,500	6,300	9,793.5	31,055
Jinsha Jiang	490,546	2,300	1,546.5	4,900
Han Shui	168,851	1,532	574.1	1,820
Jialing Jiang	159,638	1,119	694.1	2,200
Zhu Jiang	442,585	2,210	3,466	11,000
Lancang Jiang	164,766	2,354	692.9	2,200
Nu Jiang	134,882	2,013	656.7	2,000
Yarlung Zangbo	240,280	2,057	1,380	4,370

*Data for all international rivers (the Heilong or the Amur, the Lancang or Mekong, the Nu or Salween, the Yarlung or Bramaputra) include portions inside China only.

ers with abundant discharge, and drainage basins occupying about 64 percent of the country's total land area. Oceanic river systems can be again subdivided into Pacific, Indian, and Arctic drainage basins. Inland rivers, on the other hand, drain 36 percent of the total land area in China. There are a few perennial inland rivers, and large tracts have no runoff whatsoever. All inland rivers flow into saline inland lakes or die away into sandy deserts or salt marshes (Table 1.7).

As China has a vast territory with varied and complicated physical environments, surface runoff—as shown by annual runoff depth—naturally differs in different regions. As a whole, distribution of surface runoff decreases gradually from southeast to northwest (Figure 1.8) and essentially corresponds to the distribution of precipitation. Some isobaths of annual runoff depth are particularly meaningful.

1. An isobath of 50 mm annual runoff depth, which generally delimits the eastern boundary of the arid and semiarid areas, runs roughly from the western slope of the Greater Hinggan Mountains through the eastern part of the Northeast China Plain, the southern margin of the Inner Mongolian Plateau, the eastern margin of the Ordos Plateau, and up to the northern part of the Tibetan Plateau. It corresponds to a 400 mm isohyet of annual precipitation in its eastern part and a 200 mm isohyet in its western part. This isobath divides China into two major halves: the humid farming area of eastern China with abundant surface runoff, and arid pastoral western China with scanty surface runoff.

2. In eastern China, the 200 mm isobath is also an important divide. It corresponds roughly to the Qinling–Huaihe line, dividing Eastern Monsoon China into the North and the South. The latter has abundant surface runoff, generally more than 200 mm, while the former, except in some elevated areas, has less than 200 mm.

3. In the South, the 900 mm isobath is of great significance. It runs from the southern Hangzhou Estuary southwestward through a series of coastal mountains and hills to the Nanling Mountains. Southeast of this line lies the most abundant surface runoff belt in China.

4. The 10 mm isobath divides the arid area from the semiarid. In the semiarid area, a considerable amount of surface runoff still flows, whereas in the arid area, there is very little or no runoff.

TABLE 1.7
Areas of Major Drainage Basins in China

River systems and subsystems	Drainage basins	Area of drainage basins (1000 sq km)	Percentage of total land area
Oceanic system		6120.0	63.76
Pacific Ocean		5444.5	56.71
	Sea of Okhotsk	861.1	8.97
	Sea of Japan	32.6	0.34
	Bohai & Yellow Sea	1670.0	17.40
	East China Sea	2044.7	21.30
	South China Sea	825.0	8.59
	Directly into Pacific	11.1	0.10
Indian Ocean		624.6	6.52
	Bay of Bengal	558.3	5.83
	Arabian Sea	66.3	0.69
Arctic Ocean	Kara Sea	50.8	0.53
Inland system		3,480.0	36.24
	Inner Mongolia	328.7	3.42
	Gansu–Xinjiang–Qaidam	2,374.1	24.73
	Northern China	48.2	0.50
	Northern Tibetan Plateau	728.9	7.59
Grand total		9,600.0	100.00

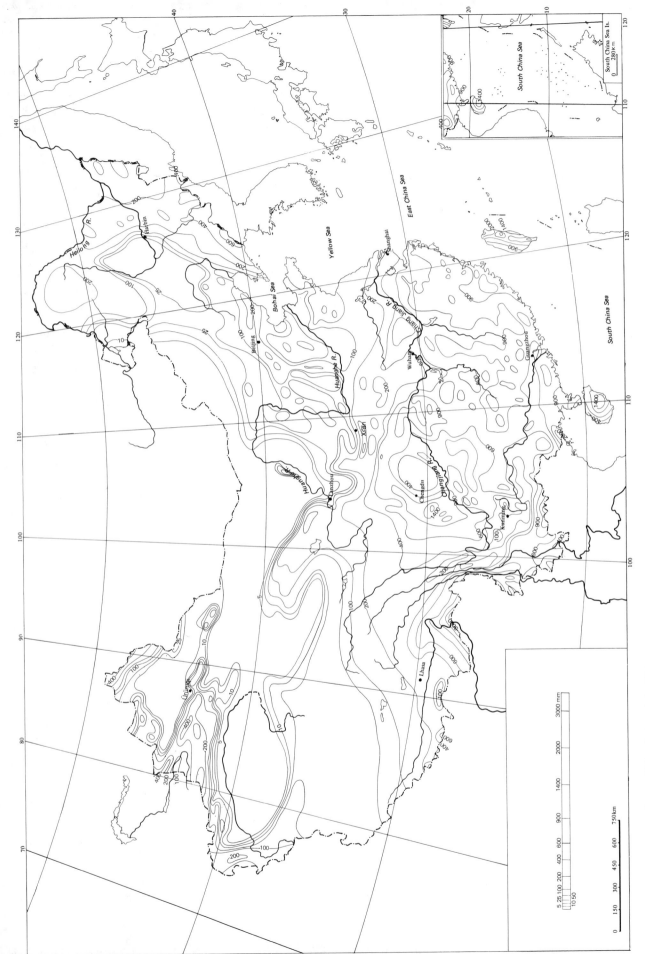

Figure 1.8 Annual runoff depth (mm) in China.

Lakes

China is also a country with numerous lakes. According to official statistics, there are approximately 2800 natural lakes, each with an area greater than 1 sq km, and a total lake area of more than 80,000 sq km. In addition, there are many artificial lakes—reservoirs—most constructed since 1949. The distribution of major lakes in China is shown in Table 1.8.

Groundwater

The vastness of China's territory and its varied natural conditions are again reflected in the formation and distribution of groundwater resources, which are distributed and concentrated mostly in several large alluvial plains (including the Northeast China Plain, the Hexi Corridor, the North China Plain, and the Middle and Lower Chang Jiang valley) and structural basins (such as the Tarim, Junggar, and Sichuan basins). In the extensive mountainous areas, geological structures and topographical conditions are quite complicated, resulting in varied conditions governing the formation and distribution of groundwater.

In arid and semiarid Northwest China, where both precipitation and surface water are scanty, exploitation of groundwater is of great significance. In some places it is the only source of water for irrigation as well as for drinking. In humid and subhumid Eastern Monsoon China, owing to rather uneven seasonal distribution of precipitation and fluvial runoff, exploitation of groundwater is also important as a supplement to irrigation during the dry season. For industrial and municipal use, groundwater sometimes has a great advantage over surface water. For example, groundwater is less subject to pollution. It is also much lower in temperature, so that it might be inexpensively used for cooling. Hence, many large cities in China, including Beijing, Xi'an, Jinan, Taiyuan, Baotou, and Ürümqi, take their municipal water supply mainly from groundwater supplies. Valuable ground hot water and mineral water resources are also widely distributed in China.

Shallow groundwater in China, chiefly based on porosity and other features of water-bearing strata, can be classified into four types:

1. *Pore water:* Contained in loose deposits, mainly distributed in the North China and Northeast China plains, on the Loess Plateau, and in piedmont plains and sandy deserts in Northwest China.

2. *Fracture water:* Contained in bedrock, widely distributed in mountain and hilly areas, and available mainly from fractures in the rock.

3. *Pore-fracture water:* Contained in permafrost regions, distributed chiefly on the Tibetan Plateau and northernmost Northeast China.

4. *Fracture-cave water:* Contained in karst regions, mainly located in Southwest and South China.

SOIL GEOGRAPHY

Vast size and complicated physical conditions make China rich and varied in soil resources. The Chinese

TABLE 1.8
Major Lakes in China (Area Exceeding 1,000 sq km)

Lake	Latitude	Longitude	Basin area (sq km)	Elevation (m, asl)	Maximum depth (m)	Total volume ($10^8 m^3$)
Qinghai	36°40′N	100°23′E	4,583	3,195.0	32.8	1,050.0
Poyang	29°05′N	116°23′E	3,583	21.0	16.0	248.9
Lop Nur	40°20′N	90°15′E	3,006	778.0	—	—
Dongting	29°20′N	112°50′E	2,820	34.5	30.8	188.0
Tai Hu	31°20′N	120°16′E	2,420	3.0	4.8	48.7
Hulun Nur	48°57′N	117°23′E	2,315	545.5	8.0	131.3
Hongze	33°20′N	118°40′E	2,069	12.5	5.5	31.3
Nam Co	30°40′N	90°30′E	1,940	4,718.0	—	—
Siling Co	31°50′N	89°00′E	1,640	4,530.0	—	—
South-Four Lakes	34°59′N	116°57′E	1,266	35.5–37.0	6.0	53.0
Ebi Nur	44°55′N	82°53′E	1,070	189.0	—	—
Bosten	41°59′N	86°49′E	1,019	1,048.0	15.7	99.0

people have studied, used, and transformed these soil resources for 80 centuries. As early as the fifth century B.C. *The Tribute of Yu* subdivided China into nine "continents" and classified their soils mainly on the basis of color. Soils were demarcated according to their fertility into three levels and nine grades; this was probably the first systematic soil classification in the world. A little later, another classic, the *Book of Master Kwan*, made a more detailed study of China's soils, classifying them into 18 types, each type with 5 fertility grades.

Although billions of Chinese farmers have laboriously worked in close contact with China's soils, little scientific research work on soils has been conducted. Modern scientific studies of China's soils started in the 1930s. At this early stage, the American school of soil science exerted great influence on the soil classification system in China; more than 10 great soil groups and 2000 soil series are identified. Since 1953, the Russian school's genetic method of evaluation has been adopted. In 1978, the current soil classification of 11 orders, 47 groups, and 139 subgroups was finally developed. Very recently, research has been started on "new" international soil classification systems, such as the American Soil Taxonomy and the FAO-UNESCO Soil Map of the World. Tentatively presented in Table 1.9 is a basis for discussing the soil geography of China. Such a result is still very preliminary. Much revision based on detailed fieldwork and laboratory analysis still needs to be done.

Chief Soil-forming Processes in China

The soil-forming process is chiefly a function of parent material, climate, landforms, vegetation, and time. In an ancient and densely populated country like China, the impact and feedback of past and present human activities are also important.

Under China's specific physical and human conditions, the following 12 soil forming processes are significant. Each soil-forming process usually gives birth to more than one soil type, and each soil type usually represents the end product of more than one soil-forming process.

1. *Weathering* is a soil-forming process under which rocks and other parent materials become decomposed and disintegrated into clay, silt, and sand particles. Thus, with weathering the soil profile starts to develop. Weathering occurs all over China and is particularly strong in humid tropical zones. Taken to its limits, the typical end results are lithosols and regosols.

2. *Leaching* is a process that involves soluble salts and other movable materials in a soil body being transported, or *leached*, from the upper horizons to a lower horizon. It occurs mainly in humid and subhumid areas where water is abundant.

3. *Podzolization* predominates in climates that are cold enough to inhibit active bacterial action but have sufficient moisture to permit large green plants to thrive. In its optimal condition, it is associated with coniferous forests. Humic acids, produced from the abundant leaf mold and humus, strongly leach the upper soil horizons of bases, colloids, and the oxides of iron and aluminum, leaving a characteristic ash-grey A2 horizon composed largely of silica. Typical end soils are podzoluvisols.

4. *Argillation* includes the chemical transformation of primary minerals into secondary minerals and clays in upper layers; these materials are then deposited in lower horizons. Typical end soils are luvisols.

5. *Laterization* takes place in a tropical or subtropical climate, where plentiful rainfall permits sustained bacterial action to destroy dead vegetation as rapidly as it is produced. In the absence of humid acids, the sesquioxides of iron (Fe_2O_3) are insoluble and accumulate in the soil as red clay, nodules, and rocklike strata (laterite). Silica, on the other hand, is leached out of the soil. Typical end products are ferralsols.

6. *Calcification* occurs mainly in semiarid and arid environments, where evaporation on the average exceeds precipitation. Rainfall is not sufficient to leach out the bases and colloids. Calcium carbonate is precipitated in the B horizon as nodules, slabs, and even dense stony layers (caliche). Its typical end products are kastanozems and chernozems.

7. *Salinization* is chiefly associated with steppe and desert environments as well as with poorly drained locations. Sulphates and chlorides of calcium and sodium accumulate in the soil. About one-fifth of China's total farmlands are estimated to be more or less affected by the salinization process. Typical soils are solonchaks.

TABLE 1.9
Correlation of Soil Types between China's Traditional Soil Classification (1973) and the FAO-UNESCO System (1977)

Soil units (FAO-UNESCO)	Soil groups of China's traditional system
1. Fluvisols (J)	*Chou tu* (wet soil), meadow soil
2. Gleysols (G)	Meadow soil, bog soil, paddy soil, irrigated oases soil, alpine meadow soil
3. Regosols (R)	Alpine frozen soil, aeolian sandy soil, purple soil, saga soil (alpine steppe soil)
4. Lithosols (I)	Soils of mountainous areas
5. Rendzinas (E)	Limestone soil, phosphocalcic soil
6. Rankers (U)	Alpine meadow soil, subalpine meadow soil
7. Vertisols (V)	*Shachiang* soil, paddy soil
8. Solonchaks (Z)	Solonchak
9. Solonetaz (S)	Solonetz
10. Yermosols (Y)	Grey desert soil, grey-brown desert soil, brown desert soil, takyric soil, alpine desert soil
11. Xerosols (X)	Sierozem, semidesert brown soil, irrigated oases soil
12. Kastanozems (K)	Chestnut soil
13. Chernozems (C)	Chernozem
14. Phaeozems (H)	Black earth
15. Greyzems (M)	Grey forest soil
16. Cambisols (B)	Burozem, drab soil, grey-drab forest soil, *mein tu* (cultivated loess), *lou tu* (cultivated old loess), *heilu tu* (dark loess), subalpine meadow soil
17. Luvisols (L)	Dark brown forest soil, burozem, yellow-brown earth, *heilu tu,* limestone soil, dry red earth
18. Podzoluvisols (D)	Bleached grey soil
19. Planosols (W)	*Baijiang tu,* yellow-brown earth, burozem
20. Acrisols (A)	Lateritic soil, red earth, yellow earth
21. Nitosols (N)	Laterite, red earth, dry red earth
22. Ferralsols (F)	Laterite
23. Histosols (O)	Peat soil, bog soil

8. *Alkalinization* is similar in process to salinization but with a higher proportion of sodium in the total salt content. Typical soils are solonetz.

9. *Gleization* is featured in poorly drained (but not saline) environments under a moist and cool or cold climate. Low temperature permits heavy accumulation of organic matter to form a surface layer of peaty material; this is the "glei" horizon, a thick layer of compact, sticky, structureless clay of bluish-grey color. The typical end products are gleysols and histosols.

10. *Humification* is essentially the slow oxidation of organic matter under a humid climate. Organic acids help in the decomposition of the minerals of the parent materials. The hydrogen ions of the acid solution tend to replace the ions of potassium, calcium, magnesium, and sodium. The typical soils are phaeozems and histosols.

11. *Leucinization* is essentially a bleaching action of upper soil horizons under seasonal flooding conditions. Iron and other colorful materials are reduced and removed either by laterally flowing water or by forming concretions in situ, with a resultant whitish layer. Its end products are planosols.

12. *Cultivation* should be considered as one of the most important soil-forming processes in China. All cultivated soils have been more or less changed from their original conditions. Especially after a long period of continuous cultivation and irrigation, some distinguished human-made soils are formed. For example, in the oases of the Hexi Corridor, after more than 2000 years of cultivation, the irrigated farmlands have been transformed into the so-called oases soils, with a fertile tilth generally more than 1–2 m deep. The widely

distributed paddy soils in southern China are another excellent example of human-made fertile and productive soil.

Major Soil Types

Under the action and interplay of these soil-forming processes, varied soil types have been formed.

1. **Fluvisols (J):** These are the soils of river valley plains, formed mainly under seasonal flood and continual alluvial deposition as well as various soil-forming processes, such as leaching, gleization, and humification. They are widely distributed along the middle and lower reaches of large rivers. In general, they are naturally fertile and have good soil moisture conditions, but are sometimes liable to flooding. Practically all of them have been cultivated, with a tilth layer more than 30–40 cm deep.

2. **Gleysols (G):** These are the soils of low depressions, usually with a high water table and impeded drainage. Gleization and humification are dominant soil-forming processes. They are widely distributed all over China, now mostly cultivated and transformed into paddy soil and irrigated oases soil.

3. **Regosols (R):** Widely distributed in sandy and mountainous areas, with a poorly-developed soil profile. Most of them are in wastelands or are slightly used as pasture.

4. **Lithosols (I):** Widely distributed on steep slopes, especially in Northwest China. With a soil profile of less then 10 cm and a humus content approaching zero, they generally are not used.

5. **Rendzinas (E):** These are soils of karst topography in humid tropical and subtropical China, with a high calcium carbonate content. On the south China Sea islands, which are essentially built up by coral reefs, a special kind of redzina (phosphocalcic soil) is developed.

6. **Rankers (U):** These soils are chiefly distributed in the southeastern border of the lofty Tibetan Plateau and on alpine meadows of Northwest China. They usually coexist with lithosols and might be regarded as a further development of the latter.

7. **Vertisols (V):** These special soils are mostly restricted to the lower reaches of the Huai He with clayey alluvial-lacustrine deposits and low depressed landforms. The chief feature of the soil profile is the existence of a blackish, clayey layer 40–60 cm thick immediately under the grey-brownish cultivated layer. This is the so-called *shachiang* layer, which is composed mainly of lime concretions.

8. **Solonchaks (Z):** These soils occur widely in steppe and desert areas where surface evaporation is higher than precipitation, and thus, salts are brought to the surface from the subsoil by the ascending capillary water. They are also distributed in patches along the coast. The salt content varies with different environments, generally increasing with increasing aridity. In extremely arid environments, a salt crust more than 3 cm thick may be formed on the ground surface; and in the Turpan–Hami Basin, where annual precipitation drops below 10 mm, nitrates with a content of 0.4–1.0 percent NO_3 are included in the soil profile.

9. **Solonetz (S):** Small patches of solonetz are scattered in northern China, usually associated with chernozems, kastanozems, xerosols, and yermosols. The most notable property of solonetz soils is their strong alkalinity (pH value of the top layer is usually higher than 9), frequently combined with salinization of the subsoil.

10. **Yermosols (Y):** These soils are widely distributed in desert areas in China. Their profiles have been only weakly developed and are usually less than 1 m thick. Humus content is low. Because soil moisture is also low, farming is not possible without irrigation.

11. **Xerosols (X):** These soils are developed in the transitional zone between semiarid and arid regions, mainly through calcification and partly by humification and salinization.

12. **Kastanozems (K):** These soils, also called chestnut soils, are extensively distributed in the steppe environment. They are developed under the interplay of calcification and humification, with a humus layer 15–25 cm thick.

13. **Chernozems (C):** Developed under temperate, subhumid environments, they are excellent agricultural soils, with a humus layer generally 20–40 cm thick. The calcareous layer usually starts 40–60 cm from the ground surface.

14. **Phaeozems (H):** These soils are developed under a temperate subhumid forest-steppe environment and are probably the most fertile soils in China. Yet, their distribution is limited to Heilongjiang

and Jilin provinces. The humus-containing layer generally has a thickness of 30–70 cm (sometimes more than 1 m), and the calcareous layer is practically nonexistent.

15. *Greyzems* (**M**): These soils are mainly restricted to the tree-clad western slopes of the Greater Hinggan Mountains and the southern slopes of the Altay Mountains. They contain a litter layer and a rich organic horizon overlying a brownish transitional B horizon.

16. *Cambisols* (**B**): These soils are at an early stage in the soil-forming process. They are widely distributed in mountainous areas. The soil profile is characterized by a top humus layer overlying a brownish transitional B horizon.

17. *Luvisols* (**L**): These soils are mainly formed within the mixed broad- and needle-leaved forest environment and are widely distributed in the Greater Hinggan and the Changbai Mountains. The typical soil profile is composed of a litter layer of 3–5 cm, then followed by a dark brown or drab argillated B horizon and the parent material layer.

18. *Podzoluvisols* (**D**): These soils are a feature of the taiga forest environment in the Greater Hinggan and the Altay Mountains. The dominant soil-forming processes are leaching, podzoliztion, and leucinization.

19. *Planosols* (**W**): These soils are the end products of intense leaching and leucinization. They are widely distributed in the northern parts of Eastern Monsoon China, the widespread *Baijiang tu* (literally, the whitish soup earth) in humid temperate Northeast China being the most famous. The most important feature in their profile is the whitish bleached E horizon overlying the argillated B horizon.

20. *Acrisols* (**A**): These soils are mainly distributed in humid, subtropical zones, under intense action of leaching, argillation, and laterization.

21. *Nitosols* (**N**): These soils are developed chiefly on basalt and red clay areas in humid subtropical regions. They are characterized by the existence of an argillated B horizon and by the absence of the bleached horizon.

22. *Ferralsols* (**F**): These soils are distributed mainly in tropical China. They are the end product of laterization, and are also influenced by leaching and humification. Their profile includes a litter layer of 2–3 cm; a grey-brownish humus layer of 10–30 cm, a reddish, oxidized B horizon with a duripan or fragipan, and finally, the reddish or brownish parent materials. Total profiles are usually quite thick, sometimes more than 3 m.

23. *Histosols* (**O**): These soils are found mainly in the marshy Sanjiang Plain in Northeast China and on the Zoige Area of the northeastern Tibetan Plateau. They are characterized by a very high groundwater table and a peat layer of from 30–40 cm to 2–3 m, sometimes even more than 10 m thick.

BIOGEOGRAPHY

The biogeographical environment of China is rich and varied, and consequently, so are the biological resources (see Chapter Two).

Vegetation

Vegetation is the sum total of all plant formations in a region. It is a major component as well as a reliable mirror of the natural geographical environment. The distribution of China's vegetation is shaped by both zonal and azonal factors. Horizontal zonal distribution of vegetation stands out clearly in China from southeast to northwest. As the distance from the sea increases and the precipitation decreases, vegetation changes gradually from forests to steppes to deserts. In the eastern forest realm, chiefly owing to areal differentiation of solar incidence and consequently a diversity of temperature conditions, there is also a conspicuous latitudinal horizontal zonal distribution of forest types. From south to north, tropical rain forest, tropical monsoon forest, subtropical broad-leaved evergreen forest, warm-temperate evergreen and broad-leaved deciduous forests, temperate mixed broad- and needle-leaved forest, and cool temperate needle-leaved taiga forest appear in a sequence. Vertical zonation of vegetation, chiefly the result of areal differentiation in elevation and consequently the redistribution of temperature and moisture conditions, is clearly developed on the Tibetan Plateau and its surrounding high mountains. It is closely interrelated with horizontal zonation; literally, vertical vegetation zonation is "stamped" with horizontal vegetation zonation, and vice versa.

The vegetation types in China are quite varied and complicated and include nearly the whole array of major horizontal vegetation types in the world, with the exception of tundra. A unique feature is the extensively distributed alpine vegetation (including alpine tundra) on the Tibetan Plateau and its surrounding high mountains. According to a recent investigation, there are 29 major natural vegetation types, 52 subtypes, and more than 600 formations in China.

Needle-leaved and Mixed Needle- and Broad-leaved Forests

These are the most important timber-producing areas in China, occurring widely in the cool temperate, temperate, subtropical, and tropical zones. They are mainly composed of *Abies, Picea, Pinus, Larix, Tsuga, Cupressus, Juniperus, Subina, Cunninghamis,* and other genera. They may be classified into the following subtypes:

1. Cool-temperate needle-leaved forest is the zonal vegetation of the cool temperate zone, mainly distributed on northern Greater Hinggan Mountains and northeastern Altay Mountains.

2. Temperate needle-leaved forest is mainly found on low mountains and hills of the warm temperate zone and the middle mountains of the subtropical zone.

3. Subtropical and tropical needle-leaved forest is mostly located on low mountains, hills, and valleys of the extensive subtropical and tropical zones.

4. Mixed needle- and broad-leaved forest is a transitional type between cool-temperate needle-leaved forest and temperate deciduous broad-leaved forest.

Broad-leaved Forests

These are the most widespread forest types in China and feature the most varied subtypes. They form zonal vegetation types, both horizontal and vertical, in warm temperate, subtropical, and tropical zones of Eastern Monsoon China. In Northwest Arid China, they are represented by the riparian forest.

1. Deciduous broad-leaved forest is the horizontal zonal vegetation type of the subtropical and middle tropical mountains.

2. Mixed evergreen and deciduous broad-leaved forest is the horizontal zonal vegetation of the northern subtropical zone.

3. Evergreen broad-leaved forest is the zonal vegetation type of the middle subtropical zone.

4. Monsoon evergreen broad-leaved forest is the transitional vegetation type between subtropical evergreen broad-leaved forest and tropical monsoon forest.

5. Hard-leaved, evergreen broad-leaved forest is a peculiar vegetation type restricted to the western part of the subtropical zone.

6. Tropical monsoon forest is widely distributed on hills and terraces in China's eastern tropical zone, ascending to 700 m in southwestern Yunnan and as high as 1000 m on the eastern slopes of the Himalayas.

8. Mangrove is mainly distributed along the coastal clay soils of Guangdong, Fujian, Hainan, and Taiwan.

9. Coral reef evergreen forest is mainly distributed on coral islands and islets of southern Taiwan and the South China Sea islands.

Shrub Formations

Shrubs are widely distributed in China, especially in temperate forested areas, although most of the shrub formations do not represent a zonal vegetation type.

1. Alpine evergreen and deciduous scrub is a vertical zonal vegetation subtype distributed widely on high mountains of temperate, subtropical, and tropical zones.

2. Temperate deciduous shrub is a secondary vegetation type arising after continuous deforestation in the subtropic forested areas.

3. Subtropical deciduous shrub is a secondary vegetation type arising after continuous deforestation in the subtropic forested areas.

4. Evergreen broad-leaved shrub is a secondary vegetation type distributed widely on hills and low mountains of tropical and subtropical zones.

5. Evergreen thorny scrub is distributed on the sandy beaches of China's tropical coast.

Grassland and Park Savanna

Grasslands and park savanna are extensively distributed over about 30 percent of China's total land area. The immense Mongolian Plateau especially has been the home of many nomadic peoples ever since Neolithic times, and its landscape is aptly described in Mongolian folklore.

1. Steppe is the zonal vegetation type of temperate semiarid land, characterized by bunch grass with a coverage of 30–60 percent.

2. Meadow-steppe is a transitional vegetation type between grassland and forest, mainly distributed in western Northeast China and eastern Inner Mongolia.

3. Desert-steppe is a transitional vegetation type between grassland and desert, with mixed bunch grass and small lowshrubs as the dominant species.

4. Park savana is a vegetation subtype of the semiarid tropical and subtropical zones, restricted to small patches in dry, hot valleys or gorges in Southwest and South China.

Deserts

Deserts are widely distributed in Northwest China and the northern Tibetan Plateau, occupying about 22 percent of China's total land area. They are characterized by sparse vegetation coverage (generally less than 20–30 percent or even less than 1–5 percent) and by a poverty of species and a simple plant community structure, with drought-resistant shrubs, lowshrubs, and small lowshrubs, predominating.

1. Semiarboreous desert is sometimes called "desert forest" and is mainly composed of *Haloxylon spp*. It is found most commonly in the Junggar Basin.

2. Shrub desert is the most widely distributed zonal desert vegetation in China. Generally, shrubs are less than 1 m in height and coverage is less than 5–10 percent.

3. Lowshrub and small lowshrub desert is extensively distributed on low mountains and gravel *gobi*, which are the two harshest desert environments.

4. Small lowshrub desert is an alpine desert, located on the Tibetan Plateau and its surrounding high mountains with elevations between 4000 and 5000 m. It is characterized by small cushion lowshrubs.

Alpine Permafrost and Cushion Vegetation

1. Alpine permafrost vegetation has developed on the upper parts of the Greater Hinggan, Changbai, and Altay mountains. It is usually less than 10–20 cm in height and less than 20 percent in coverage.

2. Alpine cushion vegetation is widespread on the Tibetan Plateau and its surrounding high mountains immediately below the eternal snow line, between 3200 and 5500 m. The dominant species are many kinds of cushion perennial grasses and small shrubs.

Meadows and Swamps

Meadows and swamp are azonal vegetation types whose habitats are determined chiefly by high groundwater tables or flooded environments.

1. Typical meadow is located on cool temperate plateaus and high mountains and on lowlands and seacoasts with a high groundwater table.

2. Alpine meadow is mainly distributed above the alpine grassland belt at elevations between 3200 and 5200 m, and is the zonal vegetation of the eastern Tibetan Plateau.

3. Saline meadow is mainly found in saline soil areas, with a groundwater table of less than 1–3 m in depth.

4. Swampy meadow is an intermediate vegetation type between swamp and meadow, mainly located in low, wet depressions.

5. Scrub-grass swamp develops on wet or flooded lowlands in the Greater and Lesser Hinggan Mountains.

6. Grass swamp is widely distributed on waterlogged or flooded lowlands, particularly on the Sanjiang Plain in Northeast China and the Zoige area on the northeastern Tibetan Plateau. The ground is densely covered with *Carex spp*. and other grasses, usually with a height of 30–50 cm and a coverage of 60–80 percent.

Zoogeography

Based on areal distribution of major terrestrial vertebrates, six zoogeographical realms have been identified in the world. They are: Paleoarctic, Neoarctic, Paleotropical, Oriental, Neotropical, and Australian. In China, two realms are represented: north of the Qinling–Huaihe line is the Paleoarctic realm; south of that line is the Oriental realm. These two realms can be again subdivided on the basis of specific habitats into seven zoogeographical regions or ecological groups of terrestrial vertebrates.

Cool-temperate Needle-leaved Forest Faunal Group

This group is characterized by a great quantity of mammals that are adapted to a cool temperate climate and taiga vegetation. They are usually winter dormant and have heavy fur. The faunal composition is rather simple. The most commonly seen mammals are deer and wild boar. Other commonly seen species are squirrel, sable, ermine, brown bear, and badger. Several well-known minority peoples live in the Greater Hinggan mountain areas and specialize in hunting. They have also successfully domesticated reindeer and some species of deer. Birds and reptiles are abundant, but amphibians are few.

Temperate Forest, Forest-steppe, and Farmland Faunal Group

On the eastern hills and mountains of Northeast China, forest and grassland-inhabiting animals are still commonly seen, such as deer, wild boar, wild rabbit, and others. Hunting is still an important occupation here. In North China, most forests have been cut down and farmlands predominate; hence, few large wild animals survive. The most commonly seen species are different kinds of rats, birds, and reptiles.

Temperate Steppe Faunal Group

The dominant mammal species are herbivorous rodents. Their populations vary greatly according to the supply of food, which, in turn, depends greatly on the amount of annual precipitation. In dry years, the animals migrate like nomads for long distances in search of feed (grass and shrub). Their population density often reaches 3,000–6,000 burrows/ha, causing great havoc in the pastureland. The control and elimination of these rats has become an urgent problem in Inner Mongolia. Herbivorous hoofed mammals also exist in great numbers; the galloping Mongolian gazelles are the most commonly seen. Their western limit coincides roughly with that of the temperate steppe. Bird species are few. Reptiles and amphibians are also rare.

Temperate Desert and Semidesert Faunal Group

Deserts also support an abundance of rodents and hoofed mammals; yet, owing to the relative scarcity of food, their populations are not so numerous as in the temperate steppe. The most commonly seen hoofed mammals are the goitered gazelle and wild ass. Birds and amphibians are few. Reptiles, on the other hand, are well adjusted to the desert habitat and are quite numerous.

Highland Forest-steppe, Meadow-steppe, and Alpine Desert Faunal Group

This faunal group, found on the Tibetan Plateau and its surrounding high mountains (not including the Hengduan Mountains), is rather poor both in species and in population numbers. Most animals live in caves and are winter dormant. Birds are numerous. Reptiles and amphibians are seldom seen.

Subtropical Forest, Scrub, and Grassland Faunal Group

This faunal group, owing to associated favorable climatic conditions and plentiful food, is quite rich both in species and in population. Seasonal and annual variations are inconspicuous. As most primary forest vegetation has been depleted, faunal composition also has been depleted and much changed as well. The dominant species of mammals in forested areas are monkeys and squirrels. In deforested hills and low mountains there are deer. Rodents live mostly in cultivated areas as do birds such as sparrows, crows, and others. Reptiles are represented by many kinds of snakes, lizards, and turtles. Amphibians, such as types of frogs, are also commonly seen.

Tropical Forest, Scrub, Savanna, and Farmland Faunal Group

This group is characterized by very complicated faunal composition and many endemic species. Practically no species can be said to predominate. Another feature is the abundance of many arboreal vertebrates, including numerous species of monkeys and other primates, bats, and carnivorous mammals, as well as amphibians (e.g., *Rhacophoridae*) and reptiles (e.g., *Draco spp.*). After deforestation, species living on the ground increase, such as deer, wild boar, and different kinds of rats. Birds are rich both in species and in quantity; they show great areal differentiation in predominant species. Reptiles and amphibians are also numerous; for example, there are 120–130 kinds of snakes on Hainan Island alone.

LAND SYSTEM

So far, our discussion has centered on individual physical elements one by one: climate, landforms, surface and groundwater, soil, vegetation, and fauna. Each is an important attribute of the physical environment. Yet, the integration of all these physical elements with the land system is what truly influences the physical environment as a whole. All economic planning and development should be based on and conditioned by the "land" as an integral total, rather than by any one individual factor.

Land Classification

The term "land" or "terrain" is broadly construed as the total physical environment of a certain section on the earth's surface, including climate, landforms, surface water, groundwater, soil, vegetation, and other physical elements. It also includes past and present human activities and their impacts on the physical environment.

Land classification is an old tradition in China's geographical studies. Since 1978, a serious and comprehensive land classification and mapping program has been in progress. This national program has two basic purposes: (1) to provide solid and detailed data on China's geographical environment, and (2) to evaluate the nation's land resources based on agricultural suitability and capability. The country is mapped at the scale of 1:1,000,000 (64 sheets in total), the major provinces and regions at the scale of 1:200,000, and the sample study areas at 1:50,000. As of 1990, about one-third of the national 1:1,000,000 land type maps had been completed, and one-third of the latter (8 sheets) have been published in color. A hierarchical scheme for land type classification and mapping has been developed.

The natural zones that are generally delimited by macro-climate conditions (temperature and moisture) as well as soil and vegetation types are the zero level, or the starting point of land classification. The Tibetan Plateau and the Loess Plateau are two exceptions, where units are delimited mainly by macro-scale landforms. Twelve zero-level major units are thus identified in China: humid equatorial zone; humid tropical zone; humid southern subtropical zone; humid middle subtropical zone; humid northern subtropical zone; humid and subhumid warm temperate zone; humid and subhumid temperate zone; humid cool temperate zone; Loess Plateau; semiarid, temperate grassland; arid temperate and warm temperate desert; and Tibetan Plateau. Within each zero-level major unit, a two-level land type classification is adopted.

The first-level land types within a zero-level major unit approximate the "land system" used by the Australian Commonwealth Scientific and Industrial Organiza-

tion (CISRO). They are identified mainly on the basis of macro- or meso-scale landforms and are listed according to the elevation of each type: from low depression through flat land, terrace, hill, low mountain, middle mountain, high mountain, to mountain top. The first-level land types are the major mapping units for the nation as a whole at a scale of 1:1,000,000. Several adjacent and genetically similar first-level land types might be grouped into a "landscape" or "natural area," which is the lowest-level regional unit in the comprehensive physical regionalization.

The second-level land types approximate "land units" of the Australian CISRO. They are generally identified and delimited by relatively homogeneous meso- or micro-scale landforms and vertical biogeographical subzones in the mountain region, and by similar soil and vegetation subtypes in the level plains. These suggest a similar land use suitability and capability and thus are best suited as the basic unit for land evaluation. Several adjacent and genetically similar second-level land types may be grouped into a first-level land type.

Land Evaluation

Land evaluation denotes the land's suitability and capability for a certain economic purpose, such as agriculture, engineering, or military uses. In China, the chief economic purpose currently is agricultural development. The basic unit for land evaluation is the second-level land type on a large-scale map and the first-level land type on smaller scale maps. Some examples of land classification and land evaluation will be given in the regional chapters.

COMPREHENSIVE PHYSICAL REGIONALIZATION

Comprehensive physical regionalization is an effort to identify differentiation among different areas on the earth's surface and to document the similarities within the same area. It reflects the total of all physical attributes and hence might serve as a guide for land use planning within these areas. Comprehensive physical regionalization is also one of the oldest traditions in Chinese geographical study. It began with the *Tribute of Yu* (fifth century B.C.), which subdivided China into nine "continents." Since 1949, physical regionalization has been considered not only as a major scientific research area, but also one of the chief aspects of regional planning, especially for agricultural development. A series of physical regionalization studies on both national and local scales has been conducted. One of the most sophisticated studies was completed in 1958 by the Working Committee on the Physical Regionalization of China of the Chinese Academy of Sciences. The following comprehensive physical regionalization is based on the 1958 scheme, with some important revisions.

Natural Realms

The most significant and differential features in China are geographical location, topography and neotectonic movement, major climatic characteristics, areal differentiation of geologic history, and human impact on physical geographical environment. Using these criteria, the country is first divided into three natural realms: Eastern Monsoon China, Northwest Arid China, and the Tibetan Frigid Plateau. This is the starting point for comprehensive physical regionalization as well as regional planning and development in China.

Eastern Monsoon China

This realm occupies about 45 percent of China's total land area, about 89 percent of China's total farmland, and about 95 percent of the total population. It has the following characteristics.

1. Location near the neighboring seas and the Pacific Ocean, means that the influence of summer maritime monsoons is strong, with sharp seasonal variations both in wind direction and in precipitation.

2. The climate is humid or subhumid, with forest as the dominant natural vegetation.

3. The chief parameter for areal differentiation is temperature, decreasing from south to north. In North and Northeast China, precipitation also decreases conspicuously from east to west.

4. Neotectonic uplift is not great; few mountains rise more than 2000 m above sea level. The mountains are essentially without modern glaciation. East of the Qinzhou–Zhengzhou–Beijing–Huma line is a broad belt of down-warping with widespread alluvial plains. (mostly below 200 m in elevation).

5. Modern geomorphological processes are predominantly normal fluvial action, and surface water is fed mainly by precipitation.

6. Owing to the absence of Quaternary continental glaciation, both fauna and flora are rich in species, and a reddish weathering soil crust is widespread.

7. With the exception of a few localities, the impact of human activities is very great. Practically all arable land has been cultivated and all natural vegetation has been modified.

Northwest Arid China

This realm is the eastern part of the immense Eurasian desert and grassland. It occupies about 30 percent of China's total land area, about 10 percent of the total farmland, and has only 4 percent of the total population. It is characterized as follows:

1. In recent geological times, there has been conspicuous differential uplifting, with the widespread formation of plateaus and inland basins of approximately 500–1500 m in elevation. In addition, a considerable portion of the area has been violently uplifted to form high mountains that surround or traverse neighboring plateaus and inland basins (e.g., Tianshan at more than 3500 m and Altay at more than 3000 m).

2. Because the area is located deep in the Eurasian continent and is surrounded by a series of high mountains, the influence of summer maritime monsoons is rather weak, and hence the climate is arid or semiarid.

3. Modern geomorphological processes consist mostly of denudation and deflation, with *shamo* (sandy desert) and *gobi* (gravel and stony desert) extensively distributed. However, along inland rivers and on piedmont plains, linear and sheet-water erosion and deposition can be quite severe after rainstorms.

4. Most drainage is inland, with few perennial rivers, which are fed by runoff and melting snow from the surrounding mountain areas. Lakes are numerous, and most are saline.

5. There has been gradual desiccation (with some fluctuation) ever since the late Mesozoic era. Both fauna and flora are rather poor in species and in population.

6. In comparison with Eastern Monsoon China, human impact is not so conspicuous. Yet, many fertile oases have been developed along the middle and lower reaches of the perennial rivers, and large tracts of grassland have been used for pasture since ancient times.

The Tibetan Frigid Plateau

This is the highest and largest plateau in the world, occupying about 25 percent of China's total land area, and less than 1 percent of both the total farmland and total population. Its features are as follows:

1. Recent large-scale uplift has given this plateau a mean elevation of more than 4000 m. The plateau is interspersed with a series of high snow-capped mountains above 7000 or even 8000 m in elevation.

2. As a result of high elevation, the atmosphere is generally thin, the temperature low, and permafrost is widespread. Solar radiation is intense, and winds are strong.

3. Most areas have inland drainage, with numerous lakes in the inland basins. The modern geomorphological processes are chiefly results of snow and ice, although fluvial action is also strong along the southeastern border, and the process of desiccation dominates the arid northwestern part.

4. Both fauna and flora are rich in species. Vertical zonation is conspicuous. On the northwestern Tibetan Plateau, desert, mountain grassland, mountain coniferous forest, alpine meadow, periglacial dwarf shrub, and continual snow appear in succession from the foothills to the mountain top.

5. Owing to the influence of strong glaciation and weak chemical weathering, soil parent materials are usually coarse and thin. Modern soil-forming processes started only after the last glaciation. Consequently, soil profiles are poorly developed, and fertility is low.

6. Natural conditions as a whole are unfavorable to human activities. Extensive distribution of farmlands and population is much lower even than in Northwest Arid China.

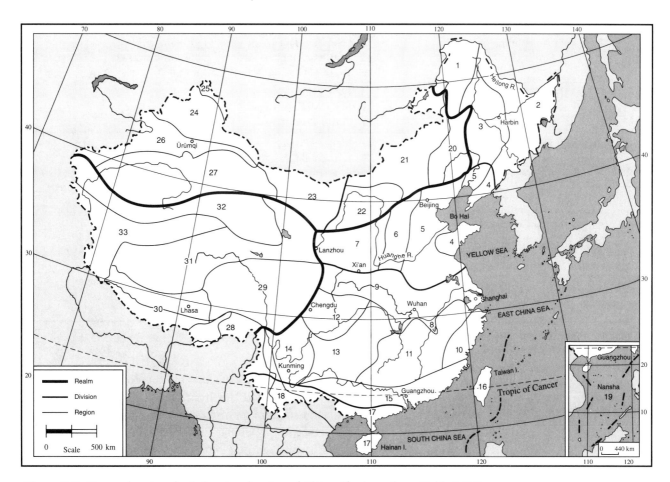

Figure 1.9 Comprehensive physical regionalization of China. (for legend, see Table 1.10)

TABLE 1.10
Natural Divisions and Natural Regions in China

	Natural divisions	Natural regions
I.	Temperate humid and subhumid	1. Great Hinggan Mts.—needle-leaved forests 2. Northeast China mountains—mixed needle- & broad-leaved forests 3. Northeast China Plain—forest-steppe
II.	Warm temperate humid and subhumid North China	4. Liaodong–Shandong peninsulas—deciduous broad-leaved forests 5. North China Plain—deciduous broad-leaved forests 6. Shanxi-Hebei mountains—deciduous broad-leaved forests & forest-steppe 7. Loess Plateau—forest-steppe & steppe
III.	Subtropical humid Central China and South China	8. Middle & lower Chang Jiang plains—Mixed forests 9. Qinling–Dabie Mts.—Mixed forests 10. Southeast Coast—evergreen broad-leaved forests 11. South Chang Jiang hills & basins—evergreen broad-leaved forests 12. Sichuan Basin—evergreen broad-leaved forests 13. Guizhou Plateau—evergreen broad-leaved forests 14. Yunnan Plateau—evergreen broad-leaved forests 15. Lingnan hills—evergreen broad-leaved forests 16. Taiwan Is.—evergreen broad-leaved forests & monsoon forests
IV.	Tropical humid South China	17. Leizhou–Hainan—tropical monsoon forest 18. Southern Yunnan—tropical monsoon forest 19. South China Sea Islands—tropical rain forests
V.	Temperate Inner Mongolia grassland	20. West Liao River Basin—steppe 21. Inner Mongolia Plateau—steppe & desert-steppe 22. Ordos Plateau—steppe & desert-steppe
VI.	Temperate and warm temperate desert of Northwest China	23. Alashan Plateau—temperature desert 24. Junggar Basin—temperate desert 25. Altay Mts.—montane grassland & needle-leaved forests 26. Tianshan Mts.—montane grassland & needle-leaved forests 27. Tarim Basin—warm temperate desert
VII.	Tibetan Plateau	28. Southern Himalayas slope—tropical & subtropical montane forests 29. Southeastern Tibetan Plateau—montane needle-leaved forests & alpine meadow 30. Southern Tibetan Plateau—shrubby grassland 31. Central Tibetan Plateau—montane & alpine grassland 32. Qaidam Basin & Northern Kunlun Mts. slope—desert 33. Ngari-Kunlun Mts.—desert-steppe & alpine desert

Natural Divisions

Based on these three natural realms, seven natural divisions are identified. A natural division is characterized by having within its borders similar temperature and moisture conditions as well as broadly similar types of soils and vegetation. Eastern Monsoon China can be subdivided according to areal differentiation of temperature conditions into four natural divisions: temperate humid and subhumid Northeast China, warm temperate humid and subhumid North China, subtropical humid Central and South China, and tropical humid South China. Northwest Arid China can be subdivided, mainly on the basis of moisture and vegetation, into temperate Inner Mongolia grassland and temperate and warm temperate desert of Northwest China. The Tibetan Frigid Plateau forms a single natural division because the whole realm is subjected to a cold environment and vertical zonation. These seven natural divisions are the chief regional units for the organization of topics in this book.

Natural Regions

Based on these seven natural divisions, 33 natural regions are identified. A natural region has not only uniform zonal features (climatic, biological, and soil), but also fairly uniform azonal features (geological and geomorphological). Hence, a natural region reflects more fully the total physical environment and is the best unit for regional planning. In Figure 1.9 and in Table 1.10, 33 natural regions are shown. Each of them will be discussed more in detail in the regional chapters.

Lower-level Regional Units

Lower-level regional units are mainly based on azonal features, and are usually "integrated" from the lower to higher units, instead of being "differentiated" from the higher to lower units. A natural subregion has rather homogeneous natural features, both zonal and azonal; hence, it is also useful in regional planning. However, owing to the unbalanced condition of scientific data, it is now usually impractical to "divide" or to "combine" a natural subregion, especially on the Tibetan Plateau. The lowest-level regional unit in comprehensive physical regionalization might be termed a "natural area," which is more or less identical with the "landscape" in land classification.

The integration and combination of the first-level land types are supposed to make up the basic, or the lowest-level, regional unit, the natural area. Then, several natural areas are combined and integrated into a subregion. However, much more in-depth fieldwork and data analysis are needed to establish a sophisticated land classification system and a complete natural area regionalization system in China.

REFERENCES

Chinese Academy of Sciences. 1979–1988. *Physical Geography of China*. 12 volumes: (1) General Survey; (2) Geomorphology; (3) Climate; (4) Surface Water; (5) Groundwater; (6) Soil Geography; (7) Plants and Vegetation (2 vols.); (8) Zoogeography; (9) Paleo-geography; (10) Historical Physical Geography; (11) Neighboring Seas. Beijing: Science Press (in Chinese).

Chinese Academy of Sciences. 1953–1959. *Comprehensive Physical Regionalization*. Beijing: Science Press (in Chinese).

Chinese Academy of Sciences. 1989. *1:1,000,000 National Land-types Classification and Mapping*. Directory and 8 color sheets (Xi'an, Hohhot, Ürümqi, Xining, Nanjing, Taiyuan, Wuhan, Hainan) Xi'an: Surveying & Mapping Press (in Chinese).

Academy of Geological Sciences. 1978. *Main Features of Geological Structure in China*. Beijing: Geological Press (in Chinese).

Chu, Coching. 1964. "Some Characteristic Features of Chinese Climate and Their Effects on Crop Production," *Acta Geographica Sinica* 30, no. 1 (in Chinese).

FAO-UNESCO. 1977. *Soil Map of the World* (Scale: 1:5,000,000). Paris: UNESCO (in English, French, Spanish, and Russian).

Hou, Xueyu, et al. 1963. "On Agricultural Development for Different Natural Regions of China," *Science Bulletin*, no. 9 (in Chinese).

Nanjing Institute of Soil Science, Chinese Academy of Sciences. 1988. *Soils of China*. Beijing: Science Press (in Chinese and English).

Vegetation of China Compilation Committee. 1980. *Vegetation of China*. Beijing: Science Press (in Chinese).

Zhao, Songqiao. 1983. "A New Scheme for Comprehensive Physical Regionalization in China," *Acta Geographica Sinica* 38, no. 1 (in Chinese).

Zhao, Songqiao. 1983. "Land Classification and Mapping in China," *Land Resources of the People's Republic of China*. Tokyo: United Nations University.

Zhao, Songqiao. 1986. *Physical Geography of China*. New York: Wiley.

CHAPTER TWO

Natural Resources

China possesses rich and varied natural resources. It ranks fourth in farmland area in the world, occupying 6.8 percent of the world's total farmland (Color Plate 5); third in grassland area, occupying 9 percent of the world's total grassland; and fifth in forest area, occupying 3.4 percent of the world's total forest (Color Plate 5). Annual runoff from China's rivers accounts for 5.6 percent of the world total, ranking sixth; and, thanks to innumerable big rivers and rugged, mountainous topography, it ranks first in hydroelectric capacity, accounting for 16.7 percent of the world total. China is also rich in flora and fauna, accounting for 10 percent each of total vascular plants and vertebrate species. Furthermore, among the 160 known mineral resources in the world, practically all have been discovered in China, with tungsten (W), antimony (Sb), zinc (Zn), titanium (Ti), vanadium (V), ferrous sulfide (FeS), rare earths, magnesite, gypsum, graphite, and others ranking first in the total world reserves, and tin (Sn), mercury (Hg), molybdenum (Mo), coal, asbestos, and talc ranking second or third. In total value of 45 major mineral resources, China ranks third (after the former Soviet Union and the United States). Yet, owing to an exceedingly high population, per capita value for many natural resources is generally far below the world average.

ARABLE LAND RESOURCES

China's inadequate supply of arable land is a critical limiting factor for food production and agricultural development. With a total population of more than 1.1 billion, about 70 to 80 percent are still engaged in agriculture. According to official 1980 statistics, there were

about 102.6 million hectares of cultivated farmland and a total population of 1.03 billion, which translates into an average of less than 0.10 ha per capita and less than 0.12 ha per farmer. In 1990, owing to large growth in nonagricultural use, the total farmland area decreased to 95.7 million ha, while population increased to 1.14 billion, resulting in an area of 0.08 ha per capita and area per farmer to 0.10 ha. The potential arable land not yet cultivated is also quite limited. I estimated in 1980, that there were only 46.9 million ha in total, and most of this land is of marginal quality. An old Chinese saying goes, "Each inch of the arable land should be optimally used."

Such limited arable land results chiefly from the overwhelmingly large proportion of unfavorable mountainous topography and the high proportion of the population engaged in agriculture. Compared with the United States, China has a similarly large land area and similar climates. However, the United States has only about one-third of its total land area in mountainous topography and only about one fourth as many people as China. Only about 3 percent of the total population of the United States is engaged in agriculture, but the United States has 80 percent more total farmland than China, 10 times more farmland per capita, and 250 times more farmland per farmer. This may be the main reason why annual food production per American farmer is now about 120 times more than a Chinese farmer (about 120 tons:1 ton).

The distribution of China's arable land resource is quite varied and uneven (Tables 2.1. and 2.2; Color Plate 5). It is an outcome of both physical conditions and historical development. About 89 percent of China's total farmland is found in the regions of best physical conditions and earliest development in Eastern

TABLE 2.1
Distribution of Arable Land Resources in China (1980)

Natural & agricultural division	Cultivated farmland (million *mu**)	Unused arable land (million *mu*)
Eastern Monsoon China	1,365.5	396.0
Northeast China	276.5	147.6
Middle & lower Yellow River	447.4	41.4
Middle & lower Chang Jiang	364.4	54.0
South China	106.9	55.0
Southwest China	170.6	98.0
Northwest Arid China	162.0	261.9
Tibetan Frigid Plateau	12.2	47.0
Total	1,539.6	704.0

*One hectare (ha) is equal to 15 *mu*.

Source: Compiled from different scientific data, not necessarily authentic.

Monsoon China, concentrated especially in the middle and lower reaches of the Yellow River and the Chang Jiang. In Eastern Monsoon China, most of the arable land has already been cultivated, with only about 22.5 percent still left unused. Unused arable lands are mainly found in the following three areas: (1) northern Northeast China, which has been developed only since the mid-nineteenth century and is still the most important reclamation area in China (please refer to Color Plate 6); (2) hilly lands in Southwest and South China; and (3) coastal beaches along the high-tide line.

About 28.3 million ha of arable lands are scattered in Northwest Arid China, mainly in the inland basins, where they are close to the most favorable land and water conditions. Some examples are the Hexi Corridor, the Elbow Plains, the Tarim Basin, and the Junggar Basin. So far, only about 10.8 million ha have been cultivated, making up about 10 percent of China's total farmland. Still unused arable land areas in this region are widespread, accounting for about 40 percent of China's total still unused arable land resource.

On the Tibetan Frigid Plateau, owing to harsh environmental conditions and late historical development, there is comparatively little arable land, whether already cultivated or still unused.

CLIMATE RESOURCES

On the other hand, China has rich and varied climatic conditions, which are quite favorable for agricultural development. The monsoon climate with its heavy precipitation and high temperature coming together in the growing season makes China's farmlands, particularly the paddy rice fields, very productive. It is one of the major factors that have enabled China to rank first in food production in the world.

Solar Radiation

The distribution of annual sunshine hours in China generally increases from southeast to northwest, inversely proportional to the distribution of annual precipitation. The Guizhou Plateau and the Sichuan Basin in Southwest China have the lowest number of sunshine hours, with an average annual rate of less than 30 percent, or fewer than 1400 hours. Hence, the Guizhou Plateau has been aptly described as being "without three successive fine days," and in the Sichuan Basin it is said that a "dog would bark at the sun." Annual sunshine hours total about 2000 in South China and in the Chang Jiang valley, but range from 2400–3000 in the Yellow River valley and Northeast China. Northwest China and the high Tibetan Plateau have the greatest amount of annual sunshine hours, generally more than 3000. The Lenghu area in the western Qaidam Basin has the highest sunshine record in China, with average annual sunshine rate of 80 percent and 3600 total annual sunshine hours. During recent years, the abundant sunshine has been gradually harnessed for home heating in Northwest Arid China and on the Tibetan Plateau.

Annual solar radiation, the chief driving force for photosynthesis, generally follows the distribution of annual sunshine hours. The Tibetan Plateau, ranging from 180–240 Kcal/sq cm, ranks first. Northwest Arid China is second with 140–180 Kcal/sq cm. While humid East-

TABLE 2.2
Distribution of Farmland in China by Province* (1990)

Province (autonomous region, municipality)	Farmland total (10,000 *mu***)	Paddy land (10,000 *mu*)	Dry farming (10,000 *mu*)
Heilongjiang	13,246.6	1,022.1	12,224.5
Jilin	5,908.9	627.8	5,281.1
Liaoning	5,200.8	805.5	4,395.3
Beijing	619.1	49.0	570.1
Tianjin	647.2	66.6	580.6
Hebei	9,834.1	210.6	9,623.5
Henan	10,399.8	596.5	9,803.3
Shandong	10,278.9	240.5	10,038.4
Shanxi	5,538.8	16.1	5,522.7
Shaanxi	5,299.5	257.2	5,042.3
Shanghai	484.8	428.0	56.8
Jiangsu	6,836.8	4,206.2	2,630.6
Anhui	6,548.3	2,772.3	3,776.0
Zhejiang	2,585.1	2,144.1	441.0
Jiangxi	3,524.3	2,989.2	535.1
Hubei	5,215.2	2,807.7	2,407.5
Hunan	4,968.3	3,948.0	1,020.3
Fujian	1,854.7	1,498.7	356.0
Guangdong	3,786.9	2,849.8	937.1
Guangxi	3,893.9	2,377.3	1,516.6
Hainan	652.6	383.0	269.6
Sichuan	9,488.4	4,833.8	4,614.6
Guizhou	2,781.3	1,167.9	1,613.4
Yunnan	4,268.1	1,469.2	2,798.9
Inner Mongolia	7,448.6	114.3	7,334.3
Ningxia	1,193.8	262.6	931.2
Gansu	5,214.6	11.4	5,203.2
Qinghai	866.4	—	866.4
Xinjiang	4,630.2	122.0	4,508.2
Tibet	333.4	0.9	322.5
Total	143,509.4	38,278.3	105,231.1

*Taiwan and Hong Kong not included.
**One *mu* equals 666.7 sq m, or 1/6 acre, or 1/15 hectare.
Source: China State Statistical Bureau, *Statistical Yearbook of China, 1991.*

ern Monsoon China generally receives solar radiation of less than 140 Kcal/sq cm, the lowest value recorded in the cloudiest Sichuan Basin and the Guizhou Plateau is less than 100 Kcal/sq cm/yr (Figure 2.1).

Temperature

Nearly all regions of China, with a few exception such as extremely high mountains, are capable of growing green plants (crop, grass, trees, etc.). The spatial differentiation in temperature is mainly represented by latitudinal zona-tion, which can be conveniently measured by the cumulative temperature during the $\geq 10°C$ period. The cumulative temperature during the $\geq 10°C$ period is the best index for cropping suitability and the most significant limiting factor for different crops in China, as shown in Table 2.3. The Physical Regionalization Working Committee of the Chinese Academy of Sciences (1959), identified six temperature zones from south to north (equatorial, tropical, subtropical, warm temperate, temperate, cool temperate); the Tibetan Plateau was not included (see Figure 1.1). The subtropical zone, gener-

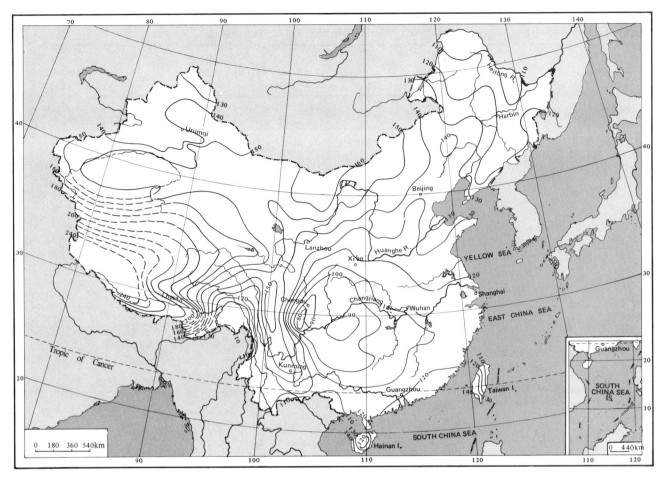

Figure 2.1 Distribution of annual total solar radiation in China (Kcal/cm²).

ally extending from 23°–34°N accounts for about 26 percent of China's total land area. This southernmost zone has a cumulative temperature during the ≥ 10°C period from 4500°–8000°C and a growing season of 250–350 days as well as annual precipitation of 750–1500 mm, making it possible to produce three crops each year. It is the best developed region agriculturally and the most densely populated area in China, accounting for 56 percent of China's total population, even though more than 70 percent of the land area is hilly or mountainous.

The vertical zonation of temperature is conspicuous in mountainous areas. Generally speaking, temperature decreases by 0.5°–0.6°C with each 100 m increase in elevation, roughly identical with the horizontal northward temperature decrease for each 100 km. Therefore, the vertical arrangement of land use (so-called vertical agriculture) should also be observed in mountainous areas.

Precipitation

As stated in Chapter One and shown in Figure 1.6, the distribution of annual precipitation in China generally decreases from southeast to northwest. Annual precipitation is abundant southeast of the Qinling-Huai He line, which is roughly identical to the 750 mm isohyet. Northwest of the 500 mm isohyet (roughly coincident with the Great Wall), there are extensive areas of semiarid and arid lands, occupying about 52.5 percent of China's total land area. In the transitional belt between the 500 mm isohyet and the 750 mm isohyet, rainfall is generally variable, often subject to both drought and flood hazards. In highly productive agricultural areas, annual precipitation is mostly concentrated in the summer half year, creating conditions favorable for crop growth, but these areas are often liable to floods and waterlogging.

TABLE 2.3
Cumulative Temperature During the ≥10°C Period and Cropping Systems in China

Temperature zone	≥10°C Cumulative temperature	Major cropping system	Major crops
Equatorial	About 9500°C	Year-round, triple cropping	Rice, cotton, sugar cane, sweet potato
Tropical	8000°–9000°C	Year-round, triple cropping	Rice, cotton, sugar cane, sweet potato
Subtropical	4500°–8000°C	Double to triple cropping	Rice, winter wheat, corn, cotton
Warm temperate	3200°–4500°C	Three crops in two years	Winter wheat, corn, millet, kaoliang, cotton
Temperate	1700°–3200°C	One crop each year	Spring wheat, corn, Irish potato, sugar beet, kaoliang
Cool temperate	About 1700°C	Marginal	Early spring wheat, Irish potato

Wind

Like solar energy, wind is abundant along the coast and in Northwest Arid China, where the average wind speed exceeds 3–4 m/sec. Wind forces are capable of being harnessed as a kind of renewable energy source, although the strong, steady winds have also caused serious eolian hazards. As of 1990, wind-driven micro-electricity generators had reached 100,000 units, with a total capacity of 12,000 KW. Da-Pan city (southeast of Ürümuqi, Xinjiang) had the largest installation, with 14 generators and a total capacity of 2050 KW.

WATER RESOURCES

Besides being a mountainous country, China also has great rivers. Rivers with their beneficial freshwater and capacity for delivering fertile alluvial soil particles have been feeding hundreds of millions of Chinese farmers for thousands of years. Chinese farmers are particularly well known for their close attachment to well-watered lowlands. Since ancient times, they have skillfully employed river systems for irrigation and navigation; their shallow-draft boats and bamboo rafts can carry loads upstream on river water less than 30 cm deep. In old China, boats were the chief communication means in southern China, while horses served the same purpose in northern China; hence, an old saying goes, "South, boat; north, horse." In modern times, rivers are also ex-tensively exploited for hydroelectric power generation and urban-industrial use.

There are three kinds of water resources: precipitation, surface water, and groundwater. We have discussed the first in the climate section; let us now briefly examine the other two.

Surface Water

Surface water resources include chiefly rivers and lakes. Fluvial runoff is an important renewable natural resource in China. According to a recent estimate, annual fluvial runoff in China totals 2630 billion cu m, as shown in Table 2.4. However, the average annual runoff depth reaches only 271 mm, whereas annual fluvial runoff per capita is less than 2500 cu m, much lower than the world average. Nevertheless, the potential hydropower resource in China, because of the mountainous topography and many large rivers originating on the high Tibetan Plateau, totals (theoretically) 680 million kilowatts (KW), ranking first in the world. In the upper and middle reaches of the Chang Jiang (Color Plate 7) and the Yellow River (Color Plate 8) the fluvial runoff is very large. As the rivers flow across the borderlands between the first, second, and third great topographical steps, they have a huge capability for generating hydroelectricity. For example, there are 24 topographic "steps" in the upper and middle reaches of the Yellow River channel, and each step might be dammed to store irrigation

TABLE 2.4
Annual Fluvial Runoff Resources in Different Drainage Basins

Drainage basin	Drainage area		Annual fluvial runoff		Average runoff depth (mm)
	sq km	% of total land area	$10^8 m^3$	% of total runoff resource	
Rivers in Northeast China	1,166,028	12.15	1,731.15	6.66	148
Rivers in N. China	319,029	3.32	283.45	1.09	89
Yellow River	752,443	7.84	574.86	2.21	76
Huai He and rivers in Shandong	326,258	3.40	597.86	2.30	183
Chang Jiang	1,807,119	18.83	9,793.89	37.66	542
Rivers along Southeast Coast	212,694	2.22	2,001.33	7.70	941
Zhu Jiang & rivers along S. Coast	553,437	5.76	4,466.27	17.81	807
Rivers in Taiwan & Hainan is.	68,160	0.71	887.36	3.41	1302
Rivers in Southwest China	408,374	4.25	2,160.84	8.31	529
Oceanic rivers on Tibetan Plateau	455,548	4.75	2,267.81	8.72	498
Arctic Basin	50,860	0.53	107.85	0.41	212
Oceanic Total	6,120,030	63.76	24,871.94	95.65	406
Inland Basin	3,679,970	36.24	1,130.70	4.35	32
China Total	9,600,000	100.00	26,002.64	100.00	271

Source: Compilation Committee, Chinese Academy of Sciences (1981). *Surface Water of China* (Beijing: Science Press).

water, to control floods and to generate hydroelectricity. Since 1949, five dams have been built, and more are under construction. The Liu-jia Gorge Dam, located about 100 km upstream from Lanzhou with a hydroelectricity capacity of 1.35 million KW, was the largest hydroelectricity producer in China before 1985. The Chang Jiang, with an annual fluvial runoff that accounts for nearly two-fifths of China's total, has an even much larger hydroelectricity capacity. The Three Gorges alone, located on the border between the upper and middle reaches of the Chang Jiang as well as between China's second and third great topographic steps, could produce an estimated 17.68 million KW of hydroelectricity if a 180 m high and 2100 m long dam is erected across the river. This would be 40 percent more than the world's current most powerful dam, the new Itaipu Dam in Brazil.

The areal distribution of fluvial runoff is quite uneven (see Figure 1.6). Most areas of fluvial runoff are concentrated in the oceanic drainage basins, accounting for nearly 96 percent of the total. The inland drainage basins, with land areas occupying 36 percent of the total land area in China, account for only 4 percent of total fluvial runoff. There are also conspicuous differences between the North and the South and among the major precipitation and runoff belts. The Chang Jiang basin is particularly outstanding with an area occupying 18.83 percent of the total land area but 37.66 percent of the total fluvial runoff resource in China.

China is also rich in lakes. Five major lake areas can be identified:

1. The Northeast China Plain, with large tracts of marshes, numerous small freshwater lakes, and a total lake area of 3722 sq km, which accounts for 4.7 percent of the total lake area in China.

2. Northwest Arid China has numerous scattered inland lakes with a total lake area of 22,500 sq km, occupying 27.9 percent of the total lake area in China. Most are terminal saline lakes of inland rivers.

3. The Tibetan Frigid Plateau also has many scattered inland saline lakes, with a total lake area of 30,974 sq km. Qinghai Lake, with an area of 4583 sq km, is the largest in China.

4. The middle and lower reaches of the Chang Jiang have numerous freshwater lakes, comprising a total area of 22,161 sq km. Poyang Lake, with an area of 3585 sq km, is now the largest freshwater lake in China.

5. The Yunnan-Guizhou Plateau has many structure-controlled, longitudinally elongated freshwater lakes, with a total lake area of 1188 sq km.

Groundwater

China has total groundwater resources of about 800 billion cu m. Shallow groundwater is mainly found in the Northeast China Plain, the North China Plain, the Hexi Corridor, northern Tibetan Plateau, and the karst areas of South China and Southwest China. There are major artesian basins in the Tarim Basin, the Junggar Basin, the Hexi Corridor, and the Sichuan Basin.

BIOLOGICAL RESOURCES

China has very rich biological resources, and during the last 80 centuries Chinese farmers have made intense use of them. Some of the resources they have used are wild plants for crop domestication, wild animals for domestication, and trees and shrubs for oasis making, "plain-forest" plantings, and other uses. (See Chapters Three and Four.) However, the negative side of human impact has also been very conspicuous, even critical, such as widespread deforestation, fauna extinction, and many biological hazards (rats, locusts, other insects, etc.). Practically no primary forests or grassland with their original fauna inhabitants still exist. (See Chapter Ten.)

Crop and Plant Resources

China has very rich flora resources. According to a recent estimate, there are 353 families, 3284 genera, and 27,150 species of vascular plants in China, accounting for 56.9 percent, 24.5 percent and 11.4 percent, respectively, of the world total.

After 80 centuries of agricultural development, Chinese peasants have domesticated and used many wild plants. The Chinese Ministry of Agriculture estimates that China has more than 1000 species of trees usable for timber, more than 4000 species of plants for medicine, more than 300 species of fruits, more 500 species of fiber plants, more than 300 species of starch plants, more than 600 species of plants that produce oil and fat, and more than 80 species of vegetables. It is particularly significant that many food crops, fruits, vegetables, and economically useful trees were domesticated for the first time in China. Some of the more familiar species include:

1. *Food crops:* millet (*Sataria italica* and *Panicum millaceum*), paddy rice (*Oryza sativa*), sorghum (*kaoliang*, *Andropogan sorghum*), buck wheat (*Fagopyrum esculentum*), barley (*Hordeum vulgare var. hexastichou*), soybean (*Glycine soya*), red bean (*Phaseolus angularis*), Japanese bean (*Stizolobium hassjoo*), and others.

2. *Vegetables:* *Dioscorea opposita* (Chinese yam), *Raphanus sativus* (turnip), *Brassica chinensis* (bok choy), *Brassica pekinensis* (celery cabbage), *Vigna sinensis*, *Allium chinensis*, *Allium fistulosum* (spring onion), *Allium sativum* (garlic), *Cucumis sativus* (cucumber), *Luffa cylindrica* (loofa), and others.

3. *Fruits:* *Malus asiatica* (Chinese apple), *Prunus armeniaco* (apricot), *Prunus ussuriensis* (pear), *Pyrus pyrifolia*, *Prunus persica* (peach), *Prunus pseudocerasus* (cherry), *Juglans regia* (walnut), *Lichi chinensis* (lychee), *Euphonia longana* (longan), *Clausena lansium* (wampee), *Diospyros kaki* (Japanese persimmon), *Hovenia dulcis* (Japanese raisin tree), *Citrus spp.*, *Fortunella spp.* (kumquats), and others.

4. *Economic crops:* *Sesamum indicum* (sesame), *Nelumbo nucifera* (lotus), *Eleocharis dulcis*, *Cannabis sativa*, *Abutilon avicennae*, *Boehmeria nivea*, and others.

5. *Medicine plants:* *Panax ginseng*, *Papaver somniferum* (opium), *Rheum officinale*, and others.

6. *Economic shrubs and trees:* *Morus spp.* (mulberry), *Camellia sinensis* (tea), *Camellia oleifera* (oil-tea), *Aleurites fordii* (tung oil), *Rhus verniciflua* (lacquer), *Sapium sebiferum*, *Illicium verum*, *Cinnamomum camphora*, *Ginkgo biloba*, and others.

In addition, many important crops and economically useful trees have been introduced into China from foreign countries at various historic times. Among these have been wheat (*Triticum spp.*), corn (*Zea mays*), sweet potato (*Ipomoea batatas*), Irish potato (*Solanum tuberosum*), cotton (*Gossypium herbaceum*), jute (*Corchorus spp.*), tobacco (*Nicotiana tabacum*), raisin (*Vitis vinifera*), banana (*Musa spp.*), sugar cane (*Saccharum officinarum*), the rubber tree (*Hevea spp.*), coconut (*Cocos nucifera*), agave (*Agave sisalova*), and many others. (See Chapter Three).

As of 1990, China had a total food cropping area of about 113.5 million ha with a total annual food production of 446.3 million metric tons, ranking first in the world.

Forest Resources

Based on China's physical conditions and historical documents, forest lands probably occupied about 40 percent of China's total land area during preagricultural times (about 80 percent of Eastern Monsoon China, 5 percent of Northwest Arid China, and 10 percent of the Tibetan Frigid Plateau). After 80 centuries of agricultural development and the accompanying ruthless deforestation, only about 1.2 million sq km of forest land are still left in China, occupying 12.7 percent of the total land area. Per capita forest land has been reduced to only 0.12 ha, and per capita annual growing forest biomass to only 10 cu m (the world averages are: 1.0 ha and 83 cu m, respectively). The types of forest land found in the mountainous areas of Northeast China, South China, and Southwest China differ according to climatic conditions. Major historical zonal forest types, from north to south, include cool-temperate needle-leaved forest (taiga), temperate mixed needle- and broad-leaved forest (Color Plate 9), warm-temperate deciduous broad-leaved forest, subtropical mixed evergreen and deciduous broad-leaved forest, tropical monsoon forest, and rain forest. Vertical zonation is also conspicuous and closely interrelated with historical zonation. The upper altitudinal limit of each forest type generally increases with the decreasing latitude. For example, the upper limit of montane cool-temperate needle-leaved forest is generally below 1000 m in the horizontal cool-temperate zone, but reaches to 1100–1800 m in the horizontal temperate zone, to 2000–3500 m in the horizontal warm-temperate zone, and to 3000–4200 m in the horizontal subtropical and tropical zones.

The distribution of forest resources by province is listed as Table 2.5.

Grassland Resources

China now has about 2.86 million sq km of grassland, accounting for 29.6 percent of the total land area. Grasslands are mainly distributed in Northwest Arid China and on the Tibetan Frigid Plateau. Major grassland types include forest-steppe, steppe, desert-steppe, alpine steppe, and park savanna (Figure 2.2). There are also many azonal grassland types, such as meadow, alpine meadow, and swamps, caused mainly by a high water table or depressed landforms. In addition, Eastern Monsoon China has large patches of secondary-growth grassland scattered in deforested areas. The distribution of usable grassland in ten pastoral provinces in 1984 is shown in Table 2.6.

Terrestrial Vertebrate Resources

According to a recent estimate, there are about 2091 species of terrestrial vertebrates in China (414 mammals, 1166 birds, 315 reptiles, 196 amphibians), accounting for about 10 percent of the world total. Many of them are endemic or principally distributed in China.

Chinese peasants have domesticated and made good use of many fauna species, such as the dog (domesticated as early as Paleolithic times), pig, sheep, goat, cattle, buffalo, horse, donkey, mule, yak, camel, chicken, duck, goose, rabbit, bee, silkworm, and others. (See Chapters Three and Four). Use has also been made of more than 70 kinds of fur-bearing wild animals. Yet, closely related to the damaging deforestation problem, fauna extinction has become a big environmental issue in China (see Chapter Ten). Since 1949, rare terrestrial vertebrates have been carefully protected according to the following categories:

1. Hunting absolutely prohibited.
2. Hunting strictly limited.
3. Hunting restricted.

Rare and protected terrestrial vertebrates in China are listed in Table 2.7.

MINERAL RESOURCES

Thanks to its vast area, mountainous topography, and complex geological history, China is rich in mineral resources, although the per capita value is invariably low for each type. As of 1990, more than 16,000 mine sites were in operation. Reserves of 148 kinds of minerals have been surveyed and assessed; more than 20 kinds rank high in proportion of world totals. The distribution of different minerals is mainly determined by geologic

TABLE 2.5
Distribution of Forest Resources in China by Province (1987)

Province (municipality, autonomous region)	Total land area (10,000 ha)	Forest land area (10,000 ha)	Total wood resource (10,000 cu m)
Heilongjiang	4,546.08	1,529.44	155,192.61
Jilin	1,888.69	607.89	71,101.76
Liaoning	1,457.39	365.27	10,855.94
Beijing	178.21	14.38	392.07
Tianjin	114.93	2.99	207.90
Hebei	1,848.79	167.68	4,809.50
Henan	1,670.00	141.99	6,821.86
Shandong	1,522.21	90.47	2,425.86
Shanxi	1,566.23	81.00	5,338.20
Shaanxi	2,059.77	447.14	27,934.63
Shanghai	59.56	0.79	61.63
Jiangsu	1,026.00	32.47	1,512.03
Anhui	1,381.65	179.16	6,975.49
Zhejiang	1,018.00	342.89	9,874.00
Jiangxi	1,667.23	546.23	30,261.08
Hubei	1,858.62	377.90	11,782.67
Hunan	2,118.35	687.23	19,887.93
Fujian	1,215.00	449.64	43,055.91
Guangdong (including Hainan)	2,120.05	587.86	23,183.30
Guangxi	2,376.00	522.82	26,587.52
Taiwan	357.60	196.95	22,183.30
Sichuan	3,660.79	681.08	115,292.83
Guizhou	1,764.71	230.93	15,940.90
Yunnan	3,826.44	919.65	132,131.38
Inner Mongolia	11,584.02	1,374.01	94,617.31
Ningxia	664.00	9.51	422.16
Gansu	4,497.34	176.90	17,305.73
Qinghai	7,215.14	19.45	2,303.18
Xinjiang	16,470.00	112.09	23,473.65
Tibet	12,284.36	632.05	143,626.16
Total	96,027.16	11,527.74	1,026,059.88

Source: Ye-jiang Hin (ed.), 1987. *Outline of Chinese Forestry.* (Beijing: Chinese Forestry Press), passim.

environments (Figure 2.3), and three types might be identified.

1. *Extensively distributed:* widely located almost all over China, but some are concentrated in favorable locations. Coal is mainly found in Shanxi, Shaanxi, Inner Mongolia, and Guizhou, but is widely distributed in other provinces. Other examples are iron, copper, and phosphates.

2. *Usually concentrated in restricted zones:* sometimes several minerals coexist in combination, such as tungsten, zinc, aluminum, and antimony. Mineral belts in South China are especially significant.

3. *Mainly restricted to local areas:* such minerals include potassium (K), which is exclusively found in the Qarhan Lake of central Qaidam Basin, Qinghai Province.

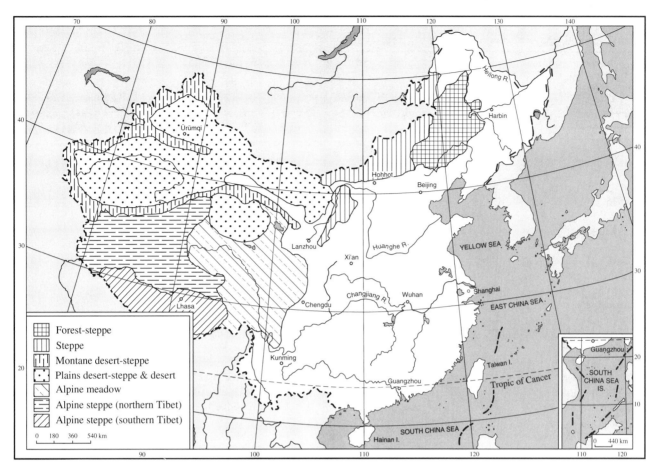

Figure 2.2 Major grassland types in China (Adapted from Institute of Geography, Chinese Academy of Sciences, *Agricultural Geography of China*, Beijing: Science Press, 1980, Map 1-2).

TABLE 2.6
Distribution of Usable Grassland in 10 Pastoral Provinces (1984)

Province (autonomous region)	Usable grassland (10,000 *mu*)
Inner Mongolia	83,557
Xinjiang	75,600
Tibet	80,100
Qinghai	48,712
Gansu	13,500
Sichuan	16,950
Heilongjiang	7,000
Jilin	238
Liaoning	1,850
Ningxia	3,937
10 province total	331,496

Source: Yu-tan, Lee *Grassland Management* (Chongqing: Sichuan Science & Technology Press, 1986), passim.

The recent estimated reserves of major minerals in China are listed in Table 2.8.

Energy Minerals

Energy minerals include coal, petroleum, natural gas, oil shale, and radioactive minerals, of which the first two are the most important in China.

Coal

Coal is the major energy source and supports the largest mining industry in China. Speculative reserves (as deep as 1500 m in northern China and 1000 m in southern China) were estimated to be 320 billion tons in 1980, with total proven reserves of 74 billion tons in 1982. In recent years, new large-scale coal mines have been developed, many of which can be conveniently exploited by open pits. Proven coal reserves reached 859.4 billion

TABLE 2.7
Rare Terrestrial Vertebrates in China

Common name	Latin name	Common name	Latin name
1. reindeer	*Rangifer tarandus*	28. white-lip deer	*Cervus alburostris*
2. moose	*Alces alces*	29. blue sheep	*Pseudois nayaur*
3. musk deer	*Moschus moschiferus*	30. Tibetan antelope	*Pantholops hodgsoni*
4. wolverine	*Gulo gulo*	31. wild yak	*Bos grunniens*
5. sable	*Martes zibellina*	32. black-necked crane	*Grus nigricollis*
6. tiger of the Northeast	*Panthera tigris*	33. tragopan pheasant	*Tragophan spp.*
7. swan	*Sygnus spp.*	34. giant panda	*Ailuropoda melanoleuca*
8. red-crown crane	*Grus japonesis*	35. lesser panda	*Ailurus fulgens*
9. mandarin duck	*Aix galericulata*	36. takin	*Budorcas taxicolor*
10. sika deer, plum flower deer	*Cervus nippon*	37. wild cattle, gaur	*Bos gaurus*
11. goral, green goat	*Naemorhedus goral*	38. slow loris	*Nycticebus coucang*
12. great bustard	*Otis tarda*	39. white-head langur	*Prebytis spp.*
13. Mongolian gazelle	*Procaprra gutturosa*	40. crested gibbon	*Hylobates concornis*
14. goitered gazelle	*Gazella subgutturosa*	41. wild elephant	*Elephas maximus*
15. ermine	*Mustela erminea*	42. great pied hornbill	*Buceros bicornis*
16. wild horse	*Equus pszewalskii*	43. green peacock	*Pavo muticus*
17. wild ass	*Equus hemionus*	44. river deer	*Hydropotes inermis*
18. wild camel, Bactrian camel	*Cameulus bactrianus*	45. long-tailed pheasant	*Syrmaticus spp.*
19. saiga antelope	*Saiga tatarica*	46. tufted deer	*Elaphodus cephalophus*
20. big horn sheep	*Ovis ammon*	47. black Muntjac deer	*Mutiacus crinifrons*
21. stone marten	*Martes foina*	48. Chinese river dolphin	*Lipotes vexillifer*
22. Tibetan snowcock	*Tetraogallus tibetanus*	49. Yangzi alligator	*Alligator sinensis*
23. eared pheasant	*Crossopilon spp.*	50. Crocodile lizard	*Shinisaurus crocodilurus*
24. beaver	*Castor fiber*	51. tiger of South China	*Panthera tigris*
25. giant salamander	*Megalobatrachus davidianus*	52. Eld's deer	*Cerrus Eldi*
26. Rhesus macague	*Macaca mulata*	53. Taiwan macaque	*Macaca cyclopis*
27. golden-hair monkey	*Rhinopithecus roxellanae*		

tons in 1990. China's annual coal production rapidly increased from 620 million tons in 1980 to 1080 million tons in 1990, ranking first in the world. (See Chapter Five).

Coal mines are now found in most parts of China, concentrating mainly on the Carboniferous-Permean strata in North China, the Jurassic strata in Northwest and Northeast China, and the Permean strata in southern China. They are especially numerous in northern China. Shanxi Province on the Loess Plateau, accounting for about 30 percent of China's total proven coal reserves, is called the "country of coal." Large-scale coal reserves have also been recently discovered in the eastern Mongolian and Ordos plateaus, where large-scale open-pit coal mines are under full scale construction. The borderland between Shanxi, Shaanxi, and Inner Mongolia is now called "The Black Triangle," and where a host of environmental problems have been occurring there as a result of coal exploitation.

Petroleum and Natural Gas

Before 1950, China was thought to be very poor in petroleum and natural gas resources, with an annual petroleum production of only 120,000 tons in 1949. Both geological survey and oil production have made great strides since the late 1950s. The first large-scale oil field (Daqing or "Great Celebration," Color Plate 10) was discovered in the northern Northeast China Plain in 1959, and China became self-sufficient in petroleum for the first time in 1965. Later on, many important oil fields have been discovered and exploited in the southern Northeast China Plain, in the northeastern North China Plain, and in the middle and lower Chang Jiang valley. These coastal oil fields, together with numerous newly discovered fields along the continental shelves of the Yellow Sea, East China Sea, and South China Sea, form a great northeast–southwest trending rich oil belt located at the inner side of the Arc Mountain System

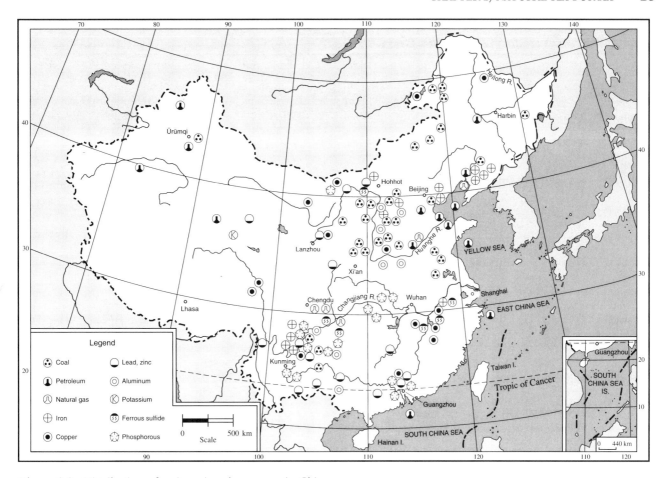

Figure 2.3   Distribution of major mineral resources in China.

(Western Pacific Rim). Numerous inland oil fields have also been discovered and are operating in the Junggar Basin, the Tarim Basin, the Hexi Corridor, the Sichuan Basin, and the Ordos Plateau, and appear to be an eastern continuation of the great Central Asian oil belt. China's annual petroleum production reached 104 million tons in 1978 and 138.3 million tons in 1990, and China became one of the leading oil producers in the world. In recent years, important new geological surveys have been undertaken along the coastal areas and the continental shelves as well as deep in the inland basins. As a result, huge amounts of oil reserves have been added, especially in the three inland basins of Xinjiang-Tarim, Turpan, and Junggar. In 1991, the total petroleum and natural gas speculative reserves in these regions accounted for one-fourth and one-third, respectively, of the national total.

Metal Minerals

China is rich in metal minerals, especially in nonferrous metals, with production of tungsten, antimony, zinc, titanium, vanadium, tin, mercury, molybdenum, iron sulfide, and rare earths ranking among the first three in the world.

Iron (Fe)

China has proven iron ore reserves of nearly 50 billion tons, ranking fifth in the world. About 95 percent of the total iron ore reserves are of low grade, with an average iron content of only 32.1 percent; high-grade iron ores (iron content above 60 percent) amount to less than 5 percent. Hence, to supply China's iron and steel industries, a certain amount of high-grade ore must be imported from foreign countries. The distribution of large

TABLE 2.8
Estimated Reserves of Major Minerals in China

Mineral	Unit of reserve	Reserve	Mineral	Unit of reserve	Reserve
Coal	100 million ton	8593.50	Magnesite	100 million ton	28.30
Petroleum	100 million ton	25.21	Gadolinium	10,000 ton	1.50
Natural gas	100 million cu m	150.00	Florine	10,000 ton	33000.00
Iron ore	100 million ton	495.70	Terralsols	10,000 ton	12.00
Manganese	10,000 ton	1400.00	Ferrous sulfide	100 million ton	128.00
Vanadium	10,000 ton	60.00	Dimond	10,000 kara	10.00
Titanium	10,000 ton	1800.00	Phosphate	100 million ton	140.80
Copper	10,000 ton	5000.00	Salt	100 million ton	1241.90
Lead	10,000 ton	200.00	Potassium oxide	10,000 ton	2213.40
Zinc	10,000 ton	500.00	Iodine	10,000 ton	18.18
Bauxite	100 million ton	14.50	Boron	10,000 ton	27.20
Nickel	10,000 ton	72.50	Barite	10,000 ton	36.30
Tungsten	10,000 ton	120.00	Talc	100 million ton	8972.00
Tin	10,000 ton	50-250	Pyrophylite	10,000 ton	10000.00
Molybdenum	10,000 ton	45.50	Clay	100 million ton	18.00
Mercury	10,000 ton	30.00	Silica	100 million ton	9.30
Antimony	10,000 ton	237.00	Dolomite	100 million ton	84.00
Gallium ore	ton	100.00	Limestone	100 million ton	103.00
Magnesium	10,000 ton	74500.00	Gypsum	100 million ton	106.00
Bismuth	10,000 ton	0.50	Asbestos	10,000 ton	5519.00
Rare earth (oxide)	10,000 ton	3600.00	Kaolinite	10,000 ton	9042.00
			Sand	100 million ton	10.90

Source: Adapted from Commission on Integrated Investigation of Natural Resources, *Handbook of National Resources in China* (Beijing: Science Press, 1990), p. 637.

iron ore bodies is restricted to a few sites, although small ore sites are found almost all over China. Large iron ore sites with proven reserves of more than 1 billion tons include Anshan–Benxi (southern Liaoning Province), Eastern Hebei, Panzihua (southwestern Sichuan Province), Wutai (northern Shanxi Province), Nanjing–Wuhu (border between Jiangsu and Anhui provinces), Baotou–Bayan Obo (Inner Mongolia), and western Hubei. Among these, only the last has not yet been exploited.

Nonferrous Minerals

The nonferrous metals include the so-called heavy metals (copper, lead, zinc, tin, nickel, antimony, mercury, cadmium, bismuth, and others), light metals (aluminum, magnesium, sodium, potassium, calcium, silicon, basium, and others), precious metals (gold, silver, platinum, rhodium, iridium, osmium, and others), rare metals (tungsten, molybdenum, vanadium, titanium, niobium, zirconium, rubidium, cesium, beryllium, gallium, indium, thallium, germanium, and others), radioactive metals (radium, polonium, terbium, palladium, ura-

nium, and others) and semimetals (silicon, selenium, boron, arsenic, tellurium, and others). These metals are widely distributed in China and usually coexist in groups. For example, at the Baotou–Bayan Obo iron mine are also found the richest niobium (Nb) and other rare earths reserves in the world; at the Panzihua iron mine are also found rich vanadium, titanium, and cobalt reserves; the Jinchuan nickel mine (in the Hexi Corridor, the richest in China) also contains copper, cobalt, and platinum reserves; and the Gejiu tin mine (in southern Yunnan Province, the richest in China) also contains lead, copper, and rare metals. As a result, important mining industries have been developed at all these sites.

Nonmetals

In China, 76 kinds of nonmetal minerals have been surveyed and assessed for their reserves. These include limestone and other building materials, iodine, bromine, and other chemical raw materials, phosphorous and other fertilizers, as well as diamonds, jade, and other precious stones. In addition, the Liaodong Peninsula, Liaoning

Province, has a huge reserve of more than 2.8 billion tons of magnisite ore, ranking first in the world.

REFERENCES

Commission on Integrated Investigation of Natural Resources, Chinese Academy of Sciences, 1990. *Handbook of Natural Resources in China*. Beijing: Science Press (in Chinese).

Compilation Committee, Chinese Academy of Sciences. 1984. *Climate of China*, Physical Geography of China. Beijing: Science Press (in Chinese).

Compilation Committee, Chinese Academy of Sciences. 1981. *Surface Water of China*, Physical Geography of China. Beijing: Science Press (in Chinese).

Compilation Committee, Chinese Academy of Sciences. 1981. *Groundwater of China*, Physical Geography of China. Beijing: Science Press (in Chinese).

Compilation Committee, Chinese Academy of Sciences. 1983, 1988. *Plant Geography of China*, Physical Geography of China (2 vols.). Beijing: Science Press (in Chinese).

Compilation Committee, Chinese Academy of Sciences. 1978. *Animal Geography of China*, Physical Geography of China. Beijing: Science Press (in Chinese).

Lee, Pan. 1984. *History of Cultivated Plants in China*. Beijing: Science Press (in Chinese).

Li, Wenyan et al. 1990. *Industrial Geography of China*. Beijing: Science Press (in Chinese).

Zhao, Songqiao. 1986. *Physical Geography of China*. New York: Wiley.

Zhao, Songqiao. 1986. "Formation and Distribution of Natural Resources in China," *Journal of Natural Resources,* 1, no.1, pp. 41–55 (in Chinese).

Zhao, Songqiao. 1984. "Arable Land Resources in China," *Natural Resources,* 1, pp. 13–20 (in Chinese).

Zhao, Songqiao. 1988. "River and Man in China," *Proceedings of the International Symposium on Water Civilization*, Toyoma, Japan (in Japanese and English).

CHAPTER THREE

Historical Background

Besides being one large country, China is also an old nation. It has had a continuous agricultural civilization for 80 centuries. Consequently, humankind has made a significant impact on the physical environment, and for most parts of China, nature and humankind have been merged and integrated into a whole. Yet, such a long history has also many disadvantages. For example, the autocratic and corrupted feudal society lasted too long in ancient China, and it has even stamped a heavy imprint on modern and contemporary China.

PREHISTORIC SOCIETY: PALEOLITHIC (ABOUT 1.7 MILLION TO 8000 YEARS AGO)

China is one of the places where humankind began. At first, the land was occupied by a slowly evolving primitive society. Groups of ancient humans (*Homo erectus*) and later groups of modern people (*Homo sapiens*) were sparsely scattered in Eastern Monsoon China. They were loosely organized by kinship groups, but without a strong family system. Each group worked and lived together, most in caves. They used crude Paleolithic tools and survived by gathering, fishing, and hunting. Their impact on the physical environment was not yet great as a whole; although by using fire, they had a significant effect on their immediate surroundings. Five human fossils and their cultural remains that have been found in China mark five stages of development in the long prehistoric period.

Yuanmou Man

Fossils of Yuanmou Man were first excavated in A.D. 1965 in a small subtropical basin (elevation 1100 m) along a tributary of the Jinsha River in the upper reaches of the Chang Jiang on the northeastern part of the Yunnan Plateau. These people lived about 1.7 million years ago. They used very primitive Paleolithic tools and probably knew how to use fire.

Lantian Man

First excavated in A.D. 1963 at Lantian (near Xi'an) on the warm temperate Loess Plateau, the Lantian people lived about 800,000 to 600,000 years before the present. Their Paleolithic tools, although still very primitive, were somewhat improved and more varied than those of the Yuanmou Man.

Peking Man

Peking Man fossils were first excavated in A.D. 1927 at Zhoukoudian (a Beijing suburb) on the northwestern margin of warm temperate North China Plain. Peking Man lived about 700,000 to 200,000 years before the present but was still *Homo erectus*, although he already had many physical features similar to *Homo sapiens*. He definitely knew how to make fire and how to maintain it. Many Paleolithic tools and animals as well as fish skeletons were discovered in these caves.

Tingcun Man

Remains of Tingcun Man were first excavated in A.D. 1954 along lower Fen River on the eastern Loess Plateau. People existed there between 100,000 and 200,000 years ago. Tingcun Man had much improved and varied Paleolithic tools compared to those of Peking Man. He also progressed gradually from living in loosely organized groups to living as members of matriarchal clans.

Upper Cave Man

At the same site where Peking Man was found, fossils of two Upper Cave people were first excavated in A.D. 1933. They lived about 18,000 years ago. They were definitely *Homo sapiens*, with much improved Paleolithic tools. In their caves, 54 kinds of fauna remains were discovered, some of which were fish fossils. The fish remains show that, besides gathering and hunting, Upper Cave Man also lived on fish. Stone arrow heads have been discovered, too, showing that the decisive weapon in primitive society, the bow and arrow, had already been invented and used. Upper Cave Man lived in matriarchal communes.

THE DAWN OF AGRICULTURAL CIVILIZATION: NEOLITHIC (ABOUT 8000–4000 YEARS AGO)

China is also one of the areas where agriculture began. Furthermore, unlike other locations of agricultural origins, which perished or disappeared, China has continued its development uninterruptedly ever since its beginning. From about 8000 years ago until about 4000 years ago, more or less coincident with the legendary period of Three Rulers and Five Emperors, early agricultural sites appeared in small patches almost all over China, especially in the middle and lower reaches of the Yellow River and the Chang Jiang. Although not yet validated by written documents, many cultural sites have been excavated and show faithfully this long prehistoric period. Geographically and agriculturally, two great farming systems stand out from the very beginning: (1) dry farmland in northern China, with the middle and lower reaches of the Yellow River as its core, and (2) paddy rice farming in southern China, with the middle and lower Chang Jiang valley and northern southeast coast as its center.

According to ancient Chinese tradition, five ethnic groups or tribe-leagues can be identified: (1) the Hua (later Han) mainly on the Loess Plateau and its surroundings; (2) the Dong Yi, mainly living along the coast of northern China; (3) the Meng, mainly in southern China, especially in middle and lower Chang Jiang basin; (4) the Chang, mainly inhabiting southwestern China and the upper reaches of the Yellow River basin; and (5) the Di, scattered on the northern border of China. These five ethnic groups gradually mingled and merged together to form the modern Chinese people.

Three cultural stages can be identified (Figure 3.1).

The Dadiwan Cultures

Including the Cishan, Peligan, and Hemudu cultures, the Dadiwan cultures might represent the earliest agricultural stage in China.[1] Dozens of cultural sites have been recently excavated, of which, the Dadiwan and Hemudu represent dry farmland and paddy rice farming, respectively.

The Dadiwan Site

The Dadiwan site is located 45 km northeast of Qin, a county in Gansu Province. It is situated in the center of the Loess Plateau where the present bioclimatic landscape is warm temperate forest-steppe. Four cultural layers (from ground surface downward) have been unearthed at this site:

1. Modern tilth layer, 0.3–1.0 m below ground surface.
2. Yangshao culture layer, 1.0–2.0 m below layer 1.
3. Dadiwan culture layer, 0.5–0.7 m below layer 2.
4. Malan loess layer, below layer 3.

The Dadiwan culture layer overlies the Malan loess layer (Late Pleistocene, more or less identical with the Würm Ice Age), and underlies the Yangshao culture

---

[1] Still earlier than the Dadiwan cultures, there might have been a cave-dwelling and knife-cultivating primitive hunting-farming system (about 8000–8500 years ago), mainly scattered in hilly southern China, such as at Fairy Cave (Jiangxi Province) and Yellow Rock Cave (Guangdong Province) cultural sites. These ancient cave-dwelling people lived by hunting but also grew a few food crops (such as taro) and vegetables (such as cucumber) in nearby areas. They cut trees with stone knives, then burned them, and sowed crop seeds with a stick amid the ash and soil. After cropping for one or two years in a spot, they moved to new sites.

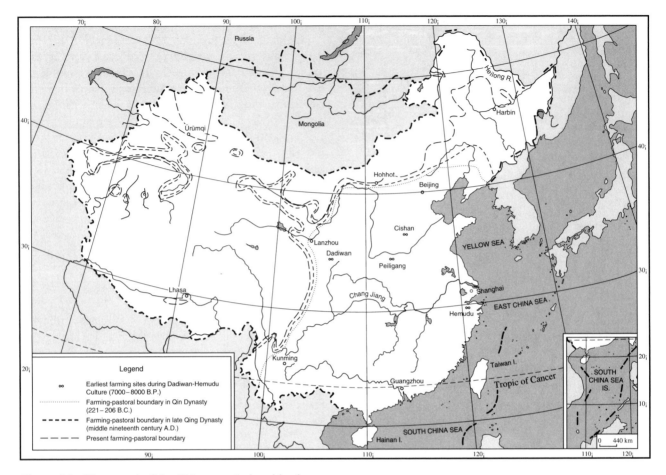

Figure 3.1   The spread of the Chinese agricultural landscape

layer. At the top of the Dadiwan culture layer, there is a diluvial or eolian statum, 20–30 cm thick, where three house sites, five tombs, and many Neolithic tools, as well as painted pottery and crop (mainly millet and rapeseed) remains have been unearthed. According to C[14] dating, the remains date from 7300–7800 years ago.

Many similar culture sites have also been excavated on borderlands of the Loess Plateau, of which Peligang of northwestern Henan Province and Cishan of southwestern Hebei Province are the most famous. It seems that during early Neolithic times, the Loess Plateau and its borderland were the origin and center of dry farming in ancient China. From here, a dry farming system was gradually developed and extended first to the North China Plain and the middle Chang Jiang valley and then to other parts of China.

The Hemudu Site

The Hemudu site is located on the coastal plain along the Hangzhou Estuary's southern bank, about 25 km northwest of Ningbo (Figure 3.1). It has an excavated area of about 40,000 sq m and an elevation of 3–4 m above sea level. Extensive lignite deposits lie underneath the surrounding paddy rice cropland, revealing its ancient lagoon and marsh environment. Its significant cultural remains include large quantities of pile dwellings, domesticated rice seeds, bone spades, pig, buffalo, and dog bones, as well as more than 50 kinds of wild animals and remains of many kinds of tropical and subtropical hydrophytes such as *Murraya paniculata L.*, *Lygodium microstuchyum*, and *L. salicifolium*.

Underneath the tilth strata (40–50 cm thick), four cultural strata appear, in order from the surface downward:

1. *First cultural strata:* about 5100–5600 years ago. From this sticky cinnamon-yellowish silt, 70–105 cm thick, greyish pottery and numerous stone utensils were unearthed.

2. *Second cultural strata:* about 5600–5900 years ago. From this sticky green-yellowish silt, 20–35 cm thick, a pile dwelling, a water well, stone utensils, and reddish pottery were unearthed, but no elephant and rhinoceros remains were found.

3. *Third cultural strata:* about 5900–6600 years ago. From this loose greyish sandy soil, 60–110 cm thick, large quantities of pile dwelling remains, bone spades, wood spades, domesticated rice, domesticated animal bones (elephant, rhinoceros, David's deer, and others) as well as greyish pottery, ivory, and lacquer works were unearthed.

4. *Fourth cultural strata:* about 6600–7000 years ago. This soft darkish silt, 100–165 cm thick, yielded large quantities of domesticated rice seeds, bone spades, pile dwelling remains, black pottery, wood paddles, wild animal bones (Asian elephant, Java and Sumatra rhinoceros, David's deer, Chinese alligator, sea turtle, land turtle, and others), and bones of domesticated animals (pig, dog, and buffalo).

The Luajiajiao cultural site and four other cultural sites along the Hangzhou Estuary's northern bank have features similar to the Hemudu Site. At all of them have been discovered large quantities of domesticated paddy rice. The rice belongs to two subspecies: *Oryza sativa L. Subsp. Hsien Ting* and *O. S. L. subsp. Keng Ting*, both originated in China. More than 30 Neolithic cultural sites south of the Chang Jiang have been discovered containing paddy rice remains. The Hemudu site might be the earliest area in China (probably also in the world) where rice was domesticated. From this evidence, domesticated rice might have spread first to the Chang Jiang basin and other southern Chinese areas, then to other parts of China and neighboring countries.

Yangshao Culture

In A.D. 1921 the Swedish geologist J. G. Andersson was the first person to excavate and recognize an important Neolithic village (Yangshao) in northwestern Henan Province. The village was dated to be about 5000–6000 years old. The Yangshao culture was widespread in the Yellow River basin, especially in its middle reaches. The Panpo (near Xi'an) cultural site was the most typical, and a museum has been founded there. Yangshao culture was a major representative of a matriarchal society. People had already acquired the skill of making stone and bone tools through the grinding process—the chief criterion for differentiating Neolithic from Paleolithic cultures. Farming (based on millet, rapeseed, and some vegetables) as well as animal husbandry (mainly the dog and pig) had been widely conducted, although gathering, hunting, and fishing were still important occupations. Primitive industries also appeared. People of the Yangshao culture manufactured bows and arrows as well as painted pottery. They knew how to spin and weave and how to build houses, thus beginning a more sedentary life.

Longshan Culture

Approximately 5000 years ago, many clans (tribes) in the Yellow River and the Chang Jiang basins entered the stage of patriarchal society one after another. Longshan cultures, including the widely distributed Longshan culture in Shandong Province, the Qijia culture in Gansu Province, and the Liangzhu culture in Zhejiang Province, are principal examples of a patriarchal commune.

By this time people had already entered the late Neolithic age. Agricultural products increased in quantity as well as in diversity. Besides millet, rice, and rapeseed, other crops such as wheat, barley, kaoliang (sorghum), hemp, and mulberry trees were grown. For the first time, the method of fermenting grain to make wine was invented. There was also a variety of domesticated animals, including horses, cattle, sheep, goats, chickens, dogs, and pigs. Sheep and goats, as well as wheat, were probably introduced from Southwest Asia.

The technology of making pottery also improved; black pottery, white pottery, and eggshell pottery were inventions of this time. Handicraft products such as jade and bone articles were developed. The progress made in the division of labor and in the exchange of commodities sped up the development of the institution of private property and the division of society into classes, which in turn precipitated the dissolution of primitive society. In political organization, this was the period of so-called military democracy, which existed in numerous clans, tribes, and tribe-leagues. Military leaders as well as political chiefs were elected. The so-called Five Emperors in ancient Chinese tradition were probably elected chiefs of the most powerful tribe-leagues.

THE EARLIEST CHINESE STATES: THE XIA, SHANG, AND WESTERN ZHOU DYNASTIES AND SPRING AND AUTUMN PERIOD (2206–403 B.C.)

The Great Yu (2206–2202 B.C.) founded the Xia Dynasty, which might be identified as the first political state in Chinese history. It was succeeded by the Shang and Western Zhou dynasties, which then broke into numerous small states in the Spring and Autumn period (or Eastern Zhou Dynasty). The political and economic center of the first three dynasties was mainly restricted to the middle and lower reaches of the Yellow River. In the Spring and Autumn Period, the middle and lower reaches of the Chang Jiang were also highly developed. Around these political and economic centers, which were under direct control of the central government, peripheral belts of semi-independent tribes or fiefs developed in relation to increasing distance away from the control of the king. Consequently, the boundaries of these ancient states are difficult to delimit. However, during the Spring and Autumn Period, these small states were usually under the nominal authority of the Eastern Zhou Dynasty and their political boundaries were more or less definite.

During this long ancient period much greater economic and social progress was made than in the primitive society. Both farming and animal husbandry were much better developed than in the Neolithic Age. Bronze rather than stone tools were used. Private property rights developed, and the division of labor as well as exchange of commodities accelerated. The primitive commune broke down as the Xia and Shang dynasties developed a slave society. The Western Zhou Dynasty started a long feudal society, which lasted until A.D. 1840 when the British and other Western powers imposed a semicolonial, semifeudal system on China.

The Xia Dynasty (2206–1766 B.C.)

The Great Yu, a member of the Hua tribe and a celebrated hydroengineer of flood control, was elected emperor in 2206 B.C. He was succeeded in 2201 B.C. by his son, Qi, and thus was founded the first dynasty (Xia), inaugurating a new epoch in Chinese political history. The Xia Dynasty lasted 471 years, with 17 successive emperors. Its territory was mainly restricted to the eastern side of Loess Plateau (southwestern Shanxi Province) and the western North China Plain (northwestern Henan Province). It had several capitals, but the main one was Anyi (modern Anyi County, southwestern Shanxi Province).

Socially and economically, the "tribal slavery system" dominated during the Xia Dynasty. All lands were state owned. People lived mainly by farming. When a clan or a tribe was conquered, people were taken as slaves and their lands were confiscated by the victor. Generally each family cultivated 3.33 ha of farmland for themselves, and 0.33 ha without any pay for the state. Handicraft industries also developed, fostering a technology for a bronze tool–making industry in a new era of Chinese civilization.

The Shang Dynasty (1766–1126 B.C.)

In 1766 B.C., the Dong Yi tribe along the lower reaches of the Yellow River under the leadership of Tang overthrew the Xia regime and established the Shang Dynasty, which lasted nearly 640 years with 30 successive emperors. Its territory was somewhat larger than that of the Xia Dynasty, including nearly all the North China Plain and the eastern part of the Loess Plateau. Owing to frequent floods in the North China Plain, the capital was moved five times during the first 370 years, and was finally fixed at Yin (modern Anyang in northern Henan Province).

Great progress was made during the Shang Dynasty. Governmental structure and army organization become quite sophisticated. Walled cities appeared. A system of owned lands and slavery was developed. The technology of raising silkworms and reeling silk as well as spinning and weaving had been mastered, and the skills of making bronze, pottery, lacquer, and wine were raised to a high level. Commerce with shell money started. A calendar and written script, appearing mainly as oracles written on tortoise shells and shoulder blades of oxen, were invented during the Shang Dynasty.

The Western Zhou Dynasty (1126–771 B.C.)

The Zhou clan was formerly distributed along the middle and upper reaches of the Wei River (the largest tributary of the Yellow River), and later moved to its lower reaches. In 1126 B.C. King Wu with his victorious army overthrew the Shang regime and established the Western Zhou Dynasty, which lasted 355 years with 12 successive emperors. Its territory was somewhat larger than that of the Shang Dynasty, enlarged especially along the northern flank of the middle and lower Chang Jiang. Its capital was essentially fixed at Hao, located to the southwest of modern Xi'an.

In order to strengthen its control on the country, the royal house of Zhou initially adopted a feudal system of fiefs whereby land and people were awarded to various dukes or princes. According to the written record, 71 states and as many as 1200 fiefs were created in this manner. Lu (in western Shandong Province), Wei (in northern Henan Province), Qi (in eastern Shandong Province), Jin (in Shanxi Province), and Yan (in northern Hebei Province) were the most important among the provinces. All lands were supposed to belong to the king, and all peasant slaves were compelled to work collectively under the "well-field" system. Agriculture was better developed than during the previous Shang Dynasty, even though irrigation, drainage, and fertilization had been previously practiced. All traditional crops, including millet, rice, sorghum, wheat, barley, beans, vegetables, melons, mulberry, hemp, and others, were grown. Another important crop—the soybean—which was all important for the nutrition and health of the Chinese peasants, was domesticated about 1100 B.C. Handicraft industries were mainly controlled by the government. The making of bronze tools was the most important. Less emphasis was given to production of pottery and silk, hemp, and woolen textiles. Commercial exchange of slaves, horses, oxen, weapons, and jade was actively pursued.

The Spring and Autumn Period (771–403 B.C.)

In 771 B.C., the rebellious fiefs of the Western Zhou Dynasty together with invading pastoral tribes, overran the core area of Zhou. The royal house had to flee eastward and established a new capital at Luoyi in what is now Luoyang, in western Henan Province. From that time the Zhou regime was known as the Eastern Zhou Dynasty although it is better known as the Spring and Autumn Period, named after Confucius's famous book, which recorded its history.

During this chaotic period, the royal house had only nominal authority over its fiefs, which were actually independent states. There were about 140 such small states, of which the most important were Jin, Qi, Lu, Wei, Yan, and Qin (in Shaanxi and Gansu provinces,

later also in Sichuan Province), Chu (in Hubei, Hunan, and Anhui provinces), Zheng (in central Henan Province), Song (in eastern Henan Province), Wu (in southern Jiangsu Province), and Yue (in northern Zhejiang Province). Gradually, the weaker states were annexed by the stronger ones. Therefore, it was a period of hegemonism as five states—Jin, Qi, Chu, Qin, and Wu—became the most powerful. Toward the end of this chaotic period, ministers within many states enhanced their power and influence. The result was that the power of many states fell gradually into the hands of a new class of landlords. For example, the once powerful Jin state was partitioned in 403 B.C. by three ministers into three states—Han, Wei, Zhao—heralding the end of the Spring and Autumn Period and the beginning of the Warring States Period.

During the Spring and Autumn Period, the ancient "well-field" farming system[2] declined, and private land-ownership came into existence. In 594 B.C., the state of Lu collected a land tax for the first time. Meanwhile, the technology of smelting iron was introduced, and iron was used to make axes, plows, and other tools. The custom of using the ox for plowing had also begun. Consequently, reclamation of large tracts of unused arable lands and construction of large-scale irrigation systems and reservoirs became possible. Two famous examples are the Que Bei Reservoir of Chu (Anhui Province) and the Kang Canal of Wu (Jiangsu Province), which was the forerunner of the Grand Canal. Handicrafts were also highly developed, including fabrication of iron and bronze tools, lacquer ware, wood construction, pottery, and textiles. On the basis of these products large-scale commerce developed, and many merchants became rich.

THE EARLY PERIOD OF FEUDAL SOCIETY: FROM THE WARRING STATES TO THE SOUTHERN AND NORTHERN DYNASTIES (403 B.C.–A.D. 589)

The very long feudal period in China started from the Warring States period in the fifth century B.C. and lasted until A.D. 1840, when the Western powers began to

[2] The ancient well-field farming system was arranged like the Chinese character "well" (井). The center square was the public land, while the surrounding eight pieces of land were privately used by peasants, who also cultivated the public land without compensation.

"open" China. This extended period might be roughly subdivided into three "cycles" or stages: (1) early period, (2) middle period, and (3) late period. During each one a grand scale of up-and-down vicissitudes in political and economic conditions occurred. Each "cycle" consisted of several feudal dynasties, and each dynasty had its small-scale ups and downs. The life-cycle model of "initial–adolescent–mature (corrupting)–old (collapsing)" might be applied to each dynasty. There is an old Chinese saying, "The world (country) will be divided after long unification, and it will be united again after long disunity." Probably an American saying, "Absolute power corrupts absolutely," can explain such a model. When each dynasty achieved absolute power, it became corrupted absolutely, thus paving the way for the rise of a new dynasty.

The early period of the feudal society came into prominence when one of the warring states, Qin, eventually unified the country for the first time in 221 B.C., although the dynasty was short-lived. Then came the Western and Eastern Han dynasties, when China reached great political and economic power, and hence the name "Han" became the symbol of Chinese nationhood.

Then came the rather chaotic period of Three Kingdoms. Subsequently the Western Jin Dynasty unified China for a short time, but soon collapsed again into an even more chaotic stage consisting of the Southern and Northern Dynasties. In A.D. 589 China was reunited by the Sui Dynasty. These nearly 1000 years of vicissitudes might be termed the ancient history of China, characterized by the appearance of a unified Chinese national state as well as the opening of the iron age. It was also the first time that nearly all the original Eastern Monsoon China between the Great Wall and the Nanling Mountains was well developed. In addition, large parts of Northwest Arid China together with Korea and Vietnam became Chinese territory (Figure 3.2).

Economically and socially, agriculture and handicraft industries progressed rapidly during the Western and Eastern Han dynasties. Iron tools and plowing with oxen were widely used, and the practice of primitive shifting cultivation (so-called knife cultivating and fire planting in northern China and fire planting and water weeding in southern China) gradually gave way to the traditional "peasant-gardener farming system." The famous Silk Road and other highways as well as sea traffic opened, and commerce and cities flourished. Population also increased. However, in subsequent chaotic periods, economic conditions deteriorated, population decreased, and probably the only bright side was that numerous nationalities mixed and fused freely, resulting in the creation of a greater and larger Chinese nation.

The Warring States Period (403–221 B.C.)

The Warring States Period evolved from the Spring and Autumn Period. At first, there were more than 20 states. After many years of bloody wars of expansion and annexation, only seven states survived: Qin, Chu, Qi, Han, Wei, Zhao, and Yan. The Eastern Zhou Dynasty itself was annexed by Qin in 249 B.C. These seven states fought, checked, and balanced one another. To cope with such a critical situation, each state was compelled to initiate reforms at one time or another. Each state tried to speed up the development of its economy and culture as well as to increase population (as work force). Each developed its own monetary system, vehicle roads, and even written script. Consequently, Chinese agricultural civilization expanded widely in Eastern Monsoon China from the Nanling Mountains (about 25° N, the southern boundary of Chu) to the Great Wall (about 40° N). Three northern border states—Qin, Zhao, and Yan—constructed the Great Wall along their northern borders for the purpose of defense against the Xiong Nu, known in the West as the Huns, a nomadic tribe-league from the north. The most thorough reforms had already taken place in Qin, and hence it became the strongest state and eventually conquered all the other states.

During this rapidly changing period, a private land-ownership system became firmly established and the newly emerged landlord class became the power base in various states. The traditional Chinese peasant-gardener farming system started to appear, and gradually it extended over all of the middle and lower reaches of the Yellow River and the Chang Jiang. Instruments of iron and plowing with oxen became popular over a wider and wider area. Irrigation construction was greatly improved. For example, Ximen Bao of Wei, channeling the water of the Zhang River for irrigation in the fourth century B.C., helped agricultural production in his state (northern Henan Province). The Dujiang Dam in the Chengdu Plain (western Sichuan Province) and the Zhenghuo Canal in the Wei River valley (middle Shaanxi Province) were among the largest irrigation projects constructed by Qin in the third century B.C. The Dujiang Dam has been operating ever since the fourth century B.C. (see Color Plate 11). According to historical documents, the average yield of millet during this period was about 1055 kg/ha.

Meanwhile, handicraft industries (such as pottery, iron wares, vehicle manufacture, and so on) progressed

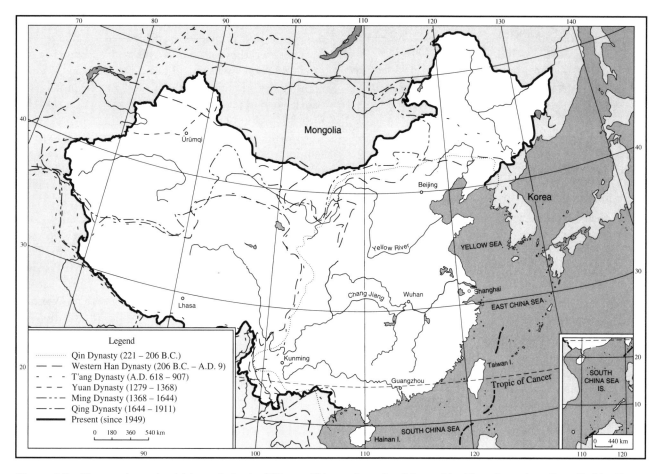

Figure 3.2 Changes in territorial boundaries in different Chinese dynasties (Mapped by Zhao Songqiao, Compiled by Deng Lang, 1992)

noticeably, and commercially oriented cities became more and more prosperous. Linzi in Qi, Handan in Zhao, Luoyang in Zhou, Ying in Chu, Ji in Yan, and Xianyang in Qin were all famous cities during this period. Most prominent was Linzi, the capital of Qi, which had a population of about 300,000 and contained six iron smelting factories. Metal coins had been introduced to facilitate commercial exchange, and each state had its own currency and highway system.

During this time, many schools of philosophy flourished, such as Confucianism, Taoism, Legalism, and Monism; each school presented its own writings and propagated its own beliefs while criticizing others. The intellectual life was described, "A hundred schools contend, and a hundred flowers bloom." Science also advanced; for example, the magnetic south-pointing needle was invented at this time.

The Qin Dynasty (221–206 B.C.)

The Qin Dynasty, from its unification of China to its collapse, lasted only 15 years; yet, it was credited as being one of the most important turning points in Chinese history. This was the first unified Chinese national state. Ying Zheng, king of Qin, called himself the First Emperor and established a huge autocratic, bureaucratic state. Qin territory included not only the original Eastern Monsoon China between the Great Wall and the Nanling Mountains, but also extended northward into the Elbow Plains of Northwest Arid China and southward to South and Southwest China and even included a part of Vietnam (Figure 3.2). Inside this huge empire, 36 (later 40) prefectures were established, and each prefecture was subdivided into a number of counties (more than 800 in total). This was also the first sophisticated administrative system in China. Additionally, a four-level hierarchical city-system was established. At the top of the hierarchy was the capital city of Xianyang with its population of about 1 million, probably the earliest city of that size in the world.

According to Qin's model, the following measures were taken to establish this unprecedented unified national state:

1. Private landownership was officially proclaimed and widely adopted.

2. A system of money and measures, written Chinese, and a road system were unified for the first time, forming the basis for present systems.

3. All weapons that had been scattered among the populace were destroyed. The first emperor also ordered the burning of books other than those approved by the Qin government. More than 400 dissident scholars were buried alive.

4. Aristocrats and rich people of all the former warring states were forced to come to live in the suburbs of Xianyang or other assigned cities.

5. A huge labor force was mobilized to link all sections of Great Wall that had been partly built by the states of Qin, Zhao, and Yan. The result was a complete, integral, colossal Great Wall. The wall started in the west at Lintao (Gansu Province) and ended in the east at Liaodong (Liaoning Province), with a total length of more than 5000 km (it was later exended to the Hexi Corridor). Its chief purpose was to keep out of the nomadic Xiong Nu (Hun) cavalry (see Color Plates 12 and 13).

6. A nationwide east–west and north–south roadway system was constructed, with Xianyang as the hub. The famous Ling Canal (near Guilin) was also constructed to link the Chang Jiang and the Zhu Jiang (Pearl River) waterway systems, which had heretofore been separate.

7. Agricultural civilization was spread to newly acquired territory.

The Western Han Dynasty (206 B.C.–A.D. 9)

Liu Bang, one of the peasant leaders at the end of the Qin Dynasty, eventually unified the country and established the Western Han Dynasty, which lasted 215 years with 13 successive emperors. The capital of the new regime was Chang'an (modern Xi'an). In political structure, the new regime followed the example of its predecessor in nearly every respect, except that it established,

besides prefectures and counties, more than 100 dukedoms and principalities, which led to a large-scale revolt. After the collapse of this revolt, Emperor Wu (141–87 B.C.) abolished all hereditary domains, and the country was administratively divided into 13 prefectures, which later developed into 103 prefectures, subdivided into 1314 counties.

During its early years, the new regime tried to maintain internal peace to recover from the damage inflicted by long civil wars. Subsequently Emperor Wu started his large-scale wars for territorial expansion and established the first major empire in East Asia (Figure 3.2). In Northwest Arid China, the strategic Hexi Corridor was wrung from the Xiong Nu (Huns) and developed as a large commercial grain base. Later, all of Xinjiang and a part of Central Asia as well as modern Qinghai Province in the northeastern part of the Tibetan Plateau became part of China. Northern Korea and northern Vietnam were also added to China. Meanwhile, the relationship among different nationalities within China grew closer. The ancient Silk Road (Figure 3.3), started from Chang'an and ended in Antioch, becoming a symbol of prosperous East–West relationships.

Emperor Wu also proclaimed, "At present, the most important job is to develop agriculture," and appointed Zhao Guo as the "minister to produce grains." Actually, a revolution in agriculture started in ancient China, and the traditional "peasant-gardener farming system" gradually became more sophisticated. The following policies and measures were installed to change agriculture:

1. Agriculture was recognized as the major occupation in the country. A small-scale private landownership system was widely encouraged. Each peasant family usually managed, with its own labor force, less than 1–2 ha of farmland, self-owned or leased from landlords.

2. Agriculture was considered a mainly self-sufficient economy. Peasants produced nearly everything they needed, except salt and a few other commodities, which were usually monopolized by the government. They also had very little to sell.

3. Manual labor was intensively used. A piece of farmland was carefully treated like a garden. Yield per land unit was rather high, but output was very low on a labor-day basis.

4. Improved iron implements and draft animals were widely used, such as a kind of plow drawn by two oxen harnessed together.

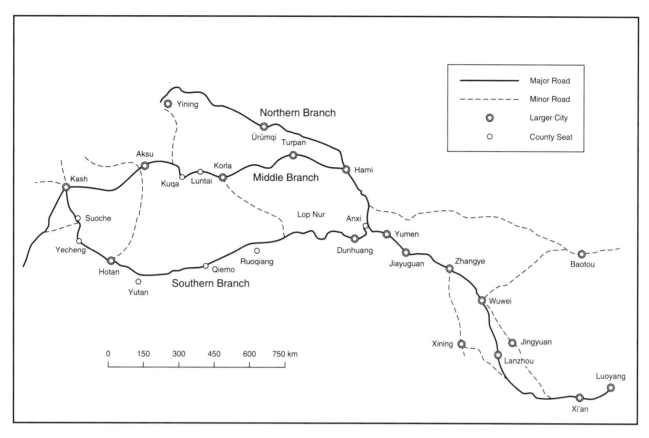

Figure 3.3 The ancient Silk Road inside Chinese territory.

5. The primitive fallow system was gradually replaced by a three-year rotating cultivation system, in which a piece of farmland was divided into three sections, each section remained unused (fallow) once in every three years to regain fertility.

6. Many new crops were introduced from Central Asia, such as grapes, watermelons, and alfalfa. Planting of tea bushes also started on a large scale.

7. A large number of irrigation works were constructed, and extensive areas of formerly unused arable lands were reclaimed.

8. Certain kinds of animal husbandry (such as pig and chicken raising) and handicraft industries (mainly textiles) were kept as sideline enterprises in peasant families, and were chiefly conducted by women. Hence, the old Chinese saying: "Man tills, woman weaves."

The population continued to increase rapidly, at the same pace as fast-growing agriculture. In A.D. 2, China had its first nationwide census (Table 3.1), recording a population of 59.6 million and a farmland area of 570 million *mu* (38 million hectares). Meanwhile, manual handicraft industries made much progress; iron, salt, and coinage were three industries conducted on a large scale under a state monopoly. Other industries such as textiles and lacquer were also well developed. Commercial and urban growth were significant. More than 10 large economic regions existed, each with one or two economic centers (cities).

The Eastern Han Dynasty (A.D. 25–220)

The Eastern Han Dynasty, like the Western Han Dynasty, emerged out of peasant uprisings and later collapsed under internal political strife, bureaucratic corruption, and more peasant revolts. It lasted nearly 200 years, with 14 successive emperors. It had its capital at Luoyang. At the zenith of its political power, it had about the same territorial extent as the Western Han Dynasty.

In agriculture, the Eastern Han Dynasty was somewhat more advanced than its predecessor, with a wider

TABLE 3.1
Population and Amount of Farmland in Chinese History

Year (A.D.)	Population (millions)	Farmland (million *mu**)	Farmland per capita (*mu*)
2 (Western Han)	59.6	576.5	9.7
105 (Eastern Han)	53.3	510.2	9.6
755 (Tang)	52.9	1,120.0	21.2
1083 (Northern Song)	25.0	413.6	16.5
1381 (Ming)	59.9	334.1	5.6
1562 (Ming)	63.7	392.8	6.2
1753 (Qing)	102.8	652.1	6.3
1812 (Qing)	361.7	728.9	2.0
1887 (Qing)	377.6	780.8	2.1
1949	541.4	1,468.2	2.7
1957	646.5	1,677.5	2.6
1971	852.2	1,510.5	1.8
1980	1,031.9	1,539.5	1.5
1990	1,143.3	1,435.1	1.3

*The extent of one *mu* in different dynasties was somewhat smaller than the present by the following ratios: (1) During Western and Eastern Han dynasties, 1:0.896; (2) During Tang Dynasty, 1:0.783; (3) During Northern Song Dynasty, 1:0.896; (4) During Ming Dynasty, 1:0.911; (5) During Qing Dynasty, 1:0.921. All data of farmland in the table have been exchanged into present *mu*, which equals 666.7 sq m, or 1/6 acre, or 1/15 hectare.

Sources: Compiled from various historial documents, not necessary authentic.

application of iron implements and ox-drawn plows. Water conservancy construction also improved. For example, the celebrated scholar and engineer, Wang Jin, made an "in-ground" river channel for the original "above-ground" lower Yellow River, which ran straight northeast to the sea and kept the area free from devastating floods for more than 800 years. A census in A.D. 105 recorded a population of 53.3 million and a farmland area of 34.01 million ha. Handicraft industries, commerce, and inland transportation remained about the same as they had been in the previous dynasty.

The Three Kingdoms (A.D. 220–280)

The Three Kingdoms represent a brief period of civil wars. At first, many warlords fought and conquered each other. Afterwards, only three warring kingdoms survived in Eastern Monsoon China—Wei in the Yellow River basin, Wu in middle and lower Chang Jiang basin, and Shu in Southwest China. Meanwhile, Northwest Arid China and the Tibetan Plateau were mainly occupied by many small principalities and were peopled by different minorities. During this chaotic period, millions of people were killed or moved southward, and millions of hectares of farmland were laid waste. Yet, for the sake of providing an assured food supply for its military, the kingdom of Wei reclaimed fields along the Yellow River and constructed irrigation works to water them. The kingdom of Wu promoted not only agricultural production in formerly undeveloped areas of southern China, but also a shipbuilding industry and marine trade along the coast. Meanwhile the kingdom of Shu paid particular attention to agricultural production in Southwest China. The irrigation works based on the Dujiang Dam were efficiently maintained. Economic development among the minority peoples in remote Southwest China was also promoted.

The Western Jin Dynasty and Southern and Northern Dynasties (A.D. 280–589)

The Western Jin Dynasty (A.D. 280–316) unified China for a short period. It was politically bureaucratic and corrupt as well as militarily weak. Soon it collapsed into an even worse condition: first, the Eastern Jin Dynasty and

16 northern kingdoms (A.D. 316–450), and then the Southern and Northern Dynasties (A.D. 450–589).

During the first period, the Eastern Jin Dynasty maintained its rule in southern China, encouraging some progress in economy and in culture, as well as a great increase of population. Meanwhile northern China was overrun by a horde of minority peoples (Xiong Nu, Xianbei, Chang, and others), which led to a sharp decrease in population but also mixing and fusing among many nationalities. More than 20 local regimes appeared in the Yellow River basin and in the Sichuan Basin, of which only 16 were of any duration. They kept on fighting among themselves in total confusion.

During the second period, southern China was ruled successively by four regimes: Song, Qi, Liang, and Chen. The capital was Jiankang (modern Nanjing), which had a population of more than 1 million. The areas south of the Chang Jiang started to become an important granary in China, and population increased rapidly.

During the same time, northern China was at first unified by Northern Wei (a tribe of Xianbei). The dynasty was later split into Eastern Wei and Western Wei, which were again transformed into Northern Qi and Northern Zhou, respectively. At last, Yang Kwang, the usurper of the Northern Zhou regime and the founder of the Sui Dynasty, unified China again and brought an end to the chaos of nearly 400 years.

THE MIDDLE PERIOD OF FEUDAL SOCIETY: FROM THE SUI AND TANG DYNASTIES TO THE NORTHERN AND SOUTHERN SONG DYNASTIES (A.D. 589–1279)

From the grand unification of China by the Sui Dynasty in A.D. 589 through the Tang Dynasty, and the Five Dynasties to the Northern and Southern Song dynasties, marked the medieval age of China. But, unlike the "dark medieval age" of Western Europe that was characterized by numerous fiefs and kingdoms, it represents a long period of vicissitudes and transition, mainly composed of the unified, autocratic dynasties. The Middle Period started with the great, powerful empires of the Sui Dynasty and early Tang Dynasty; then civil wars and warlords' dominance followed in the late Tang Dynasty and the so-called Five Dynasties and Ten Kingdoms. The Northern Song Dynasty unified China again but

with weak political and military power, and the area soon was overrun by the invading northern armies, which later occupied northern China during the Southern Song Dynasty.

Socially, the feudal society reached its norm during the Northern Song dynasty, and then gradually declined in the following invasion of Mongol and Manchu nomads. It nearly collapsed when it was attacked by capitalism and imperialism in A.D. 1840.

Economically, the traditional small-farming system and domestic handicraft industries continued to serve as the dominant mode of production. Encouraged by a strong, unified, peaceful environment, economic development was fast and stable as a whole. Peasants continued to comprise the major share of China's total population, producing most of what they needed in terms of food, clothing and other daily necessities. In regional development, southern China gradually overshadowed northern China, both in economy and in population. Paddy rice had been greatly developed in the middle Tang Dynasty. Later, double-cropping of paddy rice in the early Northern Song Dynasty increased yields. There were now more than 200 kinds of new rice varieties. Agriculture was also more effective in the North China Plain, where wheat growing and the three-crops-every-two-years system greatly increased production.

The Sui Dynasty (A.D. 589–618)

Like the Qin Dynasty, the Sui Dynasty was powerful but short-lived. The Qin–Han dynasties marked the first grand unification of China, and eventually a mighty empire was built. Similarly, the Sui–Tang dynasties represented the second grand unification of China, and an even more powerful empire was created. Furthermore, in this second period, many nationalities had been fused to form the Chinese nation, and two geographic regions—the middle and lower Yellow River basin and the Chang Jiang basin—had been merged to form the core of China. In territorial extent, the Sui–Tang empire was also larger than the Qin–Han empire (Figure 3.2).

Economically and socially, the Sui Dynasty followed the example of the Northern Wei regime by adopting the "land equalization" system. After several hundred years of devastating civil wars, population was relatively sparse and idle farmlands were relatively abundant when the Sui Dynasty came to power. The government gave every man 2.67 ha of cropland and 1.33 ha of mulberry trees (or hemp). In contrast every woman received only 2.67 ha of cropland. The cropland was to be returned to the government when a man (or woman) died. Under this free-grant land system, the amount of grain, cloth, and silk collected as taxes was very large. Shortly afterwards, both acreage and population recovered from the long chaotic period and reached a level equal to the Eastern Han Dynasty.

Agricultural prosperity led to rapid development of other areas of economic production. Emperor Yang in A.D. 605 ordered the construction of the Grand Canal. After completion, the canal was about 2000 km long and consisted of four individual canals: the Yongji, the Tongji, the Hangou, and the Jiangnan. With Luoyang as its central point, the canal extended northeastward to Zhuojun (southwest of modern Beijing) and southeastward to Yuhang (modern Hangzhou). It strengthened relationships and facilitated economic and cultural exchange between the Yellow River and the Chang Jiang basins. Like the Great Wall which was built by the first emperor of the Qin Dynasty, the canal was really grand and significant. Also like the Great Wall, it was built by sweat and blood of the peasants. Consequently, like the earlier autocratic and brutal dynasty, the Sui were soon corrupted and overthrown by peasant uprisings.

The Tang Dynasty (A.D. 618–907)

The Tang Dynasty came into being in A.D. 618 after the pacification of peasant uprisings during the late Sui Dynasty. It lasted 289 years, with 24 successive emperors. With the An-Shi Revolt (A.D. 755–763) as a turning point, the Tang Dynasty might be divided into two periods. Before the revolt, it was unified and strong, probably the mightiest empire in the world at that time with territory including nearly all of Eastern Monsoon China, Northwest Arid China, and parts of central Asia, southern Siberia, northern Korea, and Vietnam (Figure 3.2). Links with other peoples, including Turks (from the Greater Hinggan Mountains westward to the Caspian Sea), Hui Hu (Mongolia and Xinjiang), Mo He (Northeast China), Nan Zhao (western Yunnan), and Tu Bo (Tibetan Plateau), were strengthened. Hence, Tang Taizong was once proclaimed "Celestial Emperor," and his reign (Zhen Kwang, A.D. 627–649) was described as the Golden Age of Chinese history. In A.D. 755, China was administratively divided into 321 prefectures and 1538 counties, and had a total population of 52.9 million and a farmland area of 74.67 million ha (Table 3.1). But after the severe blow of the An-Shi Revolt, the dynasty was weakened by internal political strife and divided among regional warlords. After a series of peasant uprisings it eventually ended in the chaotic period of the Five Dynasties and Ten Kingdoms.

Thus, the first half of the Tang Dynasty was characterized by political unification, social stability, and economic prosperity. A land equalization system somewhat similar to that of the Sui Dynasty was adopted. In farming, the ingenious crook plow was used. Two types of water wheel were invented, one with bamboo or wooden tubes and another type for bringing water to higher ground. The development of irrigation facilities helped in the transformation of wilderness into productive fields, thus increasing agricultural output. Tea became a cash crop in many areas of southern China. Meanwhile, handicraft industries made good progress. The division of labor was minute in government-owned factories, and the number of privately owned factories increased considerably. Manufacturing of silk textiles and porcelain reached a new level of excellence. There were more than 100 copper, iron, and tin mining and smelting establishments scattered across the country.

The Tang Dynasty was also noted for its commercial activities and transportation development. Cities and towns mushroomed, of which, Chang'an (the capital, modern Xi'an), Luoyang, Yangzhou (Jiangsu Province), Jiangzhou (Hubei Province), Mingzhou (modern Ningbo, Zhejiang Province), and Chengdu (Sichuan Province) were the most famous. The center of transportation was Chang'an from which radiated all the major highways. The Chang Jiang was the most important water route in southern China, where it was a major factor in economic development that outstripped that in northern China. The Grand Canal was the major water artery between the North and the South. Economic and cultural exchange between China and many other Asian countries was greatly enhanced during the Tang Dynasty.

During the second half of the Tang Dynasty and the Five Dynasties and Ten Kingdoms, recurrent civil wars brought great misery to the people. The social economy was badly damaged by almost incessant bloody wars. Establishment of the Northern Song Dynasty in A.D. 960 reunited these separate regions.

The Northern Song Dynasty (A.D. 960–1126) and the Southern Song Dynasty (A.D. 1129–1279)

In A.D. 960, Zhao Kuangyin (Emperor Taiza) unified China and founded the Northern Song Dynasty, which lasted 166 years with 9 successive emperors. The emperor took great care to prevent the reemergence of separatist local regimes and warlords and to concentrate all power in the central government. Yet, the dynasty was politically and militarily weak and lost all border areas that the Tang Dynasty had ruled and even part of traditional Eastern Monsoon China. Its territory was somewhat smaller than that of the Qin Dynasty. The Northern Song Dynasty coexisted with four bordering regimes: the Liao (Khitan tribe) on the northeast, the West Xia (Chaung tribe) on the northwest, the Nan Zhao (Bo and Tai tribes) on the southwest, and finally the Kin (Nu Zhen Tribe) on the north, which later conquered the Liao and took the Yellow River basin away in A.D. 1126.

The territory of the succeeding Southern Song Dynasty was restricted to southern China and lasted 150 years with 9 successive emperors. Finally, all these regimes were conquered militarily by the Mongol Empire and were culturally assimilated and fused into the Chinese agricultural civilization. For example, the Liao Kingdom (A.D. 916–1125) transformed from a pastoral, slavery society into a mixed pastoral-farming, feudal society, and its tribal name "Khitan" was even used by some European languages to denote all of China (e.g., "Kitai" in Russian).

Agriculture made further progress during both the Northern and Southern Song dynasties. Especially during the Southern Song Dynasty, southern China became much more populous and more advanced economically than northern China. In the Southern Song Dynasty, population increased from 16.8 million in A.D. 1159 to 29.5 million in A.D. 1179. Water wheels equipped with wooden chains or bamboo tubes were widely used for irrigating fields, and the cultivation of paddy rice became widespread. The planting of cotton went as far south as Fujian and Guangdong, and important progress was made in the cultivation of sugar cane and tea. Reclamation of farmland, especially in montane areas and coastal lowlands, also progressed on a rather large scale.

Light manufacturing industries also advanced. The production of coal, gold, silver, copper, iron, and lead was considerable. Song porcelain was a famous handicraft product. The technology of manufacturing silk textiles and building ships was considerably improved.

Owing to unfavorable political conditions, the once-prosperous ancient Silk Road was virtually abandoned; instead, transportation and commerce flourished along the coast and big rivers. Among the best known commercial cities were Bianjing (the capital of the Northern Song Dynasty, modern Kaifeng of Henan Province), Chengdu, Xijing, Jiangling, Yangzhou, Guangzhou, and Linan (the capital of the Southern Song Dynasty, mod-

ern Hangzhou of Zhejiang Province). Kaifeng had a population of more than 1 million and commercial district of more than 6400 streets. Hangzhou had also a population of more than 1 million. The Italian traveler, Marco Polo, called it "Heaven's City" and "the most beautiful and richest city in the world."

THE LATE PERIOD OF THE FEUDAL SOCIETY: YUAN, MING, AND EARLY TO MIDDLE QING DYNASTIES (1279–1840)

In A.D. 1279, the Mongol Empire, or the Yuan Dynasty, wiped out the last resistance of the Southern Song Dynasty and marked the first time that China was entirely conquered by a minority people. After nearly 90 years of brutal, autocratic reign, the Ming Dynasty emerged out of peasant uprisings and reestablished Han China, but it was conquered again by another minority people (the Manchu) in 1644. Europeans started to come to China in the sixteenth century (middle Ming Dynasty), growing stronger and stronger, and eventually defeating the Qing Dynasty in 1840 in a dirty military action known as the Opium War. The feudal society in China, already much weakened during the Yuan, Ming, and Qing dynasties, nearly collapsed after the Opium War, and a semicolonial, semifeudal society was established.

The Yuan Dynasty (1206–1368)

The Mongols were a minority nationality dating back to ancient times. Originally they lived in northwestern Northeast China along the Ergun River (the upper reaches of the Heilong Jiang); then, from about the eighth century A.D., they spread across the Mongolian Plateau north to the Altay Mountains. They were nomads, proficient in hunting, horseback riding, and archery. During the late twelfth century, one of their leaders, Temujin, unified all the Mongol tribes and in A.D. 1206, he was elected as the Great King, or Genghis Khan, and established the Mongol Empire. Later, he and his successors started a series of conquests. The victorious Mongol army occupied vast areas north of the Yellow River in 1215, Xinjiang in 1218, Central Asia and Iran in 1219–1225, West Xia in 1227, the Kin Kingdom in 1234, Russia and a part of Poland in 1235–1244, and finally the Southern Song Dynasty in 1279. Four vassal Khan kingdoms were established: Qincha (modern European Russia and western Siberia); Ir (modern Iran and Iraq); Ogodai (central Asia and the Altay Mountains area), and Chaqadai (western Xinjiang and eastern Central Asia); the last one was closely connected with the central government.

The Mongol Empire was renamed the Yuan Dynasty during the reign of Kublai Khan (1260–1294), and its capital was moved from Shangdu (modern Dolan, Inner Mongolia) to Dadu (modern Beijing). Thus, the Yuan Dynasty held the largest territory in Chinese history (Figure 3.2), occupying not only all of Eastern Monsoon China and Northwest Arid China, but also the Tibetan Frigid Plateau for the first time.

In the very beginning, the victorious Mongol army was so brutal and barbarous that when it conquered a city or an area, practically everything was taken away or scorched to the ground and all survivors of the bloody massacre were reduced to slavery. All weapons (besides those owned by the Mongols and soldiers) were destroyed. Each 10 peasant families could own only one kitchen knife. Some heartless generals even proposed that all Chinese were useless and should be massacred and all their lands cleared for pastures. All inhabitants in China were classified into 10 unequal categories, with the Mongols as first class and the Chinese intelligentsia and beggars as the last two classes.

However, after the reign of Kublai Khan, agricultural production, handicraft industry, and cultural development gradually recovered. In 1290, the population again reached 58.8 million. More important, the grand unification of the vast Chinese area under the Yuan Dynasty paved the way for further mixing and union of numerous nationalities and helped economic and cultural exchange between Europe and Asia.

The Ming Dynasty (1368–1644)

The Ming Dynasty emerged out of Mongol tyranny and peasant uprisings in 1368 and lasted 276 years with 16 successive emperors. Its capital was at first in Nanjing, but was later moved to Beijing, which had a population of more than 1 million. Politically and militarily, it was much stronger than its Han predecessors—the Northern and Southern Song dynasties—but much weaker than the Mongol Empire. It lost most of the Mongolian Plateau, Xinjiang, and all territories beyond, but still kept Eastern Monsoon China, a part of the Tibetan Plateau, part of Northwest Arid China, and the vast territory beyond Northeast China to the Outer Hinggan Mountains (Stanovoy Range) and even Sakhalin Island (Figure

3.2). In the late Ming Dynasty, the island of Taiwan was settled by Han people. In political administration, the Ming regime became more and more autocratic and corrupted as the emperor exercised every power and privilege. The country was divided into 13 provinces, under which a hierarchy of administrative units was elaborated: prefecture, subprefecture, and county. Taxes were levied and based on the "Yellow Book" (a population census for the poll tax) and the "Fish-Scale Book" (a land tax shown in fish-scale shape).

During the Ming Dynasty, cultivated acreage of paddy rice, tea, sugar cane, and sugar beets increased by a sizable amount. The center of commercial rice production moved from the Chang Jiang Delta (emphasizing more economic crops and industries) to its middle reaches in Hunan and Hubei; and hence, an old Chinese saying: "If two Hu [Hunan and Hubei] have a good harvest, the whole country will be well fed." A number of devices—powered by oxen, people, or wind—were invented for farm irrigation. Cotton was widely planted in southern China and spread to the Yellow River basin, and finally replaced hemp as the basic material for making cloth. Silkworm raising was also popular in southern China, and Huzhou (Zhejiang Province) became very famous for the production of silk. Beginning in the sixteenth century, corn, peanuts, potatoes, and tobacco were introduced from America. Handicraft industries and commerce also progressed by leaps and bounds. There were more than 30 famous cities across the country, where centers of such industries as textiles, food, tea, and printing flourished. Along the coast, cities specializing in maritime trade developed, such as Ningbo (Zhejiang Province), Fuzhou, Quanzhou (Fujian Province), and Guangzhou (Guangdong Province).

Beginning with the middle period of the Ming Dynasty, a capitalist system of production began to appear, especially in the silk and cotton industries in the Chang Jiang Delta. Agriculture and handicraft industries became independent from each other and continued to be commercialized. Consequently, a commodity economy developed. There were several thousand textile workshops in the city of Suzhou alone, employing large numbers of workers. The specialization of labor in production terms was sophisticated, and production became large. However, the capitalist system of production, being fettered by a deep-rooted feudal system, was still in its infant stage and could grow only very slowly.

TABLE 3.2
Geographical Distribution of China's Farmland during the last 300 years (in million mu*)*

	Agricultural region	Farmland								Unused arable lands (estimated 1980)
		1661	1685	1812	1887	1949	1957	1971	1980	
I.	Middle and lower Yellow River valley	236.6	277.7	330.8	371.6	489.7	540.1	464.9	447.4	41.4
II.	Humid temperate northeast China	0.06	0.3	22.8	30.1	224.3	255.8	275.8	276.5	147.6
III.	Northwest Arid China	?	10.3	24.8	26.1	144.6	187.4	161.3	162.0	261.9
IV.	Middle and Lower Chang Jiang valley	264.3	261.1	299.4	304.5	338.1	376.8	322.7	364.4	54.0
V.	Humid Subtropical and Tropical South China	40.8	49.2	54.7	57.1	103.0	118.0	105.1	106.9	55.0
VI.	Humid Subtropical and Tropical Southwest China	7.47	9.2	58.6	58.4	166.0	191.8	168.0	170.2	98.0
VII.	Tibetan Plateau	?	?	?	?	6.7	7.6	12.6	12.2	47.0
	Total	549.23	607.8	791.1	847.8	1,472.4	1,677.5	1,510.4	1,539.6	704.9

Sources: Compiled from statistics of different periods (region), not necessary authetic.

The Early and Middle Qing Dynasty (1644–1840)

The Manchu constituted one branch of the Nu Zhen tribe and lived in Northeast China during the Ming Dynasty. In 1644 they took advantage of peasant uprisings at the end of the Ming regime and conquered China to establish the Qing Dynasty. In its early years, it pacified northern and southern China through many bloody battles and cruel persecution. It also unified Mongolia, Xinjiang, Tibet, and Taiwan, and defeated the invading Russian army in northern Northeast China. At the zenith of its political power, the area of Chinese territory included the Nansha Islands in the south, Taiwan and adjacent islands in the southeast, and northeast as far as the Outer Hinggan Mountains and Sakhalin Island, southern Siberia in the north, and the Pamirs and Lake Balkhash in the west (Figure 3.2). In addition, there was a series of vassal kingdoms, such as Korea, Vietnam, and Burma. Administratively, China Proper was divided into 18 provinces, and the borderland into six territories (Inner Mongolia, Qinghai Mongolia, Khalkha Mongolia, Tannu-Ulanhai, Xinjiang, and Tibet). Great care was taken to consolidate the unification of more than 50 nationalities. The Qing government established a Board of Minority Nationalities Affairs in the capital (Beijing), and in Southwest China multinational tribes were administered through a prefecture-county system.

The Qing regime inherited and developed further the feudal autocratic system. To strengthen its rule, the Qing government also adopted policies aimed at easing social contradictions and recovery of economic production. Farmlands laid waste during long civil wars were rapidly reclaimed, reaching 43.47 million ha in 1753 and 52.73 million ha in 1812 (Table 3.2). The total population increased with unbelievably speed, reaching 102.8 million in 1753, 361.7 million in 1812, and 377.6 million in 1887.[3]

Commerce prospered along with increases in population and agricultural production. Large textile factories developed in Nanjing, Suzhou, Hangzhou, and other

---

[3]This was partly due to a rather rapid natural growth in population under peaceful and prosperous environment, but mainly the abolition of the poll tax in 1712. Consequently, people had no more need to hide actual population growth, and thus population courts were more accurate.

cities. Progress was also made in iron smelting, copper mining, porcelain making, shipbuilding, sugar refining, and other industries. As commerce developed, nascent capitalism grew slowly but steadily.

THE MODERN PERIOD (1840–1949)

The span of approximately one hundred years from 1840 (the Opium War) to 1949 (the founding of the People's Republic of China) constitutes the modern period in Chinese history. During this period, new capitalism came from abroad and combined with old feudalism at home to reduce China to a semicolonial and semifeudal status. In this period Chinese people waged a democratic revolution led by the bourgeoisie against the Manchu feudal dynasty. Also during this period China

suffered heavy losses in territory and was even menaced by partition. However, nationalism saved China from political extinction.

During this period China also experienced a relatively large-scale northwestward shift of the pastoral-farming boundary (Figure 3.1). Concurrently there was a considerable and rapid increase in the area of farmland in almost all parts of China (Table 3.2). Three pioneer settlement belts were especially significant:

1. The Northeast China Plain, particularly its northern part

2. The southeastern border of the Inner Mongolian Plateau (Figure 3.4)

3. The Junggar Basin and the Tarim Basin, especially along the northern piedmont plains of the Tianshan Mountains (Figure 3.5)

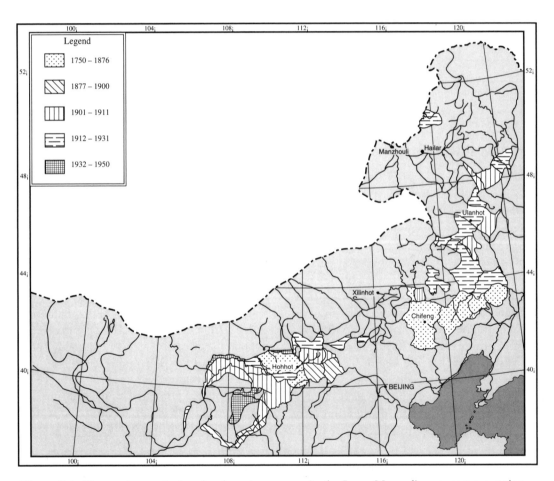

Figure 3.4 The modern agricultural reclamation process in the Inner Mongolia autonomous region (Adapted from Songqiao Zhao et al., *Agricultural and Pastoral Development in the Inner Mongolia Autonomous Region, 1958.* The Sino-Mongolia international boundary was not yet demarcated that time.)

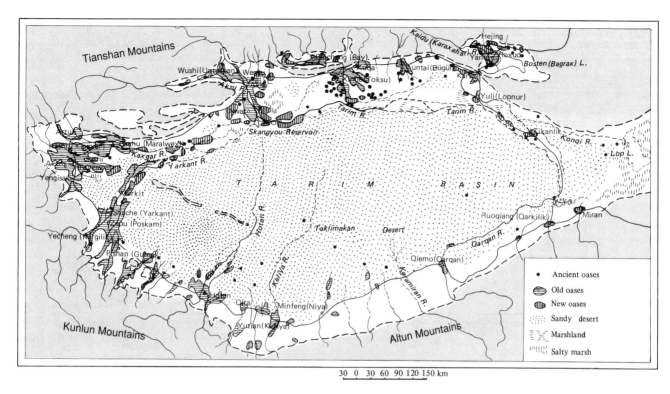

Figure 3.5 Distribution of ancient, old, and new oases in the Tarim Basin, Xinjiang Uygar-Autonomous Region.

The Late Qing Dynasty (1840–1911)

The late Qing Dynasty was a dark period of frustration for the Chinese people. A series of colonial wars—the Opium War (1840–1842), the Second Opium War (1858–1860), the Sino-French War (1884–1885), the Sino-Japanese war (1895), and the Aggression by Eight Allied Powers (1900–1901), imposed considerable hardship on the Chinese people. In addition, by a series of unequal treaties the imperialist powers imposed harsh terms on the Qing government. Consequently, the Qing Dynasty lost large tracts of territory and practically all its vassal kingdoms. For example, czarist Russia alone seized from China about 1.5 million sq km of territory (or land area equal to six times the United Kingdom). China also lost considerable independence in economic development, resulting in Chinese people becoming poorer and poorer. To combat such political and economic calamities, a series of peasant uprisings, such as the Taiping Uprising in 1851–1864, broke out, and the intelligentsia tried a series of "Westernizing movements," but all resulted in failure. Efforts to develop modern industry and transportation by Chinese capitalists also had little success. To many it seemed that the

traditional autocratic feudal society of China was too rotten to be curable. To survive under such desperate conditions, the bourgeois revolution of 1911 and the establishment of the Republic of China was a big turning point, at least giving the Chinese people liberation from the Manchu tyranny.

The Republic of China (1911–1949)

The establishment of the Republic of China in 1911 put an end to the feudal dynasties, which had lasted continuously for several thousand years. However, it did not liberate the Chinese people from deep-rooted feudalism and brutal imperialism. Soon, China again fell into incessant civil wars among warlords, and China was divided into "spheres of influence" by different imperialists.

The May Fourth Movement in 1919, which carried the banner of "Science and Democracy," and the establishment of the Chinese Communist Party in 1921 were two significant events in modern Chinese history. At first, Kuomintang (Nationalist)–Communist cooperation brought a partial unification of the country. Unfortunately, however, civil wars soon broke out again, and

TABLE 3.3
China's Agricultural and Industrial Production Value since 1949 (in million yuan)

Year	Total industrial-agricultural production value	Agricultural production value	Industrial production value		
			Total	Light industry	Heavy industry
1949	466	326	140	103	37
1956	1,252	610	642	370	272
1959	1,980	497	1,483	616	867
1967	2,306	924	1,382	733	649
1970	3,138	1,058	2,080	960	1,120
1974	4,008	1,277	2,731	1,213	1,518
1978	5,634	1,567	4,067	1,763	2,304
1980	7,077	2,180	4,897	2,309	2,588
1985	13,336	4,580	8,756	4,088	4,668
1990	31,233	7,382	23,851	11,799	12,052

Source: Compiled from official statistical sources. The inflation factor has not been eliminated.

the Japanese invasion of Northeast China in 1931 led to a full-scale bloody war in 1937, followed by the outbreak of World War II. After the Japanese surrender in 1945, civil war once again broke out, which led eventually to the founding of the People's Republic of China in 1949. Therefore, as a whole, from 1911 to 1949 the country was embroiled in bloody wars most of the time, and the Chinese people suffered unspeakable miseries.

However, it was already the twentieth century, and modern social and economic systems prevailed around the world. China could no longer remain isolated and closed. Hence, nationalism and internationalism intensely aroused a majority of the Chinese people, and modernization, highlighted by science and democracy—two slogans of the May Fourth Movement—inspired many Chinese people. This ancient country with more than 80 centuries of agricultural civilization would certainly survive and continue to flourish. For example, even under very harsh and unstable conditions, modern textile, flour, and other light industries grew rapidly in Eastern Monsoon China.

CONTEMPORARY CHINA (SINCE 1949)

The founding of the People's Republic of China in 1949 started the contemporary period. Since then, China has entered the early stage of a socialist society, featuring a rapid increase in agricultural and industrial production (Table 3.3) as well as in diverse economic structure (coexistence of traditional and modern economies). Agri-

culture is still the basis of the national economic structure, employing between 70 and 80 percent of the total labor force. Yet, industry and other nonagricultural types of production have been growing rapidly. Industrial production has surpassed agricultural production by value since 1956; the ratio between agriculture and industry in production values changed from 7:3 in early 1950 to 3:7 in the early 1980s, to 1:3 in 1990. Heavy industry started to surpass light industry in 1958. In agriculture, although the traditional farming system still dominates, the "modernization" process has been speeding up, and coupled with a series of governmental policies, agriculture has developed rapidly. However, the rapid and steady increase of population has "eaten up" most of its results.

During the last 40 years, agriculture and other economic activities as a whole have developed rapidly. However, especially in the areas of grain production and the accompanying organizational changes (Figure 3.6), four stages of ups and downs might be observed.

From 1949 to 1958

The year 1949 began a period of great economic rehabilitation and development. After more than 12 years of World War II and civil wars, the economic structure was badly shaken, and national agricultural and industrial production values in 1949 totaled only 32.6 and 14.0 billion yuan,[4] respectively. However, Chinese peasants

---

[4]The *yuan* is the Chinese unit of currency, sometimes called *renminbi* (RMB), which means "people's money." In early 1993, the official exchange rate was 5.7 yuan to one U.S. dollar.

have always worked hard, and the land reform of 1950–1952 truly enjoyed great support. The basic policy for agricultural organization at this period was collectivism, changing step by step from simple mutual aid teams to low-level cooperative farms and then to high-level cooperative farms. Agricultural output increased steadily by 8 percent each year on the average, although only a few technological improvements had been introduced. The area of farmland also reached the highest historical record in 1957 (1678 million *mu*, or 111.9 million ha). Population and industries also increased rapidly, and the long overdue industrialization of China got started.

From 1959 to 1965

The period from 1957 to 1965 included the so-called Great Leap Forward (1959–1961) and recovery. In 1958–1959 all cooperative farms were suddenly converted into communes, which were subdivided into brigades and then into production teams, with the brigade as the basic accounting unit. Agricultural production was

so disrupted that a three-year famine resulted. Total national agricultural production value decreased from 52.74 billion yuan in 1957 to 39.8 billion yuan in 1961. Other economic activities also suffered badly. One of the worst famines in Chinese history occurred. After such a disaster, a period of rehabilitation began with a series of new economic policies in which the production team became the basic accounting unit. National agricultural production values increased again to 57.76 billion yuan in 1965. The population increased rapidly, while industrial production more or less recovered.

From 1966 to 1976

The so-called Cultural Revolution began in 1966. Practically everything was disrupted. In 1967, total national industrial production value decreased to 138.2 billion yuan from a previous high of 162.4 billion yuan in 1962. Yet, national agricultural production value in 1976 still increased by 51 percent over that of 1966. It is amazing

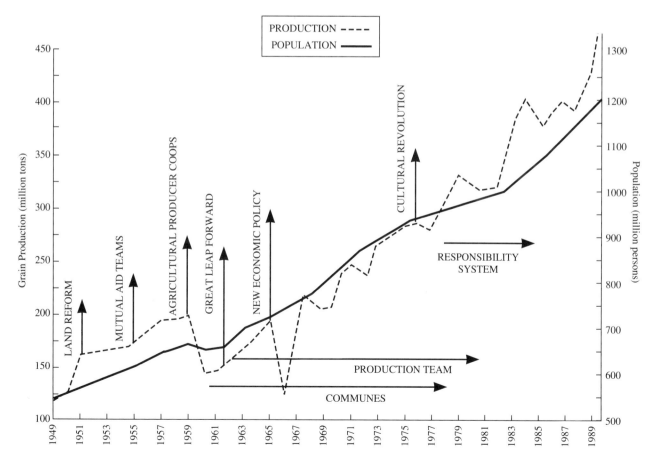

Figure 3.6 Population growth and grain production in China (1949–1990) with accompanying organizational changes

that population increased rapidly during this harsh period.

Since 1976 and Post-1978 Reforms

Following a two-year transition period, from 1976 to 1978, the present period of the Four Modernizations (modernization of industry, agriculture, national defense, and science and technology) startled in full swing. Total industrial and agricultural production values have increased very rapidly (Table 3.3). In agricultural organization, the responsibility system gradually came to prevail. Under this system each peasant family has responsibility and free decision making over a certain patch of farmland for an agreed period. Agricultural production increased rapidly, although the rate has slowed down since 1984. From 1978 to 1983, total national agricultural production values increased by 34.7 percent, food grains by 27.1 percent, cotton by 11 percent, and food oil by 102.2 percent. During these five years, China no longer imported food grains, cotton, food oils, or sugar. During the same period, multiple and comprehensive use of land, including growth of food grains and economic crops, animal husbandry, forestry, aqua-culture, and other activities, has been actively advocated. However, as population continues to increase (15.3 million in 1990), the area devoted to farmland continues to decrease (by 67,000 to 333,000 ha each year), and food demand continues to increase (by 1 to 5 million tons each year). Thus the ever-serious land–food–population problem needs to be solved urgently and effectively. This challenge will be discussed in subsequent chapters.

REFERENCES

China Handbook Editorial Committee. 1982. *History*. Beijing: Foreign Language Press.

China State Statistical Bureau. 1991. *Statistical Yearbook of China*. Beijing: Chinese Statistics Press.

Feng, Shengwu. 1985. "Origin of Chinese Agriculture as Viewed from the Dadiwan Cultural Site," *Acta Geographica Sinica*, 40, no. 3, pp. 214–223 (in Chinese).

Gong, Shido, et al. 1985. *Outline of Chinese Modern History*. Beijing: Beijing University Press (in Chinese).

Li, Be-o. 1986. *Outline of Chinese Ancient History*, Vol. 2: *From Sui and Tang to Ming and Qing Dynasties*. Beijing: Beijing University Press (in Chinese).

Li, Pang. 1984. *Developmental History of Chinese Cultivated Plants*. Beijing: Science Press (in Chinese).

Tang, Qixiang (ed.). 1982–1988. *The Historical Atlas of China*, 8 vols. Beijing: Cartographic Publishing House (in Chinese).

Wu, Weitang. 1983. "Holocene Paleogeography along Hangzhou Bay as Constructed on the Basis of Neolithic Cultural Remains," *Acta Geographica Sinica*, 38, no. 2, pp. 128–138 (in Chinese).

Zhang, Quanci. 1984. *Outline of Chinese Ancient History*, Vol. 1: *From Primitive Society to the Southern and Northern Dynasties*. Beijing: Beijing University Press (in Chinese).

Zhao, Songqiao. 1984. "Arable Land Resources and Their Development in China," *Natural Resources*, no. 1, pp. 13–20 (in Chinese).

Zhao, Songqiao, et al. 1958. *A Preliminary Study of the Location Problem of Agriculture and Animal Husbandry in the Inner Mongolia Autonomous Region*. Beijing: Science Press (in Chinese).

CHAPTER FOUR

Agricultural Development

China is essentially an agricultural country with almost 80 percent of its total population engaged in agriculture. Farming started in China as early as about 8000 years ago, and it has been continuously developed ever since. The traditional "peasant-gardener farming system" has been dominant in Chinese agricultural history. Since 1949, it has been mainly managed by socialist collective farms, and since 1978 the so-called responsibility system has dominated. State farms still account for 4.4 percent of the total farmland and 1.6 percent of the total farm labor force. China presently occupies about 6.8 percent of the world's total farmland but supports about 22 percent of the world's total population. Currently the largest grain-producing country in the world, China grew 353.4 million tons, 402.4 million tons, and 446.2 million tons of food grains in 1982, 1987, and 1990, respectively. It also ranks first in cotton, producing 3.6, 4.2, and 4.5 million tons in 1982, 1987, and 1990, respectively.

On the other hand, Chinese agriculture faces a series of challenging problems. Probably the most serious issue is the low level of modern agricultural technology and per capita production. The second is the problem of environmental dysfunction caused by overuse or misuse of many areas, resulting in heavy loss of cropland, soil erosion in grassland and forests, and devastating salinization and desertification (see Chapter Ten).

The third issue is an unbalanced agricultural structure, which overemphasizes farming while neglecting other agricultural enterprises (animal husbandry, fishing, and forestry). For example, of the total agricultural production value in 1982 (278.5 billion yuan), farming accounted for 62.7 percent, forestry for 3.9 percent, animal husbandry 16.4 percent, fishing 1.8 percent, and

sideline production (mainly rural industries) 15.1 percent. By the year 1990, total agricultural production value increased to 766.2 billion yuan, with farming, forestry, animal husbandry, fishing, and sideline production occupying 73.45 percent, 1.58 percent, 11.22 percent, 1.31 percent, and 12.35 percent, respectively. Within the farming sector, there appears to be an overemphasis on grain production while neglecting other crops (economic crops, tree crops, etc.).

The fourth problem is caused by unfavorable physical conditions, especially the mountainous topography and the uneven distribution of annual and seasonal precipitation, which adversely affects agriculture. Finally, the demands of a billion people, an overwhelming majority of them peasants, make the population–land ratio very critical, which in turn makes per capita income very low. How to enhance agricultural productivity and how to ameliorate or control these unfavorable conditions to insure agricultural sustainablility are two of the most critical agricultural problems in modern China.

CURRENT LAND USE PATTERNS

China's present land use patterns are described in Table 4.1.

Farmland

There were about 102.6 million hectares of cultivated farmland in China in 1980 and 95.7 million ha in 1990, and their distribution was quite varied and uneven. Nearly 90 percent of the farmland is concentrated in Eastern Monsoon China, with about 10 percent scat-

TABLE 4.1
China's Current Land Use Patterns

Land use	Area (in 10,000 sq km)	% in total land area
Farmland	102.7	10.7
Paddy rice	25.7	
Dry farming	77.0	
Grassland	286.0	29.8
Forest	122.0	12.7
Shrub land	14.3	1.5
Water bodies	33.2	3.5
Rocky mountains	86.0	9.0
Deserts	109.5	11.4
Glaciers & snow	4.7	0.5
Urban & rural settlements, roads	46.7	4.9
Other	154.9	16.0
Total	960.0	100.0

Source: Compiled from various sources.

tered in Northwest Arid China, and less than 1 percent in scattered patches on the Tibetan Frigid Plateau.

About one-fourth of the total farmland is productive flooded paddy lands (see Color Plate 5). It is mainly distributed in Eastern Monsoon China south of the Qinling–Huaihe line, and accounts for about 93 percent of the total paddy lands in China. It is also widely scattered in local alluvial plains, or even on terraced slopes in northern and northwestern China where irrigation water is available. Hence, Beijing, Tianjin, and Ningxia are also noted for their paddy rice production. The northernmost paddy land in the world is located at Mohe, Heilongjiang Province (about 53°31′ N), and the most elevated paddy land in the world is probably located in the intermontane basins in the southern Hengduan Mountains of Yunnan Province (about 2700 m above sea level). Since 1949, as a result of the rapid development of irrigation, the percentage of the total farmland that is paddy land increased from 23 percent in 1949 to 24 percent in 1957, to 25.6 percent in 1978, to 26.7 percent in 1990.

The nonpaddy dry farming lands (called *di* in Chinese), are three times more extensive than the paddy lands (called *tian* in Chinese) but are much less productive. Although dry farmland is widespread it is especially concentrated in Eastern Monsoon China north of the Qinling–Huaihe line, accounting for about 85 percent

of the total dry farmland in China. About 30 percent of the dry farmland has supplementary irrigation, resulting in higher productivity and a much more stable yield.

The double cropping system is an effective measure to increase sown areas without increasing farmland areas (see Figure 4.1). Such a system has been notably developed since 1949. The present northern limit of double cropping has pushed northward beyond the traditional Great Wall line, while double cropping of rice has pushed northward to 34° N, and upslope to 2424 m on the Yunnan Plateau. The northern limit of triple cropping has also pushed from 25° N to 32° N. The national average multiple cropping index increased from 130 percent in 1952, to 151 percent in 1980, to 155.1 percent in 1990. Figure 4.1 shows the distribution of multiple cropping in China. Five types might be identified.

1. Multiple cropping index above 250 percent is restricted to local areas along tropical and subtropical coasts, where a triple-cropping system involving rice-rice-sweet potato dominates.

2. Multiple cropping index from 175 to 250 is distributed widely in the eastern part of subtropical China, with the double-cropping system including rice-rice or rice-dry farmland crop dominating, partly triple cropping of rice-rice-winter wheat, or rice-rice-green manure crop.

3. Multiple cropping index from 125 to 175 is distributed widely in the western part of subtropical China and the eastern part of warm temperate North China. Double cropping of rice-corn is mainly practiced in subtropical China producing three crops in two years (corn, millet, sorghum, winter wheat, cotton, etc.) in warm temperate North China.

4. Multiple cropping index from 100 to 125 is distributed mainly in the western part of warm temperate North China. One crop per year of winter or spring wheat, millet, or a similar grain dominates, but partial double cropping is possible in low valleys.

5. Multiple cropping index below 100 percent is widespread beyond the Great Wall, consisting mainly of one crop (spring wheat, corn, sorghum, soybeans, etc.) per year, with part of the land lying fallow every other year.

After continuous agricultural development for 80 centuries, practically no more virgin land exists in China. The only notable exception is the so-called Great Northern Wilderness in Heilongjiang Province, where, for historical reasons largely virgin lands remained until 1949.

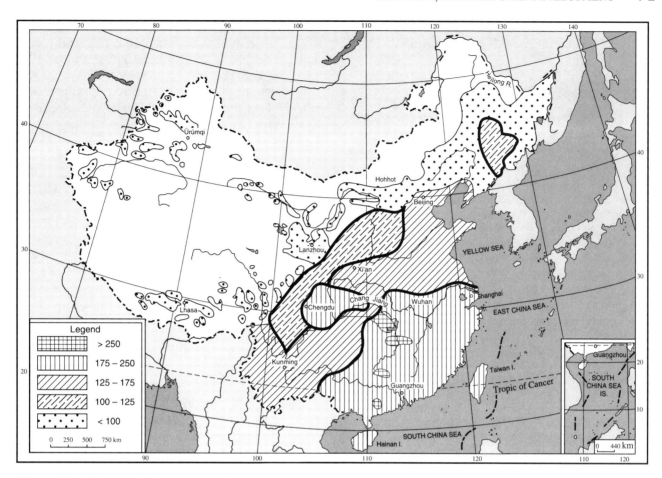

Figure 4.1 China: multiple cropping index

These lands represent the best and the largest potential reclamation area. Most other unused arable land resources are scattered in arid inland basins, along saline sea coasts, or on gentle mountain slopes. Most of them are low in fertility and marginal in reclamation quality. According to an estimate in 1980 (see Table 2.1), there remained about 700 million *mu* (about 4.7 million ha) of unused arable land resources in China, of which nearly 40 percent were in Northwest Arid China and about 20 percent in Northeast China (including Heilongjiang Province).

One of the most serious economic and social problems in contemporary China is the continuous decrease in farmland as well as in the amount of farmland per capita since 1958. Although millions of hectares of new farmland have been reclaimed each year, more is lost to nonagricultural land use. Consequently, the total area of farmland in China continues to decrease. Specifically in the case of housing and factory construction, not only is the actual plot lost, but also the surface soil of the farmland is excavated. Furthermore, most of the newly reclaimed farmlands are marginal in quality, while those occupied by nonagricultural uses are often the best farmland. Coupled with the loss of land to nonagricultural development, the phenomenal, continuous increase in China's population has pushed the per capita farmland lower and lower, from about 2.7 *mu* (0.18 ha) in 1949 to 2.6 *mu* (0.17 ha) in 1957, to 1.8 *mu* (0.12 ha) in 1971, to 1.5 *mu* (0.10 ha) in 1980, and even to 1.3 *mu* (0.08 ha) in 1990.

Grassland

According to recent investigations, China has about 2.86 million sq km of grassland. The usable grasslands in ten pastoral provinces (autonomous regions), are estimated at 2.21 million sq km (see Table 2.6 and Figure 2.2). Five grassland regions might be identified.

Northeast China and Eastern Inner Mongolia Steppe-meadow

The luxuriant steppe-meadow grassland type dominates, with a coverage up to 60–80 percent and a grass height of 60–80 cm. These lands are good pastures, suitable for cattle and sheep grazing.

Inner Mongolia Steppe and Desert-steppe Region

The typical steppe vegetation dominates in the eastern part, with a coverage around 50 percent and a grass height of 30–50 cm. The desert-steppe dominates in the western part, with a coverage of 30–50 percent and a grass height of 10–30 cm. Both are suitable for pasturing cattle, sheep, and horses. This is the best and the most extensive pasture region in China.

Northwest Desert Region

Sparse shrubs and low shrubs are scattered in the extensive inland basins and are suitable only for sheep, goats, and camels. The surrounding high mountains are endowed with montane grassland and alpine meadow, good for practicing transhumance grazing.

Tibetan Frigid Plateau Region

This region is dominated by dense, short, low-yielding alpine vegetation, suitable for yak and sheep only.

South China Montane Grassland Region

The vegetation is mainly secondary growth of shrub grassland; although growing fast, the grasses are low in nutritional quality for animal use. Generally speaking, the region would be better served by being returned to forest land.

Forest Land

Since the beginning of Chinese agricultural civilization, forested areas have been continuously reduced by deforestation. According to a 1949 estimate, forests occupied about only 8.6 percent of China's total land area. After 1949, great efforts have been exerted for afforestation, and a Ministry of Forestry was set up. As of 1980, more than 26.7 million ha of forests had been replanted. According to a detailed survey in 1974–1976 conducted by the Chinese Ministry of Forestry, there were 122 million ha of forest land in China, accounting for 12.7 percent of China's total land area. This proportion increased to 12.95 percent by the end of 1989. There are also 15.6 million ha of sparse woodland and 28.9 million ha of shrub land in China. The distribution of forest land and shrub land is shown in Table 2.5 and Color Plate 5.

Water Bodies

Chinese rivers, lakes, reservoirs, and marshes comprise a total area of about 332,000 sq km, accounting for 3.5 percent of China's total land area (see Chapters One and Two). Besides being important for fishing and aquaculture, some of the major water bodies are used for transportation (mainly the Chang Jiang and the Zhu Jiang and their tributaries) and for mineral extraction (mainly inland salt lakes).

Nonagricultural Land

These four land use types might collectively be termed as agricultural lands, and they occupy about 58.2 percent of China's total land area. The other 41.8 percent includes nonagricultural land and waste land. Currently nonusable land and waste land include chiefly rocky mountains and deserts (including sandy desert or *shamo*, and stony desert or *gobi*). They are mainly the result of the extensive mountainous topography and arid climate as well as the negative impact of human activities in China. Rocky mountains are extensive in the first and second great topographic steps, and are also found in the mountainous areas of the third topographic step. Sandy desert and stony desert, with a total area of 637,000 sq km and 458,000 sq km, respectively, are mainly found in the arid and semiarid regions (Figure 4.2). Glaciers and permanent snow are scattered on the Tibetan Plateau and its surrounding high mountains. Nonagricultural lands also include urban and rural settlements, roads and others, occupying nearly one-fifth of China's total land area; their proportion of total land use continues to increase steadily.

FARMING

China is essentially an agricultural country, and farming occupies a lion's share in agriculture. In the 1982 population census, 97 percent of China's agricultural population engaged in farming, 1.2 percent in animal hus-

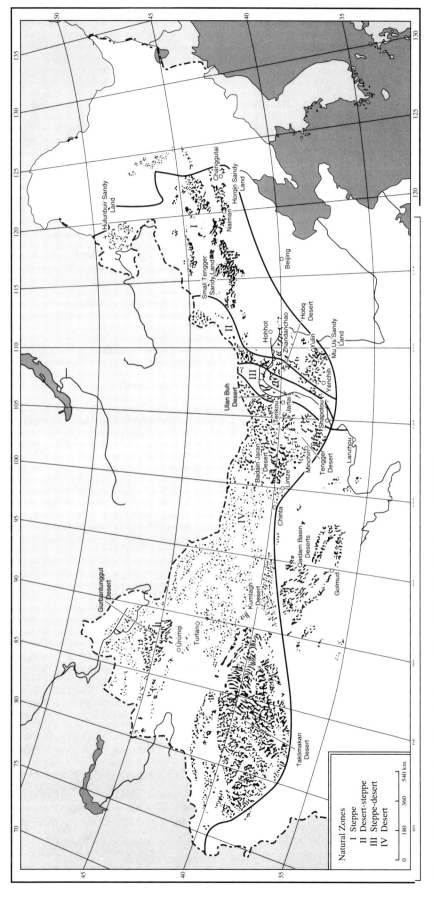

Figure 4.2 Distribution of sandy desert and sandy lands in Northwest Arid China

bandry, 0.7 percent in forestry, and 0.4 percent in fisheries.

The Farming System

China is a country of "farmers of eighty centuries," where the traditional "peasant-gardener ecosystem" has dominated ever since the second century B.C. Also, the paddy land (plain)–mulberry (dike)–fishery (pond) system in the Chang Jiang Delta and the paddy land (plain)–sugar cane (dike)–fishery (pond) system in the Zhu Jiang Delta are still among the best agro-ecosystems in the world.

Since 1949, the Chinese farming enterprise has been greatly modified and modernized. Instead of following the traditional private and small-holding landownership, it has been mainly managed by collective farms and partly by state farms. However, since 1978, the responsibility system essentially keeps the norm of the traditional "peasant-gardener ecosystem." The so-called fine agriculture system recently developed on Taiwan Island uses a small-scale farm (usually 1–2 ha, privately owned) model operated by a peasant family on a commercial bases specializing in related crops. This system yields an income (in 1989) of U.S. $7000–$8000 per capita. This farming model is a further sophistication of the traditional "peasant-gardener ecosystem," although its land uses are much more specialized and its products have a commercial orientation. The modern "petroleum agriculture" of Western countries appears unfit for China, because it relies primarily on expensive and quickly depleted petroleum as an energy source as well as on a high ratio of land area to people, which allows a farm laborer to work dozens or even hundreds of hectares of farmland. Logically the peasant-gardener ecosystem, with some important modifications, will still be the major farming system in China in the future.

Major Crops

In accord with an old Chinese saying, "food is the Heaven [first necessity] of the people," the most important crops in China have always been foods, especially grains, usually accounting for 80–90 percent of total crop land output. To date, China is the largest producer of rice, barley, millet, and sweet potatoes, the second largest producer of corn, sorghum, Irish potatoes, and soybeans, and the third largest producer of wheat in the world. However, since 1949, economic crops have also been rapidly developed. China is now the largest producer of cotton in the world, as well as the largest silk

cocoon producer, accounting for about two-thirds of total cocoon production in the world (Table 4.2).

Food Crops

In geographical distribution, four major patterns might be identified.

1. In Eastern Monsoon China south of the Qinling–Huaihe line, paddy rice dominates. It is multiple-cropped and rotated with winter wheat, winter rapeseed, winter sweet potato, winter green manure crops, and summer corn.

2. In Eastern Monsoon China between the Qinling–Huaihe line and the Great Wall, as well as in the oases of Northwest Arid China, winter wheat dominates in the southern part. It is rotated with summer corn, summer millet, summer soybeans, and other crops. Spring wheat dominates in the northern part, where it is rotated with summer millet, oat, and Irish potatoes.

3. In Northeast China (Eastern Monsoon China north of the Great Wall) one crop is grown per year, consisting of spring wheat rotating with corn, soybeans, millet, and sorghum.

4. On the Tibetan Frigid Plateau, one crop is harvested each year. *Qingke* (highland barley) dominates in higher elevations, while spring wheat is grown in local basins and low slopes.

Recently, great emphasis has been laid on the establishment and development of commercial food bases. The following 15 production locations are the most important: (a) the Songhua–Nen Plain; (b) the Three Rivers (Sanjiang) Plain; (c) Central Jilin; (d) Southern Jiangsu; (e) Northern Zhejiang; (f) the Poyang Lake Plain; (g) the Dongting Lake Plain; (h) the Chengdu Plain; (i) the Zhu Jiang Delta; (j) the Guan-Zhong Plain; (k) the Back Elbow Plain; (l) the Ningxia Plain; (m) the Hexi Corridor; (n) Northern Huai He Plain, and (o) Central Hebei. These fifteen producing locations include 365 counties, accounting for 20 percent of China's total agriculture-engaged population, 25 percent of China's total grain-growing area, and about 30 percent of China's total food grain production capacity.

Rice   China is the center of origin for rice, and it has long been the most important crop, occupying about one-fourth of China's total farmland and about 45 percent of China's total food production. It also accounts for about one-fourth of the world's total paddy land and about two-fifths of the world's total rice pro-

TABLE 4.2
Major Crops in China, 1986 and 1990

Crops	Cropping area (in 10,000 *mu**)		Annual production (in 10,000 tons)		Yield per land unit (in kg/*mu*)	
	1986	1990	1986	1990	1986	1990
All crops	216,306	222,543				
Food crops	166,399	170,199	39,151	44,624	235	262
Rice	48,399	49,597	17,222	18,933	356	382
Wheat	44,424	46,130	9,004	9,823	203	213
Potatoes**	13,027	13,681	2,534	2,743	195	201
Corn	28,686	32,102	7,086	9,682	247	302
Sorghum	2,613	2,317	538	568	191	—
Millet	4,170	3,417	454	458	102	—
Other grains	12,139	11,615	1,152	1,318	95	—
Soybeans	12,442	11,339	1,161	1,100	93	97
Economic crops	30,428	32,125	—	—	—	—
Cotton	6,459	8,382	354	451	55	54
Oil crops	17,122	16,350	1,478	1,613	86	—
Hemp, flax	1,143	743	193	110	169	—
Sugar crops	2,205	2,519	5,852	7,215	2,654	—
Cane	1,425	1,513	5,022	5,762	3,524	1,628
Beet	780	1,006	830	1,453	1,063	798
Tobacco	1,688	2,389	171	263	101	47
Other	1,810	—	—	—	—	—
Other crops	19,479	20,219	—	—	—	—
Vegetables	7,956	9,508	—	—	—	—
Green manure	6,631	6,448	—	—	—	—

*Each hectare equals 15 *mu*.
**Five units of potato equal one unit of other foods.
Source: Based on *China Yearbook of Agriculture, 1987,* and *Statistical Yearbook of China 1991.*

duction. In geographical distribution, more than 95 percent of the paddy lands are concentrated in Eastern Monsoon China south of the Qinling–Huaihe line (see Color Plate 5). There are four major cropping regions.

1. The tropical and southern subtropical zone, south of the Nanling Mountains, where long-grained nonglutinous rice is double or triple cropped, accounting for more than one-fourth of China's total paddy land.

2. Northern and middle subtropical zone, between the Nanling and the Qinling–Huaihe line, where long-grained nonglutinous rice is single or double cropped, accounting for about two-thirds of China's total paddy land.

3. The Yunnan-Guizhou Plateau, where mixed long-grain and round-grain nonglutinous rice is single cropped, accounting for about 5 percent of China's total paddy land.

4. The Sichuan Basin, where production is on terraced hill slopes producing long-grained nonglutinous rice in a single-crop system.

In North China, Northeast China and Northwest Arid China, scattered areas are single-cropped with round-grain nonglutinous rice, accounting for less than 3 percent of China's total paddy land.

Wheat This is the second-largest food crop in China, accounting for about one-fifth of the total crop land and about one-seventh of the total food production. Although widely distributed in China, wheat production is concentrated in North China's five provinces: Henan, Hebei, Shandong, Shanxi, and Shaanxi. There are many varieties of wheat, generally classified into two types based on its growing season.

1. Spring wheat is grown mainly north of the Great Wall (about 40° N) and west of the Minshan line (western Sichuan). In 1973, a record yield value of 792.5 kg/*mu* (11.89 ton/ha) was registered in an experimental station in the Qaidam Basin.

2. Winter wheat is widely grown in China, accounting for about 80 percent of total wheat production. Its northern limit has recently been pushed to 47° N (Heilongjiang Province) and its elevational limit to 4100 m (Tibet).

Corn This is a high-yield dry-farmed crop, occupying about one-half of the total dry-farmed cropland and about two-thirds of the total dry-farmed crop production. It is widely distributed in hilly lands with an annual precipitation of 800–1500 mm and a growing season of 80–150 days. A recent advancement in corn growing is the widespread use of hybrid species, occupying about one-third of total corn cropland and resulting in yield increases per land unit of 25–30 percent.

Potatoes Both sweet potatoes (about 80 percent) and Irish potatoes produce high yields even in harsh environments, and hence rank now as the third largest food crop in China. Sweet potatoes are mainly grown in southern China and usually serve as a pioneer crop in reclaiming infertile red earth wasteland. Sweet potatoes also provide an important food source for poor people. In contrast, Irish potatoes are mainly grown north of the Great Wall and serve both as a food and a vegetable for the local people. The Irish potato is considered as one of the three precious things in southern Inner Mongolia (the other two being a fur coat and oat flour).

Millet China is the earliest and largest millet-producing country in the world. Millet is a drought-tolerant and short growing-season crop, mainly grown in the North China Plain and the Northeast China Plain as well as on the Loess Plateau and the western Inner Mongolian Plateau. Its yield is rather low, and it is suitable for production only on marginal dry-farmed cropland.

Sorghum (Kaoliang) Originating in China, sorghum is tolerant of drought as well as waterlogging and is consequently grown widely in North China, Northeast China, and Southwest China. Northeast China includes about two-thirds of China's total sorghum-production area. As with corn, recent increases in sorghum production have resulted from the adoption of highly productive hybrid varieties.

Soybeans Originating in China, the soybean is classified as both a food crop and an oil crop. Although widely grown in China, production is mostly concentrated in the North China Plain and the Northeast China Plain, which, respectively, include about one-half and one-third of China's total soybean cropland. In these areas, soybeans are mainly sown in the spring. In South China, there are scattered areas of soybean cropland where it is mainly sown in the summer or in autumn.

Other Economic Crops

Other economic crops include mainly oil, fiber, and sugar crops. There are also significant economic tree crops, such as tea, mulberry, citrus fruits, and oil-tea. Special tropical and subtropical crops are grown, including rubber, sisal, and lemongrass, but their distribution is usually determined by physical conditions, as well as limits imposed by economic and social conditions. Consequently, secondary crops are usually restricted and concentrated in certain special areas.

Cotton As the major fiber crop in China, providing about 15 percent of the world's total production, cotton is mainly grown in subtropical and warm temperate climatic zones, where the cumulative temperature during the ≥10°C period is above 3000°C and 450–750 mm of water can be provided. Cotton fields in China total more than 4.7 million ha and are found in more than 1200 counties. Two major and three smaller cotton producing areas are identified.

1. *The middle and lower Yellow River valley* The North China Plain and the Loess Plateau are now the largest cotton-producing areas in China, with a little more than one-half of the total national area for cotton-growing.

2. *Middle and lower Chang Jiang valley* Although this is the second-largest cotton growing area, with about 44 percent of China's total cotton-growing area, it is the largest in total cotton production (providing about 53 percent of China's total cotton). It has also the highest cotton yield per land unit and the highest commercialized ratio of cotton production.

3. *Northwest China inland cotton producing area* includes mainly the arid, warm temperate Tarim Ba-

sin and western Hexi corridor where cotton fields are intensely irrigated.

4. *The lower Liao River valley* is a small, newly developed cotton-producing area.

5. *South China tropical area* has a nearly year-round growing season suitable for perennial cotton and kapok trees.

Food Oil Crops The peanut, which was introduced from America, today ranks first in food oil production and is grown widely in tropical, subtropical, and warm temperate climatic zones. Optimal soil conditions for peanut production are the sandy soils. Rapeseed is the largest oil crop in total cropping area. Because rapeseed can adapt to different eco-environments, it is widely grown almost all over China, and annual production is 16.2 million tons (1990). Sesame is the best quality oil crop in China. Although widely grown, production is concentrated in the Huai, Han, and Poyang basins. Oil flax is a drought-tolerant crop, of which about two-thirds is grown along either side of the Great Wall.

Sugar Crops In cropping area, sugar cane occupied about two-thirds of the total area dedicated to sugar production in 1986 and about three-fifths in 1990. In contrast, sugar beets occupied about one-third in 1986 and about two-fifths in 1990. Production areas for sugar cane are mainly along the southern and southeastern coasts, with an annual production of 50.22 million tons in 1986 and 57.62 million tons in 1990. Beet sugar production is mainly confined to temperate Northeast China, Inner Mongolia, and Xinjiang, with an annual production of 8.3 million tons in 1986 and 14.53 million tons in 1990.

Mulberry Tree (for Silk) The mulberry tree originated in China and is mainly used for feeding silkworms. China is now the largest silk cocoon producer in the world, with an annual production of 510,000 tons in 1990. Silkworms are raised in Eastern Monsoon China south of the Great Wall, where the Zhu Jiang Delta, the Chang Jiang Delta, and the Sichuan Basin are the key producing areas. To date, Jiaxing Prefecture of Zhejiang Province, Suzhou Prefecture of Jiangsu Province, Foshan Prefecture of Guangdong Province, and Nanchong Prefecture of Sichuan Province are the four major silk-producing centers in China, which collectively produce about one-half of China's total silk cocoon output. Local areas such as Hotan in the southwestern Tarim Basin also grow mulberry trees and a small silk industry has developed. Since 1949, the northern limit

of silkworm raising has pushed northward to 47° N in Heilongjiang Province. Generally speaking, silkworms are raised eight times each year in the Zhu Jiang basin and on Taiwan Island, three times in the Chang Jiang basin, and twice in the Yellow River basin.

Tea According to historical documents, tea trees were first planted during the Western Han Dynasty (206 B.C.–A.D. 9), and tea drinking became quite popular in the Tang Dynasty (A.D. 618–907). Tea was China's first export commodity and is still important in the world market. Tea gardens, with a total area of more than 1 million ha, are mainly found in Eastern Monsoon China south of the Qinling–Huaihe line, with Zhejiang, Hunan, Sichuan, and Anhui as the four main tea-producing provinces, accounting for about 60 percent of China's total production (about 530,000 tons in 1990). Tea leaves are chiefly processed into five types:

1. *Black tea:* fermented, mainly for export, accounting for about 22 percent of total production

2. *Green tea:* nonfermented both for domestic use and for export, accounting for about 44 percent of total tea production

3. *Brick tea:* compressed, mainly for minority people living in the border lands, accounting for about 25 percent of total tea production

4. *Wulong tea:* semifermented, mainly for export to Southeast Asia

5. *Jasmine tea:* mainly for domestic use, accounting for about 6 percent of total tea production

Agricultural (Farming) Regions

In accordance with physical conditions and historical background, and taking into consideration present provincial political units and their future agricultural developmental prospects, China can be delimited into seven agricultural (farming) regions (Figure 4.3). They reflect disparity in agricultural development levels, different natural conditions, and different land use trends.

The Middle and Lower Yellow River Basin (North China)

This was formerly the core region of Chinese agricultural civilization, including Hebei, Henan, Shanxi, Shandong, Shaanxi, Beijing, and Tianjin. Endowed with a favorable physical environment and a long history of agricultural development, this region has the largest concentration

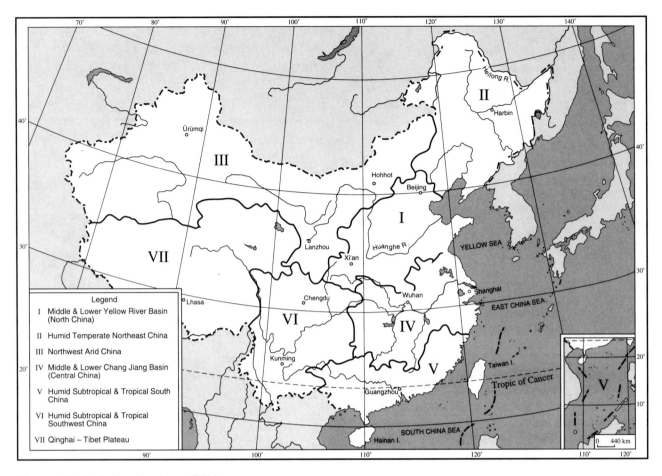

Figure 4.3 Agricultural regions of China

of cultivated land in China, with total of 30 million ha in 1980, accounting for 30 percent of the national total, and a total of 31 million ha in 1990, accounting for 32.5 percent of the national total (see Color Plate 14). There are only about 2.7 million ha of unused arable land left in this region, scattered in such areas as the coastal zone of Hebei and Shandong, the sandy land in northern Shaanxi, and the hilly area of southern Henan.

The region generally produces three crops in two years, with winter wheat, corn, sorghum, millet, and cotton as the chief crops. In the North China Plain, key problems for agricultural development are (1) establishing comprehensive measures to combat flood–drought–salinization hazards, (2) improving the irrigation–drainage system to improve the fertility of low-productive soils, and (3) increasing the use of agricultural inputs (fertilizer, pesticides, etc.). On the Loess Plateau, the most important problem is to make better use of the land to ameliorate serious soil erosion. The most obvi-

ous solution to soil erosion is to stop all cultivation on the loessic steep slopes.

Humid Temperate Northeast China

This is the pioneer settlement area in China (see Color Plate 6) including Liaoning, Jilin, Heilongjiang, and three leagues (*meng*, or prefectures) in the eastern part of Inner Mongolia. The area is suitable for cultivation, but for historical and political reasons, was little developed until the late nineteenth century. In 1887, there were only 2 million ha of farmland, constituting only 4 percent of China's total farmland at that time. Since then, both farmland and population have increased rapidly. By 1949, the farmland area amounted to 15 million ha, accounting for 15 percent of China's total, and by 1980 increasing 18.5 million ha (18.7 percent). In the category of unused arable land, this region ranks first in terms of land quality and second in acreage. It is estimated that 10 million ha are potentially reclaimable, approximately one-half of which is located in Heilongjiang.

In this region, one crop can be produced per year, with spring wheat, corn, sorghum, millet, soybeans, and sugar beets as the chief crops. Low temperature and frost, spring drought, and summer–autumn floods are the chief natural hazards. Surrounding the farming areas of the Northeast China Plain, there are tree-clad mountains—the Greater Hinggan, the Lesser Hinggan, the Changbai, and others—which are the most important timber-producing areas in China. Also in the northwestern subhumid and semiarid Northeast China Plain and on the Hulun Buir Plateau are large patches of good pastureland, as well as many lakes and swamps, where animal husbandry and fishing might be developed.

Northwest Arid China

This region includes Inner Mongolia,[1] Gansu (the Hexi Corridor), Ningxia, and Xinjiang. Although agriculture started here very early, it has been very limited and has suffered from frequent disruption. In 1685, the total area under cultivation in this arid region was about 700,000 ha, accounting for only 2 percent of China's total farmland. After 1949, with the development of irrigation systems and the planting of shelter-tree belts in this wind-swept region, the area of farmland has rapidly expanded. By 1980, farmland in this region totaled 10.8 million ha, accounting for 11 percent of the national total. Yet, cultivated land in this region still occupies only 3.3 percent of its total land area. Potentially there are still 20 million ha of unused arable land, accounting for 40 percent of the total unused arable land in China.

There are essentially two farming systems in this region. The western arid lands are dominated by irrigated oases (see Color Plate 15), mainly one crop per year, with wheat, sorghum, corn, and sugar beets as chief crops. In the Tarim Basin and western Hexi Corridor, the three crops can be grown in two years, and cotton is grown. The eastern semiarid lands are dominated by rain-fed farming, with one crop per year, and spring wheat, millet, oats, and Irish potatoes as chief crops. As a whole, the region can be classified as steppe, desert-steppe, and desert. Animal husbandry is the chief agricultural enterprise, and desertification is the chief environmental problem.

---

[1] The eastern three leagues (prefectures) of Inner Mongolia are a transitional belt; they might be included either in Northeast China or in Northwest Arid China.

The Middle and Lower Chang Jiang Basin (Central China)

This region, including Jiangsu, Anhui, Zhejiang, Jiangxi, Hubei, Hunan, and Shanghai, is endowed with excellent physical conditions as well as a long history of agricultural development, and thus has been another "core" of Chinese agricultural civilization. In 1685, a total area of 17.3 million ha was under cultivation in this region, accounting for 43 percent of the national total. By 1957, the farmland increased to 24.7 million ha, but only accounted for 23 percent of the national total. In 1980 farmland decreased to 24.3 million ha, accounting for 24.4 percent of the national total. Land use shows a sharp contrast between the hills and the plains. The plains in the Han Shui valley and around the Donting, Boyang, and Tai lakes are intensively cultivated and irrigated by a well-structured network of canals and rivers. This "watery country" (see Color Plate 16) is the most productive grain region as well as the largest commercial grain base in China. In contrast the hilly lands are extensively used and are often subject to severe soil erosion. Unused arable land in this region is limited, with a mere 3.3 million ha scattered along lake and ocean beaches and mountain piedmonts. With a very large population, the per capita farmland is generally less than one *mu* (0.07 ha). However, due to the excellent physical environment, the possibility for increasing the yield per land unit is great.

This region is generally under a double cropping system, with rice, winter wheat, corn, and cotton as the chief crops. Mountainous and hilly lands are widely distributed and are favorable for developing forestry and tree crops, although most of them are now misused and reduced to unproductive secondary grassland. Water bodies are numerous, fit for fishing and aqua-culture. Therefore, the agricultural future of this region depends on the more intensive and sustainable use of the plains as well as on the development of mountain areas and water bodies.

Humid Subtropical and Tropical South China

This region is composed mainly of Fujian, Guangdong, Guangxi, Hainan, and Taiwan. It has ample water supplies and suitable high temperatures, but is mountainous and is thus short of level land to develop farming. Historical development of agriculture is also not as long as in North China and Central China. In 1685 there were about 3.3 million ha of cultivated land in this region, accounting for 8 percent of the national total. In 1957, the area of farmland (not including Taiwan) increased to 7.9 million ha, accounting for 7 percent of the national total. And in 1980, the farmland area (not including Taiwan) decreased to about 7.1 million ha, still accounting for 7 percent of the national total. Potentially arable land in this region is very small, totaling about 3.3 million ha, scattered either along the coast or on the gentle alluvial slopes of low hills covered with red or yellow earth in the inland. The population–land ratio stress is even greater here than in Central China.

This region is generally under a double cropping or triple cropping system, with rice, sweet potatoes, and sugar cane as the chief crops. As in Central China, the agricultural future depends on more intensive but sustainable use of the level lands as well as the development of mountain areas and water bodies.

Humid Subtropical and Tropical Southwest China

This region, composed of Sichuan, Yunnan, and Guizhou, is similar to humid tropical South China; the only differences lie in its higher elevation, lower temperatures, and longer dry season. The Sichuan Basin has been often called "the heavenly endowed rich country" with favorable physical conditions and a long history of human activities. In the middle seventeenth century, however, the province suffered badly from a drastic decline in both population and farmland due to civil wars and peasant uprisings. The Yunnan-Guizhou Plateau, with relatively poor natural conditions, was not developed economically until the fourteenth century A.D. In 1887, there were 3.9 million ha of farmland in this region, 7 percent of the national total. In 1957, the farmland area increased to 12.8 million ha (7.33 million ha in Sichuan), accounting for about 11 percent of the national total. In 1980, the acreage decreased to about 11.33 million ha, but its percentage in the national total increased slightly. It is estimated that there are about 6.53 million ha of still unused arable land in this region, mainly distributed in the intermontane basins of the Yunnan-Guizhou Plateau and the low-lying valleys of southern Yunnan. The Yunnan area is a promising site for developing commercial tropical crops.

This region is generally under a double cropping system, with rice, winter wheat, and corn as the chief crops. It has a similar agricultural future to South China, but, as the topography is even more mountainous, more emphasis should be placed on sustainable "vertical agriculture" and more care should be taken for environmental protection.

Tibetan Plateau

Due to the adverse conditions associated with very high elevation, most of this plateau is not suitable for cultivation, although the upper Yellow River and its tributary Huangshui valleys in northeastern Qinghai Province were cultivated as early as the Western Han Dynasty. The Yarlung Zangbo valley in southern Tibet Autonomous Region has been farmed since the Tang Dynasty. In 1957 there were only 0.5 million ha of farmland in Qinghai (data not available for Tibet). Since 1959, the arable land resource on the plateau has been rapidly developed. By 1980 the cultivated acreage had increased to 0.8 million ha, accounting for 0.8 percent of the national total. The successful cultivation of highland barley on the terraces in the Nielami district at an elevation between 4740–4760 m (immediately below the snow line) set a new world record.

Potential cultivated land on the plateau is believed to be small, only 2.7 million ha. The suitability for expansion of farming is constrained by excessively high elevation, a very short growing season, coarse and infertile soil, and frequent natural disasters (such as frost, hail, mudflows, and landslides). A favorable factor for farming, however, is the intense solar radiation, which makes possible the production of high yields of highland barley and wheat in the areas surrounding Lhasa and Xigaze. Of necessity, animal husbandry and forestry (limited to southeastern part) will dominate the Tibetan Plateau, while farming will be restricted to local favorable areas, where the need is self-sufficiency in producing food and feed stuffs.

FORESTRY

In China, "forestry" includes two quite different aspects. One is a part of industry; its chief objective is to exploit timber resources, and it is thus somewhat similar to mining, although the wood is renewable while the minerals are nonrenewable. The other aspect is similar to agriculture, including the management and cropping of the forest. Forest management is somewhat similar to farming, although the cycle of farming usually lasts only one or a few years while that of forestry may last more than 10 or even as long as 100 years.

Current Status of Forest Development

Forest resources were quite rich in China during ancient prefarming times, and forests were even considered a nuisance in some parts of humid tropical and subtropical China. However, with the advance of agriculture and other human activities during last 80 centuries, population increased but the forest resource decreased. Forestry is now a rather weak enterprise in China, although great efforts have been made to increase forests since 1949. One of the biggest success stories in contemporary Chinese forestry is the development of the "plain forest" in the North China Plain and in other plains areas. For example, mainly through tree-crop interplanting, the area of forest coverage on the North China Plain of eastern Henan Province increased from 2 percent in the early 1950s to 10 percent in the late 1980s. Another significant success is extensive planting of oil tree crops on the hilly slopes of subtropical and tropical China. Yet, in general, Chinese forestry is now badly handicapped by management that is "too little" and "too low," which make afforestation and other measures for forestry development all the more urgent.

Compared with the world average of 22 percent forest coverage and per capita forest area of 1 ha as well as per capita forest growing stock of 83 cu m, China has only 12.7 percent, 0.12 ha, and 10 cu m, respectively. The distribution of forests in China is also uneven, with most areas concentrated in distant mountain areas of Northeast China and Southwest China, while extensive farming and pasture areas have very little forest land. Trees of economic value are also unevenly distributed. For example, oil-tea trees are mainly concentrated in two provinces, Hunan and Jiangxi, accounting for 69.3 percent of the national total, while tung oil trees grow mainly in three provinces, Sichuan, Guizhou, and Hunan. What is more, in total growing stock, mature and overmature forests occupy an overwhelmingly large portion, resulting in a very high waste rate. For example, of 7.55 billion cu m of China's total timber growing stock, mature and overmature forests account for 5.23 billion cu m (69 percent), of which, two large forest areas (Northeast China and Southwest China) account for 4.36 billion cu m (83 percent of the total mature and overmature forest).

Between 1949 and 1979, 286 large and middle-scale lumbering enterprises were established. The accumulated production of timber during these 30 years amounted to 900 million cu m and annual production increased from 5 million cu m to 50 million cu m. In the 1980s, timber production increased somewhat (Table 4.3); yet, compared with China's huge population, it is still very little.

The precious forest resource is generally over-exploited and wasted. Many productive forest areas have been burned and unwittingly turned into farmland. A pessimistic estimate forecasts that, owing to ruthless overcutting, nearly two-thirds of all national forest units will run out of suitable trees for lumber in 11 years if forest management continues to allow cutting at the current level.

Difficulty in transportation is also an important reason for maintaining a low level of forest management in

TABLE 4.3
Timber and Bamboo Production by Province, 1986*

Province (municipality, autonomous region)	Timber yield (in 10,000 cu m)	Bamboo yield (in 10,000 cu m)
Heilongjiang	1,773.97	—
Jilin	685.69	—
Liaoning	85.43	—
Beijing	6.15	—
Tianjin	—	—
Hebei	23.04	—
Henan	14.90	6.01
Shandong	7.49	—
Shanxi	12.77	—
Shaanxi	79.40	0.15
Shanghai	—	—
Jiangsu	1.99	59.14
Anhui	53.18	428.12
Zhejiang	171.01	785.74
Jiangxi	285.05	1,100.01
Hubei	119.57	603.07
Hunan	303.32	1,869.16
Fujian	610.27	742.00
Guangdong (including Hainan)	349.44	993.02
Guangxi	292.52	465.70
Sichuan	425.30	122.58
Guizhou	90.03	93.12
Yunnan	341.30	437.71
Inner Mongolia	626.99	—
Ningxia	6.47	—
Gansu	58.63	—
Qinghai	6.47	—
Xinjiang	42.22	—
Tibet	25.72	—
National total	6,502.42	7,716.05

*Taiwan and Hong Kong not included.

Source: Based on *China Yearbook of Agriculture, 1987.*

the borderlands. Consequently, taking an average, each hectare of China's forest land produces less than 2 cu m of timber as compared with 3 to 5 cu m in the developed countries.

Since 1949, large-scale afforestation work has been conducted nearly every year. By 1979, the cumulative afforested area amounted to 900 million ha. Yet, owing to low afforestation quality and low management level, only 30 percent of planted trees survived.

Forest resources are still mainly used for log timber, and only 9 percent of the wood byproducts are used as compared to nearly 50 percent in the developed countries.

Major Forest Types

Forests can be classified according to their use.

Timber Forests

In 1980, there were about 98 million ha of timber forest in China, accounting for about 80 percent of the total forest land area. About 84 percent of the timber forests are natural, while 16 percent have been planted. In the natural forests, needle-leaved species dominate. Among the planted forests, fir, pine, spruce, and larch are the dominant needle-leaved trees, and poplar and paulownia are principal broad-leaved species.

Shelter Forests

These forested areas are mainly used as wind breaks, sand protection, and soil conservation and are widely scattered in farming areas all over China. From 1949 to 1979, about 7.9 million ha of shelter forests were established. Recently, the Three Norths (North China, Northeast China, and Northwest China) Shelter Forests, the so-called Green Great Wall, have been under active construction. From 1978 to 1989, more than 9.2 million ha of shelter forests were planted, and 80.16 percent of the planted trees survived.

Economic Forests and Orchards

In 1980, there were about 8.5 million ha of economic forests in China, including food and oil tree crops, orchards, and special economic trees. Food and oil tree crops are widely distributed in mountainous areas, and as China is a mountainous country, they have bright prospects for further development. Food and oil tree crops include coconut, oil palm, oil melon, and cashew in the tropical zone, and oil-tea, tung oil, Chinese tallow tree,

chestnut, walnut, persimmon, and dates in the subtropical zones. In 1975, they had a total area of about 60 million *mu*, of which oil-tea occupied about 50 percent, followed by walnut (14 percent), tung oil (11 percent) and dates (8 percent).

China has a variety of fruit trees, including 39 families, more than 300 genera, and more than 10,000 species. In 1975, there were about 60.75 million *mu* (4.05 million ha) of orchards, of which, the six most important are apple, pear, citrus fruits, banana, grape, and pineapple. Total fruit production reached more than 5 million tons and has increased since 1975.

Certain economic trees, such as rubber (*Hevea*), lacquer, pepper, Chinese cassia tree, and Chinese wolf berry are significant for China's economy. Rubber trees have been widely planted on tropical Hainan Island and in southern Yunnan Province.

Bamboo

China is the leading country in the world for growing bamboo (Table 4.3). There are about 50 genera of bamboo in the world, of which China has 22, and more than 200 species, within the total bamboo area of about 3.1 million ha where the total number of bamboo shoots could be as many as 22 billion. Bamboo forests are widely distributed in the subtropical zone, especially in Zhejiang, Jiangxi, Fujian, Guangdong, Guangxi, Sichuan, Anhui, and Jiangsu provinces, each with more than 1 billion bamboo shoots.

Major Forest Regions

The following eight forest regions have been delimited by the Chinese Ministry of Forestry.

Cool-Temperate Needle-Leaved Forest Region

Mainly located on the Greater Hinggan Mountains, this is the largest timber-producing area in China. It has a forested area of about 15 million ha and a total growing stock of about 1.4 billion cu m. The taiga forest has its southernmost extension in the world here, with the excellent soft wood of larch (*Larix dahurica*) dominating (about 70 percent of the total forested area and 86 percent of the total growing stock). Other needle-leaved trees include pine (*Pinus sylvestris*), spruce (*Picea obovata*, *P. microsperma*), and juniper (*Juniperus dahurica*). At lower elevations, there are broad-leaved trees, including birch (*Betula platyphylla*), poplar (*Populus davidiana*), willow (*Salix rorida*), and oak (*Quercus mongolica*).

Temperate Mixed Needle- and Broad-Leaved Forest Region

This region is located on the Lesser Hinggan Mountains, the Changbai Mountains, and other mountains of eastern Northeast China. The total forested area is about 16.7 million ha, and the growing stock represents about 1.5 billion cu m, of which the Lesser Hinggan Mountains occupy 30 percent and 41 percent respectively. The dominant needle-leaved species is red pine (*Pinus koraiensis*), but it is mixed with other needle-leaved trees (*Abies halophylla*, *Picea obovati*, etc.) and many kinds of broad-leaved trees (*Tilia amurensis*, *Fraxinus mandschurica*, and *Quercus mongolica*). The altitudinal zone distribution of vegetation is prominent.

Warm-Temperate Deciduous Broad-Leaved Forest Region

Scattered widely in small patches on the Yan Shan, the Taihang Mountains, the Luliang Mountains, and other warm temperate regions, these forest areas are usually small and the growing stock low. For example, the Yan Shan forest land totals about 380,000 ha with a total growing stock of only 13 million cu m. The most commonly seen trees are various species of oak (*Quercus*), maple (*Acer*), poplar (*Populus*), birch (*Betula*), elm (*Ulmus*), and willow (*Salix*). Some coniferous trees, such as pine, juniper, fir, spruce, and larch, may also be important constituents in cooler locations.

Northern Subtropical Mixed Evergreen and Deciduous Broad-Leaved Forest Region

Forests are scattered in small patches on the Qin Ling, the Daba Mountains, the Dabie Mountains, and other northern subtropical mountains. The Qin Ling forest land is the largest, with an area of about 8.7 million ha and a total growing stock of 130 million cu m. This is the transitional belt between the north and the south, as well as between the east and the west; hence, both flora and fauna are very rich. For example, Mount Shennongjia alone is populated by 166 families, 765 genera, and 1919 species of plants.

Middle and Southern Subtropical Evergreen Broad-Leaved Forest Region

Forests are widely scattered on the hills and mountains south of the Chang Jiang. The total forest land is about 14.2 million ha and the total growing stock about 940 million cu m, accounting for about 13 percent of the national total. The zonal vegetation type appears as a profuse and luxuriant evergreen broad-leaved forest, usually with 3–7 horizons in physiognomy (2–3 horizons of high trees, 1–2 horizons of under woods, and 1–2 horizons of ground cover). The dominant evergreen trees are *Cyclobalanopsis glauca*, *Castanopsis sclerophylla*, *C. taiwaniana*, *C. fardii*, and *Schina superba*. Evergreen needle-leaved forests such as *Pinus massoniana* and *Cunninghamia lanceolata* as well as bamboo are also commonly seen; *Pinus massoniana* (horse tail pine) is the most widespread in this region, occupying about one-half of the total regional forest area. Economic tree crops, such as tea, oil tea, tung oil, peaches, oranges, and others are widely planted.

Tropical Monsoon and Rain Forest Region

Mainly found in the humid tropical zone and partly in southern subtropical zone on Hainan Island, the forested area totals 1.4 million ha and the total growing stock is 150 million cu m. Taiwan Island has 2.1 million ha of forest with 186 million cu m of total growing stock. The luxuriant tropical monsoon forest is the zonal vegetation here, and is very rich in species and high in annual biomass productivity. Even more luxuriant and varied rain forests are located in wet, hot valleys of southern Yunnan, central Hainan, and southern Taiwan.

Southeastern Tibetan Plateau Alpine Needle-Leaved Forest Region

This is the second largest timber-producing area in China, with a total forested area of about 8 million ha and a total growing stock of about 1.5 billion cu m, accounting for 7 percent and 22 percent, respectively, of the national total forest resource. Most forested areas are covered by montane mixed-needle and broad-leaved forests, the former mainly consisting of *Pinus densata*, *Tsuga dumosa*, and *Quercus aquifolioides*, while the later consists of numerous trees of the genera *Picea*, *Abies*, *Sabina*, and *Larix*. Altitudinal distribution of forests is very conspicuous. As a whole, the cold-tolerant needle-leaved forests dominate, occupying about 80–90 percent of the total forested area. Fir forest is dominant, accounting for about 45–50 percent of the total forested area. The upper forest limit of *Picea balfouriana* is 4400 m on the shady slope and *Sabina tiberita* reaches 4600 m on sunny slopes, constituting the highest tree line in the world.

Northwest Arid China Needle-Leaved Forest Region

Scattered on high mountain slopes in Northwest Arid China, with a total forested area of about 1.1 million ha and a total growing stock of about 190 million cu m, the arid needle-leaved forest region accounts for 0.9 percent and 2.0 percent of the national totals, respectively. The northern slope of the Tian Shan is the largest forested area in this region, consisting of 0.4 million ha of forest land and a total growing stock of about 90 million cu m. The dominant fir forest is generally distributed on the shady slopes between 1000–2100 m on the Altay Mountains, between 1450–2750 m on northern slope of middle Tian Shan, and between 2400–3500 m on middle Qilian Mountains. Along the middle and lower reaches of inland rivers in Northwest Arid China, narrow belts of poplar (*Populus diversifolia*) forest are found growing in the moist alluvial soils.

ANIMAL HUSBANDRY

Like farming, the development of animal husbandry in China has a very long history. For thousands of years, China has been essentially divided into two agricultural realms: the northwestern pastoral area and the southeastern farming area, delimited by the so-called farming–pastoral boundary. The Great Wall served for a very long time (from about the second century B.C. until the mid-nineteenth century A.D.) as such a boundary, and the ancient prosperous tea–horse exchange trade along the boundary served as a key link between these two agricultural realms. The pastoral area has long been the homeland for many pastoral peoples, including the Mongol Empire in the thirteenth century. With the spread of Chinese agricultural (farming) civilization, the farming–pastoral boundary has been pushed northwestward repeatedly (see Chapter Three and Figure 3.1). Yet, the pastoral area holds about 52 percent of China's total land area, while the farming area, because of its better conditions for developing agriculture (including animal husbandry), accounts for about 80 percent of China's total livestock numbers (96.3 percent for pigs and 92.4 percent for mules). The only exceptions are camels and sheep, which are mainly pastured in the northwestern pastoral area.

Current Status of Animal Husbandry Development

Both physical conditions and historical tradition are favorable for the development of animal husbandry in China. Since 1949, animal husbandry has been developing rapidly. From 1949 to 1986, the numbers of large animals, including cattle, horse, donkey, mules, and camels have increased from 60.02 million to 118.96 million, pigs from 57.75 million to 337.19 million, and sheep and goats from 42.35 million to 166.23 million. By 1990, large livestock numbers increased to 130.0 million, pigs to more than 362.4 million, and sheep and goats to more than 210 million. The total meat production of pork, beef, and mutton reached 25.1 million tons, ranking first in the world. The numbers of different livestock types at the end of 1986 are listed as Table 4.4. However, animal husbandry is still a weak department in Chinese agriculture. Its production value accounted for only 11.5 percent of total agricultural value in 1952, and 16.4 percent in 1982. Agricultural animal development has been unstable, with large periodic fluctuations. In the pastoral area, animal production still essentially follows a "natural economy," depending entirely on natural grassland for pasture. Hence, animals are destined to be "fat in autumn and summer, lean in winter, and dying in spring." Animal husbandry is under a very low

TABLE 4.4
Livestock in China, End of 1986

Livestock	Number (in 10,000)	Percentage occupied by Pastoral area	Percentage occupied by Farming area
Large livestock	11,896.1		
Cattle, buffalo	9,166.7	25.1	74.9
Horses	1,098.8	43.8	56.2
Donkeys	1,068.9	24.9	75.1
Mules	511.3	7.6	92.4
Camels	50.4	73.1	26.9
Pigs	33,719.1	3.7	96.3
Sheep & goats	16,622.9		
Sheep	9,900.9	63.6	36.4
Goats	6,722.0	29.4	70.6
Chickens, ducks, & geese	196,559.7	—	—
Rabbits	9,874.7	—	—
Bees	664.6(hives)	—	—

Source: China Yearbook of Agriculture, 1987.

level of management; for example, there is no housing and no domestic feeding for livestock during the winter. Natural hazards are frequent and damaging, especially the "white hazard" (a snow cover so thick that the livestock cannot feed on natural pastureland), as well as the "black hazard" (too little snow, so that animals cannot get drinking water). In addition to the weather hazards, numerous fierce wolves wreak great havoc on livestock, while rats and various diseases and pests do much harm to the natural grassland.

Recently, a considerable effort at modernization of animal husbandry has been conducted, such as providing housing and domestic feeding for female and young animals in the wintertime, artificial planting of grasses and feedstuff, fencing of natural grassland, establishment of pastoral production infrastructure, and processing of pastoral products. With these improvements some good results have been obtained; yet, these amelioration efforts have been far from enough.

Major Pastoral Patterns

Most animal husbandry started from nomadism, then gradually evolved to seminomadism and fixed pastoralism, and finally to rotating pastoralism and domestic feeding. All these different patterns coexist in China.

Nomadism

This is the earliest tradition of pastoralism. It still exists widely in the innermost parts of the Mongolian Plateau and the Tibetan Plateau, where annual precipitation is generally less than 300 mm and surface water is inadequate for settlement. Nomadic peoples with their animal herds wander and seek water and grass all year around. They usually have no fixed houses, but move with their simple tents which can be packed up in an hour. During each year, they usually have four major migrations (once for each season) and one to two dozen shorter moves. They generally migrate within an area with a diameter ranging from several dozen to a few hundred kilometers.

Seminomadism

Transitional between nomadism and fixed pastoralism, nomadic peoples with their livestock migrate twice to four times each year. The winter and spring pastureland is generally located on the sunny slope with access to a well and a protection stable, while summer and autumn sites are usually a few dozen kilometers away from the winter and spring site, generally with rich water and grass resources so that livestock can be fattened quickly.

In mountain and alpine areas, transhumance is considered a form of seminomadism. In this system pastoral laborers and livestock move up-hill in summer and autumn, and come down to intermontane basin pasturelands in winter and spring. The best example of transhumance in China is that of the Kazaks on the northern slopes of the Tian Shan.

Fixed Pastoralism

A home base is usually located on the margins of the area where the pastoral economy dominates. Pastoral peoples generally have fixed houses and live together in small villages, with their often overgrazed pastureland surrounding these villages. Livestock graze on these overgrazed pasturelands during daytime and return to the village at night. Animals may have to be moved ever farther away from the home base to provide sufficient feed.

Rotating Pastoralism

An innovation since 1949 and a great improvement, rotating pastoralism has now spread over wide areas on the southeastern Mongolian Plateau. Children and old people stay at a fixed home base year around, while pastoral laborers practice rotating pastoralism in the surrounding pasturelands, sometimes very far away. This is one of the best models, which will maintain human health at home while allowing livestock to grow fat in far-away rich pasturelands.

Domestic Feeding

Animals may be fed in the crop-farming area, using farm products as the chief feedstuff. Animals may also be fed in pastoral areas using supplementary feeding for the weak and young livestock in the wintertime. Very recently, following modern animal management practices in developed countries, large-scale domestic feeding of chickens and milk cows has started in suburbs of large cities at industrial installations.

Regionalization of Animal Husbandry

Based on the areal differentiation of grassland types, pastoral type, and livestock structure, four pastoral regions and eight subregions might be identified in China (see Figure 2.2)

Steppe Pastoral Region

Widely distributed in western Northeast China and eastern Inner Mongolia, this is the best-developed and the richest pastoral region in China. From east to west, two subregions are recognized.

1. *Forest-steppe subregion:* Located in the eastern part of the region, forest-steppe is the most luxuriant grassland in China, with an annual fresh grass yield of 300–450 kg/*mu*. Yet, most of the best original grasslands have been cultivated for crops during the last 100 years, resulting in a broad mixed pastoral-farming belt. Fixed pastoralism and domestic feeding are now the dominant pastoral patterns. This pastoral subregion might be further developed into a meat (beef and mutton), milk, and high-quality wool production base.

2. *Steppe and desert-steppe subregion:* Mainly distributed on the middle Inner Mongolian Plateau and the Ordos Plateau, steppe and desert steppe are the most typical pastoral areas in China, generally with *Stipa spp.* dominating in the pastureland. Nomadism and seminomadism are the chief pastoral patterns. As annual precipitation decreases from east to west, the typical steppe deteriorates into desert-steppe. The ratio of large livestock (cattle and horses) to small livestock (sheep and goats) concurrently decreases, while numbers of camels and goats increase from east to west. In the future, this subregion may be required to increase its emphasis on raising cattle and horses in its eastern part while sheep and goats could be dominant in the western part. The lush and rich Hulunbuir Steppe, which was the backyard and stronghold of the Mongol Empire in the thirteenth century, may be especially developed as the typical modernized pastoral production base.

Desert Pastoral Region

This broad region is located west of the Helan Mountains, where annual precipitation is generally less than 200 mm. Consequently, sandy desert, stony desert, rocky mountain slopes, and other barren areas are extensive, with limited areas of pasturelands consisting mainly of sparse shrubs and low shrubs. Two subregions are recognized:

1. *Mountain desert region:* Located primarily on the Tian Shan, Altay Mountains, and other high mountains, these regions are the best and the most extensive desert pastureland available. Vegetation is arranged in altitudinal zones, providing a basis for transhumance and supplementary domestic feeding as the dominant pastoral patterns. Livestock resources are rich and varied, including sheep, goats, cattle, horses, pigs, camels, and yak. Since ancient times, many famous, high-quality livestock species have been bred here, such as the Ili horse, the Altay horse, the Yangi horse, the Tacheng cattle, the Xinjiang fine wool sheep, and the Ili white pig. Hence, many improved pastoral production bases might be established in this subregion, such as the fine-wool sheep production base in Altay, Tian Shan, and Qilian mountain areas, a fat lamb production base in Altay and Ili prefectures, and a milk and meat cattle production base in Ili prefecture.

2. *Plain desert region:* Scattered in the extensive inland basins and plateaus of Northwest Arid China, seminomadism and fixed pastoralism are the chief pastoral patterns, with goats, sheep, and camels as the principal livestock species. But on the piedmont plains, transhumance dominates, while in the oases, domestic livestock feeding and pig raising are the main animal enterprises. In the future many pastoral production bases might be established in this extensive subregion, including fine-hair goat production in many areas, and camel production in the Alashan Plateau and the Junggar and Qaidam basins.

Alpine Grassland Pastoral Region

On the Tibetan Frigid Plateau there lies a special pastoral region, unique not only in China, but also in the whole world. Using the mighty Gangdise Mountains as the dividing line, two subregions are identified.

1. *Northern alpine grassland subregion:* Elevations generally range from 4500 to 5000 m, and alpine steppe and alpine desert-steppe are the dominant vegetation types with annual yield of fresh grass averaging 200–300 kg/*mu*. Livestock production consists mainly of sheep, goats, and yak, accounting for 65 percent, 20 percent, and 15 percent, respectively. Seminomadism (transhumance) and fixed pastoralism are the chief pastoral patterns. The Tibetan herdsmen also pasture a few cattle, donkeys, and pigs. Modernization of animal husbandry practices is sorely needed in this subregion. Pastoral pro-

duction of yak and sheep should be established in the near future.

2. *Southern alpine grassland subregion:* Including the Himalaya, the Gangdise, and the Nyainquen–Tanglha Mountains, this subregion is mainly composed of vertical vegetational zonation, where transhumance grazing of yak, sheep, and goats dominates. Yet, in the intermontane valleys and basins, a considerable amount of farmland has been cultivated for many years, and livestock (including cattle, donkeys, and pigs) is raised mainly by domestic feeding of feed stuffs from the farming areas.

Farming-Pastoral Region

This widely distributed region coincides with China's southeastern farming area. Livestock is raised chiefly by domestic feeding as a sideline occupation. Yet, the region produces more livestock (except camels and sheep) than the northwestern pastoral area; the variety of livestock is also much richer, including pigs, cattle, water buffalo, horses, donkeys, mules, sheep, goats, chickens, ducks, geese, rabbits, bees, and silkworms. To date, the most important animals are pigs, chickens, ducks, geese, rabbits, and bees. In the future, a milk and beef cattle (buffalo) production base might also be developed. Using the Qinling-Huaihe line as the boundary, two subregions can be identified:

1. *Northern China farming-pastoral subregion:* Compared with its counterpart subregion in Southern China, Northern China has a larger share of cattle, horses, mules, donkeys, and sheep, but it has no water buffalo. In some areas bordering the northwestern pastoral area, small-scale fixed pastoralism is also conducted, although domestic feeding still dominates the pastoral pattern. At present, as well as for the foreseeable future, pigs, cattle, and sheep are the three major livestock types. Pigs are especially important, with the major production base in the Northeast China Plain, the Guan-Zhong (Wei River basin) Plain, the Back Elbow Plain, the Ningxia Plain, the Hexi Corridor, and the North China Plain. All these animal-producing enterprises are located in major food-producing areas, and hence crops and crop residues are abundant for feed-stuffs. Chicken and rabbit raising might be also encouraged and industrialized.

2. *Southern China farming-pastoral subregion:* In its physical characteristics, this subregion is conditioned by the influences of subtropical and tropical climate, mountainous topography, rich water resources, and luxuriant vegetation. Livestock production features water buffalo and humped cattle (*Bos indicus*), and in total numbers is dominated by pigs and chickens. According to incomplete statistics, there are 43 species of pigs in this subregion. There are also many species of buffalo, cattle, sheep, goats, horses, chickens, and ducks. For the foreseeable future, the largest pastoral production here will continue to be pigs and chickens (including ducks and geese); other animals such as cattle, buffalo, rabbits, and bees might be also considered.

FISHING

Fishing also has a very long history in China. Peking Man (about 200,000 to 700,000 years ago) lived by gathering, hunting, and fishing. According to historical documents, an artificial fish pond was dug in 1142 B.C., and coastal fishing was well developed during Spring and Autumn Period (771–403 B.C.) when the state of Qi was called a "country of fish and salt." In 460 B.C., the celebrated statesman Fan Li wrote a book on fishing which might be the first book on this topic in the world. Shortly afterwards, the Chang Jiang Delta was elaborately developed for irrigation, aqua-culture, and fishing, and thus was called a "watery country of rice and fish."

Furthermore, China's geographical environment is quite favorable for the development of fisheries, both marine and freshwater. With a continental coastline of more than 18,000 km, the total coastal beach area is about 4.7 million sq km, which is supported by the immense Pacific Ocean, creating an almost limitless capacity for developing marine fisheries. Continental water bodies are also extensive, totaling about 20 million ha (including about 8 million ha of lakes), of which about 5 million ha are fit for developing an artificial freshwater fishery. The aqua-faunal resource is rich in China, with more than 2000 marine fish species in the neighboring seas. Of more than 2000 freshwater fish species, several hundred are of economic value.

Since 1949, fisheries have been developed rather rapidly in China. From a total annual catch of only 450,000 tons in 1949, production increased to 1.73 million tons in 1952, and to 3.12 million tons in 1957. However, from 1958 to 1969, the total annual catch fluctuated between 2 and 3 million tons. Then production started to increase again in the 1970s. By the 1980s, total annual catch and artificial breeding had increased rapidly, stimulated by organization of comprehensive fishery–animal husbandry, fishery–forestry, or fishery–farming production systems. In 1986, the total annual catch reached 8.24 million tons and increased further to

12.18 million tons in 1990. On the other hand, serious overexploitation and other environmental problems have started to appear. To date, fisheries are still a very weak part of China's agriculture, accounting for less than 2 percent of the total agricultural production value. Table 4.5 shows total annual catch by province in 1986.

TABLE 4.5
Total Annual Fish Catch by Province, 1986 and 1990*

Province (municipality, autonomous region)	Total annual catch (tons)		Marine (tons)		Freshwater (tons)	
	1986	1990	1986	1990	1986	1990
Heilongjiang	84,274	147,869	—	—	84,274	147,869
Jilin	38,339	70,885	—	—	38,339	70,885
Liaoning	669,542	1,073,558	631,947	1,007,118	37,595	66,440
Beijing	22,176	51,602	148	519	22,028	51,083
Tianjin	67,286	108,338	31,508	36,270	35,778	72,068
Hebei	153,063	218,553	122,994	164,880	32,069	53,670
Henan	66,074	104,753	—	—	66,074	104,753
Shandong	914,411	1,677,973	806,086	1,522,059	108,325	155,914
Shanxi	4,004	10,228	—	—	4,004	10,228
Shaanxi	8,931	20,567	—	—	8,931	20,567
Shanghai	237,062	273,583	162,394	170,438	74,688	103,145
Jiangsu	804,787	1,182,549	263,840	338,540	540,947	844,009
Anhui	207,417	291,044	—	—	207,417	291,044
Zhejiang	1,172,086	1,389,791	973,589	1,131,742	198,497	258,049
Jiangxi	192,849	306,824	—	—	192,849	306,824
Hubei	466,603	709,840	—	—	466,603	709,840
Hunan	381,747	530,082	—	—	381,747	530,082
Fujian	809,927	1,186,412	748,630	1,091,643	61,297	94,769
Guangdong	1,405,012	2,076,557	869,652	1,245,332	595,360	831,245
Hainan	—	167,464	—	145,555	—	21,909
Guangxi	211,759	323,493	131,344	202,672	80,415	120,821
Sichuan	158,391	232,561	—	—	158,391	232,561
Guizhou	13,965	22,440	—	—	13,965	22,440
Yunnan	31,160	46,041	—	—	31,160	46,041
Inner Mongolia	20,688	30,428	—	—	20,688	30,428
Ningxia	3,270	10,217	—	—	3,270	10,217
Gansu	1,160	3,562	—	—	1,160	3,562
Qinghai	4,580	3,356	—	—	4,580	3,356
Xinjiang	11,312	23,217	—	—	11,312	23,217
Tibet	—	249	—	—	—	249
Aqua-products	11,600	76,147	11,600	76,147	—	—
National total	8,235,475	12,370,203	4,753,732	7,132,915	2,381,743	5,237,288

*Taiwan and Hong Kong not included.

Sources: China Yearbook of Agriculture, 1987, and *Statistical Yearbook of China, 1991.*

Marine Fishing

Marine fishing is now the main source of fish in China, developing rapidly in recent years and accounting for 57.7 percent of the total fishery production value in l986. In the marine fishing, the natural catch is much more important than artificial breeding. The natural catch accounted for 82 percent of total marine fish production value in 1986, although the latter also developed rapidly in recent years.

Products of marine fishing include fish, lobsters, crabs, shellfish, and marine algae. A little more than three-fourths of total products are fish, of which hairtail, large yellow croaker, small yellow croaker, and cuttlefish are the most productive. Artificial breeding in marine fishing, with support especially for marine algae (mainly kelp), made great strides from the 1970s to the 1980s. The marine fishery might be divided into five fishing areas.

Bo Hai Fishing Area

Consisting of nearly closed shallow seawater fishing areas, the Liaodong Gulf, the Leizhou Gulf, and the Luan River mouth area are the principal fishing grounds. Chief fishery products include Chinese herring, Spanish mackerel, lobster, shrimp, and marine crabs. Extensive coastal beaches with great capability for developing artificial breeding also exist. Overexploitation of fish resources and pollution of seawater are two serious environmental problems.

Yellow Sea Fishing Area

This is a half-closed shallow sea with a warm temperate climate. The Yellow Sea is probably the second best developed marine fishery area in China, with numerous state-owned marine fishery bases and ports, such as Dandong, Dalian, Yantai, Shidao, Qingdao, and Lianyun. Chief fishery products include large yellow croaker, small yellow croaker, hairtail, cuttlefish, cod, Spanish mackerel, chub mackerel, Chinese herring, Pacific herring, and lobsters. Extensive coastal beaches have recently been developed for artificial breeding of shellfish, crabs, and marine algae. Overexploitation of fish resources, especially in the near-coast area, is now a big environmental problem.

East China Sea Fishing Area

This is an extensive, open continental shelf fishing area, with a subtropical climate and numerous islands and ports. It is the best marine fishery area in China, accounting for about two-fifths of the total marine catch and employing about one-half of the total number of fishermen. It produces more than two-thirds of the four principal fish catches in China—hairtail, large yellow croaker, small yellow croaker, and cuttlefish. In addition, more than 20 other economic fish species are worth catching, such as butterfish, Chinese herring, porgy, marine eel, slate cod, and shark. Shanghai and other ports are also the largest centers for processing and trading sea foods. The extensive coastal beaches are good sites for developing artificial breeding and fish culture.

South China Sea Fishing Area

This is a vast deep seawater fishing area, with a tropical climate. The chief fish products include scad, sardines, and globefish. There are also numerous other tropical fishes. Major fishing ports include Guangzhou, Shantou, Zhanjiang, and Beihai.

Pacific Ocean Fishing Area

Located mainly east of Taiwan, this area is part of the immense Pacific deep-sea fish resource. Chief fishery products include oceanic bonito, sturgeon, and mackerel, which occupy about one-third of Taiwan's total fishery production. Suao, located on the east coast of Taiwan, is the principal fishing port. Owing to the rugged topography of Taiwan's east coast, artificial breeding is limited.

Freshwater Fishing

China has long been a country with well-developed freshwater fish production. In 1986, the annual freshwater catch totaled nearly 3.5 million tons, accounting for 42.3 percent of China's total fish production. Freshwater artificial breeding was formerly limited to the Chang Jiang (Yangtze River) and the Zhu Jiang (Pearl River) deltas. Since 1949, freshwater fisheries have spread widely, and since the 1960s, production has surpassed that of the natural catch. In 1986, production reached 2.95 million tons, accounting for 84.8 percent of the total freshwater fishery production. A marvelous innovation in southern China is the breeding of fish in paddy land during the flooded time, forming a very productive ecosystem, which has farming and fishing helping each other, resulting in a bountiful production for both. There were about 760,000 ha of fish-paddy lands in 1986. The freshwater fishery can be divided into six fishing areas.

Chang Jiang–Huai He Basins Fishing Area

Located mainly in the humid, northern and middle subtropical zone, this is in the so-called watery country and includes all five of the largest freshwater lakes (Poyang, Dongting, Tai, Hongze, and Chao) in China. Consequently, it is the country's largest freshwater fishing area, producing about three-fourths of the total freshwater fish. There are more than 260 fish species in this area, of which about one-half belong to the carp family. Among the more than 50 economic fish species, carp, black carp, grass carp, silver carp, golden carp, variegated carp, hilsa herring, bream, and eel are the most important. Shrimp, crabs, shellfish, and other aqua-cultures are also important. To date, many freshwater bodies have not yet been fully utilized, and hence the capability for further development is great.

Zhu Jiang Basin Fishing Area

Mainly located in the humid, southern subtropical zone, this is the second largest freshwater fishing area, producing about one-fifth of total freshwater fish catch in China. Fishery production is concentrated in the Zhu Jiang Delta, where fish from artificial breeding accounts for more than 90 percent of the total. The paddy rice–sugar cane (or mulberry tree)–fish pond ecosystem dominates. The principal species artificially bred include carp, grass carp, silver carp, and variegated carp. Fish might be harvested two or three times each year, with a large portion of the harvest being exported to Hong Kong and Macao.

Yellow River–Hai He Basins Fishing Area

Located mainly in the subhumid, warm temperate zone, this fishing area is not yet well developed. It produces less than one-tenth of the total freshwater fish catch in China. However, it has been traditionally famous for the Yellow River carp and the Baiyang Lake crab. The fish resources (including carp, grass carp, bream, mandarin fish, and white fish) are quite rich; consequently, the potential for further development is great, and artificial breeding is now growing rapidly.

Northeast China Fishing Area

The Heilong Jiang and Liao River basins constitute a fishing area that has not yet become well developed. However, fish resources are quite rich, with more than 100 fish species; principal economic species include carp, silver carp, golden carp, grass carp, catfish, white fish, mandarin fish, sturgeon, huso sturgeon, and small-scale fish.

Northwest Arid China Fishing Area

This is an underdeveloped fishing area, occupying only 5 percent of the total freshwater area and less than 1 percent of the total freshwater fish production in China. Artificial breeding started only after 1956. Principal economic species include carp, golden carp, sturgeon, huso sturgeon, and red fish.

Tibetan Frigid Plateau Fishing Area

This is a little developed fishing area. The main cause is physical, because there are only a few freshwater bodies on the rugged and frigid Tibetan Plateau, a result of the predominantly arid and semiarid climates. Another important cause is social, inasmuch as the Tibetan people regard eating fish as disgusting. Up to now, only Qinghai Lake, which is saline, has any notable fish production, mainly the nonscaled huso sturgeon. Artificial breeding is still nonexistent on the Tibetan Plateau.

STRATEGIES FOR MODERNIZATION OF AGRICULTURE

In any country, government policies are often decisive for economic and social development. In recent years, the Chinese government has recognized that agriculture is still the basis of the national economy and food is still the core of human existence. Thus, more inputs and scientific research are needed to increase agricultural production. A series of laws and policies have been formed and put into practice, such as Land, Water, and Forest Laws for the protection and rational use of different natural resources, as well as laws implementing the responsibility system policy and the three fixation policy for farming and forestry management. All these laws and policies are necessary for productive and sustainable agricultural development. However, the laws and policies are not yet sufficiently deep and sophisticated. Further scientific and technical research for better and more rational use of all natural resources as well as for monitoring and combatting all natural hazards are much needed.

Major Constraints and Problems for Agricultural Development

There are a number of major constraints, or limiting factors, that affect agricultural development in China.

Physical Constraints

1. Mountainous topography, so that the amount of arable land resource is rather limited

2. Great seasonal and annual variations in precipitation, so that flood (mainly in late summer and autumn) and drought (mainly in spring and early summer) hazards are frequent

3. A result of both physical and human factors, soil erosion has been widespread

4. Salinization and secondary salinization are widespread in Northwest Arid China and along the coast

5. Desertification and eolian sand have imposed great havoc in Northwest Arid China

6. Other natural hazards include: frost and low temperatures in Northeast China, typhoons along southeast coasts, hailstorms and montane hazards in mountainous areas, harmful animals (rats, wolves, etc.), insects (locusts, etc.), and diseases in farming and pastoral areas.

Technical Constraints

1. Many of the irrigation facilities have become worn or damaged in recent years.

2. Effective technical measures for monitoring and combatting different natural hazards are needed.

3. Fertilizers, both chemical and organic, are needed.

4. Modern farming implements and pastoral equipment are needed. Farming and animal husbandry in remote borderlands are still using very primitive tools.

5. Agricultural management needs to be modernized as soon as possible. At present animal husbandry especially relies almost entirely on natural pastures and forested areas, which are essentially limited to timber exploiting.

Institutional and Infrastructure Development Needs

1. Scientific studies and dissemination of scientific knowledge on agricultural development needs to be greatly enhanced.

2. Industrial and transportation facilities need to be greatly modernized.

3. Illiteracy is still very high, affecting the productivity and quality of life of nearly one-fifth of the total population and nearly one-third of the rural population.

Socioeconomic

1. Comprehensive planning and improved policies for agricultural development, both national and regional, are needed.

2. Low agricultural production and meager income per capita have caused a serious poverty problem in rural China, which in turn has seriously affected agricultural development.

3. A huge and still growing population has caused a serious social and economic problem.

4. Cordial relations among all Chinese peoples should be advocated. Harmony between people and nature should be promoted.

Major Strategies for Modernization of Agriculture

To combat the serious and persistent constraints and to achieve a productive and sustainable agriculture, major strategies have been proposed. First is to maintain careful control of population growth, so that a balanced land–food–population system may be reached (see Chapter Eleven).

The economic structure should be reordered, so that industry and other nonagricultural production will be developed rapidly and the portion of agriculture-engaged population in the population will be decreased to below 30 to 40 percent.

The agricultural structure itself, also needs to be reordered to make it more comprehensive, including a balance of farming, animal husbandry, forestry, and fishing, instead of overemphasizing farming. At the same time, a comprehensive land use plan should be developed to consider all land areas of China (9.6 million sq km), instead of concentrating on farmland (about 1 million sq km) alone. The desired result is to create a "greater" agriculture (including farming, animal husbandry, forestry, fishing, and sideline industries) instead of a "small" agriculture (overwhelmingly farming) and thus comprehensively develop China's total territory. The vast mountain areas are a special landscape, where "vertical agriculture" may be developed, with intensive farming concentrated in intermontane valley plains, orchards of economic trees planted in piedmont areas, economic trees and fast-growing timber trees located on mountain slopes, and transhumance and water conservation forests or "solid water reservoirs" (glaciers and snow) on the higher slopes. The highly productive water bodies should be planned as a special land use type where fish farming (aqua-culture), irrigation farming, fisheries, and water transportation might be developed together. Salt harvesting could be developed from salty lakes and neighboring seas.

An overall plan for the limited arable land resource should be developed for intensive but sustainable use, especially for food production. As a whole, China must be self-sufficient in food supply, because with such a huge internal food demand, the world market could not supply, nor could the Chinese people afford to buy, the necessary amounts. Specific policies include:

1. Effectively protect existing farmland. Other uses that decrease farmland area will not be allowed.

2. Reclaim all remaining unused arable land, to appease somewhat the "land-hunger" plight in China. Special measures (such as sophisticated soil conservation measures) should be used on marginal lands, so that each piece of newly reclaimed land will be transformed into highly productive and sustainable farmland.

3. Increase as much as possible the land unit yield of middle and low-grade farmlands. They account for about two-thirds of China's farmlands, with the annual yield of grain of only 200–400 kg/*mu* (or 3.0–6.0 ton/ha). By using ameliorating measures that are appropriate to specific land conditions, the per land unit yield might be doubled or even tripled.

4. Use the most modern practices on high-grade lands, which occupy about one-third of China's total farmland. Even with average annual yields of grain crops of more than 400 kg/*mu* (6 tons/ha), appropriate measures are necessary to increase yields still more.

5. Enlarge the present 15 production bases of commercial grain and economic crops.

6. Apply appropriate practices for use of irrigation, mechanization, chemical fertilization, electrification, and other modern equipment to all farmlands according to their specific conditions.

7. Monitor and combat all environmental problems and natural hazards related to farming according to their specific conditions and severity.

Support for novel techniques such as hydroponics, algae culture, yeast culture, food synthesis, new crops, new species, and biotechnologies can increase China's food supply.

Modernization of animal husbandry is a high-priority need. First, because of its close link with farming, natural grassland should be protected and improved, and emergency or secondary feedstuff should be grown in local favorable sites. Second, industrialization should be closely linked with livestock production under a comprehensive management plan of pasturing, domestic feeding, and large-scale industrial installations where most of the pastoral products can be better processed before entering the market. Most of the old-fashioned pastoral tools and equipment need to be modernized.

Improved fish breeding should be established and expanded. At the same time, natural fishing areas should be protected and improved to prevent overexploitations.

Changing the present ratio between wood cutting and wood planting of 3:1 to at least 1:1 or better to 1:1.5 would establish a permanent and growing forestry production base.

Finally, regional agriculture should be carefully developed according to areal differences in physical and human conditions. (See Chapters Twelve through Eighteen.)

REFERENCES

China State Statistical Bureau. 1991. *Statistical Yearbook of China*. Beijing: China Statistical Publishing House.

China Ministry of Agriculture. 1987. *China Yearbook of Agriculture*. Beijing: Agriculture Press.

Institute of Geography, Chinese Academy of Sciences. 1980. *Agricultural Geography of China*. Beijing: Science Press (in Chinese).

Institute of Geography, Chinese Academy of Sciences. 1990. *Land Use Map of China*. Beijing: Science Press (in Chinese).

Li, Pang. 1984. *Developmental History of Chinese Cultivated Plants*. Beijing: Science Press (in Chinese).

Sin, Ye-jiang. 1987. *Outline of Chinese Forestry*. Beijing: Chinese Forestry Press (in Chinese).

Sun, Changjiang. 1989. "Major Grassland Types in China." *Chinese Journal of Arid Land Research* 2, no. 1.

Zhong, Gongfu. 1980. "Mulberry Dyke–Fish Pond in the Zhu Jiang Delta—A Complete Artificial Ecosystem of Land-water Interaction," *Acta Geographica Sinica* 35, no. 3 (in Chinese).

Zhao, Songqiao. 1984. "Distribution and Utilization of Arable Land Resources in China," *Natural Resources*, pp. 13–20 (in Chinese).

Zhao, Songqiao. 1988. *Natural Conditions and Territorial Management in the North China Plain.* Tokyo: NIRA (in English and in Japanese).

Zhao, Songqiao. 1981. "Transforming Wilderness into Farmland: An Evaluation of Natural Conditions for Agricultural Development in Heilongjiang Province," *China Geographer 2.*

Zhao, Songqiao. 1988. "Rain-fed Agricultural Development in Northwest Arid China," *Chinese Journal of Arid Land Research* 1, no.3.

Zhao, Songqiao. 1981. "Current Large-scale Reclamation in the Middle and Lower Tarim Basin and Its Impact on the Arid Environment," *Geographiche Rundschau*, March (in German).

Zhao, Songqiao, et al. 1990. *Vertical Agricultural Systems in the Hengduan Mountains and in the Qilian Mountains of the Tibetan Plateau: A Comparative Study.* Kathamandu: IDIMOD.

Zhu, Lincun. 1987. *Fresh Water Fisheries.* Beijing: Sea & Ocean Press (in Chinese).

CHAPTER FIVE

Modern Industry

China has a long history of agricultural and handicraft development, but it lags far behind many countries in the development of modern industry and secondary and tertiary production. Consequently, China suffers badly from poverty and technical backwardness coupled with a huge population. This is the chief reason why China is now put in the category of "developing" rather than "developed" countries in the world. However, since 1949, modern industry has grown rapidly in China. Especially since 1978, industry has been one of the country's "Four Modernizations."[1] Total industrial production value increased from about 14 billion yuan in 1949 to about 148 billion yuan in 1959, to about 208 billion yuan in 1970, to about 490 billion yuan in 1980, and to more than 2385 billion yuan in 1990 (Table 3.3). The ratio between agriculture and industry in annual production value has changed from 7:3 in the early 1950s to 3:7 in the middle 1980s and to 1:3 in 1990. In the 1982 census of China's total employed population, industry accounted for 13.72 percent of the labor force.

HISTORICAL DEVELOPMENT OF MODERN INDUSTRY

The history of modern Chinese industry begins in 1840, when Chinese history in general entered into its modern period (see Chapter Three). Two stages and six substages can be identified.

[1]The other three "Modernizations" are: Agriculture, National Defense, and Science and Technology.

Before 1949: "Old China"

From 1840 to 1949, most capital for China's small-scale, scattered modern industries came from foreign capitalists and the Chinese government, with only a small portion from Chinese capitalists. The distribution of these modern industries was very uneven; most were concentrated along the coast, particularly around Shanghai and Tianjin. Light industries (especially food and textiles), produced about 70–80 percent of the total industrial production by value. At the same time heavy industry was mainly restricted to mining and metallurgy. Another weak point was the dysfunction among raw materials, energy sources, capital, markets, and other factors of industrial production. For example, Shanghai, including suburbs, was the largest industrial center in Old China (especially for the textile and food industries); yet, this was also the poorest region in mineral and energy resources. Supplies of raw materials, including wool, cotton, wood, and grain, were also far from adequate.

This stage included three substages.

1840–1894

The period between the beginning of the Opium War in 1840 to the eve of the Sino-Japanese War in 1894 was the initial period of modern industrial development in China. Development was mainly controlled by foreign investors and located in their respective political "spheres of influence." For example, British investment controlled shipbuilding, silk textiles, sugar manufacture, and many other industries along the southeastern coast from Shanghai to Guangzhou. The Qing government also set up a series of "self-strengthening" industries, emphasizing the military.

Soon afterwards, Chinese national capitalists emerged and started to establish a series of small-scale modern light industries. As a whole, during this substage there were about 170 industrial enterprises in China, involving more than 100,000 workers. In production value, military industries ranked first, then came the light industries. In geographical distribution, about 70 percent were concentrated along the southeastern coast and in the middle and lower Chang Jiang valley, especially around the Shanghai, Guangzhou, and Wuhan areas.

1895–1936

Modern Chinese industry developed comparatively rapidly. Foreign and government investments dominated, but Chinese national capitalism made great strides. The number of cotton spindles increased from 830,000 in 1913 to 2.38 million in 1922, and subsequently to 5.10 million in 1936. Coal production increased from 14 million tons in 1913 to 24 million tons in 1922, and

later to 39 million tons in 1936. During this substage, textile and food industries flourished, accounting for 70 percent of the total industrial production value in 1936. In geographical distribution, the Chang Jiang Delta industrial area began taking shape for the first time, with Shanghai as its center and textiles as its chief industry. At the same time, modern industries were also developing rather rapidly along the coast of North China.

1937–1949

Devastated by the Japanese war and by civil wars, total industrial production value in 1949 decreased to only one-half of that of 1936. In 1936, there were about 120,000 modern industrial enterprises in China, of which, more than 70 percent were located in Shanghai, Jiangsu, Liaoning, Hebei, and Tianjin, while less than one-fifth were located in the extensive inland provinces (Figure 5.1).

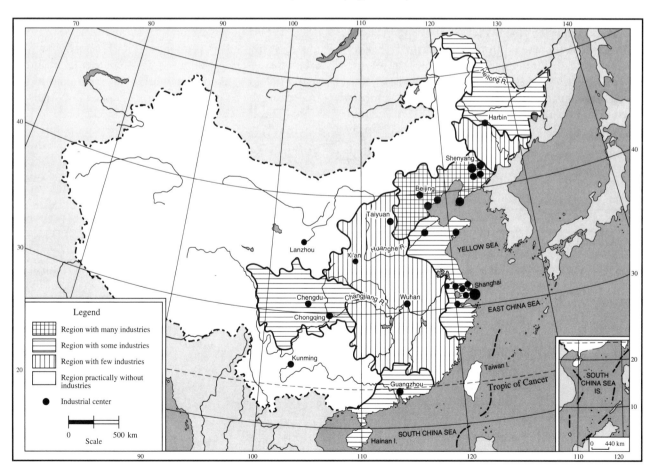

Figure 5.1 Industrial regionalization of China, in 1949

After 1949: "New China"

After the founding of the People's Republic of China in 1949, great emphasis was laid on modern industrial development, and great strides have been made. In 1985, there were about 83.48 million industrial workers and more than 400,000 industrial enterprises in China, including more than 6000 large and medium-scale factories. The percentage of industrial production value in total national production value increased from 34.5 percent in 1952 to 53.7 percent in 1985. According to official 1990 statistics, total annual industrial production value reached 2385.1 billion yuan (with an annual increase of 7.6 percent), of which the state and collective economy occupied 91.4 percent, and light industries accounted for 49.5 percent. The increase in annual production of major industrial commodities since 1949 is shown as Table 5.1.

Much has been done since 1949 to improve the modern industrial structure. First, basic heavy industries (steel and engineering) were emphasized and rapidly developed. By 1990, steel production reached 66.4 million tons, ranking fourth in the world. Second, energy industries that were the driving force in industrial development were greatly strengthened. In 1990, coal production reached more than 1 billion (1080 million) tons, ranking first in the world. The petroleum industry started from practically nothing in 1949 to a production level of 138.3 million tons in 1990, ranking sixth in the world. Third, many important industries have been founded or greatly enlarged, such as automobile and tractor assembly, oceanic shipbuilding, airplane manufacturing, and electronics manufacturing. Fourth, many traditional industries such as silk fabric, carpets, and porcelain have advanced significantly in production efficiency and quality.

Three developmental substages might also be identified in this stage.

1949–1965

During this period of rapid development and reallocation of modern industries, government stressed heavy industries over light industry, and industry was given equal or greater importance than agriculture. From 1953 to 1957, the First Five Year Plan was completed, with emphasis on the heavy industries (including steel, coal, and engineering). The first Strategic Zone for developing heavy industries was the Northeast China Plain, with Anshan as its largest center. The second Strategic Zone was along the Beijing–Wuhan Railway.

The Second Five Year Plan started in 1958 but was greatly disrupted by the Great Leap Forward. The two established strategic zones were strengthened in industrial development while establishment of two new industrial areas, the so-called Third Line, began in Northwest China and Southwest China. Investments were unusually heavy, but economic benefits were not conspicuous.

TABLE 5.1
Increase in Annual Production of Major Industrial Commodities since 1949*

Item	Unit	1949	1952	1965	1978	1985	1990
Total industrial production value	100 million yuan	140	343	1,394	4,231	8,295	23,851
Coal	million tons	32	66	232	618	872	1,080
Petroleum	million tons	0.12	0.44	11.31	104.05	124.89	138.31
Electricity	million KW/hr	43	73	676	2,566	4,107	6,180
Steel	10,000 tons	16	135	1,223	3,178	4,679	6,635
Timber	10,000 cu m	567	1,233	3,978	5,162	6,323	5,571
Cement	10,000 tons	66	286	1,634	6,524	14,595	20,971
Chemical fertilizers	10,000 tons	0.6	4.0	173	869	1,322	1,912
Automobiles	10,000	—	—	4.0	14.9	43.7	51.4
Bicycles	10,000	1.4	8.0	183.8	854.0	3,227.7	3,141.6
Cloth	100 million m	18.9	38.3	62.8	110.3	146.7	188.8
Paper	10,000 tons	11	37	73	439	911	1,330
Sugar	10,000 tons	20	45	146	227	451	582
Salt	10,000 tons	299	495	1,147	1,953	1,479	2,033

*Taiwan and Hong Kong are not included.

Source: Compiled from various official statistics.

1966–1978

Damaged by the Cultural Revolution, industrial and other types of economic enterprises showed little progress, although petroleum and a few other industries demonstrated some success.

Since 1978

A new era of rapid "modernization" and "opening up" of industrial and other economic enterprises has been underway. In accord with government policies, both light and heavy industries have been kept in balance for the first time. On average, total annual industrial production value from 1979 to 1985 increased by 10.1 percent, of which textiles, engineering, chemical engineering, and food industries increased most rapidly. Since 1982, light and heavy industries have provided about one-half of the total industrial production by value. However, the spatial disparities of industrial development deepened during the 1980s, with the coastal zone developing faster and faster, while the inland areas lagged far behind.

MAJOR MODERN INDUSTRIES

The major modern industrial categories in China are energy, metallurgy, chemicals, building materials, engineering, and light industries.

Energy Industries

China is rich in energy resources (including coal, petroleum, natural gas, nuclear energy, and solar radiation) as stated in Chapter Two. However, these resources are rather unevenly distributed, and production and consumption centers may be widely separated from each other geographically. For example, coal deposits are concentrated in North China while the consumption centers are mainly along the coast. Consequently, long-distance transportation of energy resources has long been a significant necessity as well as an economic expense. These imbalances are typified by "Northern coal moving southward," coupled with "Southern food moving northward," and thus bear significant economic and social consequences for China.

Coal

Coal is the most abundant energy source in China. Mining started as early as the sixth century B.C., and coal has been used in iron smelting ever since the Western Han Dynasty (202 B.C.–A.D. 8) and to make porcelain ever since the Tang Dynasty (A.D. 619–899). During the Ming Dynasty (1368–1644) small coal-mining sites had already been developed in many parts of China. Yet, modern coal mining started only in the 1870s. In 1913, coal production in China exceeded 10 million tons, and it reached 61.88 million tons by 1942. More than 60 percent of the coal production in Old China was concentrated in three northern coastal provinces: Liaoning, Hebei, and Shandong.

China's modern coal-mining industry has been developing rapidly since 1949 with annual production increasing from 66 million tons in 1952 to 872 million tons in 1985, and to 1080 million tons in 1990. The percentage of coal in the total energy use decreased from 96.7 percent in 1952 to 72.8 percent in 1985. In geographical distribution, besides these three northern coastal provinces, coal-mining sites are spread widely from northern China to southern China and from the coastal areas to inland basins. Large coal-mining regions include: northeastern Hebei, southern Hebei–northern Henan, western Henan, northern Shanxi, central Shanxi, eastern Shanxi, central Shaanxi, the southern Taihang Mountains area, central Liaoning, western Liaoning, eastern Heilongjiang, the Shandong–Anhui–Jiangsu border region, southwestern Guizhou, and the Helan Mountains. A very recent mining trend is the construction of large-scale open-pit coal mines on the eastern Inner Mongolia Plateau and the eastern Ordos Plateau as well as the northern Loess Plateau. The border area between Inner Mongolia–Shanxi–Shaanxi is now aptly called the Black Triangle. The economy has received a boost from large-scale coal-mining activities, but severe soil erosion and other environmental problems have become an increasing menace.

Petroleum and Natural Gas

Petroleum drilling started in China in the early twentieth century in the Mian-li oil field of Taiwan in 1904 and in the Yan-chiang oil field of Shaanxi in 1907. Later, the Yumen (Hexi Corridor, Gansu) and a few other small oil fields were discovered. However, as of 1949, annual petroleum production totaled only 120,000 tons and natural gas only 16 million cu m. Even in 1952, annual production of petroleum totaled only 440,000 tons and natural gas only 8 million cu m. In the late 1950s and early 1960s large-scale geological exploration got underway, and the Daqing (literally, "Great Celebration") oil field in Heilongjiang Province, with an annual petroleum production of 55 to 60 million tons, became the symbol of the Chinese petroleum industry. China became self-sufficient in petroleum products for the first time in 1965. Total annual production reached 125 million tons and natural gas 12.9 billion cu m in 1985, occupying a portion of the total energy source of 20.9 percent and 2.0 percent, respectively. By 1990, petroleum production had reached more than 138 million tons.

Petroleum has recently become one of the chief export commodities for China. Large-scale oil fields have been developed in Daqing, Shengli (literally, "Victory," located at the mouth of the Yellow River), Dagang (literally, "Big Port," located on the northern Hebei coast), Central Hebei, and lower Liao River Valley. A recent important discovery in western China is the existence of big oil and natural gas fields in the Tarim Basin, the Junggar Basin, the Turpan Basin, the Qaidam Basin, and eastward to the Ordos Plateau, the Loess Plateau, and the Sichuan Basin. The last one is the major natural gas production site. Large-scale exploration and construction activities are underway to develop these fields rapidly.

The oil refining industry has also been developing rapidly as new oil and gas fields are discovered. The four largest oil refineries (each with annual capacity of more than 10 million tons) are located in central and southern Liaoning, in the Heilongjiang and Jilin border area, in the Beijing–Tianjin area, and in the Shanghai–southern Jiangsu–northern Zhejiang area. Other important refinery locations are scattered in Northwest China (including Lanzhou, Yumen, Ürümqi, and Karamay). Small refineries are located in Shandong, Guangdong, and in the middle reaches of the Chang Jiang. As many refineries are located in the suburbs of big cities, air and water pollution have become a serious environmental problem.

Hydro- and Coal-fired Electricity

The first coal-fired electric power plant was built in Shanghai in 1882 with a capacity of only 12 KW. Total non-hydroelectric capacity in China reach 1.04 million KW in 1937 and increased to 1.84 million KW in 1949, of which 87.6 percent were concentrated along the coast.

Tens of thousands of electricity plants and many electric power networks have been constructed since 1949. By 1984, China's total electric capacity increased to 80.1 million KW, of which, hydroelectricity accounted for 25.6 percent. In 1990, annual electricity production reached 6180 million KW/hr, ranking fourth in the world. Six electric power systems are in service in major regions including East China, North China, Northeast China, Central China, Northwest China, and Southwest China. A recent trend is the construction of large-scale coal-fired power plants in newly developed open-pit coal-mining areas in the eastern Mongolian Plateau, the eastern Ordos Plateau, and the northern Loess Plateau, as well as construction of hydroelectric plants in newly developed large reservoir–high dam areas, such as in the Three Gorges and in other gorge areas in upper and middle Chiang Jiang and in a series of gorges in the upper and middle Yellow River. These areas and their surrounding communities will be excellent centers for energy-intensive industries in China. The poverty- and soil-erosion-stricken Loess Plateau has an especially good chance to become a rich industrialized area, while the Jiang-Han plain in the middle Chang Jiang will be developed not only as a "granary" but also an industrial "workshop" in China.

Metallurgy Industries

Since the ancient Xia Dynasty (2206–1766 B.C.), metallurgy (first bronze, then iron and other metals) has been one of the basic industries in China. The first modern iron and steel plant was founded near Wuhan in 1890. To 1949, China's steel production totaled only 15,800 tons, ranking twenty-sixth in the world. After 1949, it developed rapidly, and in 1957, steel production was 5.35 million tons, ranking ninth in the world; by 1979 production was 34.48 million tons, and by 1985 it was 46.79 million tons, ranking fifth and fourth in the world, respectively. In 1990, steel production increased to more than 66 million tons. Total production value of metallurgical industries in 1985 reached 6.64 billion yuan, accounting for 8 percent of China's total industrial production value. The iron and steel industry accounted for 4.31 billion yuan and 5 percent, respectively.

Iron and Steel Metallurgy

Iron and steel is the major metallurgical industry in China. There are now more than 1100 iron and steel enterprises in China, their distribution and allocation mainly decided by the location of raw materials (iron ore and coking coal), market and transportation facilities, and sometimes by national defense considerations (Figure 5.2). The 12 major iron and steel enterprises, located in Anshan, Wuhan, Shanghai, Baoshan, Beijing,

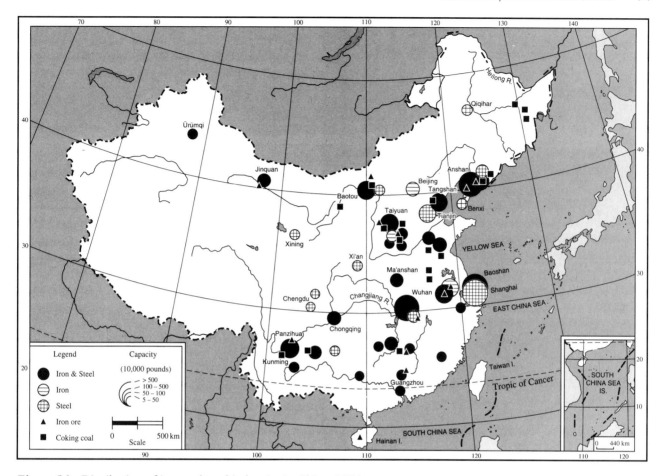

Figure 5.2 Distribution of iron and steel industries in China, 1984

Benxi, Panzihua, Baotou, Taiyuan, Ma'anshan, and Tangshan, account for more than 60 percent of China's total steel production. The largest facility is the Anshan Steel Plant, which alone produces about 7 million tons each year.

Other Metals

China is rich in metal resources (see Chapter Two). In metallurgical industries, copper (Cu), lead (Pb), tin (Sn), antimony (Sb), nickel (Ni), and mercury (Hg) among heavy metals; aluminum (Al) among light metals; tungsten (W), molybdenum (Mo), vanadium (V), and titanium (Ti) among rare metals have been better developed, usually ranking among the first five in the world. Unlike coal, most of which is found in northern China, these metal resources and their refining and fabrication industries are mainly found in southern China.

Chemical Industries

China has also a long history of chemical industries; gunpowder was invented in China in ancient times and introduced to Europe in the Tang Dynasty. Yet, not until the late nineteenth century did modern chemical industries develop. Several pharmaceutical factories were established along the coast in 1866. The first sulfuric acid (H_2SO_4) plant in China was built in Tianjin in 1876. Progress was rather slow in the late nineteenth century and the early twentieth century. However, since 1949 and especially since 1978, great attention has been paid to the development of chemical industries. From 1950 to 1983, on average, China's chemical industries increased by 17 percent each year and accounted for more than 12 percent of the national industrial production value. In geographical location, chemical industries are mostly concentrated in Shanghai, Beijing, Tianjin, Jilin, Lanzhou, and Taiyuan. Recently they have spread gradually from coastal to inland areas. In national production value, the coastal area accounted for 82.7 percent in 1950, decreasing to 64.2 percent in 1982.

Basic Chemicals

These industries include sulfuric acid, pure base, and chloric base manufacturing. They are mostly oriented to local sources of raw materials or to market opportunities, and are widely distributed in large and medium-sized cities.

Chemical Fertilizer

Developed rapidly since 1949, there are now more than 2000 chemical fertilizer enterprises in China with nitrogen fertilizer enterprises numbering more than 1300 and phosphorus about 700. In 1984, chemical fertilizer production totaled 14.6 million tons, of which nitrogen (N) fertilizer amounted to 12.21 million tons, phosphorous (P) fertilizer 2.36 million tons, and potassium (K) fertilizer 0.03 million tons. By 1990, chemical fertilizer production in China had increased to 19.12 million tons. The chemical fertilizer enterprises are mostly medium- or small-scaled, and are scattered widely in cities and towns all over China.

Organic Chemicals

Coal- and petroleum-based industries are the main organic chemical manufacturing enterprises. The rapidly developing petroleum chemical industries are usually of large or medium scale, and are generally located in the suburbs of large cities. They use ethylene as the chief raw material and had a total production of 730,000 tons in 1984.

Building Materials Industries

The building materials industry broadly includes three categories: inorganic (cement, porcelain, marble, sand, etc.), organic (plastic, carpeting, etc.), and metallic (steel, etc.). Timber is a fourth type where materials are available. These industries are based mostly on modifications of abundant raw materials and respond to market opportunities. They are widely distributed in China, especially along the coast. Since 1949, considerable emphasis has been given to development of these industries. For example, cement manufacturing, which accounts for 40 percent of total production value of the building materials industries, saw its annual production increase from 0.66 million tons in 1952 to nearly 146

million tons in 1985, and again to 210 million tons in 1990, ranking first in the world. It now has 58 large or medium-scale plants and more than 4800 small plants, scattered nearly all over China, except on the Tibetan Plateau.

Engineering Industries

The engineering industries are the basis for most other modern industries. As a consequence, they have been rapidly developed since 1949 and are now the largest modern industry in China. In 1985, there were about 110,100 engineering industrial enterprises, accounting for 24.0 percent of China's total industrial effort with a total production value of 223.5 billion yuan, which is 26.9 percent of China's total industrial production value. The highly technical automobile industry increased from practically nothing in 1949 to a production of 437,000 automobiles in 1985. In 1990, production increased to 514,000.

The engineering industries are highly varied, including machine tool, transportation equipment (automobiles, trains, trucks, bicycles, ships, airplanes, etc.), petroleum industrial machinery, mining equipment, electrical machines, and electronic machines. Such activity is mainly concentrated in 20 large cities. In 1984, the total production value of engineering industries was more than 2 billion yuan in each city; the top ten included: Shanghai (74.44 billion yuan), Beijing (28.17 billion yuan), Tianjin (25.15 billion yuan), Wuhan (13.78 billion yuan), Shenyang (13.37 billion yuan), Guangzhou (13.34 billion yuan), Chongqing (11.58 billion yuan), Wuxi (10.94 billion yuan), Hangzhou (10.09 billion yuan), and Nanjing (9.74 billion yuan).

Textile Industries

The textile industries and their products are the most important light industries as well as the most important export commodities. The small-scale home silk and hemp textile industries began as early as the Xia and Shang dynasties (2205–1126 B.C.), and the cotton textile industry began during the Northern and Southern Song dynasties (A.D. 960–1278). However, the first modern cotton textile factory was not established until 1878 in Shanghai. Soon textile industries became the largest industrial activity in China. In 1949, the production value of textile industries accounted for 45.7 percent of the total value of industrial production. Since 1949, however, modern textile products, especially cotton goods, have been further developed, and now textile factories also use chemical fibers as raw materials. Until 1984, textile enterprises accounted for 4.5 percent of the total industrial sector in China. Their total production value accounted for 15.4 percent of national industrial production, and their export value 14.7 percent of total export value. The structure and production of China's textile industries are shown as Table 5.2.

Cotton Textile Industry

This is the largest textile industry in China as well as the largest producer of cotton yarn and cloth in the world. In 1984, 5600 factories were equipped with more than 22 million spindles and about 630,000 looms. In 1990 more than 18 billion meters of cloth were manufactured. The cotton manufacturing industry depends on a cheap supply of raw material (cotton) and high market demand. Manufacturing facilities concentrate mostly in the middle and lower Chang Jiang and Yellow River valleys, especially in the Shanghai–Hangzhou and the Beijing–Tianjin areas.

Silk Textile Industry

This is the oldest and the second-largest textile industry in China as well as the largest silk and silk fabric producer in the world. In 1990, more than 530,000 tons of silk cocoons were produced. The industry is located mainly in three silk-producing areas: the Tai Lake basin (or the Chang Jiang Delta), the Sichuan Basin, and the Zhu Jiang Delta.

Woolen Textile Industry

This industry is located mainly along the coast, although most of its raw material (wool) is produced in the northwestern pastoral area. About 90 percent of the production capacity is concentrated in Shanghai, Beijing, Tianjin, and Wuxi; Shanghai alone produces 73.5 percent.

Other Textile Industries

Hemp and ramie are the other two old textile industries in China. Their location is mainly based on the availability of raw materials. Since 1949 large-scale Indian hemp textile factories have been established in Zhejiang and other provinces, ramie textile factories in Hunan and other provinces, and flax textile factories in Northeast and Northwest China. Most of the chemical-fiber textile industries have been built in recent times, and mainly use petroleum products as raw materials. There are now more than 170 enterprises, of which six are large-scale.

Other Light Industries

Paper-Manufacturing Industry

China was the first area in the world to make paper. Modern paper manufacturing started in 1891 in Shanghai. Since 1949, it has developed rapidly, with annual paper production increasing from 110,000 tons in 1949 to 9,110,000 tons in 1985. The industry is mostly small-scale and raw material–oriented, using wood as the chief raw material in Northeast China, which is also the chief timber-producing area in China. Grasses and straw are used as the main raw materials in the lower reaches of the Yellow River and the Chang Jiang, where these materials are a by-product in the major farming areas of China. In subtropical and tropical China, the lush bamboo and other plant fibers are used. Reeds also became an important pulp-making material in some swampy and lake areas, such as Dongting Lake, Bosten Lake (Xinjiang), and the swamps in the central Northeast China Plain. Owing to the shortage of wood-pulp resources, the potential for expansion of the paper-manufacturing industry is quite limited. Great efforts are underway to find new pulp-making raw materials, such as kenaf, which has recently been planted in large patches of the North China Plain.

TABLE 5.2
The Structure of China's Textile Industries (based on percentage of total production value)

Year	Cotton textiles	Woolen textiles	Hemp textiles	Silk textiles	Chemical textiles	Others	Total textile industries
1952	82.6	1.5	2.2	3.2	—	10.5	100.0
1984	73.6	7.5	2.0	8.7	5.3	2.9	100.0

Food-Processing Industry

Using farm, pastoral, and fishery products as raw materials, food processing is widely scattered in China and has developed rapidly since 1949. The enterprises are mostly small-scale and raw material-oriented, involving grain, oil, meat, tobacco, wine, sugar cane, candy, and other food sources and products. In 1985, the total production value of the food industry reached 95.1 billion yuan, accounting for 11.5 percent of total industrial production value, and ranking (after engineering and textile industries) third in China.

Salt-Manufacturing Industry

Salt making is an ancient handicraft industry in China, starting as early as Neolithic times. Unlike other handicraft industries, which were generally managed by manual workers in private homes, salt has been monopolized by the government on a large scale since the Western Han Dynasty. Since 1949, it has been further developed, resulting in a production increase from 2.99 million tons in 1949 to 20.33 million tons in 1990. Salt evaporation ponds are located mainly along the coast, especially along the flat beaches of Liaoning, Hebei, Shandong, and Jiangsu provinces. China is also the largest inland lacustrine-salt producer in the world. For example, there are more than 100 salt lakes in Qinghai Province (mainly in the Qaidam Basin), where confirmed salt reserves total more than 50 billion tons, probably accounting for 56 percent of the total inland salt reserves in the world.

Porcelain-Making Industry

Porcelain is a traditional industry in China, starting as early as Neolithic times. Since the Eastern Han Dynasty, the industry has been well developed. In 1982, China had about 1136 state-owned porcelain enterprises, earning 3.86 billion yuan for porcelain products, ranking first in the world. In national priorities, this industry has been mainly raw material– and cultural tradition–oriented, being most famous in Jingdezhen (Jiangxi Province), but also well known in Zibo (Shandong Province), Liling (Hunan Province), Tangshan and Handan (Hebei Province), and Shantou and Foshan (Guangdong Province).

Home-Use Electrical and Engineering Industries

Including refrigerators, washing machines, electric fans, bicycles, sewing machines, watches and clocks, and televisions, electrical and other home appliances have recently been developed and have contributed to the comparatively improved living standard in China. For example, annual production of bicycles increased from 14,000 in 1949 to 80,000 in 1952, to 1,838,000 in 1965, to 8,540,000 in 1978, and to 31.42 million in 1990. No wonder China is now called "a country of bicycles," just as the much richer United States is called "a country of automobiles." Furthermore, the huge population means a huge market. With better economic conditions, the market for home and personal-use products will increase, and these industries will certainly be further developed. Most are now located mainly in large cities, but they might also be located in medium and small cities in the future.

INDUSTRIAL DISTRIBUTION AND REGIONALIZATION

Most major modern industries are distributed in groups and clusters, depending on and supported by each other. They are also generally concentrated and based in cities, especially large cities. According to official statistics, at the end of 1984, there were 300 municipalities in China, (in three levels: Beijing, Tianjin, and Shanghai being provincial-level, the others being prefectural and county levels), with a total urban population of about 110 million. Of these, 295 cities had a total industrial production value of 607.8 billion yuan, accounting for 86.5 percent of the total national industrial production value. In contrast, the nine metropolitan cities each had an annual industrial production value of more than 10 billion yuan, and 20 large cities each earned 5–10 billion yuan.

Since 1949, with the priority for rapid industrial development and great areal distribution, a significant change has occurred in the geographic distribution and allocation of industrial cities. The large, old cities along the coast, including Shanghai, Beijing, Tianjin, Dalian, Shenyang, and Guangzhou, have grown to be huge, comprehensive industrial metropolises. Some old inland cities, including Wuhan, Chongqing, Xi'an, Lanzhou, Taiyuan, and Chengdu, have also grown to be large industrial cities. There is also a group of new inland industrial and mining cities, such as Ürümqi, Karamay, and Baotou. Owing to divergent geographic conditions and historical development, the geographical distribution and allocation of industrial cities is still uneven; and of 29 large industrial cities, 20 are along the coast. Three areas are especially significant.

1. *The Chang Jiang Delta:* With Shanghai as its core, this area has a total urban population of more than

15 million and a total industrial production of about 130 billion yuan (1984).

2. *The Beijing–Tianjin–Tangshan area:* With a total urban population of more than 11 million, this area has a total industrial production value of more than 60 billion yuan (1984).

3. *Central Liaoning Province:* With a total urban population of 8 million, central Liaoning Province has a total industrial production value of 38 billion yuan (1984).

THREE ECONOMIC (INDUSTRIAL) ZONES

China is currently divided into three main economic (industrial) zones as shown in Figure 5.3.

Eastern Coastal Zone

The eastern coastal zone occupies 14.3 percent of China's total land area, and its population accounts for 41.3 percent of China's total. Included in this zone are the 12 coastal provinces (municipalities, autonomous regions): Liaoning, Beijing, Tianjin, Hebei, Shandong, Jiangsu, Shanghai, Zhejiang, Fujian, Guangdong, Hainan, and Guangxi (Taiwan and Hong Kong not included). For obvious reasons, this is economically and industrially the most developed belt in China and includes most of China's modern industries, especially steel, chemicals, engineering, and textiles. Here the industrial production value of light industries is greater than that of heavy industries. In 1985, it had an industrial production value accounting for 60.3 percent of China's total. In recent years, with the establishment of special economic zones in Shenzhen, Zhuhai, Shantou, Xiamen, and Hainan Province as well as the gradual opening up of all coastal areas, economic and industrial

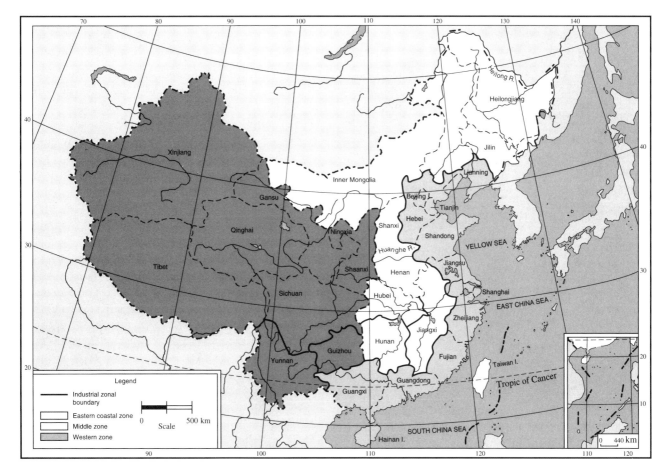

Figure 5.3 Economic (industrial) zones in China

development in this zone has been rapidly expanded. As a result it now nearly monopolizes all of China's foreign trade.

Middle Zone

Nine provinces (autonomous regions)—Heilongjiang, Jilin, Inner Mongolia, Shanxi, Henan, Anhui, Hubei, Hunan, and Jiangxi—comprise this transitional zone, which has an area occupying 29.4 percent of China's total and a population accounting for 26.7 percent of China's total. Like the east coastal zone, the middle zone is located mostly in Eastern Monsoon China, with the exception of Inner Mongolia, which belongs to the eastern part of Northwest Arid China. In economic and industrial development, this zone is less developed than the coastal zone but much more developed than the third zone. It encompasses the most important coal and metallurgical industries in China. In 1985, this zone had an industrial production value accounting for 26.9 percent of China's total. The production value of heavy industries in this zone is now greater than that of light industries.

Western Zone

Nine provinces (autonomous regions)—Shaanxi, Gansu, Ningxia, Xinjiang, Qinghai, Sichuan, Guizhou, Yunnan, and Tibet—are included in this vast zone, which includes 56.3 percent of China's total land area and 23.0 percent of China's total population. It comprises the mixed and border areas along the western parts of Eastern Monsoon China, Northwest Arid China (with the exception of Inner Mongolia), and the Tibetan Frigid Plateau. Economically and industrially, this is the least developed zone in China (with the exception of Sichuan Province), and has only a small part of China's modern industries, mostly heavy industries. Industrial cities are also very sparsely distributed. Yet, owing to its vast land area and its rich natural resources, great capabilities exist for developing hydroelectric, metallurgical, and engineering industries in the near future. Coal and petroleum extraction are also very promising in Northwest Arid China. During the Great Leap Forward and Cultural Revolution periods, great efforts and large investments were expended to establish the so-called Third Line industries in Northwest and Southwest China. However, due chiefly to mismanagement, few returns on those investments have been obtained. In 1985, this zone's industrial production value was only 12.8 percent of China's total. The production value of heavy indus-

tries in this zone is now greater than that of the light industries.

Ten Economic Regions

Very recently, another economic regionalization scheme has been proposed, dividing Mainland China into ten economic regions.

1. *Northeast China:* Including Heilongjiang, Jilin, Liaoning, and eastern Inner Mongolia, Northeast China will be developed as a heavy industrial base as well as a comprehensive agricultural (farming-forestry-animal husbandry) base.

2. *North China Coastal areas:* Including Beijing, Tianjin, Hebei, and Shandong, the North China Coastal areas will be developed as a base for high-technology industries, plus marine fisheries and cotton production.

3. *Central China Coastal areas:* Including Shanghai, Jiangsu, and Zhejiang, the Central China Coastal areas will be developed as the base of high-technology and manufacturing industries, as well as the center for finance, information, and education.

4. *South China Coastal areas:* Including Fujian, Guangdong, Hainan, and Guangxi, the South China Coastal areas will be developed as the base for export-oriented industry and agriculture.

5. *Middle reaches of the Yellow River:* Including Shanxi, Shaanxi, Henan, and central Inner Mongolia, the middle reaches of the Yellow River will be developed as the base for energy and chemical industries as well as retaining the area as an important pastoral resource.

6. *Upper reaches of the Yellow River:* Including Gansu (except the Hexi Corridor), Ningxia, and Qinghai, the upper reaches of the Yellow River will be developed as the base for energy and raw materials industries as well as a productive pastoral area.

7. *Middle reaches of the Chang Jiang:* Including Hunan, Hubei, Jiangxi, and Anhui, the middle reaches of the Chang Jiang will be developed as the base for high energy and water-consumption industries as well as for commercial grain production and processing.

8. *Upper reaches of the Chang Jiang (Southwest China):* Including Sichuan, Yunnan, and Guizhou, the upper reaches of the Chang Jiang

will be developed as a base for heavy industry as well as a center for vertical agriculture production.

9. *Northwest China:* Including Xinjiang, the Hexi Corridor, and western Inner Mongolia, Northwest China will be a base of petroleum and mining industries as well as an important area of farming-pastoral production.

10. *Tibet Region:* This is a special developing area requiring financial and technical support from other economic regions as well as considerable planning.

REFERENCES

Cannon, Terry, and Alan Jenkins, eds. 1990. *The Geography of Contemporary China*. London and New York: Routledge.

China State Statistical Bureau. 1991. *Statistical Yearbook of China*. Beijing: China Statistical Publishing House.

Li, Wenyuan, et al. (eds.). 1990. *Industrial Geography of China*. Beijing: Science Press (in Chinese).

Li, Wenyuan. 1990. "Recent Development of Industrial Geography in China." *Recent Development of Geographical Science in China*, ed. Geographical Society of China. Beijing: Science Press, pp. 197–203.

Lu, Dadao. 1987. "The Macrostrategy of Regional Development in China," *Acta Geographica Sinica*, 42, no. 2, pp. 105–114 (in Chinese).

Lu, Dadao, et al. (eds.). 1987. *Atlas of Industrial Distribution in China*. Beijing: Planning Press (in Chinese).

CHAPTER SIX

Modern Transportation and Foreign Trade

MODERN TRANSPORTATION

Transportation is an important tertiary economic activity and is also closely interrelated with primary production (such as farming and forestry) and secondary production (such as industry). All forms of transportation are indispensable in a country's economic structure as described in a Chinese saying, "Water is the life-blood of agriculture, while transportation is the blood vessel of economic structure." Another Chinese expression highlights the four basic necessities of human life: food, clothing, housing, and transportation. China has a long history that is intimately related to a comparatively well-developed ancient transportation system. In modern times, however, China lags far behind in transportation development, which retards its efforts to leave its status as a poor and "developing" country. An updated and well-developed transportation system is much needed.

Historical Development of Transportation

Ancient Transportation Development

In ancient times, China had a relative advantage in transportation development over other countries in the world. According to archeological excavations, the wood paddle was used as a motive force for water transportation more than 7000 years ago. The junk type of ship was used for transporting food grains and passengers as early as the Shang Dynasty (1766–1266 B.C.). For hundreds of years the Chinese have skillfully navigated the natural river systems for commercial transportation, and inland waterways have long been an important tradition in southern China. As early as 506 B.C., an artificial canal

was dug in the western Chang Jiang Delta. During the Qin Dynasty (221–206 B.C.), the famous Ling Canal, which connects the Chang Jiang and the Zhu Jiang drainage systems, was constructed and has operated ever since. The famous Grand Canal, with a total length of 1782 km from Hangzhou to Beijing, was completed during the Sui Dynasty (A.D. 589–618) and has henceforth served as a major water artery between southern and northern China.

Open sea transportation between China and Korea started as early as the Qin Dynasty. This sea route extended to Japan during the Western Han Dynasty (206 B.C. to A.D. 9), and later to Southeast and South Asia. During the Southern Song Dynasty (A.D. 1126–1279), when Hangzhou was the national capital, maritime transportation and seaports became very prosperous. Quanzhou, Fujian Province, was probably the largest seaport in the world at that time. During the Yuan Dynasty (1279–1368), a considerable portion of the food grain produced in the South was shipped northward by coastal navigation, which stimulated the construction of seaports in southeastern China, including Quanzhou and Guangzhou. During the early Ming Dynasty, from 1405 to 1433, seven voyages of the great navigator and messenger, Zheng He, with a huge fleet visited more than 30 coastal countries of the southwestern Pacific Ocean and the northern and western Indian Ocean. These voyages of exploration took place nearly 100 years earlier than Columbus's voyage to America.

Roads also developed very early. As soon as the Qin Dynasty unified China for the first time, a nationwide roadway network was constructed. With the capital Xianyang as the hub, this network reached modern Baotou in Inner Mongolia to the north, Lintao in Gansu

Province to the west (also the western end of the Great Wall at that time), the Shandong coast in the east, and the northern foothills of Nanling Mountains in the south. Probably this was the earliest nationwide roadway network in the world. At the same time, the ancient Silk Road started to link China with southern and southwestern Asia and eventually, with Europe (see Figure 3.3). Later, during the Tang Dynasty (A.D. 618–907), the famous Tayuling (a part of the Nanling Mountains) Road was built, which links Central China with South China.

Even pipeline transportation had its beginning in the second century B.C. in the Sichuan Basin. The pipe was made of bamboo, and the purpose was to transport natural gas to heat saltwater to extract salt.

Modern Transportation Development

The first modern railway (the Shanghai–Wusong suburb railway) was built in 1876. From 1895 to 1937 a total of 9200 km of new railways were added. Later, from 1912 to 1937, another 11,000 km of new railways were built. By 1949, there were 22,800 km in China, of which 90 percent were in Northeast China and along the coast, while more than one-third of the inland provinces had no railways at all.

Railway building has proceeded rapidly since 1949. Initially, all old railways were repaired and put into operation. Then many new railways were constructed. As of 1990, there were about 180 railway lines in China, with a total length of 53,400 km, of which 6900 km are electrified. Most railways are concentrated in the eastern part of Eastern Monsoon China (Figure 6.1). For example, more than three-fourths of the total railway length is east of the Beijing–Wuhan–Guangzhou railway. Meanwhile west of that line, especially on the extensive Tibetan Plateau and in Northwest Arid China, railways are very sparsely distributed, and two provincial capitals—Lhasa (Tibet) and Haikou (Hainan)—do not yet have

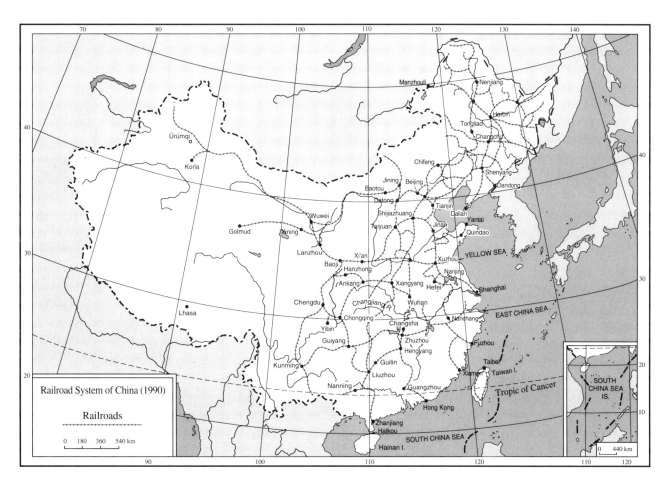

Figure 6.1 Railroad system of China, 1990. Modified and compiled by Lang Deng, 1992

any railway facilities. Furthermore, about 30 percent of the total railways are now overloaded with passengers and freight.

Modern inland waterway transportation started in the late nineteenth century, but development was extremely slow and mostly controlled by bureaucratic and foreign investors. In 1949, the navigable inland waterways totaled only 73,600 km, and almost none could accommodate large ocean-going ships. To 1990, the length of navigable inland waterways increased to 109,200 km, of which about 70 percent was concentrated in the Chang Jiang drainage system. Concurrently, many more can accommodate ocean-going ships, and many good harbors and seaports have been developed.

The first automobile was imported from a foreign country to Shanghai in 1902, and the first modern roadway—50 km long—was built from Changsha to Xiangtan (Hunan Province) in 1913. By 1936, the total roadway length in China amounted to 95,000 km, but it then decreased somewhat during the Japanese invasion and World War II. After the war roadway length increased from 80,700 km in 1949 to 1,208,300 km in 1990. All provincial capitals and all county seats (except Medog in the Tibet Autonomous Region) have been connected by roadway transportation. In Northwest and Southwest China as well as on the Tibetan Plateau, where railway and inland waterways are inadequate, roadway transportation is especially needed. Yet, most roadways are concentrated in Central China and along the coast. Furthermore, most roadways are not metalled with gravel or asphalt surfaces, and as a result are usually not operable on rainy days.

The first civil aviation company was established in 1929, and the second one in 1931. Both were controlled by foreign capital, and the total length of air routes was only 72,000 km in 1949. By 1990, there were more than 180 domestic air routes, with a total length of 150,000 km. All provincial capitals have direct air connections with Beijing. For international air traffic, agreements have been signed with 40 foreign countries.

The development of modern transportation as measured by total length, total passenger kilometers, and total freight kilometers from 1949 to 1978 to 1990 is shown in Table 6.1. It is worthwhile to point out that since 1978 when China started opening up, the rate of increase has been much more rapid.

Railways

As shown in Table 6.1, railroads are the most important type of modern transportation in China, in both passenger transport and freight haulage. Probably this is one of the most conspicuous differences between the Chinese and American transportation systems. For the latter, passengers mostly travel by automobile and airplane, although trains are still important in freight transportation. In geographic distribution, three railway networks are dominant in China (Figure 6.1).

Northeast China Railway Network

As a result of historical development, Northeast China has the greatest concentration of railway lines in China, with a total length of 14,000 km in 1990, comprising more than one-third of China's total, and a railway density of 1.7 km/sq km. The east–west Manzhouli–Harbin–Suifenhe railway which also links with the Trans-Siberian railway network in Russia, and the north–south Harbin–Shenyang–Dalian railway serve as the backbone of the Northeast China railway network, with the Shenyang–Shanhaiguan–Beijing railway connecting North China, and the Shenyang–Dandong–Pyongyang railway linking Korea. There are also many branch lines and forest railways. Major freight transportation includes the southward movement (to North China and Central China) of lumber and petroleum, and the northward movement of coal and manufactured products (from North China and Central China).

North–South Railway Network

South of the Great Wall, the busiest railways are those that link North China, Central China, and South China. Four parallel north to south trunk railways are of special importance:

1. *Tianjin–Shanghai line:* With a total length of 1470 km, this line crosses the coastal plains of North China and Central China, crossing the Yellow River at Jinan by bridge and the Chang Jiang at Nanjing by the famous bridge. This is the most economically well-developed coastal belt in China, with a very heavy commitment to passenger and freight transportation. Large amounts of coal, lumber, petroleum, and other commodities are transported southward, while food grains and manufactured products go northward.

2. *Beijing–Wuhan–Guangzhou line:* With a total length of 2300 km, this major railway line crosses

TABLE 6.1
Development of Modern Transportation in China

Type of transportation	1949	1978	1990
Total			
Passenger mileage (100 million)*	155.00	1,743.00	5,628.00
Freight mileage (100 million)	255.00	9,829.00	26,207.00
Railway			
Length (10,000 km)	2.18	4.86	5.34
Passenger mileage (100 million)	130.01	1,093.22	2,612.63
Freight mileage (100 million)	184.00	5,345.19	10,622.38
Inland waterway			
Length (10,000 km)	7.36	13.60	10.92
Passenger mileage (100 million)	15.17	100.63	164.91
Freight mileage (100 million)	63.12	3,779.16	11,591.90
Roadway			
Length (10,000 km)	8.07	89.02	120.83
Passenger mileage (100 million)	7.96	521.30	2,620.32
Freight mileage (100 million)	8.14	274.14	3,358.10
Civil aviation			
Length (10,000 km)	2.20	14.89	50.68
Passenger mileage (100 million)	1.85	27.91	230.48
Freight mileage (100 million)	0.21	0.97	8.20
Pipeline			
Length (10,000 km)	—	0.83	1.59
Freight mileage (100 million)	—	430.00	627.00

*The unit for passenger mileage is person-kilometer and for freight mileage, ton-kilometer.
Source: Statistical Yearbook of China, 1991.

the Yellow River at Zhengzhou by bridge, cuts through the Tongbai Mountain by tunnel at the border between Henan and Hubei provinces, crosses the Chang Jiang by the famous bridge at Wuhan, and cuts through the Nanling by tunnel at the border between Hunan and Guangdong provinces. This is probably the most important and the busiest railway in China. It connects with 16 other lines. Major freight includes the southward-moving industrial products of coal, steel, petroleum, and lumber, which often pass northward-moving agricultural commodities—food grains, fruits, and vegetables.

3. *Datong–Taiyuan–Jiaozuo–Zhijiang–Liuzhou–Zhangjiang line:* This line is composed of several railways, most of them newly built. It more or less parallels the Beijing–Wuhan–Guangzhou line, but is located farther west and thus serves China's third economic zone (see Figure 5.3). It has a total length of 2500 km, starting from the coal-rich Shanxi province (Datong and Taiyuan) and northern Henan province (Jiaozuo), then passing

through Hubei, Hunan, and Guangxi provinces, and arriving at Zhanjiang in Guangdong province, a seaport on the South China Sea. It crosses the Yellow River near Luoyang (Henan Province), the Chang Jiang at Zhijiang (Hubei Province), and the Zhu Jiang at Gui Xian (Guangxi).

4. *Baoji–Chengdu–Kunming line:* Starting from Baoji (near Xi'an, Shanxi Province) with its northern terminus at the great east–west trunk line of the Lianyungang–Zhengzhou–Xi'an–Lanzhou–Ürümqi route (to be discussed in the next section), this line winds across the Qinling Mountains by a series of tunnels to Chengdu (Sichuan Province), then passes through the eastern margin of the Hengduan Mountains by a series of tunnels and bridges crossing the Jinsha Jiang (upper reaches of the Chang Jiang) at Dukou. The southern terminus is at Kunming in Yunnan Province. The line has a total length of 1760 km, most of it through rugged topography. Although very difficult to build, the Baoji–Kunming line has great strategic value.

Other important north–south railways include the Chengdu–Chongqing–Guiyang line, the Beijing–Erenhot–Ulan Bator (Mongolia) line, and the Guilin–Nanning–Hanoi (Vietnam) line.

East–West Railway Network

China's east–west railway network has three trunk lines that link eastern China to western China. Inasmuch as the west-to-east-flowing rivers, the Chang Jiang and Zhu Jiang, are two major navigable waterways, there has been no need for construction of trunk railways immediately along these rivers.

1. *Lianyungang–Zhengzhou–Xi'an–Lanzhou–Ürümqi line:* This major latitudinal trunk line starts at the Lianyungang[1] seaport on the Yellow Sea and extends 3600 km westward to Ürümqi. East of Xi'an, it coincides more or less with the middle and lower channels of the Yellow River, which are for the most part not navigable. West of Xi'an, the railway generally parallels the ancient Silk Road, which historically connected China with Southwest Asia and Europe (see Figure 3.3). The Lianyungang–Ürümqi line also cuts across all important longitudinal trunk railways in China and thus forms major railway junctions at Xuzhou, Zhengzhou, Luoyang, and Xi'an (Baoji).

   Recently, the great Lianyungang–Ürümqi latitudinal trunk railway has been extended westward to the Sino-Russian border and will become the shortest Trans-Eurasian continental railway from the Atlantic coastal ports such as Rotterdam to the eastern Chinese Pacific coast. Two other extensions might be also very important in the future. One is from Turpan (near Ürümqi), crossing the Tianshan Mountains to Korla, which was formerly on the Silk Road and is now the headquarters of the newly discovered Tarim Basin oil field. With petroleum as a major impetus, a new railway network will soon be established in the Tarim Basin. Another recent westward extension of this trunk line is from Lanzhou, through Xining (capital of Qinghai Province), to Golmud in the Qaidam Basin. This line will soon extend to Lhasa and other parts of Tibet Autonomous Region, and thus fill in this gap, giving railway transportation to a very isolated region.

2. *Beijing–Baotou–Lanzhou line:* With a total length of more than 1800 km, this trunk line connects Beijing with three border provinces (autonomous regions)—Inner Mongolia, Ningxia, and Gansu. At Gansu the rail line merges with the major east–west latitudinal line.

3. *Shanghai–Hangzhou–Nanchang–Xiangtan–Guiyang–Kunming line:* This great latitudinal trunk line is composed of several railways, some of them having been built very recently. The rail line has a total length of 1135 km, connecting six provinces south of the Chang Jiang and north of the Nanling Mountains—Jiangsu, Zhejiang, Jiangxi, Hunan, Guizhou, and Yunnan.

Other important east–west railways are the Qingdao–Jinan–Shijiazhuang line, Qinhuangdao–Beijing–Datong line, and the Fuzhou–Yintang line.

Inland Waterways and Seaports

China is a country of big rivers. There are more than 50,000 rivers (each with a drainage area of more than 100 sq km) and a total river length of about 420,000 km. Over 54,000 km of these rivers is navigable. In addition, there are more than 900 navigable lakes. Practically all of these navigable waterways are located in fertile and populous temperate and subtropical plains areas and are endowed with numerous good harbors and seaports. In 1990, navigable inland waterways totaled 109,200 km, with freight haulage slightly more than the volume of railway transportation, although the total passenger distance is much less (Table 6.1). The prospect for further development of inland waterway transportation appears to be reasonably bright.

Inland Waterways

Chang Jiang   This river provides the lion's share of inland waterway transportation in China. It is regarded as "China's main street." Its main stem has a total length of 6300 km, with more than 3600 tributaries. Total navigable length reaches more than 70,000 km, of which at least 3,000 km is open to steamships all year round. Large steamships of 1000 tons can navigate below Chongqing, oceanic steamships of 10,000 tons can operate below Nanjing all year and up to Wuhan during the high-water season. It is believed that the planned Three Gorges Dam will improve the navigation facilities between Chongqing and Wuhan. The Chang Jiang basin is estimated to occupy about one-fifth of China's total land area, one-fourth of the total farmland, and one-third of the total population. About 40 percent of

---

[1]In Chinese, "gang" denotes a port. Hence, Lianyungang is also called "Lianyun Port" in English.

the total food production and 70 percent of the total rice output come from the Chang Jiang basin. This rich area is also the most economically developed region in China. With Shanghai as its core and outlet, together with a series of excellent river ports (Chongqing, Yichang, Shashi, Wuhan, Huangshi, Jiujiang, Anqing, Wuhu, Ma'anshan, Nanjing, Zhenjiang, Nantong, and others), the middle and lower reaches of the Chang Jiang are certainly one of the largest and busiest inland waterways in the world.

Zhu Jiang   This is the largest inland waterway in South China, with total freight haulage comprising about one-fifth of China's inland waterway transportation. It has a total navigable length of about 14,000 km, almost exclusively on its largest branch—the Xi Jiang (West River). Oceanic steamships of 10,000 tons can navigate only from the river mouth up to Guangzhou, the head of the delta, while smaller steamships of less than 1000 tons can go upstream to Wuzhou on the border between Guangxi and Guangdong.

Other Rivers   Although rather insignificant for inland waterway transportation, other rivers include:

1. *Huai He:*   This trunk river has a total length of more than 1000 km, of which about 700 km are navigable. Yet, so far, the river is little used.

2. *Yellow River:*   This is the second largest river in China, with a total length of 5464 km. Yet, owing to its unfavorable physical conditions, it is entirely nonnavigable in its upper reaches. From Guide (Qinghai Province) to Zhongwei (Ningxia Hui Autonomous Region), sheepskin rafts can float downstream on the yellowish water and swift current, a practice that is quite spectacular but not very practical. From Zhongwei downstream, several short sections might be navigable for small boats, but so far little use has been made of this river for navigation.

3. *Heilong Jiang (Amur River):*   This river forms part of the Sino-Russian border, with total length of 4370 km, of which 3101 km pass through Chinese territory and 2200 km are navigable. However, so far it has been only of little use. The Songhua Jiang is the largest tributary of the Heilong Jiang, with a total length of 1956 km, of which about 1500 km are navigable. Owing to high latitudes, these two rivers are frozen for 5 to 6 months each year, making sledge transportation on the ice surface important at that time.

4. *Grand Canal:*   This famous artificial waterway starts at Hangzhou, passing northward through Zhejiang, Jiangsu, Shandong, Hebei, and Tianjin, and ending at Beijing. In its design the canal crosses five big rivers: the Qiantang Jiang, the Chang Jiang, the Huai He, the Yellow River, and the Hai He. During the long historical period of feudal dynasties, the Grand Canal was important for sending food grain from southern China to imperial capitals in northern China. However, since the opening of coastal navigation and the construction of the Tianjin–Nanjing and the Beijing–Wuhan railways, the Grand Canal has been neglected and is now not navigable in many sections. Since 1949, however, portions that are seasonally navigable for small boats have increased to 1100 km, and 660 km are navigable year around.

Sea Waterways

Coastal navigation in China is traditionally divided into two systems.

1. *Northern coastal navigation:*   With Shanghai and Dalian as the two main centers, several shipping lines, including the Shanghai–Qingdao–Dalian line, the Shanghai–Yantai–Tianjin line, the Shanghai–Qinhuangdao line, the Shanghai–Lianyungang line, the Shanghai–Ningpo–Wenzhou line, and the Shanghai–Fuzhou–Xiamen line use these ports. As with the railroads, the freight commodities from north to south are petroleum, coal, steel, and lumber. Traveling from the south to the north are metal minerals, food grains, and manufactured products.

2. *Southern coastal navigation:*   With Guangzhou as the center, shipping lines serving this area include the Guangzhou–Shantou line, the Guangzhou–Beihai line, and the Guangzhou–Haikou line.

China is now open to more than 30 oceanic navigation lines, which make contact with more than 100 countries and more than 400 seaports in the world.

Seaports

To date, China has 158 seaports, of which 15 major ports are under direct management of Ministry of Communication in Beijing. Most seaports are linked together with cities, of which, fourteen (Dalian, Qinhuangdao, Tianjin, Yantai, Qingdao, Lianyungang, Nantong, Shanghai, Ningbo, Wenzhou, Fuzhou, Guangzhou, Zhanjiang, and Beihai) have been established as open

TABLE 6.2
Total Freight (import and export) of Major Seaports in China (in 10,000 tons)

Port	1952	1978	1990
Dalian	151	2,864	4,952
Yinkou	18	33	237
Qinhuangdao	181	2,219	6,945
Tianjin	74	1,131	2,063
Yantai	26	458	668
Qingdao	175	2,002	3,034
Shiju	—	—	925
Lianyungang	46	594	1,137
Shanghai	656	7,955	13,959
Ningbo	—	—	2,554
Shantou	35	153	279
Guangzhou	47	1,450	4,163
Zhanjiang	12	947	1,557
Haikou	16	76	288
Baso	—	307	431
Sanya	3	45	37
Others	—	—	5,092
Total	1,440	19,834	48,321

Source: Statistical Yearbook of China, 1991.

port-cities since 1984. There were more than 1200 ship berths in all these sea ports in 1990, of which more than 284 were capable of serving ships of more than 10,000 gross tonnage. The total freight of all seaports in 1990 reached 483.21 million tons, of which Shanghai alone occupied nearly 30 percent, as shown in Table 6.2. Shortage of deep-water and massive seaports has been one weak point in China's sea transportation system.

Highways, Civil Aviation, and Pipelines

Highways and civil aviation are the two most important means of transportation in modern industrial countries. For example, the United States especially is a "country of automobiles," where the private automobile is a necessity for nearly every American family. In contrast, present-day China is a "country of bicycles," where private cars and airplane trips are still a luxury. However, since 1949, road transportation and civil aviation have been developed rapidly. Pipeline transportation of petroleum and natural gas recently has also received high government priority for development.

Highways

Roads plus railways and inland waterways are now the three most important transportation systems in China.

In 1990, there were of 1,208,300 km of highways, nearly 23 times the total length of railways and 11 times the distance of inland waterways. Roads also rank first in total passenger distance, a little bit more than that of railways, but stand at a poor third in total freight haulage.

Roadways are generally much denser in central China and along the coast where economies are better developed and population density is high. Roadway density in central China is generally more than 20 km/sq km. In North China and Northeast China, roadway density is generally from 10 to 20 km/sq km. In all other parts of China the roadway density is below 10 km/sq km. The exception is in mountainous or sparsely populated areas where roadway transportation is particularly necessary and significant but is very sparse at present.

Two big problems restrict development of roadway transportation in China. One problem is the low quality of most existing roads, which are generally not hard-surfaced and thus are not passable when it rains. As of 1990, only five superhighways were under construction: the road between Beijing and Tanggu (140 km), the road between Xi'an and Lintong (20 km), the road between Shanghai and Jiading (20 km), the road between Guangzhou and Foshan (20 km), and the Guangzhou–Zhuhai–Shenzhen road (140 km). Another problem is the scarcity and low quality of automobiles. According to official statistics, there were only 5.51 million automobiles (in 1990) in such a populous country as China—nearly 20,788 persons per automobile. Nor can such a deplorable condition be changed much in the near future, because most Chinese cannot afford to buy automobiles.

Civil Aviation

Civil aviation has been developed from a very minimal situation in 1949 to a total route length of 506,800 km and a total passenger load of nearly 23 billion person-miles in 1990. Even so, the total freight haulage is still small (only 82,000 ton-kilometers in 1990). There are now more than 80 civil aviation airports in China, of which the Beijing Capital Airport is certainly the largest and can accommodate 3.5 million passengers each year. With increasing economic prosperity in China, civil aviation will undoubtedly develop at a rapid rate in the near future, but it seems very unlikely that it will attain such a high level as in the United States.

Pipelines

Worldwide, pipeline transportation of petroleum and natural gas now exceeds the total length of railways. In

China, the extent of pipelines has developed from practically nothing in 1949 to a total of 15,900 km and a total freight load of 12.7 billion ton-kilometers in 1990. The first long-distance pipeline in modern China was constructed in 1958 between the Karamay oil field and the Usu oil refinery in Xinjiang. Since early 1960s all large oil fields have constructed their own pipeline systems. The large-scale Daqing–Qinhuangdao–Tianjin–Beijing pipeline, with a total length of 1507 km, was completed in 1974. Soon after, the 1000-km Hebei–Anhui–Jiangsu pipeline was also completed. To date, about three-fourths of these petroleum-transporting pipelines are concentrated in Northeast China and along the coast. A major pipeline will be constructed in Xinjiang and other parts of Northwest China to serve the large new oilfields that have been discovered recently.

Pipelines for transporting natural gas are mainly concentrated in Sichuan Province, where major gas fields are distributed. In Sichuan alone, these pipelines had a total length of about 2800 km in 1990, comprising 65 percent of the national total.

CONTEMPORARY FOREIGN TRADE

In every modern country, foreign trade has been important and closely related to domestic economic development. In contemporary China, modern industry and transportation have been developing rapidly, although still not fast enough and unfortunately suffering great fluctuation; so also foreign trade. Between 1949 and 1978, the volume of foreign trade was rather small. Since the adoption of the opening up policy in 1978, there has been a great increase in the volume of foreign trade, reaching U.S. $100 billion for the first time in 1988. Even so, China accounts for only about 5 percent of world trade, despite having more than one-fifth of the world's population. There is no doubt a great potential for further development of China's foreign trade, to benefit both the world community and China itself. It seems that China will become one of the biggest markets in the world in early twenty-first century. The march of China's foreign trade since 1950 is shown in Table 6.3.

During the 1950s and 1960s, China's major trading partners were the Soviet Union and Eastern Europe. The share of Communist countries (especially the Soviet Union) in China's foreign trade in the late 1950s was almost two-thirds of the total. The break with the Soviet Union in 1960 led to a marked increase in non-Communist trading partners. Japan replaced the Soviet Union as China's main trading partner in 1965. During the period 1965–1970, China basically returned to trading patterns

TABLE 6.3
Volume of Foreign Trade, China (U.S. $100 million)

Year	Total	Exports	Imports	Balance
1950	11.3	5.5	5.8	− 0.3
1955	31.4	14.1	17.5	− 3.2
1960	38.1	18.6	19.5	− 0.9
1965	42.5	22.3	20.2	2.1
1970	45.9	22.6	23.3	− 0.7
1975	147.5	72.6	74.9	− 2.3
1978	206.4	97.5	108.9	− 11.4
1980	381.4	181.2	200.2	− 19.0
1985	696.0	273.5	422.5	− 149.0
1986	738.5	309.4	429.2	− 119.6
1987	826.5	394.4	432.2	− 37.8
1988	1,027.9	475.2	552.8	− 77.6
1989	1,116.8	525.4	591.4	− 66.0
1990	1,154.4	620.9	533.5	87.5

Source: Statistical Yearbook of China, 1991.

of the mid-1930s, with Japan, Hong Kong, and Malaysia-Singapore becoming major trading partners. The share of Communist countries in China's foreign trade fell to just over one-fifth; while the United States refused to trade with China at all.

In the period 1971–1975 (China's Fourth Five-Year Plan), with the increase in the number of countries recognizing the People's Republic of China, China's foreign trade increased rapidly, particularly that with the United States, with whom foreign trade rose enormously after the removal of U.S. government trade restrictions. By 1974, the United States was second only to Japan among China's trading partners; then came Hong Kong, West Germany, Malaysia-Singapore, Canada, Australia, France, the United Kingdom, and the Soviet Union.

Since 1978, China has been trading widely, and its foreign trade has been rising rapidly. By 1990, China traded with more than 140 countries in the world. Hong Kong, Japan, and the United States were the three largest trading partners, accounting for three-fifths of China's total foreign trade. The rank order and the total volume of exports and imports of China's major trading partners in 1990 are shown in Table 6.4.

China's balance of trade with different countries is significant. It has been generally running a deficit with developed countries but a surplus with the developing countries. As a whole, China has generally had an unfavorable trade balance. However, by 1990, it began to show an annual surplus of U.S. $8.7 billion. This is really very good news for China's economic development. Other good news included about 27.5 million tourists

TABLE 6.4
China's Major Trading Partners, 1990

Rank	Country	Total volume of exports & imports (million of U.S. $)	Percent of total exports & imports
1	Hong Kong	40,907.7	35.4
2	Japan	16,599.0	14.4
3	United States	11,767.8	10.2
4	Germany	4,971.0	4.3
5	Soviet Union	4,379.1	3.8
6	Singapore	2,832.2	2.5
7	France	2,308.4	2.0
8	United Kingdom	2,026.9	1.8
9	Canada	1,908.7	1.7
10	Italy	1,904.8	1.7
11	Australia	1,808.7	1.6
12	Netherlands	1,307.4	1.1
13	Thailand	1,193.7	1.0
14	Indonesia	1,182.3	1.0
15	Malaysia	1,176.1	1.0

Source: Statistical Yearbook of China, 1991.

TABLE 6.5
China's Major Exporting Partners, 1990

Rank	Export to	Export value (million of U.S. $)	Percent of total exports
1	Hong Kong	26,650.0	42.9
2	Japan	9,011.0	14.5
3	United States	5,179.5	8.3
4	Soviet Union	2,239.2	3.6
5	Germany	2,034.4	3.3
6	Singapore	1,974.7	3.2
7	Netherlands	908.3	1.5
8	Italy	835.0	1.3
9	Thailand	823.5	1.3
10	France	645.4	1.0
11	United Kingdom	643.0	1.0
12	Macao	505.9	0.8
13	Pakistan	494.8	0.8
14	Zaire	466.8	0.7
15	Australia	455.1	0.7

Source: Statistical Yearbook of China, 1991.

visiting Mainland China in that year, and from 1949–1990, a total of U.S. $4.89 billion in foreign investments flowing into China.

It should be pointed out that Hong Kong has been an especially important export market for Mainland China, but has reexported many Chinese goods to the rest of the world. Hong Kong has also provided transshipment and bank transaction services for Mainland China. The latter exported U.S. $2655 million of goods to, and imported U.S. $1425.8 million of goods from, Hong Kong in 1990, with a surplus balance of U.S. $1239.2 million, accounting for 14.2 percent of China's total trade surplus in that year.

Exports

Exports produce over 80 percent of China's foreign currency earnings, with the remainder from tourism, labor services, and remittances from overseas Chinese. China's exports have increased from U.S. $552 million in 1950 to U.S. $9.75 billion in 1978, and to U.S. $62.09 billion in 1990. The structure of exports in 1990 was primary products (including food, beverages, agricultural raw materials, minerals, etc.) occupying 25.6 percent, and manufactured goods (including light and heavy industries), 74.4 percent. The major source of exports has been the Eastern Coastal Zone, either from the coastal

provinces and national municipalities with a strong industrial base, such as Shanghai, Tianjin, and Liaoning, or from the coastal provinces with a sound agricultural base, such as Jiangsu, Zhejiang, and Guangdong. In recent years, the special economic zones (Shenzhen, Zhuhai, Shantou, Xiamen, and Hainan Province) and the newly opened coastal cities and seaports have contributed much to China's exports.

Hong Kong, Japan, and the United States were the top three export destinations in 1990, accounting for two-thirds of China's total exports. The rank order and export value of China's major exporting partners in 1990 are listed in Table 6.5.

Imports

China's imports have increased from U.S. $580 million in 1950 to U.S. $10.89 billion in 1978 and U.S. $53.34 billion in 1990 (U.S. $59.14 billion in 1989). Most imports to China consist of machinery (mainly used to introduce advanced technology and production equipment) and raw materials. The share of consumer and subsistence goods remains relatively small. The structure of imports in 1990 was primary products occupying only 18.5 percent and manufactured goods, 81.5 percent. Hong Kong, Japan, and the United States were still the three top sources, accounting for more than half of

TABLE 6.6
China's Major Importing Partners, 1990

Rank	Import from	Import value (million of U.S. $)	Percent of total imports
1	Hong Kong	14,257.7	26.7
2	Japan	7,588.0	14.2
3	United States	6,588.3	12.4
4	Germany	2,936.7	5.5
5	Soviet Union	2,139.9	4.0
6	France	1,633.0	3.1
7	Canada	1,478.4	2.8
8	United Kingdom	1,383.9	2.6
9	Australia	1,353.6	2.5
10	Italy	1,069.8	2.0
11	Singapore	857.5	1.6
12	Indonesia	803.2	1.5
13	Netherlands	399.1	0.7
14	Thailand	370.3	0.7
15	Spain	320.0	0.6

Source: Statistical Yearbook of China, 1991.

China's total imports. China's major importing partners in 1990 are listed in Table 6.6.

REFERENCES

Cannon, Terry, and Alan Jenkins, eds. 1990. *The Geography of Contemporary China*. London and New York: Routledge.

China State Statistical Bureau. 1991. *Statistical Yearbook of China*. Beijing: China Statistical Publishing House.

Song, Jiata, ed. 1986. *Economic Geography of China*. Beijing: Central Broadcast University Press (in Chinese).

Sun, Jinzhu, ed. 1988. *Geography of China*. Beijing: Higher Education Press (in Chinese).

Zhao, Songqiao. 1989. "River and Man in China," *Proceedings of the International Symposium on Water Civilization*, Toyoma, Japan (in Japanese and English).

CHAPTER SEVEN

Ethnic Groups

China features great ethnic diversity, the outcome of ethnic convergence and divergence in a huge territory of 9.6 million sq km over a history of 80 centuries. According to the 1982 population census, there are 56 ethnic groups in China. The dominant group is, of course, the Han with 936.7 million, or 93.3 percent of the total population in 1982. The other 55 ethnic groups together total 63.5 million, or 6.27 percent of the total population, but are scattered over more than 60 percent of China's total land area. According to the 1990 population census, the Han totaled 1042.5 million, accounting for 91.2 percent of the total population, while the other 55 ethnic groups totaled 100.9 million and 8.8 percent, respectively.[1] China is lucky compared to the former Soviet Union, where the major ethnic group, the Russians, comprised only about one-half of the total population. Consequently, with the help of an "autonomous areas" system and other enlightened governmental policies on ethnic minority groups, the current ethnic structure in China is relatively sound and stable, although a few minority problems (especially the Tibetans) still exist and should not be overlooked. Furthermore, the total minority population of nearly 100 million in 1990 amounts to more than the population of all but nine other countries of the world. No wonder the world community is so deeply concerned about China's minority problems!

HISTORICAL DEVELOPMENT OF ETHNOGRAPHY

The formation and consolidation of the Han and the present ethnic structure in China are the end products of a long historical process of evolution during the last 8000 years. Ethnic consolidation has been closely interrelated with political and agricultural development in China (see Chapter Three and Figure 3.1). The process probably started in Neolithic times (the dawn of Chinese agriculture) and appears to be divided into seven subsequent periods.

Legendary Period of Three Rulers and Five Emperors (8000–4000 years ago)

This is probably the earliest period for ethnic and agricultural development in China. According to ancient traditions and historical documents, there might have been existing five ancient great ethnic groups in China in this period.

1. The Hua, with Huang-Di or Yellow Emperor as the most distinguished political leader, lived mainly on the Loess Plateau and its surrounding areas where the earliest rain-fed agriculture may have started.

2. The Chang, with Ying-Di, the legendary God of Agriculture as their most famous political leader, lived in a broad area in the upper and middle

---

[1] The rapid increase in the minority ethnic groups during the period 1982–1990 was partly due to government policies that have given many advantages to the minority peoples. For example, the ethnic minority peoples are not subject to the rigid family planning policy. Consequently, many persons changed their identification of "Han" (in 1982) to other ethnic groups in 1990. However, as of early 1992, when the manuscript of this book was written, the details of the 1990 population census had not yet been published, to say nothing of being closely analyzed and assessed. Therefore, the population data of the 1982 census are still chiefly used in this book.

reaches of the Yellow River. These two ancient ethnic groups fought wars against each other and also intermarried. The groups eventually fused and integrated into one single ethnic group—the Hua-Xia, which is considered to be the forerunner of the Han. Today many Chinese still believe and call themselves the descendants of "Ying-Huang" (Huang-Di and Ying-Di).

3. The Dong Yi, with Vo-Hi the legendary God of Fishery and Hunting as their most famous leader, lived in the lower reaches of the Yellow River and along the coast of North China. At first they were mainly nomadic tribes engaged in pastoralism and hunting and fishing. Later, they were gradually converted to farming and merged into the Hua-Xia ethnic group.

4. The Meng, literally the "undeveloped peoples," lived over a broad area of southern China, where they especially concentrated in the middle and lower reaches of the Chang Jiang and along the Southeast Coast. They developed rice-growing agriculture for the first time in China, probably also in the world. Later, they gradually merged into the Hua-Xia ethnic group.

5. The Di, literally the "northern barbarians," lived on the northern borders of the Hua-Xia areas where they were mostly pastoral nomads. The Di were in a constant state of warfare with the Hua-Xia, but they later partly intermingled and merged.

The Earliest Chinese States Period (2206–403 B.C.)

During the bronze age of the Xia, Shang, and Western Zhou dynasties as well as in the Spring and Autumn Period, the middle and lower reaches of both the Yellow River and Chang Jiang were the political, economic, and cultural centers of China as well as the ethnic core of the Hua-Xia people. Three subcenters might be identified for this period.

The Loess Plateau

Originally the Loess Plateau was the homeland of the Hua and the Chang as well as being the first nucleus of the Hua-Xia. Here was the political center of Xia and Western Zhou dynasties, and also of the Qin and many other feudal principalities. Rain-fed farming agriculture in China was first developed here.

The North China Plain

Originally the homeland of the Dong Yi, the North China plain was the locality for the political capitals of the Shang Dynasty as well as the Qi and many other feudal principalities. Early food-procuring developments began with fishing and animal husbandry, and later rain-fed farming.

The Middle and Lower Chang Jiang and Northern Southeast Coast

These areas were originally the homeland of the Meng. In this area began the Chu, Wu, Yue, and many other feudal principalities during the Spring and Autumn Period. Rice agriculture was first developed here.

On the southern border of these three centers were scattered Meng tribes. To the north and west lived the widely scattered pastoral Di and Chang tribes, respectively.

Early Period of the Feudal Society (403 B.C. to A.D. 589)

From the period of the Warring States (403–221 B.C.) to the first unification of China by Qin in 221 B.C., Eastern Monsoon China between the Great Wall and the Nanling became agriculturally well developed, and so also did the Hua-Xia ethnic group. North of the Great Wall, the Xiong Nu (Hun), the Dong Hu, and other nomadic tribes were widely distributed. South of the Nanling lived scattered tribes of Meng and Yue.

During the Qin (221–205 B.C.), Western Han (206 B.C.–A.D. 9) and Eastern Han (A.D. 25–220) dynasties, China was politically and economically united and powerful, with political boundaries and agricultural development spreading into Northwest Arid China and the Tibetan Frigid Plateau. Since that time, China has also been culturally united, with the same written language and social heritage. Actually, China gets its name from the Qin (Chin) Dynasty, while the Hua-Xia are henceforth called Han. During this period, the Han assimilated many other ethnic tribes. One significant example was the once powerful Xiong Nu, called Huns in the West. When they were ultimately defeated, some of them moved inside the Great Wall and intermingled with the Han, some of them still stayed in Northwest China, while a greater part moved westward to Central Europe where they established the country of Hungary. Another example was the Yue tribe, who gradually became an integral part of the Han.

During the chaotic period of the Three Kingdoms, the Western Jin Dynasty, and the Southern and Northern Dynasties (A.D. 220–589), China was divided and stricken by civil wars for most of the time. Tens of millions of people perished and millions of hectares of farmland were laid waste, while many nomadic peoples invaded and imposed brutal rule on northern China. This period might be termed the "dark age" in China; yet, there were also embers amid the devastating ashes. One spark was the large-scale migration of the Han from northern China to southern China, thus providing a great push to ethnic and agricultural development there. Another was that the Han in northern China became much better intermingled and assimilated with many minority peoples. Thus, the Han not only survived but also became ethnically stronger.

Middle Period of the Feudal Society (A.D. 589–1279)

Just like the early period of feudal society, the first half of the middle period marked the powerful empires of Sui and Tang dynasties. The Han were unified and absorbed new blood from different minority peoples. For example, some of the defeated Turks, just like the Xiong Nu (Huns), moved inside the Great Wall and intermingled with the Han, while others stayed in Northwest China as the forefathers of the Uygur and Kazak, and some moved westward to Southwest Asia to establish a new country of Turkey. Even now, Chinatowns in American cities are sometimes called in Chinese "Tang streets."

During the second half of this period, including the late Tang Dynasty, the Five Dynasties, and the Northern and Southern dynasties, China was again reduced to civil wars and suffered from the invasion of many nomadic peoples. Tens of millions of people perished or moved southward. Millions of hectares of farmland were laid waste, while the Han again not only survived but also absorbed new blood from many minority peoples. Some minority peoples have also survived and continued to develop today, such as the Mongols, the Tibetans, the Hui, and the Kin who were the forefathers of the Manchu.

Late Period of Feudal Society (1279–1840)

The Yuan Dynasty (Mongol Empire, 1279–1369) marked the first time that China was entirely conquered by a minority people. Although subjected to 90 years of brutal, autocratic reign, the Han still survived and eventually overthrew the invaders by peasant uprisings, causing the Mongols to retreat to the Mongolian Plateau. During the Qing Dynasty, China was once again conquered entirely by a minority people and experienced a brutal reign with innumerable massacres of the common people and terrible persecution of the intelligentsia. The Han Chinese survived again and assimilated many minority peoples, including the conquerors—the Manchu themselves. Other minority peoples, such as the Tibetans, the Uygur, and the Hui, also survived and continued to maintain their ethnic identity.

Modern Period (1840–1949)

This was the painful period when China was reduced to a semicolonial and semifeudal society. However, during this period China experienced a relatively large-scale northwestward shift of the traditional pastoral–farming boundary by several dozens or even a few hundreds of kilometers. The Han peasants settled for the first time in northern Northeast China, southeastern Inner Mongolia, and other newly reclaimed areas, resulting in a very rapid increase of farmland area and population. From the mountainous and crowded Southeast Coast, a considerable number of poor peasants migrated voluntarily or involuntarily to Southeast Asia and other parts of the world. At present, there are more than 30 million overseas Chinese in the world, not including those Chinese descendants who have intermingled with other races and have thus lost their Chinese identity. At the end of this period, five major ethnic groups were officially recognized: Han, Manchu, Hui, Mongol, and Tibetan.

During the latter part of this period, the Japanese tried to colonize Korea and Northeast China. Their efforts resulted in utter failure, but they drove Korean peasants to settle in Northeast China, with some success. This is the origin of present-day Yanbian Korean Autonomous Prefecture of eastern Jilin Province.

Contemporary Period (Since 1949)

Since 1949, an enlightened policy on ethnic minority groups has been adopted. Theoretically, all 56 ethnic groups have equal political, economic, and social status. They are "brothers" to each other, with the most populous Han as the eldest brother. For the special benefit of the younger brothers, an "autonomous areas" system with four levels (province, prefecture, municipality, and county) has been adopted. Five autonomous regions, 62 autonomous prefectures, 71 autonomous municipalities,

TABLE 7.1
Number of Autonomous Areas, by Province (autonomous regions), 1990

Province (autonomous region)	Province level	Prefecture level	Municipality level	County level
Heilongjiang Province	—	—	—	1
Jilin Province	—	1	5	6
Liaoning Province	—	—	—	10
Hebei Province	—	—	—	6
Zhejiang Province	—	—	—	1
Hubei Province	—	1	2	8
Hunan Province	—	1	1	14
Guangdong Province	—	—	—	3
Guangxi Zhuang Autonomous Region	1	8	12	76
Hainan Province	—	—	—	7
Sichuan Province	—	3	1	54
Guizhou Province	—	3	3	43
Yunnan Province	—	8	5	74
Inner Mongolia Autonomous Region	1	8	17	71
Gansu Province	—	2	1	19
Ningxia Hui Autonomous Region	1	2	4	19
Xinjiang Uygur Autonomous Region	1	13	16	71
Qinghai Province	—	6	2	33
Tibet Autonomous Region	1	6	2	76
Total	5	62	71	589

and 589 autonomous counties have been established as shown in Table 7.1. Each of these autonomous counties may have one or more leading minority peoples, but they may not necessarily form a majority in the total population. In most of the autonomous counties Han are still the majority.

MAJOR ETHNIC GROUPS

Major ethnic groups (each with a population more than 100,000 in 1982) are listed in Table 7.2.

The Han

The Han are the largest ethnic group or "eldest brother" in China. As we have seen, the Han people have formed and evolved through the vicissitudes of 8000 years. Although now living mainly in Eastern Monsoon China, the Han are also scattered widely in Northwest Arid China and the Tibetan Frigid Plateau. As shown in Table 7.3 and Figure 7.1, the Han are the dominant ethnic group in 24 mainland provinces and municipalities. With the exception of mountainous and rugged Guizhou and Yunnan, the Han account for more than 90–95 percent of the population in most provinces and in nine of them even more than 99 percent. In the 5 autonomous regions, with the exception of Tibet (4.85 percent), the Han still account for 40–85 percent. Only in Xinjiang (in the westernmost part of Northwest Arid China) and in Tibet (in the westernmost part of Tibetan Frigid Plateau) do the Han fail to form a majority, although in Xinjiang they still account for 40.4 percent of the total population, just about the same as the Uygur.

Major Ethnic Minorities

Each of the fifteen largest ethnic minorities has a population of more than 1 million, and together they make up 89.78 percent of the ethnic minority population (1982). Five of them (Zhuang, Hui, Uygur, Zang, and Mongol) enjoy the prestige of leading an autonomous region.

The Zhuang

This is the leading ethnic group of Guangxi Zhuang Autonomous Region and the largest ethnic minority people in China. They are mainly concentrated in Guangxi, but are also scattered in the neighboring prov-

TABLE 7.2

Major Ethnic Groups in China (each with a population more than 100,000) in 1982, 1990

Ethnic group	Population (1982)	Population (1990)	Major areas
Han	936,674,944	1,042,482,187	Mainly in Eastern Monsoon China, partly in Northwest Arid China and Tibetan Frigid Plateau
Zhuang	13,383,086	15,489,630	Guangxi
Hui	7,228,398	8,602,978	Ningxia and other parts of Northwest Arid China
Uygur	5,963,491	7,214,431	Xinjiang
Yi	5,453,564	6,572,173	Western Sichuan, northern Yunnan
Miao	5,021,175	7,398,035	Guizhou, Yunnan, Hunan
Man (Manchu)	4,304,981	9,821,180	Scattered all over China
Tibetan (Zang)	3,847,875	4,593,330	Tibetan Frigid Plateau
Mongol (Mongolian)	3,411,367	4,806,849	Inner Mongolia Plateau and its borderlands
Tujia	2,836,814	5,704,223	Western Hunan
Buyi	2,119,345	2,545,059	Southern Guizhou
Korean	1,765,204	1,920,597	Eastern Jilin
Yao	1,411,967	2,134,013	Guangxi
Dong	1,142,400	2,514,014	Eastern Guizhou
Bai	1,132,224	1,594,827	Dali Prefeture (western Yunnan)
Hani	1,058,806	1,235,952	Southern Yunnan
Kazak	907,546	1,111,718	Junggar Basin (northern Xinjiang)
Dai (Tai)	839,496	1,025,128	Southern Yunnan
Li	818,000	1,110,900	Hainan
Lisu	481,884	574,856	Northwestern Yunnan
She	371,965	630,378	Zhejiang, Fujian, Guangdong
Lahu	304,256	411,476	Southwestern Yunnan
Va	298,661	351,974	Southwestern Yunnan
Sui	286,908	345,993	Southern Guizhou, northwestern Guangxi
Dongxiang	279,523	373,872	Southern Gansu
Naxi	251,592	278,009	Northwestern Yunnan
Tu	159,632	191,624	Northeastern Qinghai
Kirqiz	113,386	141,549	Southwestern Xinjiang
Qiang (Chang)	102,915	198,252	Western Sichuan

Source: Based on 1982 and 1990 population censuses.

inces of Guangdong, Hunan, Guizhou, and Yunnan. They are descendants of ancient Yue. They have been mingled freely with the Han for a very long time, and now use Chinese as both their spoken and written language. Their acculturation and assimilation processes with the Han have been nearly complete. Actually, it is now rather difficult to distinguish a Zhuang from a Han.

The Hui

This is the leading ethnic group of Ningxia Hui Autonomous Region and the second largest ethnic minority group in China. Although mainly living in Ningxia and

other northwestern provinces, they are also widely scattered all over China, especially in towns and cities. Originally some of the Hui migrated from Southwest Asia to China during the Tang Dynasty, but most of them were other ethnic groups converted to Islam. They have been closely mingled and assimilated with the Han. Now they speak and write the Chinese language and have adopted Chinese culture, but maintain Muslim customs.

The Uygur

This is the leading ethnic group of the Xinjiang Uygur Autonomous Region and the third largest ethnic minor-

TABLE 7.3
Distribution of the Han in 29 Mainland Provinces (autonomous regions, municipalities) in 1982

Province (autonomous region, municipality)	Total population	Han population	% of total population
Heilongjiang	32,665,546	31,056,708	95.1
Jilin	22,560,053	20,732,394	91.9
Liaoning	35,721,693	32,812,517	91.9
Beijing	9,230,687	8,908,480	96.5
Tianjin	7,764,141	7,600,504	97.9
Hebei	53,005,875	52,154,466	98.4
Henan	74,422,739	73,625,873	98.9
Shandong	74,419,054	74,011,440	99.5
Shanxi	25,291,389	25,227,798	99.7
Shaanxi	28,804,423	28,771,428	99.5
Shanghai	11,859,748	11,810,162	99.6
Jiangsu	60,521,114	60,410,785	99.8
Anhui	49,665,724	49,404,156	99.5
Zhejiang	38,884,603	38,723,586	99.6
Jiangxi	33,184,827	33,162,708	99.9
Hubei	47,804,150	46,025,378	96.3
Hunan	54,008,851	51,815,422	95.9
Fujian	25,873,259	25,624,151	99.0
Guangdong (including Hainan)	59,299,220	58,239,089	98.2
Guangxi	36,420,960	22,484,706	61.7
Sichuan	99,713,310	96,052,033	96.3
Guizhou	28,552,997	21,127,460	74.0
Yunnan	32,553,817	22,234,819	68.3
Inner Mongolia	19,274,279	16,277,899	84.5
Ningxia	3,895,578	2,651,354	68.1
Gansu	19,569,261	18,020,286	92.1
Qinghai	3,895,578	2,259,979	60.6
Xinjiang	13,081,681	5,286,533	40.4
Tibet	1,892,393	91,720	4.85
National total	1,003,937,078	936,703,824	93.3

Source: Based on 1982 population census.

ity in China. They are descendants of ancient Turkic people, both pastoral nomads and sedentary farmers. According to historical documents the Turk migrated in large groups from Inner Mongolia to Xinjiang around A.D. 840, then gradually formed the Uygur. They are now mainly engaged in agriculture and occupy the oases of the Tarim Basin and the Junggar Basin. They are Muslims and keep their own distinctive language and customs.

The Yi

This is the fourth largest ethnic minority group in China and the leading ethnic group for several prefectures and counties. Most live in the hilly and mountainous borderlands between Sichuan, Yunnan, and Guizhou provinces, but Liangshan Yi Autonomous Prefecture is the largest area of concentration. Until 1957, they were rather isolated and kept a barbaric slavery system. Re-

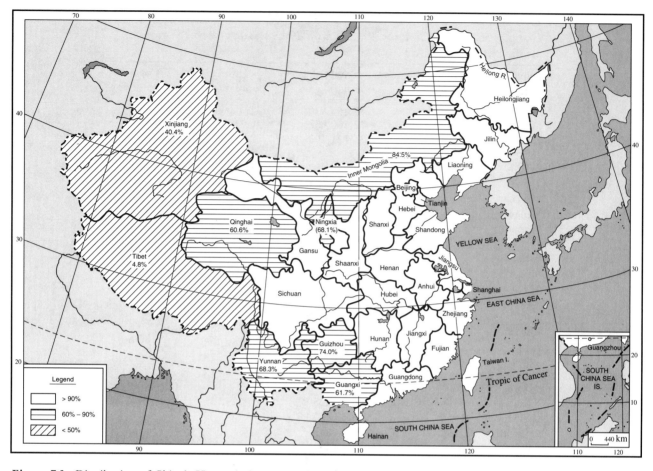

Figure 7.1 Distribution of China's Han majority among provinces, 1982

cently, they have made great progress both socially and economically.

The Miao

This is the fifth largest ethnic minority group in China. According to ancient tradition, they moved from Central China to Southwest China, and even partly to the Indochina Peninsula. They are now widely scattered in the hilly lands of Guizhou, Yunnan, and Hunan, where they still practice shifting cultivation with corn as the chief crop.

The Man (Manchu)

This is the sixth largest ethnic minority group in China. They are descendants of Qing aristocrats and soldiers, scattered almost all over China but without any specific concentrated areas. They have now nearly lost their identity and have become culturally absorbed into the Han.

The Tibetans (Zang)

The Zang are the leading ethnic group of Tibet Autonomous Region and the seventh largest ethnic minority group in China. Most live on the Tibetan Plateau and its surrounding areas, generally above 3000 m. Among all ethnic minorities in China, the extent of the Zang area is second only to the Mongol. Administratively they live chiefly in Tibet Autonomous Region, the western part of Sichuan Province (the former "Kang" area), the southern part of Qinghai Province and the border areas of Gansu and Yunnan provinces. The Zang have an ancient and glorious history, during which they have been in close contact with the Han. They created their own written language in the seventh century A.D., yet, until 1959, had been ruled by a theological serfdom system. Most of them still keep their faith in Lamaism, a sect of Buddhism, and so far keep apart from the Han and other ethnic groups. Based on principles of nationalism and humanism, the Tibetans should certainly enjoy the full privileges of autonomy, but it seems unnecessary to retreat into a theological serfdom system.

The Mongolian (Mongols)

The Mongols are the leading ethnic group of Inner Mongolia (Nei Mongol) Autonomous Region, which was the first autonomous region in China, set up in 1947. The Mongols, under Genghis Khan, established the Mongol Empire in thirteenth century. Consequently, they spread widely not only in China, but also in Central Asia and southern Siberia. Besides their homeland on the Mongolian Plateau, Mongols are also found in large groups in Xinjiang, Liaoning, Jilin, Heilongjiang, Hebei, Gansu, and Qinghai provinces. They have their own language and distinctive culture. Recently, they have been gradually adopting Han culture and getting closer and closer to the Han.

The Tujia

The Tujia are mainly found in the mountains of western Hunan and southwestern Hubei. They speak Chinese. Terraced paddy rice farming and forestry are their chief occupations.

The Buyi

The Buyi are mainly found in the Buyi-Miao Autonomous Prefecture and some other autonomous counties in southern Guizhou Province. They are closely affiliated with the Zhuang, but are less developed economically.

The Koreans

Immigrants from Korea are concentrated in the Yanbian Korean Autonomous Prefecture of eastern Jilin Province. They still keep their cultural habits and language.

The Dong

Dong live mainly on the mountainous eastern Guizhou Plateau where fir and other trees flourish. They have been famous for wood architecture since ancient times. They speak Han Chinese.

The Yao

Most Yao live in the hilly areas of Guangxi and its surrounding provinces. They are still quite undeveloped economically and live partly on sedentary rain-fed farming and partly on shifting agriculture, with corn, sweet potatoes, and taro as their chief crops.

The Bai

The Bai are concentrated around the scenic Er Lake in western Yunnan Province and have been closely connected with the Han for 2000 years. From the eighth to the thirteenth century they established the famous kingdom of Nan-Zhao, which extended its political influence far southward to the Indochina Peninsula. Now it is the site of Tali Bai Autonomous Prefecture. *Bai* means "white," the favorite color of these people, who have a high level of culture.

The Hani

The Hani are scattered on the extensive hilly areas between the Lanchang Jiang (Mekong River) and the Yuan Jiang (Red River). About one-half of the population is concentrated in the Red River Hani-Yi Autonomous Prefecture of which Geiju, the so-called "Lead Capital" of China, is the capital. Timber, mineral, and livestock resources are quite rich, and terraced farming is spectacular in this montane area.

Minor Ethnic Minorities

In the 1982 population census 13 minor ethnic minorities were identified. Each has a population of between 100,000 and 1 million, including the Kazak in northern Xinjiang and the Dai (Tai) in southern Yunnan. All together they constitute 7.86 percent of the total ethnic minority population. In the 1990 census, three of them (Kazak, Dai, and Li) were found to have a population of more than 1 million.

There are 18 minor ethnic minorities each with a population of more than 10,000 but less than 100,000 according to the 1982 population census. They include the Jingpo, the Daur, the Mulao, the Blang, the Salar, the Maonan, the Gelao, the Xibe, the Achang, the Puni, the Tajik, the Nu, the Uzbek, the Ewenke, the Benglong, the Yugur, the Jing, and the Jino. All together they represent 1.12 percent of the total ethnic minority population. But in the 1990 census, five of them (the Jingpo, the Daur, the Mulao, the Gelao, and the Xibe) had a population of more than 100,000.

There are nine minor minorities with less than 10,000 each in the 1982 population census. They include the Gaoshan, the Russian, the Baoan, the Tartar, the Darung, the Orogen, the Heshe, the Monbe, and the Lhoba. Altogether they make up only 0.04 percent of the total ethnic minority population. The Hezhe, found exclusively in the lower reaches of the Songhua

River (the largest tributary of the Heilongjiang) live entirely on fishing, forming the smallest ethnic group in China, with a population of only 1489 in 1982. The Gaoshan (literally, "High Mountain") group are mainly found in the alpine area of Taiwan, and only 1650 were found in the Chinese mainland in 1982. On Taiwan, anthropologists more clearly differentiate among them.

Finally, there are 799,705 persons in the country in 1982 whose ethnicity remained unidentified.

ETHNIC DISTRIBUTION FEATURES

The distribution of ethnic groups in China, first of all, shows the overwhelmingly dominance of the Han. In about 40 percent of China's land area, which is mostly in Eastern Monsoon China and partly in the southeastern margin of Northwest Arid China, almost all the people are Han. In the other 60 percent of the land area, Han people are intermingled with other ethnic groups in mixed settlements. In most places the Han are still the majority; for example, even in Inner Mongolia Autonomous Region, the Han comprise 84.5 percent of the total population.

The ethnic minorities are mainly distributed in the border areas and in mountainous areas, including most of Northwest Arid China, the Tibetan Frigid Plateau, and mountainous Southwest China (southwestern part of Eastern Monsoon China). They usually have a distribution core, and are also scattered widely in the surrounding areas. In special areas, there are also mixtures of ethnic minorities. For example, more than 25 ethnic minority groups, each with more than 4000 persons, coexist in Yunnan Province. Especially in the Hengduan Mountains, because of great variations in relative relief (from 500 m up to more than 4000 m) and of latitudes (from about 23° to 28°N), as well as being the crossroads of historical ethnic migrations, the area is a "museum" of human groups (also of plants and animals), characterized by conspicuous vertical and latitudinal differentiation and coexistence of ethnic groups (Figure 7.2).

The following specific distribution patterns of ethnic minorities might be observed:

1. Wide dispersion, appearing in many areas of the country. An example is the Hui, found in as many as 2308 counties and cities, while only one-sixth of the total Hui population live in Ningxia Hui Autonomous Region. They are thus widely distributed but with a low level of concentration in most areas. Another example is the Man, who are scattered in

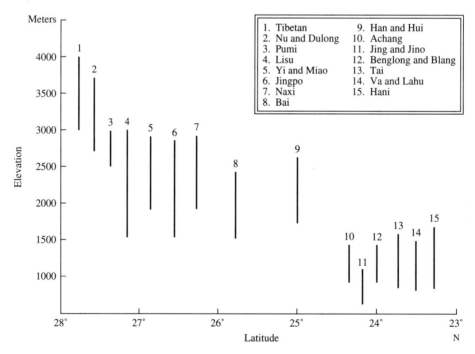

Figure 7.2 A sketch showing vertical distribution of ethnic groups in the Hengduan mountains area, Yunnan Province

2095 counties and cities, but with a relative concentration only in Northeast China, their homeland.

2. Concentrated in contiguous areas or in large regions, but also widely scattered in other areas. For example, the Dong are found in 1002 counties and cities, but 98 percent of the total population is concentrated in Guangxi. Another example is the Miao, distributed in 1568 counties and cities, but 98.9 percent of the total population is concentrated in Guizhou and the surrounding provinces. Still other examples are the Yi, distributed in 1044 counties and cites, but 99.8 percent concentrated in Sichuan, Yunnan, and Guizhou, with a particular concentration in the Liangshan Yi Autonomous Region; and the Tibetans, distributed in 1189 counties and cities, but about 46 percent concentrated in the Tibet (Zang) Autonomous Region.

3. Scattered in numerous counties but highly concentrated in a few or even in one single county. The best example is the Achang who live in 41 counties and cities, but 88.6 percent of them are concentrated in Luxi, Lianghe, and Longchuan counties in western Yunnan.

4. As a result of historical migration, concentration in several widely separated areas. The Xibe is the example for this distribution. Some live in Kaiyuan county and Shenyang city in Liaoning (as their homeland), and some in the faraway Ili Kazak Autonomous Prefecture in Xinjiang. This ethnic group mainly descended from an army dispatched by the Qing government.

REFERENCES

China State Statistical Bureau. 1982. *Population Census of China* (in Chinese).

China State Statistical Bureau. 1991. *Statistical Yearbook of China*. Beijing: China Statistical Publishing House.

China State Statistical Bureau and Institute of Geography, Chinese Academy of Sciences. 1988. *Atlas of Population of China*. Beijing: Science Press, and Oxford: Oxford University Press, (in Chinese and English).

Tang, Qixiang, ed. 1982–1988. *Historical Atlas of China*. 8 vols. Beijing: Cartographic Publishing House (in Chinese).

CHAPTER EIGHT

The Population Dilemma

China is the most populous country and the only one in the world with more than a billion inhabitants. As early as A.D. 2, the first national census in China recorded a population of 59.6 million, accounting for about one-fourth of the global population at that time.[1] According to the 1982 census, China's population reached 1,016.5 million (Figure 8.1), or about 22.4 percent of the global population in that year. In 1990 China's population soared again to 1,143.3 million, more than double the total population of seven Western industrial countries: the United States, the United Kingdom, France, Germany, Italy, Canada, and Australia (Table 8.1 and Figure 8.2). Consequently, China no doubt has the largest labor force as well as one of the largest potential markets in the world.

Yet, such a huge population imposes a tremendous stress on the physical environment and natural resources, resulting in serious economic and social problems, such as inadequate food supply, difficulties in employment, low level of income and education, and degradation of environmental quality. China is now one of the poorest developing countries in the world and ranks very low in per capita value of natural resources and economic production, even though, in total, it enjoys rich natural resources and the largest production of food grains, cotton, and coal in the world. Especially since 1949, China has been experiencing a population explosion of crisis

---

[1]According to recent world demographic studies, it took early humankind almost 2 million years to achieve a population of about 0.25 billion in A.D. 1. Then the human population doubled (to 0.5 billion) in 1650 years; doubled again (to 1.0 billion) in 200 years; and doubled again (to 2.0 billion) in 90 years; and doubled again (to 4.0 billion) in only 35 years (1941–1976); and by 1989, only 13 years later, the global population soared to 5.0 billion.

proportions, which, if not well controlled, will certainly place the survival and development of China as a nation at great risk. Because China has nearly one-quarter of the world population, such an population explosion would also create serious global problems.

HISTORICAL DEVELOPMENT OF POPULATION

China is one of the areas where humans had their beginning. In the long period of prehistoric society, small groups of gathering and hunting tribes were sparsely scattered in Eastern Monsoon China, and probably also in parts of Northwest Arid China and the Tibetan Frigid Plateau. From 8000 to 4000 years ago, early agricultural development generally coincided with small population clusters distributed almost all over China, but especially concentrated in the middle and lower reaches of the Yellow River and the Chang Jiang. Then, during the period of the earliest Chinese States—the Xia, Shang, and Western Zhou dynasties and the Spring and Autumn Period (2206–403 B.C.), China's population further increased. The middle and lower reaches of the Yellow River and the Chang Jiang were developing as the core of the Chinese nation. By the beginning of the long feudal society—the Warring States Period (403–221 B.C.)—Eastern Monsoon China between the Great Wall and the Nanling Mountains became agriculturally well developed and rather densely populated. At first there were more than 20 states, but later only seven survived. Each state tried to speed up its economic development and to increase its population and probably had several million inhabitants. Altogether China proba-

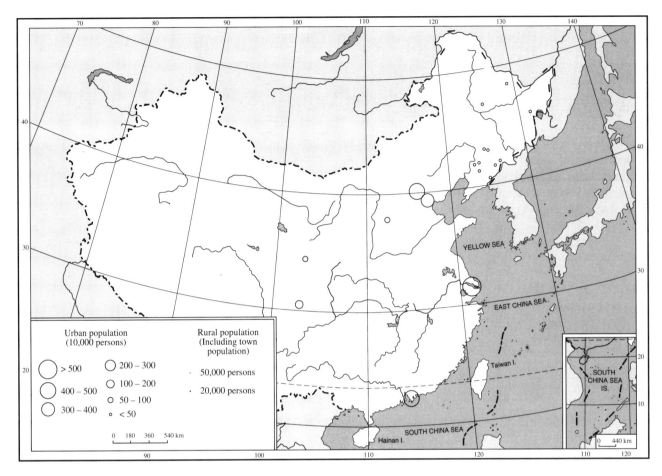

Figure 8.1 Population distribution of China, 1982

bly had 20–30 million inhabitants, but there was no trustworthy population census then.

China's first nationwide census was taken in A.D. 2 (Western Han Dynasty), recording a population of 59.6 million and a farmland area of 576.5 million *mu* (38.43 million ha). These numbers represent the general conditions of the early period of feudal society, when China was united and politically and economically strong. Subsequently, China had a series of official censuses, which marked the historical development of population in three stages (see Table 3.1).

Qin to Early Qing Dynasties (221 B.C.–Early Eighteenth Century A.D.)

This long period of feudal dynasties was characterized by three large-scale and many smaller-scale cycles of population fluctuation, with an upper ceiling of around 60 million and a lower level of about 30 million (see Chap-

ter Three). In each dynasty, the population growth stages of initial (slow growth), adolescent (rapid growth), mature (maximum growth), and old (population decrease) can be identified. The Malthusian model for population growth applies well to these large-scale and small-scale dynastic cycles.

The first rulers of each dynasty tried their best to consolidate political and economic power. They took advantage of the sparse initial population and the excess unused arable land and introduced land reform and some advances in economic development. Consequently, the population increased rapidly and reached its maximum at the dynasty's mature stage. Then came the absolute corruption of the autocratic, feudal government and the disruption of political and economic power, which caused destructive civil wars, nomadic invasions, and peasant uprisings, leading to widespread starvation. The old dynasty was eventually overthrown with about one-third or even one-half of the total population being massacred or starved to death. Subsequently, a new feudal dynasty emerged out of ashes of destruction and reduced population. For example, in A.D. 755 when the Tang Dynasty was at the zenith of its political and economic power, the population reached 52.9 million. By the time it ended and dissolved into the subsequent chaotic Five Dynasties, only two-thirds or one-half of the total population still survived. Again at the maximum population stage of the Ming Dynasty, the population exceeded 60 million (63.7 million in 1562); but after several decades of incessant Manchu invasions, peasant uprisings, and terrible drought, at least one-half of the total population had perished. Thus the once populous Sichuan Province became "empty" for a considerable time.

TABLE 8.1
Population of Selected Countries (Western Industrial Countries and Those Exceeding 100 million), 1990

Country	Population
Western industrialized countries	
Australia	16,923,478
Canada	26,538,229
France	56,358,331
Germany	78,475,370
Italy	57,644,405
United Kingdom	57,365,665
United States	250,410,000
Seven Western industrialized countries total	543,715,478
Other industrialized countries	
Japan	123,642,461
Soviet Union*	290,938,469
Nine industralized countries total	958,296,408
Large developing countries	
China	1,143,300,000
India	849,746,000
Brazil	152,505,000
Indonesia	190,136,211
Nigeria	118,819,377
Bangladesh	118,433,062
Pakistan	114,649,406

*The Soviet Union ceased to exist at the end of 1991. The largest of its successor states, Russia, has a population of about 148 million.
Source: United States Intelligence Agency, The World Factbook 1990, Washington, DC: Government Printing Office, 1990.

Early Qing Dynasty to 1949

In the early eighteenth century, after the Qing Dynasty had recovered from civil wars' damage and consolidated its political and economic power, the population increased rapidly in a unified and relatively prosperous environment. The Manchu rulers also decided to abolish the poll tax; until then, along with the land tax, the poll tax had been the chief method of raising government revenue. With its abolition people had no more reason to hide the number of their family members, and the population census increased suddenly: from the traditional upper limit of about 60 million, it jumped to 102.8 million in 1753, to 361.6 million in 1812, and to 377.6 million in 1887, accounting for nearly one-third of the global population at that time.

After 1840 China entered a modern semifeudal, semicolonial dark age. Millions of poor peasants perished from widespread natural hazards and starvation, and millions of people were massacred during a series of civil wars, foreign invasions, and peasant uprisings. For example, it is estimated that at least 20 million perished during the Taiping Uprising (1850–1860) and at least another 20 million died during the Japanese invasion and World War II. Yet, the Chinese vitality and versatility for survival and growth as well as the Chinese tradition to have as many children as possible still prevailed, and in 1949 China's total population reached 541.4 million, about one-fourth of the global population.

Contemporary China (Since 1949)

In the 1950s, the combination of the old Chinese tradition of having as many male children as possible and the new governmental doctrine of having as much manpower as possible, as well as the drive for rapid economic development and goals for improved hygiene conditions, started a phenomenal population growth, or even a population explosion (see Figure 3.5). In the 1954 census, population had already reached 602.7 million, and in 1957, it reached 646.5 million. During the Great Leap Forward and the Cultural Revolution in the 1960s, nearly everything was a mess; yet, with the exception of the so-called Three Natural Hazards Years (1960–1962), the total population continued to grow, usually by 15–20 million each year, and even more than 20 million each year from 1964 to 1973 (23.2 million in 1970). In other terms, each year's increase was nearly equal to the total population of Canada!

Since the early 1970s, in order to combat the population explosion, the government has advocated a family

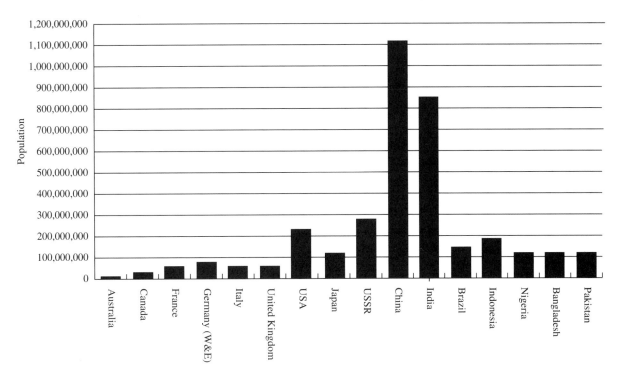

Figure 8.2 World population by country (Western developed countries and those exceeding 100 million), 1990 Data Source: CIA, *The World Factbook 1990.*

planning policy. The policy is for each couple, one child is the best, two children tolerable only in special cases, but never three or more children. Good results were achieved immediately. Both the birth rate and the natural increase rate have decreased somewhat since then. In the 1980s, population growth in China ceased to be characterized by a high birth rate, a low death rate, and a high natural growth rate. Instead, it was increasingly marked by a low birth rate, a low death rate, and a comparatively low natural growth rate.

So far, however, the population explosion has not been controlled, because the total population base is so huge, life expectancy has increased from less than 34 years before 1949 to more than 68 years after 1986, and the enforcement of family planning has been apparently relaxed in rural and border areas since 1984. China's total population broke the 1 billion mark in 1981, broke the 1.1 billion mark in 1988, and soared to 1,143.3 million in 1990. In 1990, the birth rate was 21.06 per 1000 population, the death rate was 6.67 per 1000, with a natural increase rate of 14.39 per 1000 (1.4 percent), and a net population increase of 15.3 million, nearly the total population of Australia. China's total population and birth rates, death rates, and natural increase rates from 1949 to 1990 are listed in Table 8.2.

POPULATION DISTRIBUTION

Population distribution is a function of integration among physical environment, socioeconomic conditions, and historical demographic development. The first characteristic of the Chinese case is a huge population base. About 56 percent of China's total population live in Subtropical China, a division that accounts for about 26 percent of its total land area; that amounts to more than 600 million inhabitants, or more than the total of seven Western industrial countries. Even in "wild" Northwest Arid China, an area occupying about 30 percent of China's total land surface but only 4 percent of the total national population, there are more than 40 million inhabitants, or more than Canada and Australia combined.

The second feature of China's population distribution is its relatively high density as well as its great areal variation. The national average density was 106 persons/sq km in 1982, and 119 persons/sq km in 1990. In four municipalities—Shenyang, Tianjin, Chengdu, and Shanghai—more than 34,000 persons were packed into each square kilometer in 1990; while in the large expanse of Northwest Arid China and the Tibetan

TABLE 8.2
Total Population, Birth Rate, Death Rate, and Natural Increase Rate, China, 1949–1990

Year	Total population (10,000 persons)	Birth rate (per thousand)	Death rate (per thousand)	Natural increase rate (per thousand)
1949	54,167	36.00	20.00	16.00
1950	55,196	37.00	18.00	19.00
1951	56,300	37.80	17.80	20.00
1952	57,482	37.00	17.00	20.00
1953	58,796	37.00	14.00	23.00
1954	60,266	37.97	13.18	24.79
1955	61,465	32.60	12.28	20.32
1956	62,828	31.90	11.40	20.50
1957	64,653	34.03	10.80	23.23
1958	65,994	29.22	11.98	17.24
1959	67,207	24.78	14.59	10.19
1960	66,207	20.80	25.43	−4.57
1961	65,858	18.02	14.24	3.78
1962	67,295	37.01	10.02	26.99
1963	69,172	43.37	10.04	33.33
1964	70,499	39.14	11.50	27.64
1965	72,538	37.88	9.50	28.38
1966	74,542	35.05	8.83	26.22
1967	76,368	33.96	8.43	25.53
1968	78,534	35.59	8.21	27.38
1969	80,671	34.11	8.03	26.08
1970	82,992	33.43	7.60	25.83
1971	85,229	30.65	7.32	23.33
1972	87,177	29.77	7.61	22.16
1973	89,211	27.93	7.04	20.89
1974	90,859	24.82	7.34	17.48
1975	92,420	23.01	7.31	15.69
1976	93,717	19.91	7.25	12.66
1977	94,974	18.93	6.87	12.06
1978	96,259	18.25	6.25	12.00
1979	97,542	17.82	6.21	11.61
1980	98,705	18.21	6.34	11.87
1981	100,072	20.91	6.36	14.55
1982	101,654	22.28	6.60	15.68
1983	103,008	20.19	6.90	13.29
1984	104,357	19.90	6.82	13.08
1985	105,851	21.04	6.78	14.26
1986	107,507	22.43	6.86	15.27
1987	109,300	23.33	6.72	16.61
1988	111,026	22.37	6.64	15.73
1989	112,704	21.58	6.54	15.04
1990	114,338	21.06	6.67	14.39

Source: China Bureau of Statistics, *1991 Statistical Yearbook of China*, Beijing: China Statistical Publishing House, 1991, pp. 71–80.

Frigid Plateau there are practically no inhabitants at all (Figure 8.3).

Regional Population Distribution

The areal differentiation of China's population distribution is characterized by the great diversity among the three natural realms. Within each natural realm, there is also much variation.

Eastern Monsoon China

This crowded realm occupies 45 percent of China's total land area, but nearly 95 percent of its total population live here. On the average, this realm has a population density of about 250 persons/sq km, more than seven times the world average in 1990.

The second-order diversity of regional population distribution in Eastern Monsoon China is highlighted by four major areas of population concentrations.

1. *The North China Plain and the Shandong Peninsula:* With a total area of about 500,000 sq km and a total population more than 250 million, this region contains more than 40 cities, including Beijing, Tianjin, Shijiazhuang, Jinan, and Zhengzhou. Population is especially concentrated along railway lines, along the Yellow River, the Huai He, the Hai

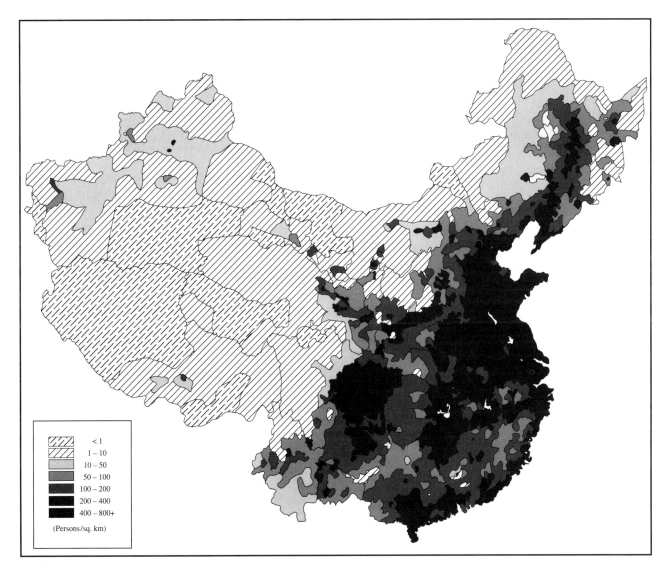

Figure 8.3 Density of population in Mainland China, 1982

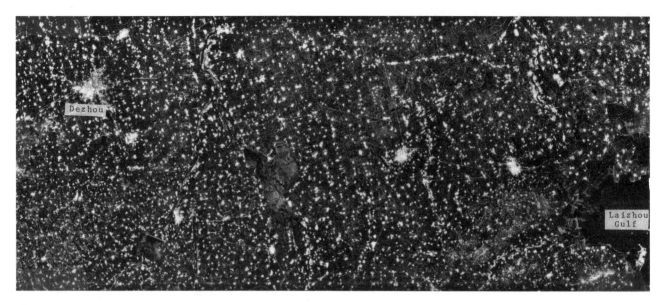

Figure 8.4 Distribution of settlements around the Dezhou area, North China plain. Each bright spot indicates a settlement. Source: Radar image (SIR-A Space Shuttle *Columbia*, November 1981)

He, and the Grand Canal, and along the coast of the Shandong Peninsula. For example, the radar image of the southern part of the North China Plain along 35° north latitude, taken by the space shuttle *Columbia* in November 1981, shows villages and cities (white spots) shining like innumerable stars in the Milky Way, with an interval between villages of only 1.0 to 1.5 km (Figure 8.4).

2. ***The Chang Jiang Delta and the coastal area along the Hangzhou Estuary:*** Containing a population more than 70 million within an area of about 90,000 sq km, this region includes some 20 cities, such as Shanghai, Nanjing, Hangzhou, and Suzhou. The population is particularly concentrated along the railways and the banks of the Chang Jiang and the Qiantang Jiang.

3. ***The Sichuan Basin:***[2] With a population of more than 70 million in an area of about 150,000 sq km, this region contains many large and medium-sized cities, such as Chongqing, Chengdu, Yibin, and Luzhou. Here population is especially concentrated in the Chengdu Plain and the Chongqing surburbs.

4. ***The middle Chang Jiang Plains:*** This region includes the Jiang–Han Plain in Hubei Province and the Dongting Lake Plain in Hunan Province. It has

an area of about 240,000 sq km and a population of more than 80 million. More than 20 cities, including Wuhan, Changsha, Zhuzhou, and Nanchang, are located here.

5. Other areas containing conspicuous concentrations are the coastal plains along Southeast Coast including the Zhu Jiang and Han Jiang deltas and coastal plains in Guangxi, Fujian, Taiwan, and Zhejiang provinces. Population concentrations are also found along the middle and lower reaches of the Wei River and the Fen River, on the Loess Plateau, and in southern Liaoning Province.

Northwest Arid China

As a whole, this is undeveloped land, with a population density of about 15 persons/sq km in 1990, much lower than the world average but still much higher than other arid and semiarid lands.

In Northwest Arid China, a great contrast in population distribution may be observed between the densely populated oases and the virtually empty expanse of sandy deserts, gravel *gobi*, and stony mountains. The oases occupy only about 3.3 percent of the total area of Northwest Arid China, but a lion's share of the population and nearly all the cities are located here. Since 1949, especially in the 1950s and early 1960s, great efforts have been undertaken to move people from the overcrowded

---

[2] The Sichuan Basin, administratively, is the eastern part of Sichuan Province, which had a total land area of 366,000 sq km and a total population of 108 million in 1990.

large cities and coastal areas to relatively underdeveloped Northwest Arid China. These efforts have enjoyed some success, although it is quite limited. For example, changes in population and ethnic composition in Xinjiang Uygur Autonomous Region from 1949 to 1982 are listed in Table 8.3.

Tibetan Frigid Plateau

With about 25 percent of China's total land area but a population less than 1 percent of the national total, this region is essentially still a "wild" land. As a whole, the population density is less than 5 persons/sq km. Except for a few farming and mining areas, the balance of the plateau is a vast expanse of virtually uninhabited land.

Population Density

As a whole, population density, like annual precipitation, decreases gradually from the southeastern coast to the northwestern interior. Yet, within both coastal and inland China, there are high-density core areas from which population density decreases with distance from the center. In Eastern Monsoon China, population density is generally more than 50 persons/sq km, although in some mountainous areas the density decreases to 10 to 50 persons/sq km. The major plains are invariably densely populated, and their density gradually increases

from north to south. The Northeast China Plain has a population density of 100–200 persons/sq km. Higher densities are found in the North China Plain, the Fen–Wei Plain, and the middle and lower Chang Jiang Plains, which generally have between 200 and 600 persons/sq km. Even higher densities occur in the Sichuan Basin, Zhu Jiang Delta, Southeast Coast plains, and western Taiwan plains, where densities between 400 and 800 persons/sq km are common. The most densely populated rural areas in China, with about 600–1000 persons/sq km, are mostly concentrated in the Chang Jiang Delta and the Chengdu Plain. The county with the highest population density in 1982 was Chenghai (Guangdong Province), with 1753 persons/sq km. From these plains to the surrounding mountain areas, the population density sharply decreases to generally 50–100 persons/sq km in hilly counties and 10–50 persons/sq km in mountainous areas.

In Northwest Arid China and on the Tibetan Frigid Plateau, the average population density of most cities and counties amounts to less than 10 persons/sq km. Most counties in the sandy desert, gravel *gobi*, and stony mountain areas have less than 1 person per sq km. The innermost centers of these hostile areas are almost entirely empty. Yet, a few cities and counties may be found where an average population density of more than 10–50 persons/sq km primarily in irrigated oases located on alluvial or dilluvial plains, such as the Hexi Corridor, the Elbow Plains, the Tarim and Manas valleys in Northwest Arid China, and the river valleys between Lhasa and Xigazê as well as the Huang Shui valley on the Tibetan Frigid Plateau.

According to 1982 statistics, over 30 percent of China's 2372 cities and counties had an average population density of more than 400 persons per sq km. The city with the highest population density in mainland China in 1982 was Shanghai, with 28,357 persons/sq km (34,035 persons/sq km in 1990). Furthermore, because of the influence of urban areas, a concentric structure has evolved in which population density declines from the city to its suburbs and further toward the surrounding rural areas. Thus, the city is not only itself a center of high population concentration, but also, by absorbing people from the surrounding rural areas, has often become a regional center of dense population. Hence, the majority of Chinese cities have an average population density of more than 10,000 persons/sq km.

TABLE 8.3
Population Growth and Ethnic Composition Change in Xinjiang Uygur Autonomous Region, 1949–1982

Ethnic group	1949	1965	1982
Total population (in 1000)	4,330.0	7,890.0	13,160.0
Ethnic groups (%)			
Uygur	75.9	52.1	45.5
Han	6.7	35.0	40.5
Kazak	10.2	6.6	6.9
Hui	2.8	3.6	4.4
Mongol	1.2	3.6	4.4
Uzbek	1.5	0.9	0.8
Xibe	0.2	0.2	0.2
Tajik	0.3	0.2	0.2
Other ethnic minorities	1.2	0.5	0.6

Source: China, official statistics.

POPULATION STRUCTURE

Sex and Age

Sex and age are two basic attributes of the population structure. They are directly related to and have a significant impact on various demographic characteristics, such as births, deaths, marriages, fertility, education, and employment.

Sex

The sex ratio of a population is the average number of males per 100 females. China has been notorious in the world for a sex ratio that reached 110 in 1947, a result of the old Chinese tradition to have as many male children as possible. This figure declined to 107.56 in the 1953 census, to 106.83 in 1964 census, and to 105.45 in the 1982 census, but rose to 106.27 in the 1990 census. Interestingly, the ratio was 107.61 for city population, 115.58 for town populations, and 104.37 for village populations in 1982. The 1980 census in Taiwan gave a sex ratio of 109.06, and the 1981 census in Hong Kong, of 109.3.

Although not pronounced, there are regional variations in the sex ratio. At the provincial level, the lowest sex ratios in 1982 were found in Tibet (99.76) and Shanghai (99.33), and the highest in Inner Mongolia (109.02), Shandong (108.51), and Hunan (108.07). At the county (city) level, 266 counties, or 11 percent of all counties and cities in China, had a sex ratio of below 100 in 1982. Low sex ratios mainly occur on the Tibetan Plateau and in the suburban and neighboring counties of large cities, such as Shanghai, Beijing, Guangzhou, Foshan, and Kunming. A total of 334 counties and cities in 1982 possessed sex ratios higher than 111; they were mainly in central Inner Mongolia, northern Shanxi, northwestern Hebei, southeastern Xinjiang, the Qinling and Daba mountain areas, and the border area between Zhejiang and Fujian.

Age-specific sex ratios are significant (Table 8.4).

The sex ratio is generally highest at birth, declining with age through adolescence and adulthood to old age, when females exceed males in number. However, in 1982 and in 1990, the sex ratio for the age category 32–59 was high, above 110; this was the result of the extremely high sex ratio of population born before 1949. After the age of 65, this high sex ratio balances out because the mortality rate among males is higher than that among females.

Age

The 1987 age pyramid in China (Figure 8.5) provides a general view of demographic development and change over the last 90 years. The lower middle part of the 1987 national pyramid expands abruptly (particularly obvious for the age group 15–24). This reflects the extremely rapid growth of population since 1949. The pyramid for ages 25–29 contracts somewhat because the so-called "Three Natural Hazards Years" (1960–1962) were marked by a series of natural disasters and social unrest. The shrinking of the base of the pyramid for the ages 0–15 is the result of China's increased efforts in family planning after the early 1970s and the consequent decrease in the birth rate.

Comparing the population pyramid of 1982 and 1987 with the 1953 and 1964 censuses (Table 8.5) reveals that fundamental changes in the age structure of China's population have taken place. After some fluctuations in the development trend after 1964, the 1982 and the 1987 pyramid obviously show the characteristics of a transition toward a mature population. It trends toward a low birth rate and a large percentage of elderly people. In the 1990 census (sample study), Mainland China's elderly population reached more than 9.8 million.

As already stated, there are great geographic variations in China's ethnic composition as well as in the level of social and economic development. Moreover, in past decade or so, the depth and scope of family planning have differed among ethnic groups, and between the

TABLE 8.4
Sex Ratio (female = 100) by Age Group, China, 1982, 1990

Year	Under 1	1–4	5–9	10–19	20–29	30–39	40–49	50–59	60–64	65–69	70 and over
1982	107.63	107.00	106.18	104.80	105.32	109.58	113.26	109.35	100.41	91.74	71.68
1990	111.68	110.24	108.24	106.16	104.98	107.38	110.32	110.94	105.89	96.14	73.30

Source: 1982 and 1990 population censuses.

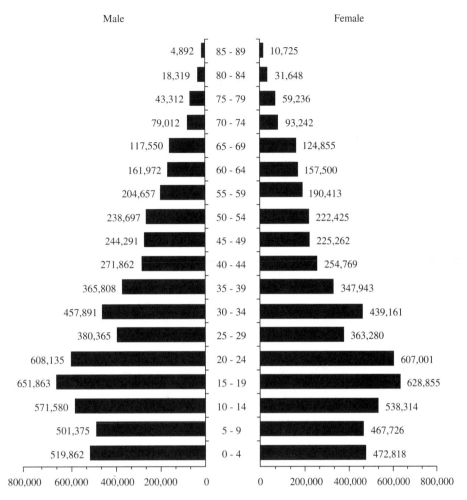

Male   Female

4,892	85 - 89	10,725
18,319	80 - 84	31,648
43,312	75 - 79	59,236
79,012	70 - 74	93,242
117,550	65 - 69	124,855
161,972	60 - 64	157,500
204,657	55 - 59	190,413
238,697	50 - 54	222,425
244,291	45 - 49	225,262
271,862	40 - 44	254,769
365,808	35 - 39	347,943
457,891	30 - 34	439,161
380,365	25 - 29	363,280
608,135	20 - 24	607,001
651,863	15 - 19	628,855
571,580	10 - 14	538,314
501,375	5 - 9	467,726
519,862	0 - 4	472,818

800,000 600,000 400,000 200,000   0   0   200,000 400,000 600,000 800,000

Figure 8.5 Age and sex pyramid of China's population, 1987 (Based on 1% sample survey, 1987)

cities and countryside, affecting the death and birth rates as well as age structures. Generally speaking, from the Han-inhabited plains in the East to the ethnic minority–inhabited plateaus and inland basins of the West, the proportion of the 15-to-64 age class decreases. The regional variation in the proportion of population over 65 years of age shows a different pattern. The variation in age level is mainly between north and south: northern China generally shows a higher proportion of older people than southern China.

TABLE 8.5
Age Structure, China, 1953, 1964, and 1982

| Year | Population (%) | | | Median age (years) | Mean age (years) |
	0–14	15–64	65 and over		
1953	36.3	59.3	4.4	22.7	26.5
1964	40.7	55.7	3.6	20.2	24.9
1982	33.6	61.5	4.9	22.9	27.1

Source: 1953, 1964, and 1982 population censuses.

Educational Level

The level of education is an important part of the quality of a nation's population. Improvement in educational level is not only a yardstick for the development of an advanced civilization, but also a necessary condition for efficient material production and effective family planning.

In modern times, China has lagged behind the developed countries in both education and economic levels. The 1982 census indicated that for every 10,000 persons in Mainland China, there were only 44 university graduates, 16 undergraduates, 663 persons with senior middle school education, 1775 persons with junior middle school education, and 3540 persons with a primary school education. In all, the proportion of the population with a primary school education or more was 68.1 percent for the whole country. The college graduate population, which is an important indicator of a region's level of higher education, accounted for only 0.44 percent, although the total number was 4.41 million. A serious contrast is that illiterate and semiliterate persons made up 31.87 percent of the total population age 12 and above.

Some improvements in educational levels were achieved in the period between the 1982 and the 1990 censuses. By 1990 there were 1.59 million Chinese with a college education, 35.39 million with a middle school education, and 42.1 million with a primary school education. In total, there were nearly 79 million Chinese with primary school education or more, or about 69.77 percent of China's total population. The number of illiterate and semiliterate people made up 22.27 percent of the total population age 15 and above; 13.01 percent of males were illiterate compared to 32.0 percent of females.

There are great regional discrepancies in the population with primary school education and over. The largest proportions with the best education are found in the three national municipalities of Beijing, Tianjin, and Shanghai, as well as in two provinces of Liaoning and Taiwan (all above 80 percent of the total population). The second highest level of education is between 70–80 percent in the provinces and autonomous regions in Northeast China, North China, Central China (except Anhui), and in South China (except Hainan). Areas with the lowest ratios are Tibet (25.5 percent), Yunnan (49.9 percent), and Guizhou (56.8 percent), all located in Southwest China or on the Tibetan Plateau. Other areas with a ratio of between 50 and 60 percent are Ningxia, Gansu, and Anhui. Great differences in educational

levels also exist among the ethnic minorities. In short, the higher educational ratios are found in the coastal areas rather than the inland areas, in the north rather than the south, in the plains areas rather than the ethnic minorities–inhabited mountain areas, and in the economically developed municipalities rather than in the rural provinces or autonomous regions. Consequently, the remote mountainous areas in Southwest China and Northwest Arid China, where ethnic minorities dominate, are usually most affected by both poverty and illiteracy.

Employment

Since China is the most populous country in the world, it follows that it also possesses the largest labor force and the largest employed population. The 1982 population census found that China's working-age population of 15 and over is 521,505,000, or 51.95 percent of the total population. Of these workers, 436,448,000 persons, or 83.69 percent, are in the age group 15–64. The total nonemployed population age 15 and over amounts to 145,157,000, accounting for 14.46 percent of the population. In short, the employment rate is very high, although not all workers are necessarily fully and efficiently employed.

The geographical variation in the employment index (the proportion of the employed population to the total population) has fairly obvious causes. It is closely related to regional variations in the level and structure of economic development and in the age structure of the population. Most counties with a high proportion of employed people (over 55 percent of the population) in Eastern Monsoon China are found along the middle and lower reaches of the Chang Jiang and the Yellow River as well as in the Sichuan Basin, and in Northwest Arid China along the Hexi Corridor. Counties with the highest proportion of employed population, over 58 percent, are located in the Chang Jiang Delta. There is also a marked difference between urban and rural areas in the proportion of the total population that is employed. The average proportion of employed people is 56.3 percent for 236 cities, 53.2 percent for towns, and 51.1 percent for villages.

The number of persons waiting for jobs in cities or towns in China in 1982 stood at 3,401,000 or 2.8 percent of the employable population, which approximates those who are economically active. This number consisted of slightly more women (53.25 percent) than men (46.75 percent). Those seeking jobs were mostly young people, age 15–24, who account for 92.46 percent.

Among them, 49.9 percent had a junior middle school education and 35.7 percent a senior middle school education. Most of them were seeking a job for the first time.

China has been essentially an agricultural country since ancient times. Even in the 1982 census, in which 15 major industrial categories were defined, 73.66 percent of China's total employed population was engaged in agriculture. This was greater than the 70.62 percent in the 1990 census. Among primary industries, 97.7 percent were engaged in farming, while those in forestry, animal husbandry, and fishing represented only 0.7 percent, 1.2 percent, and 2.4 percent respectively. The industries of mining and lumbering and production and supply of electricity, gas, and piped water accounted for 13.7 percent of China's total employed population. The other 12 categories (secondary and tertiary) include manufacturing; geological prospecting and surveying; construction; transport, post, and communications; commerce, catering, supply, and marketing of commodities; storage; management of residential buildings, public utilities, and residential services; public health, sports, and social welfare; education, culture, and art; scientific research and comprehensive technical services; finance and insurance; government, party, and public organization; and other industries. Altogether they accounted for only 12.62 percent.

According to the proportions of the population employed in each of the three industrial sectors (primary, secondary, and tertiary), five economic structure types can be identified.

1. Economic structures where the number of people employed in agriculture accounts for more than 80 percent of the total employed population. About 60 percent of the counties in China fall into this category, and are mainly found in western Liaoning, central Inner Mongolia, Shaanxi, Ningxia, eastern Gansu, Tibet, and southern Xinjiang. These counties are densely populated and mainly engaged in farming.

2. Economic structures where the number of people employed in agriculture accounts for 60–80 percent of the total employed population. About 30 percent of the counties and cities are of this type, mainly located in areas north of first type. Most of these counties are sparsely populated and depend on farming combined with animal husbandry, or mainly on animal husbandry.

3. Economic structures where the number of people employed in industry accounts for more than 40 percent of the total employed population. The number of counties and cities is small, mainly scattered in remote borderlands where mining or forestry prevails.

4. Economic structures where there is relatively balanced structure of employment. The number of people employed in industry is not more than 40 percent, or that in agriculture is not more than 50 percent. This type of structure is widespread, occurring in large cities and in suburban counties with a powerful economy.

5. Economic structures where employment is less than 60 percent in industry and agriculture combined and more than 30 percent in the tertiary sector. The number of such counties and cities remains small at China's present level of economic development. Most of them are medium-sized or small cities in southeastern China or counties in northern pastoral lands. They usually constitute small economic centers.

Family, Marriage, and Fertility

There is an interrelationship among family, marriage, and fertility. The family is the basic unit of society, and its size and composition reflect the contemporary social characteristics of a nation as well as certain historical traits of social development. Marriage as the prerequisite for family formation is a major factor that influences fertility patterns. Fertility is a basic starting point for the analysis of population dynamics and population structure as well as for population planning.

China has recently changed its cultural design from a feudal "extended" family to modern "nuclear" family.[3] The average household size in 1982 was 4.41 persons, with considerable regional variations. Relatively large average household sizes, more than five persons, were found in eastern Inner Mongolia, northern Xinjiang, the area where Gansu, Ningxia, and Qinghai provinces meet, eastern Tibet, and parts of Yunnan, Guizhou, Guangdong, Guangxi, Jiangxi, and Henan. Relatively small average family sizes (fewer than four persons) were found in the three national municipalities (Shanghai, Beijing, and Tianjin) and Jiangsu Province.

Today most Chinese households—67.4 percent—are two-generation households. The relics of the feudal extended family still account for 18.76 percent of the

---

[3]The so-called extended family in China usually denotes a household with more than two generations living together and with a family size of more than 5–10 persons.

total. The geographical distribution of these types is wide. Provinces having the largest proportion of three-generation households include Gansu (26.26 percent), Yunnan (26.22 percent), Fujian (25.57 percent), Guangxi (25.05 percent), Guangdong (24.85 percent), and Jiangxi (23.7 percent). The geographical variation in domestic household types is closely related to differences in the production system, the persistence of traditional values, and housing conditions.

In 1982, the total number of persons age 15 and over in mainland China was 665,480,612. Of this number, 28.57 percent were classified as unmarried, 63.68 percent as married, 7.16 percent as widowed, and 0.59 percent as divorced. In the 1990 sample study, 25.13 percent were unmarried, 68.16 percent were married, 6.12 percent were widowed, and 0.59 percent were divorced. The small size of the divorced population testifies to the stability of Chinese traditional family relationships. The relative proportions of men versus women who are unmarried, married, widowed, or divorced are quite different. Of the total male population age 15 or over, 32.71 have never married, 61.93 are married, 4.45 are widowed, and 0.92 are divorced. The corresponding percentages for the total female population age 15 or over are 24.22 percent, 65.52 percent, 12.00 percent, and 0.25 percent, respectively.

In 1981, the number of Chinese women of child-bearing age totaled 248,036,697, and the general fertility rate stood at 83.34 per 1000. There were more than 920 counties, or 38.2 percent of all counties and cities, with low fertility rates. Among these, 190 counties had a fertility rate of below 60 per 1000, most being found in cities, towns, or certain economically well-developed areas, such as the Chang Jiang Delta. There were 1460 counties, or 61.28 percent of all counties and cities, with a fertility rate higher than the national average. Of these, 480 counties had a fertility rate of more than 120 per 1000, most of them in economically underdeveloped areas such as Ningxia, Guizhou, and Tibet.

Regional Variations in the Population Growth Rate

In 1982, the natural increase rate for mainland China stood at 15.68 per 1000 (see Table 8.2), but there were wide variations. Population growth depends mainly on the efficiency of family planning in different areas as well as on the willingness of local inhabitants to observe the government policy. Areas with an average annual growth rate of less than 1 percent include Beijing; Tianjin; Yanji

City and Jian County in Jilin; Rongcheng, Wendeng, Mouping, and Wulian counties in Shandong; Jiande and Lanxi counties in Zhejiang; Xintian county in Hunan; and Medong, Bomi, and Lhozhag counties in Tibet. The number of areas with low growth rates is not large, but they show a healthy and promising trend in controlling population growth in China. Areas with an average annual growth rate of 1–2 percent are mainly found in densely populated and economically well-developed regions, such as the North China Plain, Chang Jiang Delta, middle reaches of the Chang Jiang, and Zhu Jiang Delta. Areas with an average annual growth rate of over 3 percent are found in Northwest Arid China, the Tibetan Frigid Plateau, and eastern Inner Mongolia. These are mainly borderland areas inhabited by ethnic minority peoples.

FAMILY PLANNING AND POPULATION CONTROL

To combat China's serious population explosion problem, family planning and other population control measures are deemed a necessity, although they are quite contrary to the Chinese tradition and have generated a lot of negative feedback. The 1953 population census recorded a total population of 602.7 million. The explosive population growth continued and even accelerated in the 1960s and early 1970s, and by 1971 China's total population reached 852.3 million.

Since the early 1970s, a family planning policy has been in force, under rather strict regulation. At first, the success of the national policy was apparent. The birth rate for the nation decreased to 17.82 per 1000 in 1979, and the natural increase rate decreased to 11.61 per 1000 (1.2 percent) in 1979. Since the early 1980s, however, the policy has become less effective, especially in the rural and border areas. The annual birth rate has risen to above 20 per 1000 again (21.04 in 1985, 23.33 in 1987, and 21.06 in 1990), and the annual natural increase has increased again to more than 15 million (18.0 million in 1987 and 16.29 million in 1990). Actually, the one-child policy has been far from strictly enforced in the rural and border areas. For example, according to official statistics, the birth rate in 1989 stood 21.85 per 1000, and first births accounted for 49.51 percent of all births, second births 31.17 percent, and third and subsequent births 19.32 percent.

On the other hand, several negative effects of the family planning policy have already appeared, some of them quite serious. First, education and other means for advocating voluntary family planning have been far from adequate. Involuntary birth control and sometimes even bureaucratically forced abortion creates serious social and moral problems, and is also against Chinese tradition. Second, there are reports that, in order to get one male child, many first-born female children have been persecuted, or even secretly killed. Third, the one-child policy usually results in a "prince" or "princess" in a family, who is spoiled not only by his or her parents but also by both sets of grandparents. The pampered child is now quite a big educational and social problem in China. Fourth, the policy has been much better obeyed by urban and well-educated families, while rural and poor families as well as ethnic minority people more or less still follow the tradition to have more children. Consequently, in the future population structure, there will be an increasing proportion of poor and less well-educated persons.

However, whether the Chinese people like it or not, for the sake of their country and the world, family planning and other population-control actions are absolutely necessary. The problem is how to make these actions more effective and how to avoid their negative effects.

REFERENCES

China State Statistical Bureau. 1953, 1964, 1982, 1990. *Population Census*. Beijing: China Statistical Publishing House (in Chinese).

China State Statistical Bureau. *1991 Statistical Year Book of China*. Beijing: China Statistical Publishing House.

Institute of Geography, Chinese Academy of Sciences. 1989. *Population Atlas of China*. Oxford: Oxford University Press.

NASA, SIR-A, Space Shuttle *Columbia*. 1981. Washington, DC: NASA (November).

United States Central Intelligence Agency. 1990. *The World Factbook*. Washington, DC: Government Printing Office.

Zhao, Songqiao. 1986. *Physical Geography of China*. New York: Wiley.

CHAPTER NINE

Urban Development

Throughout its history, China has been essentially an agrarian society, with more than 70–80 percent of the total population persuing agricultural occupations. Yet, as early as the Xia Dynasty (2206–1766 B.C.) and the Shang Dynasty (1766–1126 B.C.), walled cities developed. During the long feudal period (403 B.C.–A.D. 1840), together with political, economic, and social development, a sophisticated hierarchy of urban centers evolved, with the imperial capital as the largest city in the country. Xianyang of the Qin Dynasty (211–206 B.C.) and six other ancient capitals (Xi'an, Luoyang, Kaifeng, Nanjing, Hangzhou, and Beijing) all had nearly or over 1 million inhabitants, probably the earliest million-population metropolises in the world.[1] In modern times (1840–1949), China was reduced to a poverty-stricken semifeudal, semicolonial country, and its urban and industrial development lagged far behind the rest of the world. Since 1949, and especially since 1978, China's urbanization process again made great strides. According to the 1982 population census, there were 236 cities and 2660 towns in Mainland China, altogether housing 20.55 percent of the total population. According to the 1990 population census, there were 467 cities in Mainland China, with a total population of 335.4 million—much more than the total population of the United States—and representing 29.3 percent of China's total population. Currently, the largest-scale urbanization process in human history is going on in this most populous country in the world. However, unlike Western industrial countries, which usually have less than 10 per-cent of their total population engaged in agriculture (only about 3 percent in the United States), China's agricultural population will probably never drop below 30–40 percent.

Historical Urbanization[2]

The urbanization process in the so-called Old China (before the founding of the People's Republic of China in 1949) can be divided into two main historical periods: ancient times (before 1840) and modern times (1840–1949).

Pre-1840

During this long pre-1840 period, cities in China essentially functioned as administrative and military centers, although economic and social functions also gradually became important. As a whole, owing to the very conservative viewpoint of the feudal governments, which despised merchants and limited their commercial activities, the urbanization process could only develop very slowly.

Function and Size

In early primitive societies, clans and tribes started to build walls for military defense. During the Xia Dynasty and the Shang Dynasty, walled cities started to appear on the Loess Plateau and the North China Plain. They were

---

[1] London became a metropolis of more than 1 million only as late as 1810.

[2] This section is based mainly on the research works of Prof. Yeh Shunzhuang, Institute of Geography, Chinese Academy of Sciences.

140

chiefly used as administrative and military centers, with the strongly defended government sites located in the innermost part. Probably this was the first differentiation between urban and rural areas in China.

During the Western Zhou Dynasty (1126–771 B.C.), the country was divided into more than 1200 small, semi-independent principalities. They were consolidated to about 140 during the Spring and Autumn Period (771–403 B.C.). Each was subdivided into many fiefs. Thus, a three-level hierarchy of administrative units was formed: kingdom-principality-fief. The capital of each administrative unit was a walled city, the size of which was closely related to the administrative level and population. Economic activities and urban-rural relationships were not yet well developed.

During the Warring States Period (403–221 B.C.), only seven states survived after many years of bloody wars, conquests, and annexations. Each state then tried to speed up its political, economic, and social development. Thus, agriculture, handicraft industry, and a market economy started to grow rapidly. Urbanization processes also underwent a revolutionary change. Cities took on multiple functions, and urban-rural relationships grew closer. Some large cities even appeared such as Linzi (Shandong Province), the capital of Qi, which had a population of 300,000 and a city wall more than 20 km long. Other famous cities included Handon in Zhao (Hebei Province), Ying in Chu (Hubei Province), Xianyang in Qin (Shaanxi Province), Ji in Yan (Hebei Province), and Luoyang in Zhou (Henan Province).

During the unified and powerful Qin (211–206 B.C.), Western Han (206 B.C.–A.D. 9), and Eastern Han (A.D. 25–220) dynasties, urbanization was well developed. Walled cities were mainly administrative centers of four levels of administrative units: empire-province-prefecture-county. By the end of the Western Han Dynasty, there were 103 cities at the prefecture capital level and 1314 cities at the county seat level. These administrative centers also had a great attraction for economic and population growth. Xianyang (capital of the Qin Dynasty), Chang'an (capital of the Western Han Dynasty), and Luoyang (capital of the Eastern Han Dynasty) became the three earliest metropolitan areas in the world with nearly or over 1 million inhabitants. These unified empires with prosperous economies and transportation also encouraged commercial activities. Many large cities at that time, such as Linzi, Handon, and Chengdu, were famous for their commercial prosperity.

The political, economic, and social development in China's long feudal society as well as urban development reached its zenith during the middle years of the Tang Dynasty (A.D. 618–907). There appeared at that time a group of new cities based on handicraft industries, such as Din (textiles, Hebei Province) and Qimen (tea, Anhui Province). River and seaports also flourished, including Guangzhou, Quanzhou, Fuzhou, Wuzhou, and Ningbo in southern China, and Penlai, Laizhou, and Pinzhou in northern China. In the wild, vast Northwest China, a series of important cities also developed along the ancient Silk Road and on other strategic highways.

From the Northern Song Dynasty (A.D. 960–1126) to 1840, the multiple functions of cities became more sophisticated and their sizes enlarged. In the hierarchy of administrative units, the township was added below the county, and thus the system had five levels instead of four. The sizes of cities was usually related to the administrative level: national capitals (Kaifeng, Nanjing, Hangzhou, Beijing) generally had a population of more than 1 million; provincial and prefecture capitals usually had from 200,000 to 500,000; county seats had 5000–20,000 persons; and towns had from several hundred to 20,000. Additionally, since the Ming Dynasty (1368–1644), commercial products of farming and handicraft industries were increasingly developed, which had a tremendous impact to the urbanization process. For example, the Chang Jiang Delta had the best-developed market economy at that time. Hence, about one fourth of the large and medium-sized cities in China were concentrated there. The Zhu Jiang Delta was also significant in its market system and urban development.

Geographic Distribution

The geographic distribution of cities and towns was closely related to changing population and economic conditions. During the Xia, Shang, and Western Zhou dynasties, walled cities were mainly scattered in the middle and lower reaches of the Yellow River, most of them sited on the alluvial plains. During the Spring and Autumn Period and the Warring States periods, walled cities became widespread in the middle and lower reaches of the Chang Jiang and the northern part of the Southeast Coast. They were also built mainly on alluvial plains. Since the first grand unification in the Qin Dynasty, the spread of cities had been more or less coincident with the spread of agriculture and the expansion of Chinese territory (see Chapter Three, especially Figures 3.1 and 3.2). During the chaotic period from the Three Kingdoms (A.D. 220–280) to the Southern and Northern Dynasties (A.D. 280–589), millions of people migrated southward, and hence, the middle and lower reaches of Chang Jiang achieved about the same population size and urban density as the middle and lower reaches of the Yellow River. Nanjing became a national capital and a million-plus metropolis for the first time.

During the second grand unification of the Sui (A.D. 589–618) and the Tang Dynasty (A.D. 618–907), the urbanization process reached its highest point of the long ancient period. Urban populations comprised about 10 percent of the total population. Chang'an (modern Xi'an) and Luoyang became million-plus metropolises again, and numerous prosperous cities were scattered all over China. But from the late Tang Dynasty to the Northern and Southern Song dynasties, north China was devastated by civil wars and over run by nomadic invasions. Again, millions of people moved southward, and county seats decreased by 60 percent in North China, but more than doubled in central China. Hangzhou (capital of Southern Song Dynasty) became a million-plus metropolis for the first time, and there were numerous prosperous cities closely spaced along the Chang Jiang and the Grand Canal.

The late feudal period (1279–1840), saw the establishment of many new cities in the border provinces. For example, the Yuan Dynasty (1279–1368) was the most important period for urbanization in Yunnan province, while in the early and middle Qing Dynasty more than 100 new county seats were set up in Northeast China, Xinjiang, and Taiwan. In 1843, the urban population in China was estimated to be about 1.5 times that of middle Tang Dynasty, but because the total population was much larger, the urban population constituted only 5–6 percent of the total.

Modern Times (1840–1949)

At the beginning of modern China, the collapse of domestic feudalism and the invasion of foreign imperialism resulted in a poorly structured semifeudal, semicolonial society, which, in turn, caused very limited and unbalanced urban development. Economic factors become more important to urban development than political factors, and Shanghai (the greatest industrial center and port), rather than Beijing or Nanjing (national capitals), became the largest metropolis in China for the first time.

Owing to development of modern industries and transportation, there appeared a considerable number of large cities and ports. They were mainly located along the great rivers (such as Shanghai, Wuhan, Chongqing, Quanzhou, and Tianjin) and at good harbors along the coast (such as Hong Kong, Qingdao, and Dalian), or located at major railway junctions (such as Zhengzhou, Zuzhou, Shijiazhuang, Harbin, and Shenyang). There also appeared new mining and industrial cities, such as Fushun and Benxi (Liaoning Province), Tangshan (Hebei Province), Datong and Taiyuan (Shanxi Province), Jiaozuo (Henan Province), and Pingxiang (Jiangxi Province). Many of these large cities and ports served as the bridgeheads for foreign capitalism.

Large and extremely large cities developed rather rapidly, although small cities still dominated the urbanization process. Meanwhile medium-sized cities remained relatively undeveloped. For example, Shanghai was only a small county seat in 1843, but ten years after being opened as a seaport, its population suddenly grew to 600,000, exceeding Guangzhou as the largest seaport in China. By 1890 Shanghai became a million-plus metropolis, and soon exceeded Beijing as the largest city in China. Its population reached 3.48 million—10.8 percent of China's total urban population—in the mid-1930s. During the 1930s, four other cities (Beijing, Guangzhou, Tianjin, and Nanjing) also became million-plus metropolises.

Cities developed rapidly along the coastal areas, while others in the vast inland areas declined by comparison. In 1949, there were six million-plus metropolitan centers in China (Shanghai, Tianjin, Beijing, Nanjing, Guangzhou, and Shenyang), all located in the coastal region; four out of five of the other largest cities (Wuhan, Hong Kong, Hangzhou, and Qingdao), each with 0.5–1.0 million people, were also located along the coast. On the other hand, most medium-sized and small cities in the vast inland areas experienced a setback in urban development.

CONTEMPORARY URBANIZATION

Since 1949, stimulated by the rapid development of modern industry and transportation as well as the rapid increase in population, the urbanization process has accelerated. In the early 1950s, the total population of cities and towns was 57.65 million, comprising 10.6 percent of Mainland China's total population. In the 1964 population census, the total population of cities and towns was 127.1 million, or 18.4 percent of the total national population. The 1982 population census found a city and town population of 206.31 million, or 20.55 percent of the national population, and the 1990 population census recorded the urban population (not including towns) of 335.4 million, occupying 29.3 percent of the national population. There were 31 extremely large cities (each with a population of more than 1 million), 28 large cities (each with a population of between 0.5 and 1.0 million), 117 medium-sized cities (each with a population of between 0.2 and 0.5 million), and 291 small cities (each with a population of less than 0.2 million). Table 9.1 shows the growth of the number of cities between 1949 and 1990, and Table 9.2 lists the extremely large cities and their population in 1990.

Government policies usually have great influence on China's contemporary urbanization process. Three stages of urbanization growth can be identified since 1949.

Early Stage (1949–1957)

This was a stage of economic recovery from war damage and the planned transformation of the old urban system into a new one. The old consumption cities were changed into new production cities, and all jobless urban inhabitants were sent back to rural areas. Industrial construction, especially to develop heavy industries, were emphasized; from 1949 to 1952, the average annual growth rate of heavy industries by value was 48.8 percent, while that of light industries was 29 percent. The greatest emphasis of industrial development and urbanization was on the inland areas of Northeast China, North China, Northwest China, and central China, while the coastal zone was relatively overlooked. For example, of 825 large industrial construction projects during the First Five-Year Plan (1953–1957) only 36 percent were located in the coastal zone. As a whole, from 1949 to 1957, the number of large cities doubled (from 12 to 24), medium-sized cities increased by 50 percent

(from 18 to 27), and small cities increased by 12.7 percent (from 102 to 115); most of these increases occurred in the heavy industrial areas.

Middle Stage (1958–1978)

These twenty years were plagued by the Great Leap Forward and Cultural Revolution, and the urbanization process was overwhelmed by many difficulties. Too much economic planning and an overemphasis on heavy industries weakened urban functions and structure. The so-called Third Line construction, which overemphasized military safety but overlooked economic efficiency, made poor progress in Northwest China and Southwest China while doing great harm to the national economy and to other parts of China. Large cities grew abnormally while small cities were neglected. As a whole, the total number of cities increased from 176 to 193 during the period from 1958 to 1978, but small cities decreased from 115 to 93.

Recent Stage (Since 1978)

This new stage has been characterized by "opening up," "four modernizations," and other economic reform policies, resulting in great strides in the urbanization process. From 1978 to 1990, the total number of cities increased from 193 to 476, of which large cities including extremely large cities increased from 40 to 59, medium-sized cities increased from 60 to 117, and small cities increased from 93 to 291. In one year (1989–1990), the total number of cities increased by 17. Such phenomenal urbanization was mainly caused by five factors:

TABLE 9.1
Number of Cities, China, 1949–1990

Year	Total number	Extremely large and large cities*	Medium cities	Small cities
1949	122	12	18	102
1957	176	24	27	115
1978	193	40	60	93
1989	450	58	116	276
1990	467	59	117	291

*According to current Chinese official statistics "extremely large city" denotes a metropolis with over 1 million population; "large city," 0.5–1.0 million population; "medium city," 0.2–0.5 million population; and "small city," below 0.2 million population.
Sources: Statistical Yearbook of Chinese Cities, 1990, and *Statistical Yearbook of China, 1991.*

TABLE 9.2
Population of 31 Extremely Large Cities in China, 1990

Cities (province)	Total population* (in millions)	Nonagricultural population (in millions)
Total	79.32	62.58
Shanghai	7.83	7.50
Beijing	7.00	5.77
Tianjin	5.77	4.57
Shenyang (Liaoning)	4.54	3.60
Wuhan (Hubei)	3.75	3.28
Guanzhou (Guangdong)	3.58	2.91
Harbin (Heilongjiang)	2.83	2.44
Chongqing (Sichuan)	2.98	2.27
Nanjing (Jiangsu)	2.50	2.09
Xi'an (Shaanxi)	2.76	1.96
Dalian (Liaoning)	2.40	1.72
Chengdu (Sichuan)	2.81	1.71
Changchun (Jilin)	2.11	1.68
Taiyuan (Shanxi)	1.96	1.53
Jinan (Shandong)	2.32	1.48
Qingdao (Shandong)	2.06	1.46
Anshan (Liaoning)	1.39	1.20
Fushun (Liaoning)	1.35	1.20
Lanzhou (Gansu)	1.51	1.19
Zhengzhou (Henan)	1.71	1.16
Zibo (Shandong)	2.46	1.14
Kunming (Yunnan)	1.52	1.13
Changsha (Hunan)	1.33	1.11
Hangzhou (Zhejiang)	1.34	1.10
Nanchang (Jiangxi)	1.35	1.09
Qiqihar (Heilongjiang)	1.38	1.07
Shijiazhuang (Hebei)	1.32	1.07
Ürümqi (Xinjiang)	1.16	1.05
Tangshan (Heibei)	1.50	1.04
Jilin (Jilin)	1.27	1.04
Guiyang (Guizhou)	1.53	1.02

*Arranged according to nonagricultural population. Five large cities (Baotou, Fuzhou, Handan, Wuxi, and Datong) each had a total population of more than 1 million, but nonagricultural populations less than 1 million.
Source: Statistical Yearbook of China, 1991.

1. Rapid modernization of industry: Modern industry is the basis of modern urbanization. At end of 1984, there were 300 municipalities in China, of which 295 had a total industrial production value of 607.8 billion yuan, or 86.55 percent of the national industrial production value. Each of nine extremely large industrial cities had an annual industrial production value of more than 10 billion yuan, while each of 20 large industrial cities had 5–10 billion yuan. These large industrial cities are mostly located along the coast, with Wuhan, Chongqing, Xi'an, and Chengdu being the notable exceptions (Figure 9.1).

2. Rapid modernization of transportation and urban-rural connections has made cities the political, economic, and social cores for the surrounding regions

(hinterlands). In China's current administrative system, all national (Beijing, Shanghai, and Tianjin), provincial, and prefectural municipalities include numerous surrounding rural counties under their jurisdictions.

3. Effective reconstruction of urban economic systems: The former rigidly planned urban economic system is changing to a free market economy. In the urban economic structure, heavy industry is no longer unilaterally emphasized; instead, light industry, tertiary activities, and other economic development have been encouraged according to specific geographical and historical conditions.

4. Recent opening of coastal cities and ports has contributed much to the development of the national economy and urban growth. In 1980, four economic special zones (Shenzhen, Zhuhai, Shantou, and Xiamen) were established along the Guang-

dong and Fujian coasts. In 1984, 14 coastal ports were opened. From north to south they are Dalian, Qinhuangdao, Tianjin, Yantai, Qinqdao, Lianyungang, Nantong, Shanghai, Ningbo, Wenzhou, Fuzhou, Guangzhou, Zhanjiang, and Beihai. In 1985, the entire Zhu Jiang Delta, the Chang Jiang Delta, and southern Fujian Province became special economic zones, while Hainan Island was set up as a province and an open zone in 1988. All these special economic zones and open zones have been developing rapidly. For example, in 1982 Shenzhen (bordering Hong Kong) and Zhuhai (bordering Macao) had populations of 78,000 and 57,000, respectively. But by 1990 their populations rose to 395,000 and 366,000, respectively. Predictions are that the newly opened Eastern Shanghai Area, known as Pudong ("east of the Huangpu River"), with an area of 350 sq km and a population of 1.1

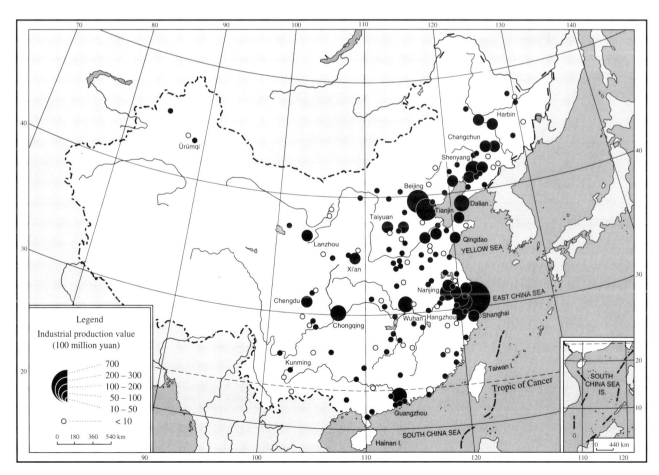

Figure 9.1 Distribution of industrial cities in China, 1984

million (1990) will probably become China's largest special economic zone in the 1990s and early twenty-first century.

5. New governmental policies since 1978, especially since 1984, to facilitate the establishment of new municipalities and new townships have greatly enhanced local economic development.[3] Such policies have been especially favorable for the development of small cities and rural towns. During the period from 1982 to 1987, the annual township growth rate averaged 34.5 percent, with a total of 9121 townships in 1987.

RURAL URBANIZATION

Since ancient times, Chinese rural society has been characterized by its traditional peasant-gardener farming system as well by its hierarchically structured rural market system and its well-developed cottage handicraft industries. By the mid-1930s, the total number of people living in market towns and mainly pursuing activities related to trade and handicraft industries accounted for about one-quarter of the total rural population. After 1949, however, the share of nonagricultural income in the rural economy dwindled. The commune and brigade enterprises initiated from 1958 to 1959 were also largely abandoned in the 1960s. Not until the 1970s did collective enterprises gradually revive. By 1976, there were 1.1 million rural enterprises staffed by a work force of 17.9 million with a total gross income of 27 billion yuan. In 1979, enterprises run by communes and brigades totaled 1.5 million, employing 29 million workers and accounting for about 10 percent of the total rural labor force.

The post-1979 agricultural reforms not only brought unprecedented agricultural production but also set the stage for rapid development of nonfarm activities and a series of rural market towns. Rural industrialization has been shown to be a good means to achieve rural urbanization. During the five-year period from 1980 to 1985, the annual growth rate of nonfarm enterprises averaged more than 20 percent. In 1986, more than 70 million people in rural China were engaged in various nonfarm activities, accounting for 19 percent of total rural employment (only 9 percent in 1978). The total production value of nonfarm enterprises in rural China reached 330 billion yuan, an increase of 18 percent from 1985 and accounting for more than 40 percent of the total output value of the rural sector. By 1988, the nonfarm labor force reached 95 million, accounting for 24 percent of total rural employment. The total production value of nonfarm enterprises reached 650 billion yuan, accounting for 53 percent of the total output value of the rural sector and 28 percent of the national output value. Few countries in the world are able to match the speed with which China has developed its rural nonfarm sector in recent years.

Such significant rural industrialization and rural urbanization have not only tremendously increased both production and income in rural areas, but also absorbed most of the surplus rural labor force and decreased significantly the proportion of China's agriculturally engaged population. Consequently, the heavy population pressure on the limited arable land resource has been greatly alleviated. Probably this will be the major approach to a Chinese type of industrialization and urbanization, and to reducing the proportion of the agriculture-engaged proportion of the total population from its present 70–80 percent to 30–40 percent in the early twenty-first century. Through accelerated rural industrialization and urbanization, the present urban distribution policy of "limited development of all large cities, the selective development of a few medium-sized cities, more development in small cities, and rapid development in rural towns and villages" will be justified. The Chinese model might also be good for the urbanization of most Third World countries.

---

[3]According to government regulations in 1955, "municipality" was limited to provincial capitals or cities with a total population above 0.1 million, while "township" was limited to county seats or towns with a total population above 2000, of which the nonagricultural population was more than 50 percent. Since 1983, any county seats and towns with more than 2000 nonagricultural residents may be considered a "township." Since 1986, any local economic centers with a nonagricultural population of more than 60,000 and with an annual total production value of more than 0.2 billion yuan may claim to be a "municipality."

REFERENCES

Cannon, Terry, and Alan Jenkins, eds. 1990. *The Geography of Contemporary China*. London and New York: Routledge.

China State Statistical Bureau. 1990. *Statistical Yearbook of Chinese Cities*. Beijing: China Statistical Publishing House.

China State Statistical Bureau. 1991. *Statistical Yearbook of China*. Beijing: China Statistical Publishing House.

Chang, Sen-dou. 1989. "The Changing Patterns of Chinese Cities, 1953–1984," in *Resources, Environment and Regional Development*, ed. C. K. Leung, Hong Kong: Hong Kong University Press.

Chang, Sen-dou, and R. Yin-Wang Kwok. 1990. "The Urbanization of Rural China," in *Chinese Urban Reform: What Model Now?* ed. R. Yin-Wang Kwok. Armonk, NY: M.E. Sharpe.

Institute of Geography, Chinese Academy of Sciences. 1987. *Population Atlas of China*. Oxford: Oxford University Press.

Kirkby, R.J.R. 1985. *Urbanization in China: Town and Country in a Developing Economy, 1949–2000 A.D.* London: Croom Helm.

Yeh, Shun-zhuang. 1991. *The Urbanization Process in China: Past, Present, and Future* (in press) (in Chinese).

CHAPTER TEN

Environmental Problems and Natural Hazards

A very large population and a very long history with their impact on China's varied physical environments result in numerous environmental problems. Natural hazards or natural disasters are those environmental problems that cause immediate loss and damage to human lives or property.

Some environmental problems and natural hazards are chiefly caused by physical factors, such as earthquakes, floods, and typhoons, and are usually catastrophic and hard to prevent or to avoid. Damage is measured mainly by loss of human lives and property. Hence, a severe earthquake that occurs in an uninhabited land, such as the middle of a desert, scarcely qualifies as a "natural hazard."

Some environmental problems and natural hazards are mainly human-induced, such as deforestation and environmental pollution. They create chronic conditions that gradually accumulate and degrade environmental quality. Still more environmental problems and natural hazards, such as soil erosion, desertification, and salinization, are caused by both human impacts and environmental dysfunction. They are usually chronic and harmful on a large scale, and they occur most frequently in ecologically fragile environments, such as arid and semiarid areas, loessic plateaus and hills, steep mountain slopes, and coastal zones where environmental changes are readily triggered and exacerbated by human action. Too often, however, the human impact serves as the dominant causal factor in environmental problems and natural hazards. For example, in a fragile arid environment, if land, water, and other resources are misused or overused, the destructive desertification process is soon triggered and greatly accelerated. On the other hand, if

these resources are rationally used, the oasis-making (or de-desertification) process will eventually gain an upper hand.

China was once called a "land of famines" and even now is still one of the countries most plagued by natural hazards in the world. According to official statistics, since 1949, about 20 billion kg of food grains and more than 3 million rooms of housing, on average, have been devastated by natural hazards each year. The severe floods in 1991 alone caused property loss worth more than 65 billion yuan. Combating these environmental problems and natural hazards has been and remains one of the most urgent problems in China.

CLIMATIC AND HYDROGRAPHIC HAZARDS

Natural hazards caused mainly by climatic and hydrographic factors are usually the most harmful to agricultural production. According to government statistics, from 1949 to 1979, about 460 million *mu* (31 million ha) of farmland, on average, were subject to and damaged by different natural hazards each year. Drought accounted for about 64 percent, floods and waterlogging about 23 percent, wind and hailstorms about 8 percent, and frost about 6 percent.

Drought

Drought is the most widespread and damaging natural hazard in China. According to historical documents, from 206 B.C. to A.D. 1949 there were 1056 severe droughts in China, nearly one every two years. Some were particularly damaging, such as that in the first half of the seventeenth century, when drought persisted for 16 successive years (1628–1644) North China was particularly hard hit. Millions of people starved to death, and the suffering helped cause a great peasant uprising, which led to the overthrow of the Ming Dynasty. Another tragic example was in 1920, when five provinces in North China were subjected to severe drought and 5 million people starved to death.

Droughts are mainly caused by the uneven annual and seasonal distribution of precipitation, not necessarily by too little annual precipitation on average. In the semiarid zone, such as eastern Inner Mongolia, where annual precipitation is scanty and seasonal variation very great, the rain-fed farming system is particularly vulnerable to drought. Here the old saying applies: "Drought occurs nine out of ten years." In the subhumid zone, such as the North China Plain, where annual precipitation is sufficient for rain-fed farming in normal years, annual and seasonal variations are extreme. Inasmuch as the farmlands are so very crowded and population density is so great, the most damaging droughts during historical times have usually happened here. Even in the humid Central and South China, because of seasonal and annual variation in precipitation, droughts are also frequent. In the arid zone, such as in the Tarim Basin, where annual precipitation is too meager for rain-fed farming, drought is not a problem in the irrigated oases if irrigation water is available and adequate. The most important strategies and measures to combat drought are promoting more effective use of available water for irrigation.

Using Currently Available Water Resources

To make more efficient use of currently available water resources, six major strategies have been adopted:

1. Building a sophisticated irrigation system so that currently available water resources can be optimally used. Especially in the arid area where no irrigation means no farming, the location and expansion of farmland should be determined by the amount of irrigation water available.

2. Reducing as much as possible the loss of irrigation water by percolation and seepage. This is especially critical in arid and semiarid areas, where the present efficient use of irrigation water resources generally reaches only about 30 percent.

3. Reducing as much as possible evaporation loss from water and soil surfaces and avoiding any kind of waste of precious water, such as overirrigating.

4. Adopting more efficient irrigation devices, such as sprinkler and trickle irrigation.

5. Selecting ecologically adapted crops and growing them in ways that use water more efficiently. For drought-frequented areas, drought-tolerant crops are preferable.

6. Adopting different irrigation systems according to areal differentiation. For example, surface water and trickle irrigation systems are appropriate in the upper part of the arid piedmont plains where the groundwater table usually lies more than 10–50 m deep, while in the middle and lower reaches of inland rivers, surface water, groundwater, and canal irrigation systems might be used.

Increasing Irrigation Water

Increasing the supply of irrigation water remains an important goal.

1. Building dams, water reservoirs, and irrigation canals to regulate and to store flood discharge. For example, during the period from 1955 to 1977, the Manas irrigation system of Xinjiang increased the utilization efficiency of its annual hydraulic discharge from less than 30 percent to more than 70 percent, and consequently its irrigation area was increased 14-fold.

2. Adopting some special agricultural systems adjusted to local environmental conditions, such as reuse of wastewater in suburban areas and better managemant of rainwater and runoff in rural areas.

3. Building underground water reservoirs and underground irrigation systems as well as developing groundwater resources as much as possible.

4. Considering transfer of water from neighboring river basins and artificial rain-making devices under certain favorable environmental and economic conditions.

Floods and Waterlogging

Floods and waterlogging are mainly caused by the interplay of natural factors such as too much water in the rainy season or low-lying areas with inadequate drainage, compounded by human mismanagement of water conservancy systems. Regions with very high population density are most affected.

One of the most flood-prone areas is the middle and lower reaches of Chang Jiang where most problems are caused by the huge amount of floodwater in the rainy season and the low-lying landforms. This area is easily subjected to flood and waterlogging, but drainage is difficult. Present water conservancy measures are far from adequate to combat these major hazards. One of the objectives for the proposed Three Gorges Dam project is to store and control Chang Jiang's floodwater. The areas suffering the most damage in the 1991 floods were also in the middle and lower reaches of the Chang Jiang.

Another even more flood-prone region is the North China Plain, which is essentially a huge alluvial delta built by the Yellow River. From 602 B.C. to A.D. 1950, there were 1573 disastrous flood-induced breaks in the dikes in the North China Plain and 26 instances of large-scale channel shifts, of which seven were exceptionally great (Figure 10.1). The catastrophic breach in the dike at Huayuankou in 1938 alone caused more than 890,000 casualties and left more than 12.5 million people homeless. Since 1949, dikes on either side of the lower Yellow River, with a total length of 1400 km, have been elevated and strengthened three times while more than 1 million persons have combated floods every flood season. No damaging floods have occurred on the Yellow River over the last 40 years. Yet, the danger of a catastrophic flood still exists, and is even increasing. Of the yearly 1.6 billion tons of sediment discharged into the North China Plain by the lower Yellow River, about one-fourth is deposited on the river bed, which is being raised at a rate of 10 cm each year.[1] The river bed of the lower Yellow River has already been raised above its neighboring plain by 5–8 m (13 m maximum). Thus the capacity of the channel to discharge floodwater is ever decreasing, while the menace of breaks in the dikes is ever increasing. For example, the highest peak flood discharge at the Huayuankou station in 1958 was 22,300 m^3/sec, while the 1982 peak flood discharge at the same station reached 15,300 m^3/sec; yet, the water gauge mark was 0.17 m higher in 1982 than in 1958.

Combating flood hazards is thus the key problem in the North China Plain for human survival and agricultural development. A sophisticated system of effective flood-control measures is much needed, including:

1. It is necessary to maintain an effective dike system and to mobilize local residents and armies to combat flood hazards on site during the flood season. A common rule is to avoid large-scale construction and investment in flood-prone areas.

2. Building a series of reservoirs seems advisable in the junction area between the middle and the lower reaches of the Yellow River, that is, between the Loess Plateau and the North China Plain. In the middle reaches of the Yellow River, two large reservoirs, the Sanmenxia and the Longmen, have already been constructed. Another key reservoir, the Xianlangti, located only 5 km upstream from the head of the huge alluvial fan of the lower Yellow River, has also been under construction since 1991 after long and heated environmental, agricultural, and economic debates. A main design feature of this last reservoir is that most of the sediment discharge of the middle Yellow River will be dropped here. In addition, more than 470 large and medium-sized reservoirs have been already built in the areas surrounding the North China Plain and should be kept in good condition.

3. To improve the river channel capacity to discharge floodwater and to transport silt sediments, the famous hydrologic engineer Pan Xiushun of the Ming Dynasty (1368–1644) devised an effective measure to narrow the river channel with dikes on either side so that the silt sediments could be carried away by the swift water current. This good tradition is still profitably used. Yet, in order to lower the bed of the lower Yellow River from its "above-plain" level to an "in-plain" level and thus to solve the flood and silt problems simultaneously, digging a new channel by making use of depressions along the lower channel seems advisable. The famous hydrologist Wang Jing of the Eastern Han Dynasty excavated a new channel for the lower Yellow River in A.D. 70, directing the flow from Kaifeng straight east into the Bo Hai at Lijin, not far from the present river mouth. For nearly 1000 years this new "in-plain" river channel was comparatively stable and kept the flood hazard relatively small. For the present flood hazard situation, the Wang Jing solution might serve as a good example. Recently, a "two channels sandwiched between three dikes" program has been also suggested.

4. Plans should be developed to divert a part of peak floodwater to neighboring depressions so that disas-

---

[1] However, in 1952, 1955, 1974, and 1983–1987, annual sediment discharge brought to the North China Plain by the lower Yellow River decreased to 0.8–1.0 billion tons, and the lower channel bed stopped rising and even eroded away slightly.

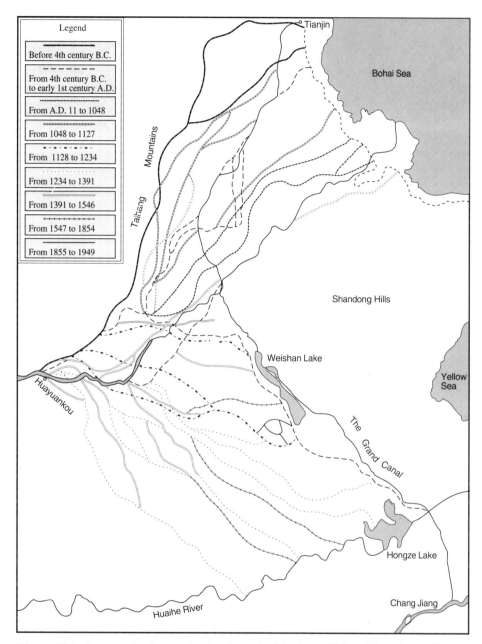

Figure 10.1 Large-scale changes in the channel of the lower Yellow River since 602 B.C.

trous breaks in dikes might be avoided and soil fertility in the flooded depressions might be improved.

5. Water and soil conservation works on the Loess Plateau should be emphasized and implemented in order to reduce the sediment discharge that comes down to the North China Plain. At present, about 95 percent of the total 1.6 billion tons of the Yellow River's annual silt sediment discharge to the North China Plain comes from the Loess Plateau.

Desiccation of Water Bodies

Many inland rivers in Northwest Arid China together with their terminal lakes have dried up in past decades. This is mainly due to ever-increasing agricultural activities in the middle and lower reaches of these inland rivers. One significant example is the lower reaches of the largest inland river in China, the Tarim River and its terminal lake, the so-called "wandering lake," Lop Nur.

Lop Nur and the Tarim River have a long evolution over historic time.

In the earliest historical records, from about the first century B.C. to A.D. 330, Lop Nur was the terminal lake of the Tarim-Konqi river system, with a water surface area of about 5000 sq km. About A.D. 330, the lower Tarim-Konqi river system shifted southeastward and emptied into a new terminal lake, Kara Koshun, while the ancient Lop Nur, together with the Loulan civilization on its northwestern bank, disappeared.

In 1921, owing to construction of a dam, the lower Tarim-Konqi rivers system flowed eastward again into the ancient Lop Nur, while the Kara Koshun dried up. The area of Lop Nur was then about 2400 sq km. In 1952, again by human intervention, the Tarim and the Konqi rivers were separated at Yuli. The Tarim turned southeastward again and emptied into the new small terminal lake of Detama, while the Konqi continued to flow eastward into a dwindling Lop Nur, which eventually dried up entirely in 1964.

In 1972, the Great West Sea Reservoir with an area of 104 sq km was built near Tikanlik. Since then, all river channels downstream as well as all terminal lakes of the Tarim-Konqi river system have dried up. Now the lake bed of Lop Nur appears like a "Great Ear" in Landsat imagery (Figure 10.2), and the area surrounding Lop Nur is now plagued by too little water and vegetation as well as too much sand and salt. An effective land restoration project is sorely needed.

In humid Eastern Monsoon China, many lakes and swamps have also dried up or greatly diminished in area as a result of large-scale agricultural use. One example is Dongting Lake in the middle reaches of the Chang Jiang, which was once the largest freshwater lake in China. It had an estimated maximum area of 14,000 sq km when the region was only slightly agriculturally developed. Dongting Lake has gradually diminshed and became very silty during the last 1000 years. By 1820 it was reduced to an area of about 6000 sq km, then to 5400 sq km by 1890, and only 4360 sq km in 1949. It now has an area of less than 2820 sq km. If effective measures are not taken, it will soon disappear.

Lowering of Groundwater Table

Recently, by overdrafting groundwater for irrigation and other uses, the lowering of the groundwater table has become quite serious in some irrigated areas. One example is the lower reaches of the Shiyang River in the eastern Hexi Corridor, where, owing to overcultivation and other misuse of irrigation water, the annual discharge of the Shiyang River decreased from more than 600 million m³ in the 1950s to less than 300 million m³ in the 1970s. The groundwater table in the Minqin oasis was lowered from about 1–3 m to more than 6–8 m beneath the ground surface. The shortage of irrigation water has become very acute since 1959, and more than one-third of the total farmland in the oasis is now underirrigated, resulting in very low and unstable yields. A considerable part of the wild shrubs and planted trees have even perished.

Another example is the North China Plain in Hebei Province, where owing to the overdraft of groundwater through extensive use of deep wells, the groundwater table has been lowered by 5–10 m in some irrigated areas. Furthermore, overtapping of groundwater in some urban areas located on alluvial coastal plains, such as Shanghai, Tianjin, Beijing, Suzhou, Hangzhou, and Ningpo, has caused localized surface collapse and sinking of the ground surface.

Tidal Waves and Tsunami

Along the coast, especially where the marine beach has been reclaimed for farmland on a large scale, the hazard of high tidal waves has been considerably increased. Along the flat, low coast in North China, tidal waves are mainly triggered by cold atmospheric fronts that occur most frequently along the Yellow River delta and Laizhou Gulf shore. On April 21–22, 1969, rising seawater invaded the Laizhou shore as far as 40 km inland. In contrast, along the rocky coast in Southeast China, tidal waves are mainly the result of strong typhoons. From A.D. 66 to 1991, there were 1687 such tidal waves. The devastating wave of July 27, 1854, in the Taizhou area of Zhejiang Province took more than 50,000 human lives.

The tsunami hazard is mainly caused by an earthquake in the neighboring sea bottom, which results in after-shock waves several dozen meters high. In Chinese historical documents, damaging tsunami waves have been recorded at least 25 times. The earliest recorded one, probably also the earliest record in the world, was reported in 47 B.C. in the Laizhou Gulf area, apparently caused by an earthquake. The most damaging one was recorded in May 22, 1781, along the west coast of Taiwan Island; it was also caused by an earthquake. The wave surge lasted 8 hours and inflicted a human death toll of more than 50,000.

Figure 10.2 Landsat image of the Lop Nur basin Xingiang Uygur Autonomous Region, 1978

Typhoons

Typhoons are one of the most significant special weather phenomena in China (as stated in Chapter One). On the average, eight strong typhoons pound the Chinese coast each year, making China one of the most typhoon-damaged countries in the world. This is essentially a natural phenomenon; there is no way to stop or avoid it. Nevertheless, as the southeastern coastal area of China is economically well developed and the population density is high, forecasting, monitoring, and protection measures are significant in lessening the damage. For example, on August 3, 1922, one strong typhoon suddenly swept through the Shantou area of Guangdong Province, taking more than 70,000 human lives. After 47 years, at about the same season and with about the same wind velocity, another typhoon swept the same area. Thanks to good monitoring and many precautionary measures, the human casualty toll was less than 1000.

Hailstorms

China is also one of the most hailstorm-damaged countries in the world. In 1987 alone, more than 2000 counties in the country reported varying degrees of hailstorm damage to a total of more than 76 million *mu* (5.1 million ha) of farmland and more than 1.08 million rooms of housing, more than 10,000 people were injured, and the death toll was more than 400 people. Hailstorms are generally most frequent in mountain areas. The high, mountainous Tibetan Plateau is consequently the most hailstorm-prone area in China. For example, Heihe (Tibet) has an average of 33.7 hailstorm days in each year, and Zage (Qinghai) averages 25.3 days.

Low Temperature and Frost

Frost damage occurs mainly in Northeast China and on the Tibetan Plateau where the annual frost-free season drops below 150 days and the accumulated temperature during $\geq 10°C$ period is below 3000°C. For example, in 1976, low temperature damage and frost caused a decrease of 4.7 million tons in food grain production in Northeast China, and in that year, this "granary" of China had a total food grain production of only 29 million tons. In southern China, these hazards inflict heavy damage on subtropical and tropical crops, such as tea, citrus fruits, and rubber trees. The lower reaches of the Chang Jiang and the Nanling Mountains area are the most seriously affected.

LAND DEGRADATION

Land degradation processes include soil erosion, desertification, salinization, and other nature-human processes that decrease land quantity and degrade land quality and fertility. In a given space and time, they are usually not as catastrophic or intense as earthquakes, typhoons, floods, and other purely natural processes, but their widespread occurrence in space and long accumulation in time make them as a whole far more devastating than the catastrophic hazards.

Soil Erosion

Soil erosion is probably the most serious land degradation problem in China. The annual soil loss caused by water erosion (not including wind erosion) totals about 5 billion tons, of which about two-fifths empty into the sea, and about three-fifths are deposited on the neighboring lowlands. In the early 1950s about 1.5 million sq km of Chinese territory were affected by soil erosion, of which about 0.4 million sq km have been more or less rehabilitated through soil conservati on measures during the last 40 years.

The Loess Plateau

This extensive area is the most notorious example of large-scale soil erosion in China, and probably also in the world. It has a total area of about 484,000 sq km, with an average erosion modulus of 3100 tons/sq km/yr. About 278,000 sq km of the Loess Plateau have been heavily eroded, and about 110,000 sq km in its northern semiarid areas are badly eroded. The soil erosion modulus ranges upward from 10,000–25,000 tons/sq km/yr, even as high as 39,000 tons/sq km/yr in local gullies. Consequently, many parts of the Loess Plateau, especially in northern semiarid areas, have been dissected into "badlands" with rugged loessic hills and gullies dominating the landscape (Figure 10.3; Color Plate 17). In recent years, the total amount of soil loss on the Loess Plateau has been around 2.2 billion tons/yr, of which about 1.6 billion tons/yr enters the Yellow River and the balance is intercepted by dams and reservoirs.

Soil erosion on the Loess Plateau can be subdivided into two types: geological (normal) and human (accelerated). Most of the geological erosion occurred before historic time and was caused by the interplay of many natural factors. The first erosion factor is the easily eroded ground surface materials, the thick-bedded loess that covers most parts of the Loess Plateau. The second factor is the concentration of annual precipitation (decreasing from 600–700 mm in subhumid southeast to 200–300 mm in semiarid and arid northwest) in the summertime (about 70 percent), which in turn is further concentrated in torrential rainstorms (about 50 percent). The third factor is the great drainage density, which has a correlation coefficient with soil erosion of 0.81. The fourth factor is the sparse vegetation cover. The semiarid steppe vegetation area in the northwestern Loess Plateau produces about 90 percent of total sediment load of the Yellow River at the Sanmenxia gauging station. It is estimated that the total geological soil erosion on the Loess Plateau might have reached 1.1 million tons/yr. in prehistoric times, or about one-half of the total present volume of eroded soil.

Accelerated soil erosion resulting from human activity has occurred in historic times. The Loess Plateau is the cradle of China's agricultural civilization. For 80 centuries millions and millions of peasants have lived on it and cultivated it. The easily eroded lands have been repeatedly misused or overused, especially by extensive cultivation and overgrazing on slopes, causing destructive soil erosion. According to recent field measurements, nonterraced farmland on a 25° loess slope produces soil erosion volume as large as 20,000 tons/sq km/yr. Consequently, the Loess Plateau has long been plagued by low agricultural production and the dire poverty of peasants, which in turn has intensified abusive overcultivation and overgrazing that causes further destructive soil erosion. An old Chinese saying goes, therefore, that "the poorer the peasant, the more loessic slopes will be ruthlessly cultivated; and the more loessic slopes are reclaimed, the poorer the peasants become."

Since the founding of the People's Republic of China in 1949, great care has been taken to promote soil conservation on the Loess Plateau, although to date, only about 100,000 sq km of heavily eroded areas have been more or less restored. A comprehensive soil-water-forest strategy and a series of engineering and biological measures have been taken.

1. Engineering measures:
   a. Slope modification, mainly by building terraces;
   b. Valley construction. Starting from the upper reaches of a river valley, a series of dams and water reservoirs have been constructed.
   c. Small-scale water conservancy construction such as irrigation ponds, underground water reservoirs, and flood irrigating-silting devices.

2. Biological measures:
   a. Soil-erosion protection can be accomplished mainly by planting trees, shrubs, and grasses on badly eroded areas.

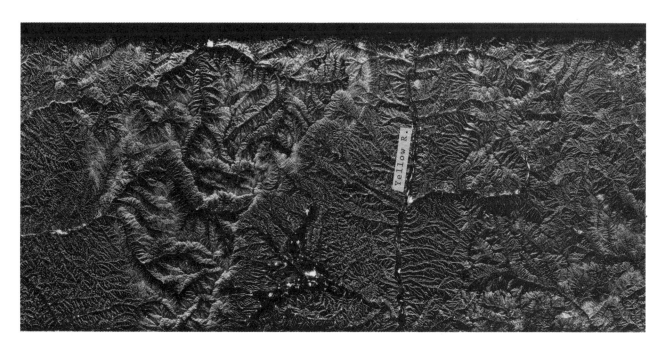

Figure 10.3 Badly dissected Loess Plateau along 30°N (Western Shanxi and northern Shaanxi). Source: Radar image, ISIR-A, Space Shuttle *Columbia*, November 1981

b. Planting tree or shrub shelter belts on farmlands and along the river channels can be useful for multiple purposes.

c. Comprehensive biological protection systems have been recently developed by the Quyu Brigade of Hegu County, Shanxi Province, on a regional scale that involves planting major tree shelter belts along the Yellow River channel, planting minor tree shelter belts on the flood plain and along the highways, and planting sand-protection forests on sandy hills and water-conservation forests on loessic hills. They have also planted shrub shelter belts on the margins of terraced farmlands and tree shelter belts on the margins of plains farmlands where grain crops are intercropped with fruits and other economically useful trees. All narrow gorges and settlement neighborhoods have been afforested and as a whole, the area has been transformed from a yellowish, sparsely vegetated badland into a green, lush mosaic.

3. Agricultural measures:

a. Increase surface roughness of farmlands to decrease sheet erosion. Deep plowing, ridge planting, hole planting, and other techniques have also been adopted.

b. Increase crop coverage to decrease gully erosion; adopt practices of intercropping, mixed cropping, and crop-grass rotation.

Central and South China Mountain Areas

The extensive mountain areas south of the Qinling–Huaihe line that are under humid tropical and subtropical climatic conditions and are also under heavy human impacts have been subject to severe soil erosion. It is estimated that the total soil loss in the upper reaches of the Chang Jiang during the last 40 years has increased from 1.3 billion to 1.57 billion tons/yr. At the Yichang Hydrological Station, Hubei Province, the average silt load of the Chang Jiang was 0.52 billion tons from 1950 to 1978, but it increased to 0.63 billion tons from 1980 to 1985. Some people even talk about Chang Jiang's being turned into "a second Yellow River" in the near future.

The granite mountaihs in South China are especially susceptible to weathering and erosion. One example is the Wuhua Territorial Management Station, Guangdong Province. Out of its total area of 23.47 sq km the granite mountain area occupies 15.93 sq km, of which about 66 percent is subject to severe soil erosion, includ-

ing 6.15 sq km in sheet erosion, 2.48 sq km in gully erosion, and 1.83 sq km in landslides. A series of soil conservation measures, both engineering and biological, have been effectively undertaken.

Another example is the granite Shenchong Basin of Deqing County, Guangdong Province, where detailed field studies have been recently conducted and instrumented by the joint China-Canada Soil Erosion Project (1987–1990). The sediment yield measured as high as 9426 tons/sq km/yr.

The key to combating soil erosion in the Central and Southern China mountain areas is to use the land according to its specific slope conditions.

A good example of soil conservation on a regional scale is in Pingnan county, Guangxi Zhuang Autonomous Region, where a 15-year (1986–2000) overall Vertical Agriculture Development Plan has been undertaken with good results both in promoting sustainable agricultural production and in effectively combating soil erosion. This county has a population of about 1 million people and a total area of about 3.0 million *mu* (0.2 million ha) distributed on either sides of the middle West River (Xi Jiang) and located roughly along the Tropic of Cancer. From mountain top to valley bottom, five vertical agriculture zones are identified (Figure 10.4).

1. *Montane forest conservation zone:* With a total area of about 1.5 million *mu* (0.1 million ha), and located mainly on mountain slopes above 200 m in elevation, this area is suitable for afforestation (pine, fir, etc.) for the purpose of soil and water conservation and timber production.

2. *Hilly economic tree zone:* With a total area of about 0.6 million *mu* (0.04 million ha) and located mainly on sloping lands between 50–200 m in elevation, this area is suitable for growing fruit and other economically useful trees such as lizhi, longan, mango, tea, and oranges.

3. *Rain-fed farming economic crops zone:* With a total area of about 0.3 million *mu* (0.02 million ha) and located mainly on gentle slopes and valley floors below 200 m in elevation, this area is suitable chiefly for highly productive economic crops such as sugar cane, tobacco, mulberry trees, and hemp. Great care must be taken to follow soil conservation measures in farming these lands.

4. *Paddy rice zone:* With a total area of about half a million *mu* (0.03 million ha) and located mainly along the valley floor below 50 m in elevation, this

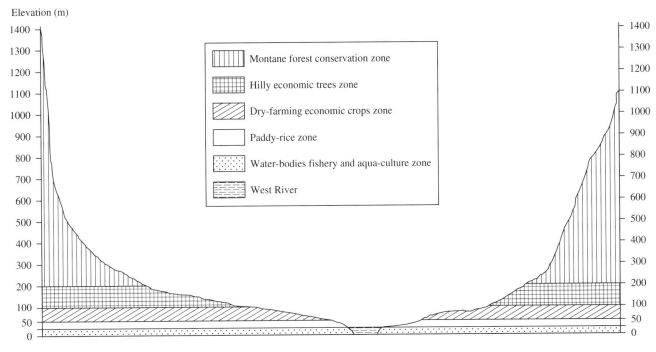

Elevation (m)

Montane forest conservation zone

Hilly economic trees zone

Dry-farming economic crops zone

Paddy-rice zone

Water-bodies fishery and aqua-culture zone

West River

Figure 10.4 Vertical structure of agricultural zones in Pingnan County, Guangxi Zhuang Autonomous Region

area is the food base for the whole county. Very intensive farming systems are employed, including double cropping of paddy rice.

5. *Fishery and aqua-culture zone:* There are about 120,000 *mu* (8,000 ha) of terrestrial water surface in the county, of which about one-half are occupied by rivers, chiefly used for irrigation and transportation. The other half includes reservoirs and ponds usable for fisheries and aqua-culture.

New Land Reclamation Areas in Heilongjiang Province

This so-called Great Northern Wilderness has been gradually transformed into the "Great Northern Granary" during the last 100 years. From 1897 through 1976, the area of farmland in Heilongjiang Province has expanded more than 1600 times and continues to increase at a high rate. The terrain is flat or undulating, consisting mainly of the Northeast China Plain. Most soils are fertile chernozem and black earth, usually with a dark upper layer 50–100 cm deep. It is now one of the largest commercial grain-producing areas in China. The newly reclaimed farmlands are mostly situated on loessic, gentle slopes where soil erosion has been rather severe. According to an estimate, about one-half of the total

farmland area in Heilongjiang Province has been subject to soil erosion, half of which has been rather severe. The slightly dark upper soil layer originally was 60–70 cm deep on gently sloping lands (generally 3°–7°), which might now be reduced to only 20–30 cm deep after 40–50 years of cultivation. Some farmlands have even had their loessic parent materials exposed. Hence, a recent soil conservation project has been to move farmlands downward to depressed meadows and floodplains while at the same time moving the planting of forest and grassland upwards to hill slopes.

Shifting Sand and Desertification

Shifting sand, together with drought, salinization, and other hazards, have caused serious desertification in Northwest Arid China, which has plagued the region for more than 1000 years, but particularly during the last 100 years. It is estimated that due to shifting sand alone, about 120,000 sq km of land became desert during historic times and another 50,000 sq km during the past 100 years. The desertification process is not as serious in arid lands as in semiarid lands. In arid lands, where farming is entirely dependent on irrigation, human activities are mainly restricted to small patches of oases, while in semiarid lands where rain-fed farming is possible but very precarious, critical environmental changes are caused by the interplay between a fragile physical environment and the heavy impacts of a growing population dependent on agricultural activities.

The Ordos Plateau

The Mu Us sandy land on the southeastern part of the semiarid Ordos Plateau has been the most notorious example of the southward march of *shamo* (sandy desert) in China (Figure 10.5). Environmental changes in the Mu Us sandy land have been very significant during historical time.

Before the Tang Dynasty (A.D. 618–907), the Mu Us sandy land offered a much more favorable physical environment, possibly because it was a vast tract of bush grassland with scattered patches of swamp jungle (*Rhamanus erythroxylon*, *Salix mongolica*, etc.). The use

of the region was mainly pastoral. In A.D. 413 the Xia Kingdom established the city of Tongfan (now known as the White City ruins in northern Chenpian District, Shaanxi Province) with a population of about 200,000 as its capital. According to historical documents, lush grassland and meadow grew in its suburbs, and rivers were clear.

Since the middle Tang Dynasty, ever-increasing human activities caused the desertification process to begin. For example, wind-blown sands began to deposit around the Tongfan suburbs about A.D. 828; when the city was finally destroyed in A.D. 904, the area had been largely transformed into shifting sand.

In A.D. 1473, the modern Great Wall was built along the southern margin of the Mu Us sandy land and served to demarcate pastoral from farming areas. Large patches of shifting sand appeared in the farming areas. In

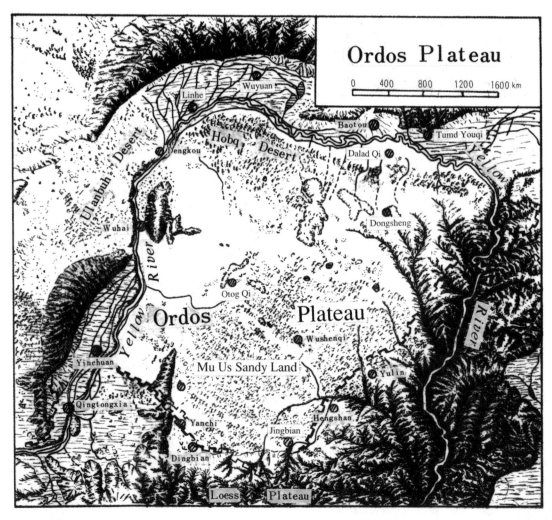

Figure 10.5   Deserts in the bend of the Yellow River (Drawn by Su Yingping)

the mid-nineteenth century, the Qing government (1644–1911) attempted to open the Mongolian "wasteland." As a result, large tracts of sandy lands in the southeastern Ordos Plateau were ruthlessly cultivated, which resulted in the devastation of grassland and the encroachment of shifting sand. Subsequently, the line dividing pastoral and farming areas moved northward to the present provincial boundary between Shaanxi and Inner Mongolia, while along the Great Wall, a 60 km wide belt of shifting sands has been formed over a period of about 300 years (from middle Ming Dynasty to late Qing Dynasty).

After the founding of the People's Republic of China in 1949, great efforts were undertaken in the 1950s to combat this desertification process. A network of tree shelter belts and sand protection was established in the southeastern part of the Mu Us sandy land. Rivers were even diverted to flow through and wash down the shifting sandy dunes to create new farmlands. For a short period the Mu Us sandy land did stop marching southward, and retreated northward instead.

Then came the Great Leap Forward and Cultural Revolution. Local pastoral inhabitants were compelled to cultivate the sandy grassland on a large scale. Large patches of lush grassland were converted into badly managed rain-fed farmlands, only to be abandoned and reduced to barren wastelands after a few years of cultivation. Such ruthless agricultural activities also caused neighboring pasturelands to deteriorate or even to be destroyed on a large scale. A field observation estimated that for each hectare of reclaimed farmland, at least three hectares of good grassland would be devastated.[2] Consequently, shifting sands extended both southward and northward. The southern border has now encroached upon the northern margin of the Loess Plateau, while the northern border has nearly merged with the Hobq Desert on the northern margin of the Ordos Plateau.

Since 1978, great efforts have been undertaken to harness the Mu Us sandy land. The key is to make better use of different land types in accordance with their specific suitability and capability. The desertification process is being checked and the oasis-making (de-desertification) process is asserting itself.

Shapotou Area

Since the desertification process is chiefly triggered and accelerated by negative human impacts on fragile arid environments, the key to combating it is good manage-

ment. Effective natural conservation programs ensure that all shifting sands are essentially fixed by water and vegetation, so that eolian erosion and deposition are prevented. However, when desertification hazards have already been triggered, both engineering and biological measures are needed. Comprehensive land use planning, based on specific local conditions and areal differentiation is necessary. For example, in the Shapotou area of Ningxia, located at the southeastern margin of the Tengger Desert and traversed by the Baotou–Lanzhou Railway, a "prevention-detention-fixation-transportation" control system was devised. The shifting sands were so effectively controlled that no accidents due to shifting sand has occurred since that busy railway began operation in 1956.

1. **Prevention:** On the surrounding borderland of the railway, a conservation program is strictly observed deep into the Tengger Desert, so that loose, shifting sand is reduced or prevented.

2. **Detention:** On the margin of the oasis, a tree and shrub shelter belt is planted for sand protection or detention, so that shifting sands from the Tengger Desert are kept outside the oasis.

3. **Fixation:** Inside the oasis, on either side of the railway (500 m wide on the northwestern windward side and 200 m wide on the southeastern leeward side), networks of checkerboards made from straw or grass, usually 1 m by 1 m in size are established. Drought-tolerant shrubs are planted in the center of each checkerboard square, so that all sand is essentially fixed (see Color Plate 28).

4. **Transportation:** On the roadbed of the railway, a flat, smooth surface is built, so that all shifting sands, if any, will not be deposited, but will be blown away.

Salinization

Most salinization is a result of low topography together with frequent waterlogging of highly mineralized groundwater and a high evaporation rate. Hence, the worst salinization occurs in the inland basins and along the sea-coast. Overirrigation without adequate drainage is the largest contributor to secondary salinization of farmland. About one-fifth of China's 100 million ha of farmland is estimated to be more or less affected by salinization. For example, in oases along the middle and lower Tarim River, more than 15,000 to 225,000 cu m/ha of irrigation water are used annually without any drainage. Thus, not only is a huge amount of precious

---

[2]According to Prof. Chen Lon-hun of Lanzhou Institute of Desert Research, Chinese Academy of Sciences.

water wasted, but also huge amounts of harmful salts are deposited on the cropland.

Another notorious example is the Back Elbow Plain along the middle reaches of the Yellow River. Within an area of about 0.2 million ha, all farmlands are irrigated but about 50.2 percent have been salinized. Of 4 million cu m of irrigation water used, only 5 percent is naturally drained, leaving a deposit of 0.8 to 1.6 million tons of salts each year even though the major irrigation water source, the Yellow River, has a mineralization level of only 0.2–0.4 percent.

Good management of irrigation water is the key to controlling secondary salinization, but drainage is an indispensable part of an irrigation system. Drainage canals can lower groundwater tables, thereby preventing salinization. In the West Elbow (Yinchuan) Plain, a drainage ditch 2.5 m deep lowers the groundwater table of a belt 200 m wide on each side by 10–30 cm. It is also important to "wash" saline soils, so that soluble salts can be leached out. In newly reclaimed saline farmlands, if irrigation water is abundant (as it is in the Yinchuan Plain), paddy rice can be grown during the first two or three years to leach out soluble salts. Other desalinization measures include deep plowing, strip farming, cultivation of green manure and salt-tolerant crops, mixing loose sand with sticky saline soils, and irrigating sandy soil with low-saline water.

On the coastal North China Plain, the interplay of natural conditions and human impacts also creates a serious salinization problem. The critical groundwater table for salinization in the North China Plain is about 2.5 m below the ground surface. Hence, saline soils are mainly concentrated in alluvial depressions (where the groundwater table is 1.5–2.5 m below the surface) and along the seacoast (less than 1.0 m). In the late 1950s and early 1960s, salinization severely reduced the productivity of more than 4 million ha of cropland on the North China Plain. Since then, an improved irrigation-drainage system has been developed and the groundwater regime has been modified by deep wells, so that the groundwater table has been lowered in many localities. The area of salinized land has now been reduced to less than 3 million ha.

GEOLOGICAL AND GEOMORPHOLOGICAL HAZARDS

As China is a mountainous country with complex geological structures (see Chapter One), the potential danger from geomorphological hazards (mountain land-slides) and geological hazards (mainly earthquakes) is widespread.

Mountain Hazards

China is not only a mountainous country, but also one of frequent rainstorms and earthquakes. Extensive mountain areas have been deforested or overgrazed. Chinese peasants have built numerous terraced farmlands on mountain slopes, and steep slopes of more than 25° are often used without terracing for rain-fed farming. Little attention has been paid to tree crops, forestry, and environmental protection. Consequently, mountain disasters occur frequently and extensively. Examples are the catastrophic rock-mud flows in mountain areas almost all over China, especially on the margins of the first and second great topographic steps. According to incomplete statistics, more than 100 counties and more than 10 mining sites in the country have been damaged by rock-mud flows, which result in thousands of human causalities and billions of yuan in property loss. The Small River basin of northeastern Yunnan Province is especially notorious for its rainstorms that trigger more than 100 rock-mud flows each year.

Slope-slips and landslides (avalanches) also occur frequently in many mountain areas. They are usually triggered by heavy rainstorms or severe earthquakes. An extreme case happened on August 25, 1933, in western Sichuan Province when an earthquake triggered a large-scale, high-speed slope-slip, throwing all of Maowen city from a 100 m high terrace headlong into the Min River, killing 8800 people.

The optimal land use pattern in mountain areas as well as the best strategy for combating mountain hazards is vertical agriculture, which is characterized by vertical zonal distribution of land use types, each of which is adjusted to its specific ecological environment. In this arrangement, its productivity is sustainable and relatively free from natural hazards. For example, the vertical agriculture system in the southeastern Hengduan Mountains is generally composed (from intermontane valley upward to mountain top) of four broad land use zones.

Farming and Multiple-use Zone

This zone is located mainly in intermontane dry valleys, which with a total area of 11,200 sq km, are widely scattered along the valley bottoms of the Jinsha (upper reaches of the Chang Jiang), the Lancang (Mekong River), the Nu (Salween River), and other large rivers. They are generally less than 2000–2500 m in elevation and receive less than 1000 mm of annual precipitation (due to the "rain-shadow" effect). Cultivated lands are mainly located intermittently on diluvial fans, on river terraces, and on gentle slopes occupying about 16 percent of the total land area. Rain-fed farming dominates, with wheat, corn, and small grains comprising the chief crops, which are usually double or triple cropped each year. About one-fifth of the farmland is irrigated for paddy rice. Chief livestock species in animal husbandry are pigs, chickens, cattle, sheep, and goats. However, fisheries are also maintained. The piedmont belt and lower gentle slopes are the best sites for developing orchards of oranges, apples, pears, chestnuts, walnuts, and other fruits.

Forestry Zone

Forests are widely distributed immediately above the dry valleys up to the tree line (about 4400 m in elevation on northern slopes and 4000 m on southern slopes). This is the second largest timber-producing region in China, but because of overexploitation and ruthless destruction for several hundred years, forests occupy only one-fourth of the total land area now. Since 1949, in the upper reaches of the Nu River, forest coverage has decreased from 30 percent to 18 percent. Environmental protection and soil conservation measures are urgently needed in this vertical zone.

Transhumance Zone

Transhumance animal husbandry is practiced on alpine shrub meadows above the tree line, up to the snow line (about 5400 m in elevation). In the wintertime, flocks are fed on farm stubble and shrub vegetation in the dry valleys. In the spring and autumn, sheep, yak, and other livestock move up and feed on the scattered montane grassland. The higher the elevation, the larger the proportion of yak in the flocks. During the summertime, alpine shrub meadows are heavily used for pasture.

Snow Zone

Above the snow line thrust the majestic snow-clad peaks and ridges. They are called the "solid water reservoir" for the neighboring rivers. They might also be used as a recreation ground, inasmuch as the mighty Gongga Mountain (7566 m) has already become famous for such a function (Color Plate 32).

Earthquakes

Most of China's frequent earthquakes are determined by geologic fault structures. The most devastating earth-

quake ever recorded in the world occurred in China. At midnight on January 23, 1556, an earthquake measuring 8.0 on the Richter scale devastated Hua County of Shaanxi Province, with a death toll of 830,000. In 1976, another disastrous earthquake of 7.9 on the Richter scale demolished the city of Tangshan (population 1 million), killing more than 250,000. According to recent statistics, since 1901, 650 earthquakes above 6 on the Richter scale have occurred in China.

Like typhoons, earthquakes are essentially a natural phenomenon, and there is no way to stop or to avoid such disasters. An earthquake is even worse than a typhoon, because it is very hard to predict and to monitor. Little or no warning can be given; hence much heavier damage occurs. However, the earthquake damage is caused less by earthquake itself than by the lack of earthquake-proofing measures. For example, the enormous number of human causalties of the 1556 earthquake was mainly caused by the collapse of loessic cave houses and the starvation that followed. However, although earthquakes are difficult to predict and to monitor in the short or medium term, they can be predicted in the long term, and thus heavy damage might be avoided. For example, the Tangshan metropolitan area is located at the junction of several deep fault lines. Thus, severe earthquakes are bound to happen in this area at certain intervals, although the exact time is difficult to tell. The best precaution is to avoid rebuilding the metropolitan area in the same location and to the same standards of construction. Unfortunately—and dangerously—the city of Tangshan, with its metropolitan population of 1 million, has already been rebuilt on the same site.

BIOLOGICAL ENVIRONMENTAL PROBLEMS

Biological environmental problems have resulted from two contradictory situations: one is "too little," such as deforestation and fauna extinction; the other is "too much," such as harmful plants and animals.

Deforestation and Forest Fires

Deforestation has been a very serious environmental problem in China. It has generally matched the spread of farming and the increase in population. Judging from China's physical conditions, supported by historical documents, forests might have occupied about 40 percent of the total land area (about 80 percent of Eastern Monsoon China, about 5 percent of Northwest Arid

China, and about 10 percent of the Tibetan Frigid Plateau) before the spread of agricultural civilization. Today, however, China is a poorly wooded country with forests accounting for less than 13 percent of the total land area. Scarcity of timber resources is one of the most acute economic problems in China. Since 1949, considerable reforestation has taken place, and the success in planting "plain forest" has been quite significant (see Chapter Three). Yet, in the major timber-producing areas, such as the Greater Hinggan Mountains and Lesser Hinggan Mountains in Northeast China, and the Hengduan Mountains in the southeastern Tibetan Plateau, logging areas are still greater than newly forested areas by a ratio of 3:1.

Forest fires are another calamity in the timber-producing regions. The unusually devastating forest fire in the northern Hinggan Mountains from May 2–5, 1987, burned 1.33 million ha of woodland.

Fauna Extinction

Similar to, and closely related to, deforestation, fauna extinction has become a major environmental problem in China. Many wild animals and birds have been exterminated or nearly exterminated. One example is David's deer (*Elaphurus davidianuus*), which was widely distributed on the North China Plain and the lower Chang Jiang valley during the Pleistocene and early Holocene. As forests were cleared and swamps dried up, deer populations were gradually eliminated. In 1900, they disappeared entirely from China.[3] Another example is wild cattle in the Qilian Mountains. One scholar in the Qing Dynasty (1644–1911) described seeing wild cattle roaming in the mountain area by the thousands, but now all have been exterminated, leaving behind only such "fossil" place-names as Yeniu ("Wild Cattle") Mountains and Yeniu Ravine.

Distribution areas of many more animal species have been restricted or isolated. For example, in Eastern Monsoon China, the panda (*Ailuropoda melanoleuca*), squirrel (*Sciurus vulgaris*), monkeys (*Macaca mulatta, Rhinopithecus spp.*) and other forest-dwelling animals have had their habitats greatly diminished as forest areas have been dramatically reduced. In Northwest Arid China and the Tibetan Frigid Plateau, hundreds of thousands of wild goats (*Procarpa gutterosa, P. picticaudata, Gazella subgutterosa*, etc.) wild deer (*Moschus spp.*), wild ass (*Equus hemonius*), wild horse (*E. przewalski*), and

wild camels (*Camelus bactrianus*) have been killed during the past few hundred years. Some of these species have been brought nearly to the point of extinction.

Harmful Fauna

Locusts are probably the most harmful species of fauna. More than 10,000 species of locust are known in the world, of which more than 800 species have been found in China, and more than 60 species have inflicted considerable damage to agricultural production. The East Asian flying locust is particularly devastating. According to incomplete statistics, during the past 2600 years (before 1949), there were more than 800 locust plagues. The North China Plain has usually been the worst affected. The locust hazard has usually been closely related to droughts and floods.

The most hideous animal is probably the rat, which is not only harmful to agriculture (including the wasteful consumption of farm products and the severe destruction of grassland and forestland), but is also dangerous to human health. There are 186 species of rodents in China, of which more than 20 are harmful rats. Two areas are especially subject to heavy damage. One is the farming area in Eastern Monsoon China where large amounts of farm products are wasted. The other is the extensive pastoral area in Northwest Arid China and the Tibetan Frigid Plateau where large grassland areas have been almost entirely destroyed by rats. Hence, on the Mongolian Plateau, rats, together with wolves and snowstorms, are considered to be the three greatest natural hazards.

Large carnivorous animals (including the wolf, tiger, and leopard) and many kinds of poisonous snakes have done great harm to humans and livestock since ancient times. With the gradual clearing of lush forest and swamp vegetation and the rapid increase in population and settlements, harm from carnivorous animals and poisonous snakes has gradually been lessened. Some harmful animals, such as the tiger, have now even become protected endangered species and have been preserved in natural reserves. Wolves, however, still inflict havoc on human life and livestock in the extensive pastoral areas of China.

Harmful Flora

In China's extensive pastoral area, several kinds of poisonous grasses exist, which have caused considerable havoc to livestock. The most notorious and the most widely distributed is horse-drunken grass or intestine-

---

[3]Very recently, a few David's deer were reintroduced from western European zoos to some Chinese zoological gardens.

broken grass, which if grazed, kills the livestock immediately. In the semiarid grassland, the more overgrazed the pasture, the more poisonous grasses will grow, sometimes even dominating the plant community. Furthermore, many kinds of weeds and some recently imported feed crops have created problems in the extensive farming area.

ENVIRONMENTAL POLLUTION AND GLOBAL CHANGES

Environmental problems that are the result of large-scale human actions and global environmental changes include environmental pollution, acid rain, global warming, and sea-level change. Many of these problems have recently been the subject of public concern and have been heatedly discussed by many of the world's leading scientists and knowledgeable public figures.

Environmental Pollution

Recently, as a consequence of rapid industrialization and urbanization as well as the large increase in energy consumption, China has suffered from "three wastes" (waste air, wastewater, waste materials). Now, environmental pollution problems have started to appear and are growing in some urban areas.

Water Pollution

According to a preliminary study in 1985, annual wastewater totaled 32.7 billion tons in China that year, of which about 80 percent drained directly from the industrial urban areas into nearby rivers and lakes, essentially without being purified. Consequently, some sections of these rivers and lakes have become polluted and the water quality is degraded. The pollutants are chiefly organic materials but mercury, cadmium, and other metals are present. The more heavily polluted areas are the industrialized regions in Northeast and North China where precipitation is not sufficient to dilute or aid in the disintegration and dispersal of the pollutants.

Air Pollution

According to official statistics, from 1980 to 1985, the total amount of industrial products in China increased by 65 percent, and coal consumption increased by 34 percent. Such increases have continued since 1985 at an even faster rate. Hence, particulates in coal smoke and sulfur dioxide emissions have recently caused serious air pollution hazards in many industrialized urban and suburban areas. Air pollution is quite serious especially in areas where the mountains encircle large urbanized areas that are crowded with heavy industries such as Lanzhou, Taiyuan, and Taibei.

Some recent scientific reports have analyzed and discussed the frequent occurrence of acid rain in the Chongqing, Guiyang, and other urban areas in Southwest China where the Third Line industrialized areas are located. Data show that the Ph value of raindrops might be as low as 3.5 to 3.7.

Soil Pollution

According to an estimate, China has now about 13 million ha of farmland irrigated directly by wastewater without being purified. Portions of these farmlands have shown symptoms of pollution by mercury, cadmium, and other heavy metals. This wastewater originates mainly from industrialized areas in Northeast and North China.

Sea-level Change

China has a continental coastline of more than 18,000 km. More than 70 percent of its large cities and more than 55 percent of its national income are concentrated along the coastal zone. Consequently, any change in sea level (whether positive or negative) will invariably have great significance for China's social and economic conditions. According to a recent estimate, the level of China's neighboring seas has risen more than 10 cm during last 100 years.

REFERENCES

Dregne, H. E. (ed.). 1992. *Degradation and Restoration of Arid Lands.* Lubbock, TX: ICASALS, Texas Tech University.

Jing, Ke. 1988. "A Study of the Relationship between Soil Erosion and the Geographical Environment in the Middle Yellow River Basin," *Chinese Journal of Arid Land Research* 1 No. 4: 289–300.

Lo, Chuyun, Sun, Sung, and Chen, Yongzong. 1988. *Physical Conditions of the Loess Plateau.* Xi'an: Shaanxi People's Press (in Chinese).

Southern China Mountain Areas Integrated Scientific Investigation Team, Chinese Academy of Sciences. 1990. *Land Rehabilitation in the Mountain Areas of Southern China.* Beijing: Science Press (in Chinese).

Sun, Guangzhong, et al. (eds.). 1990. *Natural Hazards in China*. Beijing: Academic Publishers (in Chinese).

Tang, Bangxing, and Wu, Jishan. 1990. "Mountain Natural Hazards Dominated by Debris Flow and Their Control," *Recent Development of Geographical Science in China*. Beijing: Science Press.

University of Toronto and Guangzhou Institute of Geography. 1990. *Soil Erosion and Land Management in the Granitic Region of Guangdong Province, South China*. Toronto: University of Toronto, The IDRC Soil Erosion Project (China Project).

Xiong, Yi, et al. (eds.). 1987. *Soils of China*, 2nd ed. Beijing: Science Press (in Chinese and English).

Zhang, Hualing, and Wang, Pinsheng. 1988. *Regionalization of Forestry in China*. Beijing: Chinese Forestry Press (in Chinese).

Zhang, Shen, and Tang, Yijian. 1990. "Environmental Pollution and Its Control in China," *Recent Development of Geographical Science in China*. Beijing: Science Press.

Zhao, Songqiao. 1986. *Physical Geography of China*. New York: Wiley.

Zhao, Songqiao. 1988. "Human Impacts on China's Arid Land: Desertification or De-desertification?" *Arid Lands: Today and Tomorrow*. Tucson: University of Arizona, pp. 1127–1135.

Zhao, Songqiao. 1985. "Drifting Sand Hazard and Its Control in Northwest Arid China," *Annual of Arid Zones (India)* 24, No. 3: 180–190.

Zhao, Songqiao (Chao Sung-chiao). 1981. "Transforming Wilderness into Farmland: An Evaluation of Natural Conditions for Agricultural Development in Heilongjiang Province," *China Geographer* 2: 41–56.

Zhao, Songqiao. 1988. *Natural Conditions and Territorial Management in the North China Plain*. Tokyo: National Institute for Research Advancement (in English and Japanese).

Zhao, Songqiao. 1985. "Physical Features and Economic Development of China's Mountain Environment," *Mountain Research and Development* 5, No. 4: 319–328.

Zhao, Songqiao, and Xia, Xuncheng. 1984. "Evolution of the Lop Desert and the Lop Nor," *The Geographical Journal* 150, No. 3: 311–321.

Zhao, Songqiao, et al. 1990. *Vertical Agricultural Systems in the Hengduan Mountains and in the Qilian Mountains of the Tibetan Plateau: A Comparative Study*. Kathmandu, Nepal: International Centre for Integrated Mountain Development.

Zhao, Songqiao (ed.). 1985. *Physical Geography of China's Arid Lands*. Beijing: Science Press (in Chinese).

Zhu, Zhenda, and Liu, Shu. 1988. "Desertification Processes and Their Control in Northern China," *Chinese Journal of Arid Land Research* 1, No. 1. 27–36.

CHAPTER ELEVEN

The Land–Food–Population System

Any country has two basic components: land (territory) and population (people). Land denotes the integration of all physical elements (climate, landforms, water, soil, vegetation, fauna, and so on) as well as all natural resources. Arable land resources are especially important for an agricultural country like China. A country's population includes the ethnic groups as well as the growth, distribution, and structure of all the human elements. These two basic component factors are linked and interrelated through economic development, especially food production for an agricultural country, as in an old Chinese saying: "Food is the Heaven [first necessity] of the people." Throughout history, many peasant uprisings and much political unrest started from food shortages and starvation. Therefore, the land–food–population system is the core of the environment–resource–population–development system in China. Obviously, in such a system, population is generally the most active factor.

Because the problem is so significant and so complex, and any interpretation or prediction is always risky, this chapter can only be a very preliminary discussion, which represents only my personal observation and opinion. Much more research work needs to be done, and this chapter should need revision in the near future.

PRESENT CRITICAL CONDITION

As we have seen, development of the land–food–population system in China has been a limited success. With less than 7 percent of the world's total farmland China supports more than 22 percent of the world's total population. To date, the nightmare of starvation, which had haunted the country very frequently during historic times, has disappeared under normal conditions. Yet, the system is now in a marginal, or even critical, condition. China can barely feed its huge population at a low nutrition level. In recent years, China has had to import 10–15 million tons of food each year, making it the second largest food importer in the world (second only to the former Soviet Union). On the average, food imports for each person amount to only about 10 kilograms annually. Using the annual per capita GNP as an index, China is notably one of the poorest countries in the world, reaching only U.S. $50–200 from 1950 to 1980, and only U.S. $200–300 in the 1980s, and about U.S. $300 in 1990.[1] Thus in addition to the ability to purchase foreign food, there are several additional major constraints for land–food–population development.

Population Growth

Total Population

China's population has continued to grow rapidly since 1953, and in spite of the practice of family planning, continued to grow in the 1980s. China's total population exceeded 0.6 billion in 1954, 0.7 billion in 1964, 0.8 billion in 1969, 0.9 billion in 1974, 1.0 billion in 1981, 1.1 billion in 1988, and will soon exceed 1.2 billion (probably in 1994). The total population has

---

[1] Owing to the ever-changing official exchange rate between yuan and U.S. $, it is rather difficult to measure China's per capita GNP in U.S. $. According to *Statistical Yearbook of China, 1991*, China's per capita GNP in 1989 reached 1178 yuan, equal to U.S. $313 by the official exchange rate of 3.76:1; while in 1990, it was 1271 yuan, equal to U.S. $266 by the official exchange rate of 4.77:1.

usually increased by 15–20 million each year. Consequently, the impact of so many people on the limited land and other resources becomes increasingly heavier. For example, per capita farmland has decreased from 2.7 *mu* (0.18 ha) in 1949 to 1.8 *mu* (0.12 ha) in 1971, to 1.5 *mu* (0.10 ha) in 1980, and to merely 1.3 *mu* (0.08 ha) in 1990.

Population Distribution

China's national average population density reached 106 persons/sq km in 1982 and 119 persons/sq km in 1990, more than three times the world average. Furthermore, the population is very unevenly distributed, with Eastern Monsoon China supporting more than 250 persons/sq km on the average while the Tibetan Frigid Plateau has less than 5 persons/sq km. In the densely populated coastal plains (the North China Plain, the Chang Jiang Delta, etc.), the average population density reached more than 500 persons/sq km, while large patches in Northwest Arid China and on the Tibetan Frigid Plateau are practically uninhabited. Such an uneven distribution of population makes many areas crowded with too many people, which leads to overuse and degradation of land, while some remote regions are short of human resources for economic development.

Population Structure

Sex and Age Since 1982, the population age and sex pyramid has shown the characteristics of a mature population. In 1981, the number of Chinese women of child-bearing age totaled more than 248 million and the general fertility level stood at 83.34 per thousand women of child-bearing age. The population growth peak of the 1964–1973 period led to an unusually large number of women of child-bearing age, which will in turn lead to a second peak of population growth in the late 1980s and 1990s. The percentage of elderly people has also started to increase rapidly since the late 1980s. In 1990, the number of people above 60 years old constituted about 8.6 percent of China's total population.

Employment Since ancient times, more than 80 percent of China's total employment has been in agriculture. In the 1982 population census, among China's total employed population, those in agriculture still made up 73.77 percent of the work force (70.62 percent in 1990). In recent years, modern large-scale industries and rural small-scale industries as well as other secondary and tertiary enterprises have rapidly developed, so that the percentage of people in agriculture has decreased. Yet, the natural increase among rural people engaged in agriculture still far outpaces those subtracted. The population engaged in agriculture has continued to grow rapidly, exerting greater and greater stress on arable land resources and also resulting in a reduced amount of farmland that each farmer works (about 0.21 ha in 1949, 0.15 ha in 1971, 0.13 ha in 1980, and only 0.10 ha in 1990). Recent estimates indicate that farmers as a whole spend one-third or even one-half of their time without adequate work.

Education For a long time after the Great Leap Forward and Cultural Revolution, people had little respect for science and education. Consequently, the national educational level has fallen. Evidence for this is that according to the 1982 census, 31.87 percent of the population was illiterate or semiliterate. In the rural, mountain, and border areas it is estimated that this figure might be much higher. Illiteracy is certainly a great negative factor for population quality and for economic development. Only very recently did the slogan appear, "Science and technology is the first production force," indicating that education has been gradually popularized.

Land Resources

China is a mountainous country. In the current land use pattern, farmland occupies only 10.7 percent of the total land area. Nor is the unused arable land resource extensive. According to an estimate in 1980, there were only about 46.7 million ha of unused arable land, some of which were reclaimed in the 1980s and at current rates would be practically all cultivated in the 1990s.

Since 1949, a large amount of good farmland has been taken over by nonagricultural use each year. Since 1958, total farmland has continually decreased, although new farmland has been cultivated each year. In the 1980s, 0.1 to 0.3 million ha of farmland were lost each year. In a country of more than 1.1 billion people and nearly 1 billion farmers, there were in 1990 only 95.7 million ha of farmland and 148.4 million ha of sown area (counting the one-half of the total farmland that is double or even triple-cropped).

The extensive grassland, forest, and terrestrial water bodies have been little (or not efficiently) used for producing food. Owing to overuse and misuse of land resources, land degradation problems (such as soil erosion, desertification, and salinization) are widespread and serious.

Food Production

Since 1949, and especially since 1978, China's food grain production has increased rapidly from 113.4 million tons in 1949, to 163.9 million tons in 1952, to 318.2 million tons 1980, to 353.4 million tons in 1982, then to 402.4 million tons in 1987, and recently to 446.2 million tons in 1990. Since 1949, the per land unit yield has also increased rapidly, from 68.5 kg/*mu* (1027.5 kg/ha) in 1949 to 182.5 kg/*mu* (2737.5 kg/ha) in 1980, to 209 kg/*mu* (3135 kg/ha) in 1982, to 241 kg/*mu* (3615 kg/ha) in 1987, and to 262.2 kg/*mu* (3973 kg/ha) in 1990. It seems that under the traditional peasant-gardener farming system and the present responsibility policy, it will be rather difficult to increase food production any more on a large scale. More sophisticated policies and technologies are needed.

Locational or areal differentiation of food grain production (especially commercial food grains) is quite conspicuous. So far as the productivity of farmland is concerned, three categories of farmland are broadly defined: (1) high-grade farmland, with a per land unit annual yield of more than 400 kg/*mu* (6 tons/ha), and as high as 1 ton/*mu* (15 tons/ha) in some favorable localities (such as the Shanghai suburbs); (2) medium-grade farmland, generally with an annual yield of 200–400 kg/*mu* (3–6 tons/ha) ; and (3) low-grade farmland, generally with an annual yield below 100–200 kg/*mu* (1.5–3.0 tons/ha). Each of these three categories occupies about one-third of China's total farmland. Under present scientific and technical levels, the first category probably has little more capacity for higher yields, while the second and the third categories still have a large margin of potential.

About 40 percent of China's total commercial grains come from 15 commercial production bases (in the Northeast China Plain, middle and lower Chang Jiang valley, Sichuan Basin, Wei River Plain, Elbow Plains, Hexi Corridor; see Chapter Four) where about 20 percent of China's total agriculture-engaged population lives.

One big problem in China's food production is the very low level of production per farm labor hour. It is estimated that the Chinese still depend on about 1200 hours/ha of manual labor, compared with only 10 hours/ha in the United States. Consequently, annual production of food grains per farm labor hour amounts to only 1 ton, compared with about 120 tons in the United States. In light of the urgent need of a huge population, little nongrain food is produced in China, although in total, China is the largest meat (pork, mutton, and beef) producer in the world (25.14 million tons in 1990).

Natural hazards are widespread and frequent and have brought severe blows to food production. Mismanagement of food production and storage have also caused much waste, sometimes even to the point of "having a good production but not a good harvest."

Thus, the present land–food–population system in China features a rapid increase in population and food demand, an increase of nonagricultural use of land, and a slight decrease in farmland. Despite a remarkable increase in production, food remains insufficient. The food production per capita might serve as a comprehensive index. It was 209 kg in 1949, 285 kg in 1952, 322 kg in 1980, 348 kg in 1982, 368 kg in 1987, and 390 kg in 1990. It has been barely enough for human consumption in normal years. In years of natural hazards, or as the living standard has improved and the demand for food and feed grains for meat production increases, China has had to import millions of tons of grains each year. The system is actually in a marginal or even critical condition and presents a serious challenge to China, probably also to the world. With nearly a quarter of the global population, if China fails to supply itself with food, or even economically collapses under this precarious land–food–population system, a global disaster would certainly occur, and no single country or even the UN could help.

Table 11.1 shows food and feed grain consumption (in kg) per capita per year in China and comparative

TABLE 11.1
Food and Feed Grains Consumed Per Capita (kg) Per Year in China and in the United States

Food/feed	China	U.S.A.
Food grain	269	69
Vegetables	204	112
Fruit	11	63
Meat & fish	25	103
Dairy products	3	265
Eggs	6	15
Fats & oils	6	28
Sugar	6	66
Food total	530	721
Kcal/person/day	2484	3500
Feed grain	594	1522

Source: Maria and David Pimental. 1991. "Land, Energy and Water: The Constraints Governing Optimum U.S. Population Size," *Focus,* No. 1.

values in the United States. The Chinese eat an essentially vegetarian diet, and most of China's grain production is used as human food, leaving very little for livestock feeding. In contrast Americans eat a diet rich in meat and dairy products.

PROSPECTS FOR A.D. 2000

From the 1990s to A.D. 2000, the crisis in the land–food–population system in China will become even more critical than it is now. However, it might also be the turning point as well as a transition period for China to avoid an irreversible population explosion disaster and an opportunity to get the critical land–food–population system under control. Reforms will be difficult but are required.

Developmental Constraints

Population Growth

Even with good family planning, China's total population will exceed 1.2 billion by about 1994 and 1.3 billion by 2000. The total population engaged in agriculture, even with the rapid development of rural small-scale industries, will exceed 1.0 billion in 2000. In this decade, an even greater number of women who were born during the first peak years of population growth (1964–1973) will enter their high-fertility stage, and thus accelerate the population growth rate. The population age structure will also change to a higher percentage of older people, with a total elderly population above 60 years old of more than 100 million. The costs of health care and social services will be a very heavy burden for such a poor country as China.

Land Resources

In the 1990s, nonagricultural conversion of farmland will continue even in the face of strict restrictions, while most unused arable land will be reclaimed. At best, total farmland will be kept at the 1990 level. Per capita farmland will continue to decrease somewhat. Other land resources, including forestland, grassland, and terrestrial water bodies, however, will be better used for producing food.

Food Production

The traditional peasant-gardener farming system seems to have already reached its upper ceiling of productivity,

a further modernization of agriculture (including farming, animal husbandry, forestry, and fishing) will be needed even more urgently. For increasing food production, emphasis should be laid on medium- and low-quality farmlands as well as on the commercial grain bases, such as the Northeast and North China plains, which still have great potential for increasing food production. According to a recent official estimate, total food grain production in 2000 should reach 477.5 million tons, or 366 kg per capita, slightly lower than the 1990 level. However, with a great increase in input, total food grain production might reach 500 million tons or more in 2000, with a per capita food production of about 400 kg, a little bit higher than the 1990 level.

Corrective Strategies

The following are suggestions for corrective strategies. Action should be taken before it is too late.

Family planning and other population-control measures must be more strictly observed, especially in rural areas. China cannot afford two or more children per couple. No more tolerance for big families can be permitted, even in the rural, mountain, and border areas. At the same time, public opinion and education for voluntary birth control should be greatly enhanced. The annual natural increase rate should be kept below 1.5 percent (if below 1.0 percent, so much the better), and the target for total population in 2000 should be less than 1.3 billion.

The percentage of agriculture-engaged population in the total employed population, through the rapid development of secondary and tertiary enterprises, should decrease to less than 40–50 percent (if less than 30–40 percent, so much the better), so that each farmer has enough farm work to do. While literacy in the rural areas should, of course, be improved, policies for providing public welfare for elderly people should also be implemented.

Very strict protection and very intensive use of existing farmlands should be observed, like the old Chinese saying, "Every inch of farmland should be optimally used." To make the best use of the still unused arable resources, the newly reclaimed lands should at least be kept at the 1990 per capita farmland level. With the help of the decreasing percentage of agriculture-engaged population, there will be a slight increase in the farmer per farmland ratio. Furthermore, all arable land resources will be much improved in quality and fertility, and all of China's territory of 9.6 million sq km will be rationally and gainfully used.

With the productivity of food grain per land unit and per farm laborer as well as the total production ever increasing, other foodstuffs such as meat, fish, vegetables, and fruits will also be greatly increased, so that the nutritionally low-standard vegetarian diet will be somewhat changed to a mixed meat-vegetable diet.

PROSPECTS FOR A.D. 2025

In the first quarter of the twenty-first century, China's land–food–population system will enter a crucial stage, with population control and economic development the two dominating and interrelated objectives. If population growth can be reasonably controlled and economic development greatly advanced, China will eventually become a prosperous developed country; otherwise, China would sink even deeper into poverty and misery, which even risk its very survival as a nation, and the whole world be also seriously affected.

Developmental Constraints

Most of the developmental constraints will reach their "peak" in the first quarter of the twenty-first century.

Population Growth

Three peaks of population growth will occur one by one in the first or second quarter of the twenty-first century.

1. *Total population growth peak:* From 2000 to 2030, if no stronger and more effective population-control actions are taken, China's population will keep on growing rapidly. If the present annual birth rate (2.1–2.4 percent) and annual death rate (0.6–0.7 percent) are allowed to continue, the total population will reach more than 1.6–1.7 billion in 2025–2030.

2. *Elderly population growth peak:* The elderly population growth rate would increase 2.5–2.8 times faster than that of the total population. The elderly population will exceed 0.2 billion in 2020 and reach its peak (more than 0.3 billion) in 2040. The health and social service expenses will be unbearable if China's economic development fails to advance with great strides.

3. *Working-age population growth peak:* Based on the present age structure, China's working-age (15–64 years old) population will reach its peak in

2020, with a total labor force of about 1 billion. The rural areas will feel the greatest employment pressure. If the present economic structure in rural areas does not change fast enough, the potential jobless and underemployed rural population will reach 300–350 millions, nearly one-third of the total rural labor force.

Land Resource

The land resource base will continue to be a relatively stable factor.

1. With strict conservation action, the total farmland base will not greatly decrease. On the other hand, with most of the unused arable land already cultivated, the total farmland area will also cease to increase to any great extent.

2. With the increase in total population, per capita farmland will inevitably become less and less. For example, if the total population stabilizes at 1.5 billion in 2015–2020, and the total farmland remains at its present level (95.7 million ha), per capita farmland will be only about one *mu* (0.07 ha), lower than the present (1990) level of 1.3 *mu* (0.08 ha).

   On the other hand, if the percentage of the labor force engaged in agriculture can be cut to one-half the present level, that is, less than about 40 percent of total employed population in 2015–2020, and if the total population is stabilized at 1.5 billion and the total farmland is 95.7 million ha at that time, then the per farmer land will be about 2.5 *mu* (0.17 ha), slightly higher than the present level (0.10 ha/farmer in 1990).

3. With more sophisticated environmental protection and agricultural modernization, all different types of land resources will be under much better use, and land degradation problems should be much less severe.

Food Production

Modernization of agriculture and overall land use planning will certainly produce much more food grain, feed grain, meat, fish, vegetables, fruits, and other foodstuffs. The problem is whether such an increase in foodstuffs can keep pace with, or even exceed, the growing total population. This is certainly not an easy goal.

Corrective Strategies

Several effective strategies and actions are urgently proposed with a view to attaining a prosperous, balanced land–food–population system in China by 2025.

Population Control

First of all, by an enlightened and vigorous education program as well as sophisticated and strictly executed family planning, the annual birth rate would decrease to less than 1 percent, so that zero population growth rate would be reached by about 2020, and the total population will stabilize between 1.5 and 1.6 billion.

Coupled with the Four Modernizations, the percentage of the work force engaged in agriculture would decrease to below 30–40 percent. At the same time, illiteracy must be wiped out. With improved economic and financial conditions, social security and public welfare for the still-growing elderly population will be guaranteed.

Land Management

Very strict protection and very intensive use of existing farmland will be required. With the modernization of agriculture as well as science and technology, quality and fertility of existing farmland should be continuously improved, so that it can be sustainably and productively used.

Based on overall national planning and according to specific areal differentiation of different land resources, all land resources should be optimally used, with an emphasis on the production of nongrain foodstuffs, such as meat, fish, fruit, vegetables, and oil on the nonarable land resources. Thus, the Chinese diet will change from a vegetable base to a mixed meat-vegetable diet. It will not be as high level as the American diet, which is heavily based on meat and dairy products.

Food Production

Food grains will remain the most important crops in China, and the strategy for increasing food-grain production remains the continual objective of yield per land unit. The practices of the "green revolution" and other measures should be increasingly employed. Low-grade and medium-grade farmlands should all be improved to high grade, with an annual yield of more than 400 kg/ *mu* (6.0 tons/ha). Theoretically, except for the upper ceiling of solar energy use, there is no limit for increasing the yield per land unit. Annual food grain production

might total 600 to 700 million tons in 2025 with a per capita production of 400 to 500 kg.

In the Chinese case, increasing production per unit of farm labor is also very important. On the basis of achieving high production and high farm-laborer efficiency, one important goal is to increase farmland per farm laborer. Another goal is to provide rural people with opportunities to engage in sideline production (part-time industrial or other secondary and tertiary sector jobs) if farm work is not sufficient.

Some modern special measures for producing foodstuffs, such as hydroponics, algal culture, yeast culture, production of synthetic foods, new crops and new species, and biotechnologies, should be advocated and developed substantially.

PROSPECTS FOR A.D. 2050

In the second quarter of the twenty-first century, if everything works well, China's land–food–population system can reach a balanced and prosperous stage. China will enjoy the fruits of the Four Modernizations, and may become a medium-developed country, with per capita income of more than U.S. $3000–$5000. The total population could be stabilized at about 1.5–1.6 billion, which is not beyond the carrying capacity of the land resources, if optimally used. At that time, China's total population will probably be second to India's.[2] The percentage of the labor force engaged in agriculture might decrease to less than 30–40 percent, which will certainly benefit a healthy economic structure in China as well as producing a higher per farm laborer income. The general educational level will be certainly greatly improved, with illiteracy eliminated. The elderly population will continue to increase until about 2040 and then level off, occupying about 20 percent of the total population. Yet, with improved general prosperity of Chinese society, public welfare can be guaranteed. In the future, total farmland and per capita farmland might be slightly lower than the present level, but the farmer per farmland area would be moderately higher, and all of China's 9.6 million sq km territory will be under rational and optimal use. Land degradation will cease to be a big problem. In food production, annual grain production will total more than 700–800 million tons, and the per cap-

---

[2] Although India had a total population of 853,400,000 in 1990, second to China, so far, no serious measures for population control have been taken. It is expected that India's total population will exceed 1.6–1.7 billion in the middle of the twenty-first century.

ita amount will be more than 450–500 kg, which will be enough to meet the needs of human food and livestock feed. Together with a much richer variety of foodstuffs, the general Chinese diet will be a typical mixed meat-vegetarian diet. Yet, it is still advisable to keep the old Chinese tradition, "to work hard and to live simply." The Chinese cannot afford to be luxurious even then.

REFERENCES

China State Statistical Bureau. 1953, 1964, 1982, 1990. *Population Census* (in Chinese).

China State Statistical Bureau. 1991. *Statistical Yearbook of China 1991.* Beijing: Chinese Statistics Press.

Chinese Ministry of Agriculture. 1987, 1990. *China Yearbook of Agriculture.* Beijing: Agriculture Press.

Institute of Geography, Chinese Academy of Sciences. 1980. *Agricultural Geography of China.* Beijing: Science Press (in Chinese).

Owen, Oliver S. 1980. *Natural Resource Conservation: An Ecological Approach*, 3rd ed. New York: Macmillan Publishing Co.

Pimentel, Maria and David. 1991. "Land, Energy and Water: The Constraints Governing Optimum U.S. Population Size," *Focus* 1, No. 1: 9–14.

Zhao, Songqiao. 1984. "Distribution and Utilization of Arable Land Resources in China," *Natural Resources*, No. 1: 13–20 (in Chinese).

PART TWO

Regional Geography

All physical and human factors are also interrelated in regional systems. The comprehensive physical regional system is probably the most significant and most basic, because it is comparatively stable and constant, and it features the integration of all physical areal differentiation. It is also closely related to human activities, especially agriculture. It might also serve as the basis of China's comprehensive geographical regional system. A comprehensive human (including economic, social, and political) regional system is certainly important, especially for industrial and economic development, but human factors are changing so fast in contemporary China that so far, no satisfactory comprehensive human regional scheme has been worked out. Therefore, the regional studies in this book will be mainly based on the comprehensive physical regional system of China—3 natural realms, 7 natural divisions, and 33 natural regions (see Table 1.10), with one chapter for each natural division together with its regions and subregions. The identifying numbers for natural regions and subregions in China's comprehensive physical system will be kept. However, all physical and human factors as well as their relationships and historical evolution will be treated comprehensively on equal terms. In the discussion and analysis of social and industrial development, political (mainly provincial) and traditional borders will be recognized. Especially for Northeast China, the traditional Great Wall line is adopted as the southern boundary, although southern Liaoning Province, including the Liaodong Peninsula and the Lower Liao River plain, belong to warm temperate North China rather than cool temperate and temperate Northeast China of the comprehensive physical regional system.

CHAPTER TWELVE

Northeast China

Northeast China is located in the northern part of the natural realm of Eastern Monsoon China and is delimited by Sino-Russian and Sino-Korean international boundaries on the north and east. Its western boundary is at the aridity isopleth of 1.2, corresponding roughly with the eastern boundary of Inner Mongolia Autonomous Region. The southern boundary is transitional. In the comprehensive physical regional system, it is identical with the 3200°C isotherm of cumulative temperature during the ≥10°C period that separates the temperate and the warm temperate thermal zones.

In this book, we adopt the traditional and political southern boundary of Northeast China, which corresponds roughly with the Great Wall. Administratively, this division places Heilongjiang, Jilin, and Liaoning provinces in the Northeast, with a total area of about 800,000 sq km and a population of about 99 million in 1990.

The region is the most important heavy industrial center and one of the most important bases of commercial food grains and economic crops (soybeans, sugar beets, etc.) as well as the largest timber- and petroleum-producing area in China. It is also the "new" land of China, where population and farmland area have increased rapidly during the last 100 years, but still has a large potential population carrying capacity (Figure 12.1 and 13.1).

PHYSICAL FEATURES, NATURAL RESOURCES, AND ENVIRONMENTAL PROBLEMS

Humid Temperate Climate

The climate is entirely dominated by the alternating continental and maritime monsoons. Because of its high-latitude location (from about 39° to 53 °N), it is the coolest area in China, with a cumulative temperature during the ≥10°C period of about 3200°C in the southern part, decreasing to less than 1400°C in the northwestern part. In the northern Greater Hinggan Mountains, permafrost is widespread. On the whole, winters are long and severe, with a frost-free season of less than 150 days, permitting only one crop per year. But in southern Liaoning Province, with a frost-free season of 150–180 days, three crops can be grown in two years. According to recent meteorological data, low temperature and frost rank as the prime natural hazards for agricultural development in this division. Low temperatures and frost in the spring occur once every three years, but in the summer and autumn, they may occur once every five years.

Annual precipitation decreases from southeast (Tonghua, 900 mm) to northwest (about 400 mm) as the distance from the sea increases (Figure 12.2). On

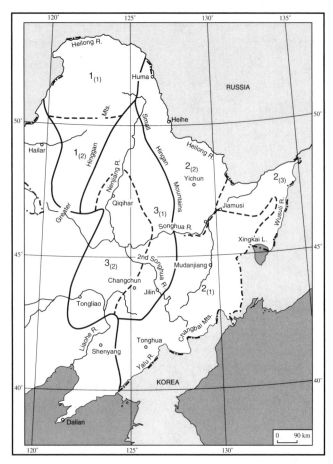

Figure 12.1 Humid and subhumid temperate Northeast China. (For legend, see Table 12.1.)

many low plains during the rainy season, there is usually too much rather than too little precipitation; drainage is a greater problem than irrigation. Relief greatly affects both precipitation and temperature, with much heavier precipitation and lower temperatures in the bordering Greater Hinggan Mountains, Lesser Hinggan Mountains, and Changbai Mountains. Therefore, the last two mountain areas have a temperate humid climate, with annual precipitation of more than 500 mm and an aridity index of less than 1.0. The northern Greater Hinggan Mountains have a cool temperate humid climate, with annual precipitation of more than 400 mm and an aridity index of less than 1.0. Generally, the extensive Northeast China Plain that is surrounded by these mountains has a temperate subhumid climate, with an annual precipitation of around 450 mm and an aridity index of 1.0–1.2. Precipitation is generally concentrated in summer and autumn, coinciding with the growing season, which is a favorable condition for agriculture. Yet, because of the flood hazard in the low plains and depressions, harvesting is sometimes at risk. Spring drought is often a problem, and supplementary irrigation is necessary.

Extensive Low Plains Surrounded by Medium and Low Mountains

This division is essentially composed of the largest plain in China—the Northeast China Plain (Photo 12.1). It is surrounded, like a huge horseshoe, by a series of north-

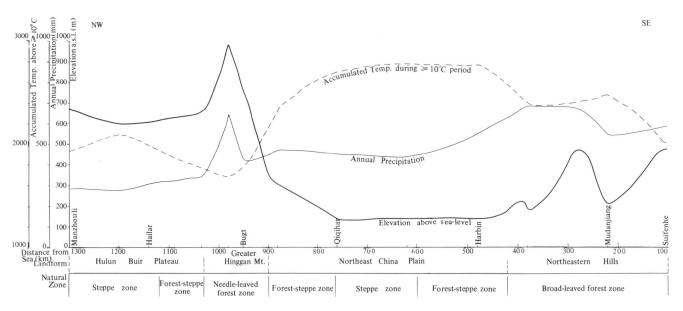

Figure 12.2 Physical profile along the Manzhouli–Harbin–Suifenhe Railway, Northeast China

Photo 12.1 The extensive Northeast China Plain, one of the largest commercial food grain bases in China.

east–southwest trending medium and low mountains. A northwest–southeast topographic profile of this division shows two humps with a saddle between: with the Greater Hinggan Mountains and the Lesser Hinggan–Changbai mountain system as the two humps and the Northeast China Plain as the saddle (Figure 12.2).

Geologically, the Northeast China Plain is a great synclinorium that has been subjected to periodic sinking since the Mesozoic era. There are rich petroleum reserves in its Jurassic sandstone beds. Geomorphologically, the plain has an undulating low surface with elevation decreasing from the peripheral piedmonts of 250–300 m to below 200 m around the confluence of the Songhua River and its largest tributary, the Nenjiang River. The surrounding medium and low mountains are generally strongly folded belts. The Greater Hinggan are geologically ancient, with generally smooth and rounded profiles. The crest line has an elevation of about 1000 m, with the steep eastern slope overlooking the Northeast China Plain. The relatively gentle western slopes descend to the Inner Mongolian Plateau. The Lesser Hinggan Mountains, uplifted as late as the middle Quaternary, are composed of low mountains and hills below 1000 m in elevation. The Changbai Mountains, however, consist of a series of northeast–southwest trending medium and low mountains, alternating with broad intermontane basins and valleys. Mount Baitou (literally "white head"), the highest peak of the Changbai Mountains, towers to 2744 m. The scenic volcanic crater lake, Tianchi (literally "heaven pond"), is located on its top (Color Plate

18). Within the Lesser Hinggan–Changbai mountain system lies the low (generally below 80 m) graben-structured Sanjiang (literally "three rivers") Plain between the Heilong River and its two tributaries, the Songhua and the Wusuli. At the foot of all these surrounding mountains, the undulating and fertile piedmont plains are well developed. They are considered to be the transitional belt between the Northeast China Plain and its surrounding mountains and the best site for agricultural development.

Bountiful Water Resources

Comparatively abundant precipitation and low evaporation rates as well as densely forested mountains ensure bountiful water resources to this division. The Heilong Jiang (Amur River) and its largest tributary, the Songhua River, and other tributaries form one of the greatest river networks in China, second only to the Chang Jiang in annual discharge. There is no deficiency of irrigation water, if needed. The swampy Sanjiang Plain is especially representative of the bountiful surface water resources. The annual runoff depth reaches 500–600 mm in the southeastern part of this division, where annual precipitation is the heaviest. Rainfall decreases northwestward to less than 200 mm in the central part of the Northeast China Plain where many small inland drainage basins and swamps are formed.

Thanks to the surrounding rugged topography, the potential for hydroelectric power is high in the upper

Photo 12.2   The Fongman Hydroelectric Station on the Second Songhua Jiang, Jilin Province.

and middle reaches of many of these swift rivers. There are many excellent sites for the construction of reservoirs. The Second Songhua River is especially famous for its Fengman Hydroelectric Station, together with its huge water reservoir, Songhua Lake (Photo 12.2). Groundwater resources are also abundant, both in quantity and in quality, as discussed in Chapter Two.

Bountiful Land Resources

Favorable climatic and geomorphological conditions also lead to the bountiful land resources in Northeast China. The Northeast China Plain and the Sanjiang Plain (Color Plate 6) comprise the largest modern pioneer settlement belts in China, and the surrounding mountains form the largest timber-producing areas.

There are now (1990) about 8.8 million ha of farmland in Heilongjiang Province alone, of which more than two-thirds are concentrated in the Northeast China Plain. Here, deep and fertile black earth and chernozem soils are widespread, and after decades of large-scale reclamation, farmlands occupy more than 50–60 percent of the total land area in some well-developed districts. Because loessic parent materials are mainly located on the gently rolling slopes, soil erosion has been rather severe on these farmlands. Therefore, a recent trend in agricultural development has emphasized the movement of farmlands downward from slopes to low-lying meadows (the so-called "dintzee") and the upward migration of woodlands and grasslands along both gentle and steep slopes.

There are now about 4.7 million ha of potentially cultivated arable land in Heilongjiang Province alone. The province ranks first in quality and second in area only to the Xinjiang Uygur Autonomous Region. These not yet cultivated arable lands are mainly located in the Sanjiang Plain (Figure 12.3) and along the lower flanks of the Greater and Lesser Hinggan Mountains.

Bountiful Biological Resources

Biological resources, both fauna and flora, are quite rich in this natural division. For years the region has been famous for timber products and "three marvels:" ginseng, marten fur, and Ula grass.[1] Even the streets of old Jilin city were paved with large timber logs before a large fire broke out at the turn of the twentieth century.

Taiga forest is found in the Greater Hinggan Mountains, with larch (*Larix dahurica*) as the chief timber resource (Photo 12.3). It is also the most important hunting ground in China. In the Lesser Hinggan and Changbai Mountains, mixed needle- and broad-leaved forests dominate, with red pine (*Pinus Koraiensis*) and hardwoods as major timber resources (Color Plate 9). In the extensive low plains are luxuriant, productive forest-steppes and meadow-steppes, which provided excellent pasture and hunting grounds before the mid-nineteenth century. Recently, many wildlife reserves (Photo 12.4) and fur farms (Photo 12.5) have been established. Fish are also abundant in the freshwater rivers and lakes.

---

[1] Ginseng is a valuable medicinal wild herb, now extensively cultivated. Marten (*Martes zibellina*) is an excellent fur-bearing animal. Ula grass (*Carex meyeriana Kunth*) is a tall grass distributed in swampy depressions, and is an excellent raw material for making sandals.

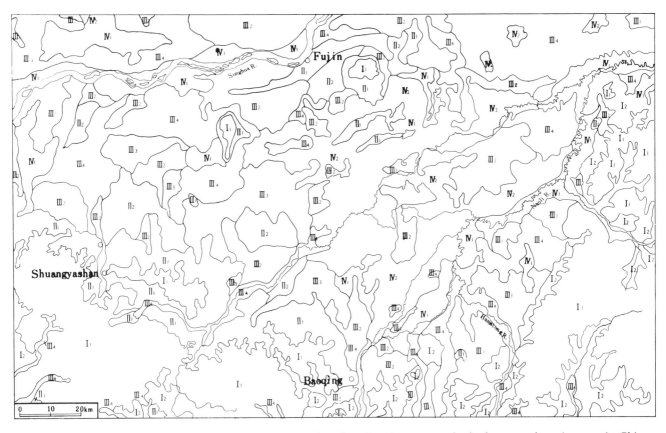

Figure 12.3 Land types in the western Sanjiang Plain, Heilongjiang Province, currently the largest reclamation area in China.

I. Broad-leaved forest — hill and low mountain

  I (1) *Quercus,* dark brown forest soil — hill and low mpuntain; I (2) *Populus, Betula* brown forest soil — hilly slope.

II. Forest meadow — terrace and gentle slope

  II (1) Lush meadow, leached chernozem — terrace and gentle slope; II (2) Gramineous meadow, chernozem — terrace and gentle slope.

III. Meadow — low flat land

  III (1) Gramineous meadow Bai-jiang (planosol) soil — low flat land; III(2) Gramineous meadow soil — low flat land;

III (3) Saline meadow soil — low flat land; III (4) Glei Bai-jiang soil — low depression.

IV. Swampy depressions

  IV (1) Gramineous *Salix* swamp; IV (2) *Carex* heavy swamp.

Photo 12.3 The greatest timber-producing area in China—the northern Greater Hinggan Mountains.

Photo 12.4   A wild water-fowl (red-crown crane) reserve in the swampy area of southern Heilongjiang Province.

Rich Mineral Resources

Northeast China is rich not only in land, water, and biological resources, but also in mineral resources. Energy and metallic minerals are especially significant.

Energy Minerals

At the present time, Daqing in the northern Northeast China Plain is the largest oil field in China, with annual production of more than 50 million tons (Color Plate 10). Important oil fields have also been found in the Liao River plain. Thus, since the early 1960s, the Northeast China Plain has been the largest oil producer in China. In Jilin and Liaoning provinces, the most important oil shale reserves in China are found, comprising 70 percent of the national total.

Coal of Jurassic and Tertiary strata is rich. The most important mines are at Fuxin and Fushun (both open-

Photo 12.5   A plum-flower deer farm at Dongfeng, Jilin Province.

pit mines in southern Liaoning) and Jixi (southern Heilongjiang).

Metal Minerals

The Anshan–Benxi area is the largest iron ore field in China, with proven reserves of more than 10.2 billion tons, about one-fifth of the national total.

Jinxi, in southern Liaoning, has largest molybdenum reserve in China, maybe in the world. In Yinkou is the largest magnesium reserve in the world.

Comprehensive Physical Regionalization

In the physical regional system, Northeast China includes two different natural divisions. North to the 3200°C isotherm of cumulative temperature during the ≥ 10°C period is cool temperate and temperate Northeast China, as shown in Table 12.1 and Figure 12.1. Southern Liaoning, which lies south of that isotherm, is a part of warm temperate North China as shown in Table 13.1 and Figure 13.1.

HISTORICAL BACKGROUND

The Soshin tribes hunted and fished in Northeast China in ancient times. The Chinese central government introduced farming into the region in the third century A.D. Later, this was the homeland of many pastoral and hunting tribes, who also fished and sometimes carried on a little bit of farming, such as Xianbei, Khitan, Nu-Zhen, and Manchu. But, as a whole, the Northeast is a "new" land for China. Until only a few decades ago, all areas north of Changchun were called the Great Northern Wilderness, an immense sea of forests on mountains and a wide sea of grass on undulating plains. In 1661, there were only 4000 ha of farmland in all Northeast China, most of which were located in southern Liaoning. Even by 1887, thirty years after the Qing government was finally forced to give up its prohibition of Han peasants moving into their Northeast China homeland, there were still only 2 million ha of farmland, which were mainly concentrated in Liaoning and southern Jilin and made up only 4 percent of China's total farmland at that time. In Heilongjiang, there were only about 5300 ha of farmland and 25,000 inhabitants in 1897. Between 1897 and 1949, pioneer settlement by small-holding farmers developed rapidly; in 1930 (on the eve of the Japanese invasion of Northeast China, then called Manchuria), Heilongjiang Province already had a total farmland area of 3.85 million ha and a population of 3.7 million. In 1949, the amount of farmland had reached a new level of 5.7 million ha. During the 30 years following 1949, farmland area increased again by more than 8.7 million ha, about 12 percent of the total land in the province. By 1990, the Heilongjiang Province had a total of 8.8 million ha of farmland and a total population of 35.4 million; the former "Great Northern Wilderness" had been transformed into the new, prosperous "Great Northern Granary" of China.

This recent agricultural development implies that the human impact on the physical environment has been less here than in most other parts of China, and that there are still abundant natural resources waiting for pro-

TABLE 12.1
Comprehensive Physical Regionalization of Northeast China

Natural region	Natural subregion	Chief environmental problems
1. Greater Hinggan Mts.— Needle-leaved forest region	1 (1) Northern Greater Hinggan Mountains	Forest fire, soil erosion, low temperature, permafrost
	1 (2) Central Greater Hinggan Mountains	Forest fire, soil erosion, low temperature
2. Northeast China Mts.— Mixed needle- & broad-leaved forest region	2 (1) Changbai Mountains	Forest fire, soil erosion, low temperature
		Forest fire, soil erosion, low temperature
	2 (2) Lesser Hinggan Mountains	Waterlogging, drought, low temperature,
	2 (3) Sanjiang Plain	frost, grassland fire
3. Northeast China Plain— Forest-steppe & meadow-steppe region	3 (1) Piedmont—Forest-steppe	Low temperature & frost, soil erosion
		Low temperature & frost, drought,
	3 (2) Plain—Meadow-steppe	waterlogging, salinization

fitable use. Northeast China is truly an El Dorado for China.

Since 1949, Northeast China has also experienced phenomenal growth of modern industry and transportation. It has been developed as the first heavy industrial base as well as the largest petroleum- and timber-producing area in China. Its railway-dominated transportation system is also the best developed.

SOCIAL AND ECONOMIC DEVELOPMENT

Agriculture

Northeast China is probably the only region in China where the three major branches of agriculture—farming, forestry, and animal husbandry—have all been well developed.

Farming

Northeast China is the most important pioneer settlement area as well one of the most important commercial food grain bases in China. Per capita farmland is also the highest, with 2.7 *mu* (national average 1.5 *mu*), or 0.18 ha, in 1980 and 2.3 *mu* (national average 1.3 *mu*), or 0.15 ha, in 1990. The potential for further farming development is also great. The former Great Northern Wil-

derness in Heilongjiang Province and other parts in Jilin and Liaoning provinces together still have more than 100 million *mu* (6.7 million ha) of unused arable land.

In the northern part of this division, the one-crop-per-year farming system dominates, with spring wheat, corn, sorghum, millet, soybeans, and sugar beets as the chief crops. Corn, sorghum, and millet together account for 70 percent of the total food grain croplands; corn fields have increased rapidly since the 1970s. The Northeast China Plain has now become the "corn belt" and "soybean belt" of China. Paddy rice is also important in local lowland, well-irrigated areas, most of it grown by Koreans. The paddy rice field in Mohe (53° 31′ N) along the Heilongjiang is the northernmost rice-growing area in the world (Photo 12.6). In southern Liaoning Province, three crops in two years are possible, and cotton can be grown.

In the future, the Northeast China and Sanjiang plains will certainly become a larger commercial food grain base. Modernization of agriculture, including overall land use planning, better use of all natural resources, and different strategies for combating various natural hazards are much needed.

Forestry

Northeast China is the largest timber-producing area in China, with a total yield of 25.5 million cu m in 1987 (17.7 million cu m in Heilongjiang, 6.9 million cu m in

Photo 12.6 The Heilongjiang (Amur River) at Mohe (53°31′ N), the northernmost point of Chinese territory.

Jilin, and 0.9 million cu m in Liaoning), accounting for about 39.2 percent of China's total timber production. The Greater Hinggan, the Lesser Hinggan, and the Changbai Mountains are the largest forestlands in China, with a total forested area of about 25.0 million ha in 1987, comprising 21.7 percent of the national total. The most important timber trees include red pine, larch, and some hardwoods. A series of forestry cities have developed in these mountain areas, of which Yichun of Heilongjiang Province is the best, being called the "capital of forestry."

However, forestry in this region is now in critical condition, even great danger. The most serious problem is mismanagement which leads to overcutting, waste, deforestation, forest fires, and other disasters. According to an estimate, the ratio between tree cutting and tree planting is 3:1. If no effective measures are taken, most forestlands will disappear within 30 to 40 years.

Animal Husbandry

In the Northeast China Plain, the extensive forest-steppes and meadow-steppes constitute a total usable grassland of about 90 million *mu* (6 million ha). Since ancient times, many pastoral peoples have engaged in animal husbandry here, with seminomadism and fixed pastoralism dominating. In the recently developed farming areas, pigs and chickens (domestic feeding) have been raised in large numbers. In the forested areas, hunting might also be considered as a form of animal husbandry. Some game species, such as reindeer (*Rangifer tarandus*) and plum-flower deer (*Cervus nippon*, Photo 12.5), have recently been domesticated.

Modern Industry and Transportation

Modern Industry

Since 1949, the first heavy industry base in contemporary China has been established in Northeast China. At first, iron and steel industries dominated, but since the mid-1960s, petroleum, engineering, and chemical industries have risen to prominence. To date, a complete and comprehensive industrial system, including engineering, iron and steel, petroleum, and chemicals, as well as coal mining, electricity, forestry, textiles, paper, sugar, and others, has been established in Northeast China. The annual industrial production value contributes about 77 percent of the total agricultural-industrial production value in the region.

In industrial location, the Shenyang–Anshan–Benxi area in southern Liaoning is the best developed area, where the largest and the second largest iron and steel enterprises in China, the Anshan Steel Company and the Benxi Iron Company, are located. Shenyang and Fushun are two large centers for metallurgical industries. The second largest industrial area in Northeast China is the Harbin–Daqing–Qiqihar belt along the Harbin–Manzhouli Railway, where highly developed petroleum, chemical, electricity, engineering, and textile industries have developed. In addition, Changchun, Jilin, Dalian (Luda), Mudanjiang, Jiamusi, and Dandong are also important industrial centers.

Modern Transportation

Railways are the major transportation network in Northeast China, with a total length of about 14,000 km, about one-fourth of the national total. Northeast China also ranks first in railway density in China, with 1.7 km/sq km. There are about 110,000 km of roadways in Northeast China, which carry about 20 percent of the total short-distance freight in the region. Other means of transportation, including river and sea waterways and airlines, are also developing, but still not rapidly enough.

Very recently, a massive seaport serving Siberia, Korea, Mongolia, and China located on the Tumen delta (the junction between Siberia, Korea, and China) has been under consideration. It might be of great value to the international development of northeastern Asia.

Ethnic Groups and Population

Ethnic Groups

Northeast China is now essentially populated by the Han, who make up 95.1 percent in Heilongjiang and 91.7 percent in both Jilin and Liaoning (1982 population census). The former ethic occupants of the land were the Manchu, who are still the sixth largest ethnic minority people in China with a total population of 4,304,981 in 1982 (9,821,180 in 1990). The Manchu have been scattered all over China and have nearly lost their identity. In 1982, there were 3,416,175 Manchu in Northeast China (1,989,989 in Liaoning Province alone), accounting for 79.4 percent of the total Manchu population in China, but comprising only 3.8 percent of Northeast China's total population. Consequently, when the Japanese invaders tried to set up a puppet state of "Manchukuo" during the 1930s and 1940s, their plan was entirely groundless and destined to be an utter failure. The obsolete term "Manchuria" should also not be used anymore in the English-speaking world.

However, there are still some other minority peoples in Northeast China. The Koreans, with a total population of 1,765,204 in 1982 (1,920,597 in 1990), were brought in by the Japanese from neighboring Korea and are mainly concentrated in the Yanbian Korean Autonomous Prefecture of Jilin Province. The Daur, the Xibe, and the Ewenke, all formerly native to Northeast China and now like the Manchu scattered all over China, also have a small population left in their homeland. The Orogen (hunting in the Greater Hinggan mountain forests) and the Hezhe (fishing in the confluence of the Heilong, the Songhua, and the Wusuli rivers) are especially well known all over China, although their numbers are very small.

Population

Together with the march of modern pioneer settlement since the mid-nineteenth century and the rapid industrialization since 1949, population growth in Northeast China has been phenomenal. Before the mid-nineteenth century, this region was essentially a land of extensive forests and grassland. Even in 1930, when the Japanese invaded, there were still only about 30 million inhabitants. But by 1982, the total population of Northeast China had reached 90.1 million, and in 1990 it reached 99.1 million.

The average population density in Northeast China is still comparatively low compared with other parts of Eastern Monsoon China, although it is already higher than Northwest Arid China and the Tibetan Frigid Plateau. In 1982, the average density in Northeast China stood at 114 persons/sq km and in 1990 about 125 persons/sq km, both a little bit below the national average.

Rural and Urban Settlements

Rural Settlement

Because agricultural development is so recent, the density and size of rural settlements in Northeast China are much smaller than those of North China, the homeland of most Han peasants in Northeast China. Especially in Heilongjiang Province, the so-called Great Northern Wilderness of only a half century ago, the distance between rural villages is usually several dozens of kilometers, while the size of each village is generally a few dozen houses. Even as late as 1953, when I travelled by train from Harbin to Hailar, a vast greenish sea of tall grasses still dominated the landscape of the Northeast China Plain, with small patches of farmland and settlements dotted sparsely along the railway, like a string of tiny islands.

The pattern of rural village distribution and the morphology of the rural villages are quite similar to those of North China. The villages are mostly composed of mud-thatch cottages and brick-tile houses. The roofs, whether of thatch or tile, generally have an angle of 5°–15°, much less steep than those of southern China where annual precipitation is much heavier, but much steeper than those in semiarid Inner Mongolian farming areas where the mud roofs are usually flat. In extremely arid Xinjiang oases, many mud houses have no roofs at all, using only grape vines for shade in the intense sunlight. These Northeastern rural villages are generally evenly located on the plain farming areas but are arranged in a linear pattern along the roadways, the river channels, and the foothill piedmonts.

Urban Settlements

With the rapid development of modern industry and modern transportation, many important cities have been developed in Northeast China, of which Shenyang, Changchun, Harbin, Dalian, Qiqihar, Anshan, and Fushun are metropolises of 1 million or more.

Shenyang   This ancient city has numerous cultural sites. It is a modern metropolis as well as the capital and economic and cultural center of Liaoning Province. Shenyang is especially significant as the largest heavy industrial center in China, with engineering and metallurgical industries dominating. It is the junction of five railways. In 1990, Shenyang had a total population of 4.54 million and a nonagricultural population of 3.6 million.[2]

Changchun   Changchun is the capital and the economic and cultural center of Jilin Province. Changchun is also the junction of three railways. Its industry specializes in transportation equipment engineering; the largest automobile-manufacturing plant in China is located here. In 1990, it had a total population of 2.11 million and a nonagricultural population of 1.68 million.

Harbin   Before the construction of the Manzhouli–Harbin Railway in 1897–1903, Harbin was sim-

---

[2] In current urban structure, each Chinese city or "municipality" usually includes one or more counties where most of the agricultural population is concentrated.

ply a small fishing village along the Songhua River. It is now the capital as well as the economic and cultural center of Heilongjiang Province. It is also the junction of five railways and the Songhua waterway route. In modern industrial development, it is famous for electrical engineering. In 1990, it had a total population of 2.83 million and a nonagricultural population of 2.44 million.

Dalian (Luda)   Located at southern tip of the Liaodong Peninsula and overlooking both the Bo Hai and the Yellow Sea, Dalian is the major seaport of Northeast China. It specializes in shipbuilding, engineering, chemical, and textile industries. Since 1984, it has become an open coastal city, with a total population of 2.4 million and a nonagricultural population of 1.72 million in 1990.

Qiqihar   Before 1949, Qiqihar was only a small city located at the northwestern border of the Northeast China Plain. It has now developed as an industrial metropolis, with engineering industries dominating. In 1990, it had a total population of 1.38 million and a nonagricultural population of 1.07 million.

Anshan and Fushun   Both are mining and heavy industrial cities and had a nonagricultural population of about 1.2 million each in 1990.

AREAL DIFFERENTIATION AND REGIONAL DEVELOPMENT

As a whole, this division will soon evolve into one of the most prosperous, comprehensive economic regions in China. Both agriculture and industry will be greatly developed. Five regions with specific physical features and economic development can be identified.

Greater Hinggan Mountains

This region is located in the northern and central Greater Hinggan Mountains. The Greater Hinggan Mountains are generally around 1000 m in elevation, with a few peaks between 1000 and 1500 m. A characteristic topographic feature is the range's asymmetrical slopes; its eastern slopes are much steeper, with conspicuous steplike terraces and erosion surfaces as well as numerous deep gorges. The western slopes are much gentler, merging with the Inner Mongolia Plateau at about the 700 m contour line. Another feature is the conspicuous longitudinal areal differentiation: north of 51° N,

granites predominate, with rounded peaks, gentle slopes, and well-preserved erosion surfaces; whereas south of 51° N, the bedrock is more varied with greater relative relief.

Climatically, this region is unique as the only cool temperate zone in China. Winters are long and severe, with a mean January temperature below −28°C and a winter season lasting more than eight months. Except in some intermontane valleys below 700 m in elevation, there is practically no summer season. The cumulative temperature during the ≥ 10°C period generally totals less than 1600°C, and the frost-free season is less than 90 days. Seasonally frozen soil during the wintertime usually has a thickness of more than 2.5 m, and there is continuous permafrost from 51° N northward and even in isolated islands south of 51° N. Annual precipitation totals about 450 mm on the eastern slopes and 350 mm on the western slopes, of which about 80 percent is concentrated in the rainy season from May to September. Because temperatures and consequently evaporation are low, the aridity index is generally less than 1.0.

Surface water resources are quite abundant. Rivers on the western and northern slopes flow into the Heilong Jiang and its headwaters, the Ergun River; on the eastern slopes, they flow into the Nen Jiang. The annual runoff depth increases from 150 mm in the south to 250 mm in the north. About 80 percent of the annual runoff is concentrated in the period from June to September.

Distribution of vegetation is determined not only by geographical location and the accompanying climatic conditions, but also by the uplift of the Greater Hinggan Mountains. As a result, this is the southernmost extension of taiga forest in the world, with the excellent softwood larch predominant. Other needle-leaved trees include pine (*Pinus sylvestris*, mostly in sandy areas), spruce (*Picea obovata*, *P. microsperma*), and at higher elevations, dwarf pine (*Pinus pumila*) and juniper (*Juniperus dahurica*). Broad-leaved trees, including birch (*Betula platyphylla*), poplar (*Populus davidiana*), willow (*Salix rorida*), and oak (*Quercus mongolica*), grow on the lower slopes. In swampy areas scattered shrubby clumps of dwarf birch (*Betula fruicosa*) and some species of willow (*Salix brachypoda*, *S. Sibirica*) dot the landscape. On mountain slopes, the most common shrubs are *Rhododendron* species. Other shrubs include *Vaccinium vitis-idaea* and *Ledum palustre*. Vertical zonation and differentiation between eastern and western slopes is conspicuous. For example, at about 50° N, broad-leaved forests predominate below 700 m; from 700 to 1000 m, the forests become the *Larix-Rhododen-*

dron type; whereas above 1000 m, the dwarf pine becomes an important component in the larch forest.

Northern Greater Hinggan Mountains

The southern boundary between this subregion (subregion 1_1 on Figure 12.1) and the next subregion is roughly demarcated at 51° N. Continuous permafrost is widespread in this subregion, as are larch forests. The dominant landscape is larch-covered medium mountains. Lumbering is, and will be, the chief economic activity in this subregion. Great care must be taken to protect and to renew these forest resources so that, for some time to come, sustainable lumbering activity can continue. Hunting is also an important occupation, especially for the Orogen and other minority groups in the area. All precious and rare fauna should be strictly protected, and if possible they should be domesticated and managed. Small patches of farmland can be cultivated in the intermontane valley plains, below 700 m in elevation. The local peasants and lumbermen are growing a small amount of vegetables and food grains for their own consumption. Effective measures for combating frost hazards and for soil conservation must be undertaken.

Central Greater Hinggan Mountains

In this subregion (1_2 on Figure 12.1), permafrost is found only in isolated islands, and larch forests are found only in patches. The landscape and land use patterns are essentially similar to the Northern Greater Hinggan Mountain subregion, with forestry being paramount. Yet, owing to a slightly warmer climate and more productive pastures, agriculture and animal husbandry occupy somewhat larger proportions of production, whereas forestry and hunting are more restricted.

Northeast China Mountains

This region is located in eastern Heilongjiang and Jilin provinces and northeastern Liaoning province. It includes three distinct physical units: the Lesser Hinggan Mountains, the Sanjiang Plain, and the Changbai Mountains. They are characterized by a series of northeast–southwest trending medium and low mountains alternating with broad intermontane basins and valleys. The highest peak, Mount Baitou, is surrounded by a basalt plateau at an elevation of more than 2600 m. The Lesser Hinggan Mountains are composed of a series of low mountains and hills. The low, flat, swampy Sanjiang Plain is a graben amid these folded mountains, with

ground surface materials composed chiefly of loessic clay.

Climatically, this is a typical humid temperate region, except for some subhumid rainshadow areas, such as the western half of the Sanjiang Plain. Because the region extends through 12 degrees of latitude, there is considerable temperature variation from south to north. For example, the growing season decreases from 150 to 110 days, whereas cumulative temperature during the ≥10°C period decreases from 2500° to 1800°C. Rainfall, on the other hand, is determined mainly by distance from the sea as well as by topographic features. The annual precipitation totals more than 800 mm in the southeast, about 500 mm in the central part, and only 450–550 mm in the Sanjiang Plain and the Lesser Hinggan Mountains. About 60–80 percent of the annual precipitation comes in the growing season.

The combined effects of climatic and topographic conditions have resulted in a well-developed river system in the region. The lofty, dome-shaped Mount Baitou, with its ample precipitation, is characterized by a spectacular annular drainage pattern; two big rivers, the Songhua and the Yalu, both originate here. Two other large rivers, the mighty Heilong and its tributary the Wusuli, flow in the northern part of this region. Annual runoff corresponds with annual precipitation; it is as high as 500–600 mm on the southern slopes of Mount Baitou, decreasing to less than 200 mm on the northern slopes and to less than 150 mm in the Sanjiang Plain. Mixed needle- and broad-leaved forests dominate the region, and both horizontal and vertical variations are prominent.

Changbai Mountains

As a humid temperate subregion, the characteristic landscape of the Changbai Mountains (2_1 on Figure 12.1) is a land of tree-clad medium mountains. These mountains consist of a series of northeast–southwest trending ranges, mostly 500–1500 m in elevation, where water and biological resources are quite rich. Many broad basins and valleys are interspersed among these mountains, such as the Mudan River valley where the famous ancient Bohai Kingdom was founded in the eighth century A.D. Since the late nineteenth century, this area has been one of the most prosperous pioneer settlement belts in China.

Vertical zonation is conspicuous, and an improved land use scheme should be based on the specific physical conditions of different altitudinal belts. Three broad altitudinal belts might be identified:

1. *Alpine tundra belt* is limited in land area, but it is unique and scenic. With an elevation of 1800–2100 m and a location immediately below the snow line, it is the highest area in Northeast China and supports special and valuable biological resources. Most of it should be reserved as a national park; one famous natural protected area has already been established.

2. *Mountain forested belts*, including the mixed forest belt, the needle-leaved forest belt, the spruce-fir forest belt, and the subalpine dwarf birch forest belt, should be mainly devoted to well-managed forestry. Restricted hunting and pasturing in the forests should be conducted. The most serious problem at the moment is deforestation, especially in the basic vegetation belt (the mixed forest belt at 500–1000 m in elevation). Deforestation must be strictly prohibited as soon as possible.

3. *Low basins and valleys* have luxuriant meadows, swamps, and other azonal vegetation types as well as rich land and water resources. Farming and animal husbandry have potential for intensive development. On either side of the larger rivers fertile floodplains and two or three steps of terraces with deep meadow soils provide excellent sites for intensive farming.

Lesser Hinggan Mountains

This subregion (2_2 on Figure 12.1) also features a humid temperate climate and a tree-clad mountain topography. Because of its higher latitude, however, temperatures are much lower and seasonally frozen soils are widespread. Furthermore, because uplift was much less and ancient erosion surfaces better preserved, the terrain is less dissected and less well drained. Consequently, there are much more swamps.

Based on geological and topographical features, the Lesser Hinggan Mountains can be subdivided again into three parts. The southeastern part has a much higher relief. It is mainly composed of low mountains and hills, with an elevation of around 500 m and an annual precipitation of about 600 mm. The dominant vegetation is mixed needle- and broad-leaved forest, with a large red pine component. It is essentially a land for lumbering, although some broad valleys such as the Tangwang valley are suitable for farming.

The middle part, located along the Heihe–Bei'an line, is mainly composed of an undulating plain, with an elevation of about 400 m and an annual precipitation of about 500 mm. The dominant vegetation is also mixed

forest, with both red pine and larch as the major components. On the whole, it is cold and swampy and is more suitable for forestry than for farming.

The northwestern part is composed mainly of hills, with an elevation of about 400 m and annual precipitation of about 450 mm. Mixed needle- and broad-leaved forest still dominates, but with a larger larch component. It should be confined to forestry except for some cultivable river valleys such as the narrow, dissected plains along the main stem of the Heilong River.

Sanjiang Plain

With an area of 42,500 sq km, the general topography of the Sanjiang Plain (2_3 on Figure 12.1) dips from southwest to northeast. The southwestern part has an elevation of 60–80 m, with ground-surface materials composed mainly of silt. Drainage is good, and marshes are not extensive. The northeastern part, however, has an elevation of 40–60 m and contains several sluggish, meandering rivers with extensive swampy floodplains. There is also a clay layer with a thickness of 3–17 m on the ground surface that makes drainage difficult and results in extensive swamps. Surrounding the plain on the western and southern sides is a series of low mountains and hills, generally between 500–1000 m in elevation, with a number of offshoot hills stretching into the margins of the plain as isolated small "mountains without roots."

Climatically, the subregion has a mean January temperature of −18° to −22°C, a mean July temperature of 21°–22°C, a frost-free season of 120–145 days, a cumulative temperature during the ≥ 10°C period of 2200°–2600°C, and annual precipitation of 500–650 mm. Because of the rainshadow effect of the surrounding mountains, the southwestern part is subhumid, while the northeastern part is still humid. Such areal differentiation is reflected clearly in land use. In the southwestern part, most lands have been cultivated, resulting in one of the most flourishing farming areas in China (Color Plate 6). In the northeastern part, swamps are extensive, but many state farms are now working efficiently to transform this wilderness into a granary.

Figure 12.3 shows the land types in the western part of the Sanjiang Plain. Most of them, except the first category (broad leaved forest—hills and low mountains), are arable, and most of them have been cultivated recently.

From the national viewpoint, this region certainly should be devoted almost exclusively to farming, although soil conservation measures must be carefully observed. On the arable plains, forestry should be restricted to shelter belts, occupying not more than 5–10 percent of the total area. On the surrounding mountains and hills forests should be dominant with no allowance for cultivation. Cultivation should go hand in hand with the establishment of a permanent farming base. Irrigation structures and systems should be established at the beginning or concurrent with reclamation; otherwise the surface water will be depleted and soil moisture will deteriorate rapidly.

Songhua–Nen Jiang Plain

The Songhua–Nen Jiang Plain is the northern part of the Northeast China Plain, sandwiched between the Greater Hinggan Mountains and the Northeast China Mountains.

Geologically, it corresponds to what is called the Songhua–Nen Jiang synclinorium, which has been gradually sinking since the Mesozoic era. The western side has been sinking more than the eastern side. Quaternary deposits about 30–50 m thick have accumulated in the depression. Such a sinking and accumulating process is still going on in the central part, the Harbin–Qiqihar–Baicheng triangle, where the largest oil field in China is located. Geomorphologically, this triangle is the lowest part of the Songhua–Nen Jiang Plain, with an elevation of only 130–140 m. Numerous lakes and swamps dot the area.

On the periphery of this depressed alluvial-lacustrine central part is a broad belt of diluvial-alluvial piedmont plains with an elevation of 250–300 m. The piedmont plains were slightly uplifted during the late Quaternary period and then dissected into a mosaic of gentle ridges, undulating terraces, and low hills, with a relative relief of less than 50–100 m. The broad, low north-northwest-trending water divide between the Songhua River and the Liao River represents the southern part of this piedmont belt. It was uplifted in the late Quaternary period and accompanied by numerous small volcanic cones.

Precipitation in the plain is less abundant than in the surrounding mountains. The annual precipitation is about 600 mm in the southeast, decreasing to about 400 mm in the northwest. The aridity index ranges from 1.0 to 1.2; hence, it is subhumid and is different from the surrounding humid mountains. The annual runoff depth also decreases from about 200 mm in the southeast to about 25 mm in the northwest.

This region also differs from the surrounding mountains in that it is a little bit warmer and has no conspicu-

ous altitudinal zonation. Winters are long and cold, with a mean January temperature of $-17°$ to $-24°C$ and a pronounced decrease in temperature from south to north. Summers are short but rather warm, with mean July temperature of $21°–25°C$, the thermal difference between south and north being insignificant. Sometimes, when the Pacific Subtropical High extends far westward and shifts somewhat northward, the weather may be quite hot, with a maximum high temperature above $35°C$. Compared with similar latitudes, this area has the greatest seasonal temperature variation in the world, showing a pronounced continentality of climate even on China's east coast. A warm summer coupled with bountiful precipitation in that season (accounting for about 60–70 percent of total annual precipitation) creates a favorable climatic environment for agriculture. Spring wheat, corn, millet, soybeans, and other crops produce a high annual yield, making this region one of the largest bases of commercial food grains and economic crops in China.

Vegetation is luxuriant, and the soil is fertile. In peripheral piedmonts, the zonal vegetation is forest-steppe, with a highly varied flora. Owing to intensive human use, few needle-leaved trees remain. The corresponding zonal soil type is black earth, usually with a humus layer more than 60–80 cm deep. There are also many azonal vegetation and soil types, such as sandy and saline soils and swamp vegetation. Near the western border, the plain gradually merges into the semiarid grassland of Inner Mongolia, which has steppe vegetation and chestnut soils.

Piedmont Area

Forming a great arc (3_1 on Figure 12.1), the Piedmont is a transitional belt between the Northeast China Mountains and the Northeast China Plain. Geomorphologically, it is essentially a gently sloping plain, composed mostly of diluvial-alluvial deposits, with a thin veneer of Quaternary loessic materials. The dominant vegetation type is forest-steppe, most of which has been turned into farmland. The zonal soil type is the fertile, deep black earth, with a top-layer humus content of 3–6 percent, generally decreasing from north to south.

For farming, this subregion is nearly ideal. Land resources are abundant, precipitation is sufficient but not excessive for crop growing; temperature conditions are generally adequate for one crop per year, although low temperature and early frost are sometimes very harmful. Thanks to good drainage, salinization and flood hazards are nonexistent. During the last 100 years, this subregion has rapidly become one of the most prosperous pioneer settlement areas in China. Future potential for agricultural growth lies chiefly in higher yield per land unit and per farm laborer, which in turn depend on improved effectiveness in the use of all natural resources and on the control and amelioration of all limiting factors, such as low temperature and soil erosion. An overall plan is much needed.

Plain Area

This central part of the Songhua–Nen Jiang Plain (3_2 on Figure 12.1) lies at a comparatively low elevation with poor drainage. Consequently, there are widespread swamps and saline soils. Geologically and geomorphologically, it is composed of Quaternary deposits 30–50 m in thickness, mostly alluvial-lacustrine and partly diluvial and eolian. Fortunately, there are large reserves of petroleum and natural gas. Compared with the Piedmont subregion, it is slightly warmer and drier, with an annual precipitation of 400–500 mm. The dominant vegetation type is meadow-steppe, characterized by the presence of drought-tolerant and salinity-tolerant grasses. The zonal soil type is chernozem, which is quite fertile but not as productive as black earth.

This is an area for comprehensive development of farming, pasturing, and forestry. To guide development, there should be overall planning to coordinate land use patterns in direct association with specific land types. For example, the meadow terrace, meadow-alluvial plain, and other good arable lands should be devoted to farming; the low swampy and saline depressions are better kept as pasture; while river margins and sandy dunes are reserved for forestry. Reeds (*Phragmites communis*), widespread in swamps and around the numerous lakes, are also an important source of paper pulp.

Liaodong Peninsula

The Liaoning Peninsula (marked 4 on Figure 13.1) is sandwiched between the Bo Hai and the Yellow Sea. Physically, it is closely related to the Shandong Peninsula, but politically and economically, it is an integral part of Northeast China.

The region consists mainly of hills below 500 m in elevation. The northeast–southwest trending Qianshan Mountains, with a total length of about 340 km and an elevation of about 500 m, serve as its backbone. The peninsula has a width of about 150 km in its northern part, narrows to about 10 km at its southern tip, and then submerges into the sea south of Dalian. The topog-

raphy also descends from north to south. The coastline extends for about 900 km, with numerous rocky islands as well as extensive marine beaches, which make good harbors and fishing grounds.

The region has a warm temperate thermal regime. Cumulative temperature during the $\geq 10°C$ period ranges from 3000°–3700°C with a frost-free season from 160–200 days. Winter wheat and fruit trees can survive without special protection in the winter. Annual precipitation totals 600–1000 mm. The zonal vegetation is broad-leaved forest. One crop per year and three crops in two years are possible. This is one of the most important fruit-, fish-, and tussah silk–producing areas in China.

Dalian (Luda), located at southern tip of the peninsula, is the major city of the region and the major seaport of Northeast China. It was occupied and exploited by czarist Russia and the Japanese for a long time. Since 1949, modern industries such as shipbuilding, engineering, and chemicals as well as sea and railway transportation have been rapidly developed. Since 1984, it has also become an open coastal city, with rapid development of foreign trade. Thus, the Liaodong Peninsula, under the leadership of Dalian, will soon become a comprehensively well-developed economic area of agriculture, industry, transportation, and foreign trade.

Lower Liao River Plain

The lower Liao River Plain (marked 5 on Figure 13.1) is the southern part of the Northeast China Plain, but climatically it is more like the North China Plain, from which it is separated by the Great Wall line. Administratively, it is a part of Liaoning Province.

This plain has been formed over a long period by alluvial deposits of the Liao River in a sinking valley. It also has rich petroleum reserves. Geomorphologically, it is low and flat, generally with an elevation of less than 50 m. In historic times, this was the earliest part in Northeast China to be cultivated by Han peasants. Yet, in its southern part, wild marshes were widespread until only a few decades ago, and the area was hence called the "Great Southern Wilderness." Now the wilderness, together with a part of the sea, has been mostly reclaimed as productive paddy lands.

Climatically, it has a warm temperate thermal regime with a cumulative temperature of 3200°–3500°C during the $\geq 10°C$ period and a frost-free season of about 180 days. Three crops can be grown in two years, and cotton is raised. Annual precipitation reaches about 600 mm. Rain-fed farming is possible, but spring drought and autumn floods are frequent, as well as low temperature and frost hazards.

This region is now one of the most industrially developed areas in China. There are three metropolises of a million or more in the region—Shenyang, Anshan, and Fushun. Shenyang, with a total population of 4.54 million in 1990, is the fourth largest city in China. All three metropolises and their suburbs are highly developed in heavy and light industries as well as railway transportation. On the other hand, environmental problems such as soil erosion, deforestation, and air and water pollution have been growing more and more serious. Because of the rapidly growing nonagricultural population, food supply is also far from self-sufficient in the region. Generally speaking, the surplus food production in Heilongjiang Province can just barely supply and compensate the food deficit in the Liaoning Province.

REFERENCES

China State Statistical Bureau. 1991. *Statistical Yearbook of China*. Beijing: China Statistical Publishing House.

Chinese Academy of Sciences. 1959. *Comprehensive Physical Regionalization of China*. Beijing: Science Press (in Chinese).

Changchun Institute of Geography, Chinese Academy of Sciences. 1981. "A Preliminary Study of Changes in the Natural Environment After the Current Large-Scale Reclamation in the Sanjiang Plain," *Acta Geographica Sinica* 36, no. 1 (in Chinese).

Institute of Forestry and Soil, Chinese Academy of Sciences. 1980. *Soils of Northeast China*. Beijing: Science Press (in Chinese).

Integrated Investigation Team of the Heilong Jiang Basin. 1961. *Natural Conditions of the Heilong Jiang Basin and Its Neighboring Areas*. Beijing: Science Press (in Chinese).

Shen, Yuancun. 1980. "Land Types and Their Transformation Measures in the Sanjiang Plain," *Acta Geographica Sinica* 35, no. 2 (in Chinese).

Sun, Jinzhu, et al. 1988. *Geography of China*. Beijing: Higher Education Press (in Chinese).

Zhao, Songqiao. 1986. *Physical Geography of China*. New York: John Wiley & Sons, Inc.

Zhao, Songqiao. 1981. "Transforming Wilderness into Farmland: An Evaluation of Natural Conditions for Agricultural Development in Heilongjiang Province," *Geographer*, no. 11.

Zhao, Songqiao, et al. 1983. *Natural Zones and Land Types in Heilongjiang Province*. Beijing: Science Press (in Chinese).

CHAPTER THIRTEEN

North China

North China is bounded by the Bo Hai and the Yellow Sea on the east and by the eastern border of the Tibetan Plateau on the west. The southern boundary follows the Qinling Mountains–Huai River line, which will be discussed in more detail in the next chapter. The northern boundary generally follows the traditional Great Wall line as discussed in the last chapter. North China has an area of about 900,000 sq km and a population of about 300 million (1990). Administratively, North China consists of Beijing and Tianjin municipalities, Shandong and Shanxi provinces, the major parts of Hebei, Henan, and Shaanxi provinces, and parts of Jiangsu, Anhui, and Gansu provinces, and Ningxia Hui Autonomous Region. Historically, it is the cradle of the Han and the Chinese agricultural civilization. It has been the political, economic, and cultural center of China for thousands of years. Of the six ancient capitals of China (Xi'an, Luoyang, Kaifeng, Beijing, Nanjing, and Hangzhou), four are located in this division. Yet, it is also the scene of many environmental problems and natural hazards, such as droughts, floods and waterlogging, soil erosion, salinization, and earthquakes. For the thousand years since the Song Dynasty, foods have been imported to North China from Subtropical China, while coal has been exported in the opposite direction.

PHYSICAL FEATURES, NATURAL RESOURCES, AND ENVIRONMENTAL PROBLEMS

The North China Platform

Geologically, the North China Platform is the Chinese mainland core. It was formed by long periods of continent building and relatively short periods of marine transgression. The geologic basement is formed by metamorphic rocks, such as gneiss, crystalline schist, slate, and phyllite. From the Cambrian to the middle Ordovician there was a long period of marine transgression when marine sediments several thousand meters thick were deposited. Within those sandstone and carbonate beds, rich petroleum reserves were formed. Subsequently a period of land denudation followed during the upper Ordovician through the middle Carboniferous. From then to the end of the Permian period, North China was covered by a shallow and fluctuating sea. Shales, sandstones, and thin beds of coal and limestone were deposited during this inundation period. Since the end of the Permian period, North China as a whole has emerged as a continent.

The Mesozoic era was distinguished by igneous intrusions, volcanic eruptions, and tectonic movements. Intensive folding and faulting accompanied by intrusion of enormous masses of granite and outpouring of andesite and rhyolite occurred in the Yanshan Mountains and Shanxi Plateau as well as the Shandong Peninsula and the Loess Plateau.

The Cenozoic era was marked by uplifting and subsidence. The mountains of the Shandong Peninsula and the Loess Plateau were regions of uplifting, whereas fluvial and lacustrine deposits were deposited in the North China Plain and intermontane basins.

An event of paramount importance to the landscape of North China was the accumulation of loess deposits during the Quaternary period. In northern Shaanxi and eastern Gansu, the loess forms a nearly continuous mantle that covers the underlying topography. This is the Loess Plateau *par excellence*. East of the Loess Plateau, loess also covers the basins and lower mountain slopes of the Shanxi Plateau, but it is not as deep. Through water erosion, loess was carried by the streams and redeposited in the surrounding plains and seas. In fact, this silty material is found nearly everywhere in North China. The significance of loess in the development of the landscape as a natural resource and an environmental problem for North China can never be overestimated.

The land surface of North China consists of four fundamental types of landforms: plains, hills, plateaus, and mountains. These types are grouped into units that conform to geological structures. On the whole, the topography descends from the plateaus and mountains in the west to low plains and hills in the east, and finally submerges under the sea. It trends generally northeast to southwest, or north-northeast to south-southwest. From east to west, four major units may be distinguished (Figure 13.1):

1. The first unit consists of hilly lands of the Shandong Peninsula, of which the scenic Tai Shan has been a

sacred mountain for China since ancient times (see Color Plate 19). This is a part of the ancient landmass and has long been subjected to continuous denudation and erosion.

2. West of the hilly lands is the great North China Plain, including the floodplains of the Huang He (Yellow River), the Huai He, and the Hai He (Color Plate 14; Photo 13.1). Most of the land surfaces are less than 100 m in elevation. They have been built of river deposits with occasional deposits of lacustrine and marine origin. The North China Plain or Huang–Huai–Hai Plain is actually a huge delta of the Huang–Huai–Hai river system.

3. The North China Plain is surrounded on the northwest, west, and southwest by mountains consisting of many parallel ranges trending northeast or north-northeast. On the ridges of the northern border

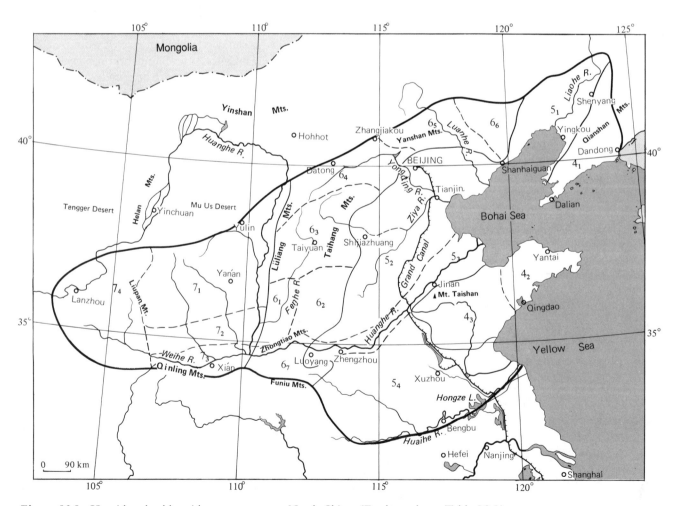

Figure 13.1 Humid and subhumid warm-temperate North China. (For legend, see Table 13.1)

Photo 13.1 The extensive Huai Plain, Anhui Province. The Huai He is also the geographic divide between northern China and southern China.

ranges, the Great Wall has been built (Color Plate 12; Photo 13.2). The average elevation of these ranges is about 1000 m. Between the mountain ranges are faulted basins. Level lands occur only in the basins and parts of the plateaus. The basins are densely populated and intensively cultivated. The mountains are rich in coal reserves and have long become the main source of coal in China.

4. West of the Lüliang Mountains is the typical Loess Plateau. Almost all the surface is covered by loess deposits, except for a few rocky mountain ranges that rise above the plateau. Originally, the plateau

surface was level, with an elevation of around 1000 m. Because of the nature of the loess deposits and human impacts during historic time, the Loess Plateau has suffered badly from soil erosion and has been dissected into a maze of gullies and hills. The chief elements of the landforms are broadly defined as *yuan* (high plain), *liang* (loessic flat ridge), and *mao* (gentle hill slope) (Figure 13.2; Color Plate 17; Photo 13.3). Chinese peasants have worked hard on this rugged topography to create a series of terraced farmlands and water reservoirs (Photos 13.4, 13.5).

Photo 13.2 The once heavily fortified Great Wall at a northern Beijing suburb.

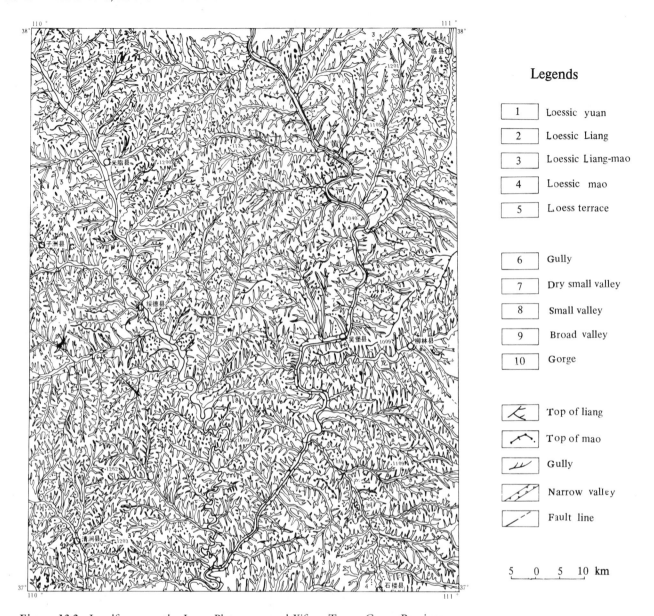

Legends

1	Loessic yuan
2	Loessic Liang
3	Loessic Liang-mao
4	Loessic mao
5	Loess terrace
6	Gully
7	Dry small valley
8	Small valley
9	Broad valley
10	Gorge

	Top of liang
	Top of mao
	Gully
	Narrow valley
	Fault line

5   0   5   10 km

Figure 13.2   Landforms on the Loess Plateau around Xifeng Town, Gansu Province

Humid and Subhumid Warm Temperate Climate

North China lies in the middle latitudes of Eastern Monsoon China. In winter, it is dominated by the Siberian-Mongolian high pressure system. The cold, dry northerly winds sweep over North China. In summer, the conditions are completely reversed. The continent is dominated by a low pressure system, and warm, moist southerly winds prevail. Although such reversals in the monsoon are apparent all over Eastern Monsoon China, nowhere else is the contrast as great as in North China.

The seasonal contrast in temperature is striking. The mean January temperature reaches 0°C in the Huaihe Plain. The mean minimum temperature at Qingdao along the southern Shandong coast, is −16.5°C. As a result, no subtropical evergreen broad-leaved trees or tree crops, such as citrus, tea, and tung oil, can be grown in North China. During the summer, the mean monthly temperature is high; everywhere it exceeds 22°C. The July mean temperature in the North China Plain reaches 28°C, and the maximum temperature can be above 40°C. The long, hot summer makes possible the cultivation of rice, cotton, and groundnuts.

Photo 13.3 Badly dissected topography on the Loess Plateau, northern Shaanxi Province.

Middle and Lower Reaches of the Yellow River (Huang He)

North China essentially represents the middle and lower reaches of the Yellow River. The Hai He and the Huai He are actually its two distributaries. All these rivers have their sources in the surrounding mountains and highlands, then flow to the lowlands and empty into the sea. The discharge of the rivers of North China is not large because of the moderate amount of precipitation in the region and the high evapotranspiration and percolation. Total discharge amounts to 150 billion cu m. The runoff depth is generally less than 200 mm and, in some parts, less than 50 mm. Considering the increasing water demands of population, agriculture, industry, and urban development, the potential shortage is evident. In recent years, underground water has been heavily exploited and even somewhat overexploited. A scheme for diverting water from the Chang Jiang is under construction.

A special problem of the hydrology of North

Photo 13.4 Terraced farmlands on the land-hungry Loess Plateau, western Shanxi Province.

Photo 13.5 Building a water reservoir in the gully area of the Loess Plateau, western Shanxi Province.

China's rivers is the enormous sediment load that originates in the loessic lands of the plateaus and mountains. The average loessic silt load of the middle Yellow River is 37.7 kg/cu m, and 60.8 kg/cu m for the middle Yongding River (a tributary of the Hai He, formerly the so-called "small Yellow River"). The total sediment load per year amounts to 1.6 billion tons for the middle Yellow River and 80 million tons for the middle Yongding River.

Vegetation and Soils

The basic vegetation type in North China is the summer green deciduous broad-leaved forest. It represents a response to the continental monsoon climate with a cold, dry winter and a warm, wet summer. The trees shed their leaves during the winter and turn to a dense, green canopy during the summer. The most commonly seen trees are various species of oak (*Quercus*), maple (*Acer*), poplar (*populus*), birch (*Betula*), elm (*Ulmus*), and willow (*Salix*). Some coniferous trees, such as pine (*Pinus*), juniper (*Juniperus*), fir (*Abies*), spruce (*Picea*), and larch (*Larix*), are also important constituents.

Conforming to the distribution of precipitation and humidity, the vegetation types change from broad-leaved trees along the coast in the east to forest-steppe and steppe on the Loess Plateau in the west and north-west. There are also differences in composition of the vegetation from east to west. More varieties of oak are found in the Shandong Peninsula than in the western

mountains. Species of pine are also different: *Pinus deniflora* is found in the east, *P. tabuliformis* flourishes in the west.

Landforms are another important factor that influences the distribution of vegetation. For example, in the mountainous region around Beijing, the lower slopes are covered by oak and pine (*Pinus tabuliformis*), and there is often a thick undergrowth of mesophytic and semi-xerophytic types. Between 1200–1800 m, some fir, spruce, and larch are found. The tops of the mountains are covered by alpine shrubby meadow.

Natural vegetation on the North China Plain has been cleared for many thousands of years for agricultural purposes, so that few examples of it can now be found. Common deciduous trees that are sometimes grown around settlements and along roads and river banks include willow (*Salix babyoanica*), poplar (*Populus canadensis, P. tomentosa*), maple (*Acer negundo*), and paulownia. The last one is now widely planted on the plain south of the Yellow River as a part of "plain forest." The common shrubs are *Vites chinensis, Zizyphus jujuba, Lespedeza*, and *Caragana sinica*. All are native to North China. *Amorpha fruticosa* is widely planted on saline soils as fodder and fertilizer; its branches are also used for weaving handicrafts.

Most of the level land on the Loess Plateau and along the river valleys is intensely cultivated. The slopes of gullies are covered by shrubs and grasses. The common shrubs are lespedeza (*Lespedeza bicolor*), *Spiraea pobescens, Vitex negundo var. Heteophylla, Zizyphus jujuba*, and *Caragana microphylla*. The predominant species of grasses are *Brothriochloa ischaeman* and *Themeda triandra var. japonica*. Toward the eastern margin of the Loess Plateau, the grass species are replaced by stipa (*Stipa gradis*, *S. krylovii*). The spread of these steppe plant types is attributed to the semiarid climate.

The distribution of soil types coincides in a general way with the distribution of vegetation. Zonal soils are represented by brown forest soils (luvisols), drab soils (cambisols), and *heilu tu* (dark loessic soil). Brown forest soils are found in the humid coastal regions of the Liaodong and Shandong peninsulas. They also appear in vertical zonation on the mountains. The altitude of the upper limit of brown forest soils increases from several hundred meters above sea level in the east to more than 1500 m in the west. Extensive areas of drab soils are found west of the brown forest soil belt. They develop under a subhumid climate and are mostly located on the piedmont plains, foothills, and mountain slopes up to a level above 1000 m in elevation. In the North China Plain, under the influence of a high groundwater table, wet soils (fluvisols) develop. Tracts of saline soils (solonchaks) are found along the coastal belt as well as in the central parts of the great plains.

On the Loess Plateau the zonal soils are dark loessic soils (calcic cambisols). Their profile has a thick upper layer of dark soil, and they are found on level land on the top of the plateau. These soils have been subjected to continual cultivation for centuries. The dark color is the result of humus accumulation. On the slopes of the rolling hills, mainly in the northern and western parts of the Loess Plateau, cultivated loessic soils develop under continual soil erosion. They are little differentiated from the parent loess material. Along the Wei and Fen river valleys, the fertile alluvial soils under intensive cultivation are stratified old loessic soils. Their soil profile has two distinctive layers: a dark upper layer developed under continuous manuring and a lighter lower layer developed under natural conditions.

Rich Energy Resources

North China is rich in energy resources. Extensive coal beds are found in the Carboniferous–Permean strata. Shanxi Province accounts for about 30 percent of China's total proven coal reserves and about 20 percent of its total annual coal production. The goal is annual coal production of 400 million tons by the year 2000. Modern large coal-mining centers also include northeastern Hebei, southern Hebei–northern Henan, west-

ern Henan, central Shaanxi, the southern Taihang Mountains, southwestern Liaoning, the Shandong–Anhui–Jiangsu border area, and others. To date, of the eight largest coal mines in China, five are located in North China (the Datong area of northern Shanxi, the Taiyuan area of central Shaanxi, the Yanzhou area of southwestern Shandong, Pingdingshan of central Henan, and Xu Xian of northern Anhui). Two of the largest commodity transportation flows in China have been the southward movement of coal from North China to Subtropical China in exchange for the northward flow of food grains from Subtropical China to North China. Coal is, and will continue to be, one of China's largest foreign exports. For example, in 1991 alone, more than 20 million tons of coal were exported from China.

Another important energy resource is petroleum. North China is located in the central part of the great oil-rich belt along the eastern Chinese coast, from the northern Northeast China Plain (Daqing oil field) southward to the Liao River oil field (southern Liaoning), then crossing the oil-rich Bo Hai (Photo 13.6), to Dagang oil field (northern Hebei coast), Shengli oil field (at the mouth of the Yellow River), North China oil field (central Hebei Province), Zhongyuan oil field (Henan–Shandong border area), and Henan oil field (southern Henan Province). These five oil fields in North China are among the eight largest in modern China.

In the upper and middle reaches of the Yellow River, where the swift river descends from the high Tibetan Plateau to the Loess Plateau, there is a series of dam sites that have potential for hydroelectric development. More than five hydroelectric plants have been already built and have supplied huge amounts of electricity to the Loess Plateau. In total, about 24 hydroelectric plants will be established on the Loess Plateau, making it very rich both in hydro- and coal-fired electricity. This is a very favorable condition for developing energy-intensive industries in this soil erosion–prone and poverty-stricken area. To date, however, lack of capital has limited this potential.

Other mineral resources include iron ore, which is mainly concentrated in northeastern Hebei Province, one of the three largest iron ore sites in China, with proven reserves of more than half a billion tons. In addition to energy resources, Shandong Province ranks first in China for gold and diamond reserves.

Photo 13.6 Oil drilling in the Bo Hai.

Comprehensive Physical Regionalization

In the comprehensive physical regional systems, North China is subdivided into four natural regions and 19 subregions as shown in Table 13.1 and Figure 13.1. In the comprehensive geographic regional system, two subregions (the Liaodong Peninsula and the Lower Liao River Plain) should be assigned to Northeast China as stated in the previous chapter.

HISTORICAL BACKGROUND

This division, as we have stated, is the cradle of Han China as well as of Chinese agricultural civilization. According to some archeological interpretations, Lantian Man lived on the Loess Plateau about 800,000 to 600,000 years ago. Peking Man lived on the northwestern border of the North China Plain about 700,000 to 200,000 years ago. Tingcun Man and Upper Cave Man inhabited eastern and northern Loess Plateau about 200,000 to 100,000 years ago. Then came the Neolithic age of agricultural civilization about 8000–4000 years ago, which coincided more or less with the legendary period of the Three Rulers and Five Emperors. Small patches of dry farmland appeared almost all over the middle and lower reaches of the Yellow River. In this period, the Hua (later Han) ethnic group was gradually formed.

During the period of the earliest Chinese states—the Xia, Shang, and Western Zhou dynasties and Spring and Autumn Period (2206–403 B.C.)—the Loess Pla-

teau and a little later the North China Plain became the political and economic core of these states. The term for this region is Zhongyuan, which means "central plain," comprising mainly the southern parts of the Loess Plateau and the North China Plain.

During the early period of feudal society (403 B.C.–A.D. 589), when China was unified and prosperous, North China continued to be the political and economic core of different dynastic empires. Xianyang and Xi'an became the capital of the Qin and Western Han dynasties, and Luoyang was the capital of the Eastern Han Dynasty. These ancient capitals might be the first three million-population metropolises in the world. The ancient Silk Road also opened. However, when China was divided and stricken by civil wars and nomadic invasions, millions of hectares of farmland were laid waste and millions of people were killed or starved in North China. Even so, most of the invading nomads were eventually assimilated into the Han. Some inhabitants of North China were also compelled to move southward and thus enhanced the political and economic development of Subtropical China. Nanjing in the lower Chang Jiang valley became the capital and a metropolis of a million people for the first time during that period.

During the middle period of feudal society (589–1279), the same population mixing and migrating phenomena continued. When China was unified under the Sui and Tang dynasties, Xi'an became the capital once again, and North China was socially and economically prosperous. Kaifeng became the capital and a metropolis of a million people during the Northern Song Dynasty. During late Tang Dynasty and the Five Dynasties period, especially when North China was overrun by nomadic invaders during the Southern Song Dynasty, millions of inhabitants of North China were killed or starved, and millions more moved southward. Hangzhou along the Southeast Coast became the capital and a metropolis of a million people for the first time, and Central China in the middle and lower Chang Jiang valley become more populous and economically better developed than North China. During this period large-scale exports of food grains from southern China to northern China via the Grand Canal began.

During the late period of feudal society (1279–1840), China was twice conquered totally by ethnic minorities, the Mongol and then the Manchu. Except for a short period in the early Ming Dynasty, the capital was in Beijing. But Central China continued to be more populous and economically better developed than North China.

In the modern period (1840–1949) and in contemporary China (since 1949), North China developed rapidly as the political center of the country. In 1812 it had a total farmland of about 22 million ha, comprising about 42 percent of the national total. In 1887 the farmland area increased to 24.1 million ha and 44 percent, respectively. In 1949 total farmland increased to 487.9 million *mu* (32.53 ha), but the proportion decreased to

TABLE 13.1
Comprehensive Physical Regionalization of North China

Natural region	Natural subregion	Chief environmental problems
4. Liaodong–Shandong Peninsulas—Deciduous broad-leaved forest region	4(1) Liaodong Peninsula	Soil erosion, low temperature and frost, drought, flood
	4(2) Shandong Peninsula	Soil erosion, drought, flood
	4(3) Central Shandong Mountains & Hills	Soil erosion, deforestation, mud flow
5. North China Plain—forest-steppe region	5(1) Lower Liao River Plain	Drought, flood & waterlogging, low temperature & frost
	5(2) Haihe Plain	Drought, flood & waterlogging, salinization, shifting sand, earthquakes
	5(3) Yellow River Flooding Area	Flood & waterlogging, shifting sand and salinization
	5(4) Northern Huaihe Plain	Flood & waterlogging, drought, salinization
6. Shanxi–Hebei Mountains—Broad-leaved forest and forest-steppe region	6(1) Southern Shanxi Basins	Drought, salinization
	6(2) Southeastern Shanxi Plateau	Soil erosion, drought, deforestation
	6(3) Central Shanxi Basin	Drought, soil erosion, low temperature & frost
	6(4) Upper Yonding River Valley	Soil erosion, drought, deforestation, low temperature & frost
	6(5) North Hebei Mountains	Soil erosion, mud flow, deforestation
	6(6) Western Liaoning Low Mountains and Hills	Soil erosion, mud flow, deforestation, earthquakes
	6(7) Western Henan Mountains	Soil erosion, mud flow deforestation
7. Loess Plateau—forest-eteppe and steppe region	7(1) Northern Shaanxi–Eastern Gansu Hills & Gullies	Soil erosion, deforestation, grassland degradation
	7(2) Northern Shaanxi–Eastern Gansu Dissected High Plains	Soil erosion, low temperature & frost, earthquakes
	7(3) Weihe Valley	Low temperature & frost, drought, earthquakes
	7(4) Middle Gansu Dissected Hills & High Plains	Soil erosion, mud flow, drought, earthquakes

33 percent of the national total because of rapid agricultural development in other parts of China. In 1980 both total farmland and the proportion decreased to 447.4 million *mu* (29.83 ha) and 29 percent, respectively.

On the whole, the historical development of North China was the earliest and the human impact on physical environment and natural resources has been the heaviest of any region in China. Hence, the environment–resource–population–development system, especially the land–food–population subsystem, has been reduced to a very critical condition, and environmental problems and natural hazards have been frequent and widespread. Effective strategies and measures for combating these environmental problems should be taken as soon as possible.

SOCIAL AND ECONOMIC DEVELOPMENT

Agriculture

North China was the cradle of Chinese rain-fed farming. To date, it is still the most important dry farmland area in China. It also has the largest concentration of farmland in China, with a total of 467.1 million *mu* (31.1 million ha) in 1990, accounting for 32.5 percent of the national total. Potential arable land resources are very limited.

The cropping system is generally three crops in two years, with winter wheat, corn, sorghum, millet, and sweet potatoes the chief food crops and cotton, edible oil (peanuts, sesame), and tobacco as major economic crops. Winter wheat is mainly grown south of the Great Wall line. Production has been increasing in recent years, but the output is still not sufficient for local consumption. Hebei remains one of the largest food-importing provinces in China. Corn production in North China continues to increase, accounting now for about one quarter of the national production. Cotton ranks first in sown area but second in national production, while peanuts, sesame and tobacco all rank first in national output.

North China has long been a land of natural hazards and of food deficiency. The North China Plain has been particularly plagued by drought, floods and waterlogging, salinization, and shifting sand, while the Loess Plateau has the worst soil erosion in the world. This is also the region with rapid growth in urban population. The crisis for the land–food–population system has, unfortunately, become all the more critical.

Yet, the North China Plain is the second largest plain in China, endowed with rich land, water, and solar radiation resources. If all these natural resources were used more efficiently, and the extreme effects of the natural hazards could be ameliorated, the potential for much higher agricultural production (mainly increased yields per land unit and per farm laborer) would certainly be very great. Hence, North China, especially the North China Plain, is now the first target area in China for increasing food production on a large scale.

Domestic livestock feeding (chiefly pigs and chickens), artificial and marine fisheries, and plain forestry are also being developed rapidly in North China, even though their proportions in total agricultural production values remain small.

Modern Industry and Transportation

Modern Industry

Based on rich mineral resources and agricultural products as well as on rapid urban development, both heavy and light industries have been developed phenomenally in North China since 1949. Future plans call for industry to be the chief economic branch in North China.

The proposed Shanxi coal-producing region (including parts of the coalfields of neighboring provinces) will be the largest coal-producing and coal-exporting area in China, probably also in the world. It will enhance the development of metallurgy, electricity, chemicals, and other heavy industries, but will also cause environmental problems. At the same time, the large oil fields in the North China Plain will promote oil refineries and other chemical industries. The entire complex will be the largest energy and chemical industry center in China.

The large iron and steel industries in the Beijing–Tianjin–Tangshan area and the Taiyuan area depend heavily on the abundant energy and mineral resources of the region and will prosper as a result of the easy access to these resources.

The large cotton textile industries have expanded from two old centers—Tianjin and Qingdao—to six new centers—Shijiazhuang, Beijing, Handan, Zhengzhou, Xi'an, and Xianyang. All major cotton textile mills are located in the cotton-growing areas. In addition there are many smaller centers.

Among industrial centers four belts are the most prominent:

1. Beijing–Tianjin–Tangshan area, with a total area of 52,000 sq km, accounts for about 9 percent of

China's total industrial production value and about 40 percent of that of North China. Chief industries include steel and metallurgy, petroleum and marine chemicals, energy, engineering, electrical equipment and electronics, and textiles.

2. Jinan–Qingdao railway belt. The chief industrial and economic center of the Shandong Province follows the Jinan–Qingdao railroad and accounts for about one-half of Shandong's total industrial production value. Chief industries of this belt include textiles, chemicals, porcelain, fertilizer, and steel.

3. Shijiazhuang–Handan. Located along the Beijing–Wuhan railway and along the eastern foothills of the Taihang Mountains, this belt is the chief industrial region of Hebei Province. Chief industries include textiles, engineering, electricity, steel, porcelain, and processing enterprises.

4. Central Shanxi, based on very rich coal mines with Taiyuan as its center, is mainly a heavy industrial center. Chief industries include steel, engineering, and coal mining.

Modern Transportation

A modern transportation network has been developed in North China since 1949. With railways and sea waterways as the backbones, this rather sophisticated network is composed of three north–south railways (Tianjin–Nanjing, Beijing–Wuhan–Guangzhou, and Datong–Taiyang–Jiaozuo), three east–west railways (Beijing–Baotou, Qingdao–Jinan–Shijiazhuang, Lianyungang–Zhengzhou–Xi'an–Lanzhou), and five seaports (Qinhuangdao, Tianjin, Yantai, Qingdao, and Shiju Port) together with their roadways, inland and sea waterways, and numerous air routes.

Railways serve mainly for the transportation and export of coal. From Datong and Zhengzhou eastward, there are already five railway links with five seaports, of which the newly built (1990) Datong–Beijing–Qinhuangdao line is the most important. The trans-Eurasia continental line is actually an extension of the Lianyungang (at the Yellow Sea coast in northern Jiangsu) and the Zhengzhou–Xi'an–Lanzhou railway, westward to Ürümqi and beyond to the Sino-Russian border, where it links with the Russian and European railway systems. It is of very great potential value.

Seaports have also made a great contribution to modern transportation in North China. Qinhuangdao is the only ice-free port in the Bo Hai and is now the greatest coal and petroleum-exporting port in China.

Tianjin, Yantai, and Qingdao are excellent old seaports. As evidence of China's newly formed interest in foreign trade, the new deep-water seaport of Shiju, located on the southern Shandong coast, has been built since 1980, chiefly for the purpose of exporting coal from southwestern Shandong province.

Ethnic Groups and Population

North China is almost exclusively inhabited by the Han, who made up about 98.5 percent of the total population in 1982 and an especially high proportion of the population in some provinces: Henan 98.9 percent, Shandong 99.5 percent, Shanxi 99.7 percent, and Shaanxi 99.5 percent.

In 1990, there were about 300 million inhabitants in this division, or about 26 percent of China's total population. Henan Province alone had a population of 86.5 million in 1990, and Shandong had 84.9 million. They are the second and third most populous provinces in China (Sichuan Province had 108.0 million people in 1990).

Rural and Urban Settlements

Rural Settlement

Closely related to overall population density, rural settlement of the North China Plain and other alluvial plains is dense, although it is relatively sparse on the Loess Plateau and in mountain areas. Village houses are generally of brick-tile with one or two floors, and a roof inclination of 5°–15°. Around and inside the villages, some broad-leaved trees are planted. Along the Huai He and other frequently flooding rivers, the villages are built on artificial terraces, the elevation of which reflects the average high-flood level. On the Loess Plateau, many houses are loessic caves, sometimes with the plateau surface as their roofs. They are supposed to be cool in summer and warm in winter, but are disastrous in earthquakes.

Urban Settlements

Closely related to rapid industrialization and urbanization in North China, large cities and modern metropolises have developed rapidly since 1949. In 1990, there were 10 metropolitan areas in North China, each with a population of more than 1 million. Three other cities—Handan, Luoyang, and Kaifeng—had a population between 500,000 and 1 million. The 10 metropolises with a population of over 1 million are:

1. *Beijing:* The capital of China for most of the time since A.D. 1279, Beijing is now also a great center of industry, transportation, education, and culture. It is also famous for its many historical, cultural, and scenic sites, including the Imperial Palace and Tiananmen Square. In 1990 it had a total population of 7.0 million and a nonagricultural population of 5.77 million, second in size only to Shanghai.

2. *Tianjin:* As one of the three national municipalities, Tianjin has the second largest comprehensive industrial base in China. In 1990 it had a total population of 5.77 million and a nonagricultural population of 4.57 million, being the third largest metropolis in China.

3. *Xi'an:* The oldest of the six ancient capitals in China, Xi'an is now the provincial capital of Shaanxi. It is famous for many historical, cultural, and scenic sites, including the tomb of the first emperor of the Qin Dynasty. In 1990 it had a total population of 2.76 million and a nonagricultural population of 1.96 million.

4. *Taiyuan:* Taiyuan is the capital as well as economic and cultural center of the Shanxi Province. It is also one of the newly built heavy industrial bases in China. In 1990 it had a total population of 1.96 million and a nonagricultural population of 1.53 million.

5. *Jinan:* Jinan is the capital as well as the economic and cultural center of the Shandong Province. In 1990 it had a total population of 2.32 million and a nonagricultural population of 1.48 million.

6. *Qingdao:* A famous seaport and industrial city along the Yellow Sea coast, Qingdao had a total population of 2.06 million and a nonagricultural population of 1.46 million in 1990.

7. *Zhengzhou:* One of the most important railway junctions in China, Zhengzhou is the capital and industrial center of Henan Province. In 1990 it had a total population of 1.71 million and a nonagricultural population of 1.16 million.

8. *Zibo:* This is an industrial city along the Jinan–Qingdao railway. It was once the prosperous ancient capital of the Qi Kingdom during the Warring States Period. In 1990 it had a total population of 2.46 million and a nonagricultural population of 1.14 million.

9. *Shijiazhuang:* The capital as well as the economic and cultural center of the Hebei Province, Shijiazhuang has rapidly developed as an industrial city since 1949. In 1990 it had a total population of 1.32 million and a nonagricultural population of 1.07 million.

10. *Tangshan:* Since this important metropolis of 1 million people was practically raized to ground by the 1976 earthquake, it has recovered rapidly and in 1990 had a total population of 1.5 million and a nonagricultural population of 1.04 million.

AREAL DIFFERENTIATION AND REGIONAL DEVELOPMENT

On the whole, North China and Central China have been and will continue to be the two core areas in China. Modern economic development including agriculture, industry, and transportation will continue to be comprehensively and rapidly developed. Some serious social and economic problems, such as the widespread environmental problems and the critical land–food–population system, should eventually be solved. At the same time, regions and subregions will be developed according to their specific physical and human conditions.

Shandong Peninsula

The Shandong Peninsula (region 4[1] on Figure 13.1) is the front door to North China, with long seacoasts and numerous seaports. The climate is much milder and more humid than interior areas at similar latitudes. On the whole, the physical and human conditions are favorable to agricultural and general economic development.

Geomorphologically, the region is dominated by undulating hilly lands. Two geomorphological units can be identified:

1. The Shandong Peninsula is composed mainly of undulating hills, mostly under 300 m in elevation. Its western margin is the peneplaned and alluvial Jiaolai Plain, which is intensively cultivated and densely populated.

---

[1] In the comprehensive physical regional system, the Shandong Peninsula is region 4 of the "Liaodong–Shandong Peninsulas—Deciduous Broad-leaved Forest Region;" hence, the number "4" is used here.

2. The central Shandong mountains and hills are composed mainly of horsts and grabens, with many peaks above 1000 m in elevation, of which the sacred Mount Taishan (1524 m) is the highest (Color Plate 19). Numerous rivers radiate away from Mount Taishan to form an impressive fluvial network. Most of the associated low mountains and hills have rounded tops and gentle slopes and are quite rich in coal reserves.

The climate is mild and humid. The mean January temperature ranges from $-4°$–$0°C$. The mean July temperature shows little areal differentiation from south to north and is generally around 25°C. The frost-free season lasts from 5.5–8.5 months, with a cumulative temperature of 3200°–4500°C during the $\geq 10°C$ period. Double cropping is generally practiced. Annual precipitation totals 600–900 mm, decreasing from the coast inland. About 60 percent of the annual precipitation is concentrated in summer. The aridity index is generally around 1.0, which represents a marginal humid condition. Because of rather high annual variability, about two thirds of the years are deficient in moisture during the $\geq 10°C$ period of plant growth. Droughts are thus frequent.

Most rivers are short and swift. The annual runoff depth ranges from 200–400 mm, with the eastern Liaodong Peninsula and central Shandong mountains attaining 500 mm. About 80–90 percent of the annual runoff is concentrated in summer and autumn. Occasional floods occur in the lowlands.

The original vegetation has been long since removed. Zonal natural vegetation is deciduous broad-leaved forest, with oak dominating. The most commonly seen coniferous tree is pine (*Pinus densiflora*). Common shrubs are *Rhododendron dauricum* and *Deutzia amurensis*. In the northern or mountainous area, mixed broad- and needle-leaved forests are also seen. The region ranks as one of the most important tussah silk–producing areas in China, with oak (*Quercus acutissima*) widely planted to feed the tussah silkworms. Fruit trees, such as apple, pear, peach, chestnut, and walnut are widely and productively grown.

The zonal soil is brown forest soil. Argillation and leaching are the chief soil-forming processes. Owing to the extensive distribution of granite and gneiss, which are composed largely of silica, as well as the large sandy tracts along the rivers and coasts, sandy soils are widespread in the region, which is planted largely in groundnuts.

The region enjoys varied land resources and well-managed agriculture. The most widespread land type is low mountains of 500–1000 m in elevation, covered with deciduous broad-leaved trees. Hills have elevations between 200–500 m, with slopes of generally more than 10°. Oak trees cover the hills, intermixed with shrubs and orchards, although some dry-farming lands have also been established on the gentler slopes.

Low hills have an elevation between 50–200 m, with slopes less than 10°, and they are largely planted with fruit trees. All mountains and hills are susceptible to severe soil erosion when the vegetation cover has been removed. Therefore, soil conservation and reforestation are of paramount importance.

Plains of various types lie below 50 m, including alluvial plains, undulating peneplaned plains, marine-eroded terraces, and plains derived from marine deposits. They have level topography and thick soils as well as favorable temperature and moisture conditions. Hence, farmlands and population are concentrated on the plains. Beaches include both marine and fluvial types. The marine beach is flat and marshy and is suitable for salt production, reed planting, or fishing. Parts of the marine beaches might be also reclaimed as farmland. The fluvial beaches are mostly composed of sandy land and are fit for planting forest shelter belts.

In conjunction with the two geomorphological units, two natural subregions can be demarcated within the region.

Shandong Peninsula

Encircled by the Bo Hai and the Yellow Sea to the north, east, and south, the Shandong Peninsula (4_2^2 on Figure 13.1) is connected with the central Shandong mountains and hills by the broad Jiaolai Plain in the west. About two-thirds of the subregion consists of undulating hills 200–300 m in elevation. Shorelines are bold and rocky; wave-cut cliffs rise abruptly from the water's edge, and isolated hilltops project out of the sea as rocky islands. There are many excellent harbors, but they are handicapped by limited hinterlands. Annual precipitation totals 700–900 mm; the cumulative temperature during the $\geq 10°C$ period is 4000°–4600°C, and the frost-free season lasts 180–210 days. Qingdao has a mean January temperature of $-1.1°C$, and an absolute minimum temperature above $-16°C$, which makes it the warmest part of North China during the wintertime. Zonal vegetation is deciduous broad-leaved forest, and

---

[2] In the comprehensive physical regional system, the subregion numbered 4(1) is the Liaodong Peninsula.

the zonal soil is a brown forest type. Practically all level land and a part of the mountain slopes have been cultivated. This is one of the major fruit-, fish-, and groundnut-producing areas in China.

Central Shandong Mountains and Hills

Located west of the Shandong Peninsula and roughly separated from the North China Plain by the 200 m contour line, the Central Shandong Mountains and Hills subregion (4_3 on Figure 13.1) is a vast area of block mountains with Mount Taishan and other high peaks over 1000 m rising majestically above the surrounding plains. Annual precipitation totals 600–900 mm, and cumulative temperature during the $\geq 10°C$ period ranges from 4000–4500°C. Zonal vegetation is deciduous broad-leaved forest with some coniferous trees at higher elevations. Zonal soils are brown forest soil and leached brown forest soil. This is mainly a land of forestry, with farming restricted to intermontane valleys. Much work in soil conservation and reforestation needs to be done here to stabilize the pattern of land use and to increase productivity.

The North China Plain

The North China Plain stretches from the Taihang Mountains and the Funiu Mountains eastward to the Bo Hai and the Yellow Sea, and from the Great Wall line southward to the Qinling–Huai He line, comprising an area of about 330,000 sq km.

The Huanghe–Haihe–Huaihe river systems are well developed and are the agents that nourish the North China Plain. The Huang He (Yellow River) is, of course, the main river in the region. It flows through the easily eroded Loess Plateau, carrying a silt load of about 1.6 billion tons annually. It then suddenly drops onto the North China Plain after passing through the Sanmen Gorge and starts building a gigantic delta of about 250,000 sq km. Hence, it is notorious for shifting, flooding, and silting in its lower reaches. The Yellow River extended its length at the mouth by 35 km during last 15 years (1975–1991).

The region is characterized by monotonous flatness. Few localities have an elevation above 50 m and a relative relief of more than 20 m. Nevertheless, from the piedmont plain of the Taihang Mountains eastward to the sea, three geomorphological and hydrologic belts can be demarcated.

1. Diluvial-alluvial inclining plains are located at the piedmonts of the Taihang Mountains. They are composed mainly of numerous alluvial fans, with a width of 10–55 km, an elevation of 50–100 m, and a gradient of 1/200 to 1/2000. Groundwater resources are rich in this belt, with the groundwater table varying from 2 to 10 m. Drainage is good, mineralization of groundwater is less than 1 gram/liter (g/l). On the margins of the alluvial fans, the groundwater table is shallow and sometimes emerges as springs. Numerous marshy lands and freshwater lakes (such as the famous Baiyang Lake) exist in the depressions between the alluvial fans.

2. Low alluvial plains are located to the east of the diluvial-alluvial plains. These are major components of the North China Plain, with elevation below 50 m and sometimes as low as 3 m. The gradient is negligible and drainage is poor. Rivers often flow sluggishly "above" the ground, resulting in frequent dam breaks and floods. Marshy depressions and shallow lakes dot the alluvial plains. Eolian sandy dunes are also formed along the river channels. The water quality is fairly good (mineralization 1–2 g/l), although the quantity is not as plentiful as needed.

3. Low coastal plains border the Bo Hai, with an elevation generally lower than 4 m. They are formed by both fluvial and marine deposits. Clay dominates the land. The groundwater table ranges from 1 to 1.5 m deep, with high mineralization of 10 to 30 g/l or more. The landforms along the coast are quite varied, including old and new deltas, sandy beaches, and dunes.

The climate is characterized by a dry, windy spring, a warm, rainy summer, a pleasant, calm autumn, and cold, dry winter. The hottest month (July) is quite subtropical, with a mean temperature of 24° to 29°C and an absolute maximum temperature above 40°C (42.6°C in Beijing). The coldest month (January) is, however, boreal, with a mean temperature of 0°C to −14°C, and an absolute minimum temperature below −20°C (−22.4°C in Beijing). Cumulative temperature during the $\geq 10°C$ period totals 3400°–4500°C (Beijing 4,056°C), and the frost-free season lasts 170–220 days. Three crops can be grown in two years, and the major crops are winter wheat, corn, soybeans, and cotton. However, owing to the limitations inherent in the severely cold winter, subtropical crops cannot survive, and no vegetables can be grown during the winter except in greenhouses.

Annual precipitation totals 500–800 mm (Tianjin 529.5 mm; Beijing 640.6 mm). Rainfall is concentrated in the summer, with winter accounting for only 3–7 percent and spring only 10–14 percent of the annual precipitation. Annual variation is generally as high as 25 percent, and the rainiest year may get more than 10 times the precipitation of the driest year. For example, Beijing had 1406 mm of precipitation in 1959 but only 168.5 mm in 1891. Therefore, spring drought and summer floods together with salinization and eolian sand often plague agricultural production in the region. According to incomplete documentary statistics, 407 droughts and 387 floods occurred in the Hai He basin between A.D. 1368 and 1949.

The region has been cultivated more than 7000–8000 years; hence, practically all natural vegetation has been destroyed or transformed. Soils, being more "conservative," are a better index for reflecting the physical environment. There are two major soil units in the North China Plain: the drab soil (cambisols) and the wet soil (fluvisols). The former is the zonal soil, with a deep solum, light texture, and good drainage, and is found mostly on the diluvial-alluvial inclining plains under good management. These soils have been excellent agricultural soils for thousands of years. Fluvisols are widely distributed on alluvial plains, with a heavier texture and usually impeded drainage and hence are plagued by salinization. Other local soil types include *shachang* soils, coastal saline soils, and meadow soils.

Haihe Plain

Delimited on the north by the Great Wall line, on the west by the Taihang Mountains, on the south by the lower Yellow River channel and bordering the Bo Hai on the east, the Haihe Plain subregion (5_2[3] on Figure 13.1) has been essentially deposited by the Yellow River and its distributary, the Hai He (Color Plate 14). It consists mainly of lowlands encircled by mountains and hills on its northern and western borders. This is one of the most important grain- and cotton-producing areas in China, with double cropping in the southern part and three crops in two years in the northern part. The Beijing area is located at the junction between the piedmont plains of the Yanshan and the Taihang Mountains and is thus sometimes called the Beijing Gulf. Distribution of major land types of this area is shown in Figure 13.3. All land types in the plain are good arable lands, now intensively used for vegetables and field crops and also extensively used for nonagricultural purposes. The surround-

ing mountains and hills are largely used for fruits, pasture, forestry, and recreation.

Yellow River Flood Area

Located mainly along the lower Yellow River, the Yellow River Flood Area (5_3 on Figure 13.1) has been frequently scoured by river flooding, and sandy dunes line the river channel. The salinization hazard is also severe.

Northern Huaihe Plain

The Northern Huaihe Plain (5_4 on Figure 13.1) is located north of the Huai He channel, which serves as the geographic divide between southern China and northern China. This subregion has the best climatic conditions in the region, but because of frequent southward collapse of dikes and flooding of the Yellow River since A.D. 1194, the original Huaihe river system has been badly deranged and drainage has been greatly impeded. The result is that, as the saying goes, "Light rains cause light waterlogging; heavy rains cause heavy floods; while no rain results in drought." Recently, conditions in this subregion have been improved through stream management and landscape modification.

Shanxi-Hebei Mountains

This region is delimited by the Taihang Mountains in the east, by the Lüliang Mountains in the west, and by the Great Wall line in the north. The area between the Taihang and the Lüliang Mountains has been traditionally called the Shanxi Plateau and has been considered as the eastern part of the Loess Plateau. But it differs from the Loess Plateau by being an anticlinorium uplifted during the Yanshan Tectonic Movement (both the North China Plain and the Loess Plateau were sinking synclinoria). Another difference is that loess covers only the basins and the lower slopes of mountains; the Loess Plateau is covered nearly everywhere. Therefore, it is preferable to combine this area with the northern Hebei Mountains to form an independent physical-geographical region.

The region consists of a series of parallel folded and faulted mountains as well as intermontane graben basins and structural valleys. They were mainly shaped during the Yanshan Tectonic Movement. On the axis of the anticlinorium, outcrops of ancient pre-Cambrain metaphorphic rocks may be found, whereas on the flanks, Cambrian and Ordovician limestones and shales and Carbonifous and Permian sandstones and shale are exposed in succession. In the latter, there are also thin

---

[3] In the comprehensive physical regional system, the subregion numbered 5(1) is the Lower Liao River Plain.

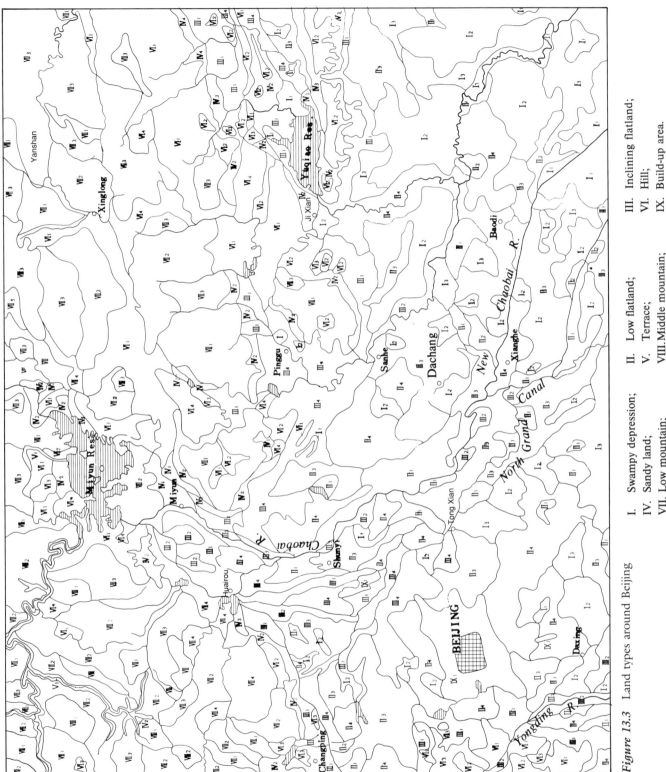

Figure 13.3 Land types around Beijing

I.   Swampy depression;   II. Low flatland;   III. Inclining flatland;
IV. Sandy land;   V.   Terrace;   VI. Hill;
VII. Low mountain;   VIII. Middle mountain;   IX. Build-up area.

limestone layers interbedded with numerous coal seams, which make this region the largest coal-producing area in China. The relief is rugged and varied, with many peaks towering above 2000 m, the highest being Mount Wutai at 3058 m. Five geomorphological units can be identified:

1. The Southeastern Shanxi Plateau includes the southern section of the Taihang Mountains and the Zhongtiao Mountains as well as the Qin He basin sandwiched between them. A series of small basins surrounded by mountains is covered by loess, which has been dissected into undulating hills.

2. The Northeastern Shanxi Plateau includes the northern sections of the Taihang Mountains, Wutai Mountain, and other block mountains. It is the highest part of the region and is the source of many large rivers.

3. The Western Shanxi Plateau is mainly composed of the north-northeast–trending Lüliang Mountains, with a length of about 400 km and highest peak at 2831 m.

4. Central basins of Shanxi Plateau include a series of Cenozoic graben basins, such as the central Shanxi Basin along the Fenhe graben and the Datong Basin in the upper Yongding River valley. These intermontane basins are the major agricultural areas on the Shanxi Plateau where the loessic materials along the basin border are dissected into terraces, and flat alluvial-lacustrine plains are common in the basin centers.

5. Hebei–Liaoning Mountains. The Yanshan Mountains are the backbone of this unit. In western Liaoning, the area is composed mainly of low mountains and hills of igneous rocks. In northern Hebei, the area consists chiefly of low and medium mountains and hills.

Climatically, the Shanxi–Hebei mountains region is a conspicuous transitional belt between the subhumid warm temperate and the semiarid temperate climates. Aridity increases from east to west on the Shanxi Plateau and from south to north along the Hebei and Liaoning mountain systems. Vertical zonation is also conspicuous. Cumulative temperature during the $\geq 10°C$ period totals 3000°–4500°C. On the Shanxi Plateau, from south to north, the cumulative temperature decreases by 340°C for each 100 km. If the relief element is added, the difference in temperature is even more prominent. For example, from Beijing (elevation 51 m) to Zhangjiakou (Kalgan, elevation 770 m), the cumulative

temperature decreases from 4046°C to about 3000°C, a sharp decrease of 550°C for each 100 km of distance between the two cities. Annual precipitation totals 400 to 700 mm, decreasing from southeast to northwest. Windward slopes receive much more than leeward slopes, and the mountainous area much more than the basins.

Rivers consist mainly of the upper reaches of the Hai He, such as the Chaobai, the Yongding, and the Ziya. The Fen He and the Qin He are tributaries to the Yellow River; whereas the Luan He and the Liao River flow into the sea independently. All these rivers generally have low discharge and uneven seasonal flow. The Chaobai River with its reservoir, Miyun, is now the most important water source for Beijing, and the Luan He has recently been diverted southward to supply a badly needed water source for Tianjin.

Distribution of vegetation and soils is also transitional. Zonal vegetation makes a transition from deciduous broad-leaved forest in the southeast to forest-steppe in the northwest. Zonal soils change from drab soils to dark loessic and chestnut soils. Vertical zonation is also conspicuous. As a rule, from the bases of the mountains up to 1200 m, warm-temperate deciduous broad-leaved forests dominate with different species of oaks (*Quercus variabilis*, *Q. acutissima*, *Q. liaodiongensis*, *Q. dentata*) being the most common. There are also other deciduous broad-leaved trees, such as *Fraxinus chinensis*, *Carpinus turczaninoii*, and *Acer mono*, and some coniferous trees, such as *Pinus tabuliformis* and *P. densiflora*. From 1200 to 1800 m, the temperate deciduous broad-leaved forests dominate, with *Betula platyphylla* and *Populous davidiana* as the major species. From 1800 to 2500 m, the forest is transformed to a cool-temperate needle-leaved type, with spruce (*Picea meyeri*, *P. wilsonii*) forest on the lower slopes (1800–2300 m) and larch (*Larix principis-ruprechtii*) on the upper slopes (2300–2500 m). The upper limit represents the tree line in North China. Finally, from 2500 m up to the mountain top, subalpine shrubby meadow predominates with common deciduous shrubs, such as *Caragana jubata* and *Spiraea alpina*, and numerous grasses, such as *Festuca ovins*, *Koleria cristata*, and *Kobresia bellardi*.

Practically all level lands, including flood plains, terraces, and platforms, have been intensively cultivated, with winter wheat, corn, millet, and sorghum as the chief crops. Cotton and tobacco can also be grown in the southern Shanxi basins. The dominant cropping system is three crops in two years. But north of the Zhangjiakou–Fengning–Chaoyang line (somewhat north of the Great Wall), the cropping system changes to one crop in one year, with spring wheat, naked oats, millet, and Irish potatoes as the chief crops. By contrast, mountains and hills are rather extensively used or even misused; most of the forest cover has been removed, resulting in severe soil erosion, although on many of the hills and some lower gentle slopes of low mountains are large areas of fruit trees, and subalpine shrubby meadows have been well used as summer-autumn pasture. Overall planning is urgently needed for comprehensive and sustainable use of the land, especially the extensive mountainous lands. Industry based on very rich coal resource seems to be the main driving force for economic development in the region.

Southern Shanxi Basins

The Southern Shanxi Basins (6_1 on Figure 13.1) include basins along the southern Fen He graben valley. The subregion features level landforms, deep soils, and a warm temperate climate, with a cumulative temperature during the $\geq 10°C$ period of 4000°–4500°C. The Yuncheng Basin has an elevation of 330–360 m, composed chiefly of alluvial-lacustrine deposits with thick salt beds in Tertiary lacustrine deposits. The famous salt-producing Xiechi Lake (elevation 324 m) is located at the southern margin of the basin.

Southeastern Shanxi Plateau

The Southeastern Shanxi Plateau (6_2 on Figure 13.1) consists mainly of mountainous and hilly lands, with numerous small intermontane basins at elevations between 800 and 1200 m. Annual precipitation totals 520–680 mm, suitable for dry farming, but level land available for irrigation is rather limited. Some forests still blanket the mountains with an average coverage of 10–25 percent.

Central Shanxi Basins

The Central Shanxi Basins (6_3 on Figure 13.1) include the Taiyuan and Xin Xian basins. The Taiyuan Basin has an area of 5050 sq km and an elevation of 700–900 m. It is bounded by steep fault scarps, both on the east and on the west, with large alluvial fans spreading along their foothills. There are also extensive loessic terraces on both the northeastern and the southwestern margins. With a cumulative temperature during the $\geq 10°C$ period of 3300°–3600°C and annual precipitation of 500–600 mm, this area is the most important agricultural and industrial center in Shanxi province.

Upper Yongding River Valley

Located at the transition between the Shanxi and the Inner Mongolian Plateaus, the Upper Yongding Valley (6_4 on Figure 13.1) includes a series of small basins along the upper reaches of the Yongding River from the Yanqing Basin in the east to the Datong Basin in the west. It is also a transitional area between a subhumid warm temperate climate and a semiarid temperate climate, which support corresponding vegetation types that also make a transition from deciduous broad-leaved forest to forest-steppe and steppe vegetation. The river valley is a stepping stone from the high Inner Mongolian and Shanxi plateaus to the low North China Plain. It enjoys a cumulative temperature during the $\geq 10°C$ period of 2500°–3000°C and an annual precipitation of 400–500 mm. In terms of human use, the valley is a transitional belt between farming and pastore. Furthermore, this is the largest coal-producing area in China and hence is suitable for comprehensive agricultural and industrial development.

Northern Hebei Mountains

Consisting mainly of low and medium mountains, the Northern Hebei Mountains (6_5 on Figure 13.1) have a subhumid warm temperate climate and cumulative temperature during the $\geq 10°C$ period of 3000°–4000°C and annual precipitation of 500–700 mm. Vertical zonation is conspicuous. The Luan He and the Chaobai River together with numerous tributaries cut through the northeast-trending ranges in deep gorges. Many reservoirs have been built at the mouths of these gorges, which provide the chief water supplies for Beijing, Tianjin, and Tangshan. Furthermore, this is the site of the Great Wall, marking the traditional farming–pastoral boundary for nearly 2000 years.

Western Liaoning Low Mountains and Hills

The Western Liaoning Low Mountains and Hills (6_6 on Figure 13.1) have a transitional climate between subhumid warm temperate and subhumid temperate.

Western Henan Mountains

The Western Henan Mountains (6_7 on Figure 13.1) are composed chiefly of the Xiaoshan, Xiong'er, Songshan, and other Paleozoic mountains in western Henan province. The often productive foothills and river valleys are extensively covered by loessic deposits. The subregion is deeply dissected by the Yellow River and two tributaries—the Yi He and the Luo He. The Xiaoshan together with the Zhongtiao Mountains in Shanxi province form the famous Sanman Gorge of the Yellow River, where a large-scale reservoir has been built and another one will be soon constructed. This is still part of North China, with a subhumid warm temperate climate and deciduous broad-leaved forests as the zonal vegetation.

Loess Plateau

The 300,000 sq km Loess Plateau is defined on its eastern margin by the Lüliang Mountains, on its western margin by the Helan Mountains, and on its southern margin by the Qinling Mountains. The northern margin, located in a transition belt, is not distinct. The Great Wall, which represents the landward limit of the moist summer monsoon as well as the traditional farming–pastoral boundary, is often used as a boundary marker because of its prominence. Administratively, the Loess Plateau includes portions of Shaanxi and Gansu provinces and Ningxia Hui Autonomous Region. With an elevation of 1200–1600 m, it is covered extensively by loess deposits from 30 to 60 m thick on the average (at its thickest it reaches 200–300 m). This is the classic zone of loess-deposited topography as well as the severest soil erosion in the world. The Loess Plateau is also notorious for low agricultural production and critical land–food–population imbalance, although it also has great potential for energy-intensive industrial development. Geologically, the loess has been deposited since the Pleistocene epoch, and three layers can be clearly identified.

1. The lower layer, called Wuchang Loess (Q1), has a rather limited distribution with a thickness of about 17 m.
2. The Lishi Loess (Q2) is most extensive, with a thickness of 80 to 120 m and constitutes the major proportion of the deposit.
3. The Malan Loess (Q3) is extensive but is only 20 to 40 m thick.

All of these types of loess are mainly eolian deposits, composed of silt, and are easily subjected to water or wind erosion. When loess is soaked with water, serious erosion might occur even on slopes as gentle as 3° to 5°, although when dry, some loess cliffs can even stand as steep as 90°.

Geomorphologically, the Loess Plateau is subdivided into three parts:

1. The southern part makes up the broad Wei He valley, which is a faulted graben.
2. The middle part is characterized by extensive flat loessic high plains, which denote a better preserved level surface with a series of deep gullies, sometimes more than 100 m deep.
3. The northern part is a loessic, hilly area composed mainly of loessic gentle slopes and ridges dissected into rugged topography (Figure 13.3).

There are also rocky island-like mountains that stand high above the Loess Plateau such as the Liupan Mountains and the Lüliang Mountains. The upper limit of the loess deposits is the so-called "loess line," which is found at about 1000 m on the Lüliang Mountains but rises to 1800 m on the eastern slope of the Liupan Mountains and as high as 2,400 m on the western slope. These rocky mountains are generally covered by forests or grasses, and hence soil erosion is limited. Even so, the potential for erosion can be high if the vegetation cover is disturbed.

This is a warm temperate thermal regime with a cumulative temperature during the ≥ 10°C period of 3200°–3600°C. Annual precipitation totals 350 to 650 mm, of which 90 percent comes in the ≥ 10°C period. Rainstorms occur frequently during the summertime and result in severe soil erosion. Moisture conditions change from subhumid in the southeast to semiarid in the northwest, with the aridity index increasing from 1.5 to 4.0. To suppress high evaporation, farmers around the Lanzhou area usually spread a "mulch" of pebbles and sand over the farmlands, forming the so-called "sand farmland."

Most of the rivers flow into the Yellow River. The annual runoff depth decreases from 50 mm in the southeast to 25 mm in the northwest. The Weihe River is the largest tributary of the Yellow River. It creates a broad, fertile valley with a cumulative temperature of 4500°–5000°C during the ≥ 10°C period, a growing season of 260 days, and an annual precipitation of 500–600 mm. It is one of the oldest farming areas in China and one of the most important commercial food grain and cotton-producing bases in China. The region was also the political, economic, and cultural center for China more than 1000 years ago.

Other important tributaries to the Yellow River are the Qian He, the Luo He, and the Wuding River. All are heavily loaded with silt, especially during the summertime. The Wuding River is so highly silt-laden that its channel changes frequently. The name "Wuding" means "always changing." These rivers are the chief agents for soil erosion and alluvial deposition in the region. Flood plains along their channels, the so-called *chuan*, although limited in area, are where most of the irrigated farmlands and settlements are concentrated.

Coinciding with moisture conditions, the zonal vegetation changes from a deciduous broad-leaved forest in the southeast to forest-steppe in the center and to steppe in the northwest. Inasmuch as the region has been cultivated for more than 7000–8000 years, practically all original vegetation has been removed. Only small patches of the deciduous broad-leaved forest are left, scattered on steep northern slopes, and on high mountain tops only a few coniferous forests remain. Environmental protection and revegetation have become a very urgent priority on the Loess Plateau.

Zonal soils are drab soils in the southeast and dark loessic soils in the northwest. Both are developed on loessic materials, with soil profiles 2–3 m thick and a humus layer about 1 m thick. Dominant soil-forming processes are calcification and humification. Cultivation also plays an important role. The dark loessic soils are in reality ancient cultivated soils, occurring generally on level, cultivated high plains and affected only minimally by severe soil erosion; they are extensively used for growing wheat, corn, millet, sorghum, and other crops. Another widely distributed ancient cultivated soil is the so-called *lou tu*, located mainly on terraces of the broad Wei He valley and developed chiefly on the drab soils. Still another cultivated soil is the so-called *min tu*, distributed in badly eroded areas and cultivated directly on loessic parent materials where a distinct soil profile has not yet developed.

Northern Shaanxi–Eastern Gansu Hills and Gullies

Located on the northern part of the Loess Plateau, this subregion (7_1 on Figure 13.1) is mainly composed of dissected gentle slopes and flat ridges. The loess grains are rather coarse and are sometimes called sandy loess. Soil erosion is severe, but recently large-scale coal deposits have been found. Zonal vegetation was temperate forest-steppe, but most of it is now destroyed. In overall regional planning goals, this subregion should be developed for comprehensive farming–pasture–forestry, with emphasis on environmental protection, and energy-intensive industrial development. At the moment, urgent measures are needed to restore the grass cover and the crop–grass rotation system and to enforce other soil conservation measures.

Northern Shaanxi–Eastern Gansu Dissected High Plains

Located south of subregion 7_1 and identified on Figure 13.1 as 7_2, this area is composed mainly of extensive level high plains and dissected gullies. Two secondary forest-covered mountainous areas are also included. The major soil types are the cultivated drab soils, which support a zonal forest-steppe vegetation. This subregion should be devoted only to dry farmland and pasture on the high plains and to foresty and pasture on the mountains. Soil conservation measures are urgently needed in both these areas.

Wei He Valley

The broad valley of the Wei He (7_3 on Figure 13.1) is composed of floodplains as well as three terraces, the so-called first *yuan*, second *yuan*, and third *yuan*. On the northern foot of the Qinling, there are still higher terraces. All these floodplains and terraces are fairly well preserved with level surfaces only along some large rivers. Zonal vegetation was temperate forest-steppe, but most has now been removed by cultivation. The zonal soil type is the drab soil. Loess deposits here generally have very fine grains, the so-called clayey loess. This subregion has long been, and will continue to be, an intensively farmed area. It was historically called "Qin's *Chuan* [valley plain] of 800 *li* [400 km]" where the capitals (Xianyang and Xi'an) of three dynasties in China (Qin, Western Han, and Tang) were located and the ancient Silk Road started. It is also being developed into an industrial belt.

Middle Gansu Dissected Hills and High Plains

This area (7_4 on Figure 13.1) is located mainly west of the Liupan Mountains and is essentially a transitional belt from a subhumid to a semiarid climate. The vegetation ranges from forest-steppe to steppe vegetation, and soils make a transition from loessic to sierozems. Soil erosion is quite severe. Rain-fed farming is still possible, but the yield is precarious. Hence, it is called the "dry land" in Gansu (the Hexi Corridor is the "oases" by contrast), one of the poorest rural areas in China. This subregion should be comprehensively used for farming-pasture-forestry, with the emphasis on environmental protection and revegetation as well as on modern industrialization based on rich hydroelectric power generated from the upper-middle Yellow River.

REFERENCES

China State Statistical Bureau. 1991. *Statistical Yearbook of China*. Beijing: China Statistical Publishing House.

Chinese Academy of Sciences. 1959. *Comprehensive Physical Regionalization of China*. Beijing: Science Press (in Chinese).

Chinese Academy of Geological Sciences. 1978. *Main Features of Geological Structure in China*. Beijing: Geological Press (in Chinese).

Department of Geography, Hebei Normal University. 1974. *The Haihe River*. Shijiazhuang: Hebei People's Press (in Chinese).

Dregne, H. E. (ed.). 1992. *Degradation and Restoration of Arid Lands*. Lubbock: ICASALS, Texas Tech University.

Institute of Geography, Chinese Academy of Sciences. 1985. *Comprehensive Development and Economic Regionalization of the Shanxi Energy Resource Base*. Beijing: Energy Resources Press (in Chinese).

Institute of Soil and Soil Conservation, Chinese Academy of Sciences. 1961. *Soils of the North China Plain*. Beijing: Science Press (in Chinese).

Liu, Dongsen, et al. 1978. *Loess in the Middle Reaches of the Yellow River*. Beijing: Science Press (in Chinese).

Lo, Chuyun, et al. 1988. *Physical Conditions of the Loess Plateau*. Xi'an: Shaanxi People's Press (in Chinese).

Shanxi Agricultural Regionalization Committee. 1981. *Interpretation and Analysis of Agricultural Physical Conditions by Landsat Imagery, Taiyuan Sheet*. Beijing: Science Press (in Chinese).

Sun, Jinzhu, et al. 1988. *Geography of China*. Beijing: Higher Education Press (in Chinese).

Wong, Fongwei. 1988. *The Land Systems on the Loess Plateau*. Ph.D. dissertation. Institute of Geography, Chinese Academy of Sciences (in Chinese).

Zhang, Weixiang. 1990. *The Land Systems and Their Economic Development in the Lanzhou Area—The Junction among Three Natural Realms of China*. Ph.D. dissertation, Lanzhou University (in Chinese).

Zhao, Songqiao. 1986. *Physical Geography of China*. New York: John Wiley & Sons, Inc.

Zhao, Songqiao. 1988. *Natural Conditions and Territorial Management in the North China Plain*. Tokyo: National Institute for Research Advancement (in English and Japanese).

CHAPTER FOURTEEN

Subtropical China

The largest and most populous division in China, Subtropical China, includes the whole of Central China and most of South and Southwest China. Administratively, it includes all of Hunan, Hubei, Jiangxi, Zhejiang, Taiwan, Sichuan, and Guizhou provinces and Shanghai municipality, as well as the southern parts of Jiangsu, Anhui, and Henan provinces and the northern parts of Fujian, Guangdong, and Yunnan provinces and Guangxi Zhuang Autonomous Region. The division totals approximately 2.5 million sq km, or an area just a little smaller than India (the sixth largest country in the world with 2.95 million sq km), but larger than Saudi Arabia (the seventh largest country in the world, 2.4 million sq km), and occupying about 26.1 percent of China's total land area (Figure 14.1). It is inhabited by more than 600 million people, accounting for about 56 percent of China's total population, or somewhat more than the total population of seven Western industrial countries (the United States, the United Kingdom, France, Germany, Italy, Canada, and Australia).

This division starts at the eastern margin of the Tibetan Plateau, coinciding roughly with the 3000 m contour line and extends eastward to the western rim of the Pacific Ocean. The northern boundary is the Qinling–Huai He line, coinciding roughly with the 0°C isotherm of mean January temperature or the 750 mm isohyet of annual precipitation. This line is probably the most significant geographic dividing line in China, showing conspicuous areal differentiation between northern China (including North China, Northeast China, and Northwest China) and southern China (including Central China, South China, and Southwest China) (Color Plate 3). The division's southern boundary is not as distinct as the other three. It will be discussed in more detail in the

next chapter. Here it is enough to point out that it lies at about 21°–22° N latitude on the Guangdong and Guangxi coasts and at 23°–25° N in southern Yunnan. An anomaly is the southern tip of Taiwan Island, which although tropical in climate and vegetation, is better combined with subtropical parts of the island to form an integral region.

PHYSICAL FEATURES, NATURAL RESOURCES, AND ENVIRONMENTAL PROBLEMS

Predominantly Mountainous Topography with Comparatively Limited Arable Land

This division is characterized by numerous mountains and hills interwoven with broad basins and alluvial valleys. Mountains, hills, and high plateaus account for more than 70 percent of the total land area (a little more than the national average), and in Yunnan Province, 96 percent. Consequently, soil erosion, mountain hazards, and other environmental problems are frequent, and the amount of arable land is quite limited, although the aesthetic combination of fantastic mountains and beautiful water bodies offers many scenic sites. From north to south and from east to west, this division is composed of eight geomorphological areas.

Qinling–Daba–Dabie Mountains

The Qinling Mountains are broad latitudinal folded mountains, with a ridge line generally ranging from 2000 to 3000 m in elevation; the highest peak is Mount

212

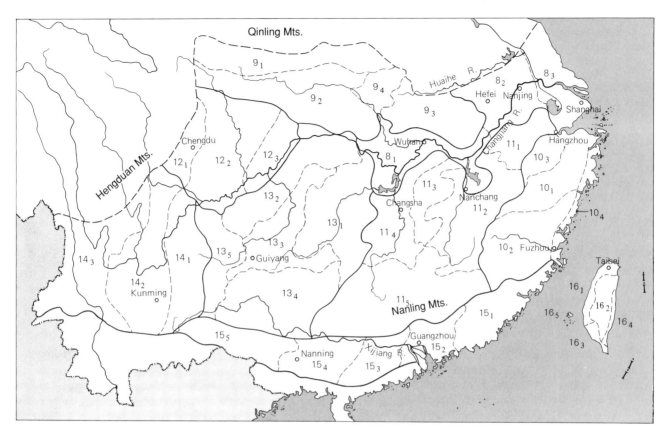

Figure 14.1 Subtropical China. (For legend, see Table 14.1.)

Taibai (3767 m) (Color Plate 3). The mountain ridge overlooks the Wei He valley from a relative relief as high as 2500 to 3000 m. It extends southeastward to the Tongbai Mountain and the Dabie Mountains, generally 500–1000 m in elevation. The Daba Mountains, located south of the Qinling, run southeastward with elevation decreasing from 2000–3000 m to about 1000 m. The highest peak here is the luxuriant Mount Shennongjia (3105 m) (Photo 14.1). The Nanyan–Xiangfan Basin is the largest inland basin in the region, with terraces and hills, mostly from 40 to 50 m in relative relief, dominating.

Middle and Lower Chang Jiang Plains

The plains of the middle and lower Chang Jiang developed along a great fault line. Three of these extensive valley plains, the Jiang–Han Plain, the Dongting Lake Plain (Photo 14.2), and the Poyang Lake Plain (Figure 14.2) are mostly located in submerged basins that formed since the Cretaceous period. Rivers and lakes are widespread, forming the scenic and productive "watery country" (Color Plate 16). The Chang Jiang Delta has a rather complicated geological history. The delta plain extended far eastward into the continental shelf during late Pleistocene recession of the sea; it then submerged and gradually silted up again, to transform Taihu Lake from a sea gulf into a freshwater lake.

Southeast Coast Mountains and Hills

The southeast coast is dominated by mountains and hills, mostly with elevations of 500 to 1000 m. They are generally northeast- or northwest-trending and composed of Mesozoic granite and igneous rocks. Amid these mountains and hills are many small graben-structured basins, with Cretaceous, Tertiary, and Quaternary beds deposited in them. Along the rocky and irregular shoreline, there are low, rolling granite hills and small patches of delta plains as well as many rocky islands, of which Zhoushan Island (524 sq km) is the largest.

Photo 14.1 Mount Shen-nongjia (3105 m), located at the borderland between Sichuan and Hubei provinces, is the highest peak in central China.

Taiwan Island Mountains and Plains

Taiwan is China's largest island; two thirds of its area is dominated by mountains and hills (Figure 14.3; photo 14.3). They are the youngest mountains in China and are still actively undergoing tectonic movement. Plains stretch chiefly along the west coast. More than 100 small islands surround Taiwan Island, of which the basaltic Penghu Islands are the most important.

South Chang Jiang Hills and Basins

This extensive area is a great amphitheater of low hills surrounded by mountains about 1000 m in elevation,

but is further enhanced by scattered small basins and strips of level plains along the rivers. There are many scenic mountains, such as the Huang Shan (Photo 14.4). Geologically, these northeast-trending mountains and hills have been controlled by the Mesozoic Yanshan Tectonic Movement with anticlines forming the ridges and synclines the valleys. Tertiary red beds deposited in basins and valleys have been largely dissected into hills.

Sichuan Basin

Surrounded by high mountains and plateau, the Sichuan Basin (Figure 14.4) is mainly composed of low mountains and hills, with an average elevation of about 500 m.

Photo 14.2 The fertile and extensive Dongting Lake plain in the middle reaches of the Chang Jiang, Hunan Province.

The fertile, well-irrigated Chengdu Plain is an outcome of downfaulting along the piedmont of the western marginal high mountains (Color Plate 11). The famous Three Gorges of the Chang Jiang (Color Plate 20) is located at the eastern border of the Sichuan Basin.

Guangxi Basin

This is the best developed karst topography area in China, probably also in the world. Arc-shaped mountains about 1000 m high are located in the middle of the basin, and together with the winding, greenish rivers, form beautiful scenic sites (Color Plate 21).

Yunnan–Guizhou Plateau

With an elevation around 1000–2000 m, this plateau is located on the second great topographic step of China. High, rugged ground surfaces cut by deep gorges (Photo 14.5) and high waterfalls (Photo 14.6) and crossed by towering mountains make up most of the region. Upper Paleozoic thick-bedded limestone strata are also widely distributed. These limestone formations have been under a warm humid environment for a long time; consequently karst topography is well developed. The high ridges and deep gorges of the Hengduan Mountains delimit this plateau from the still higher Tibetan Plateau (Photo 14.7).

Rich Humid Subtropical Climatic Resources

The subtropical, humid climate in this division offers rich climatic resources. During the winter the atmosphere at the surface is dominated by continental northern monsoons. Frequent cold waves result in rather low temperatures. The mean January temperature ranges from 2° to 8°C, with isotherms generally paralleling latitude. The absolute minimum temperature may drop below −10°C north of the Chang Jiang, below −7°C to −10°C south of the Chang Jiang, and below −4°C

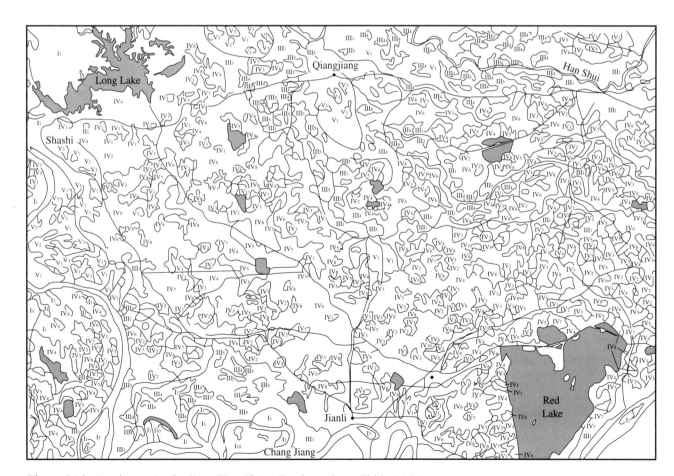

Figure 14.2 Land types in the Jiang Han Plain. (For legend, see Table 14.2.)

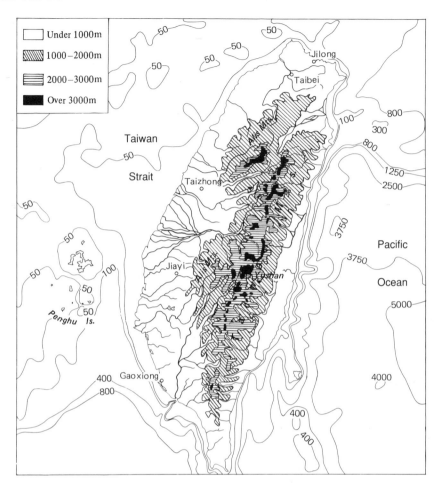

Figure 14.3 Topography of Taiwan Island and its neighboring seas

Photo 14.3 The scenic Sun-Moon Pond amid lofty mountains in central Taiwan Island.

Photo 14.4 The scenic Tiandu Peak of the Huangshan Mountains (1873 m), Anhui Province.

south of the Nanling Mountains. During the summer, maritime southeastern monsoons predominate, bringing high temperatures and at the same time, heavy rainfall, which favor productive agriculture, especially paddy rice.

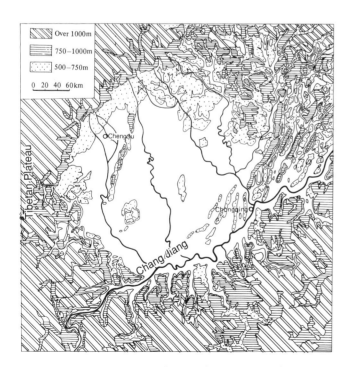

Figure 14.4 Topography of the Sichuan Basin and surrounding areas

Summertime is universally hot, with a mean July temperature around 28°C. The Yunnan–Guizhou Plateau is an exception, and is generally below 25°C. Absolute maximum temperature can be higher than the body temperature. Some examples are Chongqing (44°C), Wuhan (41.3°C), Nanjing, and Changsha which are called the four "ovens" of China because of very high summer temperatures. Spring and autumn are transitional seasons with variable weather extremes.

Annual precipitation is abundant, generally above 750 mm. Rainfall decreases from southeast to northwest and from mountain slopes to sheltered basins. For example, the windward slope of the Wuyi Mountains has an annual precipitation of more than 2200 mm, whereas the Nanyang Basin and the Hanzhong Basin have less than 900 mm. Seasonal distribution of precipitation is unbalanced, although not so extreme as in North and Northwest China. More than 70 percent of the total annual precipitation is concentrated in the summer, creating serious flood hazards along the middle and lower Chang Jiang Plains. Plum rain usually lasts about one month in the early summer or late spring along southeast coast and lower Chang Jiang valley. Typhoons with fierce winds and intense rainstorms occur frequently in the late summer and early autumn along the coast, resulting in a history of hazards. In the western part of the division, the winter dry season is conspicuous.

Based on latitudinal location and temperature conditions, three subdivisions can be identified:

Photo 14.5 The Wu Jiang Gorge on the dissected Guizhou Plateau.

The Northern Subtropical Zone

Located generally north of the Chang Jiang, the Northern subtropical zone has a mean January temperature of 0° to 5°C and a cumulative temperature during the ≥ 10°C period of 4500°–5000°C.

The Middle Subtropical Zone

This zone is generally located between the Chang Jiang and the Nanling Mountains. Here the mean January temperature ranges from 5° to 10°C, and the cumulative temperature during the ≥ 10°C period is from 5000° to 6500°C.

The Southern Subtropical Zone

Located south of the Nanling Mountains, which mark the traditional boundary between Central China and South China, the Southern subtropical zone has a mean January temperature of 10° to 16°C and a cumulative temperature during the ≥ 10°C period of 6500°–8000°C.

Bountiful Surface Water Resources

Subtropical China is endowed with abundant surface water resources, consisting of a dense river network (including irrigation and transportation canals) and numerous lakes (including reservoirs and ponds). The dendritic drainage pattern dominates. In areas with rather homogeneous bedrock, such as the Sichuan Basin, the dendritic drainage pattern is typical. Roughly parallel mountains on the Southeast Coast, on the other hand, cause a trellis drainage pattern. The density of the river network is generally more than 0.3 to 0.4 km/sq km, and even 6.4 to 6.7 km/sq km in the Chang Jiang Delta, where the most intricate river and canal network and productive "watery country" lie.

Annual watershed runoff is high. Each of the eight tributaries of the Chang Jiang, including the Gan Jiang, Xiang Jiang, Min Jiang, Jialing, Yuan Jiang, Hanshui, Wu Jiang and Yalong Jiang as well as the Qiantang and the Min rivers on the Southeast coast, has a greater runoff than the Yellow River. The Chang Jiang itself is, of course, the largest river in China. High-volume runoff combined with mountainous topography create abundant hydroelectric power potential. According to an estimate, the hydroelectric capacity of the Three Gorges Dam on the Chang Jiang will reach 17.68 million kilowatts (dam height 180 m), and that of the Wu Jiang Dam is more than 8 million KW. Even along a tributary of the Min Jiang (Fujian Province), a large, recently built hydroelectric station has a generating capacity of 600,000 KW. The hydroelectric energy sources are much needed for the development of China's modern industries and transportation.

This division also contains one of the five major lake regions in China (generally known as East Lake Region). The most specular lake group is the ancient Yunmeng Swamp Area (Figure 14.2), and the dwindling Dongting Lake is simply one of its numerous relic lakes. Other important lakes include the Poyang Lake (now the largest freshwater lake in China), Tai Hu, and Chao Hu. Most of these lakes are being silted up or reclaimed as farmlands. For the sake of flood control, freshwater

Photo 14.6 The Huangguoshu Waterfall on the dissected Guizhou Plateau, with a water head of 57 m, is the largest waterfall in China.

fisheries, and other land and water uses, overall planning must be undertaken to protect these lakes from disappearing.

Profuse and Varied Vegetation Types

Extensive land area together with favorable climatic conditions result in profuse and varied vegetation types in this division. Yet, as this is the most populous rice-producing agricultural core in China, human impact on the vegetation and soil-forming processes has been very great. All flat plains have been intensively cultivated,

with paddy rice the most important crop and human-made paddy soil the most extensive fertile soil. Mountains and hills are less intensively used, mainly for orchard and tree crops, such as tea, oil tea, and tung oil. Practically all original vegetation types have been changed. Instead, secondary evergreen broad-leaved forests, shrubs, grassland, and many trees of economic value dominate along with extensive terraced farming.

The horizontal zonal vegetation type is subtropical evergreen broad-leaved forest. Corresponding with the three major climatic subtypes, there are three major vegetation subtypes:

Photo 14.7 The scenic Yulong (literally "Jade Dragon") Mountain on northern border of the Yunnan Plateau is a range of the Hengduan Mountains, 5596 m in elevation.

Mixed Evergreen and Deciduous Broad-Leaved Forest

This is a transitional vegetation type between deciduous and evergreen broad-leaved forests and is widespread on the mountains and hills of the Northern subtropical zone. The dominant evergreen tree species are *Cyclobalanopsis spp.*, *Castatnopsis spp.*, and *Ilex chinensis*. The dominant deciduous species are *Fagus spp.* and *Platycarya strobilacea*. The zonal soil type is yellowish brown soil.

Evergreen Broad-Leaved Forest

This is the zonal vegetation type of the Middle subtropical zone. All dominant species are evergreen and are much more profuse and varied than the mixed evergreen and broad-leafed forest type. Extensive bamboo groves flourish and epiphytes also appear. The zonal soil types are red earth and yellow earth.

Monsoon Evergreen Broad-Leaved Forest

This is the transitional vegetation type between the subtropical evergreen broad-leaved forest and the tropical monsoon forest. It is chiefly found on low mountains and hills of the Southern subtropical zone. The flora are profuse and varied, the *Castanopsis* tree being the most important and widespread. There are many kinds of ferns and epiphytes. The zonal soil types are lateritic red earth and yellow earth.

Vertical zonation of vegetation and soil is also conspicuous. It will be discussed in a later section according to different latitudinal and attitudinal locations.

Rich Metal Mineral Resources

Energy resources are far less abundant in Subtropical China than in North China. One exception is the rich petroleum and natural gas reserves of the Sichuan Basin, which are considered one of the eight large oil and gas fields in China. There are also oil reserves in the Jiang–Han Plain, along the southeastern coast, and on the continental shelf of the South China Sea. Another exception is the widespread coal deposits on the Guizhou Plateau. The Pingxiang coal mine, on the border between Jiangxi and Hunan provinces, is also significant.

On the other hand, metal mineral resources are quite rich in Subtropical China. Panzihua in southwestern Sichuan Province, the Nanjing–Wuhu border area between Jiangsu and Anhui provinces, and western

Hubei Province are three of the seven largest iron ore deposits in China (each with a proven reserve of more than 1 billion tons). Nonferrous metal minerals are especially significant for their concentration in various Subtropical China locations. Among them are antinomy, zinc, and lead in Hunan Province; tungsten, copper, and cobalt in Jiangxi Province; copper in Hubei and Anhui provinces; and tin, lead, and tungsten in Guangdong Province. Most of these nonferrous metal ores occur in granite and other igneous strata. Many are among the richest in the world, including tungsten of Dayu (Jiangxi), copper of Dexiang (Jiangxi), and lead and zinc of Shuikoushan (Hunan). Gejiu in Yunnan Province, it is interesting to note, is called the "tin capital" of China.

Comprehensive Physical Regionalization

In the comprehensive physical analysis, this extensive and mountainous division is the most varied and complicated in China. There are nine natural regions and 37 subregions, shown in Table 14.1 and Figure 14.1.

HISTORICAL BACKGROUND

In historical development, extensive and populous Subtropical China can be apparently divided into three traditional divisions: Central China, the middle and lower reaches of the Chang Jiang; South China, which is the subdivision south of the Nanling Mountains; and Southwest China including the Sichuan Basin and the Yunnan–Guizhou Plateau.

Central China

Central China is located at the middle of Eastern Monsoon China, between the Qinling–Huai He line and the Nanling Mountains. Like North China, it is another development cradle of Han China and of Chinese agricultural civilization. One of the five earliest ethnic groups—the Meng—originated in the middle and lower reaches of the Chang Jiang. Even before the Dadiwan culture on the Loess Plateau, small groups of cave-dwelling and hunting-farming tribes inhabited the South Chang Jiang hills and basins (about 8000–8500 years ago). The Hemudu culture along the northern part of the Southeast Coast (about 7000 years ago) was the origin of paddy rice farming in China, probably also in the world.

During the earliest Chinese states (the Xia, Shang, Western Zhou, and Spring and Autumn Period, 2206–

TABLE 14.1
Comprehensive Physical Regionalization of Subtropical China

Natural region	Natural subregion	Chief environmental problems
8. Middle & lower Chang Jiang Plain—Mixed forest region	8(1) Hunan–Hubei Plain	Floods, desiccation of water bodies
	8(2) Lower Chang Jiang Plains & Hills	Floods, soil erosion
	8(3) Chang Jiang Delta	Floods, typhoons
9. Qinling–Daba Mountains— Mixed forest region	9(1) Qiling Mountains	Soil erosion, deforestation
	9(2) Daba–Micang Mountains	Soil erosion, deforestation
	9(3) Tongbai–Dabie Mountains	Soil erosion, deforestation
	9(4) Xiangfan–Nanyang Basin	Spring drought, autumn floods, soil erosion
10. Southeast Coast—Evergreen broad-leaved forest region	10(1) Xianxia–Kuocang Mountains	Soil erosion, floods, deforestation
	10(2) Wuyi–Daiyun Mountains	Soil erosion, floods, deforestation
	10(3) Jinhua–Quzhou Basin	Soil erosion, floods
	10(4) Coastal Hills	Typhoons, soil erosion
11. South Chang Jiang Hills & Basins—Evergreen broad-leaved forest region	11(1) Zhejiang–Anhui Low Mountains and Hills	Soil erosion, deforestation
	11(2) Central & Southern Jiangxi Low Hills & Basins	Soil erosion, deforestation, summer drought
	11(3) Hunan–Jiangxi Low Mountains & Hills	Soil erosion, deforestation
	11(4) Central and Southern Hunan Hills & Basins	Soil erosion, summer drought
	11(5) Nanling Mountains	Soil erosion, deforestation
12. Sichuan Basin—Evergreen broad-leaved forest region	12(1) Chengdu Plain	Soil erosion
	12(2) Central Hills	Soil erosion, drought
	12(3) Eastern Parallel Ranges & Valleys	Soil erosion, drought, deforestation
13. Guizhou Plateau—Evergreen broad-leaved forest region	13(1) Eastern Low Mountains & Hills	Soil erosion, deforestation
	13(2) Northern Mountains and Gorges	Soil erosion, deforestation
	13(3) Central Hilly Plateau	Soil erosion, deforestation
	13(4) Southern Hilly Plateau	Soil erosion, deforestation
	13(5) Western Mountains and Gorges	Soil erosion, deforestation
14. Yunnan Plateau—Evergreen broad-leaved forest region	14(1) Eastern Yunnan Karst Plateau	Soil erosion, spring drought, deforestation
	14(2) Central Yunnan Plateau	Soil erosion, spring drought, deforestation
	14(3) Hengduan Mountains	Soil erosion, mud flows, deforestation
15. Lingnan Hills—Evergreen broad-leaved forest region	15(1) Eastern Guangdong & Southern Fujian Costal Hills	Soil erosion, typhoons, spring drought

(continued)

TABLE 14.1
Comprehensive Physical Regionalization of Subtropical China (continued)

Natural region	Natural subregion	Chief environmental problems
	15(2) Zhu Jiang Delta	Floods, typhoons
	15(3) Western Guangdong–Eastern Guangxi Mountains & Hills	Soil erosion, deforestation
	15(4) Central Guangxi Broad Valleys & Karst Basins	Soil erosion, deforestation
	15(5) Northern Guangxi Mountains & Karst Topography	Soil erosion, deforestation
16. Taiwan Island—Evergreen broad-leaved forest & monsoon forest region	16(1) Northern Subtropical Hills and Plains	Typhoons, soil erosion
	16(2) Central Subtropical Mountains	Soil erosion, mud flows, earthquakes
	16(3) Southern Tropical Hills and Plains	Typhoons, soil erosion
	16(4) Tropical East Coast	Typhoons, soil erosion
	16(5) Penghu Islands	Typhoons

403 B.C.), Central China and North China were joined together as the core of Han China. When China was reduced to chaotic conditions, during such times as the Three Kingdoms (A.D. 220–280) and the Western Jin Dynasty and Southern and Northern Dynasties (A.D. 280–589), waves of Han emigrants moved from North China to Central China. With Nanjing as the capital, new kingdoms were established, and economic and social development proceeded rapidly.

Since the middle period of feudal society (A.D. 589–1279), but especially since the Southern Song Dynasty (1129–1279), Central China gradually exceeded North China both in population and in economic development, and Hangzhou was for a while the capital of the nation. During the late period of feudal society (1279–1840), South China's economic and demographic superiority over North China continued to grow, although during most of the period the political capital stayed in Beijing. During the Ming Dynasty (1368–1644), farming (both paddy and dry) became well developed all over Central China, including formerly undeveloped mountain areas. Development in the Chang Jiang Delta flourished especially in economic crops and handicraft industries, while the middle reaches of the Chang Jiang became the largest center of commercial food (mainly rice) production in China. In

1685, Central China had a total farmland area of 17.3 million ha, accounting for 43 percent of the national total.

During the modern period (1840–1949), Central China definitely became the economic and population center of China, and at one time also the political center. During the contemporary period (since 1949), it has remained the economic and population center of China. In 1980 it had a total of 24.3 million ha of farmland, accounting for 24.4 percent of the national total.

South China

South China has been an integral part of Chinese territory since the Qin Dynasty (221–206 B.C.). Economic and population growth in South China has been closely related to events in Central China. For example, waves of Han emigrants repeatedly came from war-stricken North China through Central China to South China. The famous Hakka (meaning literally "guest families") in northeastern Guangdong and southern Fujian migrated from far away North China in stages. In turn, most of the overseas Chinese in modern and contemporary periods emigrated from the coastal areas of South China. Since 1978, the "modernization" and "opening up" policies have also been most actively adopted in

South China. The first four "special economic zones" of Shenzhen, Zhuhai, Shantou, and Xiamen are all located in the coastal areas of South China.

Southwest China

Southwest China can be divided into two parts: the Sichuan Basin, which has been closely related with Central China, and the Yunnan–Guizhou Plateau, which is the most mountainous and the least developed part of Eastern Monsoon China. The Sichuan Basin became a part of Chinese territory as early as the third century B.C. and has been a "heavenly endowed rich land" ever since, even though it once suffered from the peasant uprising at end of the Ming Dynasty. Sichuan inhabitants in modern times have been mostly immigrants from neighboring Jiangxi, Hubei, and other provinces.

The Yunnan–Guizhou Plateau, on the other hand, was developed somewhat later than South China. For a long time, it was the "museum" of numerous ethnic minority groups and the stronghold of feudal tribes and warlords. Until the 1950s and early 1960s, when the so-called Third Line (including Southwest China and Northwest China) heavy industrial construction got started, the region had remained an undeveloped border area.

SOCIAL AND ECONOMIC DEVELOPMENT

Agriculture

Based on favorable physical conditions as well as rich natural and human resources, this natural division has the best developed agriculture in China. It can be further divided into three spatial divisions.

Central China

As we have seen, the middle and lower reaches of the Chang Jiang (Central China) are endowed with excellent natural and human resources as well as a long period of historical development. Currently, about one quarter of China's total farmland is in this region. But because of the huge population and rather limited amount of arable land, the farmland per capita is generally less than 1 *mu* (0.07 ha), less than the national average. The amount of potential arable land in the region is also very limited.

There is a distinct contrast between the mountain and plains areas. The plains are intensively used, gener-

ally under a double- or triple-cropping system. Grain crops in the "watery country" of the Chang Jiang Delta produce an annual yield as high as 1 ton/*mu* (15 tons/ha). In contrast, the mountain areas are rather extensively used, or even misused, and as a result, severe soil erosion, mountain hazards, and other environmental problems are commonplace. As a whole, this is the largest production area in China for many food crops (rice, winter wheat, etc.) and many economic crops (cotton, rape seed, hemp, etc.) as well as many tree crops (mulberry, tung oil, tea oil, bamboo, tea, citrus fruits, etc.). Domestic animal husbandry (chiefly pigs, chickens, and water fowl), forestry (chiefly management and afforestation of economic trees), and fisheries (both freshwater and marine, for natural catch and artificial breeding) are also well developed. The prospects for further agricultural development are still very bright, mainly depending on application of new agricultural technology to increase sustainable use of the plains as well as better use and conservation of mountain and water areas.

South China

This region has an ample water supply and favorable high temperature conditions, but arable land resources are even more limited than in Central China. In 1980, it had a total of 7.9 million ha of farmland, accounting for only 7 percent of the national total. Per capita farmland is generally less than 1 *mu* (0.07 ha), even as low as 0.3 *mu* in some mountainous and high population density areas, such as around Shantou in northeastern Guangdong province.

There is also a distinct contrast in the land use pattern between mountains and plains. The plains are generally under a triple-cropping system with rice, sugar cane, and sweet potatoes as the chief crops. Productivity is high. The mulberry (or sometimes sugar cane) dike–paddy field–fish pond ecosystem in the Zhu Jiang Delta (Color Plate 22) is just like a beautiful and productive garden. The surrounding granite mountains, on the other hand, have suffered badly from deforestation, soil erosion, mountain-related hazards, and other environmental problems. The future for this region, like Central China, depends on new technology for more intensive and sustainable use of the plains as well as better use and conservation measures of mountain and water areas.

Southwest China

This region is generally under a double-cropping system, with rice and corn as chief crops. Compared with South China, it has a higher elevation, lower temperature, longer dry season, and more rugged topography; both farming and fishing are less developed, but pastoral animal husbandry is better developed. For the future, more emphasis should be laid on sustainable and productive "vertical agriculture" with tree crops predominating, while giving more attention to environmental protection.

Modern Industry and Transportation

Modern Industry

In its modern industry and transportation system, this division might also be divided into three sub-divisions:

1. *Central China:* Since 1949, Central China has been developed as a high-level comprehensive industrial base in China, with metallurgy, engineering, textiles, and chemicals as the four major industries. Electrical and electronic industries are also rapidly developing. Two major industrial belts have been formed:
   a. The Chang Jiang Delta industrial belt has highly developed heavy and light industries. Shanghai is now the largest comprehensive industrial base in China, with engineering, textiles, chemicals, and electronics as the four major industries. The industrial belt along the Shanghai–Nanjing railway is also rapidly developing.
   b. The Middle Reaches of the Chang Jiang industrial belt includes three separate industrial areas: Wuhan (steel, engineering, shipbuilding, etc.), western Hubei (automobiles, hydroelectricity), and central Hunan (nonferrous metallurgy, engineering).

2. *South China:* In the so-called east coastal economic zone, South China is relatively weak in industrial development, with light industries (such as the manufacturing and processing of timber, rubber, sugar, and tea) dominating. Nonferrous minerals mining is also important. Very recently, helped by heavy investments from overseas Chinese and foreign capitalists, many light industries whose products are mainly destined for foreign export have been rapidly developed.

3. *Southwest China:* Since the 1950s and early 1960s, the so-called Third Line of construction in Southwest China has rapidly developed, with heavy industries dominating. The prospect for the Panzhihua iron and steel industry is good. Many

nonferrous metallurgical industries, including processing facilities for copper, tin, mercury, antimony, and magnesium are also important.

Modern Transportation

Since ancient times, boat and inland waterways have been the major transportation means in Central China. The Chang Jiang main channel has long been the west–east Golden Waterway, while the Grand Canal and numerous tributaries of the Chang Jiang have been important north–south waterways. In modern times, the sea waterways and a series of seaports have been developed. Among the 14 large seaports that were opened in 1984, five (Lianyungang, Nantong, Shanghai, Ningbo, and Wenzhou) are located in Central China. Shanghai is now the largest foreign trade seaport in China, and is also one of the largest ports (each with an annual freight larger than 100 million tons) in the world.

Railway transportation is also well developed in Central China. Two major west–east railways run parallel to the main Chang Jiang waterway. Three major north–south railways cross the Chang Jiang waterway at Zhicheng (southeast of Yichang, Hubei Province), Wuhan, and Nanjing, respectively. As the largest metropolis and seaport in China, Shanghai is actually served by a network of waterways, roadways, air routes, and railways.

Modern transportation in South China consists mainly of numerous sea routes and seaports, of which Guangzhou, Fuzhou, Shantou, Xiamen, and Quanzhou are the most important. Hong Kong, Gaoxiang, and other seaports in Taiwan might be also added to this category. Inland waterways are also significant; the Zhu Jiang (Pearl River) and the Min Jiang are the most important. Railways are mainly north–south trending, with large seaports as their terminus. A dense roadway network and newly developed air routes are other important modern transportation links. The Beijing–Shenzhen air route and the Hong Kong–Shenzhen Highway are some distinguished examples.

Recently developed railways are the major transportation means in Southwest China, with Chengdu, Chongqing, Guiyang, and Kunming as the four centers. Highways have been developed in mountainous areas, especially in southwestern Yunnan and western Sichuan. Most waterways are nonnavigable, and only the Chang Jiang and its tributaries within the Sichuan Basin are usable.

Ethnic Groups and Population

Central China, like North China, is almost exclusively inhabited by the Han, with other ethnic groups negligible. The Han comprise more than 95 percent of the total population (Shanghai 99.6 percent, Jiangsu 99.8 percent, Anhui 99.5 percent, Zhejiang 99.6 percent, Jiangxi 99.9 percent, Hubei 96.3 percent, and Hunan 95.9 percent).

In South China, except in Guangxi Zhuang Autonomous Region, the Han also remain an overwhelming majority (Fujian 99.0 percent, Guangdong 98.2 percent). In Guangxi, the Zhuang are the leading ethnic minority group, although the Han still make up 61.7 percent of the total population.

In Southwest China, Sichuan is also overwhelmingly inhabited by the Han, who make up 96.3 percent of the total population. On the mountainous Yunnan and Guizhou plateaus, however, numerous ethnic groups live in "vertical" distribution (Figure 7.2). In Guizhou Province, the Han represent 74.0 percent of total population, while the ethnic minority groups including Miao, Buyi, Dong, and Sui are also represented. In Yunnan Province, the Han make up 68.3 percent of the total population, while ethnic groups number more than 30, including Yi, Miao, Bai, Lisu, Lahu, Va, Naxi, Hani, Jingpo, Nu, Benglong, Jino, and others, of which the first three are most significant.

This division has not only a huge total population—more than 600 million inhabitants, but also a high population density—more than 400 persons/sq km, which is much higher than the national average. This area has been the major source of millions of emigrants moving overseas as well as to the Northwest desert lands.

However, population distribution and density reflect considerable contrasts between the intensively used plains and the extensively used mountains and hills. The most densely populated rural areas in China are found in the Chang Jiang Delta and the Chengdu Plain in the Sichuan Basin, where densities from 600 to 1500 persons/sq km are common. Most other fluvial plains and intermontane basins, such as the middle and lower reaches of the Chang Jiang, the Sichuan Basin, Southeast Coast plains, western Taiwan plains, and the Zhu Jiang Delta, have a population density of more than 400–600 persons/sq km. The numerous mountains and hills generally have a population density below 200–400 persons/sq km. Yet, unlike Northwest Arid China or the Tibetan Frigid Plateau, there is no place with a population density below 50 persons/sq km, to say nothing of uninhabited land.

Rural and Urban Settlements

In relation to the distribution and density of rural settlements, the plains of Central China and South China have similar features to those of the North China Plain. People are very densely and evenly distributed, but in the south, villages are generally clustered along the waterways (rivers and canals), while in the North, villages are mainly along the roadways. Furthermore, villages in Central and South China are usually larger than those in North and Northeast China, generally with tens or hundreds or even thousands of houses in each village. Most rural houses are constructed of brick-tile, one or two floors high with the tile roofs inclined more than 10°–15° (to drain away heavy rainfall). Recently, along the Gold Coast of South China, especially in the homelands of overseas Chinese, rural economic conditions have improved, and the rural villages have been rapidly modernized and urbanized.

Closely related to rapid industrial and transportation development, cities and metropolitan areas have grown in this division, as the Chinese say, "as fast as bamboo shoots growing in the spring." Out of 31 metropolises in China with more than 1 million people (not including Hong Kong, Taibei, and Gaoxiong), 11 are located here; and out of 28 large cities with from 0.5 to 1.0 million people, 10 are located here, including Fuzhou, Wuxi, Hefei, Nanning, Suzhou, Huainan, Liuzhou, Shantou, Ningbo, and Changzhou.

1. *Shanghai:* Besides being one of the three national municipalities, the most populous city, and the largest seaport, Shanghai is also the largest economic, industrial, and commercial center in China. It had a total population of 7.83 million and a nonagricultural population of 7.5 million in 1990.

2. *Wuhan:* Located at the crossroad between the middle Chang Jiang channel (the busiest inland waterway in China) and the Beijing–Wuhan–Guangzhou railway (the most important north–south railway in China), Wuhan is the second largest economic and industrial center in Central China, especially famous for its iron and steel production. It is also the political and cultural center of Hubei Province. In 1990 it had a total population of 3.75 million and a nonagricultural population of 3.28 million.

3. *Guangzhou (Canton):* Located at the mouth of the Zhu Jiang, it is the most important seaport and the largest economic, industrial, and commercial

center of South China as well as the political and cultural center of Guangdong Province. In 1990 it had a total population of 3.58 million and a non-agricultural population of 2.91 million.

4. *Chongqing:* As the largest economic and industrial center of Southwest China, Chongqing was the wartime capital of China during World War II. In 1990 it had a total population of 2.98 million and a nonagricultural population of 2.27 million.

5. *Nanjing* was one of the six ancient capitals of China and is now the political, economic, and cultural center of Jiangsu Province. In 1990, it had a total population of 2.5 million and a nonagricultural population of 2.09 million.

6. *Chengdu:* As an ancient city as well as the political, economic, and cultural center of Sichuan Province, Chengdu is rich in cultural and natural sights. It had a total population of 2.81 million and a nonagricultural population of 1.71 population in 1990.

7. *Kunming:* As the political, economic, and cultural center of Yunnan Province, Kunming is also famous for its scenic sites and as a "city of eternal spring." In 1990 it had a total population of 1.52 million and a nonagricultural population of 1.17 million.

8. *Changsha:* As the political, economic, and cultural center of Hunan Province, Changsha had a total population of 1.33 million and a nonagricultural population of 1.11 million in 1990.

9. *Hangzhou* was one of the six ancient capitals of China, and is now the political, economic, and cultural center of Zhejiang Province. Hangzhou is a beautiful city amid mountains, hills, rivers, and lakes, and has been famous for silk and light manufactures since ancient times. Hence, a Chinese saying goes, "Above, paradise; below, Hangzhou and Suzhou." In 1990, it had a total population of 1.34 million and a nonagricultural population of 1.1 million.

10. *Nanchang:* As the political, economic, and cultural center of Jiangxi Province, Nanchang had a total population of 1.35 million and a nonagricultural population of 1.09 million in 1990.

11. *Guiyang:* Guiyang is the political, economic, and cultural center of Guizhou Province, with a total population of 1.53 million and a nonagricultural population of 1.02 million in 1990.

AREAL DIFFERENTIATION AND REGIONAL DEVELOPMENT

On the whole, Central China will probably continue to be the most important population and economic core of China. South and Southwest China will also be the focus of greater rapid development in the future. Population control and a balanced environment–resource–population–development system are of paramount importance for the near future. In economic development, plans for industry and agriculture should both be emphasized and be kept in balance, keeping in mind that the agricultural population could decrease from its present 70–80 percent to 30–40 percent or less in the early twenty-first century. For industrial development, one of the key issues is to develop sufficient and sustainable energy sources. Thus, the proposed Three Gorges project and other hydroelectric projects are of great significance. For agricultural development, the key issues are to increase productivity while still making sustainable use of the limited level land and making better use of mountain areas and water bodies. However, as the physical environment in this division is so varied and complicated, all economic development should be based and planned according to the specific resource conditions and limitations of the different regions and subregions (Figure 14.1; Table 14.1).

Middle and Lower Chang Jiang Plain

This region is located between 28° and 34° N, with its northern boundary running roughly along the Daba Mountain–Dabie Mountain–Huaihe River line and its southern boundary zigzagging along the northern border of the South Chang Jiang Hills and Basins. It is chiefly composed of extensive alluvial plains deposited by the Chang Jiang and its tributaries. A series of lake basins stretch from the Three Gorges eastward to the sea for a total length of more than 1800 km and a total area of about 160,000 sq km. Numerous low mountains and hills encircle or dot these alluvial plains. There are three sections.

1. The middle section of Chang Jiang extends from Yichang to Wuhan and is essentially a lake basin with an area of about 80,000 sq km, of which one eighth consists of lakes. It was formerly the ancient Yunmeng Swamp area and has now been mostly drained, which has resulted in extensive low plains with elevations below 200 m (Wuhan, 27 m). The Chang Jiang flows sluggishly eastward through

many braided channels and a valley plain about 2000 m wide. Its largest tributary, the Han Shui, and each of the four large tributaries to the Dongting Lake system (Xiang Jiang, Zi Shui, Yuan Jiang, and Li Shui), have a larger annual runoff than the Yellow River.

2. The middle-lower section, located between Wuhan and Jiujiang, is a ribbon-like belt of lake basins and hills. Sometimes isolated scenic mountain peaks border the Chang Jiang, which has a much narrower channel and flows much more rapidly in this section. Tributaries are not so numerous as in the middle section, but the Poyang Lake system with its four large tributaries (Gan Jiang, Xiu Shui, Po Jiang, and Xin Jiang) enter the Chang Jiang here, so that the annual discharge of the Chang Jiang increases from 14,400 cu m/sec at Yichang (Hubei Province) to 29,700 cu m/sec at Datong (Anhui Province).

3. The lower and delta section is characterized by low elevation and a dense river network. Along the northern bank of the Chang Jiang, the elevation may drop to 2 m above sea level. The Chang Jiang channel increases in width from about 1500 m near Nanjing, to about 2000 m near Jiangyin, about 10,000 m near Nantong, and even to 80,000–90,000 m near its mouth. It empties into the East China Sea with an annual discharge of about 979.35 billion cu m and a total silt load of about 450 million cu m. This discharged sediment pushes the coast seaward at the rate of about 1 km every 60 years. The subwater delta extends eastward to 125° 30' E, about 450 km from the present mouth of the Chang Jiang. There are also many lakes and scenic isolated hills within the delta.

The region is characterized by a humid, northern subtropical climate, with high temperatures and heavy precipitation coming together during the growing season. Under these conditions, it is possible to practice the highly productive rice–rice–winter wheat (or barley) triple-cropping system. The cumulative temperature during the ≥ 10°C period totals 4500°–5000°C. Annual precipitation ranges from 900 to 1500 mm, with 50 to 60 percent of it concentrated in the summer and autumn and 30–40 percent in spring. China's widely devastating spring drought hazard is not a problem here. However, owing to the east coast location and the frequent invasion of cold waves in winter, the mean January temperature sinks as low as 0°–5°C, with the absolute minimum temperature falling as low as −5°C to −10°C, thus sometimes causing frost damage to crops. Summer is

quite hot; three out of four "oven" cities in China are located here. What is worse, excessive precipitation in the summer and autumn together with the topography and hydrology make the region susceptible to destructive floods. The flood of the Chang Jiang in 1931 was probably the most disastrous ever recorded in the world. In 1991, another disastrous flood caused great havoc in the region. Since 1949, a series of flood-control engineering works has been constructed and has shown encouraging results, but problems remain. One purpose for the gigantic Three Gorges Dam project is to control such heavy and frequent floods.

The zonal vegetation is mixed evergreen and deciduous broad-leaved forest. The zonal soil type is yellowish brown soil. However, because of more than 7000 years of agricultural development, these zonal vegetation and soil types are restricted to small patches on low mountains and hills. Soils and vegetation of the extensive plains have been intensively cultivated and turned into cultural vegetation and paddy soil. Even on the low mountains and hills, most of the original mixed forests have been destroyed and replaced by shrubs and grasses. Otherwise, these areas have been planted with economic crops such as tea, fruits, and economic trees such as masson pine (*Pinus massoniana*). The great contrast between the intensively used and densely populated plains and the rather extensively used and sparsely populated mountains is quite striking.

Hunan–Hubei (or Lianghu) Plain[1]

This subregion (marked 8_1 on Figure 14.1) coincides roughly with the middle and middle-lower sections of the Chang Jiang. It is essentially a series of alluvial and lacustrine plains. In particular it is formed by two great rivers—the Chang Jiang and Han Shui—and two lakes—Poyang and Dongting. The extensive fertile plain between the two rivers is the Jiang–Han Plain. In this subregion, human activity has long played an important role in shaping the physical environment. One significant example is the gradual dewatering and silting up of the Yunmeng Swamp and Dongting Lake (see Chapter Ten).

This subregion has long been the "rice bowl" of China. As an old saying goes, "When Lianghu has a good yield, all China will have enough food." Economic crops such as rape seed and cotton in the plains and tea, bamboo, and mulberry trees in the hilly areas are also

---

[1] "Lianghu" or Two Lake Provinces, denotes Hunan and Hubei provinces, which are located respectively south and north of Dongting Lake.

well developed. Figure 14.2 and Table 14.2 show the land types and their landform, vegetation, and soil components in the Jiang–Han Plain. Additionally, freshwater fisheries are important.

The Jiang–Han Plain is also one of the important oil fields in China. After completion of the gigantic Three Gorges Dam project, immense amounts of hydroelectric power will be available, making it possible for this subregion to become a great center for energy-intensive industries. With this potential for development in both agriculture and industry, the Lianghu Plain could certainly be one of the most prosperous areas in China.

Lower Chang Jiang Plains and Hills

This subregion (8_2 on Figure 14.1) includes plains and hills on either side of the lower Chang Jiang from Jiujiang to Zhenjiang. Plains are largely below 50 m in elevation, and hills are between 200 and 300 m, with a few peaks towering above 500–1000 m. The plains are studded with lakes, such as the Chao Hu. The plains are famous grain-producing areas in China. Hills and low mountains should be mainly devoted to forestry and tree crops, and soil conservation measures are urgently needed here.

Chang Jiang Delta

This subregion (8_3 on Figure 14.1) broadly includes all plains east of Zhenjiang. Geologically, it has been a down-warping basin since the Yanshan Tectonic Movement. Since the last submergence in the early Holocene, the Chang Jiang Delta has been gradually silted up by alluvial deposits from the Chang Jiang and the Huai He (1194–1855) as well as by extensive lacustrine and marine deposits. This extensive plain generally has an elevation below 10 m, with some isolated scenic hills of 100–200 m in elevation.

This is one of the oldest cultivated and irrigated areas in China. Except for a narrow strip of saline coastal beach, it has been almost entirely cultivated and transformed into "water country" (Color Plate 16) and "a land of rice and fish." Probably the most characteristic feature of the landscape is the innumerable rivers and canals that are the very arteries of life and transportation and also serve as an artificial drainage system. Besides being the largest industrial area, it is also the most productive grain-growing region in China, with an annual grain yield (three crops per year) near or above 15 tons/ha. It also prospers through fishing, silkworm raising, and other productive enterprises. In short, this is a show-

TABLE 14.2
Land Types in the Jiang-Han Plain, Hubei Province

I.	Fluvial-lacustrine beach and island
I-1.	Reed meadow soil fluvial beach
I-2.	Reed meadow soil river island
I-3.	Farming greyish wet soil river island
I-4.	Swampy paddy soil lake island
I-5.	Masson pine forest, brownish red soil reservoir island
I-6.	Paddy soil river island
I-7.	Meadow soil uncultivated beach
I-8.	Paddy soil lake island
I-9.	Greyish paddy soil lake island
I-10.	Greyish wet soil uncultivated beach
II.	Valley and gully
II-1.	Paddy soil interterrace gully
II-2.	Paddy soil interterrace gully
II-3.	Greyish wet soil fluvial broad valley flat land
II-4.	Paddy soil fluvial broad valley flat land
II-5.	Wet soil broad fluvial valley flat land
II-6.	Paddy soil fluvial valley flat land
III.	Alluvial tilted flat land
III-1.	Farming greyish wet soil alluvial flat land
III-2.	Farming wet soil alluvial flat land
III-3.	Paddy soil lakeside flat land
III-4.	Paddy soil wet alluvial flat land
III-5.	Paddy soil wet alluvial flat land
III-6.	Paddy soil alluvial-diluvial flat land
III-7.	Paddy soil alluvial flat land
IV.	Lacustrine flat land
IV-1.	Reed and mixed grasses swampy soil depression
IV-2.	Swampy paddy soil depression
IV-3.	Paddy soil low land
IV-4.	Swampy paddy soil lakeside land
IV-5.	Paddy soil lakeside land
IV-6.	Paddy soil lacustrine flat land
IV-7.	Submergenic paddy soil lacustrine flat land
IV-8.	Farming greyish wet soil lacustrine flat land
IV-9.	Reed meadow soil lakeside depression
IV-10.	Farming wet soil lacustrine flat land
IV-11.	Paddy soil lacustrine flat land
V.	Diluvial fan
V-1.	Wet soil diluvial fan land
V-2.	Submergenic paddy soil diluvial fan surface low land
V-3.	Paddy soil diluvial fan surface depression

(continued)

TABLE 14.2
Land Types in the Jiang-Han Plain, Hubei Province
(continued)

I.	Fluvial-lacustrine beach and island
	VI. Low terrace
VI-1.	Masson pine forest brownish red soil low terrace
VI-2.	Paddy soil flat low terrace
VI-3.	Farming brownish red soil low terrace
VI-4.	Submergenic paddy soil flat low terrace
VI-5.	Farming yellowish brown soil low terace
VI-6.	Masson pine forest yellowish brown soil low terrace
VI-7.	Masson pine forest red soil low terrace
VI-8.	Farming red soil low terrace
VI-9.	Paddy soil flat low terrace
VI-10.	Economic forest yellowish brown soil low terrace
VI-11.	Farming purple soil low terrace
VI-12.	Paddy soil tilted flat low terrace
	VII. High terrace
VII-1.	Paddy soil high terrace
VII-2.	Masson pine forest brownish red soil high terrace
VII-3.	Masson pine forest yellowish brown soil high terrace
VII-4.	Farming brownish red soil high terrace
VII-5.	Farming yellowish brown soil high terrace
VII-6.	Economic forest yellowish brown soil high terrace
VII-7.	Farming purple soil high terrace
VII-8.	Masson pine forest red soil high terrace
VII-9.	Masson pine forest purple soil high terrace
	VIII. Hill
VIII-1.	Poplar-birch secondary mixed forest red soil hill
VIII-2.	Masson pine forest yellowish brown soil hill
VIII-3.	Economic forest red soil hill
VIII-4.	Economic forest brownish red soil hill
VIII-5.	Masson pine forest red soil hill
VIII-6.	Masson pine forest brownish red soil hill
VIII-7.	Park scrub yellowish brown soil hill
VIII-8.	Bamboo forest brownish red soil hill
VIII-9.	Masson pine forest purple soil hill
VIII-10.	Tree and scrub mixed forest limestone soil hill
VIII-11.	Economic forest yellowish brown soil hill

case area for balanced development of agriculture and industry as well as for increasing agricultural production beyond the already high levels presently achieved in other regions.

Qinling–Daba Mountains

The Qinling–Daba Mountain region, with an area of about 300,000 sq km, forms a physical barrier that stretches from the eastern border of the Tibetan Plateau eastward almost to the East China Sea and divides southern China from northern China. Its northern limit is the northern slope of the Qinling (coinciding roughly with the 700 m contour line) and the Dabie Mountains, and its southern limit is the southern foothills of Micang and Daba mountains.

Vertical zonation of vegetation, soils, and land use is conspicuous. As this is the transitional belt not only between the north and the south but also between the east and the west, both flora and fauna are profuse and varied. For example, Mount Shennongjia (3105 m, Photo 14.1) alone has 166 families, 765 genera, and 1919 species of plants.

Qinling Mountains

This subregion (9_1 on Figure 14.1) includes the Qinling Mountains in Shaanxi Province and their eastward extension, the Funiu Mountains in Henan Province. The northern slopes of the Qinling are short and steep and the foothills are delimited sharply by a great fault line. One of its border ranges, Mount Huashan, is famous for its steep slopes and scenic beauty. On the other side, the southern slopes are rather long and gentle; nine separate ranges run from west to east across numerous intermontane basins and valleys.

About 90 percent of the total land area of this subregion is composed of mountains and hills, and about 47 percent is still preserved as original forest, where panda, golden-haired monkey, and other rare vertebrates still survive. Forestry should continue to be a major resource in the future, with local intermontane basins and valleys devoted to farming and economic tree crops.

Daba–Micang Mountains

Like the Qinling Mountains, this subregion (9_2 on Figure 14.1) has a tree-clad mountain landscape. Medium and high mountains occupy about 80 percent of the total land area, and low mountains and hills about 10 percent; the remaining 10 percent is plains. One significant feature is the extensive Hanzhong Basin sandwiched between the Qinling and the Daba. It occupies the upper reaches of the Han Shui and is characterized by meandering and braided stream channels with four agriculture terraces on either side. Agriculture here has been well developed since ancient times. Historically the basin has served as a great passage between the north and the south. In recent years, it has also been an important site for developing Third Line heavy industries.

Tongbai–Dabie Mountains

This subregion (9_3 on Figure 14.1) lies between the Chang Jiang and the Han Shui and is composed chiefly of dissected low mountains and hills, with elevations generally below 1000 m. Consequently, the barrier action with respect to climate is not so effective as that of Qinling. Human intervention is also much heavier, resulting in severe soil erosion and deforestation. However, croplands are more extensive, with the rice–wheat double-cropping system dominating.

Nanyan–Xiangfan Basin

The basin (9_4 on Figure 14.1) is located in a Cenozoic down-warped area. Basin deposits are on Cenozoic red beds 3000 m thick, with subsequent redeposits of early Quaternary red earth about 3000–4000 m thick. Neotectonic movements uplifted the land, which was then dissected into rolling terraces and hills with an absolute relief of 100–150 m and a relative relief of 20–30 m. The Han Shui and its tributaries flow through the basin, providing abundant irrigation water, although there are occasional severe floods. The Han Shui breaks through a narrow pass in the otherwise continuous Qinling–Dabie mountain system. It is also the path of southward-moving cold waves during winter, and an absolute minimum temperature can sink below −10°C. Annual precipitation is less than 1000 mm. It has been a significant transportation passage between northern and southern China since ancient times. Most of the basin has been cultivated, and croplands occupy 60 percent of the total land area. Soil conservation and irrigation development are two important problems here.

Southeast Coast

This region stretches northeast to southwest along the Zhejiang and Fujian coast for more than 1700 km. Its western boundary approximates the crest line of the Tianmu, Xianxia, and Wuyi mountains. The northern border coincides broadly with the funnel-shaped Hangzhou Estuary, and the southern border with the Fuqing-Yongchun-Yongding line in southern Fujian Province. With an area of about 150,000 sq km, it is characterized by hilly and mountainous topography and

numerous swift rivers as well as luxuriant evergreen vegetation. Zhejiang Province is noted for its "seven mountains, two waters, and one cropland," in other words, 70 percent of the total land area consists of mountains and hills. Compared with Zhejiang, Fujian Province is even more mountainous and land communications are more difficult. This is probably the chief reason why there are 104 local dialects in this province alone.

The climate is humid and subtropical and is quite favorable for agricultural development. Double cropping and triple cropping are generally practiced. During the cool, dry winter, isotherms run parallel to the latitudes, with a mean January temperature of 0°–10°C in the northern part and above 10°C in the southern part. During the warm, moist summer, isotherms parallel the coast, with a mean July temperature of 26°–30°C. Annual precipitation totals 1100–2000 mm, with less precipitation in the plains and along the coast. The rainy season lasts from March to June, so that unlike other parts of China, widespread spring drought is not a problem here. Typhoons are frequent from July to September, bringing torrential rain and a temporary relief from excessively hot weather, but they are a mixed blessing in that they also cause great disasters.

The density of the river network is high, usually more than 0.1 km/sq km, although most of rivers are short and swift and flow directly into the sea. Many of them have great hydroelectric potential, and some have already been profitably harnessed, such as the upper Qiantang River in the Zhejiang–Anhui border area. The drainage system is mostly of the trellis pattern, controlled mainly by geological structure and the alignment of the mountain ranges. The gradient is usually steep, and alluvial basins are dotted along the rivers like a string of pearls. The annual runoff depth ranges from 900 to 1400 mm, decreasing from southwest to northeast. The largest river is the Min Jiang, with a length of 539 km and an annual flow greater than the Yellow River. Most rivers have funnel-shaped mouths, resulting in a high tidal range. The Qiantang River is especially famous for its tidal bore; high tide may attain an amplitude of 8 m during the autumn full moon.

The zonal vegetation type is evergreen broad-leaved forest, found mainly on mountains and hills below 1000 m in elevation. Above 1000–1500 m, the vegetative cover turns to mixed evergreen and deciduous broad-leaved forest, which is also the case in the karst region. On mountains and hills below 800 m, masson pine or horse-tail pine (*Pinus massoniana*) is common. Tea plantations are especially popular along the foothills, and some of the best green tea in China is produced here. In the intermontane basins and valley plains, the land is intensively cultivated. All this natural and cultivated vegetation makes the region a vast sea of verdure, both productive and beautiful.

Xianxia–Kuocang Mountains

This subregion (10_1 on Figure 14.1), located in the northern part of the region, includes most of Zhejiang Province. It is mountainous and contains many famous scenic spots. It has been described in these terms: "Thousands of rocky peaks compete for beauty, tens of thousands of swift streams vie for velocity." The zonal vegetation is evergreen broad-leaved forest, but because of occasional invasions of cold waves and the resulting low temperatures, a mixed evergreen and deciduous broad-leaved forest grows on its northern border. Mean January temperatures range from 2.5°–6.5°C and the mean July temperature is from 27° to 28°C. Abundant annual precipitation totals 1300–1800 mm.

Vertical zonation is conspicuous. Zonal vegetation (broad-leaved evergreen forest) and zonal soil (red earth) dominate on hills and valleys below 500 m in elevation. Heavy human intervention has removed most of the natural zonal vegetation, giving way to planted vegetation and farmland. From 500 to 800 m is the belt of mixed evergreen and deciduous broad-leaved forest with yellow earth soil dominating. From 800 to 1200 m, mixed deciduous and evergreen broad-leaved forest and montane yellow earth dominate. Above 1200 m, deciduous broad-leaved forest and montane yellowish brown soil occur. Such a vertical distribution is a basis for "vertical agriculture" development. Mountains and hills above 500 m should be mainly devoted to forestry, although the extensive flat erosion surfaces might continue to be cultivated in this densely populated and land-hungry area. Valleys and hills below 500 m are intensively used for farming and economic tree crops. As a result, care must be taken to combat soil erosion, cold waves, drought, and flood hazards.

Wuyi–Daiyun Mountains

This subregion (10_2 on Figure 14.1) includes most of the mountainous and hilly lands of Fujian Province. Compared to the Xianxia–Kuocang Mountains, it is even more mountainous, with plains occupying only about 5 percent of the area. Climate and vegetation are also more tropical, with a mean January temperature of 8°–11°C, a mean July temperature of 25°–29°C, and annual precipitation generally averaging more than 1800

mm. Forestry and commercial tree crop production (including tea and bamboo) are the chief land uses in this subregion.

Jinhua–Quzhou Basin

The Jinhua–Quzhou Basin and a series of red basins along the middle Qiantang River valley are surrounded by low mountains and hills and thus combine into a large northeast–southwest trending basin, with a length of more than 200 km and a width of several dozen kilometers. Many hills interrupt the level basin, generally with an elevation of 50–250 m and a relative relief of 30–50 m. Red sandstone exposures outcrop in many places, especially in the margins of the basins, and are interwoven with the green pine trees and bamboo groves to make a very colorful landscape.

Because of the sheltered location, the climate of the basin is warmer and drier than that of the surrounding Xianxia–Kuocang Mountains subregion, with a mean January temperature of 4.6°–6.3°C, and mean July temperature of 29.5°C. Annual precipitation totals about 1500 mm and is mostly concentrated between June and August (June being the month of plum rain in the basin). Agriculture has been practiced in the basin since ancient times and now follows a triple-cropping system (rice–rice–winter wheat). This is also the most famous area in China for producing ham and preserved pork. On the surrounding low mountains and hills, the zonal vegetation is evergreen broad-leaved forest, but most of this cover has been cleared, resulting in severe soil erosion.

Coastal Hills

This narrow strip of the Zhejiang and Fujian coast (10_4 on Figure 14.1) is exposed to the direct impact of the sea. The coastline and neighboring islands are formed by a northeast–southwest trending structural line. They are usually rocky and steep, interspersed with numerous hills and drowned valleys (rias). At the mouths of many rivers lie a series of small deltaic plains where the population and farmlands are concentrated. Annual precipitation totals 1200 to 1600 mm, decreasing from the islands to inland areas. Owing to strong sea winds and frequent typhoons, evergreen broad-leaved forests are generally dwarfed. Banyan and other tropical trees are commonly seen in the southern part. In the future, this area will be suitable for the development of marine fisheries and the production of subtropical crops.

South Chang Jiang Hills and Basins

This extensive region extends from the southern boundary of the middle and lower Chang Jiang plains southward to the Nanling Mountains, and from the Xuefeng Mountain (eastern border range of the Guizhou Plateau) eastward to the Wuyi Mountains, over an area of about 300,000 sq km. The region has been socially and economically well developed ever since the late Warring States Period (403–221 B.C.).

Geomorphologically, the region is a great amphitheater of hills surrounded by low and medium mountains on all sides, except along its northern boundary where there are openings to the Chang Jiang basin and plains. Another outstanding feature is the widely scattered red basins, such as Hengyang and Changsha–Liuyang in the Xiang Jiang basin, and Ganzhou in the Gan Jiang basin. They are composed mainly of Cretaceous–Tertiary continental deposits and have been mostly eroded into hills and terraces, an absolute relief below 200 m and a relative relief of less than 100 m. Between these red basins are low mountains and hills, generally with elevations of 300–600 m. They are mostly composed of pre-Devonian metamorphic rocks and granites and are badly eroded. Some formations are also rich in metallic mineral resources. Along the large rivers, population and farmlands are concentrated on ribbon-like alluvial plains and terraces.

The climate is characterized by rainy springs and hot summers. Annual precipitation totals 1400 to 1700 mm, 40–50 percent of which is concentrated from April to June. From July to September, regional weather is controlled by subtropical high pressure, with frequent drought. Then follows a second high peak of precipitation in October or November. The mean January temperature ranges from 3° to 8°C, with an absolute minimum below −6°C. The mean July temperature generally reaches 27° to 30°C, with an absolute maximum above 38°C, which makes this area one of the hottest in China.

The river network is quite dense. Two river-lake systems (Dongting Lake and Poyang Lake) are the most important, and are located in Hunan and Jiangxi provinces, respectively. Jiangxi Province, with an area of 160,000 sq km, has more than 2400 rivers, with an average river length of 115 m/sq km. The mean annual runoff depth totals 800–900 mm. Soil erosion is very severe in the red sandstone and granite mountains where natural vegetation has long since been destroyed.

The zonal vegetation is profuse and luxuriant evergreen broad-leaved forest, and the zonal soil is thick, clayey, strongly acid red earth. The dominant evergreen tree species are *Cyclobalanopsis glauca*, *Castanopsis sclerophylla*, *C. taiwaniana*, *C. fardii*, and *Schina superba*. South of 27° 30′ N there is a mingling of some tropical species, while on the northern border there are some warm-temperate components. The upper limit of such zonal vegetation rises to 1000–1400 m in the south, dropping to 500–800 m in the north. Evergreen needle-leaved forests such as masson pine and Chinese fir as well as bamboo groves are also commonly seen. Economic trees, such as tea, oil tea, tung oil, peaches, and oranges are widely planted.

Zhejiang–Anhui Low Mountains and Hills

Located in northwestern Zhejiang Province, southern Anhui Province, and northern Jiangxi Province, this subregion (11_1 on Figure 14.1) is composed chiefly of structurally eroded low mountains and hills. Mountains are mainly northeast–southwest trending, with elevations around 1000 m. The highest and most rugged peaks are usually composed of rhyolite, granite, and other hard igneous rocks. This is the case of the famous scenic spot, Mount Huangshan (1873 m, Photo 14.4). Intermontane basins are interspersed with low hills and valleys, the latter being the most important farming areas in the subregion.

The mean January temperature ranges from 4.0° to 5.5°C, and the mean July temperature ranges from 27° to 29°C. The annual precipitation is between 1600–1700 mm. Evergreen broad-leaved forest and red earth predominate below 800 m above sea level, mixed evergreen and deciduous broad-leaved forest growing on montane yellowish brown earth are found between 800 and 1500 m above sea level, and dwarf forest and shrubby meadow predominate on a few peaks above 1500 m. This subregion is noted for its rich timber production and tree crops, including tea.

Central and Southern Jiangxi Hills and Basins

This subregion (11_2 on Figure 14.1) includes the greater part of Jiangxi Province and the Poyang Lake drainage system. It consists of a series of northeast–southwest trending low mountains and hills interspersed with red basins. It is heavily dissected by numerous rivers, and consequently hills and rolling terraces predominate, with ribbon-like alluvial plains stretching along the rivers. Loose, easily eroded Quaternary red earth covers the foothills and intermontane basins. As a result of vegetation cover destruction since ancient times, heavy soil erosion has been common.

The mean January temperature ranges from 4.5° to 6.1°C and the mean July temperature ranges from 28.7° to 30°C. The annual precipitation totals about 1400 mm. Secondary vegetation includes masson pine and oil-tea forests in the red basins and grassland and sparse masson pine forest on low mountains and hills. Small patches of evergreen broad-leaved forest are restricted to narrow valleys. In the alluvial plains and intermontane basins, farming is intensively developed. Paddy rice is the most important crop; other crops include cotton, winter wheat, and tea. Control of soil erosion and reforestation are the two most critical problems in the hill lands. Supplemental irrigation in summer and autumn is urgently needed for more intensive farming in the plains and basins.

Hunan–Jiangxi Low Mountains and Hills

Located on the border between Hunan and Jiangxi and serving as the water divide between Dongting Lake and Poyang Lake river systems, this subregion (11_3 on Figure 14.1) is dominated by north-northeast–south-southwest or northeast–southwest trending mountains and intermontane valleys. The former are mostly about 1000 m in elevation with some high peaks above 1500 m, such as Mufu Mountain (1589 m). The scenic Lushan (1474 m) is one of the best known summer resorts in China. Owing to their higher elevation, the mountains have a somewhat lower temperature and more abundant precipitation than the surrounding basins. Vertical distribution of vegetation and soil is conspicuous. Below 800 m, large tracts of masson pine, Chinese fir, and bamboo growing on predominantly red earth and yellow earth are common. Between 800 and 1500 m, a mixed forest grows on montane yellow earth. Above 1500 m, there is shrubby meadow. This is, and will continue to be, one of the most important timber and economic tree–crop producing areas in Central China.

Central and Southern Hunan Hills and Basins

This subregion (11_4 on Figure 14.1) is similar to the Central and Southern Jiangxi Hills and Basins subregion. The only differences are that it comprises the Dongting Lake instead of the Poyang Lake drainage system; it includes a greater part of Hunan Province instead of Jiangxi Province; its alluvial plains are somewhat more

extensive and hence there is a greater capability for agricultural development; and the vegetation cover is more dense and the hazards of soil erosion less menacing. Consequently, Hunan Province is one of the biggest rice bowls in China.

Nanling Mountains

The Nanling Mountains (11_5 on Figure 14.1) were once called Five Ranges from their five famous mountain ranges. The Nanling form the great geographic divide between Central China and South China, stretching from west to east more than 600 kilometers and from north to south about 200 kilometers. It is also the water divide between the Chang Jiang and the Zhu Jiang drainage systems. Yet, it is comparatively low and discontinuous, and there are many breaks where cold waves and human traffic may pass through conveniently. Therefore, it is not as effective a barrier as the Qinling Mountains between Central China and North China. On the whole, low mountains dominate the subregion, and three sections might be identified.

1. The western section consists of northeast–southwest trending peaks about 2000 m in elevation. Between Yuecheng Mountain and Haiyang Mountain lies the famous Xingan Corridor, where a canal was built more than 2000 years ago to connect the Chang Jiang and the Zhu Jiang drainage systems. The corridor is also famous for its scenic karst topography. Guilin is said to be the most beautiful scenic spot in the world (Color Plate 21), and its neighbor, Yangshuo, is supposed to be even better.

2. The central section: Mainly west–east trending, the peaks here are about 1000 m in elevation. The Beijing–Wuhan–Guangzhou railway traverses one of its passes.

3. The eastern section is the lowest section, generally below 1000 m in elevation.

In this subregion, winter lasts only one or two months, but usually brings hard frosts and occasional snow. The mean January temperature ranges from 8° to 10°C. Annual precipitation totals about 1500 mm. Subtropical evergreen broad-leaved forest grows luxuriantly, with a considerable number of tropical components on the southern slopes. The main target for agricultural development is, and will continue to be, growing subtropical timber woods and economic crops. More productive farming in intermontane basins depends on a larger and more regular supply of irrigation water.

Sichuan Basin

The Sichuan Basin, with an area of about 260,000 sq km, is one of the largest inland basins in China. Administratively, it occupies about 46 percent of the huge Sichuan Province, which had a total population of 108 million in 1990,[2] the most populous province in China, probably also in the world.

This is a typical rhombic-shaped basin that has been formed since the Indochina Tectonic Movement during the Mesozoic era (Figure 14.4). Reddish sandstone and purple shale of the Jurassic and Cretaceous periods are most common; hence, it is sometimes called simply the "Red Basin." It is demarcated roughly by the 700 m to 750 m contour line and encircled by a continuous series of high mountains. The Micang and Daba mountains on its northern border are a part of the Qinling Mountains system. The Longmen, Qionglai, and Emei mountains on its western border are the eastern border mountains of the Tibetan Plateau. On its eastern and southern borders is a series of ranges mostly 1500–2000 m in elevation. The remarkable Wushan Mountain of the Three Gorges is the most significant. The basin itself has an elevation of 250–700 m, and most of it consists of rolling hills.

Thanks to the protection provided by the surrounding mountains, the basin enjoys a much warmer winter climate than the middle and lower Chang Jiang plains, with a mean January temperature of 5° to 8°C. Summer is long and hot, with a mean July temperature of 26° to 29°C; Chongqing has experienced an absolute maximum temperature of 44°C. Annual precipitation ranges from 1500 to 1800 mm in the surrounding mountains and from 900 to 1300 mm in the basin. The relative humidity is high throughout the year, and in the western Sichuan Basin, there are more than 300 foggy days. Hence, there is an ancient saying, "A Sichuan dog will bark at the sun."

A dense concentric drainage system is developed with the Chang Jiang passing through the basin center. Numerous tributaries of the Chang Jiang are longer than 100 km; six (Jialing, Min, Tuo, Qu, Fu, and Wu) exceed 500 km. These rivers offer abundant irrigation water and

transportation facilities but are also a potential flood hazard. According to an estimate, hydroelectric capacity in the Sichuan Basin totals nearly 50 million KW. Most of these rivers meander amid intermontane valleys and sometimes cut through hills and mountains in scenic gorges, of which the Three Gorges of the Chang Jiang is the most famous (Color Plate 20). A massive dam project for multiple purposes has been approved for the Three Gorges. It will certainly bring great benefits (especially generating hydroelectricity and the ameliorating of floods) to the middle and lower Chang Jiang valleys, but it requires a huge amount of capital, and the impoundment of the high dam will drown out most of the upstream valley-bottom plains in the Sichuan Basin. Therefore, nearly 1 million inhabitants living there have to move.

Both flora and fauna are profuse and varied. Zonal vegetation in the basin is subtropical evergreen broad-leaved forest, but this has been virtually all removed, with only a few exceptional locations on mountain slopes and hills below 1500–1800 m. In addition, large patches of secondary oak forest and needle-leaved forest as well as bamboo groves persist. In combination with a vast expanse of cultivated vegetation, the green verdure of these plants interweaves with the reddish ground surface to form a colorful mosaic.

The Sichuan Basin has long been famous as an attractive and productive land in China. It has been intensively cultivated for more than 2000 years. Several kingdoms were founded here. Practically all plains and hills have been developed. Numerous irrigation ponds fed by rainfall are built on tops of hills. It now has more than 6 million ha of cropland, of which about 56 percent are paddy. It is one of the most concentrated paddy-rice-growing areas in the world.

Chengdu Plain

Located near the western border of the Sichuan Basin, the Chengdu Plain (12_1 on Figure 14.1) has an area of about 8000 sq km, which makes it the largest and most fertile plain in rugged Southwest China. It is essentially composed of eight alluvial fans, each with an elevation of 450–750 m, inclining from northwest to southeast. The plain is underlain by Quaternary sand and gravel beds, with a maximum depth of more than 300 m. Annual precipitation here totals 1000 to 1300 mm. Numerous rivers pass through the subregion, and groundwater resources are abundant.

This subregion has long been the commercial grain and rape seed oil base for Sichuan Province. The triple-

---

[2] The western half of Sichuan Province, in comprehensive physical regionalization as well as in economic and social development, is the southeastern part of the Tibetan Frigid Plateau and is very sparsely inhabited. It was once called Xi (West) Kang Province.

cropping system (two crops of rice, one crop of rape or wheat) predominates. The key factor supporting agricultural development is irrigation. The famous Du Jiang Dam irrigation system (Color Plate 11) was built in 256 B.C. to make full use of the Min and Tuo rivers. Remarkably, the system has been kept in operation without interruption ever since. Since 1949, it has been greatly improved and enlarged, with the total canal length increasing from 1100 km to 8100 km and the irrigated area from 140,000 to 560,000 ha.

Central Hills

Located in the central part of the Sichuan Basin, these low hills (12_2 on Figure 14.1) have an elevation of 250–600 m. Hills are mainly composed of reddish sandstone and purple shale, with nearly horizontal strata. They have been deeply dissected by numerous rivers, resulting in steep slopes and flat tops (mesas). In the winter, this is the warmest part of the Sichuan Basin with a mean January temperature of 6° to 8°C. Annual precipitation totals 900 to 1100 mm. Since ancient times, this has been a well-developed agricultural area specializing in growing grains, cotton, and sugar cane. Nearly all flat hill tops have been cultivated, mostly for rain-fed farming and partly for winter paddy land. Consequently, the two most urgent problems in this subregion are improvement of irrigation systems and more efficient control of soil erosion.

Eastern Parallel Ranges and Valleys

East of Huaying Mountain lies a closely folded area with anticlines as ranges and synclines as valleys. More than 30 northeast-trending ridges and valleys run parallel to each other. The elevation of the ridges increases from 700 to 800 m in the east to about 1000 m in the west. Ridges are mainly composed of reddish sandstone and purple shale and are covered by dense evergreen broad-leaved forests. The valleys are intensively cultivated. This subregion has a short, warm winter, with a mean January temperature of about 8°C. The frost-free season lasts 320–340 days without any frost at all along the Chang Jiang valley-bottom plains. The annual precipitation totals 1100 to 1300 mm. Climatically, this is a transitional area between the middle and southern subtropical zones. It is favorable for subtropical tree crops.

Guizhou Plateau

The Guizhou Plateau and its surrounding mountains, with an area of more than 400,000 sq km, is located on the second great topographic step in China. The elevation is mostly between 1000 and 2000 m, but the plateau is generally badly dissected. Consequently it was described, with some exaggeration, as being "without three *li* [one mile] of continually level land, without three successive days of fine weather, and its inhabitants each without three cents of money." Guizhou is still one of the least developed and poorest provinces in China.

The dissected plateau has a very rugged surface cut by deep canyons and crossed by towering mountains. Scattered among and encircled by these mountains and hills are high plains, the so-called *batzi*, which occupy probably only 5 percent of the total land area, but account for a lion's share of farmland and settlement. Owing to frequent wide outcrops of Paleozoic limestone, karst topography is well developed and extensive.

Climatically, the region is characterized by the absence of excessively cold winters and excessively hot summers, although rainy and cloudy days are abundant. The January temperature generally averages 5°C, and the mean July temperature is around 30°C. Cloudy, overcast weather totals more than 200 days; Meitan, with 253 cloudy and overcast days, holds the highest record in China.

Vegetation is transitional, both from east to west and from south to north. In the east, evergreen broad-leaved forest dominates; in the west, because the dry season lasts longer, a considerable portion of deciduous broad-leaved trees mingle in the forest. In the south, a monsoon forest similar to that found in the Southern subtropical zone dominates on the gentle slopes and in the valley plains. In the north, the typical vegetation is the evergreen broad-leaved forest of the Middle subtropical zone. On the extensive limestone areas, certain special types of karst vegetation dominate. They consist mainly of mixed evergreen and deciduous broad-leaved trees, but once the forest is cleared, the vegetation is reduced to sparse shrubs or grassland.

Eastern Low Mountains and Hills

This transitional belt between the Guizhou Plateau and the South Chang Jiang Hills and Basins region (13_1 on Figure 14.1) is composed mainly of low mountains, hills, and small basins with an elevation generally below 800 m. Located on the eastern border of the Guizhou Plateau, numerous tributaries of the Chang Jiang and the Zhu Jiang extend their cutting deep into the subregion, resulting in rather rugged topography. Annual precipitation totals 1200 to 1300 mm. Vertical zonation of vegetation is conspicuous. Taking Fanjing Mountain (2494 m) as an example, the evergreen broad-leaved forest is restricted to elevations below 1400 m, mixed evergreen and deciduous broad-leaved forest occupy the zone between 1400 and 2200 m, and alpine shrubby meadow vegetation predominates above 2200 m. Since ancient times, many minority ethnic groups have lived in this rather isolated subregion.

Northern Mountains and Gorges

This subregion (13_2 on Figure 14.1) is the transitional belt between the Guizhou Plateau and the Sichuan Basin. The northeast–southwest trending Dalou Mountain is uplifted on its northern border, with an absolute relief of 1300–1500 m and a relative relief of 500 to 700 m. Many gorges and canyons have been formed, of which the Wu Jiang Gorge (Photo 14.5) is the most important. Some intermontane basins are intensively developed with farmlands and dense population, of which Zunyi basin is the most famous.

Central Hilly Plateau

The central part of the Guizhou Plateau (13_3 on Figure 14.1), including the provincial capital Guiyang and its suburbs, is an undulating hilly area with an absolute relief of 900 to 1500 m but a relative relief generally below 300 m. More than 80 percent of the total area is characterized by limestone strata, and the major landforms are structural basins, block mountains, and karst topography. Many rivers have rather broad valleys and sluggish drainage where farmlands and settlements are dense. The climate is favorable for agriculture, with a mean January temperature of about 5°C, a mean July temperature of about 24°C, and an annual precipitation of between 1100 and 1200 mm. This is the Guizhou Plateau's best developed agricultural subregion. It is also an important part of the Third Line modern industrial development.

Southern Hilly Plateau

This subregion (13_4 on Figure 14.1) is located south of the Miaoling Mountains, which is the watershed divide between the Chang Jiang and the Zhu Jiang, with ridges about 1000 m in elevation. The subregion is essentially the dissected southern slope of the Guizhou Plateau, where the highest land relief is from 500 to 1400 m and

the relative relief is 300 to 700 m. In its northern part, limestone strata are widespread, and the plateau surface is deeply dissected, with an elevation ranging from 800 to 1200 m, an annual precipitation of 1200–1400 mm, and vegetation predominantly consisting of middle subtropical evergreen broad-leaved forest. In its southern part, many tributaries of the Zhu Jiang cut the subregion into low mountains, hills, and deep valleys, at elevations generally below 800 m. A conspicuous dry season followed by a wet season sustains a mid-subtropical evergreen broad-leaved forest mingled with some southern subtropical components (such as the banyan tree). Historically, this subregion is also the stronghold of many minority ethnic groups.

Western Mountains and Gorges

This subregion (13_5 on Figure 14.1) is located at the transitional belt between the Guizhou Plateau and the higher Yunnan Plateau. Most of the mountains rise above 2000 m in elevation, with slopes of more than 20°–25°. The plateau surface is preserved only in small patches on watersheds. Intermontane valleys generally have an absolute relief of 900–1700 m and relative relief of 400–600 m; the deepest gorges are more than 1000 m. The evergreen broad-leaved forest is still dominant, but montane grassland is also widespread. There is a high potential for developing forestry and animal husbandry in this subregion.

Yunnan Plateau

This region is located roughly between 24° and 28° N and 90° to 105° E, comprising an area of about 300,000 sq km. It is the transitional belt between two great natural realms in China, Eastern Monsoon China and the Tibetan Frigid Plateau. The dominant landscape is an extensive level and reddish plateau interspersed with greenish patches of intensively farmed basins surrounded by tree-clad mountains. The region is characterized, first, by a rather well-preserved undulating plateau surface and broad lake basins, mostly with elevations ranging from 1500 to 3000 m. Second, it is the southern part of the Hengduan Mountains, which feature a series of nearly north–south trending lofty mountain ranges running parallel to a series of nearly north–south trending deep river gorges. This ridge-and-gorge topography is particularly prominent north of 25° N, with a relative relief of more than 2000 to 3000 m and sometimes even more than 5000 to 6000 m. From west to east, the ridges and gorges are the Gaoligong Mountains and the

Nu Jiang (Salween River), the Nushan Mountains and the Lancang Jiang (Mekong River), the Daxue Mountains (Yunling) and the Jinsha Jiang (upper reaches of the Chang Jiang), the Mianmian Mountains and the Yalong Jiang, and the Lunan Mountains. Third, the region has extensive areas of karst topography, like the Guizhou Plateau and the Guangxi Basin. Karst is especially prevalent in eastern Yunnan where the spectacular Shilin (Stone Forest, Color Plate 23) is located. Finally, volcanic landforms have developed on the western Yunnan Plateau, of which the Tengchong area with its numerous volcanic cones and hot springs is the most significant.

The region's climate pattern is dominated by the so-called plateau monsoons—the southwestern (Indian) monsoon in the western part and the southeastern (Pacific) monsoon in the eastern part. Owing to its topographic conditions and latitudinal location, the weather is mild all year round, and the provincial capital of Kunming, with an elevation of 1960 m, is famous for its "eternal spring." Annual precipitation totals 1000–1200 mm, decreasing both from the southeast and the southwest to the north central part, although the deep valley bottoms of the Jinsha, Nujiang, and Lancang rivers have less than 1000 mm and are called "dry valleys." The division between the rainy season (May to October) and the dry season (November to April) is apparent, with winter (December to February) receiving only 5 percent of the total annual precipitation.

Vegetation is correspondingly varied and luxuriant. The zonal vegetation is evergreen broad-leaved forest, with *Cyclobalanopsis glaucoides*, *C. delavayi*, and *Castanopsis delavayi* the dominant tree species. As a result of intense human intervention, the drought-tolerant Yunnan pine (*Pinus yunnanensis*) now prevails. Vertical distribution of vegetation is conspicuous. One famous example is the snow-capped Yulong Mountain (5596 m, Photo 14.7) overlooking the Jinsha River valley, with a relative relief of more than 4000 m. Five vertical zones are demarcated: (1) the Jinsha River valley below 2000 m is covered with the semiarid subtropical shrubby savanna; (2) the basic vegetation belt (2000–3100 m) is mainly composed of Yunnan pine forest; (3) a fir forest occurs the slopes between 3100 and 3800 m; (4) alpine meadow occurs between 3800 and 4500 m; and (5) continual snow and ice appears above 4500 m.

Such conspicuous vertical distribution is also mirrored by agricultural zonation in the region. Semiarid, subtropical valleys below 1000 m might be farmed by double cropping of rice where irrigation water is available. Farmland between 1000 and 2400 m is generally under a rice–wheat double-cropping system. Farmland above 2400 m is devoted to one-crop dry farming. Above 3100 m, only forestry and alpine pastoral grazing are possible. Such vertical zonation is even reflected in the distribution of ethnic groups, with Dai, Bai, and Hani mainly inhabiting the low valleys. Tibetan, Kachin (Jingpo), Yi, and Lisu peoples live on the high plateau, while Han and Hui work the farmlands in the middle (Figure 7.2).

Eastern Yunnan Karst Plateau

With carbonate rock occupying more than 50 percent of the total land area at a thickness of more than 3300 m, karst topography is widely distributed in this subregion (14_1 on Figure 14.1). The ground surface is generally rather dry, rivers are few, and agriculture is generally restricted to rain-fed farming systems. On limestone hills and mountains, after the original vegetation has been destroyed, shrubby grassland or even bare rock tends to emerge. Conditions for plant growth on sandstone and shale outcrops are much better; they are usually covered by a thin veneer of weathered materials and Yunnan pine or oak forest. The distinction between rock mountain and earth mountain is quite significant in the subregion, and soil conservation and reforestation are needed to transform and stabilize the present poverty-stricken landscape.

Central Yunnan Plateau and Lake Basins

This subregion (14_2 on Figure 14.1) is mainly located at the watershed divide, where the plateau surface is comparatively well preserved. However, the plateau is dissected near river channels. There are also numerous faulted lake basins of which the Dian Chi near Kunming is the most scenic. These lake basins are favorable for production of rice and fish in Yunnan Province. Paddy rice occupies a larger proportion of the land than rain-fed farming. This land has a mild climate, with one of the warmest mean January temperatures (8° to 10°C) and the coolest mean July temperatures (19° to 22°C) in China. Annual precipitation ranges from 700 mm to 1200 mm, although spring drought is a problem for agriculture.

Hengduan Mountains

This subregion is composed of parallel mountains and deep gorges. North of the Baoshan–Xiaguan line (about 25° 30′ N) mountains are closely crowded together and there are almost no broad intermontane valleys or large

Photo 14.8 Downtown Hong Kong and the neighboring promontories and bays.

patches of plateau surface. South of that line, the mountain ridges become lower and the intermontane valleys broader. Two climatic factors stand out quite conspicuously. One is the barrier action of these lofty mountains. For example, Baoshan, which is located at the eastern foot of the Gaoligong Mountains, has an annual precipitation of only 903.2 mm, while Longling on the western windward slope has rainfall as high as 2595.7 mm. The second factor is the conspicuous vertical zonation. On the western slopes of the Gaoligong Mountains below 2500 m, secondary vegetation and farmlands dominate; between 2500 and 2700 m, a luxuriant evergreen broad-leaved forest prevails; between 2700 and 2960 m, there is a mixed needle- and broad-leaved forest; between 2960 and 3500 m, the needle-leaved forest predominates; while between 3500 and 3680 m, there are mainly alpine shrubs. Mountainous land makes up about 96 percent of the total area, of which about 25 percent is tree-clad. Forestry and tree crops certainly are, and will continue to be, the two major resources in this subregion.

Lingnan Hills

The Lingnan[3] Hills with an area of about 350,000 sq km, is south of the Nanling Mountains, which are traditionally considered to be northern limit of South China

[3] Literally, "Lingnan" means "south of *ling* [mountain range]." Here, *ling* means the Nanling Mountains.

as well as Southern subtropical zone. On the southeastern side, the Lingnan Hills face the Taiwan Strait, while on the southwestern side, the area is separated from the humid tropical division by a series of coastal mountains and hills.

The region is dominated by hills below 500 m in elevation. There are also a few mountains above 1000 m and a series of ribbon-like alluvial plains along the rivers. Mountains and hills are largely controlled by the northeast–southwest trending geological structural lines composed chiefly of granites and metaphorphic rocks. Guangxi is on typical karst topography. In the structural basins, such as Guangzhou, Cenozoic red beds occur. The coastline is generally rugged and irregular. There are many promontories and protected bays suitable for harbors, such as Hong Kong (Photo 14.8). The alluvial plains are recently deposited, and the deltaic plains of the Zhu Jiang and other large rivers are still growing.

The climate features a long, rainy summer and a short, dry winter. Summer lasts more than 6 to 7 months, with frequent typhoons accompanied by torrential rain, which constitute one of the most severe natural hazards in the region. In January, the mean temperature ranges from 10° to 15°C, but absolute temperature may drop below −3°C when a strong cold wave passes southward through the low and broken Nanling Mountains. It is unsafe to grow rubber trees (*Hevea*) and other tropical crops without special precautions. Annual precipitation totals 1400 to 1800 mm, with some windward slopes receiving more than 2000 mm and some secluded valleys less than 1000 mm. The seasonal variability of rainfall is rather great; spring and autumn drought as well as summer floods usually place restrictions on agricultural production. Soil erosion is severe on mountain slopes where the natural vegetation has been removed.

Abundant rainfall feeds numerous rivers that parallel the mountain ranges and broad valleys, sometimes cutting through them to create gorges. The most important river system is, of course, the Zhu Jiang, which is composed of three main tributaries. The largest one, the Xi Jiang (West River), rises in the eastern Yunnan Plateau and southern Guizhou Plateau and flows eastward across Guangxi and western Guangdong to meet two other tributaries, the Bei Jiang (North River) and the Dong Jiang (East River) near the head of the delta at Guangzhou. The Zhu Jiang then splits into a ramifying system of channels and distributaries and finally empties into South China Sea. Hong Kong and Macao are located on either side of the river mouth. There are also numerous independent rivers, of which the Han Jiang and the Jiulong are the most important, flowing into the sea at Shantou and Xiamen, respectively.

The dominant zonal vegetation is the evergreen monsoon forest, which is different from both the evergreen broad-leaved forest of the Middle subtropical zone and the rainforest or monsoon forest of the tropics. Within the region, tropical components increase from north to south. Owing to heavy human intervention, the original forests have long since been cleared and replaced. Instead, secondary forest, shrubs, and grasslands are widespread. Soil conservation and afforestation are urgent problems on mountains and hills. The low-lying alluvial plains have been intensively used, mostly for double-cropping paddy rice and highly productive economic crops, such as sugar cane, mulberry trees, and hemp. There are about 4 million ha of farmland in the region, accounting for about 11 percent of the total land area. The Zhujiang Delta, the Shantou–Chaozhou Plain, and the Zhangzhou Plain are among the most productive and densely populated areas in China. They have now been turned mostly into special economic areas.

Eastern Guangdong and Fujian Coastal Hills

This subregion (15_1 on Figure 14.1) extends northeastward along the coast and has a rugged topography. It contains many excellent seaports, such as Shantou, Xiamen, and the ancient Quanzhou. Numerous southeastward-flowing rivers cut through the mountains and hills in gorges or narrow valleys. There are also highly fertile deltaic plains; yet, given the huge population, per capita farmland is generally less than 0.5 *mu* (0.03 ha). The hard-working inhabitants must fight against both the sea and the mountains. They have made efforts to reclaim land from the sea, with considerable success. They are also making better use of mountains and hills by means of afforestation and soil conservation. This is also the most important homeland for more than 30 million overseas Chinese.

Zhu Jiang Delta

With an area of 10,000 sq km, the Zhu Jiang Delta (15_2 on Figure 14.1) is the most important farming area in South China and probably one of the most productive and sustainable ecosystems in the world (Color Plate 22). In this subregion, the growing season lasts all year, with a mean January temperature of 13° to 15°C. Annual precipitation totals more than 1600 mm. The Zhu Jiang Delta has been highly developed ever since the Qin Dynasty (221–206 B.C.) and is now the agricultural base for Shenzhen and Zhuhai as well as Hong Kong and Macao. Recently, great strides have been made in modern industry and foreign trade.

Western Guangdong–Eastern Guangxi Mountains and Valleys

This subregion (15_3 on Figure 14.1) is dominated by a series of northeast–southwest trending low mountains and hills. The Xi Jiang has cut through these mountains in narrow gorges; its tributaries on either side form broad valleys. Annual precipitation totals 1800 to 2000 mm on windward slopes and 1400 to 1600 mm on leeward sides. Evergreen broad-leaved forests and evergreen monsoon forests grow luxuriantly here; this is one of the major timber-producing areas in South China. A comprehensive "vertical agriculture" development is also significant (Figure 10.4). Soil conservation is now a growing problem.

Central Guangxi Broad Valleys and Karst Basins

Karst topography is well developed in the western and northern parts of this subregion (15_4 on Figure 14.1), and there are extensive broad valleys in the eastern and southern parts. This area is the most important producer of grain and economic crops (sugar cane, hemp) in Guangxi Zhuang Autonomous Region. It still needs more intensive management and improved irrigation systems for further development.

Northwestern Guangxi Mountains and Karst Topography

This subregion (15_5 on Figure 14.1) is the westernmost and the highest part of the region, with an elevation of 500 to 1000 m. Only the valleys of the southeast-flowing You Jiang (Right River) and the northeast-flowing Zuo Jiang (Left River) lie below 200 m, with a mean daily temperature of above 10°C nearly all year. Annual precipitation totals 1000 to 2000 mm. Agriculture is well developed. On either side of these two rivers, there are shrub- or grass-covered terraces and hills, and soil erosion is a major environmental problem. The extensive mountainous karst topography is deeply dissected.

Taiwan Island

This region is composed of Taiwan, the largest island of China, along with its more than 100 neighboring islands. Taiwan Island itself has an area of 35,760 sq km, with a north-south length of 384 km and a east-west width of 144 km at its widest point. All neighboring islands are rather small; the largest one, Penghu, has an area only of 64 sq km. Owing to the unique distribution of land and sea and the related physical and human features (Figure 14.3), Taiwan Island and its neighbors are considered as one single region with a total land area of 36,000 sq km and a total population of 20.11 million in 1989.

Taiwan is a part of the great marginal island arc of the northwestern Pacific Ocean and marks the divide between the shallow continental shelf and the deep sea basin. Taiwan's east coast, with an immediate offshore water depth of more than 2500 m, is the Chinese "window" directly facing the immense Pacific Ocean. The Taiwan Strait, with a length of about 300 km and a width of 150–250 km (the narrowest part only 130 km), is a part of the continental shelf, with a water depth generally less than 100 m.

Taiwan Island is dominated by Cenozoic mountains and hills that occupy about two-thirds of the total land area. The Central Range runs from north to south for nearly the entire length of the island. The Taiwan Geosyncline was formed during the Paleozoic era, and was concluded by the Pliocene Himalayan Tectonic Movement. The great marginal island arc of the northwestern Pacific Ocean was then formed. Since then, the island arc has been repeatedly folded, faulted, and uplifted, and the Taiwan mountains, with the Central Range as a backbone, were formed. The island is now mainly composed of four parallel mountain ranges run-ning from south to north; they are actually the continuation of the Himalaya Mountains. These are among the youngest mountains in the world, and tectonic movement is still in progress (the rate of uplift is estimated at 17 to 18 cm/100 years). There are 62 peaks higher than 3000 m in elevation; the highest one (Mount Yushan) is 3997 m. These lofty mountains contrast strongly with deep sea trenches (with depth of 3000 to 5999 m) not far off the east coast.

Between these four parallel mountain ranges, there are great parallel fault lines, contributing to the occurrence of earthquakes, landslides, and geothermal springs. There are also many intermontane lakes (Photo 14.3). Mineral resources, such as gold, silver, iron, sulfur, and coal, occur widely.

The divide between mountains and hilly areas is represented approximately by the 500 m contour line. Hills are widely distributed along the western foot of the Ali Mountains and merge westward to the coastal plains. Intermontane basins and coastal plains together account for 20 percent of island's total land area. They are densely covered with farmlands and settlements.

A long but rather monotonous coastline is another geomorphological feature of the region. In total there are about 1500 km of coastline, of which Taiwan Island itself accounts for 1100 km. Except for the northeastern corner where the Central Range meets the sea and results in a rugged coastline and abundant promontories, including the famous Jilong (Keelung) port, all of Taiwan's coastlines are rather straight. The western coast, which borders the Taiwan Strait, has a well-developed alluvial plain; the coastal beach quickly advances seaward. On average, annual advance of the coastal beach has been 35.4 m during the last 200 years. Therefore, good natural harbors are few; Gaoxiang (Kaohsiung) is the only exception. The eastern coast is largely given character by the parallel coastal range and the straight fault line; the offshore deep sea makes the formation of a depositional coastal beach difficult. Penghu Island has the most varied and irregular coastline, and Magong (Makung) is the best port in the region.

The climate is wet and hot year around. Owing to low latitudinal location (22°–25° N) and strong maritime influences, the mean annual temperature generally rises above 20°C (Taibei, or Taipei, 21.7°C). A larger part of the island north of the Tropic of Cancer belongs to the Southern subtropical zone, while a small part south of it is in the tropical zone. The mean annual precipitation for the whole island approximates 2600 mm, with the mountainous area south of Jilong recording more than 5000 mm. The highest annual precipitation in China has been recorded in Huoshaoliao, 14 km south of Jilong, which has a mean annual precipitation of 6576 mm but reached 8408 mm in 1912. In southern Taiwan, more than 80 percent of the annual precipitation falls from June to September when the southwestern monsoons and typhoons dominate. In northern Taiwan, on the other hand, the prevailing northeastern monsoon brings more rainfall during the winter.

The river network is dense but rather asymmetric. As Taiwan's major watershed divide is the Central Range, which is located somewhat eastward from the central line, the river network and alluvial plains are better developed on the western side. Owing to the small area and rugged topography, rivers are mostly small and swift. There are 151 rivers on Taiwan Island, divided into 48 river systems. Only 20 rivers have a length in excess of 50 km, with 16 of them flowing westward and 4 eastward. Deep river gorges, usually formed in the upper and middle reaches, have great hydroelectric potential. According to an estimate, the output could reach 5 million KW. Extensive alluvial fans and plains formed from river deposits are intensively cultivated.

Vegetation is luxuriant and varied. Taiwan Island has been famous for its forests and bamboo and timber production. Formerly, forests occupied about 70–80 percent of the total land area, but now the coverage is about 52 percent. Large patches of original forest and numerous economically valuable trees (more than 20 species) grow extensively up to elevations of 1600 m. In the northern and central parts, the dominant zonal vegetation type is subtropical evergreen broad-leaved forest mingled with some tropical components. The most spectacular species is the banyan tree, which grows extensively on low mountains, hills, and basins below 500 m in elevation. The southern tip of the island is characterized by tropical monsoon forest and rainforest. Dominant species in the tropical rainforest are *Myristica cagayanensis*, *Pterospermum niveum*, and *Artocarpus lenceolatus*. Vertical distribution of climate and vegetation is particularly conspicuous in the mountainous area. From low plains to alpine mountains, tropical (subtropical), temperate, and alpine climate and vegetation types appear in succession. Broadly speaking, horizontal zonal subtropical or tropical vegetation types are found below 500 m in elevation, evergreen broad-leaved forest from 500 to 2000 m, mixed forest and needle-leaved forest from 2000 to 3000 m, and alpine shrubby meadow from 3600 to 3900 m.

During the last 600 years, immigrants from the Chi-

TABLE 14.3
Annual Production of Major Industrial Commodities in Taiwan, 1990

Commodity	Unit	Volume
Cloth	100 million m	7.29
Cotton yarn	10,000 ton	20.39
Polymer fiber	10,000 ton	45.63
Bicycles	10,000	708.63
Automobiles	10,000	35.39
Sewing machines	10,000	251.47
Washing machines	10,000	23.59
Mini-computers	10,000	339.98
Recorders	10,000	812.43
Color TV sets	10,000	209.89
Cameras	10,000	1,057.14
Cement	10,000 ton	1,845.84
Coal	10,000 ton	47.21
Electricity	100 million KW/hr	823.49
Steel	10,000 ton	299.79
Paper	10,000 ton	250.88

Data source: Statistical Yearbook of China, 1991.

nese mainland (about 80 percent from Fujian Province) have repeatedly settled on Taiwan Island. In 1989, the population density reached 559 persons/sq km. The farmland area in the 1980s totaled 1.29 million ha, with a double-cropping index of 144.1 percent and with rice, sugar cane, fruits, and vegetables as major crops. Since the 1950s, agriculture (including farming, animal husbandry, fishing, and forestry) has been greatly developed, especially the so-called "fine agriculture," which is productive and sustainable and is probably a further sophistication of the traditional Chinese peasant-gardener ecosystem. It is also characterized by specialization and commercialization in farming production.

Since the 1960s, and especially since the 1970s, modern industry and foreign exports have been phenomenally developed, ranking Taiwan as one of the four "small dragons" in Asia. In 1989, total foreign trade reached U.S. $118.45 billion (exports U.S. $66.2 billion, imports U.S. $52.25 billion). In 1990, per capita GNP reached U.S. $7997. Annual production (1990) of major industrial commodities in Taiwan is listed in Table 14.3.

Northern Subtropical Hills and Plains

This subregion (16_1 on Figure 14.1) includes extensive coastal hills and plains. The mean annual precipitation totals 1500 to 2000 mm. The mean annual temperature ranges from 15° to 26°C, with an absolute minimum temperature above 4°C. Alluvial soils are thick and fertile and chiefly support paddy rice and other crops. The natural vegetation growing below 300 m is oak forest, most of which has now been removed. An evergreen broad-leaved forest is still widely distributed on higher elevations. This subregion is now the political, economic, and cultural center of Taiwan.

Central Subtropical Mountains

This subregion (16_2 on Figure 14.1) has the highest elevation on Taiwan Island, including most of the peaks above 3000 m. Consequently, it has the heaviest rainfall, with annual precipitation generally above 4000–5000 mm. It is also the most important timber-producing area. Farmland and population are comparatively sparse.

Southern Tropical Hills and Plains

Located generally south of the Tropic of Cancer and below the 500 m contour line, this subregion (16_3 on Figure 14.1) is composed mainly of two alluvial plains, the Tainan Plain and the Pindong Plain. Both have been intensively cultivated for paddy rice and sugar cane. The climate is much warmer but less humid than other subregions, with an annual precipitation around 1500 mm and an annual temperature above 24°C. The zonal vegetation is the luxuriant monsoon rainforest, with *Myritia spp*, *Sideroxylon ducliton*, *Diospyros utilis*, and *Artocarpus lanceolata* dominating. Numerous epiphytes are intermixed with the trees. Most of the original tropical rainforests have been removed.

Tropical East Coast

This subregion (16_4 on Figure 14.1) is restricted to a narrow coastal strip east of the Central Range. A longitudinal valley is sandwiched between the Central Range and the East Coastal Range, with a length of about 150 km and a minimum width of only 4–5 km. On the valley floor, the elevation ranges from 50 to 250 m. On its eastern slope, the East Coastal Range virtually plunges into the deep Pacific Ocean, with a fault scarp several hundred meters high. Climatic and vegetation conditions are similar to those of the southern tropical hills and plains.

Penghu Islands

This archipelago (16_5 on Figure 14.1) stretches north–south for more than 60 km and east–west for more than 40 km; however, it has a total land area of only 127 sq km. The archipelago is mainly composed of rocky basalt platforms where there are frequent earthquakes. The elevation nowhere exceeds 80 m. Located on the transitional belt between alternating monsoons, the area is windy year around. Annual precipitation totals about 1000 mm. Originally there were no trees, but luxuriant banyan trees have recently been planted by the local inhabitants.

REFERENCES

Cai, Yunlong. 1989. *The Land Systems and Their Economic Development on the Guizhou Plateau*. Ph.D. dissertation, Institute of Geography, Chinese Academy of Sciences (in Chinese).

China State Statistical Bureau. 1991. *Statistical Yearbook of China*. Beijing: China Statistical Publishing House.

Chinese Academy of Sciences. 1959. *Comprehensive Physical Regionalization*. Beijing: Science Press (in Chinese).

Chu, Ko-chin. 1958. "On the Delimitation of the Subtropical Zone in China," *Acta Geographica Sinica* 26, no. 2 (in Chinese).

Department of Geography, Hangzhou University. 1959. *Physical Geography of Zhejiang Province*. Hangzhou: Zhejiang People's Press (in Chinese).

Department of Geography, Kunming Teacher's College. 1978. *Geography of Yunnan*. Kunming: Yunnan People's Press (in Chinese).

Guo, Guanmin. 1980. *Physical Geography of Hunan Province*. Changsha: Hunan People's Press (in Chinese).

Hsieh, Chiao-min. 1964. *Taiwan: A Geography in Perspective*. London: Butterworths.

Liu, Wei-dong. 1990. *The Land Systems in the Jiang-Han Plain*. Ph.D. dissertation, Institute of Geography, Chinese Academy of Sciences (in Chinese).

Liu, Yinhan. 1980. "On Natural Zonation in Shaanxi Province," *Acta Geographica Sinica* 35, no. 3 (in Chinese).

Sichuan Vegetation Working Group. 1980. *Sichuan Vegetation*. Chengdu: Sichuan People's Press (in Chinese).

Sun, Jinzhu, et al. 1988. *Geography of China*. Beijing: Higher Education Press (in Chinese).

Tan, Vanyi, et al. 1980. *Physical Geography of Hubei Province*. Wuhan: Hubei People's Press (in Chinese).

Wuhan Institute of Botany, Chinese Academy of Sciences. 1980. *Plants of the Shennongjia*. Wuhan: Hubei People's Press (in Chinese).

Xu, Xianghao. 1981. *Plant Ecology and Plant Geography of Guangdong Province*. Guangzhou: Guangdong Science and Technology Press (in Chinese).

Zhang, Hunan. 1980. "The Fault Delta," *Acta Geographica Sinica* 35, no. 1 (in Chinese).

Zhao, Songqiao. 1986. *Physical Geography of China*. New York: Wiley.

Zhong, Gonfu. 1980. "Mulberry Dike–Fish Pond on the Zhu Jiang Delta: A Complete Artificial Ecosystem," *Acta Geographica Sinica* 35, no. 3 (in Chinese).

CHAPTER FIFTEEN

Tropical South China

China is essentially a country with temperate and subtropical climates. The tropical area is quite limited, occupying only about 1.6 percent of the total land area. Yet, it stretches along the Chinese southern border through more than 15 degrees of longitude from the Sino-Burmese international boundary in southern Yunnan to the southern tip of Taiwan Island. From north to south, it spreads out in the form of numerous islands dotted amid the immense South China Sea, south to Zengmu Shoal (3° 50′ N) through more than 20 degrees of latitude. Administratively, it includes Hainan Province as well as the southern strips of Yunnan and Guangdong provinces and Guangxi Zhuang Autonomous Region (Figure 15.1).

There is still some disagreement about the northern boundary of this division. The disputed area lies between 21° and 25° N. In this book we will adopt the line drawn by the Physical Regionalization of China Working Committee of Chinese Academy of Sciences in 1959, which runs westward from the southern margin of the Zhu Jiang Delta (about 22° N, not including the delta itself) through Maoming, Hepu, Chongzuo, Gejiu, Simao, and Mangshi to the Sino-Burmese international boundary northwest of Wanding. This line coincides roughly with the 8000°C isotherm of cumulative temperature during the ≥ 10°C period and the mean January temperature isotherm of 16°C. The major factor shaping the physical geographical environment of Taiwan Island is the distribution of land and sea. The tropical zone of its southern tip can be combined with its northern subtropical part to form one single natural region as discussed in Chapter Fourteen; hence, an analysis of the southern tip of Taiwan Island will not be included in this chapter.

PHYSICAL FEATURES, NATURAL RESOURCES, AND ENVIRONMENTAL PROBLEMS

This division is characterized first of all by its humid tropical landscape. It enjoys rich climatic and biological resources and is especially significant for its tropical crops and strategic value.

Humid Tropical Climates

This division is endowed with rich humid tropical climatic resources, with a cumulative temperature during the ≥ 10°C period above 8000°–9000°C, a mean January temperature above 16°C and an annual precipitation ranging from 990 to 2500 mm (Figure 15.2). The growing season lasts year-round, and paddy rice can be triple cropped, if water and labor are available. Yet, from a global point of view, most parts of this division lie at the northern margin of the tropical zone. The tropical landscape is not as typical as that of Malaysia or Indonesia, because the temperature is somewhat lower and occasional frost occurs in the northern parts of this division. Furthermore, the division is dominated by alternating monsoons, with a marked distinction between the rainy season and the dry season, quite different from the year-round humid conditions found in Malaysia or Indonesia. Hence, many typical tropical crops, such as rubber tree (*Hevea*), are usually marginal, and low temperature and frost may sometimes wreak great havoc.

This division can be again subdivided into two parts: the western part and the eastern part. The western part

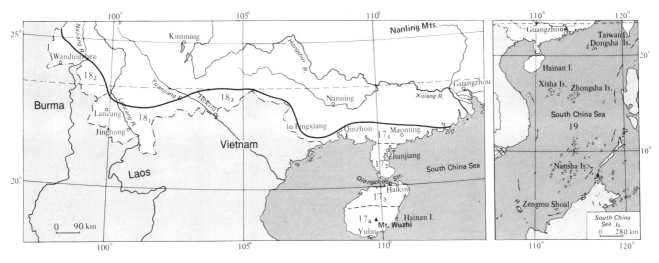

Figure 15.1 Tropical South China. (For legend, see Table 15.1.)

consists mainly of the low valleys and intermontane basins of southern Yunnan, where precipitation is derived chiefly from the Indian Ocean. Because the lofty Tibetan Plateau forms a barrier on the north and the plateau topography is so dissected, winter is much warmer, temperature inversions happen frequently, and the limit of the tropical zone stretches far north along river valleys as far as 23° to 25° N and to elevations as high as 700–900 m.

The eastern part is located along the seacoasts of Guangdong and Guangxi, as well as on the Hainan Island and numerous South China Sea islands, with precipitation deriving mainly from the Pacific Ocean. Typhoons occur frequently in the summer and autumn,

wreaking great havoc. Furthermore, because the Nanling Mountains are rather low and their topography dissected, their barrier action is not very effective, and strong cold waves may penetrate south as far as northern Hainan Island in winter. Consequently, winter temperature is much lower and the annual variation in temperature is much greater. The northern limit of the tropical zone is thus pushed southward along cold wave tracks to about 22° N.

The climate of the southern and northern parts is also distinctive. The mean temperature and absolute minimum temperature of the coldest month rises gradually from north to south. For example, Jinghong (22° 52′ N) has a mean January temperature of 15.7°C and

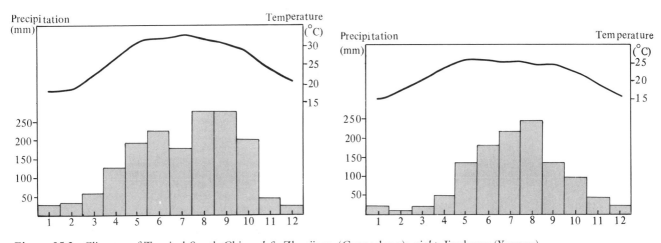

Figure 15.2 Climates of Tropical South China: *left*, Zhanjiang (Guangdong); *right*, Jinghong (Yunnan).

an absolute minimum temperature of 2.7°C; whereas Zhanjiang (21° 13' N) records 15.6°C and 2.8°C, respectively; Haikou (20° 2' N), 23.8°C and 2.8°C, respectively; Xisha (16° 50' N), 22.8°C and 15.3°C respectively; and Nansha (10° 23' N), 26.5°C and 21.1°C, respectively. Precipitation also increases from north to south. If a monthly precipitation threshold of ≤ 50 mm is used as an index for the dry season, there is no dry season in the southern part of the Nansha Archipelago, but a dry season of about three to four months does exist in the northern part of the Nansha and in the Xisha, and about three to six months on Hainan Island and the Leizhou Peninsula. Therefore, as a whole, this natural division may be divided at the Xisha Archipelago into two natural zones: the southern typical tropical zone and the northern marginal tropical zone.

Coastal and Hilly Topography

The eastern part of this division is essentially composed of hilly coasts, peninsulas, and islands, and soil erosion and mountain-related hazards are quite serious. The South China Sea islands are essentially composed of numerous small islands, beaches, reefs, and shoals, all built by coral skeletons. They are small in area. The largest island, Yongxing of the Xisha Archipelago, has an area of only 1.85 sq km. They are also low in elevation; the highest, Shidao of the Xisha Archipelago, has an altitude of only 15 m above sea level (Color Plate 24). Furthermore, more than 300 reefs and shoals are normally submerged, and only 34 islands and 8 beach areas stand above high tide for a total land area of only 12 sq km. They are divided into four archipelagos: Dongsha (East Sand), Xisha (West Sand), Zhongsha (Middle Sand), and Nansha (South Sand).

The Guangdong coast (including the Leizhou Peninsula) and the Guangxi coast together with Hainan Island are all dominated by mountainous and hilly topography. For example, on Hainan Island, with an area of 33,981 sq km, low mountains (elevation above 500 m) occupy about 25.4 percent of the area; hills (100–500 m), 13.2 percent; rolling terraces (below 100 m), 49.1 percent; flat plains, 9.6 percent; and miscellaneous, 2.7 percent.

The western part of the natural division is essentially composed of the southern part of the dissected Yunnan Plateau, which is even more mountainous and hilly. For example, in the Xishuangbanna[1] area, with an area of

[1] "Xishuangbanna" in the Dai (Tai) language means "twelve plains." The name shows that plains are very precious in these mountainous areas.

19,200 sq km, flat plains occupy only 5 percent, low and middle mountains 65 percent, and hills and terraces 30 percent.

Absolute relief exerts a great influence on the vertical zonation of climate and vegetation. In southern Yunnan especially, inversion of temperature and dense fogs often occur in low valleys below elevations of 400–500 m, with a temperature increase rate of 1.0° for every increase of 100 m (maximum record, 2.7°C/100 m). Consequently, tropical monsoon forests may be found up to 800–900 m, sometimes even above 1000 m. This is the northernmost (22.5° N) and the highest (900 m) *Hevea* (rubber tree) plantation limit in the world. Relative relief also plays an important role. Low, flat plains are usually devoted to grain crops, hill and terrace land to *Hevea* and other tropical crops, whereas low and medium mountains are mainly forested.

Dynamic Lateritic Soils

The humid tropical climate exerts a great influence on the soil-forming processes. Chemical weathering and leaching are intensive, and decomposition of organic material is rapid. Consequently, the organic content of the soil is generally low and the laterization processes predominate. The end product of laterization is called *laterite*, a porous, crumbly textured, bright reddish soil often hardening on exposure to the air and composed almost exclusively of clays and iron compounds; it is much the same process regardless of the parent materials. Yet, only in a limited area is this soil type fully developed. Most of the division's soils are at an intermediate stage of laterization. The stage may be assessed by measuring the proportion of silica to aluminum; the higher the silica content, the less laterization has taken place.

One feature of lateritic soils is their dynamic nature and the delicate balance of their fertility. These soils should not be hastily called infertile because—even if compared to the well-known fertile chernozem soil, which has a much higher humus content—the much faster recycling of nutrients in the tropics makes up for the humus content deficiency. Therefore, if the land is well managed, rapid disintegration and absorption will be balanced by a quick supplement of organic nutrients. But if the land is poorly managed or overused, soil erosion, leaching, and other depletion processes will soon dominate. In the later cases, soil fertility can be quickly degraded or even completely destroyed, and the soil becomes nearly useless for farming.

Photo 15.1 The luxuriant tropical monsoon forest in Xishuangbanna area, southern Yunnan Province.

Rich Biological Resources

Heavy precipitation and constant high temperature generate continuous plant growth and a profuse, varied flora. The luxuriant tropical monsoon forest is the typical zonal vegetation type here. Two subtypes may be distinguished: evergreen tropical monsoon forest and deciduous tropical monsoon forest. The former is found in areas with annual precipitation above 1600 mm and a short dry season, mainly in the eastern part of this division, usually with luxuriant rainforest vegetation (Color Plate 25). The latter is mainly found in the western part of this division, which has a longer dry season and annual precipitation of less than 1600 mm (Photo 15.1). However, both subtypes have similar forest physiognomy, with quite varied species and numerous tall trees as well as high annual biomass productivity. As high temperature usually coincides with the rainy season and somewhat lower temperatures with the dry season, corresponding periods have different growth rates—the luxuriant, rapid growth in the rainy season and the less luxuriant, slower growth in the dry season. The distinction between the greenish phase in summer and the yellowish phase in winter is particularly prominent.

Within such a luxuriant vegetational habitat, faunal resources are bountiful and are characterized by complicated composition and many endemic species. Arboreal and fruit-eating species of vertebrates are particularly abundant, such as many species of mammals (e.g., *Chiropheus* and *Carnivora*), of amphibians (e.g., *Hylidae*

and *Rhacophoridae*), and of reptiles (e.g., *Draco spp.*). But the most outstanding fauna is coral, whose innumerable skeletons have built up multitudes of coral reefs and islands in the South China Sea. Coral flourishes best in seawater with a temperature of 25°–30°C. Hence, it is mainly restricted to tropical seas, with the exception of the eastern coast of Taiwan Island where, owing the beneficent influence of the warm Kuroshio Current, coral is found along the coast northward into the subtropical zone (about 25° N).

Comprehensive Physical Regionalization

This division is widely scattered both longitudinally and latitudinally, although quite limited in land area. In the comprehensive physical regional system, three natural regions and 11 subregions are identified as shown in Table 15.1 and Figure 15.1.

HISTORICAL BACKGROUND

Located on the remote southern borders of South and Southwest China, this division is one of the country's least developed areas. During the long period of feudal society, when China was rather isolated from the outside world, the southern coast of Hainan Island was considered as the "Heaven's end, Earth's margin" (Photo 15.2), while the foggy low valleys of southern Yunnan were supposed to be deadly for human beings. In both

TABLE 15.1
Comprehensive Physical Regionalization of Tropical South China

Natural region	Natural subregion	Chief environmental problems
17. Leizhou Peninsula of Hainan Island— Tropical monsoon forest region	17(1) Coastal Plains of Southwestern Guangdong & Southern Guangxi	Soil erosion, typhoons, spring drought, summer floods
	17(2) Leizhou Peninsula	Soil erosion, typhoons, spring drought
	17(3) Northern Hainan Island	Soil erosion, typhoons, spring drought
	17(4) Southern Hainan Island	Soil erosion, deforestation, spring drought
18. Southern Yunnan Plateau— Tropical monsoon forest region	18(1) Southern Yunnan Low Valleys	Soil erosion, deforestation
	18(2) Southwestern Yunnan Broad Valleys	Soil erosion, deforestation
	18(3) Southeastern Yunnan Karst Plateau	Deforestation, soil erosion
19. South China Sea Islands —Tropical rainforest region	19(1) Dongsha Archipelago	Typhoons, wave action
	19(2) Xisha Archipelago	Typhoons, submergence
	19(3) Zhongsha Archipelago	Submergence
	19(4) Nansha Archipelago	Submergence

areas, the minority ethnic groups have practiced shifting agriculture since ancient times, resulting in severe deforestation and soil erosion. The widely scattered South China Sea islands were practically uninhabited before modern times, and were only occasionally used as sheltering sites for sea-going ships.

Yet, thanks to its unique geographic location and its rich natural resources, this division has developed rather rapidly since 1949. It is the major area for tropical crops in China. Many state farms and experimental stations have been set up for this purpose. Especially since 1978, when China opened up, Hainan Island and its neighboring areas have been rapidly developed, and in 1988 Hainan Island was elevated to provincial status and became the largest special economic zone in China. It had a total population of nearly 6.6 million in 1990; although compared with the Taiwan Island which has about the same size of land area and similar natural conditions, the population is still rather small (only about one-third of that of Taiwan), and the economic

Photo 15.2 "Heaven's End, Earth's Margin," the southernmost tip of Hainan Island.

development is still backward. Yet, both Hainan Island and southern Yunnan have a great capability for further development in the future.

The South China Sea islands are of great strategic significance and are valuable for oceanic transportation and fishing. There also might be rich petroleum reserves in their neighboring seas. Most of them have become a part of Chinese territory since 1945, although there are still international disputes over sovereignty.

SOCIAL AND ECONOMIC DEVELOPMENT

Tropical farming, including the cultivation of rubber trees, sisal, coffee, coconut palm, tea, and tropical fruits, has been well developed both in eastern and western parts of this division since 1949. Development efforts have been led by state farms and experiment stations. The area given to primitive shifting agriculture conducted by minority ethnic groups has been gradually decreasing, though these practices have not yet stopped. Hainan Island is now the largest rubber producer in China, accounting for 53 percent of the *Hevea* plantation area and 70 percent of the rubber production. The Xishuangbanna area of southern Yunnan accounts for the other one fourth of the *Hevea* plantation area (Photo 15.3). In 1990, the sown area in Hainan province totaled 0.8 million ha (with a double-cropping index of 141 percent), accounting for about 5.5 percent of the national total, of which food crops (chiefly rice and sweat potatoes) occupied 69.1 percent, economic crops (chiefly groundnuts and sugar cane) 21.5 percent, and other crops 9.4 percent.

Marine fishing enterprises, especially cultivated pearl raising, have been rapidly developed in the Beibu (Tonking) Gulf.

Modern industry and transportation are also developing, although they are still far from adequate. For example, no large-scale modern industrial enterprises have been set up on Hainan Island so far, and no railways have been built there. However, foreign trade has increased rather rapidly, and the continental shelf along the South China Sea is now one of the most important marine oil fields in China.

The Han are the dominant ethnic group in this division, although the central mountainous areas on Hainan Island are inhabited in large numbers by the Li and the Guangxi coast by the Zhuang. The humid tropical low valleys in southern Yunnan have long been the

Photo 15.3 A *Hevea* (rubber tree) plantation in an experimental station located in the Xishuangbanna area, Yunnan Province.

stronghold of Dai (Tai), who are also widely distributed in the Indochina Peninsula, while many other minority ethnic groups, such as the Hani, Lahu, Mulao, Blang, and Achang, live in the hills and low mountains of southern Yunnan.

So far, there are no large cities in this division. However, cities and ports are rapidly developing. Zhanjiang (northeastern Leizhou Peninsula) and Beihai (southern Guangxi coast) are two rapidly growing cities, while Haikou, Dongfang, and Sanya are three rapiding developing ports on Hainan Island. Haikou is also the capital of Hainan Province.

AREAL DIFFERENTIATION AND REGIONAL DEVELOPMENT

On the whole, this division is one of the newly developing areas in China and will be chiefly developed for tropical crop farming and foreign export trade. Yet, each of the different natural regions and subregions has its special conditions, and requirements for development planning (Figure 15.1, Table 15.1).

Leizhou Peninsula and Hainan Island

This region is located south of 21° 31′ N, including the narrow coast of Guangdong Province and Guangxi Zhuang Autonomous Region as well as Hainan Island. The region has an area of 46,451 sq km, of which Hainan Island occupies 73 percent.

The Leizhou Peninsula and Hainan Island, although separated by the narrow Qiongzhou Strait (only 15–30 km wide), have essentially similar physical conditions and economic development. Three major landform types stand out.

The extensive basalt platform and terrace, with an elevation generally below 150 m, occupies about 46 percent and 90 percent of the total land area of Hainan Island and the Leizhou Peninsula, respectively. The terrain is usually combined with many shield landform types, with a volcanic cone in the center of each shield. The basalt platform and terrace of earlier stages have been subjected to intense weathering for a long time. Whereas the reddish weathering crust is thick, the ground surface is gentle and rolling. These conditions are quite favorable for agricultural development, and farmlands are extensive. But the basalt platform of younger stages is only slightly weathered and eroded, with a rugged topography dominating. The farmers have to use rocks and gravel to build terrace walls and small patches of farmland, and grow crops on terraces and plant fruit trees along the walls. This is called "rock agriculture."

The dome mountains, with elevations generally above 500 m, are restricted to south-central Hainan Island; the highest one, at 1867 m, is Mount Wuzhi (literally, "five fingers"). This mountain system is mainly composed of granite and other igneous rocks.

Coral reefs are distributed intermittently along the coast. There are more than 120 species of reef-building corals around Hainan Island alone. The coral reefs create an excellent habitat for fish and shells. They serve as excellent wave barriers. However, if they are allowed to spread without control, they can restrict access to seaports.

Climatically, the region is controlled by alternating continental northeastern monsoons and maritime southeastern and southwestern monsoons, as well as typhoons originating in both the Pacific Ocean and the South China Sea. High temperature is typical year around, with a cumulative temperature during the ≥ 10°C period of 8200°–9200°C and a summer season that lasts 7 to 12 months. Three crops of paddy rice and other food crops can be grown per year, if irrigation water and human labor are available. Marine influences keep summertime less stiflingly hot than in the subtropical middle Chang Jiang valley. The maximum high temperature in the region never rises above 40°C, and the minimum low temperature generally ranges from 5°C to 8°C. When strong cold waves move far southward, however, the temperature may drop below 3°C, and frost may occur in the northern part. According to meteorological statistics, such severe cold waves have invaded this region seven times in the past 50 years. Therefore, great care must be taken to ameliorate low temperature effects during the winter for the planting of *Hevea* and other tropical crops in the Leizhou Peninsula and northern Hainan Island.

Precipitation is abundant, but there is a conspicuous dry season with marked areal variation. Annual precipitation on Hainan Island decreases from more than 2000 mm along the east coast (Wanning, 2151 mm) to less than 1000 mm along the west coast (Dongfang, 997.8 mm). Coupled with high temperatures, surprisingly there is a semiarid climatic region along the southwestern coast. Annual variation is also great. For example, in the rainiest year Haikou received 2282.3 mm, whereas the driest year produced only 1120 mm. Precipitation is concentrated in the rainy season (May to October), accounting for 80–90 percent of the annual total. The rainiest month has more than 400 mm of precipitation, while the driest month has less than 10 mm. Hence, both spring drought and summer floods set limitations on agricultural development.

Typhoons are familiar visitors from April through November. The strongest typhoons usually occur in September. According to statistics, from 1949 to 1978, 38 typhoons landed on Hainan Island, of which 21 had a wind velocity of more than 33 m/sec, and the strongest one (Typhoon no. 14 in September 1973) reached 61.2 m/sec. Typhoons land on Hainan Island most frequently along the middle east coast from Wanning to Wenchang, accounting for about 55 percent of the total. These landed typhoons present a grave danger to human life and tropical crops; for example, Typhoon no. 14 destroyed virtually all the houses and uprooted about 80–90 percent of the *Hevea* trees in the Qionghai area. Therefore, typhoon forecasting and the appropriate precautions and measures are of paramount importance in this region.

As on Taiwan, abundant precipitation feeds numerous rivers on this hilly island, but they are generally short and small. There are three relatively large rivers: Nandu, Changhua, and Wanquan. There are also numerous small rivers originating in the foothills; many of them are intermittent and have dry channels during the dry season.

The zonal lateritic soils, under different geological, topographical, climatic, and vegetation conditions, are further developed into various subtypes. The typical laterite is found on low hills and terraces that have different features during the rainy and dry seasons; they undergo a strong weathering-leaching process. Laterite developed on basalt is characterized by an abundance of iron.

Zonal vegetation is the luxuriant evergreen tropical monsoon forest. There are more than 1400 species of woody plants here, of which more than 800 species are tall trees and about 50 species rank as valuable timber. Shrubs and epiphytes are also profuse and varied, but grasses are comparatively few. The physiognomy of the evergreen tropical monsoon forest features multiple stories, with tall (usually 20–40 m high), uneven tree crowns within the first one to three stories; luxuriant shrubs as stories 3 to 5; and sparse grasses as stories 5 to 6. All these stories are intermixed with numerous epiphytes. Tropical rainforest is restricted to low hills and the east coast of Hainan Island where annual precipitation is more than 2000 mm and where there is no conspicuous dry season.

Deciduous tropical monsoon forest, park savanna, and sandy vegetation grow in the low hills and intermontane basins of southwestern Hainan Island where the climate is both hot and semiarid. Coastal mangrove forests grow in intermittent groves along the coast. Vertical vegetation zones include: (1) montane rainforest, located on lower slopes from 400 to 800 m where the annual precipitation totals more than 2000 mm; (2) montane evergreen broad-leaved forest, located from 1000 to 1200 m; and (3) mountain-top dwarf forest, distributed on windy mountain tops above 1300 m, with abundant mosses and lichens and dwarf trees less than 5 m in height.

As a whole, this region is rich in natural resources, but because of historical background and environmental conditions, is still far from being adequately developed. For example, Hainan Island has about 20,000 sq km of arable land, of which only 45 percent have been cultivated. The primitive shifting agricultural system still exists in some mountain areas. With a view to conserving these natural resources and using them in a more productive and sustainable way, every land type should be evaluated

and used according to its specific suitability and capability. Low, flat plains should be devoted to intensive farming; rolling terraces and hills below 500 m should be allotted chiefly to *Hevea* and other tropical tree crops; and mountain areas above 500 m could be better developed for subtropical and tropical forestry. From the national point of view, *Hevea* and other tropical crops have a special priority, and this is the best place in China for planting them. What is more, Hainan Island is now the largest special economic zone in China, and it is expected to be developed economically as fast as Taiwan Island (which has similar environmental and resource conditions) in the near future.

According to 1990 census, Hainan Province had a total population of 6.63 million, with a sex ratio of 108.4 (national average is 106.0), an annual birth rate of 24.84 per thousand (national average 21.06 per thousand), and an annual natural increase rate of 18.60 per thousand (national average 14.39 per thousand). All these indexes were slightly higher than the national averages; they might reflect the "new land" characteristics of Hainan Province. Agriculture employed 81.9 percent of the total population, about the same as the national average (79.8 percent).

Coastal Plain of Southwestern Guangdong and Southern Guangxi

This subregion (17_1 on Figure 15.1) is located on the northern margin of the humid tropical zone, with a cumulative temperature during the $\geq 10°C$ period of about 8200°C and an annual precipitation of 1450–1600 mm. Geomorphologically, it is mainly composed of plains and terraces below 100 m in elevation, interspersed with low hills. It is also the earliest developed area in this region, with nearly all natural vegetation removed since ancient times. Consequently, soil erosion is very serious and should be controlled as soon as possible. Other natural hazards include spring drought, summer floods and typhoons, and sometimes even low temperatures and frost in the wintertime.

The Leizhou Peninsula

This subregion (17_3 on Figure 15.1) is mainly composed of basalt terraces (occupying about 43 percent of the total land area), marine terraces (27 percent), and alluvial plains (17 percent); it is also dotted with diluvial plains, sandy beaches, and volcanic cones, all with elevations below 100 m. It has a cumulative temperature during the $\geq 10°C$ period of about $8000°–8500°C$ and annual precipitation of $1400–1700$ mm. It is also plagued by a series of natural hazards similar to those in the coastal plains subregion, but better land use patterns and efforts at afforestation as well as irrigation engineering have somewhat ameliorated all of them. This subregion has great prospects for future development.

Northern Hainan Island

Located north of the Chanjiang–Qionghai line (17_3 on Figure 15.1), 85 percent of northern Hainan Island is composed of extensive basalt and granite platforms below 300 m in elevation; the fertile low alluvial plain is mainly restricted to the middle and lower reaches of the Nandu River. This subregion differs from the Leizhou Peninsula in having a much larger area of basalt platform but a smaller area of terrace and plain. It is also somewhat warmer, with a cumulative temperature during the $\geq 10°C$ period of about $8400°C$ and an annual precipitation of $1500–1700$ mm. It is similar to the Leizhou Peninsula in risks of natural hazards and development potential even though the two areas are separated by the Qiongzhou Strait.

Southern Hainan Island

Located south of the Chanjiang–Qionghai line, this subregion (17_4 on Figure 15.1) occupies about 55 percent of the total land area of Hainan Island. It is mostly composed of medium mountains (elevation above 800 m), low mountains (500–800 m), and hills (250–500 m), with intermontane basins (mostly below 250 m) along the foothills. These land types overlap each other like a huge pyramid, with Mount Wuzhi (1867 m) as its pinnacle. This is the warmest subregion of the Leizhou Peninsula and Hainan Island with a cumulative temperature during the $\geq 10°C$ period of $8700°–9200°C$ and with a minimum temperature of above $5°C$. Frost is not a problem. Annual precipitation decreases from more than 2000 mm in the east to less than 1000 mm in the west, and the aridity index increases correspondingly from about 0.8 to about 1.5. Vertical zonation is conspicuous, generally with decreasing temperature at the rate of $0.6°C/100$ m, and increasing precipitation at the rate of 140 mm/100 m. Thanks to a mountainous topography, the havoc played by typhoons is restricted. Therefore, the intermontane basins in this subregion are probably the best place for developing *Havea* and other tropical crops in China. The extensive mountain slopes are also the major tropical rainforest and mountain rainforest areas in China. But the long-time clearing of natural vegetation (including shifting agriculture) has virtually eliminated forests below 500 m in elevation; only about 400,000 ha of mountain forest still survive in this extensive subregion. Therefore, natural conservation and afforestation are regarded as urgently necessary here.

Southern Yunnan Plateau

This region is located south of $23°–25°$ N, with its typical zonal vegetation (tropical monsoon forest) limited to intermonane basins and low valleys below 700–900 m in elevation. It is the southward extension of the Hengduan Mountains, with longitudinal high mountains and deep intermontane valleys paralleling each other. The area broadens from two degrees of longitude in the northern Hengduan Mountains area to about six degrees of longitude at the southern Yunnan border. In addition, the mountains become lower and the intermontane valleys broader. This natural region is thus composed chiefly of dissected plateaus and broad intermontane valleys of 700–1500 m in elevation, interspersed with middle mountains above 1500 m and low valleys below 700–900 m. A few peaks tower above 2500 m, and the lowest point is Hekou (84 m) along the Sino-Vietnam border. On the whole, the topography is rather rugged; *batze* (level plain) is restricted to intermontane basins and valleys. There are about 300 *batze* with an area larger than 1 sq km; the three largest are the Mengzi, 369 sq km; the Yingjiang, 339 sq km; and the Longchuan, 242 sq km. These level lands occupy only 6 percent of the total land area; but they contain and support most of the population and farmlands in the region.

Higher elevation and higher latitude decrease summer temperatures (generally $21°–25°C$) compared to the Leizhou–Hainan region. However, winter is slightly warmer here than at similar elevations of the Leizhou–Hainan region, with a mean January temperature of around $11°$ to $16°C$. In areas with elevations between 1300 to 1500 m, there is "eternal spring;" in areas with elevation between 900 to 1300 m, there are summer and spring (autumn) but no winter. Annual precipitation totals 1200 to 1600 mm, decreasing from both southwest and southeast to the north-central area. The windward slopes facing the Indian monsoons in the southwestern part and the Pacific monsoons in the southeastern part have the greatest precipitation in the region, with annual rainfall of 1500 to 2500 mm and 1750 to 2100 mm respectively. The rainy season (May to October) brings 80–90 percent of the annual precipitation, contrasting markedly with the dry season (November to April). The rainy season usually "bursts" in early May, and suddenly disappears in late October.

Except in the southeasternmost part, there is no direct influence of typhoons. In tropical low valleys, fog occurs frequently, with about 120 foggy days annually. Mengla, with 186 foggy days, is one of the foggiest spots in China. Fog occurs mostly in the dry season and provides a reasonable compensation for moisture deficiency at that time, but it is rather unfavorable to human health.

Surface runoff is abundant. In addition to the upper reaches of the Chang Jiang (Jinsha), there are three large international rivers (Nu or Salween, Lancang or Mekong, Yuan or Red River) flowing southward into the Indochina Peninsula. If high dams were built, a large amount of hydroelectricity and irrigation water could be produced.

This region is the "treasure garden" of flora and fauna in China. In the Xishuangbanna area alone live about 4000 to 5000 species of higher-order plants and 539 species of vertebrates. The upper limit of the tropical monsoon forest rises to 900 to 1000 m in elevation. West of the Yuan Jiang valley, owing to a longer dry season, several species of deciduous trees grow amid the evergreen tropical monsoon forest; east of the Yuan Jiang valley where the dry season is shorter, an evergreen tropical monsoon forest dominates. In low valleys below 500 m, rainforest appears. Evergreen subtropical broad-leaved forest occurs above 900 to 1000 m. All these forests have been repeatedly subject to burning and cutting for shifting agriculture since ancient times. Hence, many parts of the region are now dominated by secondary growth such as park savanna and grassland. Only about 23 to 31 percent of the original forest coverage remains. Conservation of vegetation (especially those valuable rare species) and afforestation are urgent resource management issues in this region.

Southern Yunnan is a region rich in natural resources, but they are far from adequately used. For example, Dai Autonomous Prefecture of Xishuangbanna, with an area of 19,200 sq km and an elevation ranging from 540 to 2400 m, is one of the best sites for developing tropical crops in China. The prefecture has been cultivated and developed by the Dai and other peoples since ancient times. Since 1949, the area of farmland has increased from 36,700 ha to 92,700 ha (1985), and the area of *Hevea* plantations grew from nil to nearly 30,000 ha. Yet, a series of acute problems occur in regional development. The most critical one is probably the struggle between natural conservation and locating *Hevea* planations below 900 m in elevation. From the national point of view, *Hevea* and other tropical crops should have the priority, but environmental protection must also be strictly observed at the same time. According to an estimate, lands optimally suitable for planting *Hevea* in this area total about 127,000 ha. Current yield of rubber reaches only 810 kg/ha and should be increased as much as possible. A balanced and sustainable economy should also be maintained in conjunction with the objective of a quality natural environment. The limited area of flat plains should be devoted to intensive farming; slopes and hills below 900 m can be used chiefly for *Hevea* and other tropical crops in conjunction with effective soil conservation measures; while mountain areas above 900 m should be mainly set aside for conservation and forestry.

Southern Yunnan Low Valleys

This subregion (18_1 on Figure 15.1) includes low valleys below 700 to 900 m and their surrounding mountains in southern Yunnan. The area features relatively low latitudes (mostly south of the Tropic of Cancer) and low altitudes. Consequently, the climate is hot and humid, with a mean January temperature above 16°C and an absolute minimum temperature above 10°C, while annual precipitation is above 1500 mm. During the summertime, the southwestern monsoons dominate in the western part and the southeastern monsoons in the eastern part. Evergreen tropical monsoon forests dominate in low valleys below 700 to 900 m, with patches of tropical rainforest in low valleys below 500 m, and deciduous tropical monsoon forest in some drier sheltered valleys. Mountain areas above 700 to 900 m are chiefly covered with subtropical evergreen broad-leaved forest.

Southwestern Yunnan Broad Valleys

This subregion (18_2 on Figure 15.1) is characterized by dissected plateau and broad valley topography, mostly at elevations of 700 to 1000 m. North–south mountains are found with elevations about 2000 m, and along the Longchuan and other rivers there are low valleys below 700 m. During the summertime, maritime southwestern monsoons dominate, with 85–90 percent of the annual precipitation concentrated from May to October. By contrast, the dry season is conspicuous. Owing to relatively higher latitudes (mostly 23° to 25° N) and higher altitudes, winter is somewhat cooler than in southern Yunnan, with a mean January temperature of 12° to 16°C. Therefore, this subregion is generally unfit for *Hevea* and other tropical crops, except on the warm sunny slopes of low valleys below 700 m. However, tea and other subtropical crops are at their best.

Southeastern Yunnan Karst Plateau

This subregion (18₃ on Figure 15.1) is located on the southeastern slopes of the Yunnan Plateau at elevations between 500 to 1500 m, interspersed with limestone mountains of about 2000 m. During the summer, the maritime southeastern monsoons dominate, with 80 to 85 percent of the annual precipitation concentrated from May to October. The subregion has about the same latitudinal and altitudinal characteristics as the southwestern Yunnan subregion, but it is sometimes subject to invasions of cold waves during the winter. Thus, the mean January temperature is generally lower by 1°–2°C, and the area is less appropriate for tropical crops. Here, the areal differentiation between windward and leeward slopes is quite conspicuous, with evergreen and deciduous monsoon forests dominating respectively. Heavy human intervention has reduced large tracts to grasslands or even to barren slopes. Soil conservation and afforestation measures are urgently required in these areas.

South China Sea Islands

The South China Sea is a deep sea basin, with an area of 3.5 million sq km and an average depth of 1212 m. Scattered amid this extensive sea are four archipelagos: Dongsha, Xisha, Zhongsha, and Nansha. In total, only 34 islands and beaches stand above high tide with total area of about 12 sq km. They are developed on sea-bottom terraces along the northern, western, and southern continental slopes of the South China Sea Basin. The continental shelves and slopes of the South China Sea Basin are composed of sial crust, with Paleozoic and Mesozoic granite and metamorphic rocks as a base. The coral reefs of Yongxing Island have a thickness of more than 1000 m, underlain by a reddish weathering crust 28 m thick. The latter crust might represent an ancient land surface of the Mesozoic era that was repeatedly peneplaned and submerged, resulting finally in the present sea-bottom terrace. The deep sea bottom of the South China Sea is composed of sima crust consisting mainly of basalt and volcanic eruptions. A series of sea ridges divides the deep sea basin into a northeastern shallow part and a southwestern deep part. On either border of the deep sea basin, there is a great fault line. The deep sea basin of the South China Sea might have

been formed by sea-bottom spreading since the Mesozoic era.

The South China Sea Islands are located from 3° 50′ N to 20° 42′ N. The Nansha Archipelago has an equatorial climate, and a tropical monsoon climate dominates all other parts. During the summer, the sun shines vertically overhead twice. The mean January temperature is from 21° to 26°C, with an absolute minimum temperature of 11.2°C in Dongsha, 13.9°C on Yongxing Island (Xisha), and 22.9°C on Taiping Island (Nansha). The cumulative temperature during the ≥ 10°C period totals 9150°–10,000°C, which results in a year-round growing season. The mean annual seawater surface temperature ranges from 23°–28°C, which is suitable for all tropical marine life.

With such low, flat topography, annual precipitation (1100–1500 mm) is not so plentiful as might be expected. From May to October, southeastern and southwestern monsoons prevail in Dongsha, accounting for 87 percent of the total annual precipitation. In Xisha, the precipitation is mainly derived from the southwestern monsoons that prevail from June to November. Nansha has no dry season and has an annual precipitation of 1842 mm. Owing to the small land area and the porous nature of coral reefs, there is no surface runoff on these islands. Surface water exists mainly in the form of enclosed lagoons, which are encircled by coral reefs and fed by rainfall. On Yongxing Island, the Chinese inhabitants have excavated ponds to store rainwater to develop freshwater irrigation and fishing industries. The first apparatus for converting seawater into freshwater was set up in the late 1980s in the Xisha Archipelago. There is also some fresh groundwater at a depth of about 1.5 to 3.5 m, which may be conveniently used.

The South China Sea Islands are famous for their phosphorous-rich limey soils. The parent materials are mainly corals and shells, and the soil-forming process is greatly accelerated by the humid tropical climate, luxuriant tropical rainforest, and abundant wild birds' guano. The last component speedily disintegrates into phosphate under the humid tropical climate, and then it combines with limey materials to form phosphorous-rich limey soil. According to an analysis conducted by the Nanjing Institute of Soil Science, Chinese Academy of Sciences, this soil surface layer contains 8–10 percent organic matter (sometimes as high as 57 percent), 17 to 30 percent phosphorous, and 40 percent calcium oxide. This soil is good enough to serve as fertilizer!

Biological resources are also very rich. According to a recent investigation, there are 213 species of plants (including cultivated crops) in the Xisha Archipelago alone, of which 146 species are common to Hainan Island. The major vegetation types are evergreen tropical forests, shrubs, and psammophytes on the coastal beaches. The dominant species are *Pisonia grandis* (the so-called "avoid-frost-flower"), *Guettarde specieose*, *Calophyllum inophyllum* (in trees), *Scaevvola sericea*, *Messerschmidia argentes*, *Morinda citrifolia*, *Pemphis acidula*, *Clerodendron inerne* (in shrubs), and *Ipomoes peacaprae*, *Canavalia maritina*, *Tribulus terrestris* (in grass). The most commonly seen cultivated crops are coconut palms, with many kinds of vegetables grown underneath the canopies.

This area is a paradise for birds that feed on the abundant marine life. According to a recent investigation, there are 103 species of birds living in the Xisha Archipelago alone, of which more than 60 species are commonly seen. The sula, a bird with a duck-like shape and white abdomen and red feet, is present in very great numbers. It is said that tens of thousands of such colorful birds formerly lived in the Xisha Archipelago, covering the islands like a very large "carpet of blossoming cotton." Their guano has accumulated to a thickness of more than 1 m, playing a significant role in the soil-forming process. Formerly, the guano was exported in large quantities for fertilizer.

Another rich faunal resource is marine life. One economic fish is *Caesio chrysozona*, which often appears in large shoals. Sea turtles (*Cheolonia mydas*, *Eretmochelys imbricata*, *Caretta olivacea*), *Stichopus spp.*, and many species of algae are also valuable. The coral not only builds up the South China Sea islands, but it also offers excellent habitats for different kinds of marine life, resulting in innumerable and colorful sea-bottom gardens. Each archipelago can be considered as a subregion of the South China Sea Islands.

Dongsha Archipelago

Located at about 20° N, this subregion (19_1 on Figure 15.1) is developed on the Dongsha sea-bottom terrace, which is about 300 m deep. The archipelago is composed of Dongsha Island and several submerged coral reefs. Dongsha Island, with an area of 1.8 sq km, is located in a lagoon that is surrounded by the horseshoe-shaped Dongsha circular coral reef. This archipelago is the northernmost and coolest in the region, but is also the windiest, with a mean annual wind velocity of 6.4 m/sec. It has been Chinese territory for ages, and numerous houses and temples as well as a lighthouse and a meteorological station have been established here.

Xisha Archipelago

This subregion (19_2 on Figure 15.1) is the westernmost island group in the region; it also has the largest number of visible islands (22) and beaches (4), as well as submerged reefs (5) and shoals (6). It is developed on the Xisha sea-bottom terrace, which is about 1000 m deep. Two subgroups can be recognized. The eastern subgroup is called the Xuande Islands, of which Yongxing and Shidao are the largest and the highest islands in the region, respectively. The western subgroup is composed mostly of submerged reefs and shoals. During the Ming Dynasty (1368–1644), Xisha Archipelago was called "Qi-zhou-yang" (literally, "Seven Continents' Ocean") when the famous imperial messenger and navigator Zheng He, together with his large fleet, visited seven "West Oceans" (including the Pacific Ocean and Indian Ocean) in his voyages. This was one of the important stops.

Zhongsha Archipelago

Located about 100 km southeast of the Xisha Archipelago, this subregion (19_3 on Figure 15.1) is developed on the Zhongsha sea-bottom terrace, which is separated from the Xisha sea-bottom terrace by a 2500 m-deep trough. It includes 26 submerged reefs and shoals, of which the Zhongsha Great Circular Reef (140 km long and 60 km wide) is the largest. Huangyan Island, located about 300 km southeast of Zhongsha Great Circular Reef and developed on a sea mount, is the only visible reef in this subregion.

Nansha Archipelago

Stretching far into the equatorial zone, this is the southernmost and the warmest island group in the region (19_4 on Figure 15.1). It includes 11 visible islands and 4 visible beaches, with a total land area of only 2 sq km. Taiping Island is the largest. There are also numerous submerged reefs and shoals. The Zheng He (named after the great Ming navigator) Reefs are the largest circular reefs in the whole region, and the Zengmu Shoal is the southernmost boundary of China's territory.

REFERENCES

China State Statistical Bureau. 1991. *Statistical Yearbook of China*. Beijing: China Statistical Publishing House (in Chinese).

Chinese Academy of Sciences. 1959. *Comprehensive Physical Regionalization of China*. Beijing: Science Press (in Chinese).

Geography Department, Kunming Teacher's College. 1978. *Geography of Yunnan*. Kunming: Yunnan People's Press (in Chinese).

Huang, Jingsun, et al. 1978. "Geological and Geomorphological Features of the Xisha Archipelago," *Selected Papers on Oceanography* 2 (in Chinese).

Nanjing Institute of Soil Science, Chinese Academy of Sciences. 1977. *Soils and Phosphate Mines in the Xisha Archipelago*. Beijing: Science Press (in Chinese).

Shi, Yulin. 1980. "Conservation and Utilization of Natural Resources in the Xishuangbanna Area," *Natural Resources* 2 (in Chinese).

Xu, Chunmin. 1978. "A Brief Remark on the Physical Geography of the South China Sea Islands," *Selected Papers on Oceanography* 2 (in Chinese).

Zhao, Songqiao. 1986. *Physical Geography of China*. New York: John Wiley & Sons.

Zheng, Zhaoguan. 1988. *Hainan Island*. Guangzhou: Guangdong People's Press (in Chinese).

Zhong, Gongfu, et al. 1981. "Conservation and Development of Tropical Resources on Hainan Island," *Economic Geography* 2 (in Chinese).

CHAPTER SIXTEEN

Inner Mongolian Grassland

The Inner Mongolian Grassland is the eastern part of Northwest Arid China, lying east of the Helan Mountains (Photos 16.1, 16.2). Its northern boundary is the Sino-Mongolian international boundary. Its eastern boundary corresponds with the western boundary of Northeast China. Its southern boundary, located on the southern margins of the Inner Mongolian Plateau and the Ordos Plateau, coincides roughly with the Great Wall and the 3200°C isotherm of cumulative temperature during the ≥ 10°C period. As a whole, this division has an area of about 700,000 sq km and a population of 25 million. Administratively, it includes two autonomous regions—Inner Mongolia and Ningxia—as well as a small part of Hebei Province (Figure 16.1).

PHYSICAL FEATURES, NATURAL RESOURCES, AND ENVIRONMENTAL PROBLEMS

This division features a temperate semiarid steppe and arid desert-steppe landscape. It is also characterized from southeast to northwest by a series of arc-shaped belts both in zonal (climatic–biological–soil) and azonal (geologic–geomorphological) phenomena.

Undulating Plateau Landforms

This division is mainly composed of the undulating Inner Mongolian Plateau and the Ordos Plateau. The Yinshan (Great Green Mountains, Color Plate 26) represents the southern rim of the Inner Mongolian Plateau. Since the Yanshan Tectonic Movement, which uplifted these two plateaus, this division has been comparatively stable and subjected to denudation and peneplanation for a long period, resulting in the pre-Cretaceous Mongolian and Gobi erosion surfaces. The extensive, repeated eruption of basalt during the Cretaceous, Tertiary, and Quaternary periods again enlarged the flat and undulating plateau surface and smoothed out any former irregularities. The arid and semiarid climates since the early Tertiary period have preserved all these undulating and rather undissected landforms to the present.

The middle Yellow River valley includes the Yinchuan Plain (West Elbow Plain, Color Plate 15), the Back Elbow Plain, and the Front Elbow Plain. These high plains bordering the Ordos Plateau are approximately 1000 m above sea level in elevation. Surrounding mountains that usually merge gradually into the plateaus are comparatively limited in area and seldom reach 3000 m in elevation. The West Liao River Plain, which is located east of the Greater Hinggan Mountains, generally has an elevation below 500 m.

Another geomorphological feature is the elongated structure of the landforms. For example, from Zhangjiakou (Kalgan) northwestward to the Sino-Mongolian international border (Figure 16.2), several major elongated structures appear in sequence, including the basalt platform of the Inner Mongolian Plateau margin, the denudational medium and low Yinshan Mountains, the peneplaned Mongolian erosion surfaces and *gobi* erosion surfaces of the plateau proper, and the denudational low hills with their volcanic cones and basalt platforms along the international border.

Photo 16.1 The Helan Mountains, a geographic divide between the Inner Mongolian Grassland and Northwest Desert, with *Picea* forest on the shady slope above 2500 m in elevation.

Temperate Semiarid and Arid Climate

These geomorphological features together with the relatively high latitudinal location (mostly from 38° to 50° N) result in the dominance of westerly flows in the upper atmosphere all year around, while dry, cold continental monsoons pervail in the lower atmosphere for most of the year. Warm, moist maritime monsoons penetrate only a short distance and deliver only a small amount of precipitation. This division has temperate semiarid and arid climates, with the aridity index increasing from 1.2 in the southeastern margin to about 2.0 along the Xilinhot–Baotou–Otog line, and to about 4.0 at the northwestern border. Drought, shifting sand, and salinization hazards are frequent and often devastating.

Winter is long and severe, with frequent cold waves. From November to March the weather is generally bitter cold, with a mean January temperature ranging from −9°C in the south to −28°C in the north, with a minimum temperature from −30°C to below −50°C, re-

Photo 16.2 The *gobi* shrubland on the eastern foothills of the Helan Mountains, Ningxia Hui Autonomous Region.

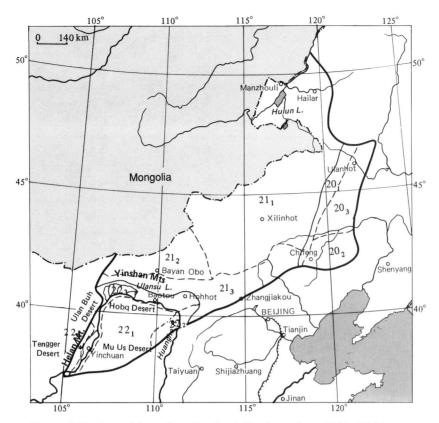

Figure 16.1 Inner Mongolian Grassland (For legend, see Table 16.1)

spectively. When the snow cover is too deep, the livestock cannot find enough grass to graze, a phenomenon called "white hazard," On the other hand, when there is too little snowfall, the livestock cannot find enough water to drink, called the "black hazard." Spring comes late and lasts about two months, beginning in April in the south and May in the north. Summer is short and warm, lasting generally from early or middle June to middle or late August with a mean July temperature ranging from 24°C in the south to 18°C in the north. Diurnal thermal variation is very great in the summer, so that the local people may even need fur coats in the morning but only light clothing at noon. Autumn is shorter than spring and may come and depart suddenly. Sometimes heavy snow falls in early or mid-September. The ≥ 10°C period lasts about 120 to 160 days, with

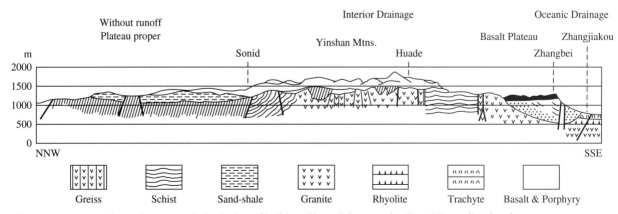

Figure 16.2 A geological-geomorphological profile from Zhangjiakou to the Sino-Mongolian border

cumulative temperature of 2000°–3000°C. Together with abundant sunshine (2800–3300 hours annually), it is adequate for growing one crop per year, subject to the danger of frequent killing frost.

Annual precipitation decreases from 400 to 450 mm in the southeast and 200 to 300 mm in the northwest, with 60–70 percent of the rainstorms concentrated in the summer (June to August). Rain usually falls suddenly in the afternoon and lasts only a short time. Rainstorms may sometimes be very heavy. For example, on August 1, 1977, a single rainstorm poured down continuously for 11 hours in the Uxin area (southern Ordos Plateau), dropping a total precipitation of 1850 mm, one of the highest records in the world. Spring and winter are usually dry, sometimes without any precipitation at all. Variation in annual precipitation is also great; sometimes there might be no precipitation at all for more than 12 successive months. Hence, in the western part of this natural division, farming is only possible with irrigation, and pastoralism remains the chief occupation in the vast nonirrigated areas. The eastern half was formerly the best and most extensive grassland in China. Now it is chiefly a transitional belt from pastoralism to dry farming that is marginal at best. In 9 out of 10 years, drought plays havoc with dry-farming yields.

In the southeastern parts of the Inner Mongolian Plateau and the Ordos Plateau where the semiarid climate changes to a subhumid climate, the physical environment is fragile and especially sensitive to change (Figure 16.3). This is a critical zone of environmental change.

Transitional Belt between Oceanic and Interior Drainage Systems

Drainage is determined by the belted distribution of precipitation decreasing from southeast to northwest as well as by the belted structure of the landforms. This overall drainage system is divisible into two subsystems: the oceanic subsystem in the southeastern peripheral area and the interior subsystem on the plateau proper. In the innermost part of the Inner Mongolian Plateau, there is no runoff at all. The great divide between oceanic and interior drainage systems runs southwestward from the western slope of the southern Greater Hinggan Mountains through the northern slope of the Yinshan Mountains to the western slope of the Helan Mountains.

The oceanic drainage system has a better developed river network, mostly consisting of the upper reaches of large rivers such as the Hailar River (upper reaches of the Heilong Jiang) and the Xar Moron (upper reaches of the West Liao River). The largest river flowing through the region is of course the middle reaches of the Yellow River, which encircles the Ordos Plateau in a great horseshoe-shaped arc. It is characterized by a string of broad alluvial basins connected through gorges and rapids. The most important alluvial basins are the three Elbow Plains, all of them well watered and intensively cultivated. This gives rise to the Chinese saying, "The Yellow River has inflicted one hundred injuries, but one benefit." Water from the Yellow River is heavily drawn upon for irrigation, so that its mean annual discharge decreases from 1019 cu m/sec at Lanzhou to 830 cu m/sec at Baotou. Another unfavorable condition is the river's northward flow to 40°27′ N latitude (upstream from Baotou), then a sudden turn eastward. It freezes over at a much earlier date at the Back Elbow Plain than upstream, and it melts much later. A high ice dam is often formed in this northern elbow of the river, and heavy flood damage ensues. Sometimes bombs must be dropped from airplanes to break up these ice dams.

There is a vast area of interior drainage. It generally has an annual runoff depth of less than 25 mm. Perennial rivers are few in number and small in discharge. They usually originate in the surrounding mountains and then dwindle away as they approach the plateau proper and disappear amid shallow depressions or flow into inland lakes. From the Hulun Buir Plateau (northeastern part of the Mongolian Plateau) southwestward to the Ordos Plateau there are more than 1000 inland lakes. They are usually small and shallow, with depth of less than 4 m. Most of them are saline or sodic, with a Ph value around 8.5, and they are widely used as sources of salt or soda. A few structural lake basins are exceptionally deep, such as Dalai Nur, with a freshwater depth of more than 10 m. In many areas there are several higher, older shorelines, showing the larger dimensions of ancient lakes.

Along the Sino-Mongolian international border, which represents the central and lowest part of the Mongolian Plateau (including Inner Mongolian and Outer Mongolian plateaus) and in the west-central part of the Ordos Plateau, there is practically no runoff. Groundwater is also scarce and available only from deep geologic strata. Here, pasturing can be conducted only during winter when some snow cover is available to provide drinking water both for the pastoralists and their livestock.

Figure 16.3 Changes in annual rainfall, 1790–1975, in the eastern part of the Hulun-Buir Sandy Land, based upon dendrochronological data; analyzed by Gong Kaofa. (1) 1790–1975 mean annual rainfall, (2) 1909–1975 mean annual rainfall.

Temperate Grassland Landscape

This division is dominated by temperate grassland landscape: the temperate steppe (Photo 16.3) east of the Xilin Gol–Baotou–Otog line and temperate desert-steppe (Photo 16.4) west of that line. It can be again divided into several subtypes that are distributed in northeast–southwest trending belts from the southeast to the northwest in a sequence as the distance from the sea increases and consequently, annual precipitation decreases. East of the Greater Hinggan Mountains lies the West Liao River Plain and its luxuriant temperate steppe vegetation, dominated by *Aneurolepidium pseudo-agropyron, Stipa gradis, S. krylonii,* and other species of grasses. This is the famous Kolshin Grassland, suitable for both farming and pasture. The Greater Hinggan Mountains mark the eastern margin of the Inner Mongolian Plateau, where the middle and southern sections are characterized by montane forest-steppe. On the eastern Inner Mongolian and Ordos plateaus, luxuriant temperate steppe vegetation appears again, of which the

Hulun Buir (Color Plate 27) and the Ujimqin grasslands are the most luxuriant. The zonal chestnut soil is quite fertile, although supplemental irrigation is necessary if it is cultivated.

The temperate desert-steppe vegetation is found on the western Inner Mongolian and Ordos plateaus. It is chiefly composed of drought-tolerant small bunch grasses and half-shrubs. The dominant grass and shrub species are *Stipa Capilata, Artemisia frigida,* and *Caragana microphylla.* They are shorter, sparser, and less nutritious than temperate steppe species. The zonal soil is brown semidesert soil, which is less fertile than chestnut soil. Irrigation is an absolute necessity for crop cultivation.

Diverse Animal Resources

Owing to the luxuriant grassland environment, the animal resources, especially hoofed animals, are quite rich. Rodents and wolves are the main undesirable animals,

Photo 16.3 A livestock-watering place on the central Inner Mongolian Plateau.

Rich Mineral Resources

This division is also rich in mineral resources. Both Inner Mongolia and Ningxia have rich coal resources. According to one estimate, Inner Mongolia alone has coal reserves of about 70,000 sq km. Several recently developed open-pit coal mines, such as Jungar in the eastern Ordos Plateau, Imin in the eastern Hulun Buir Plateau, and Helin on the eastern piedmont of the middle Greater Hinggan Mountains, will soon be mined on a large scale, with a projected annual output of 50–60 million tons each. Among minerals, the largest deposits are the iron and rare earth minerals in the Baotou–Bayan Obo area, where niobium and other rare earth reserves are supposed to be the richest in the world. Other minerals (such as chromium, copper, lead, and gold) as well as salt and soda are present in significant quantities.

Comprehensive Physical Regionalization

In the comprehensive physical regional system, the Inner Mongolian Grassland can be subdivided into 3 natural regions and 10 subregions, as shown in Table 16.1 and Figure 16.1.

HISTORICAL BACKGROUND

Human activity in this division has a long history, although not as long or as well documented as in Eastern Monsoon China. For most of its long history, Inner Mongolia has been characterized by both differentiation

although they have recently been more or less controlled. The Mongolian gazelle (yellow goat, *Procapra gutturosa*) is the most commonly seen large animal, but it has been overhunted. Birds, reptiles, and amphibians are rather few in species and in population numbers.

Photo 16.4 The desert-steppe grassland on the western Inner Mongolian Plateau.

TABLE 16.1
Comprehensive Physical Regionalization of the Inner Mongolian Grassland

Natural region	Natural subregion	Chief environmental problems
20. West Liao Basin—Steppe	20(1) Southern Greater Hinggan Mountains	Deforestation; soil erosion, rock-mud flow
	20(2) Yanshan Mountains Northern Foothills and Terraces	Drought, soil erosion; deforestation; rock-mud flow
	20(3) West Liao River Plain	Desertification; waterlogging; shifting sand; salinization
21. Inner Mongolia Plateau— Steppe and desert steppe	21(1) Hulun Buir— Xilin Gol Plateau	Desertification; grassland degradation; shifting sand
	21(2) Ulanqab Plateau	Desertification; grassland degradation; farmland depletion
	21(3) Yinshan Mountains	Soil erosion; deforestation
22. Ordos Plateau—Steppe and desert steppe	22(1) Ordos Plateau	Desertification; shifting sand; grassland degradation; farmland depletion
	22(2) Loessic Hills	Soil erosion; drought
	22(3) Elbow Plains	Salinization; shifting sand
	22(4) Helan Mountains	Soil erosion; deforestation

and integration between a pastoral society and farming communities as well as between the Han and numerous ethnic minority groups.

Pre–Qin Dynasty (Before 221 B.C.)

To date, few artifacts from Palaeolithic culture have been found in this division. However, extensive Neolithic cultural sites have been unearthed. They are characterized by well-crafted, small stone tools that people used to support their chief occupations of hunting and pasturing. In local swampy depressions, primitive rain-fed farming sites have been unearthed in which millet was the chief crop. For example, the cultural remains in Nenquan, Ningxia, indicate an agricultural history of about 7000 years, only a little later than the Dadiwan culture on the Loess Plateau.

According ancient Chinese historical documents, the Di and other pastoral tribes wandered on the Inner Mongolian grasslands before the Warring States period (403–221 B.C.). In the late Warring States Period, several well-organized tribes or leagues were formed, of which, the Hun (Xiong-nu) and the Dong Hu were the most powerful. The Hun occupied the Inner Mongolian Plateau and the Elbow Plains, as well as the Hexi Corridor and the Junggar Basin until they were utterly defeated by the Chinese army. They then moved to western Asia and central Europe in about the third and fourth centuries A.D., and eventually founded Hungary in central Europe. Some also moved southward and mingled with the Han. Generally they led a nomadic life, frequently moving to seek water and grass. The Dong Hu lived in the West Liao River basin, where they also pursued a life-style of nomadism and hunting. Other nomadic tribes, such as the Lin-hu, wandered onto the Ordos Plateau. To defend against these warlike nomadic tribes, the Chinese built the Great Wall along the southern rim of the Mongolian and Ordos plateaus. There were essentially no farming activities and no Chinese settlements on the Inner Mongolia Plateau.

From the Qin Dynasty to the Late Qing Dynasty (221 B.C.–A.D. 1840)

The Qin Dynasty (221–206 B.C.) started the first unified Chinese national state and extended its territory into the Elbow Plains for the first time. But other parts of this grassland division were still untouched (Figures 3.1 and 3.2). However, the sophisticated irrigation canal network developed during the Qin Dynasty together with the productive oasis agriculture in the Elbow Plains have continuously operated to the present (Figure 16.4).

During the unified and powerful Western Han (206 B.C.–A.D. 9) and Eastern Han (A.D. 25–220) dynasties,

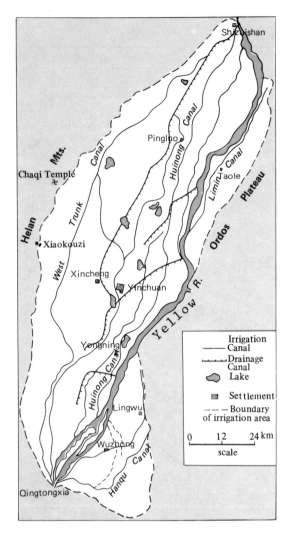

Figure 16.4 Irrigation canal system in the West Elbow Plain (Yinchuan Plain), Ningxia Hui Autonomous Region

nasties, the nomadic Mongol tribes began moving into the Inner Mongolian Plateau. The West Liao River basin was occupied by the Khitan tribes, who eventually founded the Liao Kingdom (later conquered by the Kin Kingdom) in the tenth to the twelfth centuries A.D. and engaged in both pasturing and farming. Ningxia (including the West Elbow Plain) and the western Ordos Plateau were occupied by the ancient Chang tribes who eventually founded the West Xia Kingdom and engaged in both pastoralism and irrigated agriculture.

Then came the Yuan Dynasty (1279–1368), when the nomadic Mongols established a vast empire on the Eurasian continent. The entire Inner Mongolian Grassland was under its direct control, although the Han and the Hui still engaged in irrigated agriculture in the Elbow Plains. Such an arrangement continued throughout the Ming Dynasty (1368–1644).

During the Qing Dynasty, the division once again became an integral part of Chinese territory. The nomadic Mongol still occupied Inner Mongolia and the Ordos Plateau as well as the West Liao River basin, while the Han and Hui practiced irrigated farming in the Elbow Plains.

Generally, until the mid-nineteenth century, this natural division (probably except the Elbow Plains) was considered as the "border land" lying beyond the Great Wall, which served as the traditional farming–pastoral boundary. The division was kept mainly as a pastoral land, sparsely inhabited by nomadic peoples and characterized by lush grassland vegetation. Virtually no rainfed farming was practiced. In the late fifth and early sixth centuries A.D., a folk saying vividly described the typical landscape at that time: "The sky is blue and wide, the earth is flat and vast; the grasses bow before the sweeping winds, and innumerable sheep and cattle are seen."

Modern Period (1840–1949)

Since 1840 a large-scale agricultural reclamation process (the so-called "pioneer settlement") has been taking place in eastern Inner Mongolia (also in Northeast China). As of 1949, the farming–pastoral boundary had been pushed northwestward several dozen or even several hundred kilometers from the traditional Great Wall line (Figure 3.1). The new boundary coincides roughly with the 300 mm isohyet, or the northwestern margin of steppe vegetation. Consequently, a broad northeast–southwest trending farming and mixed farming–pastoral belt has been formed along the southeastern border of the Inner Mongolia Autonomous Region, and the newly immigrating Han peasants gradually outnumbered the pastoral Mongols.

agricultural conditions continued to improve in the Elbow Plains. But soon afterwards came the chaotic period of Three Kingdoms (A.D. 220–280), Western Jin Dynasty, and Southern and Northern Dynasties (280–589). Numerous nomadic minority peoples occupied this division, except in the Elbow Plains, where agriculture was still practiced.

During the Tang Dynasty (618–907), the total area of this division became Chinese territory for the first time, although it was still peopled mostly by nomadic minority groups, of which the Turks and the Hui-hu were the most powerful.

During the chaotic period of the Northern Song (960–1126) and the Southern Song (1129–1279) dy-

Contemporary Period (Since 1949)

The first autonomous region in contemporary China, Inner Mongolia (Nei Mongol) Autonomous Region, was established in 1947. The Ningxia Hui Autonomous Region was also founded in 1954. Thus, in contemporary China, this division has been essentially under the administration of two autonomous regions, which have made great strides in social and economic development.

SOCIAL AND ECONOMIC DEVELOPMENT

Agriculture

Since ancient times, this division has been a home for many nomadic peoples. To date, pasturelands still occupy more than 70 percent of the total land area. Farmlands are mainly restricted to the Elbow Plains and mixed pastoral–farming zone in the southeastern Inner Mongolian Plateau and the Ordos Plateau. Even so, farming still produces more than 70 percent of the total value of agricultural production, while animal husbandry comprises about 20 percent. Forestry and fishing enterprises are insignificant in this division.

Animal Husbandry

All five major pastoral systems—nomadism, semi-nomadism, fixed pastoralism, rotating pastoralism, and domestic feeding—have been established in this division, with the first two dominating. Cattle, horses, and sheep are the major livestock types in the eastern steppe pasturelands, while sheep, goats, and camels are favored in the western desert-steppe pasturelands. The total number of livestock in Inner Mongolia Autonomous Region increased from 7.74 millions in 1949 to 42.54 million in 1990, including 3,850,000 cattle, 1,570,000 horses, 1,430,000 mules and donkeys, 220,000 camels (48 percent of China's total), 5,230,000 pigs, 20,750,000 million sheep, and 9,490,000 goats. In Ningxia Hui Autonomous Region, 270,000 cattle, 30,000 horses, 430,000 mules and donkeys, 30,000 camels, 2,270,000 sheep, and 900,000 goats were raised in 1990. Two areas are especially noted for pastoral development as well as for environmental problems.

The Hulun Buir Steppe The lush, productive Hulun Buir Steppe is probably the best pastureland in China and was the stronghold and backyard of the Mongol Empire in the thirteenth century (Color Plate 27). The region is located at a transition between the sub-humid forest-steppe zone and the semiarid steppe zone. The latter is dotted with extensive sandy lands and is subject to heavy wind erosion. Since the early twentieth century, the Hulun Buir Steppe has been open to modern economic development. The Manzhouli–Harbin Railway was built in 1899–1903, and since then most pine trees along the southern bank of the Hailar River have been felled, which greatly accelerated wind erosion. Excessive agricultural land development also began to cause land-degradation problems. This was especially true in 1960–1962, when the "Great Reclamation" movement was blindly implemented and about 3 million *mu* (0.2 million ha) of grassland were ruthlessly cultivated. Subsequently, the "Great Close-up" movement initiated at the end of 1962 brought great harm to the region, and even the artificial feedlots had to be abandoned. Nonetheless, such extreme activities have been controlled since the 1970s, and the Hulun Buir Steppe has once again become the best developed pastoral area in China.

The Kolshin Grassland Located in the West Liao River basin, the area enjoys the best natural conditions among China's extensive arid and semiarid lands. It has lush steppe and meadows that stretch throughout the lowlands and trees (*Pinus, Ulmus, Quercus*) are grown on the fixed sandy dunes. From the tenth to the twelfth centuries, the Liao Kingdom was established in this region, and both farming and animal husbandry were practiced. From the midnineteenth century to 1949, however, the sandy dunes were subjected to ruthless cultivation and overgrazing. In particular, rain-fed farming practices were imposed on the fixed sandy dunes without any conservation measures and thus made them vulnerable to severe soil erosion. Consequently, in and around the farmlands, pastures, and settlements, shifting sands developed from scattered spots to elongated belts, which now occupy about 10 percent of the total sandy area. In addition, the natural hazard of eolian deflation and deposition has become quite severe in and around the extensive sandy areas, so that spring sowing of crops often has to be repeated five to six times. Since 1949, the region has become an important part of the "Green Great Wall" in eastern Inner Mongolia and western Northeast China. A network of tree shelter belts has been planted to protect farmlands and pasturelands. In the future, a comprehensive farming–pastoral–forestry land use system will likely be developed.

The meadows that were formerly waterlogged in the summertime may be extensively reclaimed as good farmlands after establishing a series of water conservancy practices. Plans include planting a large network of tree shelter belts, which will serve the main objective of forestry. On the fixed sandy dunes, most of the extensively managed rain-fed farmlands will revert to grassland. Overgrazing will be carefully avoided. Improved pastures and artificial feedlots will be established. Great care will also be taken to prevent the fixed sandy dunes from degrading into shifting sands while effective measures will be adapted to ameliorate and control the existing shifting sands.

Farming

Since 1949, together with continuing pioneer settlement and large-scale Han immigration, farming and food production in both Inner Mongolia and Ningxia have developed rapidly. For example, food production in Inner Mongolia Autonomous Region increased from 2.13 million tons in 1949 to 9.73 million tons in 1990. In Ningxia Hui Autonomous Region, the total food production reached 1.9 million tons in 1990.

There are essentially two farming systems in this division. The western arid desert-steppe lands are dominated by irrigated oasis farming, one crop each year, with wheat, sorghum, corn, and sugar beets as the chief crops. The eastern semiarid steppe lands are dominated by rain-fed farming, essentially one crop per year, with spring wheat, oats, millet, Irish potatoes, and oil flax as the chief crops. Two areas are typical for rain-fed farming and irrigation oases farming respectively.

The Montane Hinterland Region Located on the Ulanqab Plateau (the middle part of the Inner Mongolian Plateau), the region (Photo 16.5) extends along the northern foothills and piedmont of the Yinshan Mountains, with an area of 37,435 sq km and a population of about 1.7 million. It slopes northward, dropping from 2000 to 1300 m. Annual precipitation also decreases northward, from 400 to 250 mm, of which 65–70 percent falls from June to August. The frost-free season lasts 90–120 days. Steppe vegetation dominates. The region's northern boundary is roughly coincident with the boundary between the steppe and desert-steppe zones, or the boundary between the Yinshan northern piedmont and the Inner Mongolian Plateau proper. It is also roughly coincident with the 250 mm isohyet.

Pioneer settlement began here only in 1932. It is typical of the mixed pastoral–farming belt for its very crude rain-fed farming system. Today, farmlands account for 27.3 percent of the total land area, forests only 1.9 percent, while pasturelands occupy nearly 70 percent. In production value, however, farming contributes 50.5 percent, animal husbandry 35.2 percent, forestry 3.3 percent, and sideline production 10.0 percent of the total agricultural production value. About 80–90 percent of the farmlands are located on hill slopes, and about 52 percent of the total land area is susceptible to severe soil erosion. Only 9 percent of the total farmlands receive supplemental irrigation, and virtually no chemical fertilizers are used. Five crops, including spring wheat, naked oats, Irish potatoes, oil flax, and rape seed, account for 80 percent of all croplands; spring wheat ranks first (44.5 percent). About 10–20 percent of the farmlands lie fallow each year. In 1979, the region produced 607,000 tons of food grains, with an average farmland yield of only 863 kg/ha and only 1075 kg per farm laborer. Nevertheless, this is one of the most important commercial food grain and edible oil seed bases in the Inner Mongolia Autonomous Region.

In order to increase low, unstable agricultural yields and combat rapidly deteriorating environmental quality, the following measures are urgently needed:

Photo 16.5 Rain-fed dry farming on the northern foothills and piedmont plains of the middle Yinshan Mountains, Inner Mongolia Autonomous Region.

1. Redistribution and relocation of farmlands and pasturelands. A large proportion of rain-fed farmlands on hill slopes should be abandoned and returned to pastureland. In addition, farmlands should be concentrated and more intensively managed in the inland river valleys and local basins where moisture and soil conditions are much more suitable and supplemental irrigation water is available. Together with other agricultural measures, such as crop rotation and salinization control, supplemental irrigation has the potential to triple the food yield per hectare, at least.

2. Farming technology needs to be modernized by such inputs as mechanization, proper use of manure and chemical fertilizers, development of new adapted crops, and genetic engineering of existing crops for better adaptation to increase yields and respond more effectively to management practices.

3. Animal husbandry especially needs to be modernized. The traditional methods of pastoral management, which depend entirely on natural grassland and manual labor, should be revolutionized. For example, natural pasturelands should be fenced and protected, then improved by a series of agricultural measures including reseeding, weed control, and managed grazing. Animal husbandry should be managed like a modern industry, by incorporating controlled grazing and supplemental feeding and modern pastoral products processing and manufacturing.

4. Forestry should be used mainly for the purpose of environmental protection. In valleys and basins, a network of tree (shrub) shelter belts may be planted, but the area of woodlands should not occupy more than 5–10 percent of the total land area. On hill slopes, only sparse, low-growing shrub shelter belts are required.

5. Modern industries based on mining and agricultural–pastoral products, along with modern transportation systems, need to be developed.

6. Much more scientific research is needed.

7. Educational programs are needed for those engaged in animal husbandry and crop agriculture as well as all members of their families.

The West Elbow Plain (Yinchuan Plain) The West Elbow, or Yinchuan, Plain (Color Plate 15) includes administratively 11 counties of the Ningxia Hui Autonomous Region, with a total area of about 17,000 sq km. Geologically and geomorphologically, it is a graben filled by diluvial-alluvial deposits, with an elevation ranging from 1090 to 1300 m, descending from southwest to northeast. The middle Yellow River flows through the plain and supplies both bountiful water and rich land resources. Climate is temperate and arid, with an annual precipitation of 200–300 mm.

As early as 215 B.C., the Qin Dynasty sent an army into the region to build irrigation canals and reclaim farmlands along the Yellow River. Shortly afterwards, the oases-making process was undertaken on a much larger scale, and a sophisticated network of canals was completed (Figure 16.4). The region was further developed and its farmlands enlarged during later dynasties. The region became the core area and Yinchuan the capital of the West Xia Kingdom (A.D. 982–1227). During this time the oases-making process was much accelerated. Since 1929, it has again served the core area of the Ningxia Province (Ningxia Hui Autonomous Region since 1954). There are about 5 million *mu* (0.33 million ha) of farmland (all irrigated) in the region, of which paddy rice fields occupy about 40 percent. Other major crops include wheat, corn, kaoliang, millet, soybeans, and rape seed usually on the basis of one crop per year. Unused arable land resources are still extensive, although waterlogging and salinization are the chief limiting factors for their reclamation.

Forestry and Fishing

Both forestry and fishing have but limited development in this division. However, the upper slopes of the Helan Mountains and the southern section of the Greater Hinggan Mountains[1] are partly clad with coniferous forests, and in some better developed farming and pastoral areas, many tree shelter belts have been planted. Fishery enterprises have been somewhat developed in the middle reaches of the Yellow River as well as in some large freshwater lakes, such as the Ulansihai in Back Elbow Plain and the Hulun Nur on Hulun Buir Plateau. According to official statistics, there are 12.38 million *mu* (0.82 million ha) of terrestrial water surface in the Inner Mongolia Autonomous Region, of which 7.76 million *mu* (0.51 million ha) might be used for artificial fisheries, but to date only 6.95 million *mu* (0.46 million ha) have been actually used. There are about 100 kinds of edible fish in Inner Mongolia, but carp is the most important.

---

[1]The entire northern section of the Greater Hinggan Mountains is densely clad with taiga forest, but it is geographically a part of Northeast China, rather than the Inner Mongolian Grassland, although administratively it is now a part of Inner Mongolia Autonomous Region.

Modern Industry and Transportation

Modern Industry

Before 1949, there were no modern industries in Inner Mongolia and Ningxia, except for a few manual workshops producing furs in Baotou, Hohhot, and Yinchuan. Practically all consumer goods had to be imported. For example, in the deep reaches of the Inner Mongolian Plateau, one small box of matches might be exchanged for a fat sheep, and one piece of brick tea could equal the value of a riding horse.

Since 1949, modern industries have been gradually developed. In the 1950s and early 1960s, some large-scale modern industries were established, based mainly on rich mineral resources. One example is the Baotou Steel Company, which is based on the Bayan Obo iron ores and nearby coal mines. From the mid-1960s to the mid-1970s, many small and medium-scale industries were developed, including chemical fertilizers, coal mines, electricity, and textiles. Since the late 1970s, using local agricultural and pastoral products as a base, many light industries have been organized, such as textiles (especially woolen textiles), food (featuring milk, meat, and sugar), and fur processing. Among the heavy industries, three large-scale open-pit coal mines in Imin, Helin, and Jungar are the most significant.

The distribution and structure of modern industries have also undergone great changes. In the 1950s and early 1960s, only a few modern industries were scattered in some political centers, such as Hohhot, Yinchuan, and Baotou. Since then, a network of industrial sites and cities has been established, of which two industrial belts are the most important.

1. **Baotou–Hohhot belt:** This is the major industrial belt in Inner Mongolia Autonomous Region, and features the Baotou Steel Company as one of the largest iron and steel producers in China. It is developed along the Beijing–Baotou Railway, stretching for more than 300 km from east to west in the fertile Front Elbow Plain. Here the major industries include iron and steel, coal mining, textiles, and food industries.

2. **Yinchuan–Shizuishan–Wuhai belt:** This is the major industrial belt in the Ningxia Hui Autonomous Region (Wuhai is located just across the border in Inner Mongolia Autonomous Region). It is developed along the Baotou–Lanzhou Railway. Major industries here include coal mining, coal-fired and hydroelectricity, chemical fertilizers, manufacturing industries, and woolen textiles.

Modern Transportation

In 1949, only four railways extended independently into Inner Mongolia from North China and Northeast China, the Beijing–Baotou Railway being the most important one. There was no railway at all in Ningxia. Roadways were also few and badly managed, with a total length of only 1557 km on the Inner Mongolian Plateau and 1020 km in Ningxia. Water and air traffic were nearly nonexistent and in most areas, transportation depended on horse, ox, and mule.

From 1950 to 1966, railways and roadways were constructed on a rather large scale, including the Jining–Erenhot Railway (leading to Ulan Bator), the Baotou–Lanzhou Railway, and the Baotou–Bayan Obo Railway. The grass checkerboard sand-protection project in the Shapotou area, southern Ningxia, where the Baotou–Lanzhou railway passes through the southeastern margin of the Tengger Desert (Color Plate 28) is internationally known. The total length of roadways in Inner Mongolia increased to 25,688 km in 1966. Since 1975, the Beijing–Tongliao Railway and numerous roadways were constructed, and the Beijing–Hohhot–Yinchuan–Lanzhou airline began operations for the first time. Nevertheless, modern transportation in this division is still far from well developed.

Ethnic Groups and Population

Ethnic Groups

Three major ethnic groups live in this division: the Han, the Mongol, and the Hui.

1. **Han:** There are now about 19 million Han in this division. Although only 2 percent of all Han live in this division, they make up 84.5 percent of the total population in Inner Mongolia Autonomous Region and 68.1 percent of the total population in Ningxia Hui Autonomous Region. Most of them came originally from North China, and a small portion emigrated recently to Ningxia Hui Autonomous Region from Zhejiang and other southeastern coastal provinces.

2. **Mongol:** There are about 3.4 million Mongols in China, of which 90 percent live in Inner Mongolia Autonomous Region. They are now the leading mi-

nority ethnic group in the region. They dominate in the extensive pastoral areas and mix with the Han in the pastoral–farming belt.

3. *Hui:* There are nearly 6 million Hui scattered all over China, but only one-sixth of them live in Ningxia Hui Autonomous Region. They are now the leading minority ethnic group in Ningxia Hui Autonomous Region, generally in mixed settlements with the Han.

4. Other minority ethnic groups in this division include the Man, the Daur, the Ewenke, and the Koreans. Most are concentrated in separate small areas. For example, most Ewenke live in the Ewenke Autonomous Banner (county) of the Hulun Buir League (prefecture).

Population

The population problem in Ningxia Hui Autonomous Region is about the same as in China in general: the growth rate is too rapid and there is a critical land–food–population imbalance. But in Inner Mongolia Autonomous Region, the condition is somewhat different. Here, population pressure has not been so acute, and in the first half of the twentieth century, owing to very poor hygiene conditions, there was even population decrease in Mongolia. However, since 1949, both natural increase and new immigration have increased Mongolian numbers rapidly, while family planning has been rather loosely enforced in the region. The population problem is growing more serious.

Rural and Urban Settlements

Rural Settlement

In the extensive nomadic and seminomadic areas, there are few settled villages and houses. The nomads move incessantly with their livestock and their tents, which can be packed up in an hour. In each banner (county), there is usually only one fixed site—the Lamaist temple, where the county government is also located. In other pastoral types—fixed pastoralism, rotating pastoralism, and domestic feeding—there are small fixed rural villages scattered widely on the plateaus and plains. Each village is usually made up of a few or a few dozen simple earthen houses. In the farming areas, the rural villages are larger (usually a few dozen earthen houses) and are less widely spaced (usually a few dozen kilometers). Compared with the densely clustered rural villages on the North China Plain, where the rural villages are usually only 1.0–1.5 km apart, the Inner Mongolian grassland is indeed wide and wild.

Urban Settlement

There were some famous ancient cities in this division, such as Hohhot and Yinchuan. Since 1949, these ancient cities have been enlarged. Many new cities have also appeared, such as the coal-mining cities of Wuhai and Shizuishan and the international border city of Erenhot. Three cities are now the most significant urban settlements in this natural division:

1. *Hohhot (literally "blue city" in Mongolian):* Located in the Front Elbow Plain and at the southern piedmont of the Yinshan Mountains, Hohhot was first founded in A.D. 1579 as the capital of a Mongol principality. It has been the capital of Inner Mongolia Autonomous Region since 1952. It is now an industrial center for textiles, food processing, and other industries as well as a central area for many cultural and scenic attractions. In 1990, it had a total population 0.89 million and a nonagricultural population of 0.65 million.

2. *Yinchuan (literally the "silvery plain"[2]):* Located in the West Elbow Plain and at the eastern piedmont of the Helan Mountains, Yinchuan was the capital of West Xia Kingdom for more than 200 years. It is now the political, economic, and cultural center of Ningxia Hui Autonomous Region. It is also famous for many cultural and scenic sites.

3. *Baotou:* Located between the Front and Back Elbow plains, Baotou was formerly a market for farming and pastoral products as well as a center for transportation. The population was about 60,000 in 1949. The establishment of the large-scale Baotou Steel Company in 1954 has stimulated other modern industrial developments in the Baotou area. It is now the largest modern city and the only metropolis with at least 1 million people in this division. In 1990 it had a total population of 1.2 million and a nonagricultural population of 0.98 million.

---

[2]The name was given due to the silvery reflection caused by heavy salinization.

AREAL DIFFERENTIATION AND REGIONAL DEVELOPMENT

As a whole, this division is farming–pastoral oriented, with modern industrial and transportation development in a few urban areas. However, different regions and subregions have generally had different developmental trends.

West Liao River Basin

Located east of the southern Greater Hinggan Mountains, the West Liao River Basin is the only region is this division to be characterized by low plains and wide-spread farmlands. It is surrounded by mountains and hills on the northern, western, and southern sides, but the eastern side is open to the Northeast China Plain. Consequently, it has a horseshoe geomorphic configuration, with an elevation decreasing from about 1200 m in the west to 120 m in the east.

This region enjoys the best temperature and moisture conditions in Northwest Arid China, with a cumulative temperature during the $\geq 10°C$ period of 1400–3200°C and annual precipitation of 300–600 mm. Summer rainfall provides about 80 percent of the total annual precipitation, which is favorable for crop growth but makes low depressions vulnerable to flooding. Spring is dry and windy. In conjunction with widely distributed sand beds, large patches of sandy dunes have formed, of which about 10 percent are shifting sands. This region is essentially composed of the Kolshin Grassland.

Southern Greater Hinggan Mountains

This subregion (20_1 on Figure 16.1) has an elevation of 1000–1500 m and a relative relief of 100–500 m. Annual precipitation totals 400–500 mm. Vertical zonation of vegetation is conspicuous, with coniferous forests on the higher slopes (1300–1700 m above sea level) and deciduous broad-leaved forests on the lower slopes (below 1300 m); while luxuriant grassland and farmland (corn as the chief crop) are located in the intermontane basins and piedmont plains. As a whole, this subregion should be mainly devoted to forestry and pasture. The protection of natural vegetation and afforestation are two urgent needs. Local favorable sites with better climatic and topographic conditions, such as intermontane basins and piedmont plains, may be cultivated for food grain crops.

Yanshan Mountains Northern Foothills and Terraces

The western part of this subregion (20_2 on Figure 16.1) is dominated by the Yanshan Mountains, generally with elevations between 1500 and 1800 m. The eastern part is mainly composed of low mountains, hills, and terraces, with elevations between 500 and 700 m, generally covered with thin loessic soils. Annual precipitation totals 500–600 mm in the western part, decreasing to 400–500 mm in the eastern part. Owing to severe soil erosion and heavy human intervention, almost all the natural grassland has been removed. Bare basalt platforms and shifting sand dunes are widely present. In future development programs, protection of vegetation and other soil conservation measures should be greatly emphasized.

West Liao River Plain

This subregion (20_3 on Figure 16.1) is essentially identical with the Kolshin Grassland.

Inner Mongolian Plateau

The Inner Mongolian Plateau stretches from east to west through 14 degrees of longitude. It runs from the western foothills of the southern Greater Hinggan Mountains to the eastern border of the Ulan Buh Desert. It also stretches from south to north through 10 degrees of latitude from the Yinshan to the Sino-Mongolian international boundary. Geomorphologically, the region includes the Inner Mongolian Plateau and the montane arc of the Yinshan, both uplifted since the Quaternary period, with elevations ranging from 1500–2200 m for the Yinshan Mountains to 1000–1500 m for the Inner Mongolian Plateau. The Yinshan has a steep southern slope overlooking the Elbow Plains (Color Plate 26), while the Inner Mongolian Plateau generally has a rolling plateau surface and inclines from the southern margin northward to the plateau proper. There are also many scattered local depressions.

Owing to its rather high latitude and altitude as well as its openness on the northern side, this region becomes the highway of cold waves during the winter, with a much lower temperature than other parts of the world at similar latitudes. The mean annual air temperature ranges from $-2°C$ to $-6°C$, becoming colder from southwest to northeast. Annual precipitation ranges from 400 mm on the southeastern border to 200 mm on the northwestern border. The 300 mm isohyet roughly divides the eastern steppe zone from the western desert-steppe zone (Figure 16.1).

As a whole, this region has been and will continue to be used mainly for pastoral development. In the eastern steppe area, marginal pioneer settlements have been occupied ever since the mid-nineteenth century, where they have been the cause as well as the recipients of widespread drought and desertification problems. Environmental protection is an urgent problem. Rich mineral resources (coal, iron, etc.) provide an opportunity for developing industry and transportation.

Hulun Buir–Xilin Gol Plateau

This eastern part of the Inner Mongolian Plateau (21_1 on Figure 16.1) generally has more favorable environmental conditions, with steppe vegetation dominating. The Hulun Buir Plateau is basically a graben basin with a vast rolling plateau surface of 550 to 700 m in elevation and an annual precipitation ranging from 250 to 400 mm. Its historical as well as social and economic development have already been discussed. The Xilin Gol Plateau is composed chiefly of volcanic hills and basalt platforms along the Sino-Mongolian border, an immense peneplaned plateau surface in the middle, and the Hunshandake Sandy Land in the south. Its social and economic development is essentially similar to that of the Hulun Buir Plateau.

Ulanqab Plateau

This is the central part of the Inner Mongolian Plateau (21_2 on Figure 16.1). Located between the Yinshan in the south and the Sino-Mongolian international boundary in the north, the Ulanqab Plateau descends northward from about 2200 m to about 900 m. It is essentially an uplifted, peneplaned plateau (the so-called Mongolian erosion surface), having four or five stepped erosion surfaces (mostly overlain with stony *gobi*) that are composed mainly of Tertiary red sandstones. Hence, the area bears the name Ulanqab which means "red cleavage" in Mongolian. The climate is arid, with annual precipitation ranging from 200 to 300 mm (decreasing westward) and an aridity index of 2.0–4.0 (increasing westward). Zonal vegetation is a transitional type between steppe and desert-steppe. The marginal pioneer settlements and future prospects in the Montane Hinterland Region have already been discussed.

Yinshan Mountains

The Yinshan (21_3 on Figure 16.1) comprises one of the great geographic divides in China; the areal differentiation between "up mountain" (Inner Mongolian Plateau) and "down mountain" (Elbow Plains) is quite conspicuous. The Yinshan itself is dominated by desiccation and denudation processes. The crest lines generally have an elevation of 1800 to 2000 m. The southern slope of the western section is a steep fault scarp that overlooks the Front Elbow Plain with a relative relief of more than 1000 m. On the other hand, the northern slope of the western section is much less steep and merges into the Inner Mongolian Plateau through a broad belt of hills and intermontane basins. The eastern section is much lower and less rugged; the dominant landscapes are large basins studded with smaller basins and barren basalt platforms. Vertical zonation of vegetation is conspicuous. There are coniferous forests on higher slopes, while temperate semiarid steppe dominates the lower slopes and foothills. Farmlands have been developed in large tracts during the last 100 years and are located mostly on gentle slopes and intermontane basins but sometimes even on steep slopes and hilltops, resulting in severe soil erosion. Overall planning and better management for both grasslands and farmlands are much needed.

Ordos Plateau

This region is encircled on the north by the Yinshan, on the west by the Helan Mountains, and the south by the Great Wall (Figure 10.5). It is essentially composed of the rolling Ordos Plateau together with its surrounding medium mountains and high plains. Climatically and biologically, it is a transitional zone between the semiarid steppe and the arid desert-steppe. The middle Yellow River encircles and traverses the region in a great arc, furnishing bountiful irrigation water and fertile soils. Yet, owing to meager rainfall, other perennial rivers are few, and the lakes are mostly saline or sodic. Areal differentiation inside this region is prominent.

Ordos Plateau

This subregion (22_1 on Figure 16.1) is roughly demarcated by the Great Wall on the south and by the Yellow River on the other three sides. Geologically, it has been stable for a very long time, with undisturbed level strata and without any igneous activity. During the Mesozoic submergence, a broad synclinal basin was formed, and thick sandstones, conglomerates, and shales were deposited in it. Since the Quaternary, it has been uplifted to its present elevation of 1200–1600 m, with Zhuozi Shan (Table Mountain, 2149 m) as the highest peak. As a whole, it is an undulating denudational plateau that is covered by large-scale eolian landforms. The east–west Hobq Desert with an area of 16,000 sq km is located on its northern arid border. The Mu Us Sandy Land is located on the semiarid southeastern border. It has an area of 25,000 sq km, of which fixed, half-fixed, and shifting sand each comprises about one-third. There is also a series of deflated low depressions between these two sandy areas that have much better quality water and other more favorable physical conditions.

Winter is severe and long, controlled by cold, dry northwestern monsoons, with mean January temperatures of −10°C to −13°C. Summer is short but warm, with a mean July temperature of 20–23°C. Annual precipitation totals 300–400 mm in the eastern part, decreasing to 200–300 mm in the west. Seasonal and yearly variations in weather are great, resulting in marked divergence in the productivity of the grassland. East of Otog, zonal vegetation is steppe, whereas west of it is desert-steppe. Ecologically, both are mainly composed of xerophytes and psammophytes. This is China's most critical area vulnerable to environmental change and desertification, and consequently, the most urgent present problem is to make rational use of the land and other natural resources so that the desertification process can be reversed (see Chapter Ten).

Loessic Hills

The subregion (22₂ on Figure 16.1) is restricted to a small area in the northeastern Ordos Plateau. It is a transitional belt between the Loess Plateau and the Ordos Plateau, with an elevation of between 1200 and 1500 m and annual precipitation of about 400 mm. In the last 100 to 200 years, it has been actively cultivated and overgrazed, resulting in severe soil erosion as well as very low agricultural production. What is worse, the area already has been dissected into numerous barren hills, with a relative relief of 100–200 m, a total gully length of 5000–7000 m/sq km, and a surface erosion rate of 1–2 cm/yr. Therefore, soil conservation measures are of paramount importance here. Farmlands on steep slopes should be abandoned, terraced, and transformed back into productive grassland and woodland; fertile valley bottoms may continue to be used as farmlands, but modern agricultural technology should be applied.

Elbow Plains

This subregion (22₃ on Figure 16.1) is sandwiched between the Ordos Plateau and the Helan–Yinshan mountain systems. It includes three fertile high plains along the middle Yellow River: the West Elbow Plain (Yinchuan Plain), the Back Elbow Plain, and the Front Elbow Plain. Geologically and geomorphologically, these high plains are a series of grabens filled by diluvial-alluvial deposits, with a depth of about 1000 m in the western and northern Back Elbow Plain. This subregion inclines generally from southwest to northeast.

Protected by the Helan Mountains and the Yinshan on the west and north, the Elbow Plains are also a little bit lower in elevation than the Inner Mongolian and Ordos plateaus. The mean January temperature ranges from −9°C to −14°C, and the mean July temperature from 21°C to 24°C. In the West Elbow Plain, cotton can be grown under irrigation. Annual precipitation ranges from 300 to 450 mm in the Front Elbow Plain to 200–300 mm in the Back and West Elbow Plains. Rainfed farming is possible in the Front Elbow Plain, but yields are rather precarious. In the other two plains, irrigation is an absolute necessity for agricultural development. The minimal precipitation is not only far from adequate for crops, but is even harmful because it induces salinization and soil surface crusting.

As early as the third to second centuries B.C., the Qin and Han dynasties sent armies and colonists first to the West Elbow Plain and shortly afterwards to the Front and Back Elbow Plains. Extensive farmlands and sophisticated irrigation canal systems were built (Figure 16.4). The area was turned into the "land of rice and fish," comparable to the fertile, rich lower Chang Jiang valley. With the improvement of irrigation and drainage systems as well as amelioration of drought, salinization, eolian hazards, and other limiting factors, this subregion can be further built up as a large new commercial grain base in Northwest Arid China.

Helan Mountains

The Helan Mountain range (22₄ on Figure 16.4) is also one of the great geographic divides in China, dividing the grassland from the desert as well as delimiting oceanic and interior drainage systems. This longitudinal mountain system was first folded and uplifted during the Yanshan Tectonic Movement and uplifted again to its present altitude during the Himalayan Tectonic Movement. Neotectonic movements have also been quite violent; the Helan Mountains are still uplifting, and earthquakes occur frequently. The crest lines have a general elevation ranging from 2000 to 3000 m above sea level (the highest peak is 3556 m). Like other border mountains that surround the Inner Mongolian Plateau, the Helan Mountains have an asymmetric profile, with steep eastern slopes and much gentler western slopes. When viewed from the West Elbow Plain, the Helan silhouette looks like a galloping horse, hence the Mongolian name, "Helan."

Modern geomorphic processes are dominated mainly by desiccation and denudation, with gravel *gobi* dominating the landscape (Photo 16.2). Only a small patch of alpine shrubby meadow remains on the mountain crest. Patches of needle-leaved forest also survive on the upper slopes above 2500 m (Photo 16.1). Protection of natural vegetation and afforestation are certainly two most important ameliorating measures that need to be undertaken in the subregion.

REFERENCES

Agricultural Geography of Inner Mongolia Compilation Committee. 1982. *Agricultural Geography of Inner Mongolia*. Hohhot: Inner Mongolia People's Press (in Chinese).

China State Statistical Bureau. 1991. *Statistical Yearbook of China*. Beijing: China Statistical Publishing House.

Department of Geography, Inner Mongolia Normal University. 1965. *Physical Geography of Inner Mongolia*. Hohhot: Inner Mongolia People's Press (in Chinese).

Dregne, H. E. (ed.). 1992. *Degradation and Restoration of Arid Lands*. Lubbock: ICASALS, Texas Tech University.

Integrated Investigation Team of Inner Mongolia and Ningxia. 1980–1981. (1) *Geomorphology of Inner Mongolia*; (2) *Climate and its Relationship with Agriculture and Animal Husbandry in Inner Mongolia*; (3) *Water Resources and Their Utilization in Inner Mongolia*; (4) *Soil Geography of Inner Mongolia*; (5) *Vegetation of Inner Mongolia*. Beijing: Science Press (in Chinese).

Sand Control Team, Chinese Academy of Sciences. 1984. *Report on the Integrated Investigation of the Mu Us Sandy Land*. Beijing: Science Press (in Chinese).

Sun, Jinzhu. 1976. *Physical Conditions and Their Transformation in the Elbow Plains*. Hohhot: Inner Mongolia People's Press (in Chinese).

Sun, Jinzhu, et al. 1988. *Geography of China*. Beijing: Higher Education Press (in Chinese).

Zhao, Songqiao. 1986. *Physical Geography of China*. New York: John Wiley & Sons.

Zhao, Songqiao. 1988. "Human Impact on Northwest Arid China: Desertification or De-desertification," *Chinese Journal of Arid Land Research* 1, no. 2.

Zhao, Songqiao. 1989. "Recent Advances in China's Arid Land Research," *Chinese Journal of Arid Land Research* 2, no. 1.

Zhao, Songqiao. 1990. "The Semi-arid Land in Eastern Inner Mongolia—An Area of Critical Environmental Change," *Chinese Journal of Arid Land Research* 3, no. 3.

Zhao, Songqiao. 1991. "The Oases-making Process (De-desertification) in China's Desert Lands," *Chinese Journal of Arid Land Research* 4, no. 2.

Zhao, Songqiao, et al. 1958. *A Preliminary Study on the Locational Problem of Agriculture and Animal Husbandry in Inner Mongolia*. Beijing: Science Press (in Chinese).

CHAPTER SEVENTEEN

Northwest Desert

The extremely arid desert in Northwest China extends eastward to the Helan Mountains and southward to the border mountains of the Tibetan Plateau: the Kunlun, Altun, and Qilian mountains. On the western and northern sides, it is defined by the Sino-Russian and Sino-Mongolian international boundaries. This division has an area of about 2.1 million sq km, occupying 22 percent of China's total land area, but contains only about 2 percent of the national population. Administratively, it includes Xinjiang Uygur Autonomous Regions (13 prefectures), the Hexi Corridor (3 prefectures) of Gansu Province, and the Alashan Plateau (Bayan Nur League) of Inner Mongolia Autonomous Region (Figure 17.1).

PHYSICAL FEATURES, NATURAL RESOURCES, AND ENVIRONMENTAL PROBLEMS

Arid Climate

The first characteristic of the deserts of Northwest China is that the climate is extremely dry. Annual precipitation decreases westward from about 200 mm along the Helan Mountain piedmont plain to the driest part of China, the eastern Tarim Basin, with an annual precipitation of less than 25 mm (only 3.9 mm at Toksun in the Turpan Basin). It increases westward slightly to 70 mm along the Sino-Russian border. Rainfall is also sporadic; usually there is none for more than six successive months, then suddenly one storm might produce one half or even two thirds of the total annual precipitation. Consequently, sunshine and solar radiation are quite abundant, with generally more than 3400 hours of sunshine and 130–155 Kcal/sq cm of solar radiation annually.

The Alashan Plateau and the Junggar Basin have a temperate thermal regime, with a frost-free season of 150 to 200 days and a cumulative temperature during the $\geq 10°C$ period of 3000° to 3500°C. The Tarim Basin has a warm temperate thermal regime, with a frost-free season of 200–230 days and a cumulative temperature of 4000°–4500°C. All over these regions, winters are long and severe, and thermal variations, both annual and diurnal, are enormous. The highest temperature in China (47.6°C) was recorded at Turpan and one of the lowest (−51.5°C) at Fuyun, less than 500 km due north of Turpan. On the surface of a sand dune in the Gurbantünggüt Desert, an extreme temperature of 83°C was recorded in 1956 on a field trip of the Chinese Academy of Sciences.

Strong winds blow frequently. In the winter, cold, dry northwestly and northeastly winds predominate. In summer, there are frequent atmospheric disturbances producing "hot easters." Consequently, Anxi in Gansu Province and Toksun in Xinjiang Autonomous Region, are both called the "wind reservoir of the world" because of wind velocities above 18 m/sec that blow 35 and 72 days per year, respectively. The Junggar Gate, which is located on the northwestern margin of the Junggar Basin, has 155 days of strong winds each year.

Plateau and Inland Basins Geomorphology

This division is essentially composed of the Alashan Plateau (the western part of the Inner Mongolian Plateau, including the Hexi Corridor) and two great inland ba-

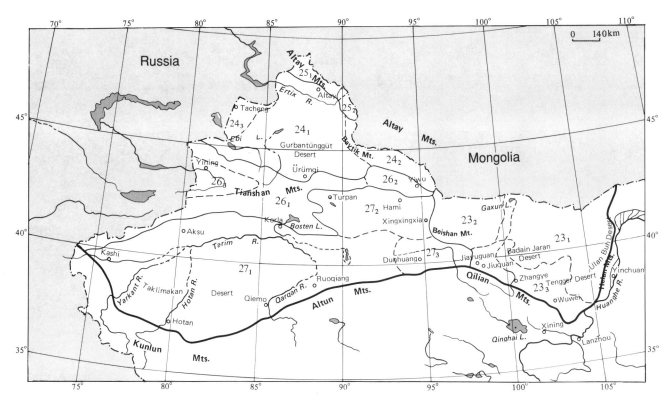

Figure 17.1 The Northwest Desert (For legend, see Table 17.1.)

sins, the Junggar and the Tarim. All are surrounded by high mountains: the Altay, the Tianshan, the Kunlun, the Altun, and the Qilian.[1] On the whole, the ground surface is level or undulating and consists of rather coarse materials (chiefly sands and gravels). Under an extremely arid climate, they form the wild expanse of yellowish sandy desert (*shamo*, Color Plate 29) and greyish gravel desert (*gobi*, Photo 17.1), together occupying about 45 percent of the total area of this division. The surrounding mountains stand out conspicuously and exert a great influence on the desert environment. The highest peak of the Tianshan, Mount Tomul, towers up to 7435 m above sea level. Most ridges are also high above the snow line. The snow-capped Mount Bogda rises to 5445 m, with the scenic Tianchi (Heaven Pond) amid luxuriant coniferous forest on its northern slope (Color Plate 30), while to the immediate south lies the Turpan Basin which contains the lowest elevation on the China mainland (−155 m).

The Junggar and the Tarim basins generally have an elevation from 500 to 1500 m and dip gradually from the surrounding mountains and their piedmonts to basin centers, where the largest and second largest sandy deserts in China, the Taklimakan, and the Gurbantünggüt, are located. From the surrounding mountains to the basin centers, a series of distinctive land types appear in succession as the elevation decreases (Figure 17.2):

1. Extremely high mountains, more than 5000 m in elevation, mainly under eternal snow and snow-accumulation processes (Photo 17.2)

2. High mountains, generally 3000–5000 m, mainly under the process of erosion

3. Denudational mountains and hills, generally less than 3000 m

4. Peneplaned stony level land (denudational stony *gobi*) (Photo 17.3)

5. Diluvial fan (gravel *gobi*)

6. Diluvial-alluvial plain (sandy gravel *gobi*)

7. Alluvial plain (clay and silt level land)

8. Alluvial-eolian plain (fixed, half-fixed, and shifting sand dunes)

---

[1] The Kunlun, the Altun, and the Qilian mountains are the border ranges of the Tibetan Plateau. They will be discussed in the next chapter.

Photo 17.1 The depositional gravel desert (*gobi*) on the southern piedmont plain of the Tianshan Mountain. A modern highway follows the route of the ancient Silk Road through this region.

9. Alluvial-lacustrine plain (chiefly salt crust and *yardang*) (Photo 17.4)

The Alashan Plateau has an elevation of 1000 to 1500 m. The highest peak of the Mazong Mountains rises to 2791 m, and is still under the process of desiccation. The region is chiefly composed of a series of northeast–southwest or east–west trending denudated, peneplaned mountains and hills. Inselbergs and stony *gobi* predominate in the former; diluvial gravel *gobi*, and diluvial-alluvial sandy gravel *gobi* chiefly comprise the latter (Figure 17.2B). In the southern and eastern margins of the Alashan Plateau, some extensive sandy deserts prevail, including the Badain Jaran, the Tengger, and the Ulan Buh.

Interior Drainage

There are almost no perennial rivers fed by local runoff in this desert division. Only intermittent streams and a few large rivers that originate in the surrounding high mountains flow into the arid areas. All these rivers terminate in interior drainage with only one exception: the Ertix River in the Junggar Basin. The upper reaches of these rivers are located in the surrounding mountain areas and have numerous tributaries and rich discharges. As soon as they flow out of the mountains, both their tributaries and discharges diminish quickly. Water qual-

ity also deteriorates. Finally, the rivers die out in the lower reaches, either flowing into salty inland lakes or disappearing into salt marsh. The largest inland river in China, the Tarim River, has lost its lower reaches and its terminal lakes; Lop Nur and Taitima Lake have been completely dry since 1972.

The distribution of groundwater is quite uneven. There are rich groundwater resources along perennial river channels and high mountain piedmont plains, but they are very poor in most other areas. On the front margin of the large piedmont plains, good, rich groundwater often emerges in springs. This is sometimes called the "spring line" and serves as the site of cities and highways; the famous Silk Road along with many ancient cities were essentially located along this "spring line" (Color Plate 13; Photos 17.5, 17.6).

The most widely distributed soils in this division are yermosols, xerosols, and solonchaks, all with poorly developed soil profiles and high salt content. Consequently, they are generally unfavorable for agricultural use, and a series of improvement measures, such as leaching by irrigation, drainage, and salinization control must be taken if they are to be used as farmland.

Despite these problems, along modern and ancient rivers as well as in the lower part of the diluvial-alluvial plains, there are considerable areas of rather fertile soils, chiefly azonal soils, such as fluvisols and gleysols. Under

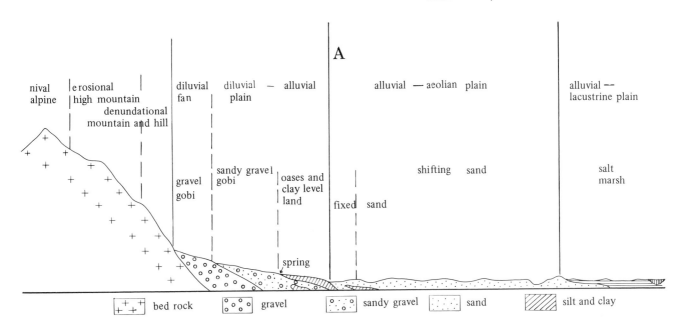

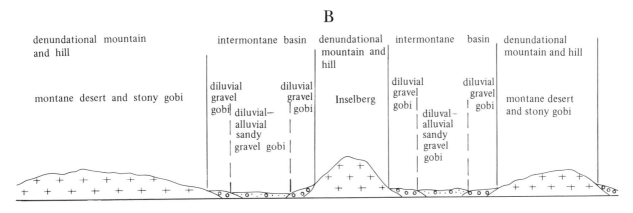

Figure 17.2 Physical profiles in China's deserts: (A) Inland basin type; (B) Plateau type.

proper management these might be cultivated. There are now about 4 million ha of farmland in this division, with about 12 million ha of potentially cultivated farmland, or nearly 30 percent of the total potential arable land resource in China.

Sparse Desert Vegetation

The zonal desert vegetation is sparse, generally less than 10–30 percent in coverage, with large tracts of less than 1–5 percent. In certain areas, such as gravel *gobi* along the Kunlun Mountains piedmont plain, the shifting sand sea in the central Taklimakan Desert, and the peneplaned stony *gobi* in the Gaxun Desert, there is practically no vegetation at all for tens or even hundreds of kilometers. Furthermore, owing to the unfavorable natural conditions for plant growth, it is extremely difficult or even impossible for vegetation to become reestablished once it has been destroyed.

The desert vegetation is mainly composed of shrubs, including species of the *Chenopodiaceae*, *Compositae*, and *Zygophyllaceae*. Paralleling the correlation of differ-

Photo 17.2 The Tianshan No. 1 Glacier, located on the ridge of the Tianshan Mountains south of Ürümqi, about 3600–4000 m in elevation.

ent land types, there are five major desert vegetation types:

1. ***Mountain and hilly desert:*** Small half-shrubs predominate. The upper limit of this type is found from approximately 1800 to 2000 m on the northern slopes of the Qilian Mountains and the southern slopes of the Tianshan, and as high as 3200–3600 m on the northern slopes of the Kunlun Mountains.

2. ***Gravel desert (gobi):*** Distributed widely, gravel deserts can support only very sparse half-shrubs and small half-shrubs.

3. ***Sandy desert (shamo):*** Widespread sandy deserts may support half-shrubs, shrubs, and ephemeral grasses and small herbs but the water-holding capacity of desert sands is low and offers only a high-risk environment for vegetation.

Photo 17.3 The Wind City (formerly called "Devil's City"), a citadel-like landform on denudational stony *gobi*, northwestern Junggar Basin, Xinjiang Uygur Autonomous Region.

Photo 17.4 The *yardang*, caused by wind deflation, northeast of the Lop Nur dried basin.

4. ***Clay and silt desert:*** Rather restricted in distribution, clay and silt desert provides moderately favorable environment for half-shrubs and ephemeral vegetation.

5. ***Saline desert:*** Distributed widely in low depressions, saline desert's chief vegetation is fleshy, salt-tolerant, small half-shrubs; most are species of the *Chenopodiaceae* family.

There are also several azonal vegetation types.

1. ***Riverine forest:*** Distributed mostly along modern and ancient river channels, with poplar (*Populus diversifolia*) as the predominant species.

2. ***Saline shrub:*** Composed mostly of *Tamarix spp.* and *Nitraria spp.* that usually grow in clumps on the periphery of shifting sandy areas adjacent to saline water sources.

3. ***Saline meadow:*** Distributed mainly on the lower reaches of alluvial-diluvial plains, with a shallow sa-

Photo 17.5 The ruin of the ancient Yang Guan ("Sun's Gate"), located at the westernmost part of the Hexi Corridor, was the starting point of the ancient Silk Road to cross the extensive Taklimakan Desert.

Photo 17.6 A distant view of the famous One Thousand Buddhas Grotto, western Hexi Corridor.

line groundwater table and luxuriant salt-tolerant grasses.

4. ***Cultivated vegetation (oasis):*** The cultivated oases flourish with luxuriant cultural vegetation and stand out conspicuously amid the surrounding vast expanse of greyish or yellowish desert.[2]

Diverse Desert Fauna

Desert fauna, like steppe fauna, are characterized by the dominance of rodents and hoofed animals, but because of meager food supply, population numbers are low. Their special adjustments to an extremely arid environment, such as the cave shelters and winter dormancy of rodents, ability to migrate to search for water and grass and to escape from the enemies of the hoofed animal, are essential for their survival. The dominating rodents are *Meriones spp.* and *Allactage spp.* The former live mainly in the *gobi*, whereas the latter live both in sandy and stony deserts. The most commonly seen hoofed animals are the yellow goats (*Gazella subgutterosa*), which usually run in small herds. Sometimes small groups of wild ass (*Equus hermonius*) may also be seen.

Reptiles, especially *Lacertiformes*, are relatively abundant in the desert environment. Commonly seen snakes are *Eryx miliaries* and *Psammophis lineolatus*.

Birds and amphibians are seldom seen. Probably the dominant bird species is *Galerida cristana*, but usually only one or two of these birds appear within a distance of a kilometer; sometimes there are none at all for dozens of kilometers.

Oases stand out conspicuously amid a vast empty expanse of open sand or *gobi*. In these oases, birds and other vertebrates are more abundant, and human activities bring in many new animals foreign to the original desert habitat. These include sparrows, swallows, small domestic rats, and others.

Rich Mineral Resources

This extensive division is endowed with rich mineral resources, which are good incentives for developing modern industry and transportation. Since 1949, 118 kinds of minerals have been discovered in Xinjiang alone, of which 6 kinds rank first among the reserves for all 31 provinces and regions of China.

Petroleum

In this division is located one of the two richest oil belts in China. This major oil belt, continuing from Southwest Asia and Central Asia, stretches from the Tarim Basin and the Junggar Basin eastward through the Hexi Corridor to the Loess Plateau, the Ordos Plateau, and the Sichuan Basin. The Yumen oil field (Hexi Corridor) was discovered in the 1930s, and the Karamay oil field

---

[2] "Desert" in Chinese means "wide expanse." The sandy desert is called *shamo*, while the gravel desert is called *gobi*.

(Junggar Basin) in the early 1950s. Both became major petroleum-producing areas in China at that time, although their annual production was rather small. Since the early 1960s, the major oil-producing areas in China have shifted eastward to another oil belt, the Northeast China Plain and the coastal zone. But recently, oil exploration efforts are shifting back to the Tarim, Junggar, and Turpan basins. These inland basins could be the major petroleum-producing areas in China again in the near future.

Coal

The extensive, rich underground "coal sea" in China includes the Loess Plateau, the Ordos Plateau, and the Inner Mongolian Plateau as well as the desert areas of the Alashan Plateau and the Junggar Basin. In potential coal reserves, Xinjiang Uygur Autonomous Region ranks first in all the Chinese provinces and regions.

Metal Minerals

In the central Hexi Corridor of Gansu Province and Altay Prefecture of Xinjiang Uygur Autonomous Region are the largest nickel and copper reserves in China, accounting for 75 percent of the total national reserve. Reserves of iron and chromium are also rich in the Tianshan and the Altay Mountains areas. The latter is also famous for its gold mine, which has been exploited since as early as the Tang Dynasty. In Mongolian, *altay* means "gold."

Nonmetallic Minerals

Salt, soda, gypsum, mica, and many other nonmetallic minerals have been found in this division. The Hotan area in the southwestern Tarim Basin has long been famous for jade mining and carving.

Comprehensive Physical Regionalization

Areal differentiation within China's desert division is quite conspicuous, chiefly because of divergent landforms and ground-surface materials. Five natural regions and 14 subregions are identified in Table 17.1 and Figure 17.1.

HISTORICAL BACKGROUND

In historical development, this division is somewhat similar to the Inner Mongolian Grassland.

Pre–Western Han Dynasty (Before 121 B.C.)

As in the Inner Mongolian Grassland, few remains of Palaeolithic culture have been found in this division, while Neolithic culture sites characterized by small stone tools and pastoral-hunting economies are widely distributed. On the northern and southern piedmont plains, Neolithic sites have been discovered that yielded color porcelains with bones of cattle, horses, and sheep as well as millet cake. The ancient people at that time probably engaged in pastoralism as well as in primitive farming.

In the late Warring States Period (403–221 B.C.), the Hexi Corridor, the Alashan Plateau, and the Junggar Basin were peopled by the nomadic Hun (Xiong-nu), Usan, and Yue-zi, while in the Tarim Basin, the Turk (later Uygur) settled in a series of oases around the rim of piedmont plains, where they mainly engaged in irrigated farming. At that time, each larger oasis became a "kingdom." These irrigated oases have a history of agriculture of at least 3000–4000 years, with the earliest date not yet known. In 138 B.C., and again in 119 B.C., when the celebrated Zhang Chin was sent as an ambassador to visit the "West Domain" (including Xinjiang and Central Asia), he discovered 36 "kingdoms" there.

From Western Han Dynasty to Late Qing Dynasty (121 B.C.–A.D. 1840)

In 121 B.C., the Chinese army took over the Hexi Corridor for the first time and established four administrative prefectures: Wuwei, Zhangye, Jiuquan, and Dunhuang. Irrigated agriculture flourished along the middle and lower reaches of the three main inland rivers (the Shiyang, the Black, and the Shule), of which the middle reaches of the Shiyang and the Black were particularly well developed and thus gave their names to "Silvery Wuwei" and "Golden Zhangye," respectively. Ever since then, the Hexi Corridor has been the largest commercial grain base in Northwest Arid China. In A.D. 2, China's first national census recorded that the Hexi Corridor had 35 counties and a total population of 280,021.

From the Hexi Corridor, the ancient pioneer settlement also extended into the lower reaches of the Black River (Inner Mongolia) and into the lower reaches of the Tarim River (Xinjiang), so that a series of oases was linked to form the famous Silk Road (Figure 3.3). Later, more oases were created. In 60 B.C., the "West Domain" was proclaimed a Chinese province, with its capital at Uli (modern Luntai). However, both the Junggar

TABLE 17.1
Comprehensive Physical Regionalization of the Northwest Desert

Natural region	Natural subregion	Chief natural hazards
23. Alashan Plateau— Temperate desert region	23(1) Alashan Plateau Proper	Shifting sand, desertification, grassland degradation
	23(2) Mazong Mountains	Soil erosion, grassland degradation
	23(3) Eastern and Middle Hexi Corridor	Desertification, shifting sand, salinization
24. Junggar Basin— Temperate desert region	24(1) Junggar Basin Proper	Desertification, shifting sand, salinization
	24(2) Nomin Gobi	Desertification
	24(3) Emin Valley	Drought, salinization, grassland degradation
25. Altay Mountains— Montane grassland & needle-leaved forest region	25(1) Northwestern Altay Mts.	Soil erosion, deforestation, grassland degradation
	25(2) Southeastern Altay Mts.	Soil erosion, deforestation, grassland degradation
26. Tianshan Mts.— Montane grassland & needle-leaved forest region	26(1) Middle Tianshan Mts.	Soil erosion, desertification, grassland degradation
	26(2) Eastern Tianshan Mts.	Soil erosion, desertification, grassland degradation
27. Tarim Basin— warm temperate desert region	27(1) Tarim Basin Proper	Shifting sand, desertification, salinization, deforestation
	27(2) Turpan–Hami Intermontane Basins	Desertification, salinization, shifting sand
	27(3) Western Hexi Corridor	Desertification, shifting sand, salinization

Basin and the Alashan Plateau were still wild and pastoral and were peopled very sparsely by nomadic minority ethnic groups.

Modern Period (1840–1949)

Just like Inner Mongolia, large-scale pioneer settlement has taken place in Xinjiang since the mid-nineteenth century. Old oases in the Tarim Basin and in the Hexi Corridor have been enlarged, and new oases in the Junggar Basin have been created. According to historical documents, Xinjiang (including the Tarim Basin and the Junggar Basin) had 944 trunk irrigation canals and nearly 1.8 million *mu* (0.12 million ha) of farmland in 1908. In 1949, Xinjiang had a population of nearly 4 million persons.

Contemporary Period (Since 1949)

The Xinjiang Uygur Autonomous Region was established in 1956, as was the Bayan Nur League (Inner Mongolia). Together with three prefectures in the Hexi Corridor (Gansu Province), social and economic development has progressed with great strides.

SOCIAL AND ECONOMIC DEVELOPMENT

Agriculture

Similar to the Inner Mongolian Grassland, this division has long been a land of nomadism, but as the desert pastureland is much lower in quality than the grassland, animal husbandry has been less productive. On the other hand, irrigated farming started much earlier in this division and is much better developed.

Farming

This is the most typical area of oasis farming in China. Nearly all farmlands are irrigated, and rain-fed dry farming is essentially nonexistent. In Xinjiang, farmland occupies only 2.5 percent of the total land area but produces 65 percent of the total agricultural production value. There are three important farming areas, or oasis belts, in this division.

The Hexi Corridor With an area of about 200,000 sq km, the Hexi Corridor is sandwiched between the Qilian-Altun Mountains (South Mountains, or Nan Shan) and the Mazong-Longshou Mountains (North Mountains, or Bei Shan). Three physical belts and eight major land types might be identified (Figure 17.3):

1. The northwest–southeast trending South Mountains are the northeastern border ranges of the Tibetan Plateau, composed of high mountains with ridge lines of 4000–5000 m high. They form a huge "wet island" in China's arid lands and have an annual precipitation of more than 300–500 mm, with Wushaoling (3035 m) receiving 358.8 mm. All three major river systems in the Hexi Corridor originate here. The terrain is rugged and the climate is cold, making farming very limited here.

2. The Corridor Plain stretches nearly 1000 km from the Wushaoling (Photo 17.7) northwestward, with a width of 10–50 km. It is blocked and interrupted by the Yangzhi Mountain and the Black Mountain and is consequently divided into eastern (Shiyang River basin), middle (Black River basin), and western (Shule River basin) sections. The corridor plain is mainly composed of diluvial-alluvial deposits with

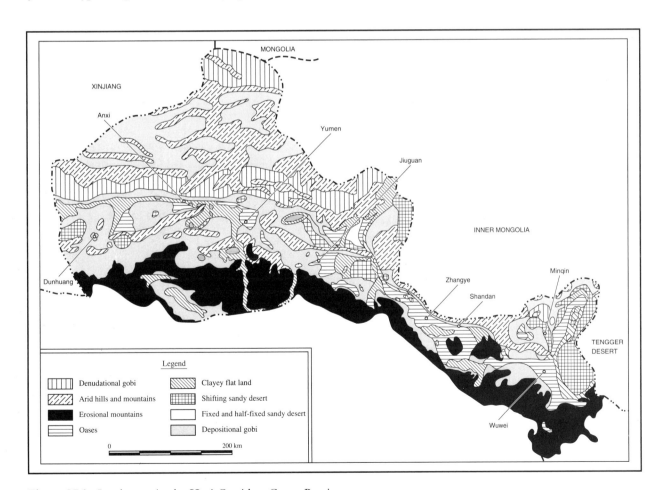

Figure 17.3 Land types in the Hexi Corridor, Gansu Province

Photo 17.7 The Wushaoling, the eastern end of the Qilian Mountains and the starting point of the Hexi Corridor, Gansu Province.

an elevation of from 1000 to 1500 m. Arable land resources are abundant. But the climate is dry, with only scanty and sporadic rainfall that decreases from the southeast to the northwest as the distance from the sea increases (Wuwei 162.3 mm, Zhangye 124.8 mm, Jiuquan 85.7 mm, Yumen 56.8 mm, Anxi 40.6 mm, Dunhuang 43.6 mm). If cultivated, crops must be irrigated at least two to four times during the growing season. Hence, the distribution of oases is largely determined by available irrigation water, which is generally most abundant in the middle reaches of the three inland rivers.

3. The North Mountains, composed of northwest–southeast trending ranges, reach elevations between 1500 and 2000 m. Barren denudational hills and stony *gobi* are widespread, leaving little room for oasis-making.

The oasis-making process began in 121 B.C. Since then, oases have become the largest commercial grain base in Northwest Arid China. The magnitude of this oasis-making process (de-desertification) has fluctuated somewhat. It was greater when China was united and strong and smaller when the country was split and weakened. Since 1949, the total area of irrigated farmlands has been more than doubled. With a total population of about 3.5 million, there are now nearly 5 million *mu* (0.33 million ha) of irrigated farmland in the Shiyang River basin, nearly 4 million *mu* (0.27 million ha) in the Black River basin, and about 1 million *mu* (0.07 million ha) in the Shule River basin.

The Tarim Basin Since 1949, the oasis-making process has been accelerated in Xinjiang. In the past 40 years, more than 2 million ha of new oases have been opened up and more than 200 state farms established. Especially along the middle and lower reaches of the Tarim River, a large-scale reclamation project has been launched since 1955. By 1990, farmlands more than doubled. However, such reclamation projects have also brought adverse impacts on the fragile, extremely arid environment, especially salinization and desertification.

The Turpan–Hami Basin might be considered as a part of the Tarim Basin. It has long been a typical example of using the *karez* (underground) irrigation system to turn barren gravel *gobi* into productive oases.

The Junggar Basin The large-scale oasis-making process started in the Junggar Basin only since the mid-nineteenth century. However, the Shihezi Reclamation Area of the middle reaches of the Manas River is now the best example of turning the sandy desert into oases in Northwest Arid China (Figure 17.4). This reclamation project occupies an area of 24,000 sq km, of which mountains and hills constitute 25 percent, plains (including *gobi*, salt marsh, and sandy desert) 45 percent, and oases 30 percent. From south to north, the relief decreases gradually from 900 m in the Tianshan foothills to 300 m in the southwestern margin of the Gurbantünggüt Desert. Until about 200 years ago, the region was still primarily a grazing area. In 1949, it had a total population of about 50,000 and a total farmland of 30,000 ha. Modern large-scale reclamation efforts have been implemented since 1956, and in 20 years, the pop-

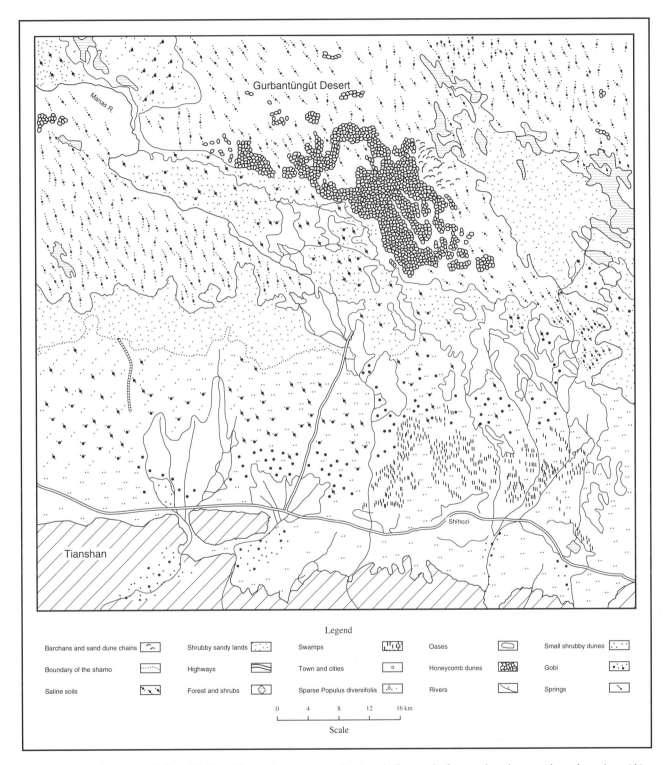

Gurbantüngüt Desert

Manas R.

Tianshan

Shihozi

Legend

Barchans and sand dune chains	Shrubby sandy lands	Swamps	Oases	Small shrubby dunes
Boundary of the shamo	Highways	Town and cities	Honeycomb dunes	Gobi
Saline soils	Forest and shrubs	Sparse Populus diversifolia	Rivers	Springs

0   4   8   12   16 km

Scale

Figure 17.4   The Manas Valley, Xinjiang Uygur Autonomous Region, before and after modern large-scale reclamation: (A) in 1955; (B) in 1977.

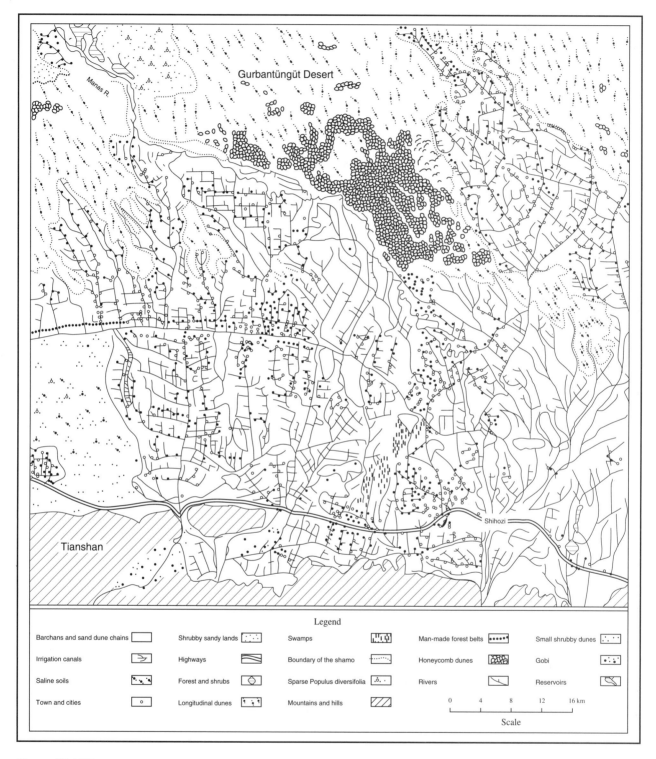

Figure 17.4(B)

ulation has increased 16-fold and the farmland 10-fold (Color Plate 31).

Animal Husbandry

Xinjiang is also famous for its pastoral development. According to an estimate, the usable grassland area in Xinjiang totals 50 million ha, of which, 60 percent are mountain grassland, with conspicuous vertical zonation. Consequently, the major pastoral pattern is transhumance, with livestock moving up the mountain slopes to make good use of mountain grassland in the summer and autumn and coming down to desert basins for winter and spring grazing. On the Alashan Plateau, seminomadism is the major pastoral pattern. In the oases, domestic feeding is also practiced. Major livestock breeds are sheep, goats, cattle, horses, and pigs. Since ancient times, many high-quality livestock species have been bred in Xinjiang, such as the Ili horse, the Tacheng cattle, the Xinjiang fine wool sheep, and the Ili white pig. On northern slopes of the Qilian Mountains in the Hexi Corridor, animal husbandry has also been well developed since ancient times.

Forestry

As a whole, forestry is little developed in this desert division. In Xinjiang Uygur Autonomous Region, annual timber production amounted to only 4.2 million cu m in 1986. There are two forest types.

1. Mountain forests are mainly distributed on the northern slopes of the Tianshan (elevation: 1500 to 2700 m) and the Altay Mountains (elevation: 1200 to 2300 m), where 760,000 ha of coniferous forests grow, accounting for 31 percent of Xinjiang's total forest area but 97 percent of the total forest growing stock. On the northern slopes of the Qilian Mountains (elevation: 2600 to 3500 m), 100,000 ha of *Picea* forests grow. In contrast, the northern slopes of the extremely arid Kunlun Mountains support essentially no trees.

2. Plain forests, including again two types:
   a. The broad-leaved riverine forests are mainly composed of poplar (*Populus diversifolia*). There are about 700,000 ha of such forests in Xinjiang, of which 64 percent are located in the Tarim Basin.
   b. Sparse shrubs and half-shrubs are scattered widely in desert areas. The best area is the Gurbantünggüt Desert's fixed and half-fixed

sandy dunes, which are mainly stabilized by *Haloxylon spp.*

Fishing

Fishing enterprises are little developed in this division. According to official statistics, there are about 1 million ha of terrestrial water bodies (including rivers and lakes) in Xinjiang, with another 50,000 ha of reservoirs. There are also more than 50 kinds of edible fish species, but the annual catch is very small (4580 tons in 1986, 3356 tons in 1990). Nothing can be reported about artificial breeding of fish in this division.

Modern Industry and Transportation

Modern Industry

Before 1949, modern industry in this division was restricted to one small-scale oil field and refinery in Yumen (Hexi Corridor) and another small-scale oil field development in Karamay (Junggar Basin). Since 1950, modern industries based on mineral resources have developed rapidly. The Yumen and Karamay oil fields were enlarged in the mid-1950s and became the largest oil fields in China at that time. Later, many state farms in Xinjiang started to establish industries, such as iron and steel, textiles, coal mining, food processing, and others. In the 1960s, two large-scale industrial enterprises, the Jiuquan Steel Company and the Jincheng Copper and Nickel Company, both in the Hexi Corridor, were established. From the mid-1960s to the 1970s, many medium- and small-scale industries, including those producing chemical fertilizers, coal, electricity, and textiles, were developed. Since 1978, based on farm and pastoral products, many textile and food industries also have been developed. Among the heavy industries, oil refining and oil products reprocessing have been established rapidly and have now become the most important industries in Xinjiang.

The structure and distribution of modern industries have undergone great changes. In the 1950s and early 1960s, there were only a few modern industries scattered in Ürümqi, Karamay, and Yumen. In the 1960s and 1970s, especially after 1978, a network of industrial cities and industrial enterprises was formed, of which two industrial belts are the most important:

1. *Tianshan Northern piedmont plain industrial belt:* Extending about 400 km from Ürümqi westward to Shihezi and to Karamay, facilities in this belt produce about 70 percent of the total industrial

output value in Xinjiang Uygur Autonomous Region. This also happens to be the most important farming area in Xinjiang, with significant production of cotton, sugar beets, and other economic crops. The industrial structure is dominated by heavy industry, accounting for about two thirds of the total industrial value. The most important heavy industry is oil production and refining, accounting for about one third of the total industrial production value. Other heavy industries include coal mining, chemical engineering, and manufacturing. Light industries are also developing, in such areas as textiles, carpets, and sugar.

2. **Central Hexi Corridor industrial belt:** This industrial belt accounts for about 20 percent of the total value of industrial production in Gansu Province. Major industries include Yumen oil drilling and refining, the Jiuquan Steel Company, and the Jincheng Copper and Nickel Company.

Modern Transportation

In ancient times, this division was served by the famous Silk Road, and Xinjiang became the "front door" of China. In modern times, however, it has lagged far behind in transportation. There was practically no railway or air service before 1962, and only 3361 km of badly managed roadway in all of Xinjiang Autonomous Region at that time.

In 1966, the first railway (from Lanzhou to Ürümqi) and the first air route (from Beijing to Ürümqi) were constructed, while roadway mileage increased to 23,000 km. Since 1978, the development transportation system has accelerated. In 1983, the railway from Ürümqi was extended southward across the Tianshan Mountains to Korla (headquarters of the newly discovered Taklimakan oil field), and in 1990, a railway was extended westward to the Sino-Russian border, to complete the new trans-Eurasia continental railway from Rotterdam (in western Europe) eastward to Lianyungang on the Yellow Sea. Road transportation has also been improved. Air traffic has increased very rapidly to include several international air lines and project Ürümqi as the "front door" of China once again.

Ethnic Groups and Population

Ethnic Groups

Since ancient times, this extensive division has been the battlefield as well as the fusion ground for numerous ethnic groups. Today, the Han and the Uygur and 45 other minority peoples live here.

1. **Han:** About 10 million Han live in this division. The Hexi Corridor, with its 3.5 million people, has long been overwhelmingly peopled by the Han. Since 1949, the Han population has increased rapidly in this division. For example, in Xinjiang, the Han increased from less than 0.3 million in 1949 (6.7 percent of the total population) to 2.8 million in 1965 (35.0 percent of the total population) and to 5.3 million in 1990 (40.4 percent of the total population).

2. **Uygur:** This is the third largest ethnic minority group in China, with a total population of nearly 6 million in 1990. They are principally concentrated and become the leading ethnic minority group in Xinjiang Uygur Autonomous Region, which had a total population of 13.16 million in 1990. Between 1949 and 1965, the Uygur population in Xinjiang increased from 3.3 million to 4.1 million, and then to 5.99 million in 1990. However, their percentage of the total population decreased from 75.9 percent in 1949 to 52.1 percent in 1965 and to 45.5 percent in 1990.

3. **Other minority peoples:** In Xinjiang, besides the Han and the Uygur, there also live the Kazak (6.9 percent of the total population), Hui, Mongol, Uzbek, Xibe, Tajik, and 39 other ethnic minority groups. In the Hexi Corridor, there also live many minority peoples: Tibetans, Uygur, Kazak, Dongxiang, and Tu, of which, the Tibetan, Uygur, and Kazak are the leading ethnic minorities in one autonomous county each. On the Alashan Plateau, the Mongol are the leading ethnic minority people in the Bayan Nur League (prefecture).

Population

The total population increased rapidly in Xinjiang from 4.3 million in 1949 to 13.16 million in 1990. Yet, the land is vast (more than 1.6 million sq km), and the average population density reaches only 8 persons/sq km, with extensive areas virtually empty. Compared to the small total population, the arable land is rather abundant. There were about 3.2 million ha of farmland in 1990, about 3.6 *mu* (0.24 ha) per person, nearly three times the national average. Besides, there are still more than 1.1 million ha of potentially arable land. Therefore, the land–food–population system here is much less critical than in China in general. However, family planning and other population-control measures should now be taken seriously before it is too late.

The Hexi Corridor as the largest commercial food grain base and one of the most important industrial belts in Northwest Arid China has also experienced rapid population growth since 1949. It now produces about 70 percent of the total commercial food grains in Gansu Province and has a new immigration project of 200,000 persons under consideration.

Rural and Urban Settlement

Rural Settlement

In the wild desert lands, rural settlements are even more sparse than in the grasslands. In the grasslands, horses are a good transportation animal, covering several dozens of kilometers of distance each day. But in the desert, horse-riding is generally not good enough, and it is better to use an automobile or a camel to cover long distances. What is more, in large expanses of shifting sand, gravel *gobi*, and rocky mountains, there might be no village at all for hundreds of kilometers.

In oasis belts, such as in the middle and lower reaches of the Tarim, Black, Shayang, and other larger inland rivers, rural settlements are generally composed of a few dozen earth houses. They are located a few dozen kilometers apart and have similar aspects to those in the Elbow Plains or the Northeast China Plain.

Urban Settlement

Similar to the Inner Mongolian grassland, this division has a series of ancient and rebuilt cities as well as many newly founded cities. So far, there is only one million-population metropolis (Ürümqi). The following cities are comparatively more significant:

1. ***Ürümqi:*** Located on the northern piedmont plain of the Tianshan with an elevation about 900 m, the old walled city of Ürümqi was first founded in 1760 as a county seat. It became a provincial capital in 1884, and has been the capital of Xinjiang Uygur Autonomous Region since 1956. Its population increased from less than 100,000 in 1949 to nearly 1.05 million in 1990. It is now an industrial as well as political and cultural center, and its suburbs are famous for many scenic spots, such as the Tianchi (Heaven Lake, Color Plate 30), the Tianshan No. 1 Glacier (Photo 17.2), and the Turpan Basin (Photo 17.8).

2. ***Kashi (Kashgar):*** Kashi is located at the western border of the Tarim Basin. It was China's "front door" on the Silk Road and was one of the 36 ancient "kingdoms." It now has about 140,000 inhabitants, of which two thirds are Uygur. Kashi is famous for quality agricultural products and beautiful traditional arts as well as its market square and the Edegar Muslim temple.

Photo 17.8 The ruin of an ancient Guihe, Turpan Basin, Xinjiang Uygur Autonomous Region.

3. *Hotan:* Located at the southwestern border of the Taklimakan Desert, Hotan is also one of the largest oases along the ancient Silk Road. Hotan has been famous for its carpets and jades since ancient times, and since the 1950s also for its silk fabrics.

4. *Shihezi:* Newly founded in the early 1950s, Shihezi is the headquarters of the Shihezi Reclamation Area and is also an industrial center for textiles, foods, and other light industries.

5. *Jincheng:* Located on the wild gravel *gobi* in the central Hexi Corridor, Jincheng is a newly established mining and industrial city, specializing in nickel and copper metallurgy.

AREAL DIFFERENTIATION AND REGIONAL DEVELOPMENT

Future projections are that this division will rely on petroleum and other heavy industries as the driving economic force, while irrigation farming, animal husbandry, light industry, and transportation will be important, but subsidiary, economic strengths. Environmental protection and measures for combating natural hazards (desertification, shifting sand, salinization, and others) should be carefully undertaken. Probably in the first quarter of the twenty-first century, this division will be developed as a strategic backyard of China. However, development trends for different natural regions and subregions should be based on their specific physical and human conditions.

Alashan Plateau

The Alashan Plateau is the easternmost part of China's desert division, with the Helan Mountains and the Qilian Mountains as its eastern and southern borders. Its northern boundary is the Sino-Mongolian international boundary, and its western boundary coincides roughly with the boundary between Inner Mongolia Autonomous Region and Xinjiang Uygur Autonomous Region. This is exclusively an arid land with an aridity index greater than 4.0 and relative humidity usually less than 10 percent. Geomorphologically, it is the southwestern part of the Inner Mongolian Plateau, with denudational medium mountains of 2000–2500 m in elevation interspersed with depositional intermontane basins of 1000–1500 m. Its drainage is entirely interior, and it contains large tracts without any runoff at all. Soils are mainly composed of yermosols and solonchaks, and vegetation consists chiefly of very sparse shrubs and half-shrubs. Consequently, land types (Figure 17.2B) are mainly montane desert, denudational stony *gobi*, diluvial gravel *gobi*, and shifting sand, all of them unfavorable to agricultural development and human settlement.

There is conspicuous areal differentiation within this region. From south to north, the elevation decreases gradually, resulting in a drier climate and diminishing vegetation as well as a sparser population.

Alashan Plateau Proper

The Alashan Plateau Proper (23_1 on Figure 17.1) is an ancient, stable platform that consists of a series of northeast–southwest or east–west trending ranges interlocked with depositional basins. The southernmost range is called the Heli–Longshou Mountains. The intermontane basins generally represent the plateau surface, which is mostly covered with denudational stony *gobi* and diluvial gravel *gobi*. Three large border basins, however, are occupied by extensive sandy deserts: the Badain Jaran, the Tengger, and the Ulan Buh. The Badain Jaran Desert is the second largest shifting sandy desert in China, with an area of about 40,000 sq km, of which shifting sand occupies about 83 percent. Its highest sand dune reaches 420 m, probably the highest in the world.

Along the lower reaches of large interior rivers, ribbon-like fertile alluvial plains have been used as irrigated farmland since ancient times. For example, the lower reaches of the Black River and its delta around the Juyan Lake were actively cultivated as early as the second century B.C.

On the whole, this subregion is unfavorable for agricultural development. It should be mainly reserved for extensive pastoral land use. Some exceptions are the local fertile plains with available irrigation water where regional planning and scientific farming should be encouraged. Mineral and salt extraction industries also have potential.

Mazong Mountains

This subregion (23_2 on Figure 17.1) is geologically a part of the ancient Alashan–Mazong Massive. It is composed of four northeast–southwest trending mountain ranges in a row. Most of these ranges have an elevation between 1500 and 2000 m, and the process of desiccation dominates. Barren denudational mountain desert and stony *gobi* are widely distributed with a well-developed darkish desert varnish. Thus, it is called the Black Gobi, one of the wildest and most desolate areas in all of

China. In the intermontane basins, however, natural conditions are somewhat better; widespread depositional gravel *gobi* land surface is covered with sparse vegetation, which can be used as pasture. Under low intensity of use some minerals are also exploited in this subregion.

Eastern and Middle Hexi Corridor

The eastern and middle sections of the Hexi Corridor (23_3 on Figure 17.1) belong to this region (its western section is a subregion of the Tarim Basin region). This subregion is probably the most favorable area of China's entire desert division for agricultural and industrial development.

Junggar Basin

The Junggar Basin is triangular with the Tianshan and the Altay Mountains as two limiting sides and the western (Sino-Russian border) remaining relatively open. Like the Alashan Plateau, this is a temperate desert. Yet, it differs by being rather open to the moist westerly winds through two gaps, the Ertix Valley and the Junggar Gate. Consequently, it is less arid, with annual precipitation of 100 to 300 mm, decreasing from west to east. There is also much greater snowfall and snow cover during the winter season, which helps increase the growth of natural vegetation. Geomorphologically, the Junggar Basin differs from the Alashan Plateau by having a lower elevation (500–1000 m) that decreases from northeast to southwest. The lowest point is 189 m near Ebi Lake. Therefore, in spite of higher latitude and colder winters, it is favored with warmer summers, and a frost-free season of about 160 days. Another difference is that it is an inland basin rather than a plateau. The distribution of land types consists of depositional *gobi* around the marginal piedmont plains and the Gurbantünggüt Desert in the basin center.

Areal differences within this region are highlighted by the divergence between the Junggar Basin proper with its western and eastern borders. Thus, three natural subregions can be identified.

Junggar Basin Proper

This subregion (24_1 on Figure 17.1) has an area of about 180,000 sq km, of which gravel *gobi* and sandy desert occupy 72,000 and 60,000 sq km, respectively. It can be subdivided into two parts. The northern basin, between the Altay Mountains and the Gurbantünggüt Desert, is characterized by thin Cenozoic beds and widespread *gobi* and eolian landforms. The southern basin, with very thick Cenozoic deposits, includes the extensive Gurbantünggüt Desert and the widely distributed *gobi* on the northern piedmont of the Tianshan. Between the sand desert and the gravel *gobi* lies a relatively narrow belt of clayey and silty soils on the plain that corresponds roughly to the "spring line" and its neighboring oases of the Hexi Corridor. Most farmlands, roadways, and settlements in the Junggar Basin are concentrated along this fertile and well-watered belt.

Conditions of hydrography, soils, and vegetation are also slightly better than those on the Alashan Plateau. The Ertix River, with an annual runoff discharge of about 10 billion cu m, is the only river in China that flows into the Arctic Ocean. All the inland rivers together have another 10 billion cu m or so annual runoff discharge. In the Gurbantünggüt Desert, shifting sand formerly occupied only 3 percent of the total area, but the sand-covered area increased rapidly to 10–15 percent during the Cultural Revolution. It has now become one of the major environmental problems in the region. The widespread fixed sand areas have a shrubby vegetation cover of 30–50 percent and the half-fixed sand areas about 20 percent; both types of sandy area provide good winter pasture. The extensively distributed yermosols, if well irrigated, can be turned into good farmlands. It is estimated there are about 4 million ha of arable land not yet used in the Junggar Basin.

On the whole, this subregion is best suited for pastoral development, and one of the best pastoral systems is transhumance. Large-scale agricultural reclamation, which started only 200 years ago, has also been successfully undertaken since 1955. One of the outstanding examples is the middle and lower reaches of the Manas River (Color Plate 31; Figure 17.4). Recently, petroleum and other industries have also been developed along the northern piedmont of the Tianshan and have already become the leading economic components of the subregion.

Nomin Gobi

Located on either side of Baytik Mountain (highest peak, 3479 m) along the Sino-Mongolian border, the Nomin Gobi region (24_2 on Figure 17.1) is essentially composed of several small inland basins. The climate is extremely arid. The lowest point, Nom Lake (elevation: 500 m), has an annual precipitation of only 12.5 mm. The landscape is dominated by denudational stony *gobi* and diluvial gravel *gobi*, with glittering desert varnish and very sparse vegetation coverage (less than 5 percent). There are only a few inhabitants, engaged in very extensively managed pastoralism.

Emin Valley

Located along the Sino-Russian border and west of the border mountain range (2000–3000 m in elevation) of the Junggar Basin, the valley (24_3 on Figure 17.1) at its eastern margin is about 1000 m, then lowers to only 400 m at the Tacheng suburb. The broad valley plain belongs climatically to the desert-steppe zone, with an annual precipitation of about 300 mm and a frost-free season of about 125 days. It is well watered and luxuriantly covered with meadow and swamps, and it can be used for growing wheat and forage crops. On the mountain slopes, shrubby-steppe, meadow-steppe, and alpine meadow are luxuriantly distributed, all of which are good pasture.

Altay Mountains

The Altay Mountains stretch from northwest to southeast more than 2000 km along the Sino-Russian-Mongolian border. Only the southern slopes of this mountain system's middle section lie inside Chinese territory, with a length of about 500 km and an elevation of more than 3000 m at the crest line. The highest peak, Mount Youyi (literally "Friendship," 4374 m), is located on the northwestern margin of the region, and its southeastern tip merges into the vast level expanse of black *gobi*.

This is a geologically ancient folded belt that appeared for the first time after the Caledonian Tectonic Movement. During the Himalayan Tectonic Movement, it was sharply uplifted and faulted, resulting in four prominent topographic steps from the Ertix Valley northeastward to the Sino-Mongolian Border. Remnants of multicyclic erosional surfaces are still visible, with elevations of 2900–3000 m, 2600–2700 m, 1800–2000 m, and 1400–1600 m, respectively. The snow line is about 3200 m high.

As both latitudinal and altitudinal locations are rather high, the area has low temperatures and comparatively plentiful precipitation. On windward (western) slopes, the annual precipitation totals more than 250–500 mm. Therefore, the area is the source of many rivers in the Junggar Basin, including the Ertix and the Ulungur.

Coinciding with vertical zonation of geomorphic and climatic conditions, vegetation and soil are arranged in vertical belts that reflect the major areal differentiation in this region. From the foot to mountain top, they are:

1. **Desert-steppe:** from the foot of the mountains to about 800–1450 m high, with its upper limit ascending from northwest to southeast. The dominant species are *Artemisia spp.* and *Stipa effusa*.

2. **Shrub-steppe:** The shrub-steppe upper limit ascends from 1200 m (in the northwest) to 1900 m (in the southeast). The most commonly seen species are *Spiraea hypericifolia*, *Artemisia frigida*, and *Festuca ovina*. The plant coverage is usually greater than 50 percent, and this shrub-steppe is an important spring and autumn pasture.

3. **Montane needle-leaved forest:** The upper needle-leaved forest limit ascends from 2100 m (in the northwest) to 2300 m (in the southeast). Predominant tree species are *Larix sibirica* and *Abies sibirica*, with a total wooded area of nearly 1 million ha. This is one of the most important timber-producing areas in Northwest Arid China.

4. **Subalpine grassland and meadow:** The upper limit ranges from 2300 m (in the northwest) to 2600 m (in the southeast). Dominant grass species are *Festuca rubra*, *F. ovina*, *F. kirilovii*, *Poa altaica*, *P. sibirica*, and *P. alpina*, all yielding high-quality pasture. Vegetation coverage may be as high as 95 percent, making it one of the best summer pastures in China, although it is not yet fully used.

5. **Alpine meadow:** The upper limit ranges from 3000 to 3500 m. In the northwestern Altay, it is alpine shrub-meadow, dominated by *Betula rotundifolia* and many kinds of lichens and mosses. In the southeastern Altay, it is alpine meadow, composed mainly of *Cobresia spp.* and *Carex spp.*, with a vegetative cover of more than 90 percent.

6. **Alpine cushion vegetation:** This low alpine vegetation, composed mostly of lichens and mosses, is found immediately below the snow line.

The best use of this region is for shorter duration transhumance, coupled with some local mining. Environmental protection is of paramount importance to ensure that no grassland degradation occurs.

Using moisture as the chief diversifying criterion, two subregions might be identified in the Altay Mountains.

Northwestern Altay Mountains

The higher elevation and prevalent moisture-bearing winds of the northwestern Altay Mountains (25_1 on Figure 17.1) result in much heavier precipitation and lower limits of the various vertical vegetation zones.

Southeastern Altay Mountains

With less precipitation and higher temperature, this subregion (25₂ on Figure 17.1) is much more desiccated than the northwestern part. For example, the upper limit of desert-steppe ascends to 1400 m. Montane needle-leaved forest is also much more restricted in area and does not grow in the southeastern tip of the Altay Mountains.

Tianshan Mountains

The Tianshan Mountains, one of the greatest mountain systems in the world, stretch from west to east over a total distance of about 2500 km, with a width of from 100 to 400 km. Only the middle and eastern sections lie inside Chinese territory, dividing Xinjiang into two distinct regions: the Junggar Basin and the Tarim Basin. The Tianshan Mountains within Chinese territory are composed of more than 20 parallel ranges, interspersed with graben-structured and rhomboid-shaped intermontane basins, over a length of about 1700 km and a total area of about 244,000 sq km.

Geologically, this is an ancient folded belt, first folded during the late Caledonian Tectonic Movement. As a result of the Indochina, Yinshan, and Himalaya tectonic movements, the area was repeatedly folded, faulted, and uplifted in the eventful formation of the modern, lofty Tianshan Mountains. There are four vertical belts of modern geomorphic process that appear in succession:

1. **Belt of eternal snow and modern glaciation (Photo 17.2):** Above 3800 to 4200 m in elevation, this is the largest modern area of glaciers in China. There are 6896 glaciers, which usually terminate at elevations between 3000 and 4000 m, sometimes even moving as far downslope as 2500 to 2800 m.

2. **Belt of snow accumulation and ancient glaciation:** This belt is located between 3000 and 3800 m in elevation. Glaciers existed here during the Pleistocene, but have retreated since the Holocene. Snow accumulation is now the dominant geomorphic process, with seasonal snow cover lasting more than 10 months in some places.

3. **Belt of fluvial erosion:** Located at elevations between 1000 and 3000 m, this is the vertical zone of heaviest precipitation, generally more than 500 mm

annually, or even more than 1000 mm (highest record 1130 mm). Fluvial erosion results in very rugged topography.

4. **Belt of desiccation (denudation):** This belt is generally located below 1000 m where annual precipitation is less than 100–200 mm.

The Tianshan Mountains area is like a huge elongated "wet island" amid the vast expanse of extremely arid deserts. More than 200 rivers originate here, of which the Ili River and the Aksu River are the largest. According to recent studies, the annual runoff water discharge of all these rivers totals 43.9 billion cu m. In addition, the total water reserve of modern glaciers on the Tianshan Mountains (not including the eternal snow) is estimated at 360 billion cu m—truly a huge "solid reservoir."

Vegetation distribution shows conspicuous vertical zonation. Six major vertical zones are recognized. The upper limit of each vertical zone varies somewhat according to the exposure of the slope as well as longitudinal and latitudinal locations.

1. **Temperate montane desert:** below 1100 m in elevation; mainly sparse *Artemisia spp.*

2. **Montane steppe:** located between 1100 and 2000 m, mainly *Artemisia terrealbae*, *Festuca ovina*, and *Stipa spp.*

3. **Montane forest-steppe:** located around 2000 m in elevation, small patches of *Picea* forest on shady slopes and grassland of *Poa spp.* and *Artemisia spp.* on sunny slopes. This is a good summer pasture area.

4. **Subalpine needle-leaved forest:** located between 2000 and 2700 m, consisting of large patches of *Picea* forest on shady slopes (Color Plate 30) and luxuriant grassland on sunny slopes. The former is good timber, whereas the latter is excellent summer pasture.

5. **Alpine meadow:** located between 2700 and 3700 m, dominated by *Carex spp.*, *Alchemilla vulgaris*, with *Bromus inermis* and *Poa pratensis* also common. This is an excellent summer and autumn pasture, frequented by the Kazak nomads who practice transhumance.

6. **Alpine cushion vegetation:** located between 3700 and 3900 m, dominated by lichens and famous for the beautiful snow lotus that blooms in the late summer.

On the whole, this region should be mainly used for

forestry and transhumance, with some local mining. Environmental protection should be emphasized.

Middle Tianshan Mountains

This subregion (26_1 on Figure 17.1) is the major part of the Tianshan region in China.

Eastern Tianshan

This subregion (26_2 on Figure 17.1) is restricted to a small part of the Tianshan Mountains east of Bogda Mountain, with a width of about 100 km and a crest line elevation below 4000 m. Precipitation decreases gradually from west to east, and upper limits of vertical vegetation zones correspondingly ascend higher. For example, the upper limit of *Picea* forest lies at 1700 m on the Bogda Mountain (about 89° E), ascends to 2350 m on Barku Mountain (about 91° E), and disappears entirely near Yiwu (about 95° E).

Ili Valley

The Ili River empties into the Lake Balkhash of Central Asia; only its upper reaches lie inside Chinese territory. The Ili Valley (26_3 on Figure 17.1) is a broad valley plain consisting several fanlike terraces. It is surrounded by mountain ranges except on the western side, where warm, moist westerly winds rush in. Therefore, the climate is less arid than that of the Junggar Basin, is warmer in winter, but cooler in summer (owing to higher elevation). The frost-free season lasts from 160–210 days. Annual precipitation ranges from 280 to 470 mm, decreasing from west to east. Spring and autumn are the rainy seasons, accounting for about four-fifths of the annual precipitation, which makes dry farming possible and popular. The Ili River has an annual runoff discharge of 12.3 billion cu m, which ensures that there is no lack of irrigation water if it is needed. On the surrounding mountain slopes, luxuriant montane steppe, montane forest-steppe, and alpine meadows are extensive. These excellent pastures have been famous for their high-quality horses ever since the second century B.C. This subregion could be established as one of the commercial grain bases as well as one of the pastoral production centers in Xinjiang.

Tarim Basin

This gigantic, rhomboid-shaped inland basin is surrounded by the Tianshan, Kunlun, Altun, and other lofty mountains, with a maximum length of nearly 2000 km (including the western Hexi Corridor) and a maximum width of 520 km. This is also the innermost core of China's desert landscape, with annual precipitation of less than 90 mm. Owing to its comparatively low latitude and altitude as well as being closely surrounded by lofty mountains, it is unique as the only warm temperate desert in China. Three crops every two years may be grown if irrigation water is available.

The Tarim Basin is on an ancient massif, encircled and demarcated by many deep faults. According to recent geomagnetic surveys, the ancient massif base is buried to a depth of 19 km in its central part. In its border downwarped area, both marine and terrestrial deposits of Palaeozoic, Mesozoic, and Cenozoic sediments have a maximum thickness of more than 10 km. Most of them are excellent petroleum-bearing and groundwater-bearing beds.

Tarim Basin Proper

This inland basin subregion (27(1) on Figure 17.1) is nearly all mountain-locked, with only a narrow corridor plain, about 70 km wide, between the Altun Mountains and the Kuruktag,[3] which merges eastward into the western Hexi Corridor. It has an area of nearly half a million sq km, of which sandy deserts occupy about 331,000 sq km (Color Plate 29) and gravel *gobi* (Photo 17.1) about 105,000 sq km. The surface slopes from southwest to northeast. The Tarim River is a good indicator of the general topography; its channel has an elevation of about 1300 m in the southwestern Tarim Basin, and then flows northeastward to its terminal lake, Lop Nur (Figure 10.2), which is 780 m high, the lowest point, or "sink," in the Tarim Basin.

All rivers originate in the surrounding high mountains, providing a total annual discharge of about 37 billion cu m. If rainfall and runoff were sufficient, all these rivers might be integrated into one single fluvial system—the Tarim–Konqi–Qarqan river system. However, at present, all rivers originating from the Kunlun Mountains (except two headwaters of the Tarim River, the Yarkant and the Hotan) die out amid the immense stony and sandy deserts. Even the Tarim River itself is now chiefly fed by the Aksu River, which originates in the Tianshan. Ultimately, the Tarim River flows into its terminal lakes of Lop Nur, Karakoshun, and Taitema, known as the "wandering lakes." All have dried up since 1972 (see Chapter Ten).

Land types in the Tarim Basin are distributed in

---

[3] In Uygur, *tag* means "mountain."

concentric belts around the basin (Figure 17.2A). Immediately below the surrounding mountains lie the diluvial gravel *gobi* and alluvial-diluvial sandy gravel *gobi*, which are located on the piedmont plains. Below them are the narrow belts of fertile, well-watered, clayey and silt level land and oases. Next is the immense Taklimakan Desert, 85 percent of which consists of shifting sand dunes with narrow ribbons of fixed and half-fixed sand dunes on its peripheries as well as some corridors of oases that penetrate deeply into the Taklimakan Desert along large inland rivers.

From the land use point of view, the most important land types in this region are certainly the oases and their neighboring arable clayey and silt level lands. According to the reclamation process, oases in the Tarim Basin might be classified into three categories (Figure 3.5): ancient oases (such as Loulan), old oases (developed before 1949), and new oases (cultivated since 1949). The resent oases are mostly located in the middle and lower reaches of the Tarim River; more than 140,000 ha of farmland have been reclaimed here since 1955. For the sake of further agricultural development, great care must be taken to control salinization and shifting sands as well as to improve the effective use of irrigation water.

During the 1980s, a very big event occurred in the Tarim Basin: the discovery and production of a increasing amounts of petroleum. In the future, probably the largest economic enterprises here will be oil production and refining, with related heavy and light industries. To support the increased population brought into the area by industrialization, irrigated farming and transhumance pastoralism will also develop rapidly.

Turpan–Hami Intermontane Basin

This subregion (27_2 on Figure 17.1), sandwiched between the Tianshan and the Kuruktag, is an area of extremes. Toksun has the lowest annual precipitation record in China (3.9 mm). Turpan city has the highest maximum temperature record in China (47.6°C; unofficially, 48.9°C). The Turpan Basin is also famous as a "wind reservoir;" a maximum wind velocity of 50 m/sec was once recorded. A new electricity-generating technology using wind power has been developing. Ayding Lake with an elevation of 155 m below sea level is the lowest point on the Chinese mainland. Denudational stony *gobi* and diluvial gravel *gobi* are extensive in both the Turpan and the Hami basins, and a vast expanse of denudational black *gobi* dominates the neighboring Gaxun Desert. This is one of the most concentrated areas of *gobi* in the world.

Since ancient times, this subregion has been a great political and economic center in Northwest China. There are many famous ruins in this subregion, including several capitals of ancient kingdoms (Photo 17.8). The Uygur inhabitants are particularly famous for their *karez* (underground) irrigation canals, several or even several dozen kilometers long, which lead and conduct precious water from the faraway Tianshan Mountains to irrigate and transform the wild gravel *gobi* into a luxurious garden of grapes, melons, and other crops. Turpan grapes and Hami melons together with Uygur hospitality are famous throughout China. According to statistics, in early 1980s there were 1158 *karez* canals in the Turpan Basin alone, with a total length of more than 3000 km and an annual discharge of 777 million cu m.

Western Hexi Corridor

The western section of the Hexi Corridor (27_3 on Figure 17.1) is similar to its middle and eastern sections, except that it is somewhat lower in elevation (generally 1000–1200 m) and farther away from the sea. Consequently, it is drier (annual precipitation is 40–50 mm) and warmer (the frost-free season is about 200 days and the cumulative temperature during the $\geq 10°C$ period is 3300°–4000°C). Long-fiber cotton can be grown here if irrigation water is available. This subregion has been intensively cultivated for more than 2000 years and has fertile agricultural soil (although rather restricted in area) more than 2 m deep. Located here is the terminus of the westernmost section of the Great Wall and the starting point of the ancient Silk Road, which crosses both northern and southern margins of the immense Taklimakan Desert (Color Plate 13). This subregion is imbued with stark scenic beauty and ancient cultural splendors, such as the One Thousand Buddhas Grotto (Photo 17.6), the Yang-Guan (Sun Gate, Photo 17.5), the Singing Sand Mountain, and the New Moon Spring. No doubt this is an area of great interest to thoughtful and curious tourists.

REFERENCES

China State Statistical Bureau. 1991. *Statistical Yearbook of China*. Beijing: China Statistical Publishing House.

Dregne, H. E. (ed.), 1992. *Degradation and Restoration of Arid Lands*. Lubbock: ICASALS, Texas Tech University.

Editorial Board. 1980. *Agricultural Geography of Xinjiang*. Ürümqi: Xinjiang People's Press (in Chinese).

Integrated Investigation Team of Xinjiang, Chinese Academy of Sciences. 1965–1978. (1) *Soil Geography of Xinjiang*; (2) *Groundwater of Xinjiang*; (3) *Surface Water of Xinjiang*; (4) *Geomorphology of Xinjiang*; (5) *Agriculture of Xinjiang*; (6) *Animal Husbandry of Xinjiang*. Beijing: Science Press (in Chinese).

Lanzhou Institute of Desert Research, Chinese Academy of Sciences. 1980. *An Outline of Chinese Deserts.* Beijing: Science Press (in Chinese).

Sun, Jinzhu, et al. 1988. *Geography of China.* Beijing: Higher Education Press (in Chinese).

Zhao, Songqiao. 1986. *Physical Geography of China.* New York: John Wiley & Sons.

Zhao, Songqiao. 1985. *Physical Geography of China's Arid Land.* Beijing: Science Press (in Chinese).

Zhao, Songqiao. 1981. *Desert Lands of China.* Lubbock: ICASALS, Texas Tech University.

Zhao, Songqiao. 1987. "Human Impact on Northwest Arid China: Desertification or De-desertification?" *Chinese Journal of Arid Land Research* 1, no. 2.

Zhao, Songqiao. 1988. "Desertification and De-desertification in the Hexi Corridor," *Chinese Journal of Arid Land Research* 1, no. 2.

Zhao, Songqiao. 1989. "Recent Advances in China's Arid Land Research," *Chinese Journal of Arid Land Research* 2, no. 1.

Zhao, Songqiao. 1990. "Recent Geographic Discoveries and Research Advances in the Tarim Basin," *Chinese Journal of Arid Land Research* 2, no. 1.

Zhao, Songqiao. 1991. "The Oases-making Process (De-desertification) in China's Desert Lands," *Chinese Journal of Arid Land Research* 2, no. 1.

Zhao, Songqiao, and Xuncheng, Xia. 1984. "Evolution of the Lop Desert and the Lop Nur," *The Geographical Journal* 150, no. 3.

CHAPTER EIGHTEEN

Tibetan Plateau

The dominant characteristics of the Tibetan Frigid Plateau, one of the three natural realms of China, are its very great altitude, very rugged topography, and very conspicuous vertical zonation as well as a frigid climate. So far, only one natural division has been identified, although it is subdivided into six natural regions (Figure 18.1, Color Plate 4). It is located on China's first great topographic step and is sometimes called the "roof of the world." It is surrounded by a series of lofty mountains, such as the Himalaya Mountains with the highest peak in the world, Mount Qomolangma (Color Photo 2) on the southwestern border, the Kunlun and Karakoram mountains on the northwestern border (Photo 18.1), the Hengduan Mountains on the southeastern border (Color Plate 32), and the Altun and Qilian mountains on the northeastern border. There are also many east–west or northwest–southeast trending, extremely high mountains inside the plateau, such as the Gandise, the Nyainqentungulha, and the Tanggula (Color Plate 7). The Tibetan Plateau has an area of 2.5 million sq km, about one-fourth of China's total land area. Nevertheless, it includes only 0.8 percent of China's total population and 0.8 percent of China's total farmland. Historically and administratively, it is divided into three main parts: (1) the Zang (Tibet), or western half, now the Tibet (Xizang) Autonomous Region, with an area of about 1.23 million sq km, a total farmland of 0.22 million ha (1990) and a total population of 2.2 million (1990); (2) Qinghai (literally, "Blue Sea"), or northeastern part, an independent province for a long time, with an area of about 0.72 million sq km, total farmland of 0.58 million ha (1990), and a total population of 4.46 million (1990); and (3) the Kang, or southeastern part, once an independent province (Xi Kang), now the sparsely populated western part of Sichuan Province, mainly including two Tibetan Autonomous Prefectures (Garze and Aba). In addition, the northernmost borderland of Yunnan Province, the southwesternmost borderland of the Gansu Province, and the southernmost borderland of the Xinjiang Uygur Autonomous Region are also physically parts of the Tibetan Plateau, which is generally delimited by the 3000 m contour line.

The relative recency of the Himalayan Tectonic Movement, the violence of recent uplift, and the vastness of the land area and the low latitudinal location all combine to make the Tibetan Plateau's physical geographic environment complicated and unique. This is the youngest, largest, and highest plateau in the world, with many other extremes, such as the highest farmland and upper forest limit in the world as well as the largest and most numerous lakes in China. It also displays the close interrelation of horizontal and vertical zonation. Sometimes it is also called the "third pole" of the world. Many geographers and other scientists as well as tourists have expressed strong interest in this natural realm, and many multidisciplinary scientific investigations have been conducted here since 1949. Nevertheless, scientific information about this extensive area is still far from adequate. What is more, until 1959, the Zang-inhabited area had long been subjected to the tribal serfdom system and was wrapped in mysterious Lamaism. Many social and economic conditions are rather difficult to understand and to evaluate. Therefore, we can now only present a broad outline in this book.

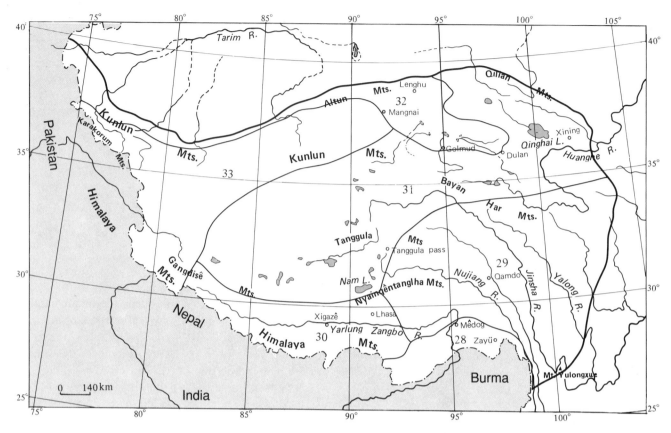

Figure 18.1 The Tibetan Plateau (For legend, see Table 18.1.)

PHYSICAL FEATURES, NATURAL RESOURCES, AND ENVIRONMENTAL PROBLEMS

Since the late Miocene epoch, the physical geographic environment of the Tibetan Plateau has undergone tremendous changes. The major factor determining such tremendous changes, besides the worldwide Quaternary glaciation and its impact on global climatic fluctuation, is undoubtedly the violent uplift of the area from near sea level to an average of more than 4000 m in elevation. The modern physical geographical environment of the Tibetan Plateau is briefly analyzed in the following discussions.

Roof of the World

The ancient, low, undulating late Tertiary erosional surface, which was once widely distributed in Eurasia and other continents, was uplifted in this part of the world to 4500–5000 m above sea level to form the high surface of the Tibetan Plateau. Consequently, the geomorphic processes and landforms have been repeatedly rejuvenated; in fact, this is the youngest and largest geomorphic realm in the world. In its southeastern parts, different kinds of rejuvenated landforms are badly dissected to create a very rugged topography (Figure 18.2). On nearly all riparian longitudinal profiles there appear three conspicuous knickpoints, which represent three cyclic stages of rejuvenation. In the middle and lower reaches of many large rivers, the valley-within-valley landform is commonly seen. Owing to prominent areal differentiation in moisture conditions from southeast to northwest and consequently great divergence in the intensity of erosion, the deeply dissected southeastern parts of the Tibetan Plateau, where the erosional process dominates, contrast strongly with the central and northwestern parts where desiccation and snow-accumulation processes dominate. In these latter parts, an undu-

Photo 18.1 Mount K2 of the Karakorum Mountains, 8611 m in elevation, is the second highest peak in the world.

lating and relatively undissected high plateau surface prevails under frigid and arid conditions, and the drainage system turns from oceanic to interior.

This "roof of the world" is also the source area for many mighty rivers in East and South Asia. In its northeastern parts (Qinghai), the most important one is certainly the largest river of China, the Chang Jiang, and its many tributaries. Its headwater, the Do River (Color Plate 7), with icy water all year around, originates from the main peak of the Tanggula Mountains (6600 m). It flows across the southeastern parts of the Tibetan Plateau in deep gorges. The Yellow River also originates

nearby (Color Plate 8). At first it flows sluggishly eastward, and then cuts a series of deep gorges on the border between the Tibetan Plateau and the Loess Plateau where many hydroelectric stations have been constructed (Photo 18.2). On the southeastern part of Tibetan Plateau, two other great rivers—the Nu (Salween) and the Lancang (Mekong)—originate and flow into the Indochina Peninsula. On the southwestern part of the Tibetan Plateau, the Indus and the Yarlung Zangbo (which forms the upper and middle reaches of the Brahmaputra River, Photo 18.3) originate. From the northwestern part of the Tibetan Plateau, the headwaters of China's largest interior river, the Tarim, originate. On this "roof of the world" is also the largest number of lakes in China, as well as the largest one, Qinghai Lake (in Mongolian, Koko Nur) and the highest one, the Nam Co (in Tibetan, literally the "Heaven Lake;" Photo 18.4). Such a high and rugged topography results in limited arable land and frequent mountain hazards and hailstorms as well as severe soil erosion.

Frigid Climate

High elevation also results in low temperature everywhere on the Tibetan Plateau (excluding the southern slopes of the Himalayas, which are physically not a part of the Tibetan Plateau). The elevation is at least above 2500 to 3000 m, and on the northwestern part (Qiantang Plateau or Chantang Plateau) the average elevation is above 4500 to 5000 m, while numerous extremely high mountains tower above 5000 m to 6000 m or even above 7000–8000 m. Therefore, in spite of rather low latitudes and intense solar radiation (140–190 Kcal/cm^2/yr, the highest in China), the mean January temperature ranges from $-10°C$ to $-15°C$, and the mean July temperature (the lowest in China) is roughly equal to the mean January temperature in Subtropical China. There is no frost-free season in areas above 4000 m (the average elevation of the Tibetan Plateau), and all extremely high mountains are generally wrapped in glaciers and eternal snow. Even in the local farming areas, where the elevation is generally below 3000 m, low temperature and frost hazards are common.

Another climatic feature is the great diurnal and seasonal variation in temperature. Great thermal differences exist between winter and "summer," but diurnal variation is even greater. During daylight, there are also great thermal differences between sunny and shady sites. Tibetan farmers are often seen working on their farmlands

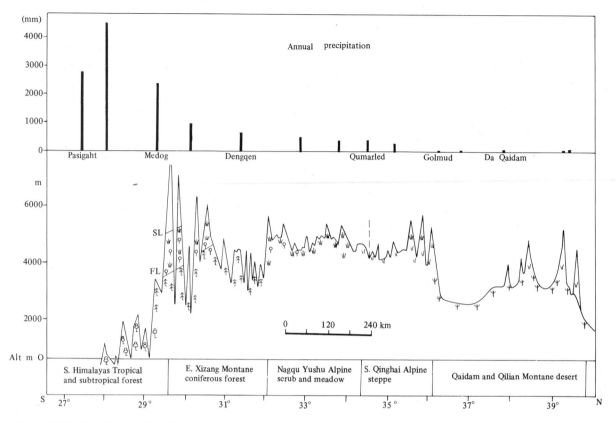

Figure 18.2   Physical profile of the Tibetan Plateau along 32° N

with bare arms under brilliant sunshine, only to rest in the shade wearing heavy fur coats.

The Dominating Snow-Accumulation Process

High elevation and frigid climate together with relics of Quaternary glaciation have led to widely distributed glaciers and permafrost on the Tibetan Plateau. Existing glaciers have a total area of about 47,000 sq km, more than four-fifths of the total glacial area in China. There are two modern glaciation centers on the Tibetan Plateau: the temperate maritime type located in the southeast, and the cold continental type in the northwest. There are also numerous isolated alpine valley glaciers in the Himalayas and other high mountain areas.

Permafrost is widespread in areas of the central and northwestern Tibetan Plateau. On the highly uplifted Qiantang Plateau, permafrost may have a total thickness of 80 to 90 m and a seasonally active layer of 1 to 4 m in vast continuous expanse, forming a huge "permafrost

island" within the low latitudinal permafrost-free belt in the world. Permafrost also presents a serious problem for the construction of the Golmud–Lhasa railway.

Thus, snow-accumulation processes dominate on the Tibetan Plateau. Great diurnal and seasonal thermal variations make freezing and thawing action frequent and extensive. Mechanical weathering plays an important role in geological denudation. Different types of periglacial landforms are also common.

The soil-forming process is also characterized by its youth with minimal soil profile development and soil minerals that are but weakly altered. Coarse soil texture and very strong freezing-thawing action are other outstanding soil genesis features. All represent unfavorable conditions for agricultural development.

Diverse Floral and Faunal Distribution

Both flora and fauna on the Tibetan Plateau are represented by two distinct systems. In the frigid-arid central and northwestern parts, fauna pertains to the palaeo-

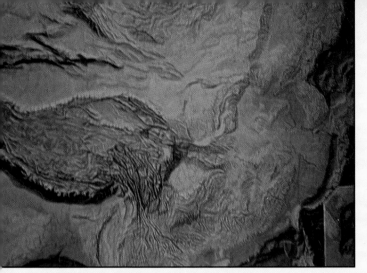

A satellite view of China's topography.
(Plate 1)

Mount Qomolangma (Mount Everest) of the Himalaya Mountains, located on the border between China and Nepal, 8848.13m in elevation, being the highest peak in the world.
(Plate 2)

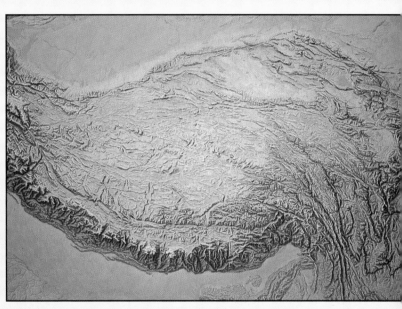

A satellite view of the lofty Tibetan Plateau.
(Plate 4)

The majestic Mount Taibai, 3767m in elevation, is the highest peak of the Qinling Mountains, which are the most important geographic divide in China, dividing northern China from southern China.

(Plate 3)

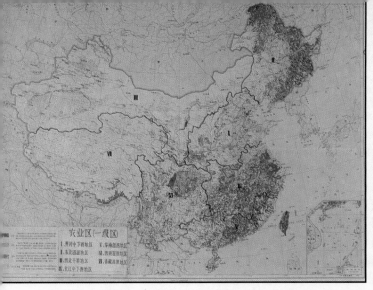

A land use map of China's paddy land (red), dry farm-land (orange), and forest (green).

(Plate 5)

The Sanjiang (Three Rivers) Plain, currently the largest reclamation area in China.

(Plate 6)

The icy headwaters of the Chang Jiang, the Do Do River originates at the main peak of the Tanggula Mountains, 6600m in elevation.

(Plate 7)

Ngoring Lake, headwaters of the Yellow River, has an elevation of 4300m and an average depth of 20m (maximum depth 30.7m).

(Plate 8)

The colorful and luxuriant mixed needle- and broad-leaved forest on the Lesser Hinggan Mountains.

(Plate 9)

A night view of the Daqing Oil Field, the largest oil field in China.

(Plate 10)

The Du Jiang Dam irrigation area, western Sichuan Basin, was first constructed in 256 B.C. and has been operated ever since.

(Plate 11)

The Shanhaiguan, or the Gate between Mountain and Sea, is the first fortress of the Great Wall.

(Plate 12)

The Jiayuguan is the last fortress of the Great Wall, located in the western Hexi Corridor. It is surrounded by extensive gravel *gobi*.

(Plate 13)

The extensive and productive Hai He Plain, Hebei Province. The Hai He is a distributary of the lower Yellow River.

(Plate 14)

The irrigation farming in the West Elbow Plain (Yinchuan Plain), Ningxia Hui Autonomous Region.

(Plate 15)

The Chang Jiang (Yangtze) Delta, a "watery country" and a "land of rice and fish."

(Plate 16)

A typical *liang* (loessic flat ridge) and *mao* (gentle hillslope) topography on northern Loess Plateau; near Yan'an, Shaanxi Province.

(Plate 17)

The Tianchi (Heaven Pond) near the top of the Changbai Mountains, a typical volcanic lake with a maximum water depth of 373 m.

(Plate 18)

Sunrise on top of China's ancient sacred mountain, Tai Shan, Shandong Province.

(Plate 19)

The famous Three Gorges of the Chang Jiang at the eastern border of the Sichuan Basin. This is the lower, or Xiling Gorge.

(Plate 20)

The beautiful Guilin landscape, northeastern Guangxi Province, features blue karst hills and green meandering rivers.

(Plate 21)

The productive and sustainable ecosystem of mulberry (or sugar cane) dike–paddy field–fish pond in the Zhu Jiang (Pearl River) Delta, Guangdong Province.

(Plate 22)

The fantastic Shilin (Stone Forest) on the eastern Yunnan Plateau is probably the most typical "karst forest" topography in the world.

(Plate 23)

The highest island of the South China Sea Islands—Shidao of Xisha Archipelago is only 15m in elevation, composed exclusively of coral reefs.

(Plate 24)

The luxuriant tropical rainforest on low mountain slopes, central Hainan Island.
(Plate 25)

A distant view of the Yinshan mountains (Great Green Mountains); the southern rim of the Mongolian Plateau.
(Plate 26)

The most luxuriant grassland in China—the Hulun Buir Steppe. In the 13th century, it was the backyard of the Mongol Empire.
(Plate 27)

The grass checkerboard sand-protection along the Baotou-Lanzhou Railway in the Shapotou area, Ningxia Hui Autonomous Region.
(Plate 28)

The wild, shifting, sandy desert of the Taklimakan, located in the center of the Tarim Basin, with an area of about 330,000 sq km. This is the largest sandy desert in China and the second largest in the world.

(Plate 29)

The scenic Tianchi (Heaven Pond) and its surrounding coniferous forest on the northern slope of the Tianshan Mountains.

(Plate 30)

The Shihezi Reclamation Area in the middle Manas valley, Junggar Basin, Xinjiang Uygur Autonomous Region, is a typical modern example of turning a sandy desert in a productive oasis.

(Plate 31)

Mount Gongga, 7556m in elevation, is the highest peak in the Hengduan Mountains. Yak and Tibetan tents are in the foreground.

(Plate 32)

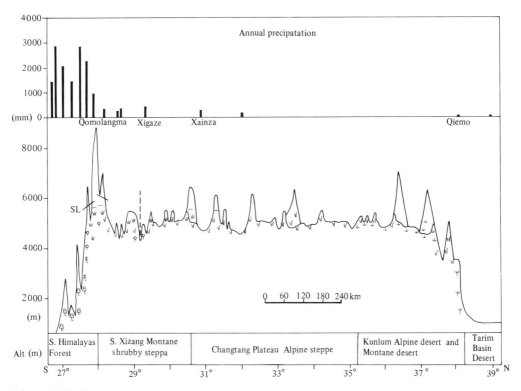

Figure 18.2 B

arctic realm, and flora relates to the Tibetan Plateau subregion of the panarctic region. Forests do not exist, and shrubs are dwarfed. In the less frigid and more humid southeastern parts, fauna pertains to the oriental realm and flora are classified as the Chinese Himalayan

forest subregion of the panarctic region. At lower elevations, the vegetation becomes much more luxuriant, and needle-leaved forests occur in large stands.

The surrounding lofty mountains, according to their orientation, geographic location, and other features, play

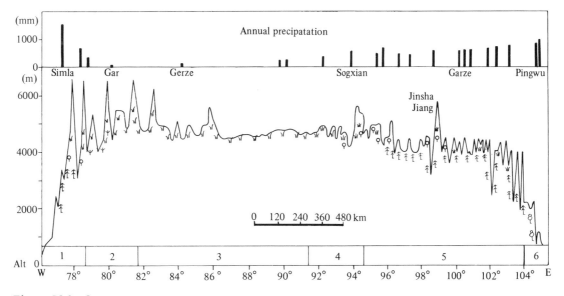

Figure 18.2 C

Photo 18.2 The Longyang (literally "Dragon-Sheep") Gorge of the upper Yellow River. A large-scale hydroelectric station is under construction.

an important role. The extremely high Himalayas with their west–east orientation and southern marginal location, serve as an effective barrier between the Tibetan Plateau and the Indian subcontinent. They bar practically all tropical and subtropical faunal and floral elements. The west–east trending Kunlun–Altun–Qilian mountain system is also a barrier between the Tibetan Plateau and Northwest Arid China, yet, owing to their somewhat lower relative relief and numerous mountain passes, their barrier action is not as effective as the Himalayas. Many common species of fauna and flora appear in both the Tibetan Plateau and Northwest Arid China. Thus, the Qaidam Basin on the northern border of the Tibetan Frigid Plateau realm might also be considered a

part of Northwest Arid China. The Hengduan Mountains on the southeastern border of the Tibetan Plateau, consisting of a series of parallel north–south trending high mountain ranges and deep river gorges, serve as highways along larger rivers and thus facilitate migration and intermingling among different species of fauna and flora. Furthermore, owing to the Tibetan Plateau's great relative relief and consequently very conspicuous vertical zonation as well as its being an excellent asylum for fauna and flora during Quaternary glaciation, many pre-Tertiary relic species survive in the area (Photo 18.5). This is also the distributing center for many modern species, such as *Rhododendron spp.* among flora and *Carruian spp.* among fauna.

Comprehensive Physical Regionalization

Both horizontal and vertical zonation are conspicuous on the Tibetan Plateau. These two factors are closely interrelated, and their integration determines the conspicuous, yet complicated, physical regionalization of the Tibetan Plateau.

Horizontal differentiation is chiefly expressed in terms of moisture response which, in turn, is mainly caused by the combined effect of mountain-barrier action and atmospheric circulation. As most mountain ranges on the Tibetan Plateau follow a west–east direction and serve as a series of barriers against moisture-bearing maritime monsoons, annual precipitation decreases successively from more than 1000 mm on the southeastern border to less than 200 mm on the northwestern border. Correspondingly, aridity increases from humid and subhumid to semiarid and arid. As a result of the Tibetan Plateau stretching for more than 12 degrees latitude from south to north, latitudinal divergence of temperature exists as well. The upper limit of the forest belt and the elevation of the modern snow line on the northern slopes of the middle Qilian Mountains are both lower by 600–1000 m than those on the southern slopes of the middle Himalaya Mountains.

Vertical zonation is certainly the most significant areal differentiation on the Tibetan Plateau; it often overshadows horizontal zonation, although it is also stamped with the features of the latter. Two systems of altitudinal zones can be identified: the maritime (humid and subhumid) and the continental (semiarid and arid). The former occurs mainly on the southeastern Tibetan Plateau and features intense fluvial erosion, strong biochemical weathering, acid soils, and mesophytic types of vegetation. The spectrum of altitudinal zones is composed

Photo 18.3 A highway bridge crosses the sluggish Yarlung Zangbo (upper reaches of the Bramaputra River). This is the core area of Tibet Autonomous Region.

chiefly of a montane needle-leaved forest belt, with alpine scrub and meadow belts distributed above it. By contrast, the continental system is extensive on the central and northwestern Tibetan Plateau, and is dominated by desiccation and snow-accumulation processes, intense mechanical weathering, alkaline soil, and xerophytic vegetation. The spectrum of altitudinal belts is composed mainly of montane steppe and montane desert, with alpine meadows on the higher slopes.

By integration of all this vertical and horizontal areal differentiation, six natural regions can be identified on the Tibetan Plateau (Table 18.1, Figure 18.1).

HISTORICAL BACKGROUND

According to available historical documents, the Tibetan Plateau was sparsely inhabited by the Chang, the Ti, and

Photo 18.4 The Nam Co (literally "Heaven Lake") on the Qiantang Plateau (northwestern Tibetan Plateau), 4718 m in elevation, is the highest salt lake in China.

Photo 18.5 The Wanglang Natural Reserve is located at the southeastern margin of the Tibetan Plateau. A panda is climbing up a tree.

other nomadic peoples before the second century B.C. They were chiefly nomads but also practiced some farming. As early as the third century B.C., the ancient Chang began farming in the alluvial plains of the northeastern Tibetan Plateau, including the broad Huang Shui and Datong River valleys (both are tributaries of the upper Yellow River). In the early Western Han Dynasty (206 B.C.–A.D. 9), Chinese political influence and agricultural civilization entered both the Hexi Corridor and the northeastern Tibetan Plateau, and farmlands were greatly expanded. The great divide of the Sun-Moon Mountain line (just east of Qinghai Lake) between the sown and the pastoral, as well as between oceanic and interior drainage, formed and has persisted ever since.

In the Sui (A.D. 589–618) and early Tang (A.D. 618–907) dynasties, China was once again unified and strong. The Chinese army defeated the Tayuwen tribes, who were partly farming and partly pastoral and had established their kingdom on the northeastern Tibetan Plateau from the fourth to the seventh centuries. From 609 to 681, the Han took over the area and expanded farming in these broad valleys. But soon afterwards, the Tu Bo (the ancestor of the modern Zang) with their pastoral civilization (also growing highland barley, or *qingke*, in low valleys) conquered practically all of the Tibetan Plateau, including the eastern Qilian Mountains and the northern Hengduan Mountains. This was the

TABLE 18.1
Comprehensive Physical Regionalization of the Tibetan Plateau

Natural region	Chief natural hazard
28. Southern Himalayan Slopes—Tropical & Subtropical montane forest region	Montane hazards, soil erosion, deforestation
29. Southeastern Tibetan Plateau—Montane needle-leaved forest & Alpine meadow region	Montane hazards, soil erosion, hailstorms, deforestation
30. Southern Tibetan Plateau—Shrubby grassland region	Soil erosion, drought, montane hazards, grassland degradation
31. Central Tibetan Plateau—Montane & alpine grassland region	Montane hazards, soil erosion, drought, grassland degradation
32. Qaidam Basin & Northern Kunlun Mts. Slopes—Desert region	Salinization, shifting sand, strong wind
33. Ngari–Kunlun Mts.—Desert-steppe alpine desert region	Drought, soil erosion, strong wind

Photo 18.6 The Budala (literally "Holyland of Buddhism") Palace, built in the seventh century and located on a hilltop of a northwestern Lhasa suburb. It has 11 floors with a total height of 110 m.

golden age of Tibetan history. King Chizunlun of Tu Bo married the Chinese princess Wen-cheng and introduced Chinese agricultural civilization on a large scale. Probably farming areas along the middle reaches of the Yarlung Zangbo were established in this period. The majestic Budala Palace, a 110 m high brick building with 11 floors (Photo 18.6), was also built at that time. It is said that its gold roof can be seen from 20 km away. However, the Tu Bo kingdom was soon split into numerous small tribes dominated by serfdom.

During the Yuan (1279–1368), Ming (1368–1644), and Qing (1644–1911) dynasties, the entire Tibetan Plateau became a part of Chinese Empire (Figure 3.2). In the Ming Dynasty, farmlands were greatly increased on the alluvial plains of the northeastern Tibetan Plateau (in late Qing Dynasty farmlands were also extended to the gentle slopes of Qilian Mountains), totaling about 50,000 ha, of which about 40,000 ha were concentrated in the Huang Shui valley. Many new settlers, including the Han, Hui, Tu, and Sula, were recruited from neighboring provinces and mixed with the Tibetan people in settlements. During the same period, pastoral Mongol people invaded the area, reaching south of the middle Yellow River (they were somewhat pushed back by the Tibetans in the late Qing Dynasty). However, all other parts of the Tibetan Plateau (including Zang, Kang, and southern Qinghai) were still mainly inhabited by Tibetan tribes and chiefly engaged in pasto-

ralism (except in the middle reaches of the Yarlung Zangbo). All these feudal imperial governments adopted a "divide and rule" policy. Under these governments, the Tibetan Plateau was divided into numerous small tribes and districts, with feudal chieftains autocratically ruling generation after generation, resulting in stagnation of all political, economic, and social development. Especially in the Zang-inhabited areas, mysterious Lamaism and tribal serfdom have dominated and stifled nearly all opportunities for development in improvement of individual welfare.

During the Republic of China (1911–1949) and even until the 1950s, these deplorable conditions were essentially unchanged. The harmful "divide and rule" policy was still untouched, although both the Qinghai and Kang (also called Xi Kang, or western Kang) areas were organized into provinces. Lamaism and the tribal serfdom system in the Zang-inhabited areas were still kept. What was worse, numerous civil wars raged. A few thousand pastoral Hazark also migrated from the Junggar Basin to the western Qilian Mountains and north Qaidam Basin. Only since the Kang rebellion in 1957, especially since the Zang rebellion in 1959, have the social and economic conditions been greatly changed. Still many political, economic, and social problems have not yet been solved.

SOCIAL AND ECONOMIC DEVELOPMENT

Agricultural Development

Agriculture is still the major economic activity on the Tibetan Plateau. For example, in 1989, the gross production of agriculture and industry in Tibet Autonomous Region totaled 1.7 billion yuan, of which 80.45 percent was in agriculture. The same year, total population in Tibet Autonomous Region reached 2.16 million, of which 86.11 percent were rural.

Animal Husbandry

Nomadic pastoralism has been the chief agricultural activity on the Tibetan Plateau since ancient times, while farming has been limited to local areas in low valleys and basins, generally below 3000 m in elevation. According to government statistics, there were more than 487 million *mu* (32.5 million ha) of usable grassland (occupying about 95 percent of the total land area), 5.54 million large livestock, and 16.77 million sheep and goats in Qinghai province in 1990. In comparison, Tibet Autonomous Region had 801 million *mu* (53.4 million ha) of usable grassland, 6.12 million large livestock, and 16.08 million sheep and goats. The yak is the typical livestock species of Tibetan animal husbandry. It is mainly adapted to 3000 to 6000 m in elevation. Yaks supply the daily necessities to the Tibetan people, including milk, meat, and wool. The darkish, rectangular Tibetan tent is also made with yak wool, which is one special component of the Tibetan landscape and can be distinguished significantly from the whitish, dome-shaped tent (made with sheep wool) on the Mongolian Plateau as well as on the Mongol-inhabited areas of the northeastern Tibetan Plateau. Furthermore, just as the camel is the "ship of the desert," the yak is the "ship of the plateau."

Farming

Farming has been conducted on the Tibetan Plateau since ancient times, but the harsh physical environment and undeveloped human conditions limit its area and production. In 1990, there were only 8.66 million *mu* (0.58 million ha) of farmland in Qinghai Province and 3.33 million *mu* (0.22 milliom ha) in Tibet Autonomous Region, occupying only 0.6 percent and 0.23 percent of the national total farmland, respectively. Major farming areas, besides the southern slopes of Himalaya Mountains which are actually beyond the Tibetan Plateau, are restricted to three types of locations: (1) the Yellow River and its tributary Huang Shui valleys on the northeastern Tibetan Plateau, with a general elevation of 2500–3000 m, where the valley plains are mainly irrigated farms, and on scattered rain-fed farming areas on the surrounding mountain slopes; (2) the middle Yarlung Zangbo valley on the southern Tibetan Plateau, in areas of around 3500–4000 m where the rain-fed farming system is practiced. The highest farmland (highland barley) production reaches 4760 m, immediately below the snow line, which is certainly the world's record; (3) the piedmont plains of the southern Qaidam Basin on the northern Tibetan Plateau, at elevations generally between 2600 to 3000 m that are exclusively limited to irrigated farming on land reclaimed very recently by a group of state farms.

The dominant cropping system is one crop per year, with wheat (both spring and winter), highland barley (*qingke*), peanuts, and rape seed as the four major crops. As the rain-fed farming system is generally under very poor management, crops yields are very low. Even in 1991, when the average crop yield of Tibet Autonomous Region reached the highest in its history, the value was still only 1800 kg/ha.

Food grain production is not yet self-sufficient. For example, in 1989, the gross output of grain production in Tibet Autonomous Region was about 549,900 tons (averaging 256 kg per capita). The gap between demand and supply was about 141,000 tons, which had to be transported to the region by the badly managed roads from the Sichuan Basin thousands of kilometers away. To provide the grain, the government had to spend 80 million yuan as a subsidy.

Forestry

The Hengduan Mountains area is the second largest timber-producing area in China. Most mountain slopes are covered by mixed broad- and needle-leaved forests and pure needle-leaved forests. The mixed forests consist chiefly of *Pinus densata*, *Tsuga dumosa*, and *Quercus aquifoliodes*, while the latter contain numerous trees of the genera *Picea*, *Abies*, *Sabina*, and *Larix*. The upper forest limit of *Picea balfouriana* is 4400 m on the shady slope, compared with *Sabina tibetica* at 4600 m on the sunny side. These constitute the highest forest tree lines in the world.

In this area, annual timber production reaches more than 2.5–3.0 million cu m. The chief problem facing forestry is overcutting. It is estimated that forests originally covered more than one half the total land area in the Hengduan Mountains, but several thousand years of overexploitation and ruthless destruction have reduced the forests to only about one fourth of the original area. Environmental protection and afforestation are much needed in the Hengduan Mountains.

Modern Industry and Transportation

Besides agriculture, other types of economic activity are insignificant on the Tibetan Plateau, and modern industry and transportation are almost negligible.

Modern Industry

No large-scale modern industries have been developed on the Tibetan Plateau. Probably the only exception is the petroleum and other minerals (potassium, boron, salt, etc.), mining, and refinery industries in the Qaidam Basin, where a network of asphalt-metalled roads has also been built since the early 1980s.

Modern Transportation

Limited by a remote borderland location and many harsh physical conditions, the Tibetan Plateau has long been noted for its inaccessibility. There is at present only one single railway on this extensive plateau, starting from Lanzhou (capital of Gansu Province), passing through Xining (capital of Qinghai Province), and ending at Golmud. Lhasa and Haikou are now the only two provincial capitals in China without a railway connection. Since the 1950s, there have been two long-distance west–east highways: one across the Kang area, connecting Lhasa with Chengdu (capital of Sichuan Province), and another across Qinghai Province, connecting Lhasa with Xining and Lanzhou. Both are major trade routes. There are also strategic roadways, linking Lhasa with outposts along the international boundaries. Air routes between Lhasa, Xining, Lanzhou, Chengdu, and Beijing have been opened since the early 1980s. There are no navigable inland waterways on the Tibetan Plateau.

Ethnic Groups and Population

Ethnic Groups

The current distribution of ethnic groups on the Tibetan Plateau is an end product of historical development as we have seen. Qinghai Province is now populated by a mixture of many ethnic groups. The Han still have a majority, making up 60.6 percent of the total population. The Zang are about 19.4 percent of total population, and most live in southern Qinghai Province, where the elevation is generally above 4000 m. In contrast to Qinghai Province, Tibet Autonomous Region is comparatively simple in ethnic structure, with the Zang making up about 94.4 percent of the total population, while the Han comprise only 4.9 percent. This is the only exception in China to the Han generally forming the overwhelming majority (even comprising 84.5 percent of the total population in Inner Mongolia and 68.1 percent in Ningxia). Based on the 1982 population census, the distribution of ethnic groups in Qinghai Province and Tibet Autonomous Region is shown in Table 18.2.

Population

Since 1949, with improved social and economic development on the Tibetan Plateau, the population has increased rather rapidly. In 1990, the total population of Qinghai Province reached 4,456,946, and that of Tibet Autonomous Region was 2,196,010, increases of 14.4 percent and 11.6 percent, respectively, since 1982. However, population density is still far below the national average, only about 6 persons and less than 2 persons per sq km, respectively.

AREAL DIFFERENTIATION AND REGIONAL DEVELOPMENT

This extensive and lofty division has a significant political and strategic value to China. Economically, it has been

TABLE 18.2
Distribution of Ethnic Groups in Qinghai Province and Tibet Autonomous Region, 1982

	Total population	Han	Zang	Mongol	Hui	Sula	Man	Hazark	Tu	Others
Qinghai	3,895,706	2,359,979	754,254	50,456	533,750	60,930	3,048	1,497	128,930	2,862
Tibet	1,892,393	91,720	1,786,544	116	1,788	—	95	5	52	12,073

and will continue to be a land of pastoralism, with local intermontane valleys and basins devoted to farming, in order to be self-sufficient in food and vegetables. Modern industry and transportation should also be greatly developed as appropriate. All social and economic development of different regions, however, should be based on and adjusted to their specific natural and human conditions.

Southern Himalayan Slopes

This region (28 on Figure 18.1) includes mainly the southern slopes of the East Himalaya and the Kangrigarbo Mountains. Physically, it is not a part of the Tibetan Plateau itself, and politically a considerable part (south of the so-called McMahon line) is now occupied by India.

The main Himalayan ranges have crest lines of more than 6000 to 7000 m, with numerous summits over 7000 to 8000 m. But the East Himalaya is much lower, only 7756 m at its highest peak, Namjagbarwa. There are several glaciers formed from oceanic storms. Erosional and depositional landforms associated with glaciation are found mainly in the valleys below the snow line. In the upper reaches of the rivers and their tributaries, U-shaped glaciated valleys are well developed. As a result of recent river sculpture, the valley form changes from a wide trough to deep gorges. In general the fluvial erosion process dominates. It is characterized by intense dissection and deep gorges with typical V-shaped valleys as well as by the steepness of the valley walls. The Yarlung Zangbo cuts its way in a great bend through the mountain ranges around the foot of Namjagbarwa. From Paiqu, where the river enters the gorge, the elevation decreases from about 2800 m to about 600 m when the river reaches Xirang, a distance of about 240 km. A very large hydroelectric capacity is available, if there is such a need.

The strong moisture-laiden southern monsoons bring abundant precipitation to the southern slopes of the Himalayas. The climate is warm and humid, which differs entirely from the dry, cold climate on the Tibetan Plateau proper. In most of the valleys and hills where the elevation is below 2500 m, the mean temperature of the warmest month varies from 18°–25°C and that of the coldest month from 2°–16°C. There is a dependable frost-free season below 1000–1200 m. The region is the most humid section of the Himalayas. Mean annual precipitation varies from 1000 to 4000 mm in the districts below 2500–3000 m. The highest precipitation belt in the East Himalayas is generally found at altitudes between 1500 and 2500 m where the annual rainfall is about 2000 to 3000 mm.

The vegetation types vary greatly. At lower altitudes, below 1000–1200 m, there are tropical evergreen and semi-evergreen rainforests in which trees of the genus *Dipterocarpus*, *Dysoxylum*, *Terminalia*, and *Shorea* dominate. Once the primeval rain forest is cleared, dense bamboo groves may extend and remain as secondary growth. In the Yarlung Zangbo valley, the tropical evergreen rain forest grows at least as far up as Singing (450 m) and the semi-evergreen rain forest extends to Medog (1000 m).

The lower montane evergreen broad-leaved forest belt occupies the largest part of the vertical zonation. It consists chiefly of evergreen *Fagacae*, among which the genera *Castanopsis* and *Cyslobalanopsis*, heavily clogged with mosses, are dominant. This belt usually features mist forest or mossy forest, corresponding with the belt of highest precipitation. Tree ferns are common; the number of lianas and epiphytes is very diverse. Zayu, bordered by the Yunnan Plateau on the southeast, has a wide expanse of pine forest (consisting mainly of *Pinus yunnanensis*) because of its lighter precipitation and an obvious dry season.

The higher montane needle- and broad-leaved mixed forest belt includes various types of vegetation, such as the hard-leaved forest of *Quercus semecarpifolia*, the moisture-loving forest of *Chulka dumosa*, and the Himalayan endemic forest of *Pinus griffithii*. A good number of species and genera of *Abies* (*A. spectabilis*, *A. delarayi*, *A. georgei*) dominate the montane coniferous forest belt. The forest of *Betula utilis* and dwarf *Rhododendron* shrubs are frequently found near the upper forest limit, which varies in altitude from 3700–4100 m.

Above the forest belt, plant communities of alpine scrubs and meadows cover the terrain. The former consist chiefly of *Rhododendron*, *Salix*, and *Cassiope*; the latter, mainly of *Carex*, *Juncus*, *Kobresia*, and *Polygonum*. A variety of alpine flowers bloom, and during their short growing season, they create a sensationally colorful landscape.

On the whole, natural resources are quite bountiful. Abundant forest resources include various kinds of timber and rare plants. Tropical and subtropical fruits, such as oranges and bananas, grow at lower altitudes. Tea as well as temperate fruits, such as apples, pears, and peaches, can also be planted in the region.

Farmlands, limited by rugged topography, stretch mainly along the river valleys, especially in the Zayu River basin. Rice, African millet, maize, and wheat are the leading crops. Farming is still carried out by primitive shifting agriculture, relying on slash-and-burn cultivation, which results in widespread soil erosion and deforestation. Yak and sheep are pastured in the alpine belt, whereas cattle graze at the middle and lower altitudes.

In the future, the tropical and subtropical forests and other biological resources should be more profitably used, and the planting of rice, tea, and other crops extended. Environmental protection is also important.

Southeastern Tibetan Plateau

This natural region (29 on Figure 18.1) comprises mainly the middle to northern parts of the Hengduan Mountains, or the Kang area. The region consists of a series of high mountain ridges sandwiched between deep river gorges. The mountain ranges trend nearly north to south. From west to east, they are: the Nyainqentanglha, the Taniantawen, the Ningjing, the Chola, the Shaluli, the Daxue, the Zheduo, and the Qionglai. The Nu Jiang (Salween River), the Lancang (Mekong River), the Jinsha (Chang Jiang), and their numerous tributaries lie in between. The ridges cut deeply into the southeastern Tibetan Plateau in parallel gorges with the elevation of valley floors varying between 2000 and 4000 m. Above the ridges, peaks tower as high as 5000–6000 m, where glacial and periglacial landforms are common. The undulating residual surfaces of the southeastern Tibetan Plateau are fragmentary, with altitudes about 3500 to 4500 m generally tipping from north to south.

This region features sharp fluvial landforms. In the northern part (north of 30° N), the rivers flow in a nearly northwest–southeast direction with a slight gradient. Terraces and floodplains occur in a number of broad valleys. Southward from 30° N, the rivers turn to a north–south orientation, and are characterized by deepcut gorges, steep valley walls, swift torrents, and steep river gradients. The terraces and floodplains almost disappear in the river bottom, while mountain hazards including mudflows, landslides, and slope slips are frequent.

During the summer, usually from June to September, the region is under the influence of monsoons, both from the southeast (Pacific monsoon) and from the southwest (Indian monsoon). Annual precipitation totals 400 to 1000 mm, decreasing northwestward from the periphery to the interior. Vertical changes in temperature are obvious. The mean temperature of the warmest month is 12°–18°C in the valley with an elevation of 2500 to 4000 m, and only 6° to 10°C in the high mountains or plateau surfaces of 4000 to 4500 m. Hailstorms occur as often as 20 to 25 days per year; this is one of the heaviest hail hazard areas in China.

The altitudinal change in soils is quite prominent and also quite different between windward and leeward mountain sides. Taking the Mount Gongga (7556 m) as an example (Figure 18.3, Color Plate 32), on its eastern (windward) slope, the Dadu River valley bottom is composed of red and yellow earths, then upwards, from 1300 to 2300 m, is montane drab soil; from 2300 to 2800 m, montane brown soil is the rule; from 2800 to 3400 m, highly organic alpine meadow soil dominates; from 4600 to 4900 m, immature alpine tundra soil covers the bedrock; and above 4900 m (the snow line), only eternal snow covers the bare rocks; while on its western slope, the first two altitudinal belts are missing, and the snow line stands at 5100 m. Montane drab soils are good arable soils, and are developed on narrow terraces, diluvial fans, and lower slopes of dry valleys at elevations under 3000 to 3600 m. They are characterized by a thin coarse texture and are alkaline to neutral in pH. Other soils are also closely correlated with geomorphological, climatic, and vegetational conditions.

The region has one of the richest alpine floras in the world. Vertical zonation in vegetation types is very conspicuous. At the floor of warm and dry valleys, which are generally under 2400 m in elevation and suffer from rainshadow and foehn effects, thorny shrubs consisting of *Opuntia monacantha*, *Acacia farnesiana*, and *Pistacia weinmannifolia* are the dominant species. Most areas are covered by montane mixed needle- and broad-leaved forests and pure needle-leaved forests. From the periphery to the interior, forests occur continuously or in large patches. Above the tree line, alpine scrubs and meadows are usually found on the divides and ridges.

The southern part of the region is rich in forest resources. The volume of timber growing stock is about 500–800 cu m/ha. Some of the special products include such medicinal commodities as musk, the tuber of elevated gastrodia (*Gastrodia elata*), the bulb of fritilaria, Chinese caterpillar fungus (*Cordyceps sinensis*), and several mushroom species. Fruit trees, such as apple, pear, peach, and walnut, may be grown at lower altitudes.

Farmlands are relatively few and are chiefly concentrated on the terraces and alluvial fans in the dry valleys. Highland barley, wheat, peas, and potatoes are the main crops. Corn may be grown at lower altitudes. Animal husbandry still plays an important role in the region. Yak, sheep, and goats make up the bulk of the livestock. Transhumance is widely practiced. Livestock are driven

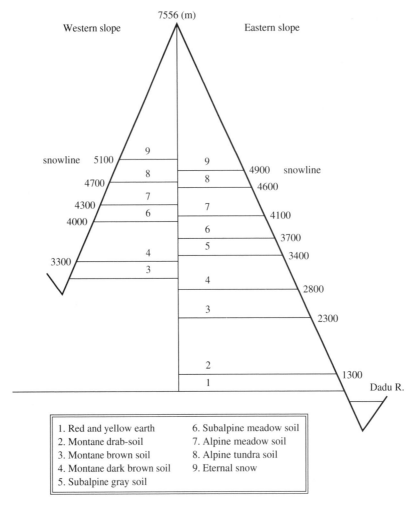

Figure 18.3   Vertical zonation of soils on Gongga Mountain (drawn by Yu Dafu)

into the alpine belt after the snow melts and returned to the valleys and foothills in the cold season. Water resources abound in the gorge areas; the further development of small, scattered irrigation and hydroelectric projects is promising.

Southern Tibetan Plateau

This is the core region (30 on Figure 18.1) of the Zang-inhabited areas. It lies between the Himalayas in the south and the Gangdise–Nyainqentanglha ranges in the north. The vast intermontane basin is mainly drained by the Yarlung Zangbo while its northwestern part feeds the upper reaches of the Indus River.

The Himalaya Mountains are highest in the middle section where there are numerous lofty peaks. Besides Mount Qomolangma, five peaks rise above 8000 m and more than 40 peaks are above 7000 m. All of these high peaks provide a favorable basis for glacial action. The southern slopes of the mountain system are much steeper than the northern slopes and tower abruptly from 6000 to 7000 m above the Ganges Plain of India, while the northern slopes descend gradually to a series of fault basins and valleys on the Tibetan Plateau. The Gangdise–Nyainqentanglha Mountains trend from west to east. They also have a steep south slope and gentle slopes on the northern side, which borders the Qiantang Plateau.

The Yarlung Zangbo, traversing from west to east along the great graben at the southern foot of the Gangdise–Nyainqentanglha ranges, is a large river with the highest altitude in the world (Photo 18.3). In the broad valley of its upper stream (the Maquan River), there stretch broad alluvial plains with scattered barchan sand dunes. In the middle reaches of the Yarlung, broad valleys and depressions alternate with narrow gorges. In the broad valleys, there are innumerable braided channels as well as a series of piedmont plains, diluvial fans, and several steps of terraces; deposits of eolian sands are also widespread.

Owing to the more southerly latitude and the lower altitude, the region has a higher temperature than other parts of the Tibetan Plateau. The mean temperature of the warmest month ranges from 10° to 16°C and the coldest from 0° to −10°C. As a result of the great climatic barrier of the mighty Himalayas, annual precipitation decreases from 500 mm in the east to 200 mm in the west, and the aridity index increases from 1.5 to 3.0. In the valleys of middle Yarlung Zangbo, 70–80 percent of precipitation occurs at night, resulting in abundant sunshine. The gross annual radiation totals 160–190 Kcal/sq cm; this is one of the highest records in China. Lhasa is known as the "City of Sunlight," with 3400 hours of annual sunshine.

The predominant vegetation is montane shrub-steppe and alpine steppe. The broad basin and lower slopes below 4400 to 4600 m are mainly covered by montane steppe, consisting chiefly of *Stipa bungeana*, *Aristida triseta*, *Pennisetem flaccidem*, and *Orinus thorolda*. In the middle reaches of the Yarlung Zangbo, the montane shrub-steppe dominates, consisting of *Sophora moorcroftiana* and other shrubs. Above altitudes of 4400 to 4600 m, the alpine steppe prevails, consisting chiefly of *Stipa purpurea*, *Artemisia welbyi*, *A. younhusbandii*, and *A. stracheyi*. In the basins and valleys of the northern foothills of the Himalayas, where annual precipitation drops to 200–300 mm, dwarf shrubs of *Caragana tibetica* and *C. versicolor* are scattered in the alpine steppe belt. The upper limit of the alpine steppe belt reaches an altitude of 5000–5200 m. Above this, alpine meadow and cushion vegetation occur. The former consists chiefly of *Kobresia pygmaea* and *Carex montiis-everstii*, and the latter is dominated by genera of *Androsace*, *Arenaria*, and *Astragalus*.

Land types include mainly alpine meadow–high mountain, shrubby steppe–high plain, and meadow–level land. The last two types are chiefly located in the middle reaches of the Yarlung Zangbo, constituting the major farming and settlement areas in Tibet Autono-mous Region. The farmlands in this region make up about 60 percent of Tibet's total. The fields stretch on the terraces along the river and on the lower part of the alluvial-diluvial fans. The elevation varies between 3300 and 4200 m. There are some irrigation facilities. The main crops are highland barley, winter and spring wheat, peas, and rape seed, generally one crop per year. The upper altitudinal limit is very high on the northern slopes of the Himalayas—4760 m for highland barley and 4200 m for winter wheat.

An analysis of the ratio of potential evapo-transpiration to precipitation shows that 4500 cu m/ha of water is needed to irrigate winter wheat in a normal year. Soil fertility deficiency is another limiting factor for agricultural development. Amelioration of soil nutrient conditions with fertilizers and extension of irrigation fa-cilities are necessary to improve productivity. It is also advisable to plant forest shelter belts for soil conserva-tion and shifting sand control. In the western and higher pastures, the land is chiefly used for grazing; overgrazing and grassland degradation are sometimes big problems, and measures for environmental protection are neces-sary.

Central Tibetan Plateau

This region (31 on Figure 18.1) stretches across the central Tibetan Plateau from southwest to northeast, including administratively the middle part of Tibet Au-tonomous Region and a major part of Qinghai Province.

The high Qiantang Plateau (literally, "northern upland") is sandwiched between the Kunlun Mountains in the north and the Gangdise–Nyainqentanglha Moun-tains in the south. This extensive, desolate upland, with an elevation of 4500–4800 m, is characterized by an intermontane basin (the Tibetan Plateau surface) and is studded by numerous inland lakes, such as the Nam Co (Photo 18.4) and Siling Co. Most of the lake basins are of fault origin, with extensive lacustrine plains and piedmont depositions. Glaciers appear on the surround-ing high peaks above 6000 m.

The upper reaches of the Chang Jiang and the Yel-low River, at an elevation of 4200 to 4700 m, are on a slightly dissected rolling plateau that stretches between Tanggula Mountains in the south and eastern Kunlun Mountains in the north. The mountain ranges trend generally east–west and have a relative relief below 500 m. The rivers also flow eastward.

The eastern Qilian Mountains, which rise to nearly 4000–5000 m above the Hexi Corridor, consist of a series of parallel ranges that extend from west–northwest to east–southeast. There are many intermontane basins and valleys, with an elevation of 2500–3000 m in northeastern Qinghai province, including the Qinghai Lake basin, the broad valleys of the Yellow River and its main tributaries (such as the Huang Shui), where the most important arable land resources of the Tibetan Plateau are located. Qinghai Lake lies at an elevation of 3200 m, with an area of 4400 sq km; it is the largest lake in China. The northeastern margin of Qinghai, with an elevation of around 2500 m, is generally covered by a mantle of loess; soil erosion occurs constantly, and dissected hills and terraces are extensive.

As a whole, this region has a semiarid climate. Annual precipitation varies between 100 and 400 mm, decreasing from east to west. Strong winds blow frequently in winter and spring. On the plateau areas above 4000 m in elevation, the mean temperature of the warmest month varies between 6°–10°C. There is essentially no frost-free season, and hence, no farming.

On the Qiantang Plateau and the upper reaches of the Chang Jiang and the Yellow River, the main vegetation type is alpine steppe, consisting chiefly of *Stipa purpurea, S. subsessiliflora var. basiplumosa,* and *Carex moorcroftiana.* Above the alpine steppe belt occurs the alpine meadow of *Kobresia pygmaea.* Valleys and basins are covered by marshy meadows consisting of *Kobresia littledalei* and *Kitibetica.* The saline meadow, consisting of *Aneurolepidium dasistachyum* and *Pollygonum sibiricum,* occurs in northern and western parts of the Qiantang Plateau; while the prostrate shrubs of *Hippophae* and *Myricaria* are sparsely scattered on the gravel *gobi.*

The montane steppe prevails in the eastern Qilian Mountains, consisting mainly of *Stipa krylovii, S. breviflora,* and *Artemisia frigida.* Above this belt, the montane forest steppe belt contains needle-leaved forest, consisting of *Picea crassifolia* and *Sabina przewalski.* Above the montane forest steppe belt there are alpine scrubs and meadows; the former are composed of *Rhododendron, Caragana jubata, Potentilla fruticosa,* and *Salix spp.,* and the latter of *Kobresia* and *Pollygonum.* Around Qinghai Lake, the luxuriant alpine steppe mainly consists of *Stipa purpurea.*

The frigid Qiantang Plateau and upper reaches of the Chang Jiang and the Yellow River are exclusively used for grazing sheep and yak. Owing to low productivity and harsh climatic conditions, better land and herd management is necessary to combat the damage of drought, low temperature, and strong wind.

At lower altitudes in northeastern Qinghai Province, physical conditions are more favorable for agricultural development, and the land has been cultivated since the third century B.C. Spring wheat, highland barley, and rape seed are the leading crops. The surrounding mountain areas provide extensive pastures, and sheep, yak, and horses make up the bulk of the herds. Future development should include better grassland management, such as rotation of grazing, preparation for winter forage, protection of pasture from overgrazing, and a program to combat rodent damage. To enhance farm production, irrigation and fertilizers are needed.

Qaidam Basin and Northern Kunlun Mountain Slopes

This region (32 on Figure 18.1), which includes the Qaidam Basin, the western Qilian Mountains, the Altun Mountains, and the northern slopes of the Kunlun Mountains, extends in a nearly east–west direction. It is the transitional area between two natural realms in China—the Tibetan Frigid Plateau and Northwest Arid China. This region, especially the Qaidam Basin, is characterized by a temperate desert, but it is still considered part of the Tibetan Plateau, mainly on the basis of its high elevation and geological formations as well as its temperature and moisture conditions.

The Qaidam, an oval shaped basin at an elevation of 2600 to 3000 m, is a graben. It inclines from northwest to southeast. The inland basin can be visualized in the form of a series of concentric belts, proceeding from the surrounding mountains through the piedmont plains to the playa lakes at the center. Consequently, a series of land types (denudational mountain and hills, denudational and depositional *gobi,* sand dunes, *yardang,* and salty marshes) appear in succession (Figure 18.4, Table 18.3). *Yardang,* formed by eolian deflation on the Tertiary loose strata, are widespread in the northwestern part of the Qaidam Basin, which is the most extensive *yardang* area in China. The southeastern part of the Qaidam Basin is covered by the diluvial-alluvial facies of the Quaternary period. In general, the diluvial-alluvial piedmont plains stretch along the foothills and are composed mainly of gravel *gobi.* Shifting and half-fixed sand dunes are scattered on them. At the outer fringe of the piedmont plain, where the underground water level is high or emerges as springs, salty soils, or salty marshlands appear; this is also the belt of newly cultivated farmlands. The center of the basin is covered by an extensive alluvial-lacustrine plain of sandy loam or clay. It is an area of comparatively low elevation, about 2600–2700 m, and is studded with numerous playas and

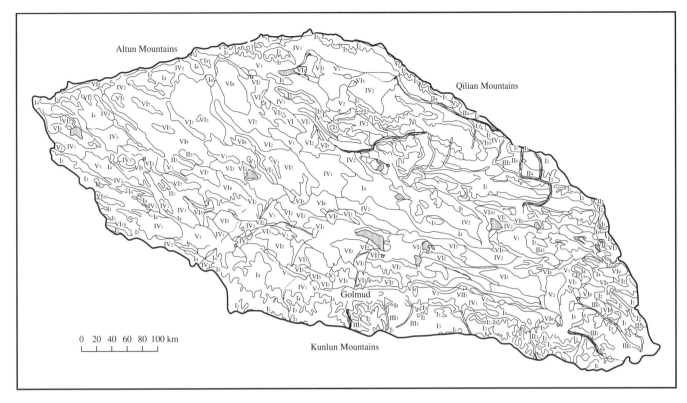

Figure 18.4 Land types in the Qaidam Basin, Qinghai Province (For legend, see Table 18.3.)

salty marshes where mineralized sinks are located and are often covered by a vast area of salt crust of the sulphate-chloride type. This is one of the richest salt-mining areas in the world; more than 97 percent of China's potassium reserves are located in the Qarhan and surrounding areas; even the 60 km highway that crosses the Qaidam Basin center is paved with blocks of solid salt. Lithium, boron, bromine, iodium, manganese, and other minerals are also all very rich in these salt lakes and marshes. Petroleum reserves are also abundant in the Qaidam Basin.

The western Qilian Mountains consist of a series of ranges and intermontane valleys and basins that trend in a nearly northwest–southeast direction, with a crest line altitude of about 4000–5000 m as contrasted with the elevation of intermontane valleys between 3000 and 3500 m. The Altun Mountains, with an altitude of 3600–4000 m, run from east–northeast to west–southwest. The Kunlun Mountains turn to a nearly east–west direction, and in their middle section, high ridges reach over 5000–6000 m.

Climatically, this region is the driest part of the Tibetan Plateau. Annual precipitation in the Qaidam Basin decreases from 100–200 mm in the east to only 10–20 mm in the west. The annual aridity index increases from 6.0 to 50.0. The climate here is also characterized by a cool summer and a cold winter, with frequent strong winds in the spring and winter. The mean temperature of the warmest month is 10°–18°C, while the coldest month varies from −10° to −15°C, with an absolute minimum temperature of −30° to −35°C. The gross annual radiation is as high as 160–180 Kcal/sq cm, and the annual sunshine totals 3000–3600 hours, which somewhat compensates for the low temperature, the major limiting factor for agricultural production here. The state farms in the Qaidam Basin are famous for their high yield of spring wheat even under harsh natural conditions. A record high for one crop of spring wheat of 792.5 kg/*mu* (11.9 ton/ha) has been reported.

The desert vegetation consists chiefly of extremely drought-tolerant shrubs and half-shrubs, such as *Ephedra przewalski*, *Salsola abrotamoides*, *Sympegma regelii*, and *Artemisia spp.* Barren lands of hills, *gobi*, shifting sand dunes, and salty marshes occur in large patches. The upper limit of montane desert lies at an altitude of 2500 to 3000 m and is sometimes even as

TABLE 18.3
Land Types in the Qaidam Basin, Qinghai Province

I	Mountain and hill	I-1	Eternal snow and cushion vegetation
		I-2	Alpine meadow and shrub meadow
		I-3	Alpine steppe-meadow
		I-4	Coniferous forest
		I-5	Montane steppe
		I-6	Montane desert
II	Terrace	II-1	Steppe terrace
		II-2	Meadow-steppe terrace
		II-3	Desert-steppe and desert terrace
		II-4	Alpine steppe terrace
		II-5	Alpine meadow terrace
III	Valley and gully	III-1	Steppe valley and gully
		III-2	Meadow-steppe valley and gully
		III-3	Desert valley and gully
		III-4	Alpine steppe valley and gully
		III-5	Alpine meadow valley and gully
IV	*Gobi* (gravel desert)	IV-1	Alluvial-diluvial sandy gravel *gobi*
		IV-2	Diluvial gravel *gobi*
		IV-3	Denudational stony *gobi*
V	*Shamo* (sandy desert)	V-1	Shifting sandy desert
		V-2	Semifixed sandy desert
		V-3	Fixed sandy desert
VI	Level land	VI-1	Salt lake
		VI-2	Salt marsh lowland
		VI-3	Salt meadow lowland
		VI-4	Saline marsh–meadow lowland
		VI-5	Saline meadow lowland
		VI-6	Takyr level land
		VI-7	*Yardang* and badland
		VI-8	Salt desert level land
		VI-9	Desert-steppe and steppe level land
		VI-10	Alpine-steppe level land
VII	Oasis	VII-1	Irrigated farming

high as 3600 to 3800 m in the western Kunlun Mountains. Above this area appears the montane steppe. The alpine desert, consisting of *Ceratoides compacta*, prevails around Har Lake and Yema South Mountain. A number of lowlands are covered by saline meadow, consisting chiefly of reeds (*Phragmites*) and *Aneurolepidium*.

The principal oases of the Qaidam Basin, just as in other inland basins of Northwest Arid China, are located along the margin of the piedmont plain where rivers flow out of the surrounding mountains. As groundwater emerges, it can be used for irrigation. Just as in other desert lands, no irrigation means no farming. The main crops are spring wheat, highland barley, potatoes, rape seed, sugar beets, and peas. Salinization control is an important measure for agricultural development. However, the future of economic development in the Qaidam Basin is expected to rely mainly on mining and other industries.

The vast areas of desert, montane steppe, and saline meadow are extensively used for grazing camels, sheep, and yak. For further development of animal husbandry, it will be necessary to set up yearly reserves of forage and feeds.

Ngari–Kunlun Mountains

This region (33 on Figure 18.1) is located on the northwestern border of the Tibetan Plateau. It includes the western Ngari area and the southern slopes of the western Kunlun Mountains.

The Ngari area is composed of the upper reaches of the Indus River and the broad basin of Banggong Lake, with elevations varying between 3800 and 4500 m. The area is encircled by the West Himalaya, the Gangdise, and the Karakorum Mountains. All these mountains have crest lines higher than 5500 to 6000 m. Because of the extremely arid climate, only small glaciers appear on a few peaks, and there is little forest coverage.

The western Kunlun Mountains, with an elevation of more than 6000 m, follow a nearly west–east direction on the northwestern rim of the Tibetan Plateau. The range is a center of glaciation, with a glaciated area of more than 4000 sq km.

Between the Kunlun and the Hoh Xil Mountains, streches a series of west–east trending lake basins with elevations between 4800 and 5100 m. The denudational piedmonts are connected with the lacustrine plains. The snow-accumulation process prevails, and there is permafrost everywhere. At the bottom of ancient lakes or lacustrine basins, the alpine desert soil contains residual carbonate or chloride salts.

The Ngari area is rather warm in summer. The mean temperature of the warmest month varies from 10° to 14°C, and that of the coldest month from −10° to −14°C. Owing to the climatic barrier of parallel ranges in the southwest, the annual precipitation varies from only 20 to 100 mm.

Montane desert steppe and montane desert prevail in the Ngari area, consisting chiefly of *Stipa glareosa*, *Ceratoides compacta*, and *Ajanta fruticulosa*. The upper limit of the montane desert, consisting of *Ceratoides latens*, reaches an elevation as high as 4600–5200 m. In the alpine belt of the southern part of the region, alpine shrub-steppe occurs, consisting primarily of *Stipa purpurea* and *Caragana versicolor*.

In the western Kunlun Mountains area, the zonal vegetation of the extensive lacustrine plains is alpine desert, in which *Ceratoides compacta* and *Ajania tibetica* are species endemic to the Tibetan Plateau. The diluvial fans are mainly covered by *Carex moorcroftii*, but *Ceratoides compacta* and *Stipa subsessiliflora var. ba-*

sinpalmosa are also included. In the northwestern part of the Kunlun Mountains, alpine desert consisting of *Ajania tibetica* dominates in the intermontane basins at elevations between 4700 and 5200 m. Such an alpine desert is characterized by a sparse cover of dwarf plants. The Akesayqin (literally, "white desert") is an extensive area of disputed sovereignty between China and India. This is essentially a barren land without any flowering plants.

The main soil types are montane desert-steppe soil and montane desert soil. They are characterized by indistinct differentiation in profile development, marked gravel pavement at the surface horizon, low content of organic matter (lower than 1 percent), and slight eluviation of calcite ($CaCO_3$). Owing to thick recent deposition, many soil profiles remain undeveloped.

On the whole, the region is now used extensively for grazing sheep and goats, with the exception of the lower valleys in the southern part, where small areas of farmland have recently been developed with irrigation. The great obstacles for developing animal husbandry are lack of water, insufficient winter and spring pasture, and a long, severe winter. Modernization of both farming and animal husbandry as well as environmental protection are urgently needed.

REFERENCES

Agricultural Geography of Qinghai Compilation Group. 1979. *Agricultural Geography of Qinghai*. Xining: Qinghai People's Press (in Chinese).

Chengdu Institute of Geography, Chinese Academy of Sciences. 1980. *Agricultural Geography of Sichuan*. Chengdu: Sichuan People's Press (in Chinese).

Chengdu Institute of Geography, Chinese Academy of Sciences. 1983. *Geographic Investigation on Gongga Mountain*. Chongqing: Science and Technology Document Publishing Office (in Chinese).

China State Statistical Bureau. 1991. *Statistical Yearbook of China*. Beijing: China Statistical Publishing House.

Chinese Academy of Sciences. 1959. *Comprehensive Physical Regionalization of China*. Beijing: Science Press (in Chinese).

Chinese Academy of Sciences. 1980. *Environment and Ecology of the Tibetan Plateau*, 3 vols. Beijing: Science Press (in Chinese and English).

Chinese Academy of Sciences. 1984. *Agricultural Geography of Tibet*. Beijing: Science Press (in Chinese).

Chinese Academy of Sciences. 1986. *Special Issue of the Hengduan Mountains Scientific Expedition*. Beijing: Science Press (in Chinese).

Huang, Fensun. 1985. *A Brief History of the Tibetans*. Beijing: Races Press (in Chinese).

Jin, Zhou (ed.). 1982. *Tibet: No Longer Medieval*. Beijing: Foreign Languages Press.

Liu, Yanhua. 1991. *Land Systems and Sustainable Development of Agriculture in the Southern Tibetan Plateau*. Ph.D. disertation, Institute of Geography, Chinese Academy of Sciences (in Chinese).

Qinghai Bureau of Agriculture and Forestry. 1984. *Farming Regionalization of Qinghai Province*. Xining: Qinghai People's Press (in Chinese).

Schweinfurth, U. 1957. "Die Horizontale und Vertikale Verbreitigung der Vegetation in Himalaya," *Bonn Geographische Abl.*, heft 20 (in German).

Sun, Jinzhu, et al. 1988. *Geography of China*. Beijing: Higher Education Press (in Chinese).

Zang, Mingtao, et al. 1982. *The Roof of the World: Exploring the Mysteries of the Qinghai–Xizang Plateau*. Beijing: Foreign Languages Press.

Zhang, Rongzu, et al. 1981. *Physical Geography of Tibet*. Beijing: Science Press (in Chinese).

Zhao, Songqiao. 1986. *Physical Geography of China*. New York: John Wiley & Sons.

Zhao, Songqiao, et al. 1990. *Vertical Agriculture Systems in the Hengduan Mountains and in the Qilian Mountains of the Tibetan Plateau: A Comparative Study*. Kathmandu: International Centre for Integrated Mountain Development.

Zhao, Songqiao, and Yuancun Shen, 1989. "Physical Conditions and Agricultural Development in the Qaidam Basin," *Selected Papers of the ISEUNRAA*. Ürümqi.

Zheng, Du, et al. 1985. *China's Qinghai–Xizang Plateau*. Beijing: Science Press (in Chinese).

APPENDIX

A Glossary of Geographic Place-names

A

Aba	阿坝
Abag Banner	阿巴嘎旗
Abgyag Glacier	阿札贡拉冰川
Aihui	爱辉
Ailao Mountain	哀牢山
Aksayqin (Akesaichin)	阿克赛钦
Aksu	阿克苏
Aksu River	阿克苏河
Alashan (Alxa) Plateau	阿拉善高原
Ali (Ngari)	阿里
Ali Mountain	阿里山
Along	阿龙
Altay Mountains	阿尔泰山
Altun Mountains	阿尔金山
Anda	安达
Andir River	安迪尔河
Anhui Province	安徽省
Ankang	安康
Anqing	安庆
Anshan	鞍山
Anshun	安顺
Anxi	安西
Anyang	安阳
Aomen (Macao)	澳门
Awa Mountain	阿瓦山
Ayding Lake (Aydingkol)	艾丁湖

B

Back Elbow Plain	后套平原
Badain Jaran Desert	巴丹吉林沙漠
Baicheng	白城
Baihe River (Bai He)	白河
Baiku Lake	佩枯湖
Bailingmiao	百灵庙
Bailong River (Bailong Jiang)	白龙江
Baingoin	班戈
Baiyang Lake	白洋淀
Bangong Co (Bangong Lake)	班公湖
Banpo Village	半坡村
Banyan Gol	巴彦高勒
Baoding	保定
Baoji	宝鸡
Baoqing	宝清
Baoshan	宝山
Baotou	包头
Barkan	巴尔康
Barku Mountain	巴尔库山
Batang	巴塘
Bayan Har Mountains	巴颜喀喇山
Bayan Nur	巴彦淖尔
Bayan Obo	白云鄂博
Baytik Mountain	白塔山
Bei'an	北安
Biebu (Tonkin) Gulf	北部湾
Beidaihe	北戴河
Beihai	北海
Beijiang River (Bei Jiang)	北江
Beijing (Peking)	北京
Beilun River	北仑河
Beishan (Mazong) Mountains	北山
Bengbu	蚌埠
Benxi	本溪
Bijie	毕节
Black River (Ruoshui)	黑河（弱水）
Bogda Mountain	博格多山
Bohai Sea (Bo Hai)	渤海

Bomei	波密	Damxung	当雄
Bose	百色	Dandong	丹东
Boshula Mountain	伯舒拉山	Dan Xian	儋县
Bosten Lake	博斯腾湖	Da Qaidam	大柴旦
Buir Nur	贝尔湖	Daqing (Taching)	大庆
Buyun Mountain	步云山	Daqing Mountains (Yin Shan)	大青山（阴山）
		Datong (Anhui Province)	大通（安徽省）

C

Cangzhou	沧州	Datong (Shanxi Province)	大同（山西省）
Central China	华中	Datong River	大通河
Changbai Mountains	长白山	Daxia River	大夏河
Changchun	长春	Daxiang Mountain	大相岭
Changde	常德	Daxue Mountains	大雪山
Chang Jiang (Yangtze River)	长江	Dayu Mountain	大庾岭
Changsha	长沙	Dedu	德都
Changshu	常熟	Delingha	德令哈
Changtang (Qingtang) Plateau	羌塘高原	Delun	吉伦
Changzhi	长治	Dengkou	磴口
Changzhou	常州	Dengqen	丁青
Chanjiang	昌江	Dexiang	德兴
Chaobai River	潮白河	Dezhou	德州
Chaohu Lake (Chao Hu)	巢湖	Dianchi Lake (Dian Chi)	滇池
Chaor River	绰尔河	Diaoyu Island	钓鱼岛
Chaoyang	朝阳	Dinghai	定海
Chaozhou	潮州	Dianyue	定日
Chengde	承德	Dobson Nur	达布逊湖
Chengdu	成都	Do Do River	沱沱河
Chenghai	澄海	Dongfang	东方
Chengxi	辰溪	Donghai Sea (East China Sea)	东海
Chenzhou	彬州	Dongjiang River (Dong Jiang)	东江
Chifeng	赤峰	Dongsha Archipelago	东沙群岛
Chin Xian	晋县	Dongsheng	东胜
Chola Mountain	雀儿山	Dongting Lake	洞庭湖
Chongming Island	崇明岛	Doqen Lake	多庆湖
Chongqing	重庆	Du'an	都安
Chongzuo	崇左	Dujiang Dam	都江堰
Chunghaitze	中海子	Dukou	渡口
Cishan	磁山	Dulan	都兰
		Dunhuang	敦煌
		Duolun	多伦

D

		Dupang Mountain	都庞岭
Daba Mountains	大巴山	Duyun	都匀
Dabie Mountains	大别山		
Dadiwan Culture	大地湾文化		

E

Dadong	大塘	East China Sea (Dong Hai)	东海
Dadu River	大渡河	Ebi Nur (Ebi Lake)	艾比湖
Da Hinggan (Greater Hinggan) Mountains	大兴安岭	Ejin Banner	额济纳旗
Daiyun Mountain	戴云山	Ejin (Juyun) Lake	居延海
Dakong	大港	Elbow (Hetau) Plains	河套平原
Dalian (Dairen)	大连	Emei Mountain	峨嵋山
Daliang Mountains	大凉山	Emin River	额敏河
Dalou Mountain	大娄山	Erenhot	二连
		Ergun River	额尔古纳河

Er Lake	洱海
Erlang Mountain	二郎山
Ertix River	额尔齐斯河

F

Fangshan	房山
Fankou	樊口
Feihe River (Fei He)	淝河
Fencheng	汾城
Fenghuo Mountain	风火山
Fengman	丰满
Fengning	丰宁
Feng Xian	凤县
Fenhe River (Fen He)	汾河
Five Linked Lakes	五大连池
Foping	佛坪
Foshan	佛山
Foziling Reservoir	佛子岭水库
Friendship (Youyi) Peak	友谊峰
Front Elbow Plain	前套平原
Fuchun Jiang (Fuchun River)	富春江
Fuding	福鼎
Fuhe River (Fu He)	抚河
Fujian Province	福建省
Fujiang River (Fu Jiang)	涪江
Fujin	富锦
Fuling	涪陵
Funiu Mountain	伏牛山
Fuqing	福清
Fushun	抚顺
Fuxian Lake	抚仙湖
Fuxin	阜新
Fuyun	富蕴
Fuzhou	福州

G

Gandis Mountains	冈底斯山
Ganguan Island	甘泉岛
Ganhe River (Gan He)	甘河
Ganjiang River (Gan Jiang)	赣江
Gansu Province	甘肃省
Ganzhou	赣州
Gaoligong Mountain	高黎贡山
Gaoxiong (Kaohsiang)	高雄
Gaoyou Lake	高邮湖
Gar	噶尔
Garze	甘孜
Gashun Lake	嘎顺湖
Gaxun Desert	嘎顺戈壁
Gejiu	个旧
Geladangdong Mountains	格拉丹东山
Gerze	改则

Gold-Silver Island	金银岛
Golmud	格尔木
Golog	果洛
Gongga Mountain	贡嘎山
Grand Canal	大运河
Greater Hinggan (Da Hinggan) Mountains	大兴安岭
Great Wall	长城
Guangdong Province	广东省
Guangxi Zhuang Autonomous Region	广西壮族自治区
Guangyuan	广元
Guangzhou (Canton)	广州
Guanting Reservior	官厅水库
Guan Xian	灌县
Guco	古措
Guiji Mountain	会稽山
Guilin	桂林
Gui Xian	贵县
Guiyang	贵阳
Guizhou Province	贵州省
Guohe River (Guo He)	涡河
Gurbantünggüt Desert	古尔班通古特沙漠
Gutian River	古田溪
Guyuan	固原, 沽源
Gyangze	江孜
Gyaring Lake	扎陵湖

H

Haifeng	海丰
Haihe River (Hai He)	海河
Haikang	海康
Haikou	海口
Hailar	海拉尔
Hainan Island (Province)	海南岛 (省)
Haiyan Mountain	海洋山
Hami	哈密
Handan	邯郸
Hangzhou	杭州
Hangzhou Estuary	杭州湾
Hanjiang River (Han Jiang)	韩江
Hanshui River (Han Shui)	汉水
Hanzhong	汉中
Haoshaoliao	火烧寮
Har Lake	哈拉湖
Harbin	哈尔滨
Hefei	合肥
Hegang	鹤岗
Heihe River (Black River)	黑河
Heilong River (Heilong Jiang, Amur R.)	黑龙江

Hekou	河口	Jiading	嘉定
Helan Mountains	贺兰山	Jialing River (Jialing Jiang)	嘉陵江
Hemudu Culture	河姆渡文化	Jiamen	金门
Hangduan (Traverse) Mountains	横断山脉	Jiamusi	佳木斯
Hengshan Mountain (Heng Shan)	恒山	Ji'an	吉安
Hengyang	衡阳	Jiangdezhen	景德镇
Hebei Province	河北省	Jiang-Han Plain	江汉平原
Henan Province	河南省	Jiangsu Province	江苏省
Hepu	合浦	Jiangxi Province	江西省
Hexi Corridor	河西走廊	Jiangyin	江阴
Himalaya Mountains	喜马拉雅山	Jiao–Lai Plain	胶莱平原
Hobq Desert	库布齐沙漠	Jiaozuo	焦作
Hohhot	呼和浩特	Jiaxing	嘉兴
Hoh Xil Mountains	可可西里山	Jiayuguan	嘉峪关
Hong Kong	香港	Jilin Province	吉林省
Hongze Lake	洪泽湖	Jilong (Keelung)	基隆
Hotan	和阗	Jinan	济南
Hotan River	和阗河	Jincheng	金昌
Huade	化德	Jinggang Mountain	井冈山
Huaihe River (Huai He)	淮河	Jinghoug	景洪
Huainan	淮南	Jingle	静乐
Hualian	花莲	Jingpo Lake	镜泊湖
Huanghai (Yellow) Sea	黄海	Jinhua	金华
Huanghe (Yellow) River	黄河	Jining	集宁
Huangshan Mountains (Huang Shan)	黄山	Jinsha River (Jinsha Jiang)	金沙江
Huangshi	湟水	Jinta	金塔
Huangyan Reef	黄岩岛	Jin Xiǎn	金县
Huan Xian	环县	Jinzhou	锦州
Huashan Mountain (Hua Shan)	华山	Jiufeng Mountain	鹫峰山
Hau Xian	华县	Jiujiang	九江
Huayuankou	花园口	Jiuling Mountain	九岭山
Hubei Province	湖北省	Jiulong River	九龙江
Huizhou	惠州	Jiuquan	酒泉
Hukou	湖口	Jixi	雞西
Hulan River	呼兰河	Junggar Basin	准格尔盆地
Hulin	虎林	Junggar Gate (Alataw)	准格尔门(阿拉山口)
Hulunbuir Plateau (Grassland)	呼伦贝尔草原	Juyun Lake (Ejin Nur)	居延海
Hulun Lake (Dalai Nur)	呼伦池		
Huma	呼玛		

K

Hunan Province	湖南省	Kaidu River	开都河
Hunchun	珲春	Kaifeng	开封
Hunshandake Sandy Land	浑善达克沙地	Kaiyuan	开原
Hutao River	滹沱河	Kanas Lake	喀纳斯湖
		Kangding	康定

I, J

		Kangrigarbo Mountain	岗日嘎布山
Ih Ju League	伊克昭盟	Kangringboqe, Mount	康仁波钦峰
Ili River	伊黎河	Kara Holshun (Black City)	黑城
Inner Mongolia (Net Mongol)	内蒙古	Karamay	克拉玛依
Jashan Mountain	夹山	Karchin Glacier	卡钦冰川
Jarga Plateau	若尔盖高原	Kashi (Kashgar)	喀什
Jartai Salt Lake	吉兰泰盐池	Kaxgar River	喀什噶尔河
Jarud Banner	扎鲁特旗	Keriya River	克里雅河

Kolshin (Horqin) Grassland	科尔沁草原
Kolshin (Horqin) Sandy Land	科尔沁沙地
Konqui River	孔雀河
Korla	库尔勒
Kuecang Mountain	括苍山
Kunlun Mountains	昆仑山脉
Kunming	昆明
Kuqa	库车
Kuruk Mountain (Kuruktag)	库鲁塔格

L

Laizhou Gulf	莱州湾
Lancang	澜沧
Lancang (Mekong) River	澜沧江
Lantian Man	兰田人
Lanzhou	兰州
Laobie Mountain	老别山
Laoshan Mountain	崂山
Ledong	乐东
Leizhou Peninsula	雷州半岛
Lenghu	冷湖
Lesser Hinggan (Xiao Hinggan) Mountains	小兴安岭
Lesser Wutai Mountain	小五台山
Lhasa	拉萨
Liangcheng	凉城
Liangshan	凉山
Lianyungang (Lianyun Port)	连云港
Lianyun Mountain	连云山
Liaodong Peninsula	辽东半岛
Liaohe River (Liao He)	辽河
Liaoning Province	辽宁省
Liaoyang	辽阳
Lijiang	丽江
Liling	醴陵
Linfen	临汾
Lingjiang River (Ling Jiang)	灵江
Lingling	零陵
Linhe	临河
Lingwu	灵武
Lintao	临洮
Lintong	临潼
Lishi Loess	离石黄土
Lishui River (Li Shui)	澧水
Litang	里塘
Liupan Mountains	六盘山
Liuyang	浏阳
Liuzhou	柳州
Loess Plateau	黄土高原
Longchuan	陇川
Longling	龙陵
Longmen Mountain	龙门山

Longshou Mountain	龙首山
Longyang Gorge	龙羊峡
Lop Lake (Lop Nur)	罗布泊
Luanhe River (Luan He)	滦河
Lüda (Dalian)	旅大
Lufeng	陆丰
Lüliang Mountains	吕梁山
Luan Mountain	路南山
Luntai	轮台
Luohe River (Luo He)	洛河
Luoyang	洛阳
Lushan Mountain	庐山
Luzhou	泸州

M

Ma'anshan	马鞍山
Magong	马公
Malan Loess	马兰黄土
Manas River	玛纳斯河
Mangnai	茫崖
Mangshi	芒市
Mangui	满贵
Manzhouli	满州里
Maoming	茂名
Mapam Yum Co	玛旁雍湖
Maquan River	马泉河
Markit	麦盖提
Mazong (Beishan) Mountains	马宗山
Medog	墨脱
Meitan	湄潭
Mei Xian	梅县
Mengding	孟定
Megla	勐腊
Mengzi	蒙自
Miaodao Archipelago	庙岛群岛
Miaoling Mountains	苗岭
Micang Mountain	米仓山
Minfeng (Niya)	民丰
Minjiang River (Min Jiang)	岷江
Minqin	民勤
Minshan Mountain	岷山
Miyun	密云
Mohe	漠河
Mori	木里
Mudanjiang	牡丹口
Mufu Mountain	幕府山
Mu Us Sandy Land	毛乌素沙地
Muztagata, Mount	慕士塔格峰

N

Nagqu	那曲
Nam Co (Nam Lake)	纳木湖

Namjag Barwa Mountain	南迦巴瓦山
Nanchang	南昌
Nanchong	南充
Nandu River	南渡江
Nanhai Sea (South China Sea)	南海
Nanjing (Nanking)	南京
Nanling Mountains (Nan Ling)	南岭
Nanning	南宁
Nanping	南平
Nansha Archipelago	南沙群岛
Nantong	南通
Nanwei Island	南威岛
Nanxiong	南雄
Nanyang	南阳
Naqa	纳曲
Neijiang	内江
Nei Mongol (Inner Mongolia)	内蒙古
Nenjiang River (Nen Jiang)	嫩江
Nganglaring Lake	昂拉仁湖
Ngari (Ali)	阿里
Ngoring Lake	鄂陵湖
Ningbo (Ningpo)	宁波
Ningxia Hui Autonomous Region	宁夏回族自治区
Ninjing Mountains	宁静山
Niuzhuang	牛庄
Nomin Desert (Nomin Gobi)	诺明戈壁
Nom Lake	淖毛湖
Northeast China	东北
Northeast China Plain	东北平原
North China	华北
North China Plain (Huang–Huai–Hai Plain)	华北平原（黄淮海平原）
Northwest China	西北
Nujiang River (Nu Jiang, Salween R.)	怒江
Nyainqentanglha Mountains	念青唐古拉山

O

Ondormiao	温都尔庙
Ordos Plateau	鄂尔多斯高原
Orqen	鄂伦春
Otog banner	鄂托克旗
Oujiang River (Ou Jiang)	瓯江

P

Pacific Ocean	太平洋
Paikü Lake	佩枯湖
Pamir Plateau	帕米尔高原
Pearl (Zujiang) River	珠江
Peligan Culture	裴李冈文化
Penghu	澎湖
Pingdingshan	平顶山

Pingdong	屏东
Pingjiang	平江
Pingliang	平凉
Pingluo	平罗
Pingnan	平南
Pingshan	平山
Pishan	皮山
Pojiang River (Po Jiang)	鄱江
Poyang Lake	鄱阳湖
Puma Yum Co	普莫雍湖
Pumqu Valley	朋曲谷地

Q

Qaidam Basin	柴达木盆地
Qamdo	昌都
Qarhan Salt Lake	察尔汗盐地
Qarqan River	车尔成河
Qianhe River (Qian He)	泾河
Qianligang Mountain	千里冈山
Qianshan Mountain (Qian Shan)	千山
Qiantang Jiang	钱塘口
Qiemo	且末
Qilian Mountains	祁连山脉
Qimantag	其曼塔格
Qingdao (Tsingtao)	青岛
Qinghai Lake (Kuku Nur)	青海湖
Qinghai Province	青海省
Qinghai–Xizang (Tibetan) Plateau	青藏高原
Qingtang (Changtang) Plateau	羌塘高原
Qinhe River (Qin He)	沁河
Qinhuangdao	秦皇岛
Qinling Mountains (Qin Ling)	秦岭
Qinzhou	钦州
Qionglai Mountain	邛崃山
Qiongzhong	琼中
Qiongzhou Strait	琼州海峡
Qiqihar	齐齐哈尔
Qira	策勒
Qogir, Mount (K-2)	乔戈里峰
Qomolangma, Mount (Mt. Everest)	珠穆朗玛峰
Quanzhou	泉州
Qujiang River (Qu Jiang)	渠江
Qumarleb	曲麻莱
Quwu Mountain	屈吴山
Quzhou	衢州

R

Raohe	饶河
Riyue (Sun-Moon) Mountain	日月山
Riyue (Sun-Moon) Pond	日月潭
Ruoshui River (Black River)	弱水（黑河）

Ruijin	瑞金	Suide	绥德
Ruoqiang	若羌	Suifenhe	绥芬河
		Suzhou	苏州

S

Sanggan River	桑干河
Sanjiang (Three Rivers) Plain	三江平原
Sankeshu (Three Trees)	三棵树
Sanmen Gorge	三门峡
Sanshui	三水
Sanya	三亚
Second (Di'er) Songhua River	第二松花江
Serling Co (Serling Lake)	奇林湖
Shaanxi Province	陕西省
Shache (Yarkant)	莎车
Shaluli Mountain	砂鲁里山
Shangdong Province	山东省
Shanghai	上海
Shanshan	鄯善
Shantou	汕头
Shanxi Province	山西省
Shaoquan	韶关
Shaoyang	邵阳
Shapotao	沙坡头
Shanshi	沙市
Shenhang Island	深航岛
Shennongjia, Mount	神农架
Shenyang	沈阳
Shenzhen	深圳
Shidao Island	石岛
Shihezi	石河子
Shijiazhuang	石家庄
Shijiu Port	石臼港
Shiquan River	狮泉河
Shiyang River	石羊河
Shizuishan	石嘴山
Shuangyashan	双鸭山
Shuikoushan	水口山
Shule River	疏勒河
Shunde	顺德
Sichuan Basin	四川盆地
Sichuan Province	四川省
Simao	思茅
Siping	四平
Sog Xian	索县
Songhua Lake	松花湖
Songhua River (Songhua Jiang)	松花江
Sonid Banner	苏尼特旗
South China	华南
South China Sea (Nan Hai)	南海
Southwest China	西南
Stone Forest	石林

T

Taba (Daba) Mountains	大巴山
Table Mountain	桌子山
Tacheng	塔城
Taching (Daqing) Oil Field	大庆油田
Taihu Lake (Tai Hu)	太湖
Taibai, Mount	太白山
Taihang Mountains	太行山
Taihe	泰和
Taijinar Lake	台吉纳尔湖
Tainan	台南
Taiping Island	太平岛
Taishan Mountain (Tai Shan)	泰山
Taiwan Island	台湾岛
Taiwan Strait	台湾海峡
Taiyuan	太原
Taizhong	台中
Taklimakan Desert	塔克拉玛干沙漠
Tangshan	唐山
Tanggu	塘沽
Tanggula Mountains	唐古拉山
Tangwang River	汤旺河
Taniantaweng Mountains	他念他翁山
Taohe River	洮河
Taoyuan	桃源
Tarim Basin	塔里木盆地
Tengchong	腾冲
Tenggar Desert	腾格里沙漠
Three Gorges (Chang Jiang Gorges)	长江三峡
Three Rivers (Sanjiang) Plain	三江平原
Tainchi Lake (Heaven Pond)	天池
Tianjin	天津
Tianlinlao Mountain	田林老山
Tianmu Mountain	天目山
Tianshan Mountains (Tian Shan)	天山
Tibetan (Qinghai–Xizang) Plateau	青藏高原
Tieling	铁岭
Tikanlik	铁干里克
Tingcun Man	丁村人
Toksun	托克逊
Tomul, Mount	托木尔峰
Tongbai Mountain	桐柏山
Tonghua	通化
Tongliao	通辽
Tumen River	图们江
Tuojiang River (Tuo Jiang)	沱江
Turpan Basin	吐鲁番盆地

U

Ujimqin	乌珠穆沁
Ulan	乌兰
Ulan Buh Desert	乌兰布和沙漠
Ulanhot	乌兰浩特
Ulanqab	乌兰察布
Uliangsu Lake	乌梁素海
Ulungur Lake	乌伦古湖
Ulungur River	乌伦古河
Urho (Wind City)	乌尔禾 (风城)
Ürümqi	乌鲁木齐
Usu Uxin Banner	乌审旗

V, W

Vachin Mountain	梵淨山
Wanding	畹町
Wanning	万宁
Wanquan River	万泉河
Wan Xian	万县
Weifang	潍坊
Weihai	威海
Weihe River (Hebei Province)	卫河 (河北省)
Weihe River (Shaanxi Province)	渭河 (陕西省)
Weishan Lake	微山湖
Wenchang	文昌
Wenquan	温泉
Wenzhou	温州
West Elbow (Yinchuan) Plain	西套平原
West Liao (Xi Liao) River	西辽河
White Head (Bai Tou), Mount	白头山
Wuda	乌达
Wudang Mountain	武当山
Wuding River	无定河
Wugong Mountain	武功山
Wuhai	乌海
Wuhan	武汉
Wuhu	芜湖
Wujiang River (Wu Jiang)	乌江
Wuliang Mountain	无量山
Wushan Mountain (Wu Shan)	巫山
Wushao Mountain (Wushao Ling)	乌鞘岭
Wusuli River	乌苏里江
Wutai Mountain	五台山
Wuwei	武威
Wuxi	无锡
Wuyiling	乌伊岭
Wuyi Mountains	武夷山
Wuyuan	五原
Wuyur River	乌裕尔河
Wuzhi (Five Fingers) Mountains	五指山
Wuzhou	梧州

X

Xar Moron River	西拉木伦河
Xiaguan	下关
Xiamen (Amoy)	厦门
Xi'an	西安
Xiang'an	兴安
Xiangfan	襄樊
Xiangjiang River (Xiang Jiang)	湘江
Xiangride	香日德
Xiangquan River (Langqen Zangbo)	象泉河
Xiangtan	湘潭
Xianxia Mountains (Xianxia Ling)	仙霞岭
Xianyang	咸阳
Xiao (Lesser) Hinggan Mountains	小兴安岭
Xiaoshan Mountain (Xiao Shan)	淆山
Xichang	西昌
Xiechi Lake (Xie Chi)	解池
Xifeng	西峰
Xigaze	日喀则
Xi Liaohe River (West Liao River)	西辽河
Xijiang River (Zhu Jiang)	西江 (珠江)
Xilin Gol	锡林郭勒
Xilinhot	锡林浩特
Ximeng	西盟
Xingkai Lake	兴凯湖
Xining	西宁
Xinjiang River (Xin Jiang)	信江
Xinjiang Uygur Autonomous Region	新疆维吾尔自治区
Xin Xian	忻县
Xinxinxia	星星峡
Xinyang	信阳
Xiong'er Mountain	熊耳山
Xiqing Mountain	西倾山
Xirang	希浪
Xishi Archipelago	西沙群岛
Xishuangbanna	西双版纳
Xiushui River (Xiu Shui)	修水
Xixabangma, Mount	希夏邦马峰
Xizang (Tibet) Automonous Region	西藏自治区
Xuande Archipelago	宣德群岛
Xuefeng Mountains	雪峰山
Xuwen	徐闻
Xu Xian	宿县
Xuzhou	徐州

Y

Yadong	亚东
Yalong River (Yalong Jiang)	雅砻江
Yalu River	鸭绿江

Yamzho Yum Co	羊卓雍湖
Yan'an	延安
Yanbian	延边
Yancheng	盐城
Yanchi	盐池
Yanding	永定
Yangshuo	阳朔
Yangzhou	扬州
Yanji	延吉
Yanjiang River (Yan Jiang)	沅江
Yanqing	延庆
Yanshan Mountain (Yan Shan)	燕山
Yantai	煙台
Yanzhi Mountain	焉支山
Yanzhou	兖州
Yarkant River	叶尔羌河
Yarlung Zambo (Yarlung River)	雅鲁藏布江
Ya Xian	崖县
Yecheng	叶城
Yellow Dragon Mountain	黄龙山
Yellow River (Huang He)	黄河
Yellow Sea (Huang Hai)	黄海
Yenchang	运城
Yibin	宜宾
Yichang	宜昌
Yichun	伊春
Yihe River (Yi He)	伊河
Yilan	宜兰
Yilehuli Mountan	伊勒呼里山
Yichuan	银川
Yingde	英德
Yingjiang	盈江
Yingkou	营口
Yingtan	鹰潭
Yinhe River (Yin He)	颖河
Yining	伊宁
Yinshan Mountains (Yin Shan)	阴山
Yiwu	伊吾
Yongchun	永春
Yongding River	永定河
Yongjiang River (Yong Jiang)	甬江
Yongle Archipelago	永乐群岛
Yongning	永宁
Yongxing Island	永兴岛
Youjiang River (Right River)	右江
Youyi (Friendship), Mount	友谊峰
Yuanjiang River (Red River)	元江·沅江
Yuanling	沅陵
Yuanmou	元谋

Yuecheng Mountain	越城岭
Yueyang	岳阳
Yuli	尉犁
Yulin	榆林，玉林
Yulong Mountain	玉龙山
Yumen	玉门
Yumenguan	玉门关
Yunling Mountains	云岭
Yunmong Swamp Area	云梦泽
Yunnan Province	云南省
Yushan Mountain (Yu Shan)	玉山
Yushu	玉树
Yutian (Keriya)	于阗

Z

Zage	扎格
Zayü	察隅
Zengmu Reef	曾母暗沙
Zhangbei	张北
Zhanguangcai Mountains	张广才岭
Zhangjiakou (Kalgan)	张家口
Zhangye	张掖
Zhangzhou	樟州
Zhanjiang	湛江
Zheduo Mountain	折多山
Zhegu Lake	哲古湖
Zhejiang Province	浙江省
Zhenghe Reefs	郑和群岛
Zhengzhou	郑州
Zhenjiang	镇江
Zhicheng	枝城
Zhijiang	枝江
Zhongba	仲巴
Zhongsha Archipelago	中沙群岛
Zhongtiao Mountain	中条山
Zhouhe River	沽河
Zhoushan	舟山
Zhuhai	珠海
Zhujiang River (Zhu Jiang, Pearl River)	珠江
Zhumadian	驻马店
Zibo	淄博
Zigong	自贡
Zishui River (Zi Shui)	资水
Ziwu Mountains	子午岭
Zoige	若尔盖
Zomo Lake	淖毛湖
Zuli River	祖厉河
Zunyi	遵义

INDEX